ITIL® Service Management

Implementation and Operation

ITIL® Service Management

Implementation and Operation

Ahmad K. Shuja

CRC Press
Taylor & Francis Group
Boca Raton London New York

CRC Press is an imprint of the
Taylor & Francis Group, an **informa** business
AN AUERBACH BOOK

CRC Press
Taylor & Francis Group
6000 Broken Sound Parkway NW, Suite 300
Boca Raton, FL 33487-2742

Version Date: 20120213

International Standard Book Number: 978-1-4200-8939-4 (Hardback)

Visit the Taylor & Francis Web site at
http://www.taylorandfrancis.com

and the CRC Press Web site at
http://www.crcpress.com

To my ever-loving family

ADDITIONAL ITSM IMPLEMENTATION & SUPPORT MATERIAL

Additional support material related to implementing business service and IT service management can be acquired from www.xceedure.com. This material includes a sample IT service catalog, presentation templates, other process-specific implementation books as well as planning and assessment tools.

Contents

PART IV OPERATING BUSINESS SERVICE MANAGEMENT

Foreword

Industrial enterprises, and society at large including government and non-profit organizations, have always sought ways to control the allocation of their resources towards specific goals, and to control the performance of activities towards particular outcomes. Without going into the history of the industrial enterprise, at a certain point in time the focus of managers moved from the quality of materials and labor to the quality of the process. For decades, success factors were defined in terms of how well the process was designed, implemented, executed and controlled. During this era the ideas and principles of process definition, process reengineering, process maturity became the staple of almost every organization around the world. The belief that well-managed and mature processes, combined with advanced automation and control using information technology, will produce better and more predictable outcomes has literally shaped organization structures, metrics and management styles.

For the most part, and for most organizations, this belief has been rewarded with better results. However, process excellence is necessary but not sufficient, especially if the very notion of value is changing from the customers' perspective. The world has changed much in the last ten years in terms of the output of the processes. Services are increasingly the form in which new value is being demanded, as opposed to tangible and intangible assets (e.g., packaged software) that customers own and maintain. Therefore, a majority of business processes are now part of service delivery or service production systems. This means the product-based process mindset originally created during the golden years of manufacturing, needs to be updated with an outcome-based "sense for services".

While much of the now mature process mindset requires no change (after all, mature service industries such as airlines, banking, and telecommunications borrowed heavily from industrial engineering and manufacturing systems), there are new design principles, new rules for measurement and, of course, new ways of judging improvement versus transformation. In the services domain, customers care even less about how, for example, an IT organization manages its network of servers or its portfolio of applications. All they care about is the actual delivery or support process they have to participate in to fully access and enjoy the benefits of a service.

By the very definition of services, many of the technical aspects of an operation are anyway abstracted or hidden from the customers and users of IT. Also, the production and consumption of services are more or less inseparable (or tightly-coupled). These two characteristics of a service-oriented enterprise make customers more sensitive to benefits and costs: customers more readily sense a decrease in benefits and more readily perceive an increase in costs. This makes the job of "IT service managers" much harder than their counterparts in other domains.

The good news is that the discipline of service management and the associated body of knowledge have grown and matured considerably over the last decade, as almost a natural outcome of more and more services being produced and consumed in every sector and segment of every major economy. The advent of service-based delivery models such as cloud computing, Software-as-a-Service (SaaS), and Infrastructure-as-a-Service (IaaS), will only make service management a more important capability than ever before. A service-oriented approach to service management may sound like a tautology; it is unfortunate the ground reality in terms of what most organizations need.

The notion of radical change and transformation is most appealing (almost romantic), and for some organizations nothing less would make a difference. For most organizations, however, large and rapid change may not only be destabilizing and risk-prone but also entirely needless. Therefore, before committing to any such substantial change or transformation, organizations must be absolutely certain nothing less will do; incremental and iterative change will fall short of the overarching business imperative.

With well-defined increments and a series of well-managed iterations, an organization can achieve more or less the same outcomes or advantage as more radical change and transformation that is almost big-bang in nature. The challenge of course is defining those increments and managing those iterations. It is best to first attain a certain level of organizational maturity in terms of a set of core service management processes that are "capable and lean". Then increments can be defined in terms of some capability or functional component of a process, measurable or verifiable in terms of one or more outcomes. Iterations can be defined in terms of betterment or improvement of the outcomes which are driven either by commitments made to customers or the organization's governance, risk and compliance (GRC) mandates. That is, a set of well-defined metrics should be used to determine what increments and how many iterations are required as part of a tactical plan or roadmap to fully execute a service-based IT strategy.

Every organization is a store of knowledge, skills and experience. How such valuable stocks are used to achieve certain goals and objectives partly depends on the "social habits" of the enterprise. In today's business environment, purely internal efforts or initiatives completely insulated from the knowledge, insight and expertise of external partners, vendors and consultants, are increasingly rare. Similarly rare are efforts and initiatives that do not engage internal human capital and knowledge assets, even if they are part of an outsourced contract or arrangement. An incremental and iterative approach to excellence in service management allows a judicious combination of internal and external assets, including public frameworks, standards, methodology and tool sets.

Achieving service excellence is a non-trivial undertaking with failure and underperformance just as common as success. This book does a thorough job in explaining how to assure desired outcomes. It's incremental and iterative approach to implementing service management is fortified with enterprise architecture principles and methods thereby ensuring performance levels enterprise-wide.

Majid Iqbal
Author ITIL v3 Service Strategy

Preface

Welcome to *ITIL® Service Management: Implementation and Operation*. In this book, I address some of the key questions that most Information Technology Infrastructure Library (ITIL) practitioners and IT managers are trying to answer today. These mostly relate to implementing business service management by leveraging ITIL v3 guidelines in ways that cause the least disruptions, are seamless to business customers, and enable IT to deliver business value in the most effective, visible, efficient, and incremental manner. To ensure that strategic efforts like service management implementation are able to survive all the risks (management shuffles, loss of sponsor, etc.), it becomes even more important to effectively and continually communicate measurable business value to all business and IT stakeholders.

ITIL v3 provides a detailed set of guidelines on some of the core concepts related to IT service management. The overall ITIL v3 literature provides a discussion of how mature IT organizations operate to manage IT services throughout their life cycle. ITIL v3, however, does not provide detailed discussion and guidelines on how to achieve the desired maturity that may be required to manage IT services.

ITIL v2 provided a process-centric approach (single, multiple, or all processes) to achieving process improvements. ITIL v3 takes a service life cycle approach. This book focuses primarily on how IT organizations can get the most returns on their IT service management implementation investments in the least possible time. The content and structure of this book is designed to address this need.

This book is based on the experiences and lessons learnt from real world service management implementation projects/initiatives. Accordingly, I will be including "Practical Tips" as and when appropriate to further re-enforce the core concept and how it may be applied in your respective organizations/projects.

Author

Ahmad K. Shuja (www.shuja.info), Co-Founder & President of Xceedure Inc. (www.xceedure.com), is an accomplished and passionate ITIL v3 Expert, Enterprise Architecture (EA), and Business Process Management (BPM) consultant and practitioner who has helped his clients with envisioning, defining, implementing and institutionalizing these practices such that "measurable" business benefits can be realized early on in order to keep the "momentum" going. Ahmad has a proven track record of enabling enterprises to realize their business vision through an effective management of IT services, innovative use of emerging technologies, and creation of business-aligned IT organizations. He has both been a hands-on ITIL/IT Service Management/Solution architect as well as a mentor and manager. He has expertize in complementing domains including EA and BPM and the respective supporting tools like Tibco, ARIS, Lombardi, and others as well as frameworks like TOGAF & Zachman. He has developed as well as led the development of tailored EA/BPM/ITSM frameworks, methods and processes to enable his clients to realize highly anticipated process enablement, asset re-use, optimal asset utilization and overall IT governance related benefits. Ahmad has established and managed EA/BPM/ITSM functions as well as mentored process owners and architects at some of the most reputable companies globally. A renowned author and a technology management expert who turns challenged low-performing IT organizations into cost-effective high-performing business partners through the institutionalization of a service-oriented customer-focused practices.

Ahmad holds graduate degrees from Massachusetts Institute of Technology (MIT), University of Oxford, and University of Toronto. He also holds numerous professional certifications, including ITIL v3 Expert ITIL v2 Service Manager (aka ITIL v2 Master), ITIL v3 Intermediate/ITIL v2 Practitioner, Project Management Institute (PMI) Project Management Professional (PMP), Software Engineering Institute (SEI) Certificate in Capability Maturity Model Integration (CMMI), and Certified RUP Specialist, to name a few. Ahmad is the author of "Rational Unified Process: Reference and Certification Guide", and "ITIL® Service Management: Implementation and Operation". He has published a couple of IT Service Management papers and also speaks at professional forums.

Content and Structure of *ITIL® Service Management: Implementation and Operation*

Part I ITIL v3 and Organizational Transformation

Chapter 1 Introduction

This chapter provides an overview of business service management, why it is important, why IT leadership and practitioners need to think about it now, and what the bottom-line value is for the business. We also discuss business services, technical services, and IT services.

Chapter 2 Integrating IT with Business

At the core of business service management is the integration of IT with the businesses that it aims to enable. In this chapter, we learn more about the role of IT in enabling businesses to achieve their objectives in a more effective manner.

Chapter 3 Service Management Implementation Overview

This chapter discusses some of the key challenges faced by business enterprises today and how business service management can help address those challenges. We learn what it really means to implement business service management and what some of the critical success factors are. We discuss how business service management is likely to impact the overall organizational culture and some of the major risks associated with such endeavors.

Part II Iterative and Incremental Approach to Implementing Business Service Management

Not everything in your IT organization is equally important; the 80/20 rule applies here. We learn about an approach that will enable you to achieve the desired IT improvements in a manner that will minimize the risks of failure, maximize returns on IT improvements and related investments, and optimize opportunities to achieve strong business–IT integration.

Chapter 4 Iterative and Incremental Service-Oriented Service Management Implementation: An Introduction

This chapter provides an introduction to an iterative and incremental approach that will enable you to identify risks associated with service management implementation and manage them in an effective manner. We discuss what can be done to make IT improvements visible to your customers and other businesses that you support.

Chapter 5 Discipline: Project Management

In this chapter, we discuss the core activities that must be performed so that the appropriate management of the project is in place to ensure that the desired capabilities and improvements are delivered within agreed costs and schedule targets.

Chapter 6 Discipline: People and Organization

Achieving business service management will impact all aspects of the organization and, most important, the people within the organization. We discuss how the organization and people aspects of business service management implementation can be optimally managed and the associated core activities.

Chapter 7 Discipline: Continual Service Improvement Institutionalization

Continual service improvement is at the core of aligning and realigning IT services with the evolving business needs. In this chapter, we discuss all that must be done to ensure that functional continual service improvement capabilities are institutionalized within the organization over the course of the business service management implementation project.

Chapter 8 Discipline: Business Service Improvement and End-to-End Business Service Management Implementation

At the core of achieving business service management is the continuous improvement of business services to align with evolving business needs. We discuss what it means to achieve end-to-end business service management and the associated activities that must be performed.

Chapter 9 Discipline: Service Management Process Improvement

Service management processes underpin the overall service quality. In this chapter, we discuss how service management process improvements can be prioritized and achieved so that they make a direct and positive impact on the quality of business services.

Chapter 10 Discipline: Business Service Management Technology Architecture and Integration

Automation plays a critical role in ensuring consistent quality and enforcing enhanced processes. Business service management relies heavily on processes and, without appropriate enabling tools, it will be a challenge to achieve this. In this chapter, we talk about how technology architecture and appropriate integrations can be achieved.

Chapter 11 Discipline: Business Service Management Technology Delivery

This chapter discusses what activities need to be performed and when to ensure that the right technology is delivered to enable business service management at the right time.

Chapter 12 Iterative and Incremental Service-Oriented Service Management Implementation Life Cycle: Phases and Iterations

This chapter introduces the different phases that can exist within the business service management project and how those can be aligned with service and process improvements.

Part III Planning and Implementing Business Service Management

Chapter 13 Business Service Management Roadmap

In this chapter, we discuss the first step in planning the business service management implementation—development of the overall business service management implementation roadmap.

Chapter 14 Business Service Management Implementation Planning

In this chapter, we discuss all that needs to be done to plan the business service management implementation.

Chapter 15 Implementing Business Service Management

In this chapter, we learn about the key aspects of implementing business service management. These aspects will enable us to maintain our focus in the right direction during the implementation phase.

Part IV Operating Business Service Management

Chapter 16 Operating Business Service Management

Business service management operation is what creates value for the customers and businesses. If implemented appropriately, business service management should enable the IT organization to effectively manage its processes, people, and technologies to deliver the needed services in the most cost-effective and predictable manner.

Chapter 17 IT Service Management, Enterprise Architecture, and Service-Oriented Architecture—Effective Enablement of Business Service Management

In this chapter, we discuss business service management and associated emerging topics like enterprise architecture and service-oriented architecture and how these do and do not relate to business service management. We see how these can be positioned to compliment the business service management implementation effort.

Audience

This book is intended to provide guidelines to all those IT professionals who are involved in envisioning, managing, and operating IT service management. This book will provide extensive guidance to the:

- Chief Information Officer
- Head of IT
- IT service management project stakeholders including project and program managers
- Process owners (change managers, configuration managers, service level managers, etc.)
- ITIL consultants and practitioners
- Students of IT management and related disciplines

I

ITIL v3 AND ORGANIZATIONAL TRANSFORMATION

Chapter 1

Introduction

The only constant is change
And our nature is to resist change

Welcome to *ITIL® Service Management: Implementation and Operation*. This book will address some of the key questions that most Information Technology Infrastructure Library (ITIL) practitioners and IT managers are trying to answer today. These questions primarily relate to implementing business service management (BSM) by leveraging ITIL v3 guidelines in ways that cause the least disruptions, are seamless to business customers, and enable IT to deliver value in the most effective, visible, efficient, and incremental manner. To ensure that strategic efforts such as service management implementation are able to survive all the risks, including management shuffles, loss of sponsor, etc., it becomes even more important to effectively and continually communicate measurable value to all business and IT stakeholders.

This book will not focus on the ITIL v3 content—what it is, what processes it involves, and so on. You can learn those details about ITIL v3 in five official ITIL v3 books: *Service Strategy*, *Service Design*, *Service Transition*, *Service Operation*, and *Continual Service Improvement*. I plan to discuss, in detail, everything that we need to know about implementing service management by leveraging guidelines provided in ITIL v3 literature. By the end of this chapter, you will be able to answer the following questions:

- What is BSM and how does it relate to IT? Why is it important? Why now? Why not now? What does it really do for the business? What if we do not implement BSM? We will discuss the term IT service management (ITSM) and how it is related to BSM, if at all.
- What is the difference between business services, technical services, and IT services? We will examine what these terms mean and if there is any relationship between them.
- What is the nature of business enterprises and why is BSM critical to their success? In answering this question, we will look at what business enterprises are and consider a range of different perspectives.
- How have business enterprises evolved in the Information Age? After establishing a level of understanding about business enterprises, we will briefly review how they have evolved and we will see how this evolution relates to IT.

- What are the transformation drivers that are inspiring business enterprises to fundamentally transform their businesses in this Information Age?
- What is the role of IT in enabling business enterprises to efficiently operate in this new and ever-changing environment and to achieve their business goals? After achieving a comprehensive understanding of business enterprises and their ongoing transformations, we will discuss the role of IT in those transformations and the expectations of the business enterprises.

An Overview of BSM

BSM requires relating the business performance to IT operations performance (i.e., assessing and measuring the performance of IT in relation to the performance of the business). For example, let us look at a very simple example of change management. Introducing changes in the IT environment are costly, risky, and require a lot of effort. The main question to ask is: "What do these changes do for the business?" Instead of measuring the number of changes that were successfully implemented, we will take a step further and measure the impact (financial, reputation, customer satisfaction, throughput, business service and product delivery, accuracy, etc.) of these changes on the businesses and its customers.

We all know that it is recommended to perform cost-benefit analysis for every change, and most IT organizations that I have encountered do try to develop something like a business case: Were customers able to realize the envisioned benefits as a result of the planned IT changes? Therefore, to realize the true value of achieving BSM, IT must be able to measure its performance as it relates to business performance. This will further enable IT to target future improvements that create the most value for the business.

BSM is a means to an end, that is, enabling businesses to achieve greater profits, faster growth, compliance with regulatory requirements, or other business goals through an innovative and effective use of IT. BSM is a journey, not an end itself. It is a culture in which serving the business and managing IT to deliver the needed services at agreed levels are the key objectives. BSM will involve innovative use of information and communication technologies (software, business applications and services, the Internet, hardware, networks, and other tools) to automate the right processes, targeting the service improvements that make the most impact, improving IT processes to ensure that services are managed and delivered as committed, and continually aligning and realigning IT organizations to better integrate with businesses and customers.

Traditionally, IT has been regarded as a cost center. Some even go to the extent of making remarks like, "IT is a necessary evil. We cannot live with them and we cannot live without them." It is this very reason that the IT budget is almost always the first one to be slashed whenever there is a need to cut down costs. To enable you to have a better appreciation of why IT is perceived like this, here is a brief scenario that we will all be able to relate to because we all use cell phones. Visualize the following key services that we use as customers of a cell phone company:

- **Registering for cell phone service**. When you register for cell phone service, you may visit their sales office, call customer service, or use an online service if they have one. Imagine that you call or visit the sales office and you are given a list of departments that you should call to sign up and activate your service:
  - Network management
  - Finance management
  - Device activation
  - Billing and account management

You call each of the departments to ensure that the right cell phone service is activated for you and that you will be billed for the service you have registered for.

- **Billing.** When you start using the service and receive a bill, it does not show you the specific charges. To make matters worse, you do not know what to expect in the next bill and you feel that you do not have any control over costs. You use 100 minutes and discover that you pay the same fee as your friend who used 500 minutes.
- **Service warranty.** Imagine that you would like to make a call and are in the service area. You receive a message that service is not available to you.
- **Service utility.** The service does not perform as advertised when you use it. For example, you save your voice messages, but when you try to retrieve them, you are unable to do so.
- **Customer service.** Reaching customer service becomes a complete project. You never know how long you will have to wait when you call. When you do get connected, your needs are not addressed. In fact, you are told that customer service will get back to you, but they never do. When you call them to follow-up, they have no record of your previous call or its resolution. In other cases, they may ask you to contact another department because your request is something that they cannot do.

Now, I will ask you one question: If you were this customer and you had the option to switch to another service provider, would you? If you did not have the option to change your service provider, would you do all that you could to reduce your costs? I will be surprised if your answer is anything other than "Yes."

In most IT organizations operating at a low level of service management maturity, the above symptoms are not uncommon. I can summarize the pain points as follows:

- **Lack of transparency.** Businesses and customers do not understand what they are paying for and why. Commonly, IT personnel will not clearly understand their costs and expenses. To make matters worse, they may not even understand who their customers are.

Practical Tip: In one of the global financial firms where the term "IT Tax" was very well known and common amongst the customer / user base, those business units that were not heavy users of IT services were pushing / lobbying for outsourcing IT. Their core rationale was based on the fact that their respective business units were being over-charged for basic IT services such as Email and Internet and that they were able to get the same set of services at about 1/10th of the cost. Note here that your customers / users evaluate your services in terms of value delivered vs. cost incurred. If your customer's perceptions are that the services that you deliver cost more than the value they generate, your customer's may be already looking for alternatives.

- **Lack of control and IT tax.** Continuing on the above-mentioned challenge, matters become much worse when neither IT nor its customer base knows how to control IT-related costs. If IT does not understand what they do, why they do it, or who they do it for, it is a much greater challenge to understand the IT costs, be able to control those costs, and spend in areas where the returns are maximized. Consider the following statements about managing, controlling, measuring, and defining (Case and Spalding, 2007):

> You cannot manage what you cannot control.
> You cannot control what you cannot measure.
> You cannot measure what you cannot define.

In environments where IT costs are not understood and cannot be rationalized or controlled, they are spread across the customer population regardless of utilization or subscription. This means that customers are essentially taxed for the IT services that they use–aka "IT Tax."

- **IT talk**. Businesses, in most cases, do not care about the technology; they need to be able to perform their business processes more efficiently and do their work faster. IT that does not understand who their customers are and what those customers need, often end up with the IT talk and forget about the core business needs. This is the environment where discussions concern tools and technologies and not business problems, opportunities, and requirements.

Now, keeping that discussion and your customers in mind, what do you think about this statement:

> We need to transform our IT organization from a cost center to a business organization that is perceived by businesses and customers as a value-added, enabling business partner.

I will ask you to pause here for a moment, take a deep breath, and give it some thought. What does it mean for an IT organization to be managed as a business? You will need to ask some core business questions:

- Do we know who we are?
- Do we know who our customers are?
- Do we know what they need?
- Do we know what we offer?
- Do we know how much it costs us to produce what we offer?
- Are our customers willing to pay the price for our services or products?
- Does our offer match our customers' needs?
- What can we do to improve whatever we offer?

IT needs to think like a business; we produce IT services that we want to sell.

Now, let me turn the picture around and see IT from the customers' perspective. If you were IT's customer, what kind of organization would you like as your business partner? The answer that you get is going to have some key characteristics. For an IT organization to become a business partner, it is critical that we, as IT managers and leaders, ask the following questions:

- Is IT able to understand customers' needs and pain points and is it able to do something about them?
- Is IT able to deliver what it promises (i.e., both service warranty and service utility)?
- Does IT clearly understand core business processes, the gaps and opportunities, and the IT capabilities necessary to address those needs?
- Can IT see beyond organizational boundaries and enable core business processes that span across existing business applications and departments, and also across geographies? For example, completing a mortgage process from its initiation to final disbursement (in the case of approval) or logging (in the case of denial) may involve a wide variety of departments (marketing, sales, credit, real estate assessment, risk, legal, disbursement, and potentially others) and their underlying business applications. BSM means that IT will be able to

achieve a thorough and clear understanding of this level of business process definition (not in silos) and manage their resources to best enable the end-to-end business processes.

- Is IT able to offer customers enough information about their costs and the ability to control those costs?
- Is IT able to measure and report service quality in business terms? For instance, if IT enables supply chain management processes, can it measure how much revenue its services have helped businesses generate because of availability and performance? If IT offers customers video conferencing capabilities, can it help customers understand how many costs (travel, lodging, etc.) they have been able to avoid because they were able to conduct their meetings using video conferencing services?

When IT services are linked to the business processes that they enable, it becomes possible to measure IT service performance in business terms and provide reports that will help businesses make wise investments. In a mature organization where BSM is a norm, IT should be able to identify where business processes are weak or broken and be able to improve those processes before enabling them. If business processes are not designed correctly, then IT will be automating broken processes.

BSM is about IT capabilities to manage business services. For IT to manage the business services, it needs to be integrated with the business. BSM is about achieving business–IT integration through end-to-end (i.e., from business processes down to infrastructure components) management of all components that are used to enable business processes. End-to-end management includes:

- Clear identification and mapping of business processes that IT is supposed to enable.
- Clear identification of all components that make up a business service (i.e., an IT service that enables a given business process).
- Development of a complete value chain that relates IT components to business processes that they support.
- Impact-based management of IT components. This means that each IT component is managed based on the value that it delivers to the business. Not all components are equally important. If there is one component that is part of the value chain that enables the supply chain management process, then it will need to be more effectively managed than, for example, the one that is part of the chain that processes batch reports.

ITIL v3 provides a comprehensive set of guidelines that can be used to achieve BSM, which enables business enterprises to leverage IT to its maximum potential in enabling processes so that:

- IT performance can be measured in terms of business performance.
- Continual improvement becomes part of the culture enabling business enterprises to continually improve their products and services.
- Adaptability to changing competitive landscapes becomes a norm.

Achieving the right balance of governance, efficiencies, effectiveness, innovation, organization, transparency, traceability, and management is critical to implementing BSM. If implemented appropriately, BSM will enable end-to-end traceability between business vision and strategy: the business processes needed to achieve the vision, the business services that enable those business processes, the technical services that realize the business services, and the technology components that implement technical services. This concept, also known as BSM, is shown in Figure 1.1.

Let us first clearly understand the key terms that we mentioned above.

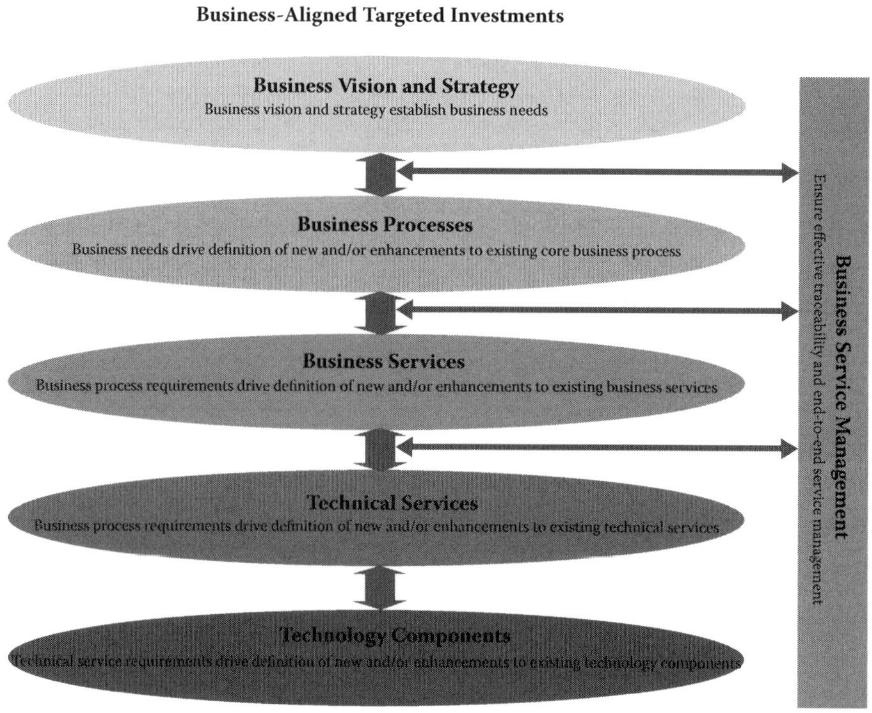

Figure 1.1 Traceability and end-to-end service management.

Business Vision and Strategy

Clear understanding of business vision and strategy is going to go a long way in enabling IT organizations to align their respective capabilities (processes, people, partners, and technology) to enable business enterprises to meet their stated visions. From this understanding of business vision, core business processes can be defined to implement these visions.

Business Processes

Business processes serve at the core and implement the products and services that business aims to deliver. It is at this level in high-maturity organizations that IT partners with the businesses to design the most innovative ways to enable processes. In fact, IT needs to play a role in optimizing business processes to ensure that the right technology capabilities are deployed to enable the right processes at the right levels.

Business Services

Business services enable business processes. These are commonly defined *for* customers and need to be defined *with* customers in mind. These are the services that the customers of the IT organization are able to understand.

Technical Services

Technical services realize business services. Technical services, as the name suggests, are internal facing and are not normally visible to the customer. One or more technical services may be required to realize a given business service and technical services may be shared across multiple business services.

We will discuss business services, technical services, and IT services in greater detail in the next chapter. In addition, there are a few terms that may be new to you here such as service catalog, service level management (SLM), service level agreement (SLA), operational level agreement (OLA), and others. We will discuss these terms and others later in this book.

Technology Components

Technology components implement technical services. Examples of these include software, application, hardware, network, database, and other components.

Service Tree

Service tree is an important concept and will prove very helpful throughout this book. Let us discuss in detail what we mean by service tree and how it relates to end-to-end service management. An example is shown in Figure 1.2.

Practical Tip: Service Tree becomes extremely helpful when you are trying to communicate to the senior level business and IT management stakeholders why certain investments need to be made in some IT services in order generate greater business value. In my consulting experience over the years, I have been able to use Service Tree to represent a variety of important business as well as IT perspectives. For instance, you can begin to rationalize why you need to make improvements for certain IT components and how do they map to the overall value generated for the business.

The service tree shows a logical relationship between the various components that exist within IT and provides an important platform to start thinking about end-to-end BSM. Note that many relationships exist among the various layers. For example, there may be one or more technology components required to implement one technical service, and there may be one or more technical services that exist to realize one business service, and there may be one or more business services that exist to enable one business process. The ability to establish such relationships will enable organizations to truly align their business and technical services to enable business enterprises to meet their visions. To demonstrate this concept, let us look at one of the most common IT-performance measurement attributes—availability. Thorough end-to-end implementation of a service tree will enable business enterprises and IT organizations to start managing services and underpinning components to enable business process in the most effective and efficient manner. As shown in Figure 1.3, business process and business service level availability needs can really drive how we invest in building our IT capabilities.

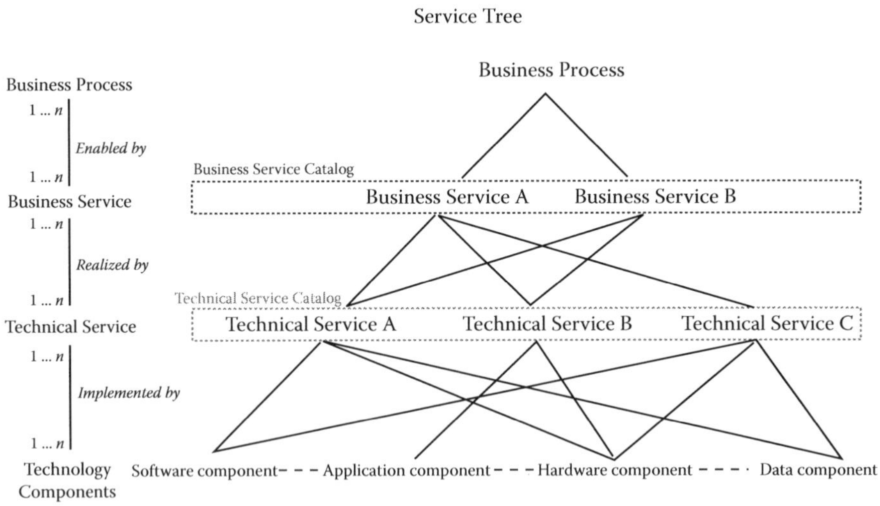

Figure 1.2 Service tree.

As shown in Figures 1.3 and 1.4, business service A has an availability target of 98%. This will give the IT organizations availability targets for technical services that realize business service A. IT organizations can plan accordingly for each of the underlying technical services.

Let us discuss a real-world example. This will further clarify the service tree concept and its importance. Figure 1.5 shows a complete value chain for the supply chain business process. In this example, we assume that the business enterprise needs 99% availability of the supply chain business process. This availability target needs to be justified by the returns on the investments made to enable this process at the desired targets. However, an important and critical driver is defined

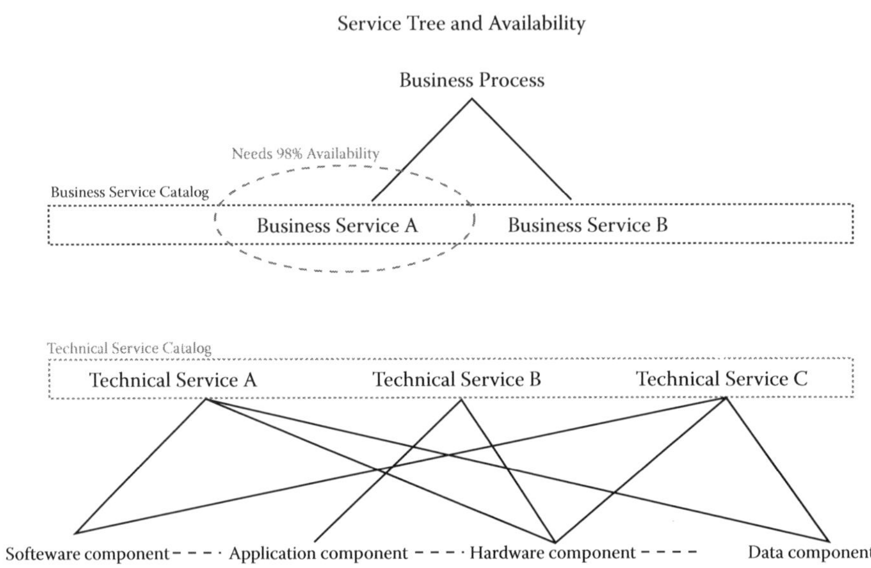

Figure 1.3 Service tree and availability.

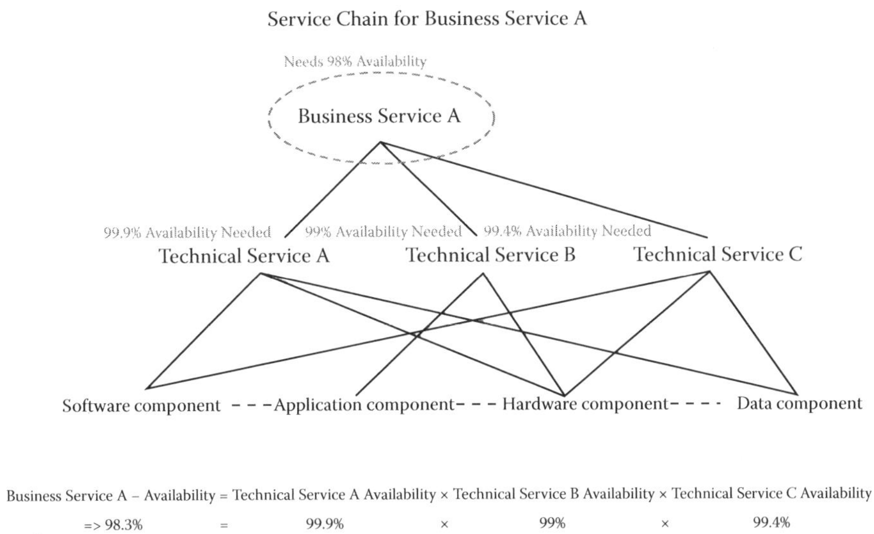

Figure 1.4 Service chain.

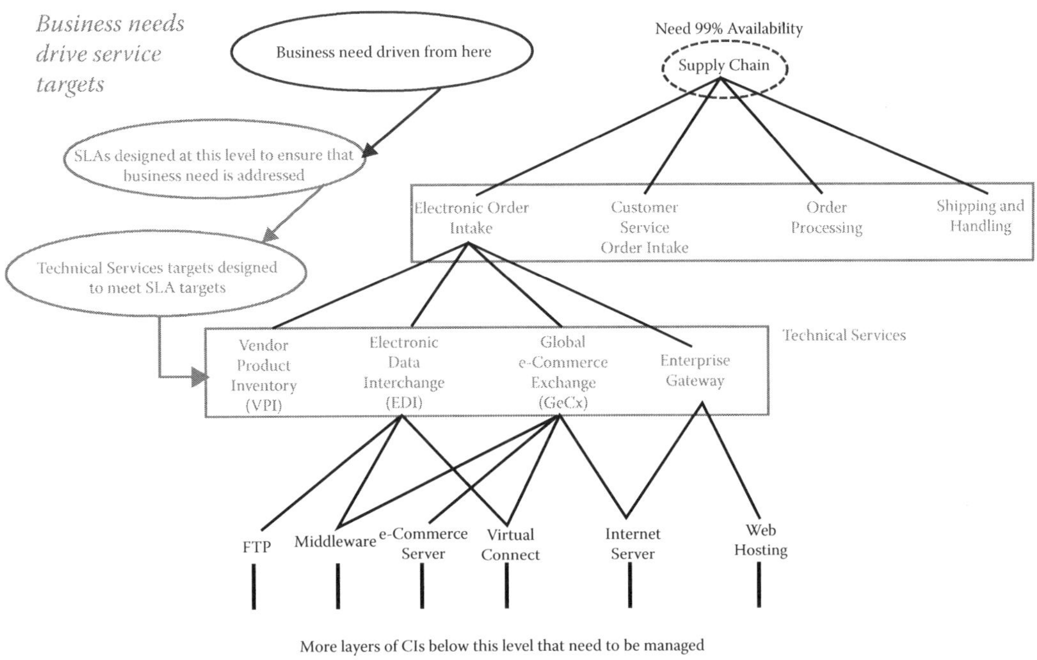

Figure 1.5 Value chain for a supply chain business process.

Practical Tip: Practical application of Service Tree to demonstrate how you may be able to trace a particular business need right from a particular business process to supporting business services through to technical services and other downstream configuration items.

here for the respective investments that will be made in building IT capabilities. In a true BSM environment, business needs are driven at the business process level. These needs shape how IT capabilities are designed and implemented. SLAs are established between business services and business processes to ensure that IT meets business needs. Technical services are developed to meet the SLA targets. We will discuss greater implementation details in Part II and Part III of this book. However, it is very important to clearly understand this concept early on.

End-to-End BSM

We have now seen the term *end-to-end service management* a couple of times. Let us now make sure that we have a thorough understanding of what this is all about. As you can see in Figure 1.6, the service tree is at the core of end-to-end service management discussion.

End-to-end service management means that each component (configuration item) of the service chain is appropriately managed to ensure that agreed targets are met so that businesses and customers are able to achieve their objectives. For this to happen, the following should be in place:

- Clear and concrete definition of business and related technical services in the service catalog
- Thorough definition and understanding of service level requirements

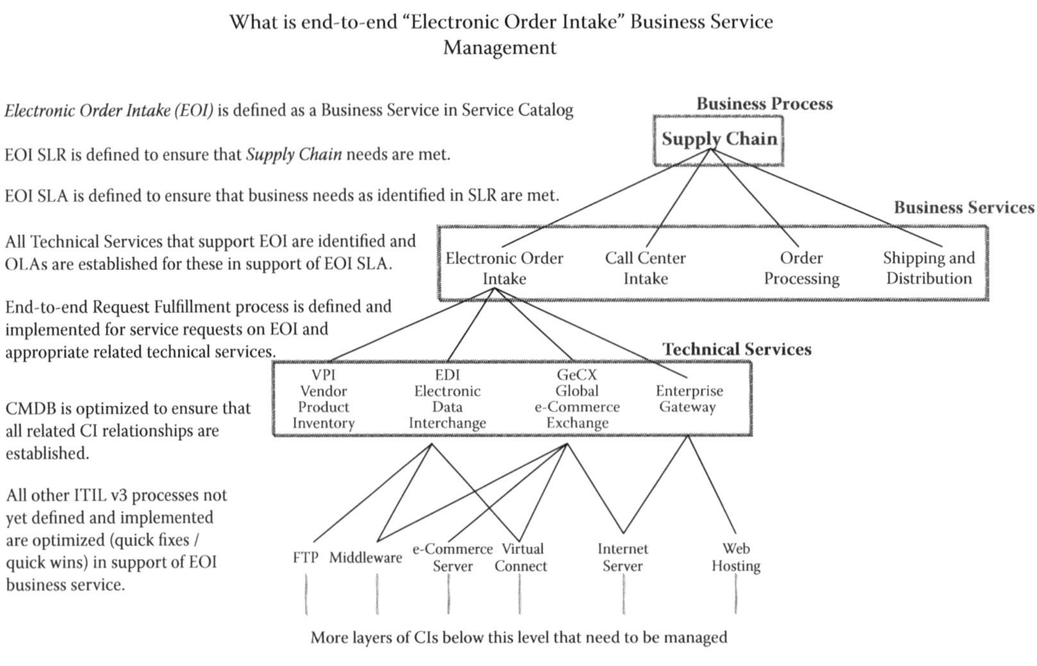

Figure 1.6 End-to-end service management.

- Development of other components related to service design (in ITIL v3 terms, service design package)
- Definition and agreement of necessary SLM components (SLAs and OLAs) to ensure that business needs captured in service level requirements and agreed on in SLAs are met
- Identification of high-volume, low-risk requests that can be placed on the business and technical services in the catalog and implementation of end-to-end request fulfillment for these requests
- Optimization of a configuration management database to support the end-to-end service management involving creation of appropriate configuration items (CIs), documentation of related details, and building appropriate inter-CI relationships
- Refinement and optimization of all other ITIL v3 process to support the identified services—ideally in a targeted fashion so that quick wins are achieved

Implementation of this end-to-end service management is discussed in greater detail in Part II and Part III of this book.

The Nature of Business Enterprises and BSM

This book is about implementing BSM based on guidelines provided by ITIL v3. Implementing BSM is a challenging task and, in most cases, may need major cultural shifts to happen to make it successful. To build an appreciation of why BSM is critical and what factors need to be kept in mind, we will take a step back and look at the nature of business enterprises and how BSM can enable these enterprises to grow and prosper in the most effective and efficient manner. Let us discuss business enterprises from a range of important and interesting perspectives.

Business Enterprise: A System of Systems

A living organism is not only a conglomeration of separate elements but a definite system that possesses organization and wholeness (Bertalanffy, 1951). A system is also defined as "an organized or complex whole; an assemblage or combination of things or parts forming a complex or unitary whole." Such system definitions seem to adequately fit the typical business enterprise. Business enterprises can be viewed as a man-made living system. These systems exist in a larger environment where they are constantly interacting and dynamically interplaying with other systems such as the environment itself within which they exist and with their respective customers, competitors, labor and nonprofit organizations, suppliers, governments, and many other similar systems. Like any living system, a business enterprise is a system of other interrelated systems that need to work in organized harmony and collaborate to accomplish the business vision and goals. These goals encompass both business–enterprise-specific goals as well as those of individual participants.

In another related discussion, Johnson et al. (1964) provided another interesting and common analogy in which they compare an organization to the human body: the skeletal and muscle systems represent the operating line element, the circulatory system is a necessary staff function, and the nervous system is the communication system. In this sense, an organization is represented as a self-maintaining structure, one that can reproduce (i.e., organic growth within business enterprises). Just as streamlined operation of each system within a living system is important for efficient and effective operation of a larger living system, it is critical that all systems within a given business enterprise system operate in harmony to effectively achieve the desired business goals.

This is precisely what BSM does for an IT service provider i.e., BSM enables IT service provider to ensure that relevant IT assets are managed in such a harmonized manner that achieves optimal utilization and maximizes value creation.

Business Enterprise: The Only Constant Is Change, and Our Nature Is to Resist Change

Business enterprises in today's world influence the environment in which they operate and are influenced by a range of external factors such as government regulations, competition, associations (with other systems) working toward maintaining healthy environments, and so on. In responses to these, business enterprises always find themselves in situations where they need to respond to these external influences to achieve a state of dynamic equilibrium and maximize profitability. In a way, whenever a business enterprise is under stress from these external systems, it will take necessary steps to minimize this stress. The Le Chatelier principle states that a stable system under stress will move in the direction that tends to minimize the stress. This movement may mean undertaking business process reengineering and other related initiatives with a goal of making necessary modifications in the way business enterprise is managed. These modifications may be made at different levels. These levels are as follows:

- *First level.* The first level of modification is simply *no modification*. If the changes in the environment do not apply to or impact the given business enterprise, then it does not need to undertake any modification. This needs to be carefully assessed and planned since it may just be a matter of resistance to change. If modification is warranted by the business circumstances, then resistance should not be the factor to prevent that modification from taking place.
- *Second level.* The second level of modification is *adjustment*. Adjustment is the use of existing features to respond to the change in the environment. This can be likened to minor modifications of inputs and outputs of existing activities. In terms of business enterprises, such adjustments may be undertaken whenever less critical issues are identified as a result of an internal or external audit. There may be other efficiency-related drivers that can potentially motivate a business enterprise to undertake such adjustments to fill gaps and achieve some quick wins.
- *Third level.* The third level of modification is *adaptation*. Adaptation is the development of new capabilities to respond to the change. This can be likened to the addition and subtraction of activities and data to the diagrams as well as changing their relative positions. For business enterprises, it may mean that they are required to make substantial improvements in their business processes to achieve their objectives. In comparison to adjustment, where quick fixes are made to fill gaps, adaptation modifications normally result in the development of new features for the existing systems or the development of new systems.
- *Fourth level.* The fourth level of modification is *evolution*. Evolution is change in the genetic structure of the model. This can be likened to performing business process reengineering to radically change the processes and, therefore, the model. Evolution is usually considered to be occurring slowly over a long period. The use of the term here applies only to radical change, not to the time span of the change. Such changes mean transformations for enterprises. One recent example of evolution is how the emergence of e-commerce and the Internet has truly changed the way businesses are conducted.

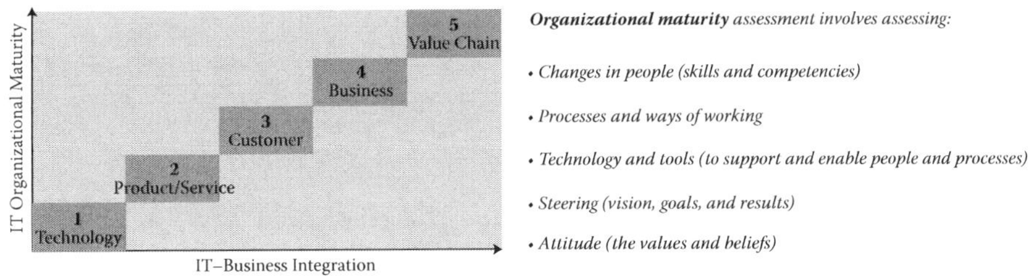

Figure 1.7 Organizational maturity levels.

The level of modification that may be required is determined by a range of external as well as internal factors. These include:

- *External and internal pressures.* External pressures may range from compliance related from regulatory bodies to social responsibility and competition. In some cases, internal pressures may be shaped by external pressures and may require business enterprises to be more innovative, efficient, profitable, or adaptive. We will discuss these pressures in detail later in this chapter in the "Aligning Transformational Drivers" section.
- *The business enterprise's organizational maturity.* Another important factor that may impact the modification level required depends on the business enterprise's current state organizational maturity level. According to ITIL v3 literature, there are the several levels of organizational maturity. For a greater discussion on these, please refer to ITIL v3 literature (Figure 1.7).

Business Enterprise: Lives through a Complete Life Cycle

Business enterprises can be viewed as living systems; they are born, go through an infancy stage, grow and mature to a full business enterprise, and, if not managed appropriately, die. Just like a living system, a business enterprise also goes through a life cycle. There are very distinct life cycle phases that characterize the needs and capabilities of a business enterprise organization. Studies show that organizational changes follow a predictable pattern that can be characterized by developmental stages. These stages are sequential in nature, occur as a hierarchical progression that is not easily reversed, and involve a broad range of organizational activities and structures. One interesting question that is frequently asked is, "Do successful organizations need to change or do only the ones that are facing challenges need to change?" Interestingly, for successful organizations, change is the only constant. Organizations that are successful are successful primarily because they have been able to see a need to modify, as discussed in the previous section, and undertake appropriate steps to adjust, adapt, or evolve. As business enterprises modify the core processes to efficiently and effectively enable the business to grow as it is supposed to, IT organizations must align and deliver the right capabilities in an effective fashion (Shpilberg et al., 2007).

Organizations are fundamentally impacted by external environmental circumstances as well as internal factors. Business enterprises are successful because of their ability to foresee the changes in their environment and make necessary modifications in an efficient manner. These modifications, if made under the right circumstances, enable business enterprise organizations to make fundamental changes and evolve to their next life cycle phase. The relevant questions for us include:

- *How is IT related to these external and internal circumstances?* BSM, if implemented correctly, will enable the business enterprises to respond efficiently and effectively to ever-changing external and internal circumstances in an agile fashion. In Part II of this book, we will discuss in detail how BSM implementation will build this capability.
- *What can IT do to enable a business enterprise to achieve a state where it is able to realize its goals in the most effective and efficient manner?* In the Information Age, businesses are increasingly dependent on IT to enable their core processes. We will learn about BSM and business process management in greater detail in Chapter 2.
- *How can IT be as adaptive as the business enterprise needs to be? What can IT service management do to enable establishment of adaptive IT?* In Chapter 10, we will learn more about BSM in production. We will learn how an IT organization can be as adaptive as it needs to be and how continual iterative and incremental improvements and business–IT alignments will play a critical role in achieving this objective.

Evolution, Transformation, and Governance

Evolution is a process that has consistently improved extraordinarily complex organizations (organisms)—sometimes in remarkably short periods (Hooker, 1995). Similarly, business enterprise organizations have constantly been evolving throughout the Industrial Revolution to the recent information revolution. During the past decade, business enterprise organizations have experienced some of the most significant evolutions in the ways in which businesses operate and are managed. These evolutions resulted in an exponential growth in the opportunities available to business enterprises. If such evolutions take place in the absence of necessary governance, business enterprises face unforeseen stresses. To react to these stresses and challenges, business enterprises are driven by external and internal forces to undertake modifications. If the required modifications, as discussed earlier, are significant enough, they can result in large strategic transformational efforts. We will discuss some of the key transformational drivers later in this section. Let us briefly discuss the origin of these transformational drivers.

The emergence of the Internet has not only transformed inter- and intra-business relationships, but also business-to-customer relationships in revolutionary ways. In the late 1990s, IT began to be viewed as the major vehicle and the Internet as the key channel to transform the post–Industrial Revolution era in major ways. During pre-Internet times, business enterprise organizations focused on leveraging the power of computers, databases, and networks to better run their everyday operations and to better manage internal resources. The emergence of the Internet opened up a vast range of opportunities for entrepreneurial leaders to leverage this new technological capability in innovative ways and to build fortunes. As success stories found their way to public media, a perception started to take form that can be summarized as follows:

> Well, this IT is magical and can really help us solve all our problems. Let's invest and build IT systems and hope for the best. And, most importantly, let the experts be as innovative as they can be. We all know that governance and controls don't really help entrepreneurs. So let's keep those roadblocks out for now.

The result of this "magical IT" perception was that business enterprises of all sizes decided to make huge investments, without much governance, in building IT systems. The IT job market was booming. In the early 2000s, major efforts were undertaken by organizations of all sizes to be early adopters in this new world of Internet and IT. The dot.com era emerged, but did not last long. We all know what happened in the Silicon Valley: The bubble was followed by its bust. A few investors made fortunes, but most faced huge losses. When business enterprises encountered such environmental pressures, they moved in the opposite direction, which resulted in a drastic reduction in IT investments. Downsizing and layoffs followed the bust. One of the most damaging strategic impacts of this bust was a major reduction in IT investments. This created another set of challenges for business enterprises: Poor life cycle management of IT systems led to deteriorating performance of IT departments. Reduced investments in IT, coupled with business growth, led to ever-increasing complexities and reduced productivities. When faced with these and other related challenges, business enterprises reverted to analyzing what really happened.

The discussion above can be summarized in the *governance spectrum* shown in Figure 1.8. From the governance perspective, business enterprise organizations went from the extreme right, less governance than needed, to the extreme left, more governance than needed. Achieving balance is critical and we are now seeing that organizations are striving for that.

Governance needs to be business-aligned, balanced, and managed as "business-as-usual." Governance is not necessarily bad, nor does it necessarily prevent innovations. In fact, if implemented appropriately, governance becomes the enabler of greater effectiveness and efficiencies. The right level of governance will ensure that the investment opportunities in building IT capabilities are appropriately evaluated and that intelligent decisions are made that will create the most returns. We are now seeing emerging standards such as ISO/IEC-20000, Control Objectives for Information and Related Technology, ITIL, Capability Maturity Model Integration for Services Constellation, and others that are intended to provide guidelines and frameworks for organizations to implement the right level of governance to maximize profitability.

Business enterprise organizations are striving hard to find ways to leverage IT in innovative ways and that is expected to enable them to do more, better, faster, and cheaper. The right level of governance enables organizations to make carefully planned targeted investments so that IT capabilities are developed that enable enterprises to realize their business goals. Earlier in this chapter, we discussed the service tree concept and the inherent business process–business service–technical service–technology component traceability that it provides. In very simple terms, the service tree may function as a foundation for defining the right level of governance.

We know that governance needs to be implemented appropriately at all levels of an organization. The governance approach will depend on the level at which it is being implemented. At a

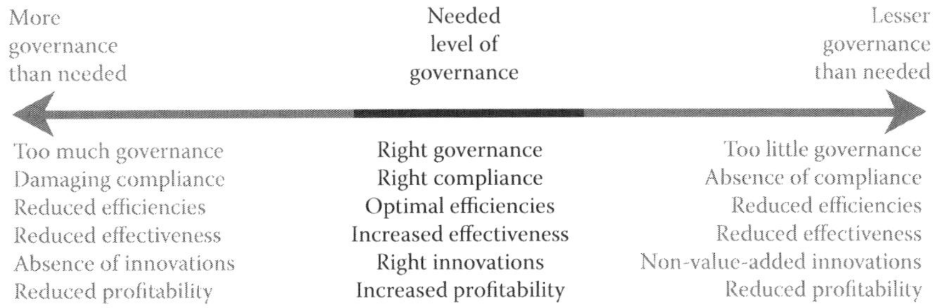

Figure 1.8 Governance spectrum.

Practical Tip: Having worked in some of the most regulated industries, I have first hand experienced situations whereby, in order to ensure that my organization delivers the desired business results, we defined the "Needed level of governance" at levels which were more liberal compared to other instances where we had to be more conservative. In other words, there is no single level of governance that will address all situations. You will have to consider the mandate of the organization/team, assess the risks, and custom define governance that will enable that organization/team to achieve it's intended vision in the most effective and efficient manner.

strategic level, IT strategy needs to be aligned with business strategy. At a program level, governance will need to ensure that the right programs are identified and selected so that the IT strategy can be realized. Within a program, governance will need to ensure that programs are managed appropriately and that they lead to a solution that enables business processes in a manner that satisfies the business needs in the most effective manner. When in production, governance needs to ensure that IT delivers on the commitments made to the businesses. In summary, governance will be needed at each level within an organization.

Different levels of governance shown in Figure 1.9 are:

- *Strategic governance* ensures that the IT strategy is completely aligned with the business strategy and that IT services are developed that support business services and enable business processes.

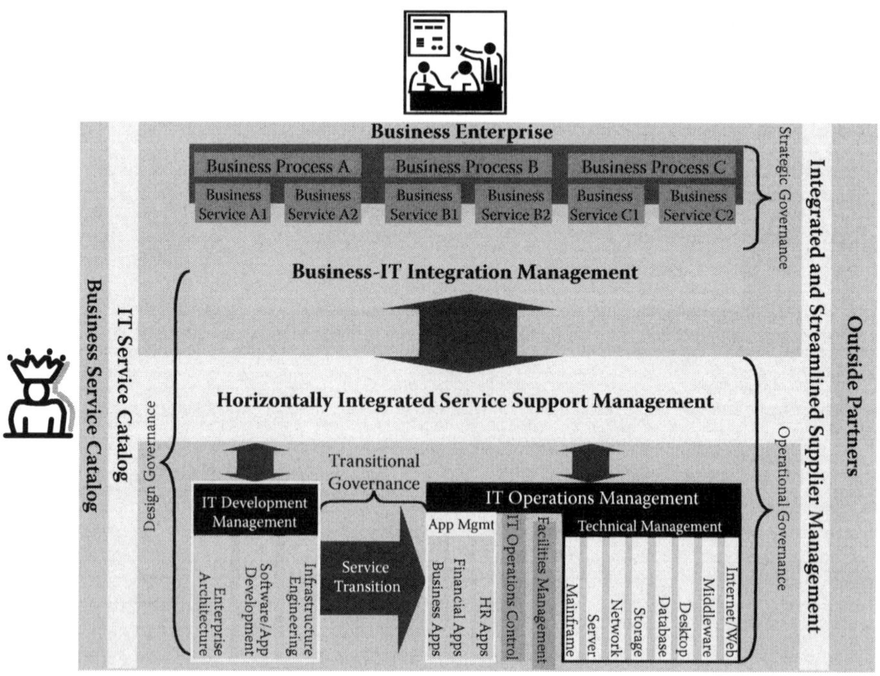

Figure 1.9 Governance at different levels.

- *Design governance* ensures that IT services are architected and designed in line with business needs. This may be implemented through appropriate program and project management functions.
- *Transition governance* ensures that when IT services are developed, they are transitioned to the operational environment in a controlled and coordinated fashion.
- *Operations governance* ensures that IT continues to deliver its services as agreed and expected.

Aligning Transformational Drivers

Requirements from the respective regulatory bodies across different industries (Securities and Exchange Commission, Basel II Framework, Food and Drug Administration, Public Company Accounting Overview Board, and Sarbanes–Oxley, among others) require respective business enterprises to launch program after program to address them. In most cases, the requirements arise independent of each other. This often creates a scenario where business enterprises respond to requirements in an uncoordinated and siloed manner. This trend, especially prevalent in larger business enterprises, forces individual organizational units to undertake separate and sometimes competing compliance programs to address regulatory requirements. A holistic approach to implementing governance is necessary. To maximize the returns on investments made on improving governance, we should clearly understand the key transformational drivers, how they are related to governance, and how we can align them effectively.

Transformational drivers, depending on particular business needs, are those that fuel most transformational efforts within medium to large business enterprise organizations. By nature, these transformations aim to fundamentally transform the way businesses are run and IT is managed and operated. Otherwise, these would be incremental improvements. Figure 1.10 graphically

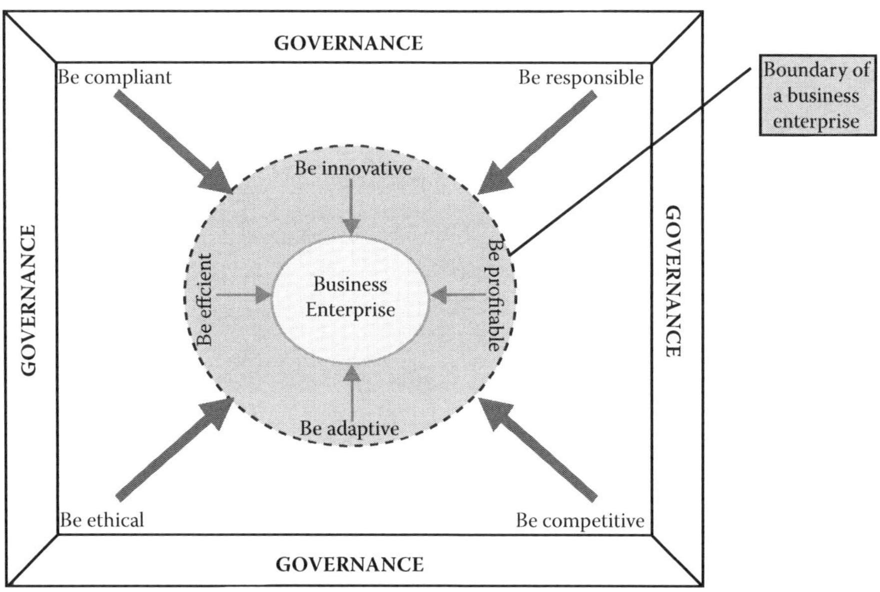

Figure 1.10 Transformational drivers.

shows some of the key internal and external transformational drivers. Note that governance plays the most critical role across all of these drivers, from inception to final implementation.

Business enterprises are constantly under a wide range of external and internal pressures that shape their respective transformational strategies. The following are some of most significant internal and external drivers that play an important role and, therefore, need to be managed effectively.

External Drivers

The following external drivers affect an organization's strategies.

Be Compliant

Business enterprises operate in a larger community and need to comply with the law and regulations of the land. Most recently, we have seen emergence of compliance standards such as SOX to put regulations and governance around financial systems.

Be Responsible and Ethical

These drivers are different from the economic ones. It is interesting to see how business enterprises leverage social responsibility efforts to their financial advantage. How important is social responsibility? How are enterprises responding? What benefit, in terms of financial gains, do these enterprises expect? Let us look closely at what some of the largest corporations are doing. Corporations such as Bank of America, Aetna Life and Casualty Company, Shell Petroleum, and Chase Manhattan Bank are responding to social responsibilities and have begun to include *social audits, social action reports,* and *social balance sheets* in their annual reports. Although the form, content, and sophistication of such accountings vary considerably, they assess, typically, company performance with regard to racial and ethnic minorities, women, the environment, underdeveloped nations, consumers, employees, and the general community (Epstein, 1976).

Be Competitive

Business enterprises operate in a competitive world. To be successful, they need to operate efficiently to keep the operating costs low and effectively to maintain the quality of products and services that they offer.

Internal Drivers

Often, transformations are needed not only to address the needs generated as a result of external forces, but also to respond to internal drivers that may or may not be linked to the external ones. We normally see business enterprises combine a range of drivers to strategize and achieve the desired transformations. Some of the significant internal drivers are discussed below.

Be Profitable

The motive of any business enterprise is financial gain; the method is essentially purchase and sale. The aim and usual outcome is an accumulation of wealth (Walter, 1991; Walker, 1968; Nussbaum,

1968; Marx, 1979). Accumulation of wealth, according to Veblen, serves as the fundamental objectives of a business enterprise. Investments are made for profit, and industrial plants and processes are capitalized on the basis of their profit-yielding capacity (Veblen, 1996, p. 90). This is of particular interest to us. Integrating IT with the business and enabling efficient processes is at the core of ensuring effective service management.

Be Innovative

There is a growing recognition among economists that the innovation process is key to understanding the economic development and that business enterprise is an organization that is central to the innovation process. Yet, despite considerable research that draws inspiration from the seminal insights of Joseph Schumpeter, "innovation economists" have yet to expound a rigorous and relevant theory of innovative enterprise. In my experience, I have sometimes seen businesses drive innovation and, at other times, advances in technology drive innovations in the business processes. For example, John Reed of Citi had this vision, "Citi never sleeps." Automated teller machines did not exist then. His vision drove technology innovation and led to their development. Figure 1.11 shows how business innovation drives technology innovation and how the ultimate impact is the creation of business value.

Innovations in technology drive innovations in businesses (Figure 1.12). An excellent example of such technological innovation has been the emergence of the Internet, a technology initially developed for defense collaboration purposes that brought revolutions across the business world.

Closely related to innovation is the subject of "learning organizations," which means that organizations constantly learn from their experiences and employ those experiences to achieving greater business gains. According to Nevis et al. (1995), while companies do not usually regard learning

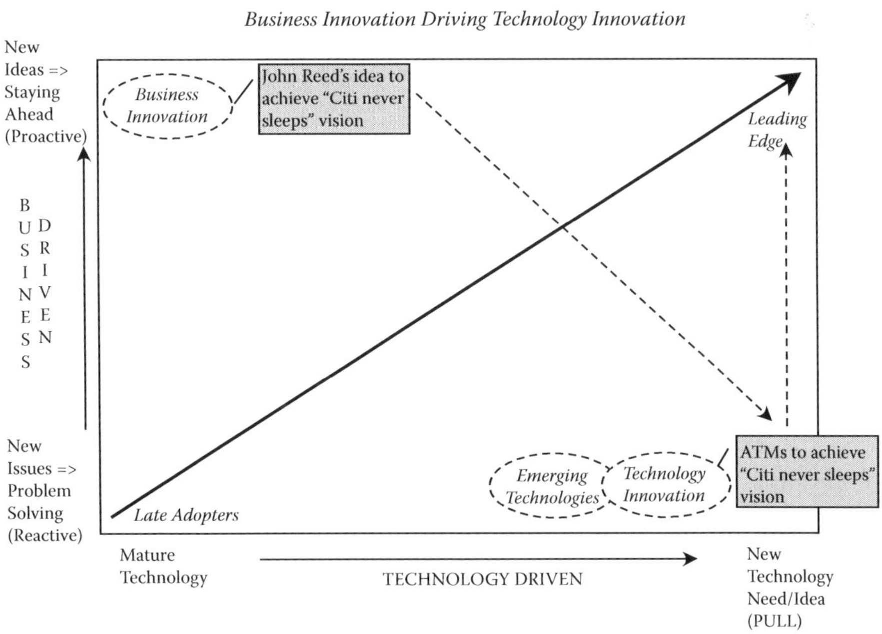

Figure 1.11 Business innovation drives technology innovation.

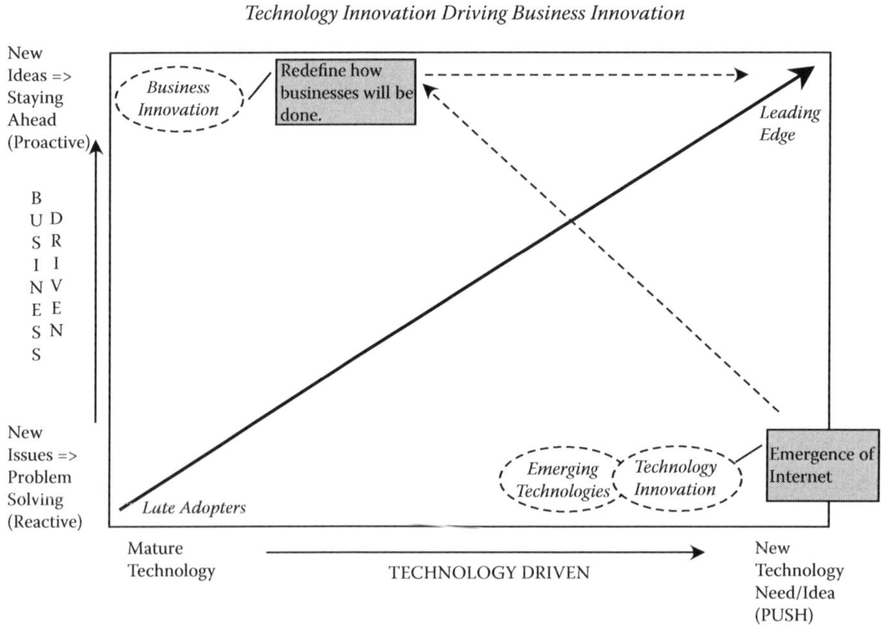

Figure 1.12 Technology innovation drives business innovation.

as a function of production, their research on successful firms indicates that three learning-related factors are important to their success:

1. Well-developed core competencies that serve as launch points for new products and services
2. An attitude that supports continuous improvement in the business' value-added chain
3. The ability to fundamentally renew or revitalize.

These factors identify some of the qualities of an effective learning organization that diligently pursues a constantly enhanced knowledge base. This knowledge allows for the development of competencies and incremental or transformational change. If implemented appropriately, BSM can provide a tremendous platform upon which business enterprises are able to emerge as true learning organizations.

Summary

In this chapter, we learned about service management and how it relates to IT. To build a better appreciation of why organizations need to view Business Service Management as a means to achieving Business Service Management, i.e., when all components are managed to enable business processes in the most effective and efficient manner. We have also seen over the past decade or so, how the emergence of the Internet provided the platform for IT to truly evolve the way business enterprises conduct their respective businesses. With this evolution, there is more need than ever before to integrate business and IT in ways that generate true business value, leading to the creation of innovative products and services. Under such demands, BSM provides the right set of competencies to achieve the much-needed business–IT integration.

References

Bertalanffy, L. V. 1951. General systems theory: A new approach to unity of science, *Hum. Biol.* 23: 303–361.

Case, G., and G. Spalding. 2007. ITIL v3 Continual Service Improvement, Office of Government Commerce. The Stationary Office, UK.

Gibson, J. L., J. M. Ivancevich, and J. H. Donnelly Jr. 1994. *Organizations: Behavior, Structure, Processes.* CA: McGraw Hill/Irwin.

Hooker, C. 1995. *Philosophical Psychology* 8(3): 287–299.

Johnson, R. A., F. E. Kast, and , J. E. Rosenzweig. 1963. *The Theory and Management of Systems,* New York: McGraw-Hill Book Company, Inc.

Johnson, R. A., F. E. Kast, and J. E. Rosenzweig. 1964. Systems theory and management, *Mange. Sci.* 10(2): 367–384.

Nussbaum, F. L. 1968. A history of the economic institutions of modern Europe: An introduction to Der moderne Kapitalismus of Werner Sombart (Reprints of economic classics). New York: A. M. Kelley.

Marx, K. 1979. Kapital, Das (Everyman's Library; no. 848). Duttan Adult.

Quinn, R., and K. Cameron. 1983. Organizational life cycles and shifting criteria of effectiveness: Some preliminary evidence. *Manage. Sci.* 29: 33–51.

Shpilberg, D., S. Berez, R. Puryear, and S. Shah. 2007. Avoiding the alignment trap in information technology. *MIT Sloan Manage. Rev.* 49: 51–58.

Service Design, p. 263.

Plambeck, J. A. 1995. Le Chatelier Principle (1850–1936). http://dwb.unl.edu/Teacher/NSF/C09/C09Links/www.chem.ualberta.ca/courses/plambeck/p101/p01101.htm.

Veblen, T. (1996). *Social Science Classics Series: The Theory of Business Enterprise.* (3rd Ed). New Jersey: Transaction Publishers.

Walter, B. 1991. *Economic Studies.* New York: Scholarly Pr.

Walker, F. A. 1968. The Wages Question: A treatise on wages and the wages class (Reprints of economic classics). New York: A. M. Kelly.

Chapter 2

Integrating IT with Business

In this chapter, we will learn more about the role of IT in enabling businesses to achieve their business objectives in a more effective manner. When we speak about enabling business through IT services, business service management (BSM) is difficult to avoid. As discussed, BSM requires relating the business performance directly to IT operations performance. In other words, is IT delivering the right services at the right levels to its customers so that the desired business performance is achieved? This business performance can be measured in terms of revenue, profitability, customer satisfaction, etc. To relate IT performance to business performance, IT must define appropriate Critical Success Factors or CSFs and necessary Key Performance Indicators or KPIs that provide visibility into its contributions to business success. For example, in the case of an online retail business, one of the KPIs may be the level of availability of online order processing systems during the holiday season. If business requires its online order processing processes to be available at 99.999% during the holiday season, did IT deliver the desired services at that level? Such measurements will enable targeting of improvements that create the most value for the business. It is important to appreciate that BSM is a means to an end, that is, enabling businesses to achieve greater profits, faster growth, compliance with regulatory requirements, or any other business goals through an innovative and effective use of IT. BSM refers to a culture in which serving the business and managing IT to deliver the needed services at agreed levels are the key objectives. BSM will involve innovative use of software to automate the right processes, targeting the right service improvements that make the most impact, improving IT processes to ensure that services are managed and delivered as committed, and continually aligning IT organization to better align with businesses and customers.

Having discussed the BSM, let us now look at what happened in the IT industry over the past decade or so. We have witnessed how the emergence of the Internet impacted core business processes. We have seen large business initiatives to reengineer core business processes to exploit the opportunities that IT and the Internet have to offer. Look at the following examples of industrial evolution: eBay has redefined and created new boundaries for bidding processes; Amazon is continually evolving how it serves the retail market; and insurance companies have defined new ways to sell and manage insurance policies. All of these innovations required tremendous reengineering of the fundamental ways in which these business enterprises carry out their businesses and deliver their products and services to their customers. Such advancements have put a great deal of pressure on IT to grow and evolve to support business growth and evolution and not necessarily only to provide back-end support. Such expectations from businesses and customers have put IT in the spotlight and IT management and practitioners are being challenged to deliver more, better, faster, cheaper, and in ways that advance achievement of core business objectives. To mature an IT organization to a point where IT services actually enable and support business processes and IT performances are measured in terms of business performance, BSM is implemented based on the guidelines provided by the Information Technology Infrastructure Library (ITIL v3). Business enterprises where IT services enable business processes, and IT performances are measured in terms of business performances, are known as IT-enabled business enterprises. In my consulting engagements with some of the key financial and pharmaceutical companies, I have witnessed first-hand an evolution in the ways business managers and leaders view IT. In most forward-looking and innovative business enterprises, business management has started to appreciate business capabilities that IT can help achieve. At one of the town hall sessions, a senior business manager discussed future business capabilities that he was visualizing for his business unit and expressed those capabilities in terms of IT services. That was an amazing indication of how businesses have started to appreciate the potential value that IT can offer in enabling business processes. This is good news for those IT managers and leaders who have long waited for the day when IT could become a value-added partner of their respective customers and businesses. Those senior and mid-level IT managers who still believe that IT is a back-office function, and that IT teams do not need to understand business processes, need to change the way they think about IT before it is too late. If you are not delivering value to your customers and businesses, then someone else will come in and fill that vacuum.

In this chapter, we will learn about the various IT organizational maturity levels and what it really means for IT to become a value-added business partner. There are still enterprises where neither business nor IT management views IT as a potential value-added business partner and statements such as, "We are just in a support role," "We are just a cost center," "We know what we need to deliver and our customers don't need any more," and so on, are common in those environments.

In today's business enterprises and across a range of industry verticals—from manufacturing, energy, retail and distribution, construction, entertainment, pharmaceutical, to financial and other service industries—IT can truly evolve into a value-add business partner. In becoming a value-add business partner, IT must attain a comprehensive understanding of business strategies, core business processes that will implement those strategies to deliver the right products and services to its customers, and specific business services that IT needs to deliver to its business customers to enable those core business processes. This will require IT to focus on aligning its strategies to integrate with business needs, and on further improving its efficiencies, so that it is able to most effectively deliver what is needed.

In my experience, in most environments where IT organizations are not viewed as business partners, it is mostly because the IT organization lacks understanding of its customers, their businesses, and what they really need from IT. Peter O'Neill, a researcher at Forrester Research, rightly states in his paper that the greatest inhibitor of achievement of higher levels of BSM maturity is the reluctance of IT staff to change their *modus operandi* to become more business-centric (O'Neill et al., 2007). It may not be unreasonable to state that, unfortunately, in low-maturity IT organizations, IT becomes its own enemy.

This chapter is about business–IT integration. By the end of this chapter, you will have achieved a comprehensive understanding of key service management concepts and will be able to answer the following critical questions:

- How are IT service management (ITSM) and BSM—concepts that have already been discussed in Chapter 1—related or not related? What do these concepts have to do with the emerging business–IT integration buzzword?
- Is ITSM, BSM, or business–IT integration right for us? How do we position our IT organization? What factors should we consider when setting up our IT vision?
- What is meant by *aligning business and IT strategies*? How do we actually achieve that? How does aligning business and IT strategies help IT become more effective and efficient?
- What are business processes? How do these relate to business services? Is IT service the same as business service? Is technical service something different from IT service?
- What does it mean to enable business processes? How should we go about achieving that?
- What is the big picture of business–IT integration?

ITSM, BSM, and Business–IT Integration

There are a lot of different perspectives and definitions of ITSM and how it actually relates to BSM. Where does ITIL come in and how do they all relate to each other?

According to Evelyn Hubbert, ITSM aids the change of an IT organization from a support group to a service group in which ITIL processes are introduced (Hubbert, 2008). For most IT organizations, such a change is transformational and requires reorganization from siloed, technology-focused teams into process- and service-oriented groups. ITIL v3 defines a set of good practices (compared to best practices, which assume ideal circumstances and which may differ from one organization to another) that enable the delivery of high-quality, low-cost IT services to the lines of businesses. Using ITIL guidelines, IT organizations are able to implement processes that enable them to manage the services they provide from end to end. This encompasses conception of a need, identification of an IT service to meet that need, architecture, design, deployment, operations, and retirement. This capability is ITSM. According to Hubbert (2008), ITSM supports the change of an IT organization from a technology silo into an organization that leverages processes to deliver IT services to its customers. Business relationship management or account management functions are introduced and a service management tier is developed. Before we get into detailed discussion of BSM, let us see how different practitioners and researchers define it. According to Forrester, "Business service management dynamically links business-focused IT services to the underlying IT infrastructure."

A business-focused IT service may be a specific IT service or part of a business process, but it must support a significant, visible business metric for a business owner. In the context of BSM, an IT service is not a business service if it is not visible to a business user or stakeholder outside of IT (O'Neill et al., 2007). Business–IT integration occurs when all IT efforts and investments are solely focused on creating business value for its customers. More and more IT organizations and business enterprises are realizing that business–IT integration is a state where a business makes the best use of its IT resources and capabilities to enable enterprises to meet their respective goals and objectives. BSM is not the end goal; it is the vehicle by which to achieve business–IT integration. Business–IT integration is the end goal and BSM provides the means to that end. IT organizations aspiring to become business-integrated, value-add partners with their customers can achieve that vision through implementing BSM. ITSM provides the most critical foundation to achieve BSM.

It is important to note that BSM is not about implementing a single silo process or function, such as establishing a service desk function or implementing incident or change management. BSM requires that appropriate ITIL v3 processes (depending on organizationally specific business needs, priorities, IT maturity, etc.) are implemented or improved to enable the IT organization to manage the delivery of needed services at agreed levels to ensure that the desired business results are realized.

In IT-specific terms, BSM is the capability of an IT organization to align and re-align and to manage its underpinning IT components (application, software, hardware, network, and others) such that measurable business value is created.

Figure 2.1 shows that the quality of service management processes (e.g., change management, incident management) determines the quality of services that the IT organization is able to deliver. Consider the following scenario. If e-mail is one of the services that you deliver to your customer, the amount of time it will take you to create a new e-mail account for a new employee will be based on how well your request fulfillment processes are executed by the fulfillment teams. Your efficiency and effectiveness in delivering your services to your customers is determined by the maturity of your underlying service management processes.

BSM enables the achievement of business–IT integration, that is, IT delivers high quality business services at expected levels consistently to its end users. In addition, BSM ensures that IT performance is measured based on the performance of its businesses and customers. BSM prerequisites, according to Forrester/O'Neill are infrastructure resource mapping, business process mapping, end-to-end management, and dynamic linking of processes to infrastructure.

Let us look at another BSM view. Cappelli (2006) views BSM as a tool that helps IT present a more business-oriented view of IT service quality and communicate the results in a language that

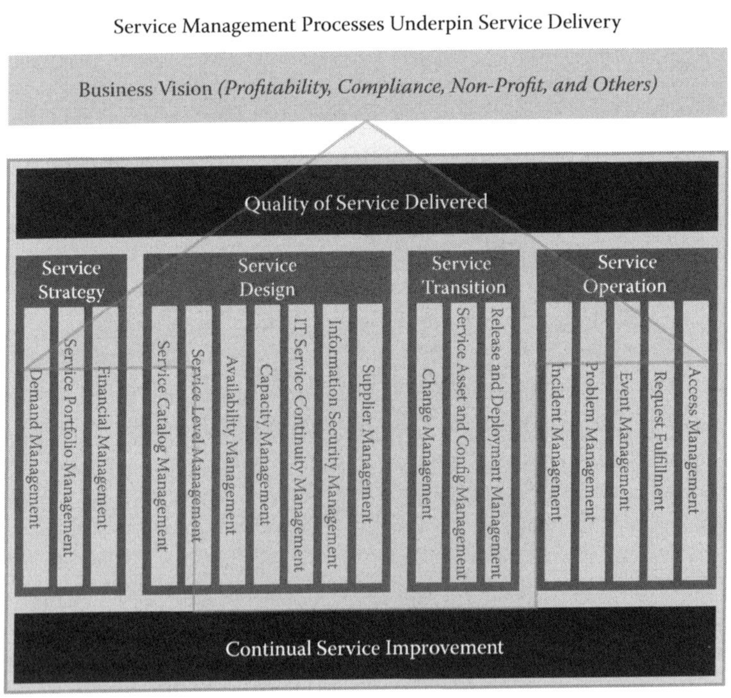

Figure 2.1 Service management processes underpin service delivery.

businesses and customers can better understand. BSM can help drive both agility and innovation when IT services are reported to the customer in real time, with corresponding business processes and even financial data. Creating valuable business-oriented IT service views is a complex process that starts with detailed conversations between the IT organization and its business unit customers to:

- First, understand the critical business processes and vital business functions.
- Second, define the high-priority, business-oriented IT services that are required to enable those business processes.
- Finally, document the relevant service-level expectations based on business impact or cost of a business process outage.

Cappelli (2006) further defines BSM as a "category of IT operations management software products that link the availability and performance status of IT infrastructure components to business-oriented IT services that enable business processes." At its core, BSM is about providing the capability to manage technology as a business service, rather than as individual IT infrastructure components. BSM is more than just a tool. It is a way of managing each IT component so that it delivers measurable business value.

According to Forrester (O'Neill et al., 2007), "Business service management dynamically links business-focused IT services to the underlying IT infrastructure." A business-focused IT service may be a specific IT service or part of a business process, but it must support significant, visible business metric for a business owner in the context of BSM. An IT service is not a business service if it is not visible to a business user or stakeholder outside of IT (O'Neill et al., 2007). ITIL provides the guidelines to achieve BSM. According to IDC research (Evergreen Systems, Inc., 2006), a survey of 11 different global organizations from across different industries and geographies shows that a 30% overall improvement in efficiency was achieved as a result of implementing numerous ITIL processes and improving those already in place. Specific improvements, with the percentage of improvement, include:

- Incident management and service desk support: 40.5%
- Server management and support: 30.9%
- Change management: 28.4%
- Network infrastructure management and maintenance: 23.1%
- Configuration databases maintenance: 22.8%
- Applications management: 10%
- Problem management: 9.4%
- Service level management: 8.5%
- Increase in average number of network devices controlled per full time employee: 57%
- Average reduction in headcount growth: 12.2%

Other significant gains include the following:

- Three-year cost of investment: $2.1 million
- Annual cost savings and increased revenue: $14.5 million
- Net present value of three-year savings: $26.7 million
- Payback period: 11.8 months
- Return on investment (ROI) over the 3-year life of project: 422%

Another key recent success includes a $500 million savings for Proctor & Gamble, as well as a 6–8% reduction in operating costs and a 15–20% reduction in technology personnel (Ferrarini, 2007).

Gartner Research (2006) also surveyed 350 senior IT executives in 2005 and determined that "There was a strong positive correlation between those not using ITIL, and the degree to which respondents felt their infrastructure was under-funded. It is therefore believed that this reflects their focus on creating a service driven organization, the need to be competitive and achieve greater maturity."

Figure 2.2 shows the conceptual organizational architecture that represents the core principles that should underpin the achievement of larger BSM goals. The illustrated organizational architecture aims to enable IT organizations to achieve BSM through the delivery of high-quality business process–aligned business services in a cost-effective and efficient manner. Please note that the BSM implementation exposes managed business services that enable specific business processes and are visible to and understandable by business users and business customers.

Most IT organizations that are at lower maturity levels—those that are technology focused—exhibit the characteristics of technologically siloed organizations. BSM is not entirely achieved by implementing BMC's ITSMv7 (one of the key IT Service Management tool vendors) or any other service management tool. A tool or technology is one critical component that helps enforce the desired behavioral changes necessary to achieve the larger cultural transformation. I mention this specifically because I have seen good intentions end in not-so-successful projects. A chief information officer of one of my clients (a large multinational company) approved about $12 million for the first phase of such a transformation effort. The key objective was to transform the

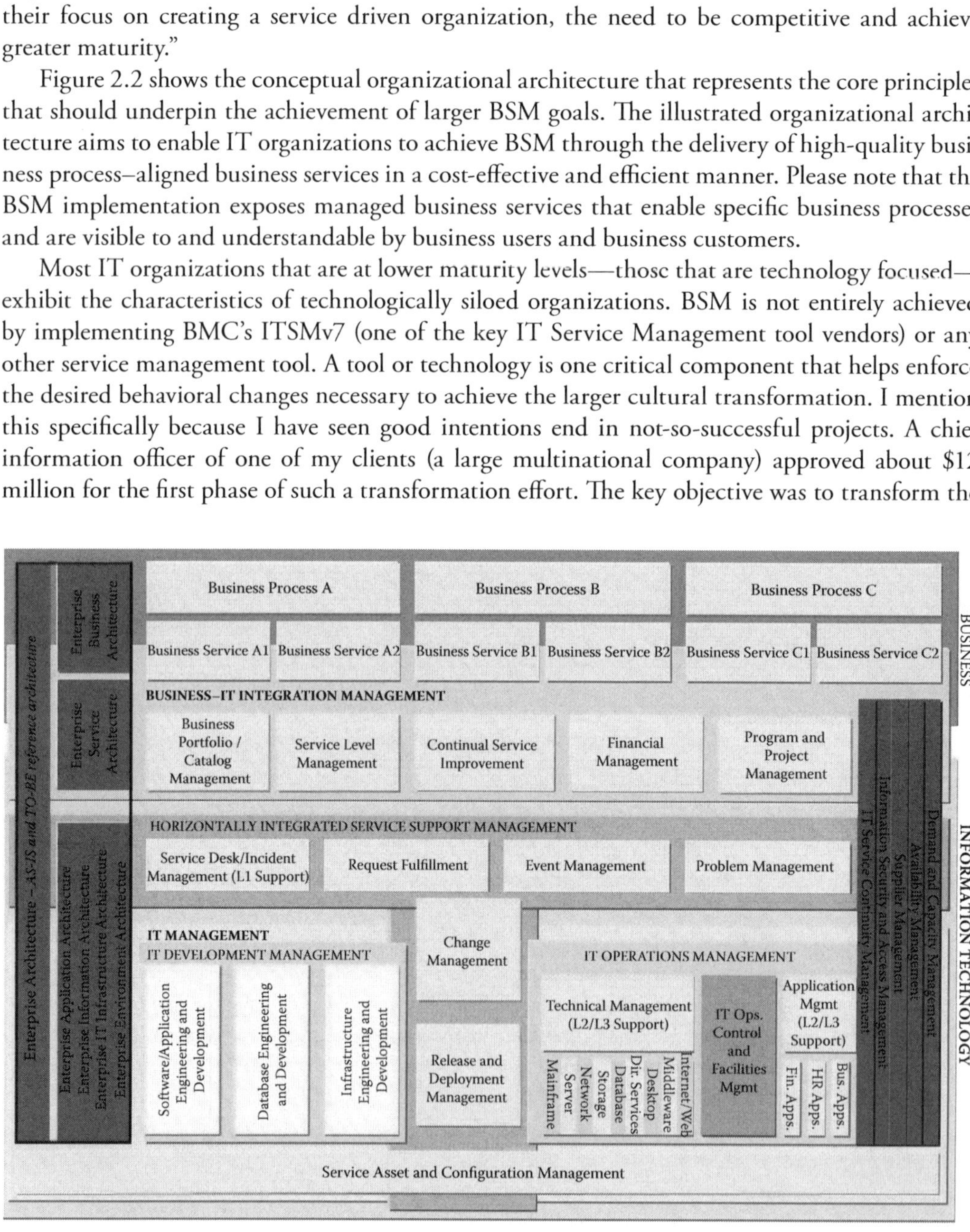

Figure 2.2 Conceptual organizational architecture to support business service management.

technology-aligned IT organizations into business-aligned, service-oriented BSM organizations. Mismanagement ended this effort, envisioned as a multiyear undertaking, in less than a year because the project team was unable to demonstrate tangible and quantifiable benefits to keep the momentum going. The key factors that led to the failure of this major initiative included:

- Lack of appropriate ITIL v3 and BSM expertise
- Bringing tools before processes
- Lack of appropriate program management and governance
- Inappropriate assignment of overall organizational transformation efforts to technologists
- Effort inappropriately driven by tool vendors
- Inappropriate management of key organizational transformation aspects (vision and strategy, governance, people, processes, tools and organization)

When the project team and management realized that ITSM and BSM were more than just deploying ITIL-compliant tools, it was too late. Upon realizing what actually happened, the organization undertook a major effort to realign organizational roles and responsibilities to match the processes implemented by the tool. When the organization and teams began to use the tool, it was discovered that the tool had performance and capacity issues. In summary, the initiative that was envisioned to help transform the technology-based organization to a business-focused organization was mismanaged to the extent that it became a firefighting exercise or, colloquially, "putting lipstick on a pig." Deploying what our vendors call an "ITIL v3–compliant" tool into a low-maturity organization will not change anything. In fact, it will inflict tremendous damage on the overall transformational effort. Once again, it is important to appreciate that tools are important parts of enforcing the process and that tools are not the only aspect. Depending on organizational process maturity and readiness, it may actually not be beneficial to put a tool in place in the beginning.

It is an important lesson to learn that there is no silver bullet for transforming a technology-focused organization to one that is business-focused. It requires a consistent, well-thought-out and well-planned approach that migrates a given organization, in small incremental steps, to a higher-maturity level, business-aligned, and business-focused IT organization. IT organizations that only focus on tools, or any other single aspect, normally spend millions of dollars without realizing the true benefits of BSM and lose the all-important sponsorship to continue on this transformational journey.

Positioning IT Organization and Establishing the Vision

In my mind, it is very clear that IT is there to enable businesses and customers to achieve their respective business objectives. Businesses and customers really do not care whether it is a UNIX platform, Windows, a blade server, or some other new, more powerful box. They care about how much more efficient and effective they are in doing what they need to do to deliver what they need to deliver to their end customers. The extent to which a business enterprise is able to exploit IT capabilities to achieve its business objectives is determined by the maturity of its IT organization. ITIL v3 provides a set of good practices for an organization to build IT capabilities so that it is able to deliver what the organization's customers are looking for. Figure 2.3 (ITIL v3 Continual Service Improvement) shows an organizational maturity model. It ranges from a technology shop (i.e., level 1) to a value-chain, value-add partner (i.e., level 5).

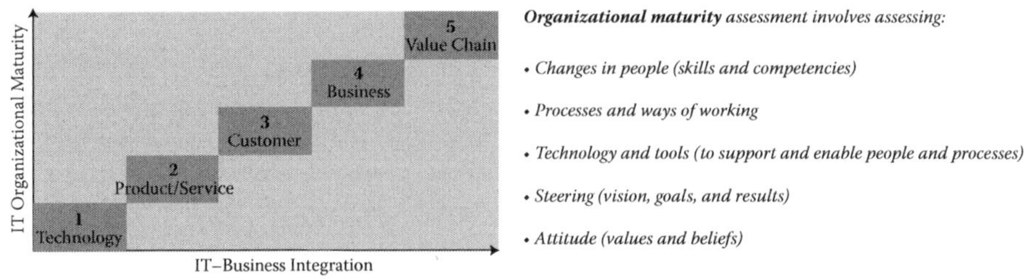

Figure 2.3 Organizational maturity model.

Before discussing IT organization positioning, let us briefly discuss what these different levels represent and that the maturity cannot be achieved in one step. Instead, maturity is achieved one level at a time and requires consistent effort.

Level 1: Technology

IT organizations at maturity level 1, *technology*, demonstrate the following characteristics:

- They are technology-focused and technology-aligned.
- There is a lack of appreciation of which technology components enable which business services. IT staff members largely look at technology components as top-end or lower-end (i.e., great memory, multiprocessor, high-speed, high-end technology, etc.).
- IT investments are primarily made based on technological aspirations rather than business enablement and return on investments. New technologies are acquired because they are new and may have some business uses.
- Technology domains are managed in technology silos. For example, problems are prioritized and resolved based on technology focus, not because of the potential impact of these problems on business or customer priorities.
- IT organizations plan and deliver their services largely in a vacuum without a comprehensive appreciation of the business needs.
- IT organizations largely find themselves in a reactive mode of operating.

Level 2: Products/Services

IT organizations at maturity level 1 are technology-focused. They understand what each technology is capable of, but lack understanding of how these technological capabilities may benefit their customers or businesses. The next level of maturity is *products/services*. What that means is that the IT organization is now able to understand what services or products (that may be used by customers or businesses) are produced by these technologies. IT organizations at maturity level 2 exhibit the following characteristics:

- IT organizations understand the products or services that are created or delivered by their technology components.
- There is a better understanding of which technology components deliver what services.
- Organizations are still largely technology-driven because of a lack of understanding of business and customer needs.

To summarize, IT organizations at maturity level 2 understand the products and/or services that they deliver. However, they lack a clear and comprehensive appreciation of whether these products or services are actually aligned with business needs. In addition, at maturity level 2, IT organizations may not understand whether the products or services that they produce have any customers. They ask questions such as, "Is there anybody who is going to pay for the products or services that we produce?" In ITIL v3, the service catalog provides a list of products and/or services that you currently produce and deliver. We will discuss this in greater detail later in the book.

Level 3: Customers

IT organizations at maturity level 2 have a clear understanding of the technology that they have and the products and/or services that those technological capabilities are able to deliver. However, if they do not understand the market they are trying to serve and the needs of their customers that they are trying to address, they may actually be producing products or services for which their customers are not willing to pay. They may be making investments in building the technological capabilities that actually produce the products or services that are not required.

At maturity level 3, *customers*, IT organizations are able to clearly understand their customers and what they actually need. At this level of maturity, IT organizations are able to identify the gaps between the products or services that they produce and the products or services that customers actually need. Based on this, IT organizations are able to improve and define services so that the actual customer or business needs are met.

Level 4: Business

With the concrete understanding of technology capabilities, products and/or services produced, and the needs of the customers and/or businesses, IT organizations are able to run IT as a business at maturity level 4. Some of the characteristics are as follows:

- IT organizations clearly understand the market (customers and/or businesses) that it is trying to service.
- IT organizations understand their distinctive capabilities and in what services they are able to provide differentiating services at competitive prices.
- Customers/businesses have control over IT-related costs and what they want from IT, and they appreciate the value delivered.
- IT organizations are no longer a cost center. In fact, IT organizations are able to compete with other outside (in case of internal IT organizations) IT vendors and demonstrate that they are able to provide higher-quality services and lower costs. This is organization maturity level 4.

Level 5: Value Chain

IT organizations at maturity level 5 clearly understand the value chain, that is, how IT services enable business processes and ultimately create value for the end-customers (customers of their customers and/or businesses). These IT organizations are able to clearly relate their IT services to business processes and business products/services. At this level, IT organizations actually become value-added partners. Some of the characteristics are as follows:

- IT organizations intimately understand their business, vision, and strategy.
- IT organizations appreciate the key challenges that present risk to the business vision.
- IT organizations understand what services they provide and how those services enable their respective business partners.
- IT organizations are able to plan and build new and innovative IT services that help mitigate business risks and position the business for success and higher profitability in the marketplace.

Having discussed the various maturity levels, the next important question to ask yourself is what level is appropriate for your business and customers. Do all IT organizations aspire to become value-added business partners with their customers? One can simply argue that if any of the core business process is automated or enabled by some level of IT services, then IT is perhaps playing a critical role in the success of that business. Other relevant aspects that may be considered in determining the relative importance of IT are as follows:

- **Reports and dashboards.** Are reports and dashboards generated by using IT systems? Are these reports used by senior management to make important business decisions? Are these reports used by IT senior management to plan IT improvements?
- **Computational needs.** Do businesses, customers, or end users depend heavily on IT systems to perform complex, large-volume data analytics and calculations? Do these computations provide business-critical information? Can businesses be profitable without such computational capabilities? Are IT systems used to store the results of these computations?
- **User base.** What percentage of total employees in the company (in the case of an internal IT service provider) or in the customer's company (in the case of an external IT service provider) depend on IT for completing their everyday tasks?
- **Business challenges.** Are business challenges associated with lack of proper IT services? Do customers/businesses face challenges if IT does not deliver the right products/services at the right levels?
- **Communication and collaboration.** Do customers use IT for collaboration- and communication-related activities?
- **Business process enablement.** Is IT used to enable all or part of business processes?
- **Support IT services vs. enabling IT services.** Finally, is IT used in a support function or is it viewed as an enabling function? Do customers/businesses believe that IT is there solely to support their work through e-mail, storage, telephone, and other basic support services? Or, is IT used to enable businesses to better provide their products/services to their end customers? For example, in a manufacturing business, does the business depend on IT for their supply chain management processes?

To achieve organizational maturity level 3 or above, a comprehensive effort to improve service management processes needs to be planned and implemented. If an organization is currently at maturity level 1, then achieving maturity level 3 or above will mean more cultural transformation than any other single factor. In the process, the overall IT capability—the ability of an organization to achieve the most business benefits from its IT resources—is enhanced.

Is Business–IT Integration Right for Us?

This is an important question for business as well as IT leadership. It really depends on the maturity of both businesses and IT organizations. I have come across business leaders who have a clearer picture of how they can leverage IT in achieving their business successes than the IT leadership does. In low-maturity organizations, integrating IT with the business means cultural and organizational transformation. Such transformations require changes across all aspects—process, people, organization, technology, and partners—of the IT organization and, therefore, do not come without high inherent risks of failure. In most cases, such transformational efforts are high-budget, high-risk, and high-return endeavors and warrant a critical review of whether this is something that needs to be undertaken. According to a survey of IT directors and managers from across 90 companies carried out by Evergreen Systems at the September 2006 itSMF National Conference, top priorities that drove ITIL projects included service quality, efficiency/cost reduction, and IT/business alignment. On the other hand, resistance to organizational change and unproven business value were rated as the most significant barriers to ITIL initiatives adoption (Evergreen Systems, 2006).

A business case should be developed with a clear ROI and other relevant metrics. Even with an overall business plan, all new transformational projects require executive sponsorship and long-term funding. Achieving BSM by implementing ITIL v3 is a complex endeavor and, if not envisioned and planned appropriately, it may end in disaster. In my experience, those BSM projects that do not have a clear strategy in the beginning are most likely to show little or no business value. Improvements may be realized in small pockets, but not at the business level.

Development of an ITIL/BSM strategy is not unlike the development of any organizational change undertaking in a large organization. Accordingly, it should be conceived, planned, and executed as if the organization is going to go through an organizational change. Kotter (1990) recommended a well-ventilated approach to such organizational change management. Key components are:

- Establishing a sense of urgency
- Creating a coalition
- Developing a clear vision
- Sharing the vision
- Empowering people to clear obstacles
- Securing short-term wins
- Consolidating efforts
- Keeping the effort moving forward
- Anchoring the change

The first six months of the transformation are the most critical. Effective planning, governance, risk, and change management will play an important role in demonstrating the value to be realized and keeping the momentum going. We will learn how such successes can be planned and achieved later in this book.

Aligning Business and IT Strategies

In business enterprises with low-maturity IT organizations, IT is traditionally perceived to be a necessary evil and treated as a cost center because of the following key business reasons:

- IT costs are taxed across all businesses/customers, regardless of whether a particular business/customer uses any of the things provided by IT or not. These things are normally not well understood in low-maturity organizations and may not actually qualify as something that is delivering value to the customers. Therefore, they may not be services.
- Businesses/customers really do not understand what their IT organization does for them and, in most cases, may not have visibility into what they are paying for and why.
- Businesses/customers have no control over whether they get what they want.
- Businesses/customers view IT as a necessary evil because they know that they need certain things from IT and that they will not be able to function without those things. In other cases, the existing IT organization/service provider is the only option available and businesses/customers do not have any choice.
- Businesses/customers believe that IT does not know what they do and what pains they go through on a daily basis. In addition, businesses/customers believe that they will have to go through a painful journey to have IT enable their business processes.
- IT is perceived as disconnected from the business and as a spender that does not itself understand what it costs them to create their services.
- Business/customers believe that IT makes promises and rarely delivers.
- Last, if businesses/customers could, they would get rid of IT in a split-second.

I can just continue down this list. You get the point. These are the real pain points of most businesses and customers that have to deal with low-maturity IT organizations. The most unfortunate part of this is that continuing disappointments in IT have largely led businesses/customers not to believe in IT. The result may be that, under these conditions, if you go to your business partners with revised service level agreements (SLAs), they will not even sit down to look at them. The most common reaction that business relationship managers or account managers get is, "You don't know our pain points." This is not an exaggeration and is based on my experiences with real clients. The key question is, "How do you go about creating that trust again?" On the IT side, we must realize the following facts:

- *Understand what you do for your customers and how well you do it.* First, and most important, you need to clearly understand what you do for your customers. This will involve interviewing business customers, end users, and IT stakeholders. You will need to quickly establish a clear understanding of your customers' pain points on all that they receive from you.
- *Stop that bleeding immediately.* When you understand what you do for your customers and their pain points, plan (as part of the larger BSM implementation) to address the pain points immediately and achieve quick wins.
- *Plan to achieve business–IT integration.* In strategic terms, one important reality is that if IT does not align its strategy with the overall business strategy, then it will continue to be a cost center and perceived as a necessary evil. IT organizations must plan a long-term transformation to become a value-added business partner if they are to survive the competition from outside IT service providers.

According to Samuels (2006), achieving business alignment and demonstrating the business value of IT remain top CIO issues. Those IT organizations that are unable to demonstrate business value and tangible returns will face continuing pressures from business leadership to deliver. To realize the much-anticipated business value, IT organization has to integrate with the business to effectively support and enable business processes.

Business Process and Business–IT Integration

The concept of business processes is nothing new. Business processes have existed since the dawn of business enterprises. Garvin (1998) presents a process view of an organization and defines processes as collections of tasks and activities that together—and only together—transform inputs into outputs. Within organizations, these inputs and outputs can be as varied as materials, information, and people (Garvin, 1998, p. 33). Process theories have appeared in organizational theory, strategic management, operations management, group dynamics, and studies of managerial behavior. The few scholarly efforts to tackle processes as a collective phenomenon either have been tightly focused on theoretical, methodological statements, or have focused primarily on a single type of process theory (Mohr, 1982; Monge, 1990; Van de Ven, 1992; Van de Ven and Huber, 1990). Yet when the theories are taken together, they provide a powerful lens for understanding organizations and management (Garvin, 1998, p. 34). From the discussions, organization and processes of an enterprise affect each other.

A business exists because it creates and delivers those products and services that are needed by its customers. For the automotive industry, these products are cars and other vehicles. For banks, it may be a range of banking products and services such as personal accounts, mortgages, personal loans, and so on. The activities and steps that need to be executed to develop and deliver these products and services are logically grouped into business processes. Those processes that result in the creation of core business products and/or services are called business processes. The more efficient the business processes are, the greater throughput the business will have, thereby increasing its profitability. Before the emergence of the Information Age, businesses used other means to improve their productivities. For example, the original process that resulted in the manufacturing of automobiles did not have an assembly line. Instead, individual stations were used. As shown in Figure 2.4, the introduction of the assembly line by Ford Motor Company between 1908 and 1913 transformed the way in which automobiles were manufactured. Similarly, in recent years, the emergence of information technology and the Internet created tremendous opportunities for the business leaders and entrepreneurs to exploit these new channels to transform their business

The old-fashioned way—limousines are assembled at individual stations by a Pittsburg manufacturer, 1912.

End of the assembly line. The Ford Model T is joined to its chassis at the Highland Park plant.

Figure 2.4 Automobile manufacturing business process innovation. (From Evergreen Systems, Inc., 2006, "Developing the Business Case for ITIL Part 2," http://www.eyewitnesstohistory.com/ford.htm)

processes and introduce new ones. eBay, Amazon, Google, almost all financial services companies, and many others are great examples of those enterprises in which *business is IT and IT is the business.* These and other similar companies have exploited IT to the point that IT is integrated into their respective business processes.

Therefore, although business processes are not something new, the interdependencies between the success of the business processes and the effective delivery of IT services is definitely something new. In the case of the automotive industry, raw materials include the automotive parts (engine, transmission, body parts, electrical system, and so on) and the assembly line business processes consume these parts to produce a complete, operational vehicle at the end of the assembly line. Similarly, in the case of IT, the IT components (applications, software, hardware, servers, networks, and so on) are the raw materials that feed IT processes. The end result of these IT processes result in the creation of IT services. For these services to be valuable to their consumers, it is absolutely critical that these are aligned with the respective needs of the customers.

> Using people, processes, partners, and products (tools), IT managers must establish a comprehensive understanding and a logical picture of all business-critical IT infrastructure components such that an end-to-end view of IT services that directly enable business processes can be established. Through this understanding of how IT components enable business processes, IT management will be able to appropriately manage IT components and make investment decisions such that business value of IT is optimized.

For them to be valuable, the IT organization must learn to communicate in terms of business metrics and customer satisfaction. In the magazine *Optimize*'s CIO effectiveness survey of more than 700 chief executive officers (CXOs), 7 out of 10 CXOs say that the most important criterion in considering the effectiveness of a CIO is the CIO's ability to support company-wide business strategies (Samuels, 2006). Not simply metrics, but business metrics, are critical in building awareness of all the value-added IT achievements. According to *CIO Insight*'s July 2006 survey on business value and ROI for IT, only six out of ten companies measure the business value of IT (Alter and Davis, 2006). "CFOs and boards of directors will continue to insist on metrics such as ROI and return on capital," says Ian Campbell, CEO of Nucleus Research. "Return tends to be the driver for all investment decisions" (Alter and Davis, 2006). According to Gartner Research, "Convincing the financial director to fund technology projects is perhaps the most important part of an IT director's role. Indeed, spending initiatives are largely funded on the perception of the value expected by the business sponsor" (Alter and Davis, 2006).

Business Processes, Business Services, and Technical/IT Services

We have briefly discussed the role of business processes when it comes to aligning IT with the business. Let us now further discuss how these business processes are related to business services. Figure 2.5 shows the relationship between business process, business service, technical service, and technology components.

A restaurant is a good non-IT example. Think about the menu. It is put together in a language that allows customers to understand what dishes can be ordered and what to expect from each (a brief description). Imagine a restaurant that is serving a hotel; the room service menu may be different from the restaurant menu. Now, let us see some IT-related examples. When you ask

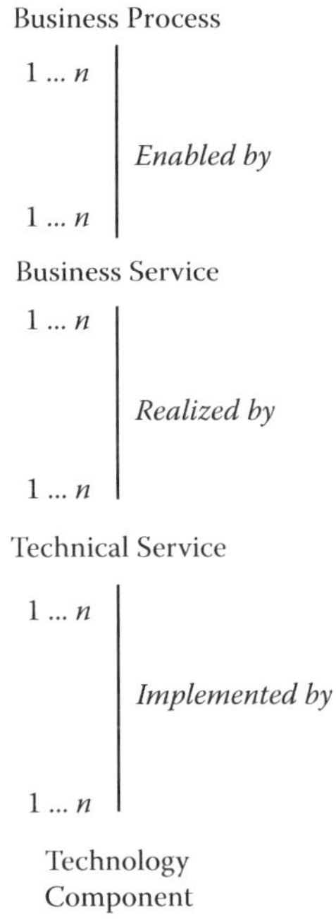

Figure 2.5 Business processes and services.

for high-speed Internet service, you do not normally ask for the number of servers, routers, and other infrastructure components you need. On the other hand, if you are providing infrastructure services and your customers are application service providers or application development organizations, the business services may be more technical in nature.

The point is that business services are what your customers are able to relate to. What constitutes a business service depends on what business you are in and who your customers are. Remember the restaurant example. Their end customers are those people who come to the restaurant to have dinners and lunches. But these restaurants are themselves someone's customers (e.g., those parties that provide ingredients). Therefore, business services presented to the customers will vary depending on your particular business and your customer segments. Note that there may be more than one business service required to enable a given process, and business services may be shared across a range of business processes. Both business services and technical services are types of IT services (Figure 2.6). An extensive comparison between business and technical services is provided in Table 2.1. We will discuss some other examples in detail later in this section.

Technical services realize business services and, as the name suggests, are internal facing and not normally visible to the customer. One or more technical services may be required to realize a given business service and technical services may be shared across multiple business services. Continuing with the same high-speed Internet service example, some of the technical services that realize this service may involve connectivity, Web-server hosting, ftp, and other technical services and these may be shared by other business services as well. In Part V: Emerging Trends, we will learn how emerging technologies such as service-oriented architecture can be leveraged to effectively and efficiently design and implement these technical services. Table 2.1 gives a comprehensive comparison between business and technical services.

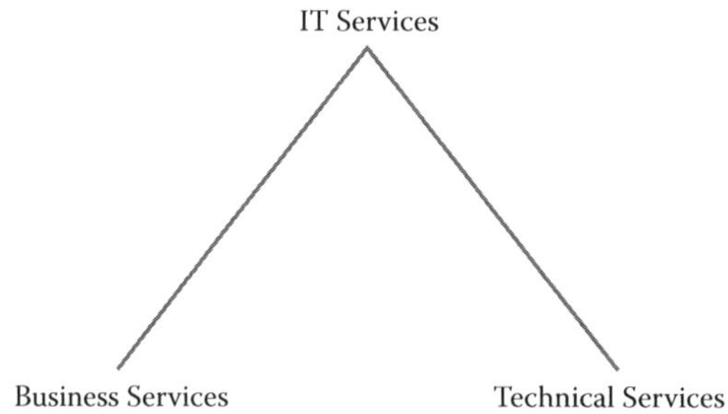

Figure 2.6 Both business services and technical services are types of IT services.

We have defined the business services and technical services above. So, you may ask me what I think about IT services. As stated before, both business services and technical services are types of IT services. The former is higher-level, business-focused, customer-friendly, and comprises one or more technical services. The latter is inward-focused (for the consumption of IT developers and managers), technical in nature, and largely shared and/or reused to support other business services.

Enabling Business Processes

In almost all cases, business expectations from IT can be categorized as follows:

Core business services. These are the services that most businesses use to keep their operational businesses running. These include services such as e-mail, telecommunication, back-up and

Table 2.1 Business Services vs. Technical Services

Business Services	*Technical Services*
Are business customers facing and form part of business service catalog view of Service Catalog?	Are IT partners/IT professionals facing and form part of Technical Service Catalog view of Service Catalog?
Can be easily understood and related to by business customers	Cannot be readily related to (in most cases) by business customers
Map onto and support customer's business processes	Support business services and are mostly shared across different business services
Should underpin business processes	Should underpin the Business Service Catalog and not form part of customer view
Provide a basis for service and service management process improvement efforts	Are largely improved in support of improving the business services
Provide a basis for implementing SLM. The Business Service Catalog enables the implementation of proactive/preemptive SLM thereby maturing it into Business Service Management	Provide a basis for building relationships between services, SLAs, OLAs, and other underpinning agreements and components. This further enables identification of the technology required to support a business service and the support groups that support the components

recovery, voice and/or video conferencing, and so on. These may not directly enable any specific core business processes but are definitely essential to keeping the businesses going. Almost all IT organizations are expected to provide these and probably other core IT services. Standard services that are common across organizations and industries are discussed in the sample service catalog shown in Appendix A. We will discuss this in greater detail later.

Business-specific business services. The second set of services are those that directly impact the ways a business executes its business processes and develops and/or delivers its products and services to its end customers. Discovering and aligning business services requires a clear identification and mapping of business processes. Higher-maturity IT organizations are now aiming to build better appreciations of what their customers' businesses really do. This business knowledge enables IT organizations to:

- Achieve comprehensive understanding of those business processes that truly enable business enterprises to generate revenue and be profitable. Without these business processes, business enterprises would go out of business. Examples of this are retail banking, where online banking is a must, and the manufacturing industry, where supply chain management is at the core.
- Identify areas for business process improvement to ensure that IT is enabling efficient business processes and not the broken ones. Enabling inefficient business processes results in wasted investments. This is a sensitive area and needs to be carefully managed. Normally, business processes should be owned and, therefore, improved by the business units and not IT. However, if IT discovers that a certain business process is inefficient or broken, it is critical to communicate this to the customers/businesses and share the resulting impact so that appropriate improvements can be made before automation.
- If IT organization is able to clearly understand business processes, it will be in a position to propose to the businesses/customers innovative ways in which IT can enable these business processes. Accordingly, business services are designed and developed that enable achievement of business objectives.

BSM ensures the enablement of business processes by effectively managing all enabling IT components end-to-end and measuring performance of these components in relation to business performance. According to O'Neill et al. (2007), those IT organizations that are attempting to present their business value more positively are the ones that are beginning to develop true BSM capabilities. They aim to achieve this by:

- Understanding the metrics their business users use to decide if IT is providing value
- Linking these metrics and associated business services to IT infrastructure components

Business Service Management and Business Process Management

Business services enable the business process and are what business customers, in most cases, relate to. Implementing end-to-end BSM will involve the following key activities:

- Identifying and defining the business service in the service catalog
- Defining the service level requirements for the business service

- Defining and agreeing on the SLA necessary to ensure that the needs identified in service level requirements are met
- Defining and identifying all technical services that support the business services in the service catalog
- Identifying, defining, and agreeing upon all necessary operational level agreements for these technical services
- Defining and implementing end-to-end request fulfillment processes for all appropriate requests that can be placed on these services
- Optimizing the configuration management database to represent the relationships between all the configuration items that ensure successful delivery of the business service
- Implementing all other ITIL v3 processes to ensure that this business service is managed end-to-end

Achieving BSM will require IT organizations to align different IT teams (infrastructure, application development, operations, etc.) and components to achieve the envisioned business–IT integration. The separation between application and infrastructure results in a disconnect between business needs and end-to-end management of those needs from the fulfillment perspectives—applications teams architect, design, and develop applications to satisfy functional needs (termed *utility* in ITIL v3) and, in most cases, when these applications are deployed, there are mismatches in network and server capacity resulting in unforeseen outages due to lack of what ITIL v3 defines as *warranty*. These outages cause disruptions, not only for business customers, but also for IT teams. Such events result in increased costs of delivering IT services, reduced productivity, and increased customer dissatisfaction. BSM aims to implement end-to-end management for IT services provided by the IT organization with the goal of addressing the challenges mentioned above.

Factors Impacting Service Management Implementation

As discussed, BSM implementation is more about cultural transformation than anything else. It is a major shift in the way IT organizations plan, produce, deliver, and manage their products and services. According to Cappelli (2006), most BSM-critical success factors are about people and processes, not technology. Some of the critical success factors that impact service management implementation include:

- *Senior business and IT management commitment.* This is the most critical factor in achieving successful implementation of BSM.
- *Return on investment.* BSM implementation requires significant investments and successful business leaders do not make investments if they do not see reasonable and justifiable returns. IT improvements that do not actually impact the value that businesses and customers receive are not wise investments.
- *Communication, communication, and communication.* Marketing and communication are the most critical components of trying to implement BSM. IT has traditionally been weak in sharing the success stories. Businesses and customers typically only communicate with IT when something breaks down. Communicating good news as well as bad to the customer is critical. Most of the time, we focus on only the bad and leave the good out. As IT organizations embark on making improvements to products and services that they produce, communication planning and execution is critical. The service level management process provides

means and ways in which service target achievements should be shared. In addition, business relationships, or account management functions can prove very useful in communicating with the businesses and customers, identifying and defining services, and negotiating SLAs. Scorecards, dashboards, heat-maps, and other displays must be made available to customers all the time. This is critical to maintaining IT credibility.

- *Business drivers and needs that require IT organizations to improve the way they deliver their services to the businesses.* This will require IT organizations to make major investments in improving the quality of services that they provide.
- *Objective self-assessment.* Realistic IT self-assessment to establish current state service management and process maturity is critical. This will enable the leadership and service management project teams to make better estimates on the level of investments required before pursuing BSM projects.
- *Personnel performance management.* KPI and metrics should be very thoughtfully established. Performance metrics should be introduced that encourage IT personnel to be responsible for the delivery of end-to-end services. Such metrics will encourage cross-organizational teams to collaborate and work toward common objectives.
- *Not everything is important.* Not every IT component is critical. Use business impact as a guide to identify the critical components and guide the prioritization. Focus on those 20% of the components that make 80% of the revenues. Focus on those that result in the improvement of end-to-end service quality. Select the right metrics that tell you what you want to know about the service quality. Those IT organizations that start a big, all-encompassing BSM initiative with the goal of defining IT service dependency relationships for all lines of business and millions of IT components, and the intention of achieving 100% monitoring coverage of all IT components in the IT infrastructure rarely make it to the end (i.e., successful achievement of BSM). This is primarily because such a large effort results in a highly complex project that takes years to implement and generally leads to disillusionment and failure. The more successful deployments break up the project into smaller business-focused (not IT-focused) components. Focus in successful efforts is continually maintained on defining and monitoring only a few critical IT services and underpinning IT components, then expanding after achieving critical successes. These initial successes are used to keep the momentum going. If your company has a disaster recovery plan, it may be a good source of important information as you prioritize which services are more critical and the respective underpinning IT components. This will also enable effective improvement in component monitoring capabilities. Redundant monitoring is removed and gaps in monitoring are identified and appropriate remediation plans can be created.

Measuring Business–IT Integration

So we understand now what is meant by BSM and some of the critical success factors. Measurements are at the core of enabling IT organizations and leadership to assess how well IT organizations are supporting their respective businesses and customers. We will focus on indicators that help IT organizations appreciate the extent to which they understand their customers' businesses and the level of support that they provide to their customers to achieve their business objectives.

Some of the performance indicators of business services that will enable the assessment of BSM are listed here. Each indicator comprises a range of recommended metrics and measurements.

Depending on your particular drivers to achieve BSM, you may decide on a subset of these metrics.

- Quality and maturity of business and technical services (IT services)
- Business process enablement and support
- Business–IT integration

Quality and Maturity of Business and Technical Services (IT Services)

This indicator aims to measure the quality and maturity of IT services. It allows the IT organization to see how mature their internal technical processes are. These processes include the service management processes (the ITIL v3 processes such as incident management, change management, and so on) as well as business and technical service processes (e.g., those processes that implement online order processing services or document management services). Measurements include:

- Quality of IT organization's processes, products, people, and partners
- Average response times to changing business goals and needs
- Percentage of IT resources involved in operations (keeping the lights on) vs. new development
- Percentage of IT budget spent on developing new IT services and capabilities compared to the total IT budget
- Percentage of IT budget spent on managing existing IT services
- Ratio of IT budget spent on developing new services to managing existing services
- Percentage of IT services (business or technical services) provided by supplier (i.e., outsourced)
- Percentage of IT services that use standard technology components and other standards
- Quality of technical documentation and other training manuals
- Level of technical expertise
- Ratio between the total number of employees within the IT organization to the total number of non-IT employees within the business organization
- Level of dependence on external resources (e.g., consultants and vendors or suppliers)

Business Process Enablement and Support

This indicator shows the extent to which the services provided by the IT organization enable and support business processes. Some of the metrics and attributes of this indicator include:

- IT understanding of core business processes of their customers/businesses
- Percentage of revenue generated through the use of business services
- Cost of unavailability of business services on revenue
- Percentage of business processes that rely on business services
- Number and percentage of users that depend on business services to perform their day-to-day job functions
- Quality of information and data to support decision-making
- Business and customer perception of IT
- Level of support to the management of the organization. This may include the percentage of key business decisions that are made based on the information and knowledge processed and provided by business services

Business–IT Integration

These metrics and indicators enable us to understand how well IT is integrated with the business. These include:

- IT understanding of business strategies
- Percentage of IT projects (per year) that are business-driven, are initiated by IT, and are a result of alignment of business and IT strategies. These projects are considered innovative and will result in enabling core business processes and addressing core business needs/pain points. These projects must be conceived within IT.
- Percentage of IT projects (per year) that are business-driven and are initiated by the business. These projects must be conceived with business
- Percentage of investments made in IT development compared to the total investments across the business enterprise (applies to internal IT service provider)
- Percentage of IT budget of the total revenues of the business enterprise

There are other metrics that are related to specific ITIL v3 processes (e.g., change management, service asset management and configuration management have their own metrics). Relevant ITIL v3 literature should be used to understand, identify, and select specific metrics to measure the maturity of these processes.

Summary

We have discussed the key characteristics of IT organizations at various maturity levels and learned about how the different maturity levels of IT organizations impact the value delivered to businesses and customers. We have also discussed the importance of aligning IT strategies with business strategies and the role of business processes in enabling such alignment. With this understanding of BSM, business services, business process, and business–IT integration, we will discuss the business-focused approach to implementing BSM in the next chapter.

References

Alter, A., and Z. Davis. 2006. *July 2006 Survey: What's the Value of IT? At Many Companies, It's Just Guesswork.* http://www.cioinsight.com (accessed July 12, 2006).

Cappelli, W. 2006. *Business Service Management: Technologies and Processes for IT/Business Alignment.* Gartner Symposium/ITxpo, Palau de Congressos de Catalunya, Barcelona, Spain.

Evergreen Systems, Inc. 2006. "Developing the Business Case for ITIL Part 2." Evergreen Systems, Inc. http://www.xlr8-technologies.com/cms/admin/assets/evergreensys/assets/whitepapers/BusValITILPrt2.pdf.

Ferrarini, E. 2007. *Introduction to ITIL: Early US Adopters Show Business Value.* http://www.enterpriseleadership.org/blogs/Articles/2007/12/03/introduction-to-itil-early-us-adopters-show-business-value (accessed March 12, 2008).

Gartner Research. 2006. *The Information Technology Infrastructure Library Improves Infrastructure Investment.* http://www.gartner.com/DisplayDocument?ref=blog&id=491590 (accessed June 9, 2006).

Garvin, D. A. 1998. The processes of organization and management, *Sloan Management Review*, 39(4): 33–50.

Hubbert, E. 2008. *Why IT Service Management Should Matter To You.* http://www.forrester.com/rb/Research/why_it_service_management_should_matter_to/q/id/46464/t/2 (accessed September 16, 2008).

Kotter, J. 1990. *A Force for Change: How Leadership Differs from Management.*
Mohr, L. B. 1982. *Explaining Organizational Behavior.* San Francisco: Jossey-Bass.
Monge, P. R. 1990. Theoretical and analytical issues in studying organizational processes, *Organizational Science,* 1(4): 406–430.
O'Neill, P., T. Mendel, and R. Iqbal. 2007. *Business Service Management: Early Birds Are Catching the Worm, But IT Still Doesn't Get It.* http://www.forrester.com/rb/Research/business_service_management_early_birds_are_catching/q/id/41458/t/2 (accessed March 2007).
Samuels, M. 2006. *Push Your IT Value or Suffer Suspicion,* VNU Network, VNU Business Publications, 2006.
Van de Ven, A. H. 1992. Suggestions for studying strategic process: A research note, *Strategic Management Journal,* 13: 169–188.
Van de Ven, A. H. and G. Huber. 1990. Longitudinal field research methods for studying processes of organizational change, *Organizational Science,* 1(3): 213–219.

Chapter 3

Service Management Implementation Overview

We have learned about the evolutions and transformations that most business enterprises go through over the course of their life cycle. Over the past decade, we have witnessed the evolutions caused by the emergence of the Internet and IT. Immediately after the dot.com bubble burst, business enterprises have, justifiably, gone through a state of denial (IT is a necessary evil; IT is not important; IT is back-office, etc.) by attempting to outsource as much of IT as possible. When companies such as ebay.com, amazon.com, and many others demonstrated how IT and the Internet enabled them to emerge as leaders in their respective verticals, others that were previously in denial have started realizing that IT could enable their businesses to capture new markets, enter new regions, offer value-added services and products to their customers, be more profitable, generate greater wealth for their shareholders, and other benefits. Procter & Gamble reported savings of more than $500 million through an innovative use of IT and implementation of service management. Amazon.com has shown that it is possible to not only survive, but to be profitable, during tough economic times. There is an increasing degree of dependency between the core business processes of business enterprises and the capabilities provided by the Internet and IT. As a result of this dependency, IT organizations have found themselves under increasing pressures from the businesses and customers that they support to evolve their organizations and ensure tighter business–IT integration.

Information Technology Infrastructure Library version 3 (ITIL v3) provides a unique set of guidelines that creates a view of how mature IT organizations should provide effective business service management (BSM). ITIL v3 is unique in the sense that it spans a wide range of IT industry practices, standards, and disciplines to bring all into a larger perspective, that is, business–IT integration. ITIL v3 enables IT organizations to plan and implement their transformations and improvements to achieve BSM. We understand that business enterprises evolve and that process evolution is always one of the key components of such change. For these evolutions to be efficient and successful, business enterprises continue to depend on and look toward IT for support. In such situations, IT organizations are expected to be agile and able to respond to ever-changing business environments and competitive drivers. However, the challenge for lower maturity level (organizational maturity level 2 and lower) IT organizations is that they always find themselves reacting to such business demands and they do so in a way that is not efficient and causes a lot of disruptions such as service outages, slow response capability, expensive changes, lack of alignment between the needs and the solution, etc. Because these IT organizations are largely disconnected from their businesses and customers, they are unable to appreciate and proactively plan to build the right IT capabilities to support and enable business evolutions in a timely manner.

Depending on the role that IT plays in enabling the core business processes, the rate of IT evolution may be critical to the overall business success and profitability. For some business enterprises, implementing service management may be transformational and embarking on such a journey may sometimes be more about cultural transformations than any other single factor. It may need a major shift in how people think about and manage IT. These shifts may include:

- IT is for the business, not for IT.
- Targeted technology capability investments to maximize business profitability.
- Firefighting is not rewarded, proactive fire prevention is rewarded.
- We will thrive, not just survive.

Cultural transformation, an aggregate of small behavioral transformations over time, is achieved through:

- Well-aligned business and IT vision and strategies
- Clear definition of enterprise architecture standards and governance policies
- Thoughtful management of changes in people's attitudes and ways of thinking
- Careful planning, management, and incremental implementations of a range of continual service and service management process improvements
- Business–IT organizational realignments
- Knowledge Management throughout the course of BSM implementation and operation

These critical aspects of implementing BSM are graphically represented in Figure 3.1.

Cultural transformation is, therefore, easier said than done. Business enterprises have been struggling to leverage ITIL guidelines and achieve the transformations necessary to realize the highly anticipated effectiveness and efficiency business–IT integration benefits.

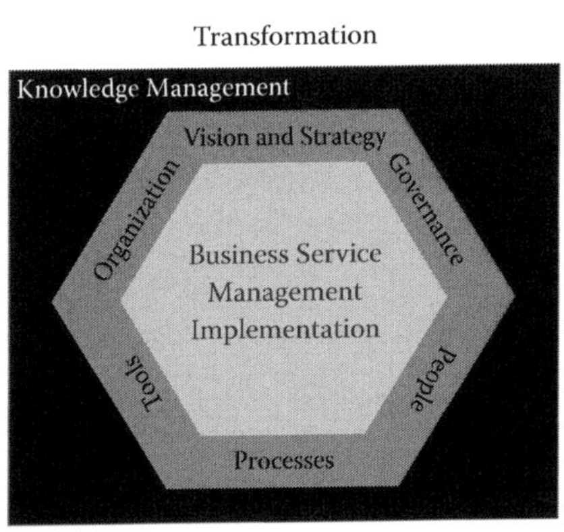

Figure 3.1 BSM implementation hexagon.

It is important to note that such transformation—*normally a higher degree of change with greater impact*—does not happen overnight and requires consistent, incremental, and ongoing improvements. BSM implementation is no exception. What makes such transformations even riskier is the lack of organizational knowledge about all that is necessary to make these efforts successful. It is absolutely critical to realize that ITIL v3 is more than just IT infrastructure and operations management, and that BSM sometimes means a major shift in the way IT is managed and operated and also in the manner that it delivers its services to the customers. ITIL v3 and BSM are about integrating IT with the business and ensuring traceability from business processes through to business services, technical services, and all the way down to individual technology components (infrastructure, application, software, hardware, databases, middleware, etc.).

Implementing BSM will very likely impact each and every aspect of the business enterprise organization. In fact, depending on the organizational baseline maturity level, implementing service management may be revolutionary and it may take some time before the undertaking organizations start realizing the benefits. To make matters worse, organizational tolerances to wait for these transformational benefits to come through have been declining. In efforts to see the returns sooner, some organizations have considered options to outsource BSM without completely realizing what this means. There is a detailed discussion on outsourcing BSM in Chapter 10.

Implementing BSM is expensive, risky, and difficult, and requires a consistent and well-planned approach. Many of the questions that IT managers have asked me over the years pertain to keeping the momentum going in the midst of ever-changing organizational and business environments. Two of the most common questions are, "How do we implement BSM and demonstrate the value-added benefits before our next management shuffle?" and "What do we do when this shuffle happens and we lose the support?" The answer to these questions is simple. To keep the senior management sponsorship alive and to survive the frequent management shuffles and excite the larger organization about this transformational change, we must demonstrate the business value created as early as possible and help the senior management and the larger organization see one small slice of our BSM vision at a time. Under such business and organizational pressures, faster turnaround coupled with effective and efficient management of continual improvement efforts may be the answer.

How can IT organizations go about delivering incremental and iterative value to business customers through steady and ongoing improvements in an agile fashion? Parts II and III of this book are dedicated to answering this question in great detail. This chapter, however, will provide an overview of BSM implementation and management of such efforts. By the end of this chapter, you will be able to answer the following questions:

- *What are the increasing challenges that business enterprises face?* We will discuss how organizations that manage their business services will look, and we will see the common challenges faced by organizations that do not manage their services effectively.
- *How can BSM help and what does it mean to implement it?* After clearly building an appreciation of the challenges faced by not managing the services, we will discuss what BSM can do to address the identified challenges.
- *Why is it difficult to implement BSM?* Implementing BSM is not easy. It takes commitment, resources, willingness to change, and discipline. We will discuss some of the factors that need to be in the forefront of BSM implementation efforts.
- *What are the key components of BSM implementation? What are the critical steps involved in implementing BSM?* We will discuss some of the key components of successfully implementing BSM and the high-level steps needed to implement it. More detailed discussion of these components and steps is provided in Part II of this book.

- *What are the BSM implementation critical success factors?* We will learn about some of the most critical factors in successfully implementing service management.
- *What is the most appropriate approach for implementing BSM so that it improves our success probability?* Based on our understanding of the most critical success factors, the most appropriate approach addresses those critical factors and ensures successful implementation of BSM.
- *What are the common challenges and risks and how should they be managed?* We will conclude the chapter by identifying and discussing some of the most common challenges and risks that need to be carefully managed.

BSM at a Restaurant

Let us continue with the restaurant example that we started in the earlier chapters and discuss restaurant BSM in greater details (Figure 3.2). Most of us have experienced dining at a variety of restaurants. With obvious exceptions, after we go through the initial settling-in steps, we are presented with a menu that presents the following:

- Special featured items.
- Meals grouped by categories such as appetizers, pizza, specialties, etc.
- Individual meal items with relevant details such as the name of the item, a brief description, and pricing information.
- Other relevant information on potential exceptions is normally provided by the server.

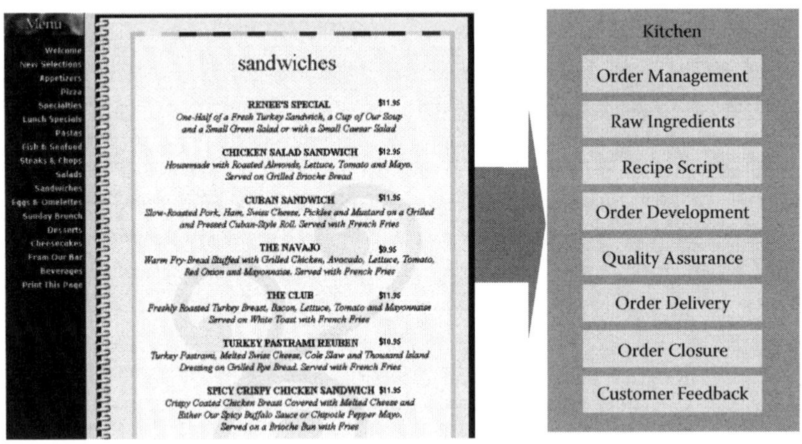

Service Management question to ask:

- What if there is no menu?
- What if there is no clear definition on how to place an order?
- What if you are asked to reach out to the Chef and explain to him/her what you need?
- What if multiple members from the kitchen reach out to you to further understand what you need?
- What if you ordered the *Cuban* and received the *Club*?
- What if it takes longer than usual to receive your order?
- What if there is no price available?

Figure 3.2 Service management at a restaurant.

If I ask you to rank your experience at a particular restaurant, what factors will you consider? We all appreciate that there are personal preferences. However, there are certain elements of the experience that are absolutely critical and largely common. These include:

- The way we are received, welcomed, and shown to our tables
- The hospitality of the server and the presentation of the menu
- Clarity of the items described in the menu
- Pricing information
- Timely delivery of the order
- Appropriate follow-up to ensure satisfaction
- Overall customer care and attitudes
- If there are issues with the order, proper management of complaints

In most cases, restaurants will not accept orders outside of the menu items. Have you tried ordering Indian curry at a McDonalds? In short, restaurants define and maintain their respective menus in order to achieve the following:

- Clearly define their customers/market that they plan to serve.
- Ensure that customers clearly understand what items the restaurant offers.
- Based on historical data and demand, ensure that the appropriate quantity and quality of required ingredients are ordered and acquired.
- Ensure that the right staff (chef) with the right skills and experiences (competencies) are hired to prepare and offer the items listed on the menu.
- Ensure that recipes (processes) for the items in the menu are clearly documented and well maintained for quality and consistency and more.

In the case of a restaurant, the menu helps determine what people require, what processes need to be defined, what tools are necessary, and what partners and suppliers will have the ingredients necessary to prepare the items. Think about what the kitchen would do if there was no menu. Now, let us look at some situations that lead to a negative overall experience. These may include:

- What if there is no menu? Imagine the experience and the steps that you would need to go through to explain what you want and then for the kitchen to agree on a one-on-one basis how to fulfill your request. Keep in mind that there are restaurants where every order may be custom-made or prepared by the customers themselves. Even in those restaurants, there will be menus but the menus will list ingredients and recipes instead of prepared meals.
- What if there is no clarity on how to place the order? Do you go to the kitchen yourself? Do you place the order at the bar or at reception?
- What if there are no servers and you are asked to reach out to the chef directly? Imagine the impact that it will have on the kitchen and its productivity?
- What if you are approached by multiple members of the kitchen team to gain further understanding of what you need? Even if you eventually receive exactly what you were expecting, will you be happy and satisfied as a customer?
- What if you ordered one item and received a totally different item?
- What if you were kept in a never-ending waiting period and, every time you inquire, you are told that it will be ready soon?
- What if the price is not clear?

Having applied BSM to a restaurant environment, let us discuss what it might look like at a high-maturity IT organization. Following that, we will discuss the challenges faced by less mature IT organizations and how those challenges can be addressed by implementing BSM.

BSM at a Mature IT Organization: The Target State

In this section, we will discuss the state that any organization aspiring to implement BSM is hoping to achieve. In order words, we are already setting the vision of how a mature IT organization should look post-BSM implementation.

You have already been introduced to the service tree concept in Chapter 1. Here, we will extend it further and see what it really means to have a service tree. In the example shown in Figure 3.3, we see that there is only one business process that needs to be enabled. In the real world, you will see that there will be a set of core business processes.

Any given business process will need one or more business services to enable it and business services can be shared across multiple business processes. If we go down one level, we will see that one or more technical services are needed to realize a given business service and these are mostly shared by one or more business services. If you take the service tree represented in Figure 3.3 and document the business services and technical services provided by the IT organization, that becomes your service catalog. This is graphically represented in Figure 3.4.

As shown in Figure 3.4, new market drivers lead to the development of new or refined business processes. From an IT perspective, these new business processes will create new demand for IT to develop and deliver the needed capabilities in the form of new business services. In most organizations, such endeavors to deliver new capabilities/new business services are achieved through proper program and project management. Similarly, if there are any business processes that are being retired and the demand for associated business services is going to diminish, plans should be made to manage the retirement of those business services and relevant (unshared) components. For example, if Amazon.com decides to offer its customers the ability to sell their items through a bidding process, this will require the design and development of new "bidding" and related business processes. This will mean that IT will need to plan and implement associated respective business services to enable

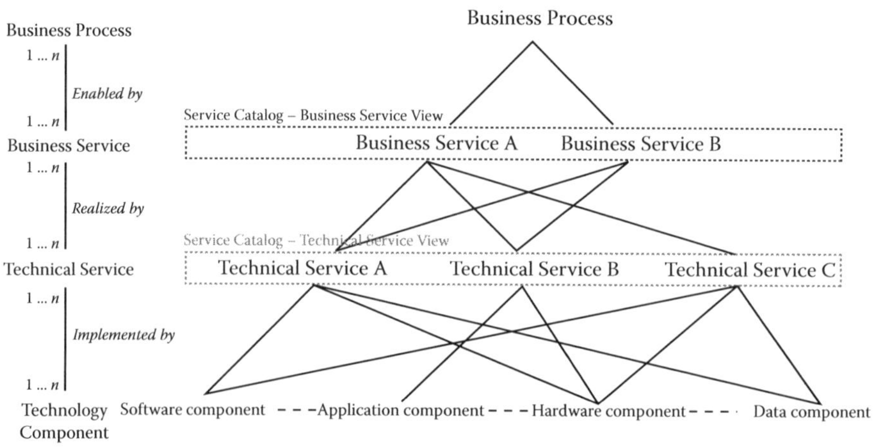

Figure 3.3 The service tree.

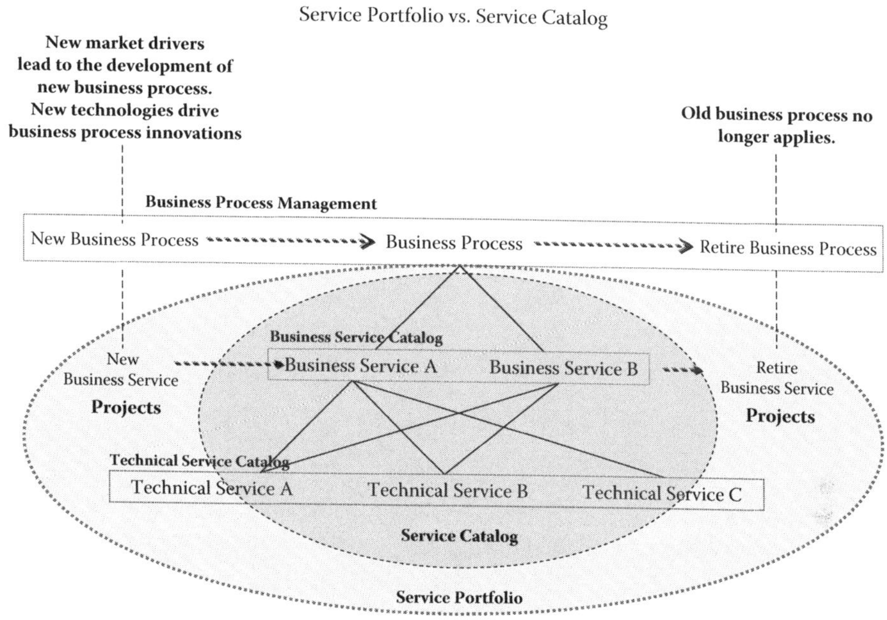

Figure 3.4 Service portfolio and service catalog.

the "bidding" and related business processes. Depending upon the service level requirements (SLRs) the "utility" or "fit for purpose" as well as the "warranty" or "fit for use" aspects of the service are realized through the appropriate architecture and design of new/desired business services.

The service catalog is a menu of items (business services and technical services) offered by the IT organization. If there are any business services on the service catalog that do not add value or enable any of the business processes, that is an evidence of a potential "leak" within the IT organization and the IT organization must assess whether it should continue to offer those services or not. According to ITIL v3, the service catalog should contain all operational, those that are soon going be operational, and retired services. This may be tailored to organizationally specific needs. For example, I have had clients who chose to include only those retired services that could be reactivated if the need arose. Another scenario that may require for retired service(s) to be included in the service catalog is if there are customers who are still using some/all of the "retired" services and those services will need to be supported. These "retired" services primarily included those services that were retired because of diminishing demand. The IT organization still had the capabilities to reactivate those services. I also had some clients who used their service catalog as a source to market new and upcoming services. They included services that were going to be offered soon (within 4 weeks). It depends on how the organization wants to use its service catalog but the purpose remains the same: to clearly communicate what the IT organization offers to businesses and customers and to ensure that these business services are aligned with business processes. On the other hand, as shown in Figure 3.4, the service portfolio includes all retired, operational, and future services.

Having gained this understanding of the service portfolio and service catalog, let us see how these are used in different roles within a business enterprise. Figure 3.5 shows how various roles may leverage the service portfolio and service catalog. Management (business and IT) may use the service portfolio to strategize for new services and plan to retire old services. Customers (business and IT) may use the business service view of the service catalog to place requests for services, to

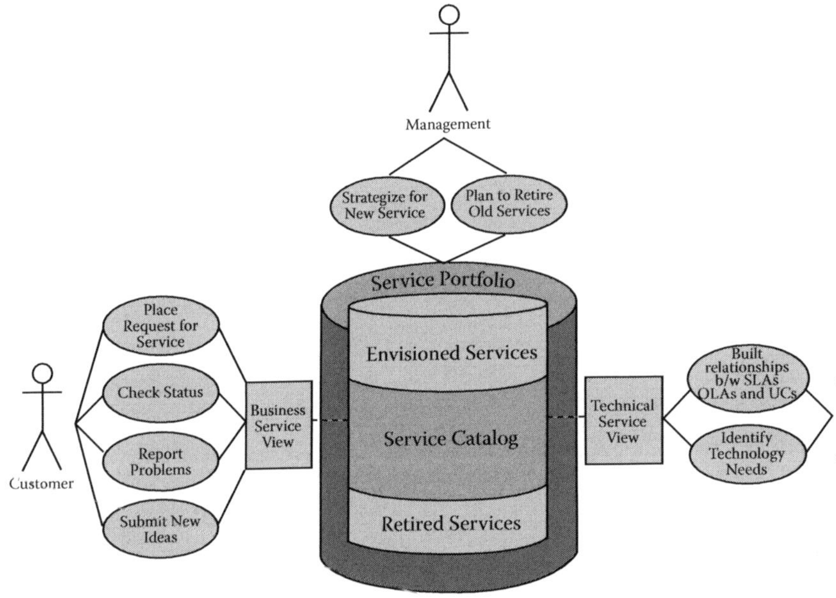

Figure 3.5 Main uses of the service portfolio and service catalog.

check the status of a request for service, to report service problems (issues/incidents), and to submit new ideas. Depending on the role of the customer, he or she may be provided with a different view into the service catalog and may even see different offerings and tiers together.

IT may use the technical service view of the service catalog to build relationships between service level agreements (SLAs), operational level agreements (OLAs), and underpinning contracts (UCs) and to identify technology needs. Let us look at an example of request initiation and routing. Figure 3.6 shows a vision where the service catalog serves as a gateway into IT, just as a menu at a restaurant serves as a gateway into the kitchen. If a service is not in the service catalog, it is because there is not sufficient incentive to offer that service. All IT activities in the service catalog must contribute to building and delivering new services, maintaining, operating, and improving existing services, or retiring those services that are no longer needed.

The service catalog shows all of the services provided by IT. Customers can choose to call the service desk to initiate the request or use the interactive (online) service catalog to do the same. You will notice that there are a small number of clearly defined request types that can be initiated by the customer using the service catalog. These may include the following:

- Opening a new account
- Changing an existing plan
- Reporting a problem
- Submitting a new idea

Depending on organizational needs and the type of service, there may be more or fewer types of requests. The message is simple:

> *The service catalog is the gateway into the IT and should list all services provided by the IT and the types of requests that can be placed on those services.*

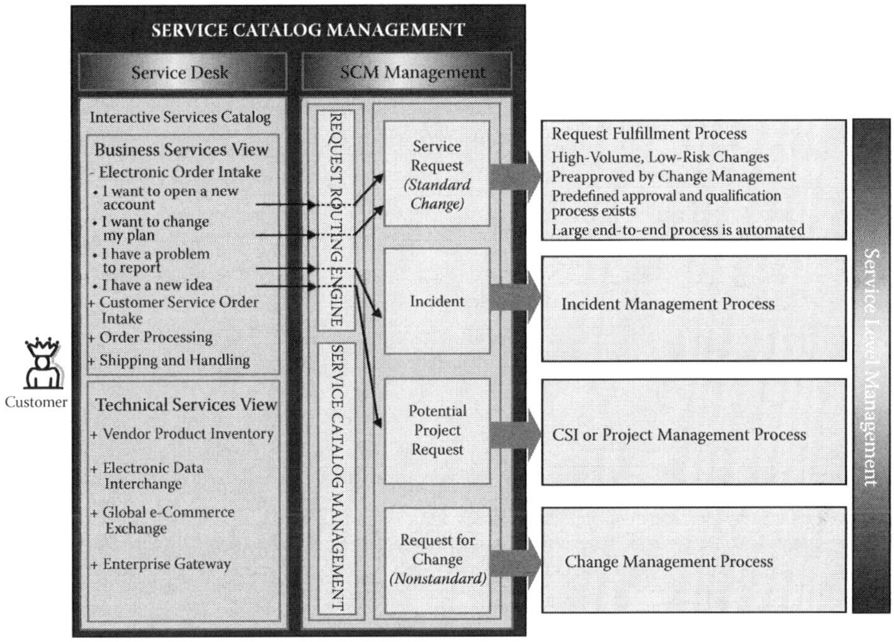

Figure 3.6 Request initiation and routing.

Depending on the type of the request submitted, the request routing engine performs request classification and categorization and routes the requests to the appropriate process. Note that this request routing engine may be as simple as a spreadsheet or as intelligent as a rule-based workflow engine.

Mature IT organizations are able to leverage their service catalog to align its technical capabilities to meet the expectations established using the service catalog and service level management processes. We will discuss these processes in greater details in Parts II and III of this book.

All services listed in the service catalog need to be managed to ensure that they deliver the desired level of utility and warranty to the customers of these services so that these services are deemed valuable and serve as a means of delivering value. The capability of an IT organization to manage and deploy its resources and ensure that the services it offers deliver the desired value is called service management. Some of the key goals that should be achieved by implementing service management are:

- Service level requirements of services listed in the service catalog must be clearly documented and understood.
- Service level management must ensure that achievable targets are established.
- Request fulfillment must ensure that high-volume, low-risk requests are managed effectively and efficiently in as automated a manner as possible.
- The service desk must be the single point of contact for the customers.
- Configuration management systems (tools and databases) must be optimized to ensure that the quality of data available is sufficient to support decision-making.
- Configuration item (CI) relationships must be established so that they support the end-to-end management of services. Auto discovery tools are limited in their capabilities. CI

relationship development and the capturing of useful information is mostly a manual effort. For a medium to large organization, it means significant investments. Targeted efforts focused on value creation are necessary. We will discuss this in much detail in Part II of this book.
- Change management and release and deployment management processes are optimized to ensure that changes are effectively planned and efficiently deployed into the production environment. For high-impact services in the service catalog, custom change models may be defined.

Practical Tip: Remember, processes are only as important as the services/products that they underpin.

- Incident models are defined for critical services to ensure that those services may be brought back to operations (in case of an incident) as soon as possible.
- Event management capabilities are developed for those critical IT components that are supporting critical business services.

The main message here is that *not everything is equally important.* Keep the *80/20 Rule* in mind when planning to implement service management: Improve the 20% of services that make 80% of the impact. The end goal of service management implementation is to identify the value chain for a given business process and ensure that all CIs that implement that value chain are managed

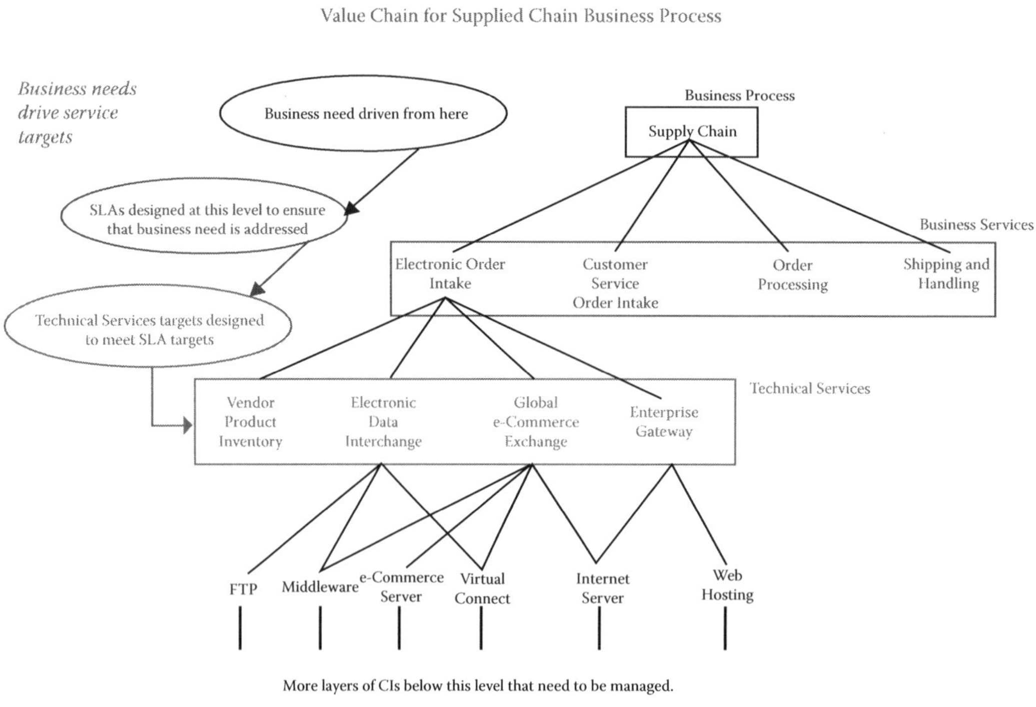

Figure 3.7 End-to-end service management.

effectively. This will enable IT to manage customer expectations and deliver IT services at the desired levels. Figure 3.7 shows an example of a value chain for a supply chain business process.

A supply chain is a business process that is enabled by four business services: electronic order intake, customer service order intake, order processing, and shipping and handling. Each of these business services may be further realized by one or more technical services. In the example mentioned above, the electronic order intake service is realized by vendor inventory product (VPI), electronic data interchange (EDI), global e-commerce exchange, and enterprise gateway technical services. Each of these technical services may be implemented by one or more technology (hardware and software) components. As shown in the figure, business needs from the top must drive all IT activities in terms of improvements across supporting technical services and components.

Challenges Faced by Less Mature IT Organizations

In the past few years, we see trends that suggest that management of IT, as a discipline, is on its way to achieving the next level of maturity. When we talk about a business using IT in a traditional manner, this means that they have:

1. Kept their infrastructure engineering and operations functions somewhat separate from application development and operations.
2. Managed technology, not the business.
3. Thought, planned, and managed in a siloed fashion.

I am witnessing a trend whereby most established (with a legacy environment in place) business enterprises that have been using IT in a traditional manner are now undertaking major transformational and improvement initiatives to bring alignment across different IT components in an effort to achieve the highly desired Business–IT Integration benefits discussed in Chapter 2. The separation between application and infrastructure resulted in a disconnect between business needs and the end-to-end management of those needs from the fulfillment perspectives—applications teams architected, designed, developed, and implemented applications to satisfy functional and nonfunctional application needs in somewhat of a vacuum. When these applications are deployed in production, mismatches happen and negatively impact the customer experience with IT products and services.

A close integration between application and infrastructure architecture, engineering, and development is absolutely critical to successfully meeting the business needs in an effective and efficient manner. For example, if an application is designed for 99% availability driven by business needs, it may not actually be available if the network has a lower or same availability level.

Practical Tip: A global business enterprise deployed a single-sign on (SSO) application without thoroughly analyzing the demands and capacity requirements, both at application and infrastructure levels. When it was put in production, other departments saw the benefits and began migrating to the SSO platform to take advantage of the benefits. Soon after deployment, the SSO platform was supporting more than 4000 business applications, which it was never implemented to do. The lack of capacity planning in this case resulted in the outage of the SSO platform and the unavailability of all of the business applications, which impacted the business's bottomline tremendously.

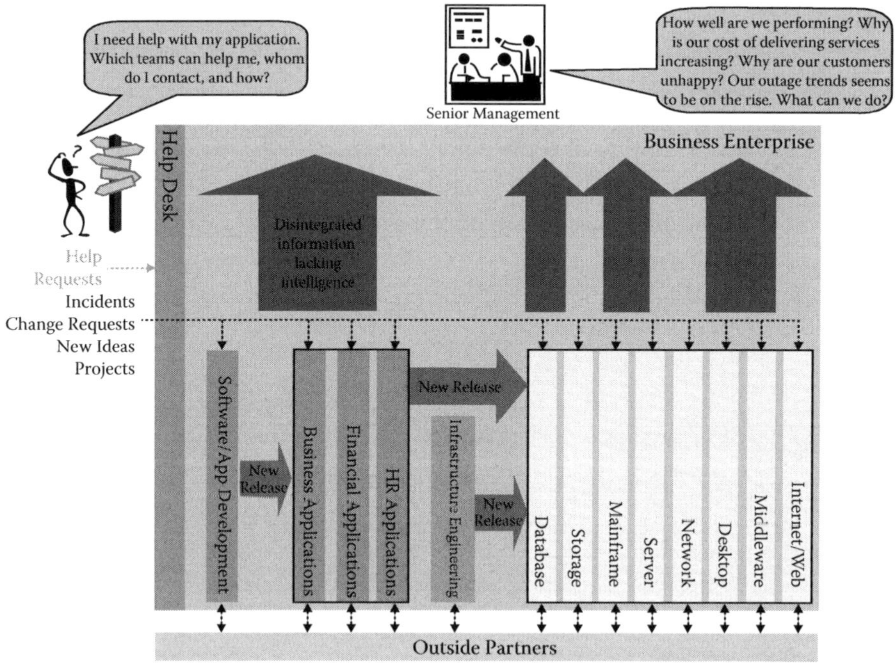

Figure 3.8 Siloed enterprises.

If architected in a vacuum, these applications will very likely be mismatched to network and server capacity resulting in unforeseen outages. These outages cause disruptions not only for business customers, but also for IT teams. In fact, if not governed and managed appropriately, this can transform the organizational culture to one where firefighting is a norm and is encouraged and rewarded. In financial terms, this results in increased costs of IT services, reduced productivity, and increased customer dissatisfaction.

Let us elaborate on the siloed organizations and the challenges associated with such structures. As discussed, most IT organizations today operate in a siloed environment, depicted in Figure 3.8. Applications are engineered and developed in an effort to address the functional requirements and the nonfunctional, application-related requirements. Infrastructures are engineered, developed, and managed with the aim of managing technology components within those infrastructures. There may exist more than one release channels into production. Senior leadership and management, both within the businesses and within IT, receive largely disconnected information that does not enable intelligent decision-making.

> *In the middle of such chaos, unfortunately, you also come across leaders who are unable to appreciate the new generation of challenges that their business enterprises face and want to force obsolete ways of managing IT. Combinations of these and other similar barriers lead to mismanagement and, ultimately, a non-delivery of those exact services that IT exists to deliver and that are required by our business customers.*

This cycle creates an overall negative impact on what IT stands for and promises to deliver—that is, enabling business processes in an effective and efficient manner. In this chapter, we discuss these challenges and review, at a high level, how BSM can address these and related challenges.

In Part II of this book, we will discuss implementation and related details. Let us now discuss the range of silos that exist and, in most cases, are detrimental to the services delivered by IT.

Siloed Engineering and Development

In most established, although not necessarily mature, IT organizations today, there seems to be a damaging common trend where the organization of IT (application, software, network, mainframe, databases, etc.) developments is concerned. Commonly, you see a software development organization that is responsible for architecting, engineering, and developing new applications or new releases of existing applications. You also see infrastructure engineering that is mandated to architect and engineer infrastructure-related components. The question is, "What happens when applications are developed in a vacuum without engaging the infrastructure?" Here is what happens: When these applications are released into production, the infrastructure may not be designed to provide the capacity to ensure the response times and availability targets (warranty) needed by the businesses. This mismatch causes unforeseen scenarios that, in most cases, lead to outages in critical business processes.

Siloed Technology Management

Most companies today are still managing their respective technologies in a siloed environment. What does it mean to be managing technology in silos and what is the resulting impact? Note that, while the answer presents the worst-case scenarios, there are business enterprises where these scenarios are real and you may be able to relate a combination of these to actual situations.

Looking at Figure 3.8, we can easily identify the following:

- New software and applications are developed in a silo and released independently to production.
- New releases to existing software may be managed within specialty areas and releases may be deployed independently.
- New infrastructure releases may be rolled into production via a separate channel.

Each time a release is put into production, a change is introduced to the environment and, if not managed and governed appropriately, this can lead to damaging outages. This siloed technology management poses a range of challenges. Some key examples follow.

Mismanagement of Service Availability

Figure 3.9 shows what happens when technology components are managed in silos. Each silo may be performing at 99% availability; however, when we look at the business service level, the performance may not be what is needed by the business.

Misalignment with Business Needs

In most cases, we have more work and fewer resources. That is why prioritization plays such a key role in running a profitable business. An important question to ask is, "How do we prioritize our work in IT?" In a high-maturity organization—operating at an organizational maturity level of 4 or 5—almost all investments in IT are made to improve business capabilities and perform its core business processes more efficiently and effectively. In business enterprises where technology

Component	Example	Component Availability	Net Availability
Business Process	Supply Chain	N/A	99% × 99% × 99% × 99% × 99% × 99% × 99% = 93%
Business Service	Electronic Order Intake	99%	99% × 99% × 99% × 99% × 99% × 99% = 94%
Technical Service	Electronic Data Interchange	99%	99% × 99% × 99% × 99% × 99% = 95%
Technology Components	Middleware	99%	99% × 99% × 99% × 99% = 96%
	Database	99%	99% × 99% ×99% = 97%
	Operating System	99%	99% × 99% = 98%
	Network	99%	– 99%

Figure 3.9 Siloed component management.

is managed in silos, one of the major challenges is that technology managers managing individual components are often managing them in a vacuum. For example, if network operations is operating in a silo, then chances are that network components are being managed at the respective component levels and without much insight into the role that each component plays in the delivery of associated business services and which business processes are impacted if these are not managed appropriately.

Siloed Request Management

With siloed engineering and development and technology management, it is no surprise that there may exist multiple channels for routing different types of requests placed on IT by the customers. This results in confused and dissatisfied customers and ultimately impacts the business's bottom-line. If you are running an internal IT organization, you should still think of users as customers and strategize, plan, and manage the delivery of services appropriately. Imagine that you call your cell phone service provider to change your service plan and are advised to contact the billing department, account management, the network services department, and others to fulfill your request. It would be no surprise if you chose to change your service provider. Similarly, we need to manage our internal users as customers and think about and manage IT as a business to align ourselves with the business needs and to integrate with the businesses and emerge as a value-added business partner.

Siloed Reporting and Communication

Siloed technology and request management lead to multiple, often disconnected and disintegrated, reporting and communication channels. Senior management and leadership teams base their decisions on the information provided to them. If this information is provided in a manner that does not represent IT accurately, it will negatively impact the decision-making capability and, ultimately, the business.

Siloed Visions and Leadership

Siloed engineering, development, and management lead to siloed visions and leadership. This is the last thing you want if you are responsible for delivering IT services to the customers. Unfortunately, I have come across leaders who have been operating in this siloed fashion for so many years that they find themselves incapable of thinking otherwise or they may prefer to have small domains. Ironically, in most of corporate America, there is a notion that the more people managed, the greater the scale of responsibility, and the larger the compensation. This encourages the wrong behaviors in managers and leaders who want to retain their small empires for the sake of being recognized as having greater responsibilities and not because it is in the best interest of the business. Leadership needs to appreciate the impact of siloed vision and bring the range of silos together for the success of the larger business.

Siloed Supplier Management

I have seen that siloed engineering, development, and management will lead to siloed supplier management. As shown in Figure 3.8, each siloed organization establishes its own relationships with outside partners and suppliers. Having these siloed relationships leads to the following negative impacts:

- Deepens the silos beyond organizational boundaries where the outside partners and suppliers agree to provide the levels of services that may satisfy the needs of a given silo but may not satisfy needs of the larger business needs.
- Minimizes the potential volume-based, enterprise-wide, cost benefits.
- Leads to higher than necessary complexities in the portfolio of solutions provided by outside partners and suppliers.

Who Is Impacted by This Siloed Approach?

The businesses and customers, as well as the IT organization, are impacted if IT is managed and operated in silos. If businesses are not realizing their true potential because IT is unable to deliver on its commitments, then they will likely face losses and this will ultimately impact IT negatively. This does not suggest that all business enterprises, irrespective of their specific business needs, should be horizontally integrated. Relationships with outside partners should be managed in a way that satisfies the needs of that particular business.

What Can BSM Do to Help?

BSM aims to implement end-to-end management for business services provided by the IT service provider, with the goal of addressing the challenges mentioned above. It is important to appreciate that how BSM is implemented depends entirely on a given organization, the business needs, and the associated challenges. Although there is a definite set of capabilities that can be achieved by appropriately implementing BSM, these capabilities will vary from implementation to implementation. We will now discuss some of the capabilities that BSM implementation should focus on building.

Business–IT Integration

We covered this topic in greater detail in Chapter 2. To summarize, business–IT integration will enable IT to become a value-added business partner. Instead of reacting to emerging business needs, business–IT integration enables IT to proactively identify new and innovative ways to enable the core business processes. Business enterprises can then maximize the IT-enabled growth potential.

Efficient Management of Services

Both business and technical services (discussed in Chapters 1 and 2) are optimally managed from strategy and planning through to transition, operation, and continual improvement to ensure that they meet business needs. Efficient service management leads to effective IT, enables effective customer expectation management, and results in improved customer satisfaction ratings.

Appropriate Organizational Alignment

If implemented appropriately, BSM implementation will enable IT to identify and agree on a set of organizational principles. These principles should serve as the foundation for building the appropriate organizational structures. Note that, over the course of the BSM implementation program, the IT organization is continually aligned to better address the particular business needs. This alignment is achieved through small, incremental, and iterative steps.

Greater Traceability between IT Capabilities and Business Goals

BSM enables the establishment of traceability between business processes and business and technical services through to lower level technology components. This traceability enables IT to build its capabilities to meet specific business needs.

Greater Transparency

Greater traceability enables visibility into how different business and technical services and other components are performing. This transparency enables IT to be proactive in managing the services it offers.

Clear Definition of Channel(s) Available to the Customer to Engage IT

BSM implementation will ensure that appropriate channels are defined and implemented so that customers are able to place varying types of requests and demands on IT in an effective and efficient manner.

Right Level of Governance

If implemented appropriately, BSM will ensure that appropriate governance is implemented at all levels—from strategy to implementation and operation. In addition, continual service improvement (CSI) will ensure that targeted improvement investments are made.

Difficulties Associated with Implementing BSM

Let us now discuss some of the challenges that organizations face when implementing BSM. This will develop further appreciation of why it is critical to iteratively and incrementally build slices of our BSM vision over time. Note that the extent of difficulties associated with implementing BSM depends on the current state (baseline) of maturity of both the business enterprise and IT organizations. For those that are at lower maturity levels, this may mean a fundamental shift in the ways in which business enterprises and IT organizations operate. Major difficulties may include the factors discussed in the following subsections.

Cultural Shift and Organizational Change

For organizations that have lower maturity levels, BSM implementation may lead to a fundamental shift in the way in which IT delivers its services to the customers and how customers engage IT in providing the specific services. Fundamental shifts leading to transformations do not happen overnight and need a consistent and steady approach to incrementally and iteratively improving the services provided by IT organizations.

Technology Management vs. Business Management

In many established organizations (not necessarily mature), IT is viewed and managed as a back-office cost center. According to the ITIL v3 Organizational Maturity Model, shown in Figure 3.10, those IT organizations that operate at the technology management level are maturity level 1 organizations.

In most cases, such technology management cultures encourage teams and departments within an IT organization to operate in silos (siloed engineering and development, siloed technology management, siloed request management, siloed reporting and communication, siloed vision and leadership, and siloed supplier management) discussed earlier in this chapter.

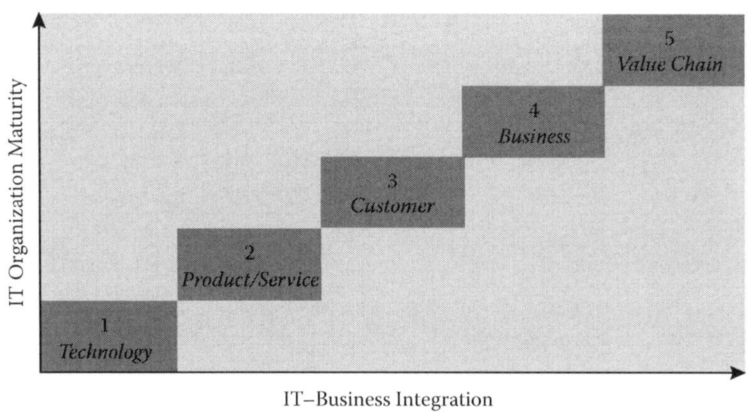

Figure 3.10 Organizational Maturity Model.

Maturity level 4 IT organizations manage their respective technologies to integrate with the business needs. A shift from being a technology management maturity level 1 organization to a business management maturity level 4 organization usually is a major one and requires transformations in the way that IT thinks, plans, and delivers its services to its customers. Such transformations do not happen in a big-bang step. Instead, it requires thought leadership, focus, organization, and management to achieve these overall cultural transformations in small, targeted, ongoing incremental steps.

Service Management vs. Technology Management

IT components (software, hardware, applications, networks, servers, etc.) need to be managed to ensure that the respective services that these components support are appropriately managed to meet the business needs. It takes only one weak link, as depicted in Figure 3.11, to break the value-chain. One weak component is all that is required to cause an outage in a critical business service.

To relate this idea to BSM, let us look at the service tree once again as shown in Figure 3.3. Business processes are enabled by one or more business services. Business services are realized by one or more technical services. Technical services are implemented by one or more technology components. In a less-mature organization, these components are managed in silos, as shown in Figure 3.8. The end result is that each of the components that make up a given business service is managed in silos. Therefore, a break in one component breaks the entire service chain.

A real-world service chain example, using the service tree concept, is shown in Figure 3.7. A supply chain business process is enabled by four business services: electronic order intake, customer service order intake, order processing, and shipping and handling. Business services, in turn, are

Figure 3.11 One weak link.

implemented by one or more technical services, and so on. To ensure that a supply chain business process is available as agreed with the customers, it is absolutely critical that the IT organization is able to manage all components that make up that supply chain business process. End-to-end BSM is the only effective and efficient way to guarantee that all components that implement a given business service are managed consistently and to ensure that business services are managed so that related business process needs are met.

When teams and departments within an IT organization do technology management, they do so in silos and that may lead to a creation of a potential weak link. For IT organizations to migrate from being technology management to service management may sometimes be a challenging task.

Balancing Resources between Firefighting and Innovation

The chances are that the resources of a low maturity level organization are engaged in firefighting most of the time. When initiatives such as BSM implementation are undertaken, special attention should be given to the number of additional resources that may be necessary to successfully deliver on new initiatives. In most cases, consultants may be an appropriate option. Higher maturity levels will enable organizations to dedicate more resources to innovation and fewer resources to keeping the lights on.

Lack of In-House BSM and ITIL Expertise

Whenever transformational efforts are undertaken, it is critical to have subject matter experts advise and assist in implementing related components. For effective and efficient implementation of BSM, it is critical that ITIL experts are appropriately identified, acquired (if necessary), and engaged. It is recommended that appropriate ITIL training is designed and delivered to the internal resources as the service management implementation program progresses. This will enable

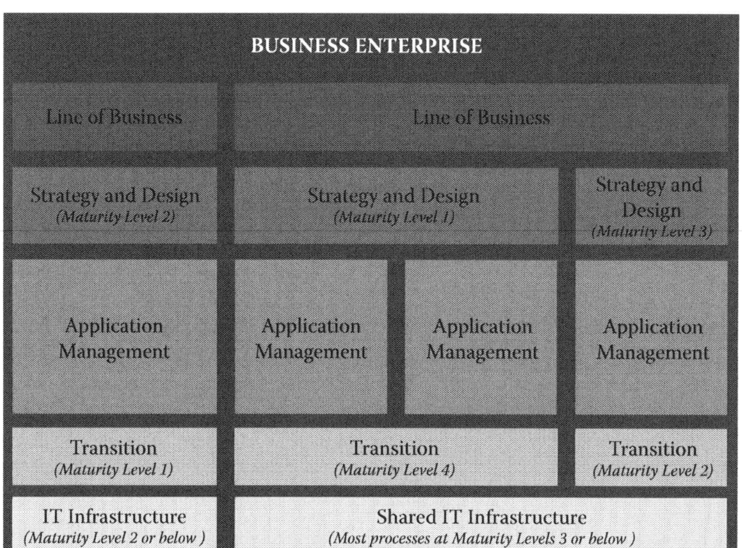

Figure 3.12 Varying maturity levels.

the organization to build in-house expertise that will be much needed when it is time to operate service management.

Multiple Independent Silos and Varying Maturity Levels

As shown in Figure 3.12, in most medium- to large-sized organizations, there may be multiple independent business-aligned IT organizations, and each may be at a different maturity level. How should BSM implementation be planned and executed to ensure that associated complexities and risks are appropriately managed and that focused business service improvements are implemented?

Efforts Required to Improve Service Management Processes

Mature service management processes provide the necessary foundation required to ensure that business services are managed effectively. Improving service management processes may have major impacts on the way people and teams within an IT organization perform their day-to-day jobs in managing technologies. Figure 3.1 graphically shows the different aspects that need to be managed to ensure successful implementation of BSM.

Longer Turnaround Times

In ITIL v3, there are more than 18 service management processes. Traditional service management implementation practices offer process-centric approaches (discussed in detail in the next section). Service management process improvement focus may take longer to mature from process maturity level 1 to level 3 or level 4, thereby pushing the anticipated BSM-driven business benefits further down; business benefits require that service chains for business processes are managed end-to-end as shown in Figure 3.7. My experience in working with a variety of clients across industries has taught me that if it takes too long to demonstrate the business value of making significant investments in improving IT, the sponsorship is likely to dry up and, between management shuffles, the entire transformation will be at risk. We need a more innovative approach to deal with these challenges.

ITIL v3 and Common BSM Implementation Practice

ITIL v3 is a collection of best practices of managing IT. It comprises more than 18 processes across the five phases of a service life cycle: service strategy, service design, service transition, service operation, and CSI.

- *Service strategy*
  - Service portfolio management
  - Financial management
  - Demand management
- *Service design*
  - Service catalog management
  - Service level management

  - Capacity management
  - Availability management
  - IT service continuity management
  - Information security management
  - Supplier management
- *Service transition*
  - Change management
  - Service asset and configuration management
  - Release and deployment management
  - Knowledge management
- *Service operation*
  - Event management
  - Incident management
  - Problem management
  - Request fulfillment
  - Access management
- *Continual service improvement*

This covers the seven-step CSI.

For each of the process areas, ITIL v3 literature provides guidelines on the following:

- Purpose/Goal/Objective
- Scope
- Value to business
- Policies/Principles/Basic concepts
- Process activities, methods, and techniques
- Triggers, inputs and outputs/interfaces
- Metrics
- Challenges, critical success factors, and risks
- Other related topics such as tooling, organizational, and more

ITIL v3 literature explains what activities need to be executed within each process area, what roles should perform those activities, and what this process will look like when implemented. As discussed, the literature also explains the scope, risks, critical success factors, key performance indicators (KPIs), and other related process details. It is then up to the business enterprises to take this literature and implement it. This is where the challenge lies. A good analogy may be that if I tell you what San Francisco looks like while we are sitting in New York, but I don't tell you how to get there, you can choose to go by road, train, plane or foot. Similarly, ITIL v3 tells us how an IT organization should look if it implements ITIL, but it does not really tell you in any detail how to implement ITIL.

As anticipated, organizations have been struggling to leverage ITIL guidelines and achieve transformational improvements to realize anticipated effectiveness, efficiency, and business–IT integration benefits. Implementation expertise may exist within largely expensive consulting services firms. They make millions helping organizations implement BSM. This book shows you better, more innovative, and more practical approaches to implementing BSM yourself.

To date, companies have taken a more process-oriented approach, that is, they identify which process(es) have the most gaps and then try to improve those processes. This approach comes with a range of challenges including:

- Longer turnaround times
- Siloed process-centric approaches lacking cross-process business- and service-oriented thinking
- Higher risks of losing sponsorship
- Potential lack of alignment between improvement-related investments and business needs

To make matters even more complicated, implementing BSM impacts each and every aspect of an organization. Depending on the organizational baseline maturity level, implementing service management may even be revolutionary and take years before the organizations start realizing the benefits. Worse, organizational tolerance to wait for these transformational benefits to come has been declining. We need an iterative and incremental, service-oriented, agile method to go about delivering business value through steady and ongoing business-specific improvements.

In summary, ITIL v3 guidelines tell us what needs to be implemented for each of the above-mentioned processes. But, it does not tell how to go about implementation. It gives a picture of how the end-state should look, but it does not tell how to get to that end-state. With all the challenges, business-related and others, on the landscape, organizations need guidance. They try to adopt ITIL guidelines by following a process-oriented approach. ITIL v2 provided guidelines on three distinct types of these approaches: single-process approach, multiple-process approach, and all-process approach. Companies follow the same process-oriented approach when it comes to implementing BSM. The traditional process-specific approach has been graphically illustrated in the upper half

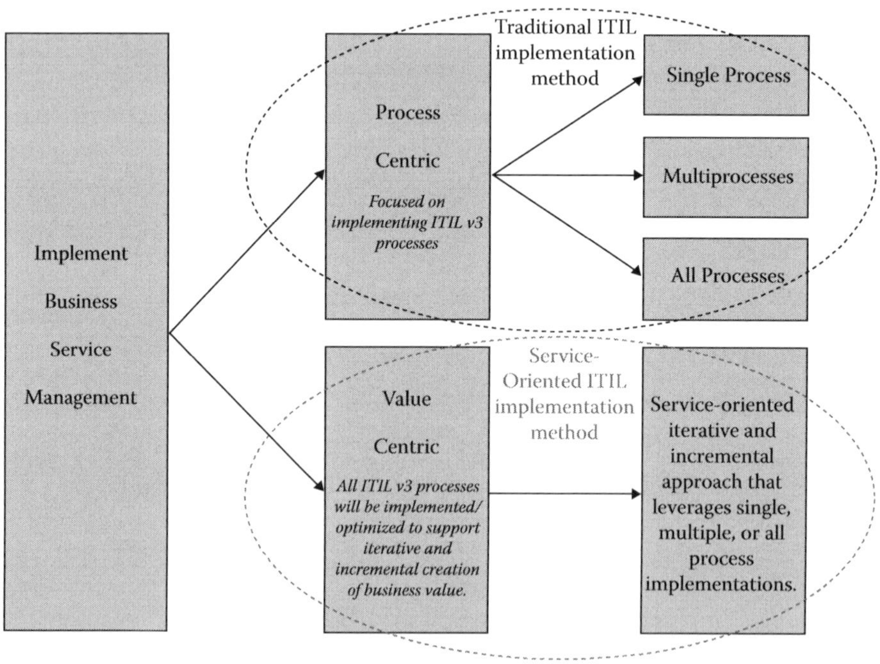

Figure 3.13 Service management implementation approaches.

of Figure 3.13. Single-, multi-, and all-process approaches have been around since ITIL v2. Most companies still approach ITIL implementation from the perspectives of implementing processes and maturing them. We will discuss the challenges that companies tend to face in adopting this approach and how a more iterative and incremental business value-centric approach may have greater probability of success in today's ever-changing and all-demanding environment.

Problems Associated with the Traditional ITIL Implementation Method

Longer Turnaround for Potential Return on BSM Investments

There are always returns on improvements made. The question is how to maximize that return, not only for IT, but also for the overall business. Depending on organizational maturity, there are some processes that may bring potential returns in terms of improving efficiencies in those process areas. However, to make these improvements real for the business, so that the business can see immediate impact on investments made in improving IT processes, improvement-related investments need to be made with business needs in view.

Let us discuss service asset and configuration management as an example. One of the core components of this process area is the configuration management database (CMDB). Depending on the size of the organization, this CMDB may contain millions of records. To be at process maturity level 4 or 5, CMDB should provide information on all IT assets that exist and the interrelationships (e.g., which application is installed on which server, which network does this server belong to, what network components support the delivery of services provided by this server, etc.). Since most of these relationships cannot be captured automatically, for a medium- to large-sized organization, it may take years and millions of dollars before a CMDB is mature. If it is done in a traditional nontargeted manner, it will be like boiling an ocean. There are obviously more business-critical CIs than others; some support more critical business services than others. Pareto analysis must be performed and targeted business-value, service-oriented improvements must be implemented in an iterative and incremental fashion. Otherwise, if organizations do go down the path of improving CMDB and other individual processes to higher maturity levels without putting the larger business context in view, there may be many years before business realizes the true benefits.

Nontargeted Improvement Investments

Process improvement–specific investments may produce some desired efficiencies within IT, but mostly these are not felt by the business. There may be cost savings, but not necessarily value-added improvements. To maximize the return on improvement investments, these investments must be aligned with business goals and efforts should be targeted to specifically improving those IT components that result in maximum improvements for the business. If the service catalog is the source of information on all services that IT offers to its customers, then use that as the platform for planning and improving services. Identify those services that make the most impact on the business, and plan service and service management process improvements for those services. This will ensure that all IT improvement investments are made in a targeted manner.

Ineffective Risk Management

Traditional process-specific approaches may lead to ineffective risk management across a range of areas. Two of the critical areas are service improvement risks and architecture and integration risks.

Service improvement risks—Focusing on service management process improvements without attempting to leverage those improvements to improve the business services that support the core business processes will push service management implementation business benefits forward. Such a situation may put the entire initiative and the sponsorship at risk.

Architecture and integration risks—Focusing on individual process-silos with limited cross-process, cross-service, and cross-organization integration visibility will likely push major architecture and integration risks forward. Implementing BSM by leveraging service management process improvement for selected prioritized services early on in the program will enable the organization to see a slice of the BSM vision in action. This slice will give a view of what IT will look like at the end of the effort and will further enable the IT organization to gain support and sponsorship and build excitement among the teams to embrace the BSM ways of thinking and operating.

Key Service Management Implementation Components

As shown in Figure 3.14, the main end-state goal is to achieve business–IT integration. Achieving this state means that the IT organization has a value-added partnership with the customer and the businesses that it supports.

Three key components that will be essential to achieving the business–IT integration goal are discussed in the following subsections.

Service Improvement

Service improvements will be implemented at two levels: business services and technical services. As shown in the service tree in Figure 3.3, business services enable business processes. It is critical to assess the customer pain points and desires early on in the project. Based on that analysis, the most business-critical processes should be identified. The business services that support those

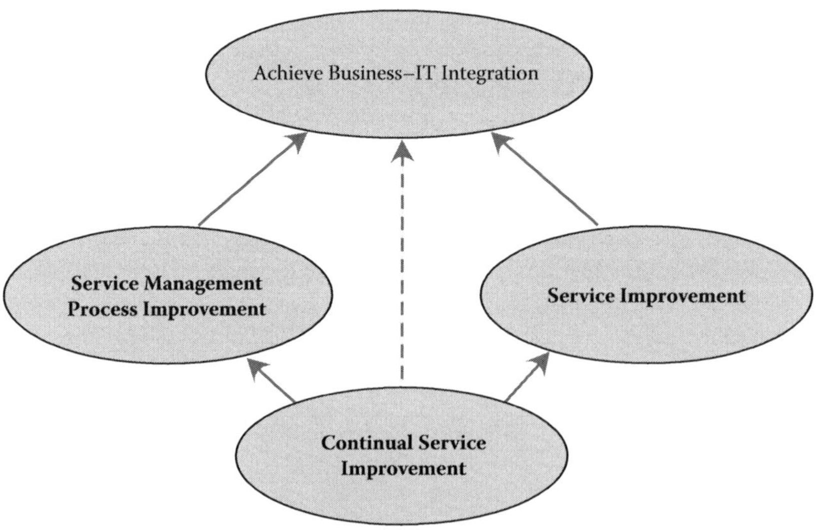

Figure 3.14 IT service management implementation components.

business processes are appropriately prioritized for service improvement efforts. These services drive the downward improvements (i.e., which technical services should be improved) and so on.

Service Management Process Improvement

There are more than 18 service management processes in ITIL v3. Depending on the key improvement drivers, as well as some process interdependencies, these processes are improved and implemented.

Continual Service Improvement

As shown in Figure 3.14, CSI is the most critical component of implementing service management. If implemented and institutionalized appropriately, CSI can become an engine of cultural transformation. ITIL v3 describes it as an essential part required to "keep the momentum going." Figure 3.15 shows some of the key CSI inputs, outputs, and main activities. These are key inputs, key activities, and outputs.

Key Inputs

- Service performance data—Provide information on how different services as listed and defined in the service catalog are performing against the targets agreed on in the SLAs and OLAs.
- Service management process performance—How are service management processes performing? These are based on predefined KPIs and will require process-monitoring capabilities.
- New requirements—CSI should function as a sole organization that solicits new ideas and other requirements (security, regulatory, etc.) from across the organization.

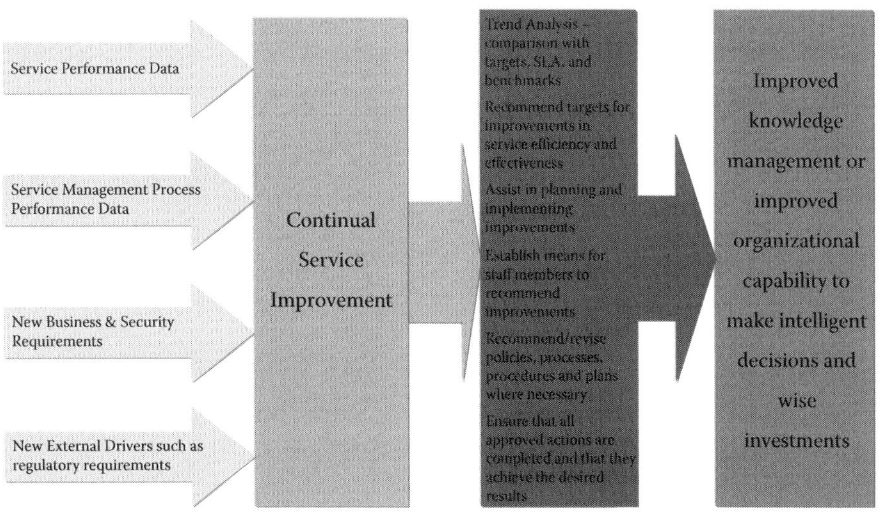

Figure 3.15 CSI—key inputs, outputs, and value creation.

Key Activities

- Trend analysis—This may include comparisons with targets, SLAs, and benchmarks.
- Recommended improvement targets—What are achievable targets for improvements?
- Planning and implementing—Depending on how CSI is implemented, it may make significant contributions in planning and implementing improvements.
- Channel for new ideas—CSI may provide a main channel to staff members to submit new ideas for improving services and service management processes.
- Revise policies, processes, and procedures—CSI will play a central role in managing policies, processes, and related procedures. We will learn how CSI can leverage business process management practices to effectively and efficiently deliver the most value.
- Ensuring improvement implementations—It is a good practice for CSI to ensure that improvement implementations are delivered. This will impact the related KPIs.

Output

Through the inputs identified and activities performed, the key and most valuable output that CSI provides is the improved organization capabilities to make intelligent decisions and wise investments.

CSI is one of the most critical components of BSM implementation. We will discuss planning and implementing aspects of CSI in great detail in Parts II and III of this book.

Summary

In this chapter, we have learned about the challenges that organizations face today and how service management can enable organizations to address and manage these challenges. We have also discussed the common implementation approaches and why it is difficult to implement service management. We have discussed why implementing BSM means transformation for most established (though not necessarily mature) organizations. Increasing pressures on IT from the customers to deliver value sooner means that such transformations must deliver business value sooner to ensure that the momentum is maintained and sponsorship stays alive. Traditional process-centric service management implementation mostly comes with delayed value creation and ineffective risk management. An iterative and incremental approach to implementing BSM will enable organizations to improve service management processes and to create immediate business value that positively impacts the business bottom-line profitability. In Part II of this book, we will discuss how BSM can be implemented in an iterative and incremental manner.

Reference

Shuja, A. 2008. *Iterative and Incremental Service-Oriented Service Management Implementation,* itSMF Conference, Madrid, Spain. 13th May, 2008. http://209.85.229.132/search?q=cache:yGP8xPGfl6kJ:www.uc3m.es/portal/page/portal/congresos_jornadas/congreso_itsmf/Iterative%2520and%2520Incremental%2520Service-Oriented%2520Service%2520Manag.pdf+iterative+and+incremental+service-oriented+service+management&cd=1&hl=en&ct=clnk.

II

ITERATIVE AND INCREMENTAL APPROACH TO IMPLEMENTING BUSINESS SERVICE MANAGEMENT

Chapter 4

Iterative and Incremental Service-Oriented Service Management Implementation: An Introduction

We have discussed the challenges associated with implementing business service management (BSM) using IT Infrastructure Library version 3 (ITIL v3). We know that initiatives such as BSM implementation are long term and need consistent support and sponsorship to be successful. We have also discussed the need to create business value quickly and to manage all enterprise changes (process, organizational, architectural, and integration changes) and related risks effectively.

In this chapter, I introduce an approach that will enable the organizations embarking on BSM to effectively demonstrate the value of implementing such improvements and to achieve rapid returns on the investments. The way to realize the returns on such investments quickly, while managing and optimizing associated risks effectively, is to manage these implementations in a business-focused, service-oriented, iterative, and incremental manner. The key focus of these improvements should not be on achieving and measuring IT improvements, but rather on improving customers' experiences and businesses' perception of the value of IT services. Measurements must be made so that the business impact of these improvements may be calculated. The results of these improvements, measured in terms of business impact, must be appropriately communicated to the businesses and customers to ensure that the journey continues through any management shuffles. This chapter will answer the following questions:

- *What is iterative and incremental service-oriented service management implementation (i2-SOSMI)? What is the purpose of this approach?* We will learn about an innovative approach to implement BSM.

- *What does it mean to implement BSM incrementally?* We will discuss how we can implement one "slice" of BSM at a time and reap the potential value it will generate for the larger organization.
- *At the core, what activities are required to implement BSM incrementally?* We will learn what core activities are performed, at a high-level, to implement BSM incrementally. We will have detailed discussions on these activities in Chapters 5 and 6.
- *What is i2-SOSMI architecture? What is the content and life cycle of i2-SOSMI?* We will learn about the approach in terms of the overall architecture and the key components. We will introduce the concept of disciplines, phases, and iterations.
- *What are some of the main BSM implementation patterns available?* If BSM is the target state for the organization, there are multiple paths available to get to that destination. This chapter includes a brief introduction to those approaches. Detailed discussions will be provided in Chapter 6.

Introduction

The i2-SOSMI methodology is an iterative and incremental risk-driven approach to implementing BSM. It is inspired by and leverages some of the industry's leading software development practices (iterative and incremental software development approaches such as the Rational Unified Process, SCRUM, and others) and the core v3 *Continual Service Improvement* (CSI) seven-step process.

Just like any other methodology, the i2-SOSMI provides a rich set of guidelines (process-specific work breakdown structure templates, workflows, document templates, and other important implementation concepts) that are expected to facilitate the implementation of BSM. However, it must be customized to the specific organization's BSM needs and objectives.

Purpose of i2-SOSMI

The i2-SOSMI methodology aims to:

- Address the challenges that organizations face in implementing BSM.
- Ensure that targeted service management process improvements are made.
- Deliver continual and incremental business value in a consistent, steady, and ongoing manner.
- Effectively manage risks associated with implementing BSM such as organizational, architecture, integration, and process-related risks.
- Ensure that service management process improvements are targeted on improving the business bottom-line by integrating improvements with improving and effectively managing the businesses services.

Implementing One "Slice" of BSM Vision at a Time

At the core of the i2-SOSMI is a focus on enabling the undertaking organization (referred to as the "subject organization") to implement one "slice" of the BSM vision at a time and to continue delivering these slices every 6 months or so. Visualize these slices as incremental improvements that are very well planned and targeted to achieve specific, well-defined, and measurable business and customer improvements. Such a focus will further ensure that the momentum, support, and sponsorship of achieving BSM are kept alive.

Implementing a slice of BSM will need all key service management components, which include continual service improvement, service management process improvement, and service improvement, and will need to be implemented in an integrated manner. However, before we get into those details, let us first understand what it really means to implement a slice of the BSM vision.

What Does It Mean to Implement a Slice of BSM?

Figure 4.1 depicts a close-to-the-real-world situation where less mature organizations are divided into clear silos. This creates some potentially negative impacts.

- *Lack of clarity on roles and responsibilities*
  There are situations (business process A, business service A, and technical service E) where roles and responsibilities are not clearly defined. Each silo is managing its own components without much visibility on how their respective areas impact or do not impact the business profitability. In some cases, you will even see significant overlaps in the responsibilities of different departments within the larger IT organization.
- *Lack of visibility into critical components*
  Because of this lack of cross-silo visibility, there is a lack of understanding on which components are more critical to the business. In some larger low maturity organizations, you will often see multiple configuration management databases and multiple instances of numerous

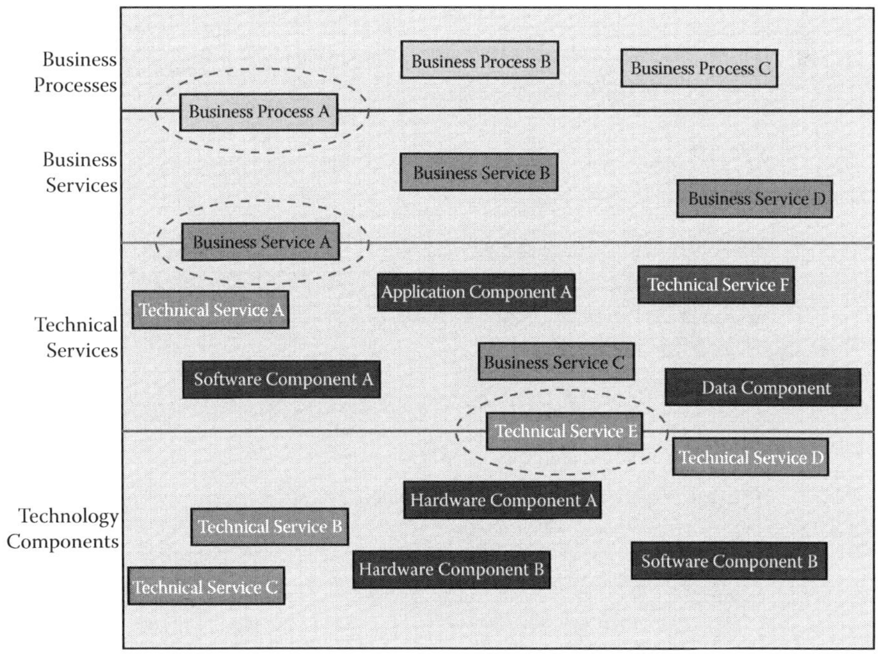

Figure 4.1 A low-maturity level IT organization.

service management processes (Change Management, Incident Management, and so on). When it is time to prioritize where to make improvements, such decisions are mostly made in a vacuum leading to obvious impacts on potential returns on those investments.

The i2-SOSMI provides guidelines to enable organizations to improve service management processes and to leverage these improvements to effectively and efficiently enable the core business processes. Targeted investments are made to improve those components of the service chain that enable the business-critical processes. Parallel service management processes and service improvements are implemented to not only improve IT management capabilities but also to demonstrate how those improvements in IT processes and management impact the business profitability. This is one factor that seems to play a most critical role in fueling the continued sponsorship and support. Investments made in IT improvements where it is difficult to relate to the bottom-line business profitability are the first ones to be impacted in case of budget squeezes or management shuffles.

Figure 4.2 shows a BSM slice implemented for business-prioritized process. Underneath that process, all service management components are improved for both service management processes and business services.

Targeting the service management process and service improvements on those critical components that enable a business process means that all related business services, technical services, software, application, data, and hardware components are improved to ensure that we are able to meet the agreed targets documented in service level agreements (SLAs). It is important to note that documenting and agreeing on targets is the easy part; the challenging part, and where most of us feel the heat, is when it comes time to meet the agreed targets. Such targeted improvements will enable us to be clear about achievable targets and to agree to terms that can be met.

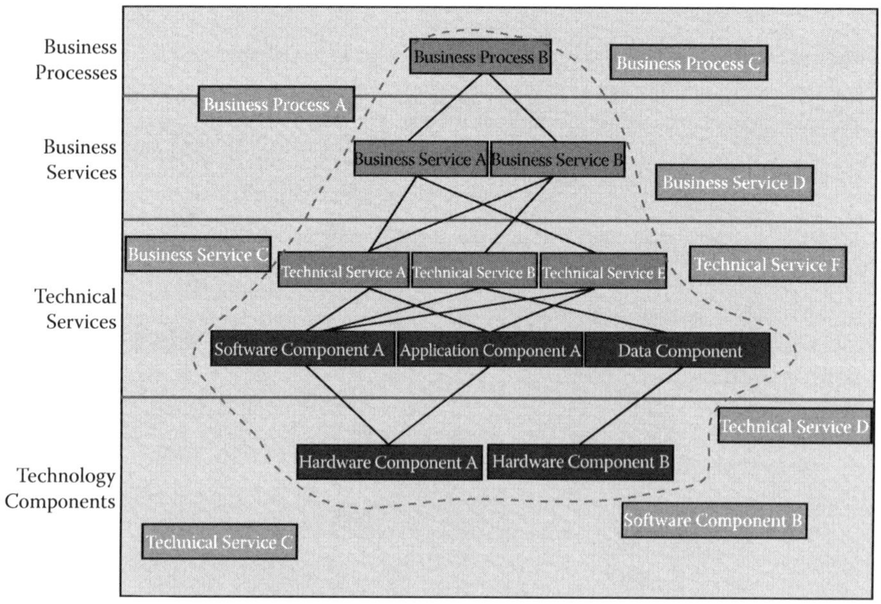

Figure 4.2 A "slice" of business service management.

Expected Benefits

If managed correctly, implementing a slice of BSM at a time is expected to achieve the following:

- Immediate returns on service management improvement investments
- A demonstration to the larger organization of what the end state will look like
- Early identification and appreciation of potential architectural and integration risks
- Sustained support and sponsorship
- A service-oriented, end state–operational "slice" of the organization (people, process, and tools)

From a practical implementation perspective, this last benefit is very important to appreciate. For this slice of BSM, all the organizational capabilities will be delivered for selected business processes and services. This will include all potential roles, both within the service management process (process owner, process manager, etc.) and the service management areas (business service manager, service delivery manager, technical service owner, etc.), new tooling capabilities, process performance monitoring and analytical capabilities, and so on. It will enable organizations to see how new technologies such as service-oriented architecture can be leveraged in building shared, reusable service components and can be demonstrated through proof-of-concepts. It is, therefore, crucial that this slice represents how the envisioned transformed organization will look at the end of this initiative. Key components of the BSM implementation are represented in the BSM implementation hexagon in Figure 4.3.

The i2-SOSMI Architecture

Enabling organizations to incrementally implement one slice of BSM at a time is at the core of i2-SOSMI methodology. This is:

- Business-focused (prioritized based on the most critical business processes)
- Service-oriented (by ensuring implementation of the means of delivering value to businesses and customers)
- Iterative and incremental (targeted measurable improvements are achieved one small step at a time)

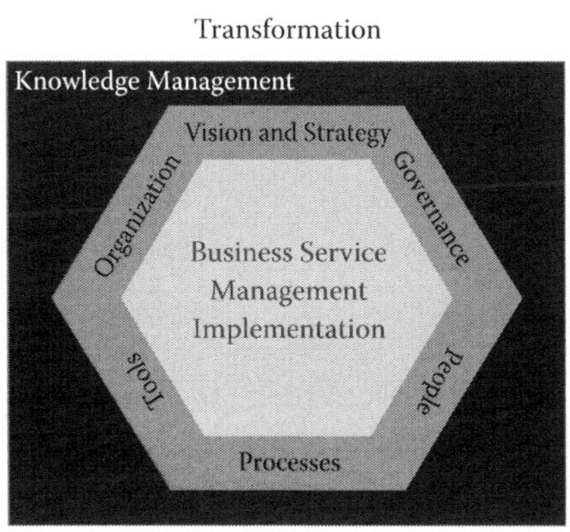

Figure 4.3 A BSM-implementation hexagon.

Let us now see how this methodology is architected and why.

The i2-SOSMI provides a set of comprehensive guidelines that the subject organization will need to successfully implement BSM based on ITIL v3. The i2-SOSMI v2 consists of seven disciplines and four phases. Content is represented in work streams and life cycle is represented in phases. Each phase consists of three iterations: visualize, architect, and realize. We will discuss each of these iterations in greater detail. In summary, there are three key i2-SOSMI architectural components:

- Disciplines
- Phases
- Iterations

Figure 4.4 shows the i2-SOSMI architecture with all these key components graphically represented.

The i2-SOSMI life cycle progresses from left to right. As the project progresses through the phases, greater organizational maturity is achieved through continual, steady, and ongoing improvements. As shown in Figure 4.4, there are four phases: foundation, design, align, and integrate. Note that as the project progresses through the phases and organizational maturity improves, the planned, targeted, and proactive process and service improvements become greater and are managed under CSI (BSM-aligned, continual service and process improvements). At the same time, the "quick wins and quick fixes" type of reactive, ad-hoc, and unplanned improvements become fewer and fewer.

You will also notice phases named across the vertical axis as well. In front of each phase, you will notice *Service Management Process Improvement* and *Business Service Improvement and End-to-End Business Service Management Implementation*. It shows that within each phase, both service management processes and business services are improved. In other words, you are ensuring that you are able to immediately leverage the service management improvements implemented to deliver business value by improving the business services. *Service Management Process Improvement* and *Business Service Improvement and End-to-End Business Service Management Implementation* are two of the seven disciplines and will be discussed in greater detail later in this book. The vertical box named *Disciplines Critical to Business Service Management Implementation* represents that activities from across the seven disciplines are performed across all phases of the project. Let us now briefly discuss each of the i2-SOSMI architectural components.

Disciplines

In this section, we will learn about some of the most important areas that need to be considered when planning to implement BSM. Depending on the organizational maturity of service management practices, there may be a need to consider other areas as well. However, there are some areas that are critical to the successful implementation of BSM. These critical aspects are captured in the form of disciplines and each discipline will describe those critical aspects in the form of activities performed, roles that perform those activities, inputs that are required to successfully achieve objectives, and outputs produced as a result of these activities. In i2-SOSMI, the content that is related to these aspects is captured with each of the disciplines and this content is discussed in terms of activities performed and outputs produced.

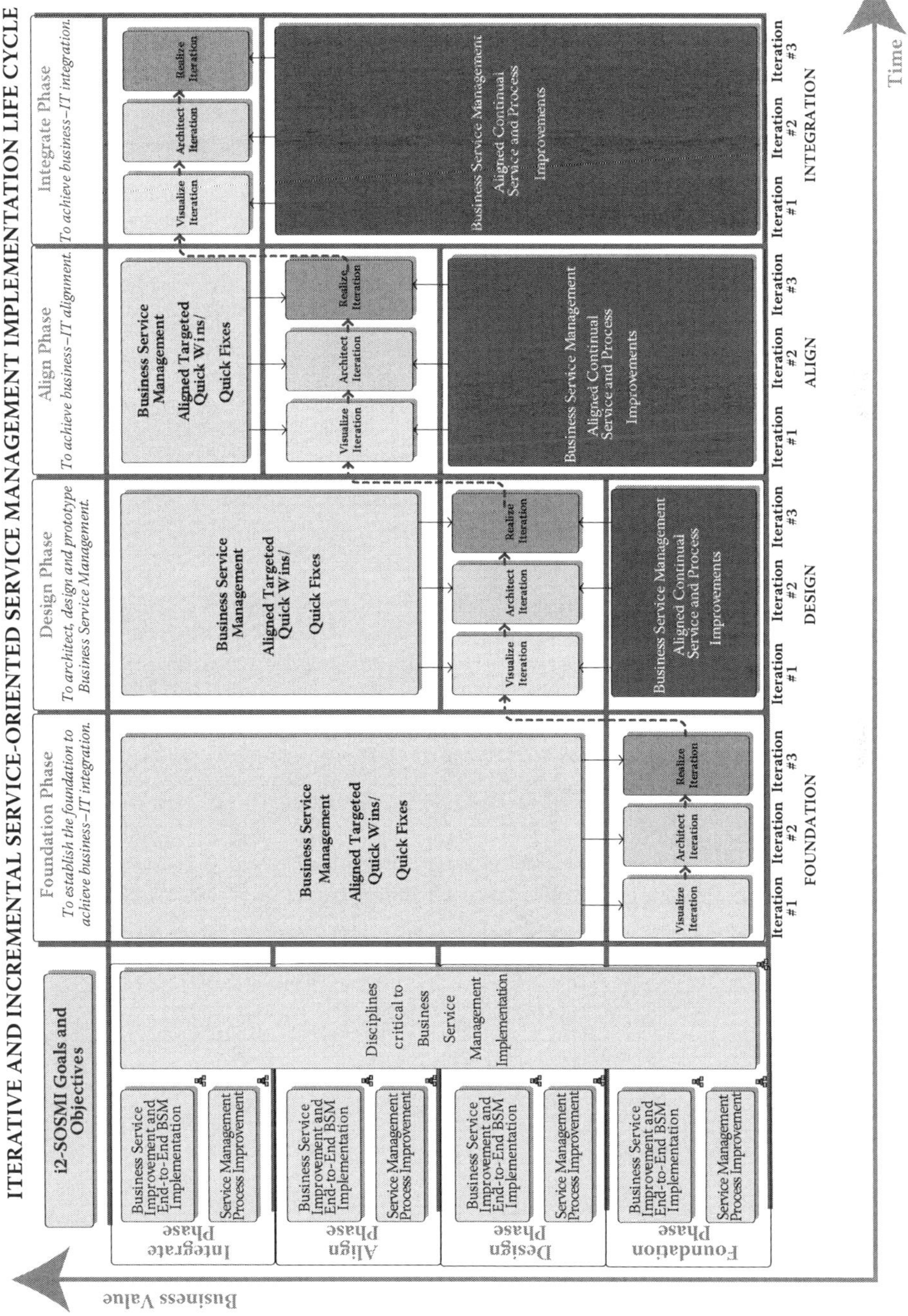

Figure 4.4 The i2-SOSMI architecture.

Meaning of the Term "Discipline"

Let us start by looking at the term *discipline*. According to the *Merriam-Webster Dictionary*, the term *discipline* is defined as follows:

- From the Latin *disciplina*—teaching, learning, from *discipulus*
- To bring (a group) under control
- A field of study
- A rule or system of rules governing an activity

According to Shuja and Krebs (2008), the term *discipline* has been historically used in relation to learning, teaching, controlling, and governing. In relation to controlling, discipline is also defined as a controlled behavior expected to produce a specific improvement. It is also defined as a pattern of behavior made up of a set of rules and methods. As a concept, *discipline* is primarily derived from iterative and incremental software development practices such as the Rational Unified Process (RUP) and defined as a categorization of activities based on similarity of concerns and cooperation of work effort. A discipline is a collection of activities that are related to a major "area of concern" (or "a field of study," as discussed above) within the overall project. In i2-SOSMI, just like in RUP, an activity is a process element that supports the nesting and logical grouping of related process elements, thus forming breakdown structures. We will see in Chapter 6 that, from the life cycle perspective, activities will be carried out concurrently from across different disciplines.

However, these activities are separated into distinct disciplines to effectively organize content, which makes comprehension and thereby learning easier. In addition, since the skill sets needed to perform the tasks in one area of concern are probably similar, logical grouping of these activities simplifies how different roles are organized. This enables us to organize a small set of roles in a way that they are aligned to one another along discipline lines (Shuja and Krebs, 2008). We will also see in detail how these related activities are governed and performed in an organized manner, not in isolation, and not in a haphazard fashion. In fact, there is a recommended sequence that should be followed to achieve optimal performance and maximize productivity and predictability. It is important to note that, although disciplines propose a recommended sequence of activities, these are truly performed in parallel with activities from other relevant (based on where you are in the project life cycle) disciplines. The benefits provided that logically group the i2-SOSMI activities into distinct disciplines are:

- Easier to comprehend the activities.
- Proves very useful when tailoring a given discipline to meet the specific needs of the organization.
- Different roles are able to better and more effectively understand their respective responsibilities.
- Enables project managers to more effectively monitor and control these activities.

The i2-SOSMI Disciplines

The iterative and incremental service-oriented service management implementation (i2-SOSMI) methodology effectively enables IT organizations to rapidly implement BSM in ways that will

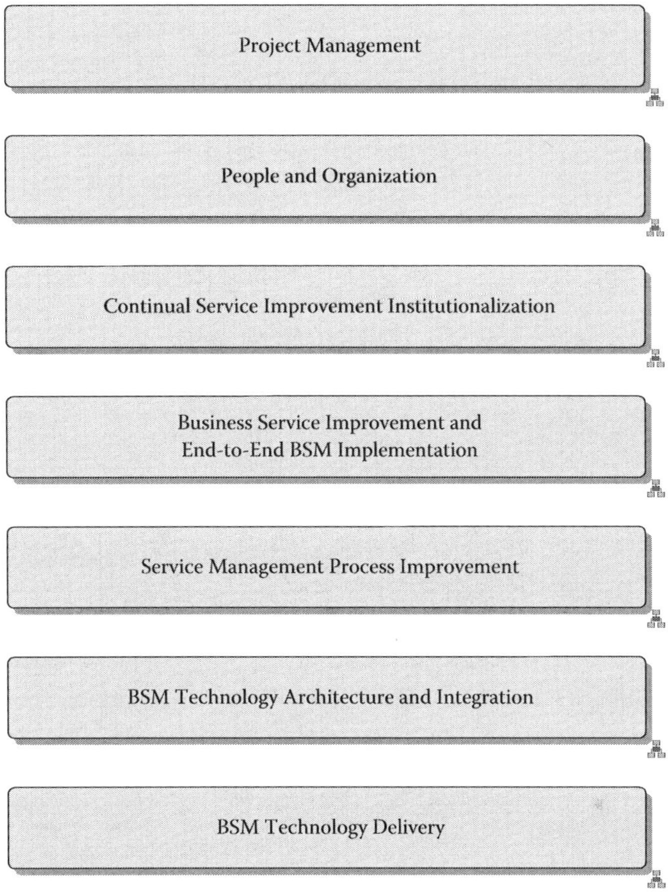

Figure 4.5 The i2-SOSMI disciplines.

maximize the returns and will minimize the associated risks. There are seven disciplines (also known as key areas or work streams) as shown in Figure 4.5.

These include:

1. Project Management
2. People and Organization
3. Continual Service Improvement Institutionalization
4. Business Service Improvement and End-to-End Business Service Management Implementation
5. Service Management Process Improvement
6. Business Service Management Technology Architecture and Integration
7. Business Service Management Technology Delivery

Figure 4.6 shows the i2-SOSMI work breakdown structure.

Let us now briefly discuss each of these disciplines.

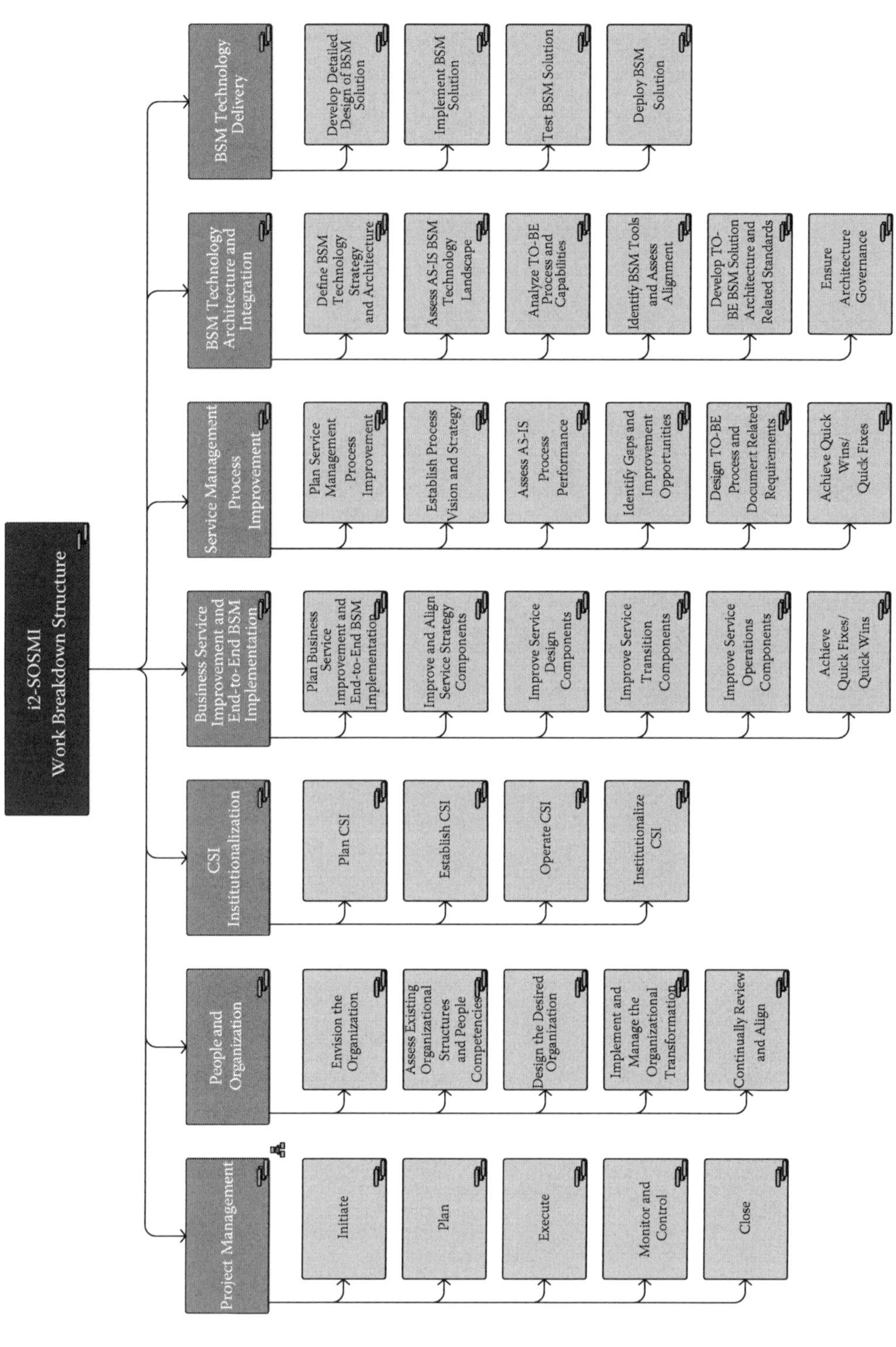

Figure 4.6 The i2-SOSMI work breakdown structure.

Project Management

The project management discipline is based on guidelines provided by the Project Management Institute's *Project Management Body Of Knowledge* (PMBOK). It specifically focuses on project management activities that are required to be carried out to plan and implement BSM.

People and Organization

BSM is more about organizational and cultural change than any other single factor. It is people who make up an organization and represent a specific culture. If it is about people changing their behaviors and attitudes, then organizations will need to make dedicated plans to ensure that the correct people are identified, selected, and trained to make this organizational transformation a success. If you have identified, trained, and developed the correct people, the next task is to organize them appropriately to minimize conflicts and stream collaboration. In this discipline, we will discuss the required activities to ensure that the correct people and organization are developed to support the BSM.

Continual Service Improvement Institutionalization

CSI, according to ITIL v3, must enable the organizations to keep the momentum going. In most organizations, there are functions and teams that focus on quality improvement and related areas. ITIL v3 introduces this concept of continual improvement, which in its true sense requires an environment that motivates people to continue to thrive instead of just survive. CSI must drive this cultural transformation.

As we implement BSM, it is critical to establish CSI culture across the organization. CSI implementation may take a range of different forms. However, the function remains the same (i.e., to enable the organization to keep its momentum of continual improvements). In early phases and iterations of the BSM implementation project, we will be focusing on establishing the foundation for CSI. As we go through the project, CSI must mature so that, toward the end of the project, CSI emerges as an established function. Therefore, CSI discipline will provide comprehensive guidelines on planning and establishing CSI practices across the organization. Once we effectively manage services, we are able to achieve the following:

- Clearly understand how services are performing against established targets.
- Collect all relevant data and trends showing service usage patterns, potential breaks across weak links, and other related information.
- In-depth analytics can be performed on the data collected to identify opportunities for improvements.
- Better appreciation of changes in business needs and organizational capabilities to meet those needs. This will further enable the organization to better do capacity and demand management.

The above information will enable organizations to continually monitor service performance and proactively identify opportunities for improvements. To achieve this, CSI needs to collaborate closely with service level management. We will learn in Chapters 5 and 6 how the role of CSI evolves over the course of a BSM implementation project.

In addition to continually improving services, CSI must drive the service management process improvements. In fact, these service management process improvements will underpin and enable any desired service improvements. For example, if you are currently able to create a new account for e-mail service in 5 business days and you need to reduce it to 3 business days, you will most likely need to improve the underpinning request fulfillment process for new e-mail account creation. Once the service management processes (ITIL v3 processes) are initially developed (managed and delivered under the Service Management Process Improvement discipline) and are brought under management, the following will be possible:

- Thorough understanding of operational processes
- Process performance monitoring against established key performance indicators (KPIs)
- Collection of high-quality process performance data
- Trend analysis
- Identification of opportunities for improvements

CSI institutionalization is critical to achieving sustainable, long-term service improvements and must be managed appropriately.

Business Service Improvement and End-to-End BSM Implementation

IT creates and delivers services to its businesses and customers. Through these services, IT must deliver value to its customers. If these services are not perceived as valuable to their respective customers, then there is a break in the value chain and the likelihood that customers are going to be unhappy is very high. Services enable IT organizations to measure the value they create. The i2-SOSMI's main focus is on ensuring that all improvement (people, process, and technology) opportunities are identified, managed, and realized so that the results of these improvements are visible to the customers and benefits can be measured in business terms. Service improvement enables organizations to implement service management on existing services.

The Service Improvement discipline ensures the high-impact service improvement focus as an integral component of the overall BSM implementation project. Services should be selected and prioritized from the service catalog (developed as one of the key Foundation Phase deliverables). These services can include business or technical services. It is, however, strongly recommended that services that are selected are business services. This will further ensure that each underpinning technical service and other components that need to be improved are improved in a targeted fashion and in support of a larger business service. This will also enable the organization to demonstrate the business benefits of improving a given business service through service level achievements and improved service management. Now, imagine a maturity level 1 organization where the notion of BSM may be truly an alien one. In such cases, first, we may need to bring services under management. Once under management, we will be able to continually improve these services based on KPIs.

End-to-end BSM (process, tooling and integration, people, and partners) implementation refers to the effort of bringing services under management for the first time. We can call it initial service management development effort. This is performed in each phase for a prioritized set of services. End-to-end BSM is what implements an incremental slice of our vision.

In summary, this discipline enables organizations to implement service management on existing services and provides guidelines on planning and establishing CSI practices.

Service Management Process Improvement

The quality of the product or service produced depends on the quality of the underpinning processes that result in the creation of that product or service. This discipline focuses on the initial development of service management processes. The later continual improvements on these processes are managed and achieved under the CSI. How efficiently and effectively an IT organization is able to fulfill requests for new services or changes to existing services depends on how well the IT teams and departments responsible for fulfilling those requests are able to identify, process, and complete those requests. We will discuss the key concepts related to developing and managing processes just like you manage any other asset within your organization in Chapter 9 (Service Management Process Improvement). The i2-SOSMI ensures a strong alignment between service management process improvement and service improvement so that

1. Improvement investments are identified, prioritized, and decided in a business-focused and targeted fashion.
2. All improvements realized as a result of the investments contribute optimally toward improving the services delivered to customers.

The key purpose is to ensure that improvements are made visible to the customers and businesses to enable creation of positive perceptions about the business value delivered through IT services. Therefore, in short, this discipline will enable organizations to develop new processes. It leverages industry process development and improvement best practices and provides ITIL v3 service management, process improvement, work breakdown structure.

In summary, this discipline enables organizations to develop new processes.

BSM Technology Architecture and Integration

Whenever individual processes are improved and associated tools are implemented in silos, the end result will be a siloed solution and integration across those processes and underlying support tools will most definitely become a project of its own. This discipline will ensure that architecture and integration standards are established for BSM implementation. It is based on process-integration needs to support BSM. This discipline ensures that architecture and integration standards are established for BSM implementation and that appropriate governance is provided to ensure an end-to-end BSM solution. Note that there are service management tools available in the marketplace. However, for these tools to enable organizations to achieve end-to-end BSM, they need to be integrated with existing tools (where appropriate), aligned with organizational needs, and configured to support any special process needs.

Tools and enabling technologies play a critical role in enforcing respective processes in efficient manners. In this discipline, we will discuss the activities that should be planned and executed to ensure that appropriate technologies are correctly architected and integrated to deliver the desired capabilities required to enable end-to-end BSM.

There are two main aspects related to this discipline: architecture and integration and governance.

- *Architecture and integration*
  This aspect concerns architecting the right solution to ensure end-to-end BSM. Enabling BSM means breaking through the organizational silos and building cross-department, enterprise-wide integrated solutions. All activities that are required to be performed to ensure that the right BSM solution is architected are managed and executed in this discipline.

- *Governance*
  This aspect is about ensuring that the architected solution is developed and implemented according to the architecture. Any related standards are developed and enforced.

BSM Technology Delivery

This discipline is about implementing and delivering the BSM solution in compliance with the architecture.

i2-SOSMI disciplines are important part of the methodology. We will discuss these disciplines in detail in this part of the book. As discussed, there are seven disciplines (also known as key areas or work streams) as shown in Figure 4.5. These include Project Management, People and Organization, Continual Service Improvement (CSI) Institutionalization, Business Service Improvement & End-to-End Business Service Management (BSM) Implementation, Service Management Process Improvement, BSM Technology Architecture & Integration and BSM Technology Delivery. A recommended sequence is discussed for each of the seven disciplines that should be performed to maximize efficiencies and predictability. It is important to note here that these specific sequences are not performed in isolation. In fact, we will see in Chapter 12 how activities from across different disciplines may be performed concurrently to produce the business value in an incremental manner. In addition, these disciplines will enable the related roles to clearly understand and appreciate all the work that they are responsible for. As discussed earlier, the concept of disciplines is not new and just provides an established means to organize the work that needs to be performed in specific field of study. Activities within each of these disciplines provide a generic guideline. These will need to be tailored depending upon a range of factors. According to Shuja and Krebs (2008), these factors may include project complexity, organizational maturity, organization culture, regulatory compliance and policy requirements, development type, and organization size.

Initiatives that have enterprise-wide cultural impact are the most challenging to manage and success and failure of these efforts are determined by the way changes in peoples' attitudes and behaviors are managed.

Each chapter on discipline (from Chapter 5 to Chapter 11) aims to answer the following business service management implementation related questions:

- What are some of the most critical aspects of successfully implementing business service management? *These critical aspects are captured in the form of disciplines and each discipline will describe these critical aspects in the form of activities performed, roles that perform these activities, inputs that are required in order to successfully achieve objectives, and outputs produced as a result of these activities.*
- What are some of the core activities that need to be carried out in order to implement business service management? *Activities are at the core of each discipline.*
- What are the key roles that need to be engaged in service management implementation? What are their core responsibilities? *We will discuss the RACI (Responsible-Accountable-Consulted-Informed) assignments for each of the activities.*
- What is the recommended sequence in which these activities should be carried out? *For example, in most organizations, you need to have an approval from the senior management on the program roadmap and the charter before you are able to proceed. This sequence of activities will be discipline specific and will contribute towards building the project lifecycle that will be discussed in Chapter 12.*

- What are some of the key artifacts that are produced and managed within each of these disciplines? *These artifacts are the outputs produced as a result of activities performed within each discipline.*
- What are any other specific practical guidelines to ensure that objectives of each of these disciplines are successfully met? *We will discuss important business service management concepts from implementation perspective here. ITIL v3 publications provide a detailed discussions on ITIL v3 but not necessarily on how to achieve business service management using the guidelines provided in ITIL v3 .*
- How can organizations that do not currently manage business services transform their technology-focused management practices to align with business needs in the most effective and efficient manner? We will discuss aspects related to each discipline.

Key Components of the i2-SOSMI Disciplines

We will learn in detail what activities need to be performed within each of these disciplines to ensure that BSM is implemented effectively. As mentioned, a recommended sequence is discussed for each of the seven disciplines that should be performed to maximize efficiency and predictability. It is important to note here that these specific sequences are not performed in isolation. In fact, we will see in Chapter 12 how activities from across different disciplines may be performed concurrently to produce the business value in an incremental manner. In addition, these disciplines will enable the related roles to clearly understand and appreciate all the work that they are responsible for. Activities within each of these disciplines provide a generic guideline. These will need to be tailored depending on a range of factors. According to Shuja and Krebs (2008), these factors may include project complexity, organizational maturity, organization culture, regulatory compliance and policy requirements, development type, and organization size.

For each discipline, we will discuss the following key components:

- Objectives
- Work breakdown structure
- Workflow
- Roles
- Artifacts
- Key concepts

Let us discuss each of these in greater detail.

Objectives

Each discipline is composed of a specific set of objectives that must be met. These objectives will drive the activities that need to be performed and outputs that need to be produced.

Work Breakdown Structure

According to the Project Management Institute (PMI), the project's work breakdown structure (WBS) provides the relationship among all the components of the project and the project deliverables. WBS, according to PMI, is a deliverable-oriented, hierarchical decomposition of the work to be executed by the project team to accomplish the project objectives and create the required deliverables. It organizes and defines the total scope of the project. Each descending level represents an increasingly detailed definition of the project work. You will see that i2-SOSMI adopts a slightly different view of WBS. Discipline WBS in i2-SOSMI represents the activities-oriented, hierarchical decomposition of the project effort specific to the respective discipline. Each descending level represents an increasingly detailed definition of the project work.

Workflow

Discipline workflow is a semiordered sequence of activities performed by specific roles to achieve a particular goal (Shuja and Krebs, 2008). This semiordered nature of discipline workflows emphasizes that the discipline workflows cannot present the real nuances of scheduling real work, for they cannot depict the optionality of activities or iterative nature of real projects (Shuja and Krebs, 2008). Yet, they still have value as a way for us to understand the process by breaking it into smaller areas of concerns. It is important to appreciate that the sequence of activities in each of the workflows is based on best practices such as PMBOK, ITIL v3, Enterprise Architecture, and others. It should, by no stretch of the imagination, be taken as a mandatory sequence.

Roles

A role is a definition of responsibilities of an individual or a team. This describes a role played by an individual or team within the project. Each role may be realized by many individuals or teams, and each individual or team may perform many different roles.

Artifact

Related to each activity are the artifacts, which are either produced or refined depending on when the activity is performed during the project life cycle. Artifacts are normally required to perform any given activity and as a result of performing this activity, one or more artifacts may be created, read, updated, or deleted. Artifacts do not necessarily have to be documents. Artifact can also be an executable application, component, or system.

Key Concepts

All key concepts related to the discipline will be discussed in this section. For example, in the *Business Service Improvement and End-to-End Business Service Management* discipline, we will discuss concepts related to implementing BSM.

Phases

Phases represent the life cycle aspect of the i2-SOSMI approach to implementing BSM. There are four phases in the i2-SOSMI:

- *Foundation*
  The *foundation* phase aims to establish the foundation required to achieve business–IT integration.
- *Design*
  The *design* phase aims to architect, design, and prototype BSM.

- *Align*
  The *align* phase enables the organization to achieve business–IT alignment.
- *Integrate*
  The *integrate* phase achieves the envisioned business–IT integration and delivers BSM for the organization.

Iterations

Each iteration within i2-SOSMI focuses on improvements across a wide range of areas as they relate to business services as well as service management processes.

Figure 4.7 shows the key aspects of a process. These aspects must be planned, designed, and implemented to ensure that the process is institutionalized. These are generic aspects and are as follows:

- *Organization and People.* Process refinements will impact the people and organizations that may be responsible for executing those processes.
- *Control and Governance.* Processes must be controlled through relevant policies, objectives, and ownership.
- *Tools and Enabling Technologies.* Enabling technologies help in not only enforcing agreed processes, but also in executing those processes in an effective and efficient manner.
- *Measurements and Improvements.* To improve those processes on a continual basis, it is critical that appropriate measurements are designed and performed and improvement opportunities are identified and implemented.

Each phase must consider all the above-mentioned key aspects and iterations must ensure that these are appropriately implemented. Let us now discuss i2-SOSMI iterations. As shown in Figure 4.4, each phase consists of three iterations.

Visualize Iteration

The goal of this iteration is to establish a clear vision for specific objectives that will be achieved during that given phase and to ensure that the established vision is achievable. A key deliverable of

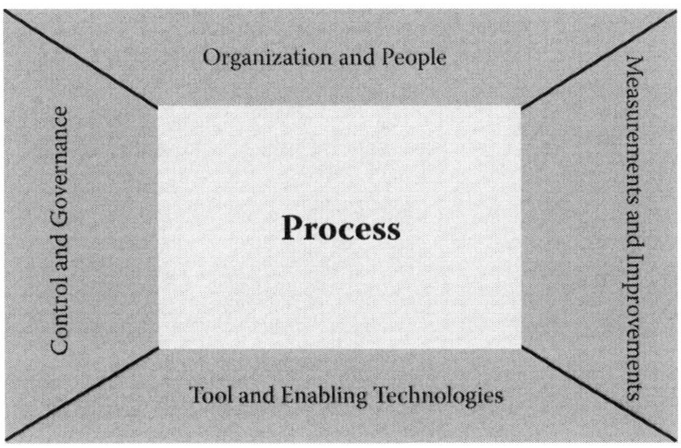

Figure 4.7 Key process aspects.

this iteration should be an executable prototype (for both process development and improvement, as well as business service implementation).

Architect Iteration

The goal of this iteration is to build upon the *Visualize* iteration by further refining the service management processes along with the key aspects to support the planned service improvements. With regard to tooling, more (prioritized) functionality is added to the prototype. By the end of this iteration, beta release (or QA build) should be ready.

Realize Iteration

The goal of this iteration is to deliver the improvements that were identified during the first iteration by deploying the first baseline release of the solution.

We will discuss each of these disciplines and phases in greater detail in Chapters 5 and 6. As mentioned, each phase consists of three iterations. At the core of this architecture are the iterations. Let us now discuss some of the key activities performed within each iteration.

High-Level i2-SOSMI Iteration Activities

Figure 4.8 shows the high-level activities carried out within each iteration of the BSM implementation program. Note that each iteration ends with the delivery of tangible business-value. Also,

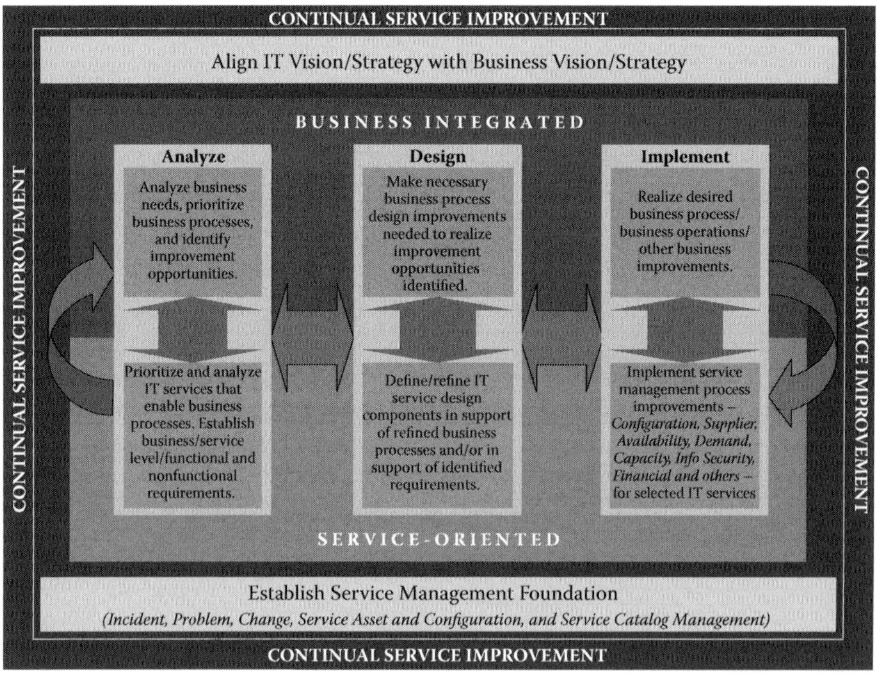

Figure 4.8 High-level i2-SOSMI iteration activities.

note the importance of alignment with business and IT vision and strategy at the top and development of the service management foundation at the base. Let us now discuss these key activities in detail.

Align with Vision and Strategy

At the top of Figure 4.8, you will see "Align IT Vision and Strategy with Business Vision and Strategy." This means that there needs to be a continual alignment with larger business and IT visions and strategies. Each iteration begins by revisiting and ensuring that a continual alignment between deliverable of the given iteration and the business and IT strategy exists. If executed appropriately, BSM strategy should further refine the larger IT strategy.

Establish Service Management Foundation

As the name suggests, this foundation is absolutely critical to effective and efficient implementation and management of business services. As shown in Figure 4.9 (Shpilberg et al., 2007), alignment and efficacy are both required to achieve IT-enabled growth. In ITIL terms, for a business enterprise to realize IT-enabled growth, it is essential that IT organization is able to effectively management entire service lifecycle from Service Strategy through to Service Operation and Continual Service Improvement. The i2-SOSMI iteration ensures that improvements in both directions are implemented to achieve IT-enabled growth for a critical business process or service (depending on organizational priorities and situations).

Assuming that the subject organization is presently operating at organizational maturity level 1, service management foundation development will consist of four core service management

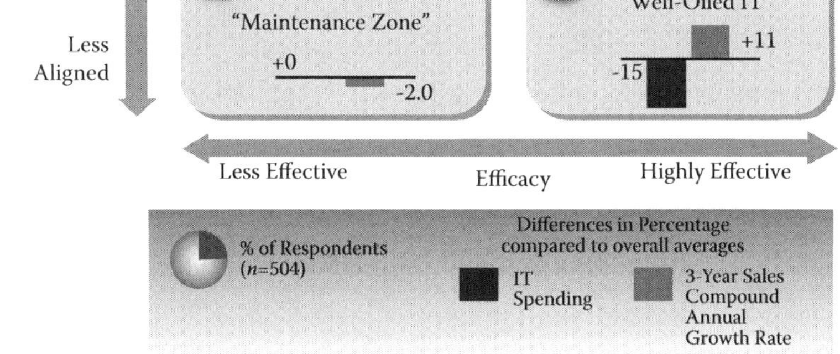

Note: Based on 504 responses from 452 companies
Source: Bain Analysis

Figure 4.9 Alignment and efficacy (Shpilberg et al., 2007).

processes. These include incident management, problem management, change management, service asset and configuration management, and service catalog management. Let us try to understand what it means to establish this foundation.

Incident Management, Problem Management, and Change Management

Establishing incident, problem, and change management processes will include the following:

- Common, consistent, and standard processes defined for the organization
- Clear roles and responsibilities established
- Process operational and management organizations defined (process operational organization executes the process and process management organization—*likely to be part of CSI*—managing ongoing process performance monitoring and improvements)
- Tool implemented
- Appropriate training provided and support materials produced
- Well-defined process KPIs established
- Processes rebaselined

Service Asset and Configuration Management

Establishing service asset and configuration management will include the following:

- Define a consistent and standard service asset and configuration management process.
- Depending on the organization, establish a common CMDB. It may be a single repository or a federated environment.
- Create and migrate known configuration item (CI) records perform auto discovery.
- Establish clear roles and responsibilities.
- Define process operational and management organizations (*likely to be part of CSI*).
- Provide appropriate training and support materials.
- Establish well-defined process KPIs.
- Baseline the CMDB and bring it under change management.

Service Catalog Management

The service catalog plays an important role in providing the foundation to implement BSM. The service catalog serves the function that a menu serves in a restaurant (Figure 4.10).

Without a menu, how can a kitchen plan what ingredients to have, what recipe scripts to produce, what resources to acquire, what expectations to manage, what economies to plan, and so on? Without a service catalog, how can an IT organization identify the IT capabilities to develop, the targets to establish, and the expectations to manage? The service catalog provides a single source of all the operational (and soon-to-be operational) services that are provided by the IT organization. The service catalog will drive how business process and services are prioritized and will drive how specific improvements are implemented across a range of service management processes such as service level management, capacity management, availability management, request fulfillment, service asset and configuration management, and others. As shown in Figure 4.11, key related uses of the service catalog may include the following:

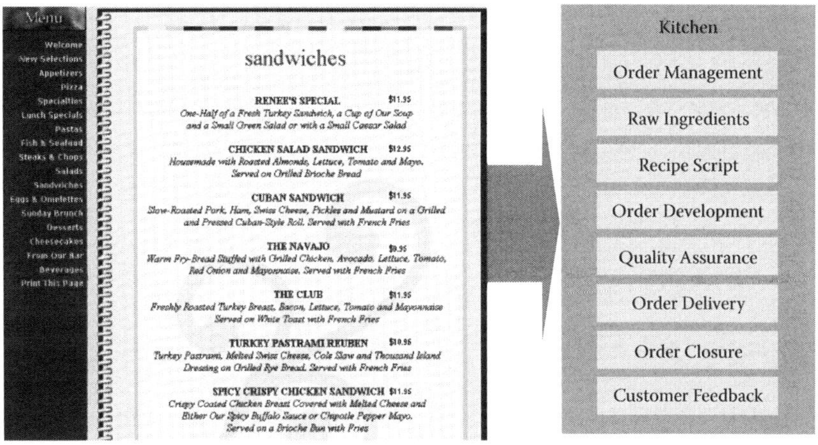

Service Management questions to ask:

- What if there is no menu?
- What if there is no clear definition on how to place an order?
- What if you are asked to reach out to the Chef and explain to him/her what you need?
- What if multiple members from the kitchen reach out to you to further understand what you need?
- What if you ordered the *Cuban* and received the *Club*?
- What if it takes longer than usual to receive your order?
- What if there is no price available?

Figure 4.10 Service management at a restaurant.

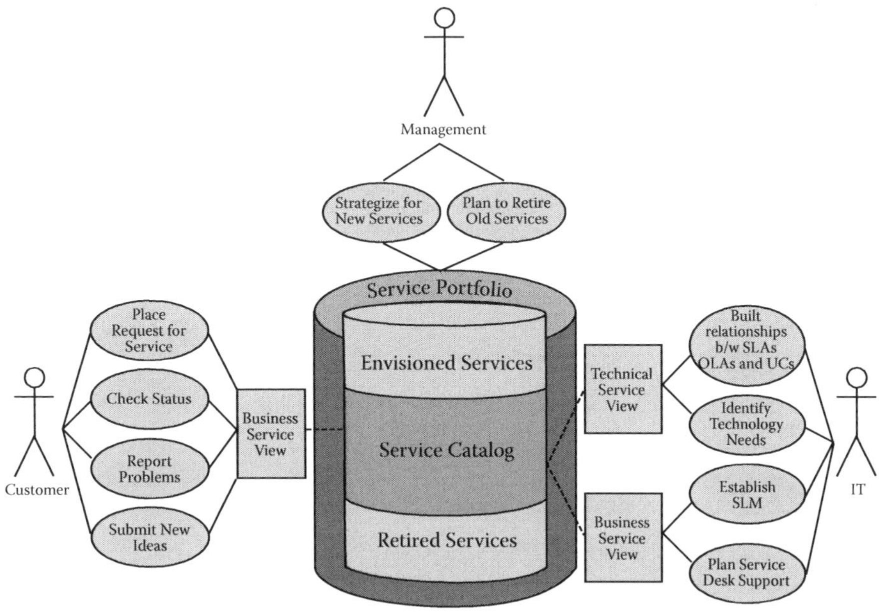

Figure 4.11 Potential uses of the service catalog.

- A customer may use the service catalog to place a request for service, check the status of a request, report problems, and submit new ideas.
- IT may use the service catalog to establish service level management, plan service desk support, identify technology needs, and build and manage relationships between SLAs, operational level agreements, and underpinning contracts.

Core Repeatable Activities

The following core activities are performed in each iteration.

Analyze

Each iteration focuses on specific business needs. To ensure that needs are understood and addressed objectively, key associated business processes are prioritized and enabling business services are identified. Note that the service catalog needs to be established as part of the service management foundation. This service catalog is then used to identify and prioritize the business and technical services that need to be improved. To maximize business benefits, it is recommended that prioritization should be carried out at the business services level and technical services should be improved to improve the selected business services. In almost all cases, there may be one or more technical services required in order to realize a given business service and each technical service may be shared by one or more business service. These business service and technical service relationships are shown at a high level in the service tree discussed earlier and shown in Figure 4.12. To improve a given business service, improvements will be implemented within the underpinning technical services. In short, the following key activities should be performed:

- Analyze business needs, prioritize business processes, and identify improvement opportunities.
- Prioritize and analyze IT services that enable business processes.
- Establish business/service level/functional and nonfunctional requirements.

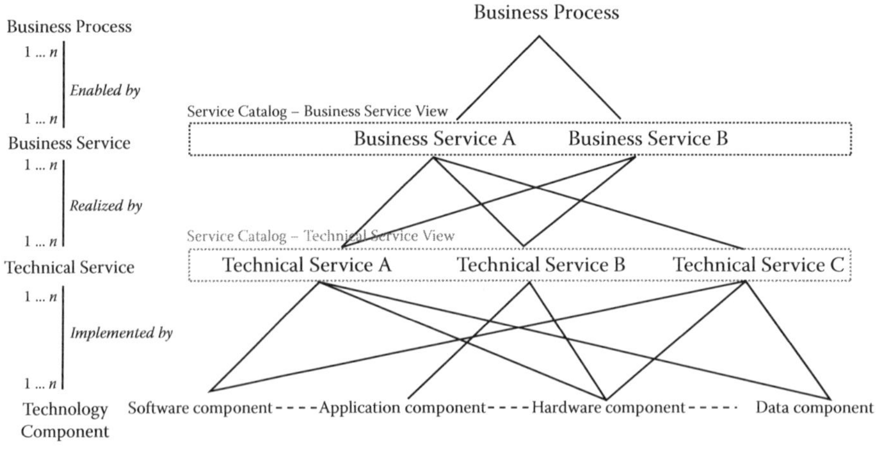

Figure 4.12 The service tree.

Quantifiable improvement opportunities are identified that will be delivered by the end of that iteration at business process and business service levels. Service level requirements (SLRs) are understood and associated and SLAs are established and agreed upon.

Design

The following key activities should be performed:

- Make necessary business process design improvements needed to realize improvement opportunities identified.
- Define/refine IT service design components in support of refined business processes and/or in support of identified requirements.

Implement

As per the SLRs and SLAs, business and technical services are improved to ensure that agreed targets are met. To improve the quality of business and technical services, the IT service management processes will need to be improved. The following activities should be performed:

- Realize desired business process/business operations/other business improvements.
- Implement service management process improvements – *Configuration, Supplier, Availability, Demand, Capacity, Info Security, Financial & others* – for selected IT services.

Each iteration will result in service and service management process improvements. The quality of CI that supports the prioritized business service is optimized and CI interrelationships are established.

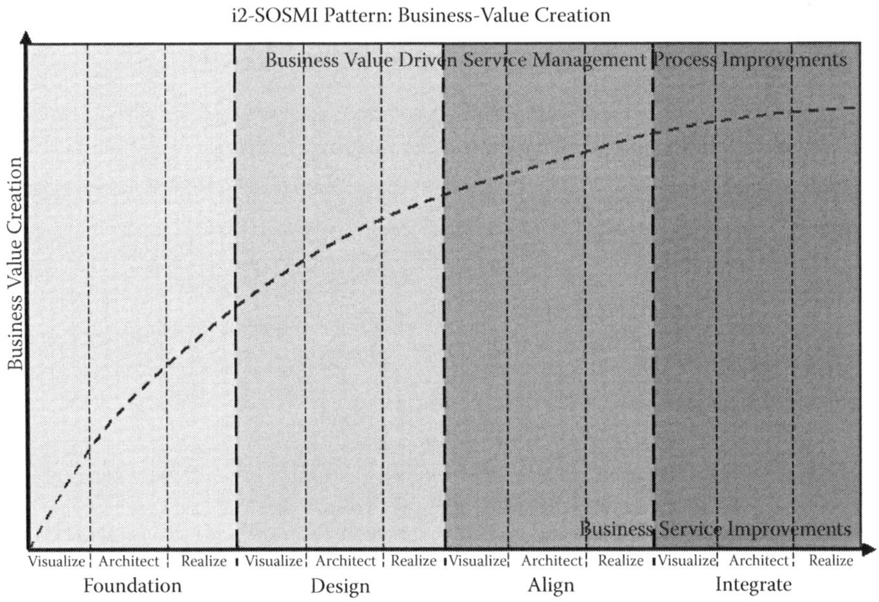

Figure 4.13 A business-value creation graph.

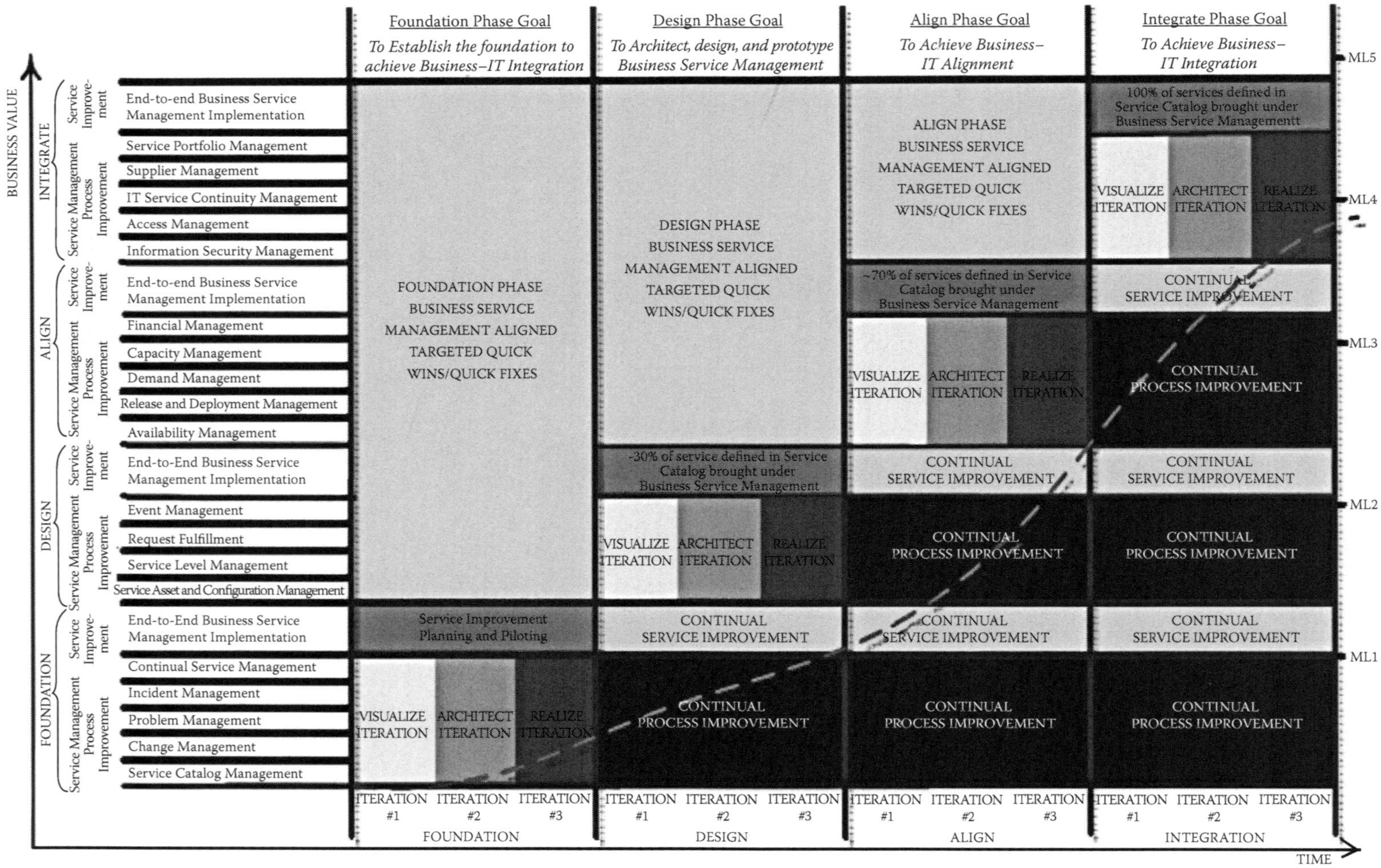

Figure 4.14 The business-value creation life cycle.

This ensures that an optimizing repository such as CMDB does not become an "ocean-boiling" task and is performed in a targeted fashion that will ensure achievement of concrete business results.

The i2-SOSMI Patterns

Depending on the key drivers for implementing BSM, a specific pattern may be leveraged. Each pattern lays out a specific sequence in which ITIL v3 processes should be implemented. Note that these are just patterns and aim to provide a starting point for the subject organization. It is important to note that these patterns and associated graphs are based on my experience and are representation of my professional opinion. In addition, these just represent the most common paths/drivers that organizations may pursue. There may be unique situations that require organizations to define their own approaches/patterns. These specific/unique patterns will need to take into account organizational key drivers/imperatives and define how service management processes should be grouped and sequenced i.e.,

1. Which processes need to be improved first?
2. What sequence we will need to improve these processes in?

Additional discussion and potential sequences for "Compliance & Regulation" pattern is shown on Figure 14.4 and for "Hybrid Pattern" on Figure 14.5. The following patterns are developed for i2-SOSMI.

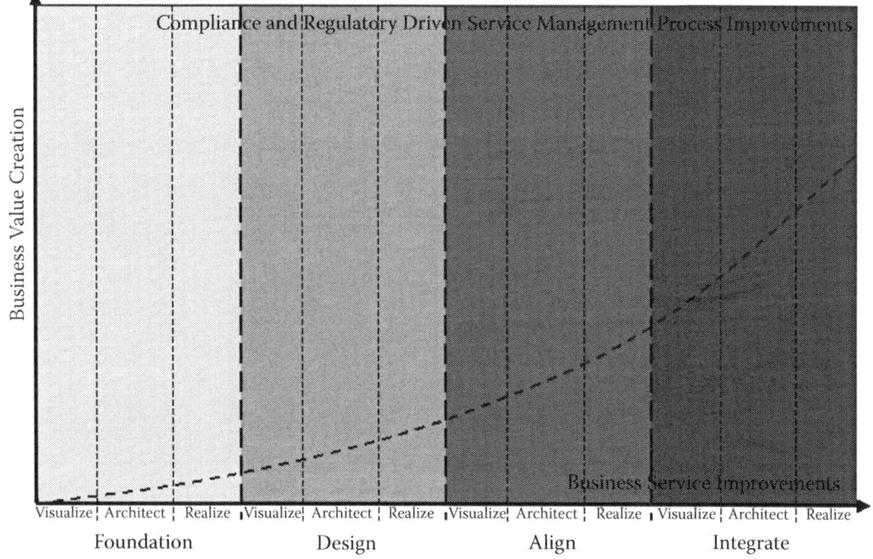

Figure 4.15 A compliance and regulation improvement graph.

Practical Tip: i2SOSMI Patterns represent the results that I was able to see companies deliver. Earlier in i2SOSMI project (assuming that organization is at lower maturity levels), as you start to make improvements (both quick wins as well as planned/targeted service and service management improvements), you will see that significant business improvements are realized. However, as your organization gains higher maturity levels, you will see that you will need to institutionalize more statistical methods (like Six Sigma) to identify and realize improvements. It is also important to appreciate that 80/20 rule (20% of services actually contribute towards 80% of the revenue) still holds.

The i2-SOSMI Pattern: Business-Value Creation

If the key driver for an organization is to become a business-value partner, then a business-value creation pattern will provide an appropriate starting point. Figure 4.13 shows the business-value creation graph for a business value–driven service management process and business service improvements.

The recommended life cycle for this pattern is shown in Figure 4.14. We will discuss this in greater detail in Chapter 6.

The i2-SOSMI Pattern: Compliance and Regulation Improvement

This pattern provides guidelines around implementing and improving the processes that enable an organization to address any pressing compliance-related concerns (Figure 4.15). This pattern recommends a different sequence in which ITIL v3 processes are implemented and improved.

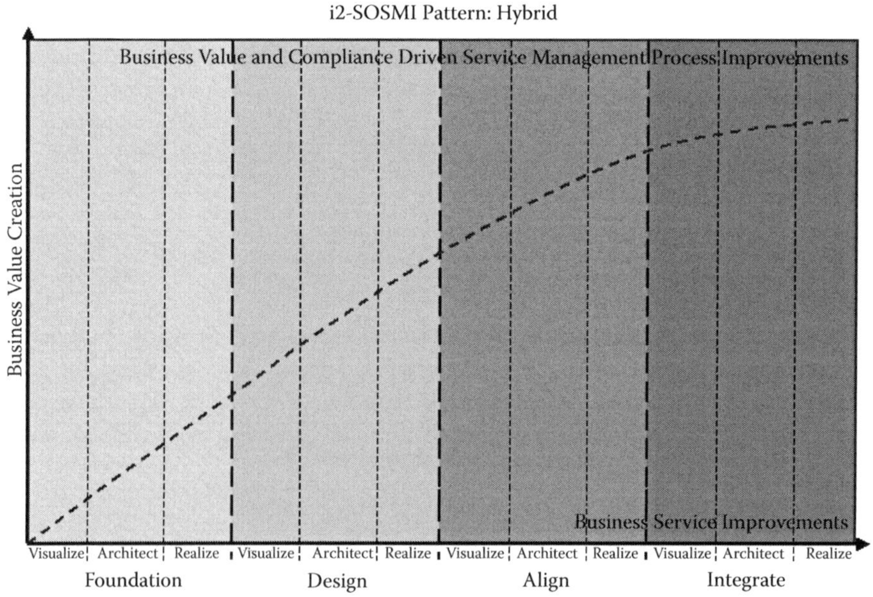

Figure 4.16 A hybrid graph.

The i2-SOSMI Pattern: Hybrid

This combines the above two patterns (i.e., a balance between business-value creation and compliance and regulation) (Figure 4.16).

Summary

In this chapter, we achieved a high-level understanding of the i2-SOSMI methodology. In the remaining chapters of Part II of this book, we discuss the i2-SOSMI methodology in detail. The message here is that all IT-related improvements must be business-focused and should enable you to measure the return on investments made on such improvements in business terms. It is critical to align these improvements with selected prioritized business processes that make the most impact on the businesses' objectives. It is neither important nor sensible to try to achieve end-to-end BSM for all business services. The 80/20 rules applies (i.e., 80% of business value is most likely generated by 20% of business services).

References

Merriam-Webster Dictionary. http://www.merriam-webster.com.

Shpilberg, D., S. Berez, R. Puryear, and S. Shah. 2007. Avoiding the alignment trap in information technology. *MIT Sloan Manag Rev* 49(1), 51–58.

Shuja, A., and J. Krebs. 2008. *Rational Unified Process: Reference and Certification Guide*. New York: IBM Press.

Chapter 5

Discipline: Project Management

According to the Project Management Institute *Project Management Body of Knowledge®*, project management is the application of knowledge, skills, tools and techniques to project activities to meet project requirements. It is accomplished through the application and integration of project management processes of initiating, planning, executing, monitoring and controlling and closing. In this chapter, we will discuss how project management is performed specifically in Business Service Management implementation projects and some of the core deliverables that should be produced.

It is important to note that Project Management is a discipline that applies to domains other than IT. For instance, each project whether related to IT, construction, or any other domain will need to create and manage project plans. However, the content of these plans will be different. In order to provide specific Project Management guidance related to Business Service Management implementation, this chapter offers the following:

1. Establishes the foundation of project management that will support the overall i2SOSMI approach for planning and managing Business Service Management implementation discussed in Part III of this book.
2. Based on my experience in implementing Business Service Management, I have created custom templates provided in Appendices B and C of this book that will support the reader of this chapter in applying generic project management principles to Business Service Management domain. These appendices include the following:
   a. Business Service Management Project Charter Template
   b. Business Service Management Project Management Plan Template
   c. Business Service Management Implementation Project Communication Strategy & Plan Template

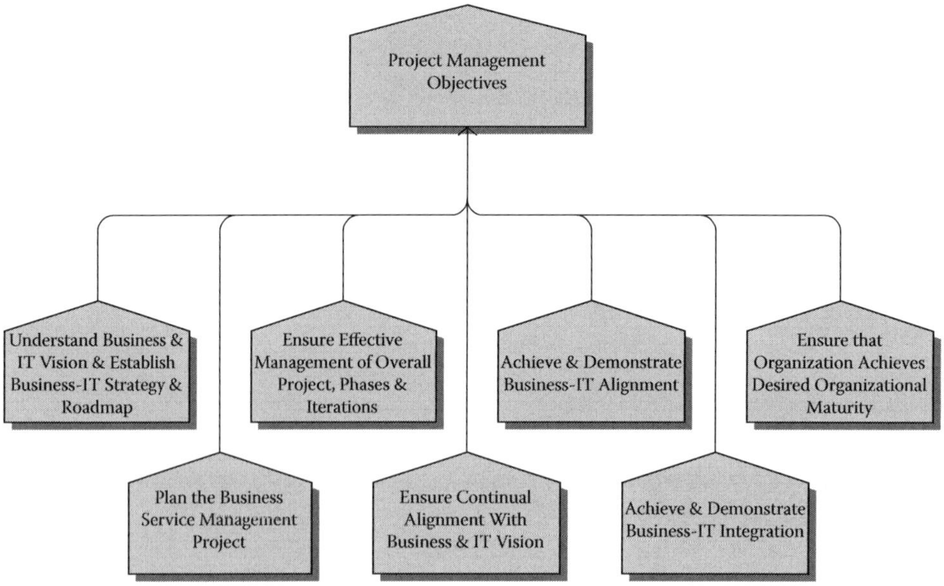

Figure 5.1 Project management objectives.

Purpose

Purpose of Project Management discipline is:

- To provide a framework for managing service management implementation programs and projects
- To provide practical guidelines for initiating, planning, executing, monitoring, and controlling and closing the programs and projects
- To provide a framework for establishing the service management vision and for ensuring that appropriate activities are performed to realize that vision

Objectives

Some of the key Project Management objectives are as follows (see Figure 5.1):

- Understand Business & IT Vision & Establish Business-IT Integration Strategy & Roadmap
- Plan the Business Service Management Project
- Ensure effective management of overall project, phases, & Iterations
- Ensure Continual Alignment with Business & IT Vision
- Achieve & Demonstrate Business-IT Alignment
- Achieve & Demonstrate Business-IT Integration
- Ensure that organization achieves desired Organizational Maturity

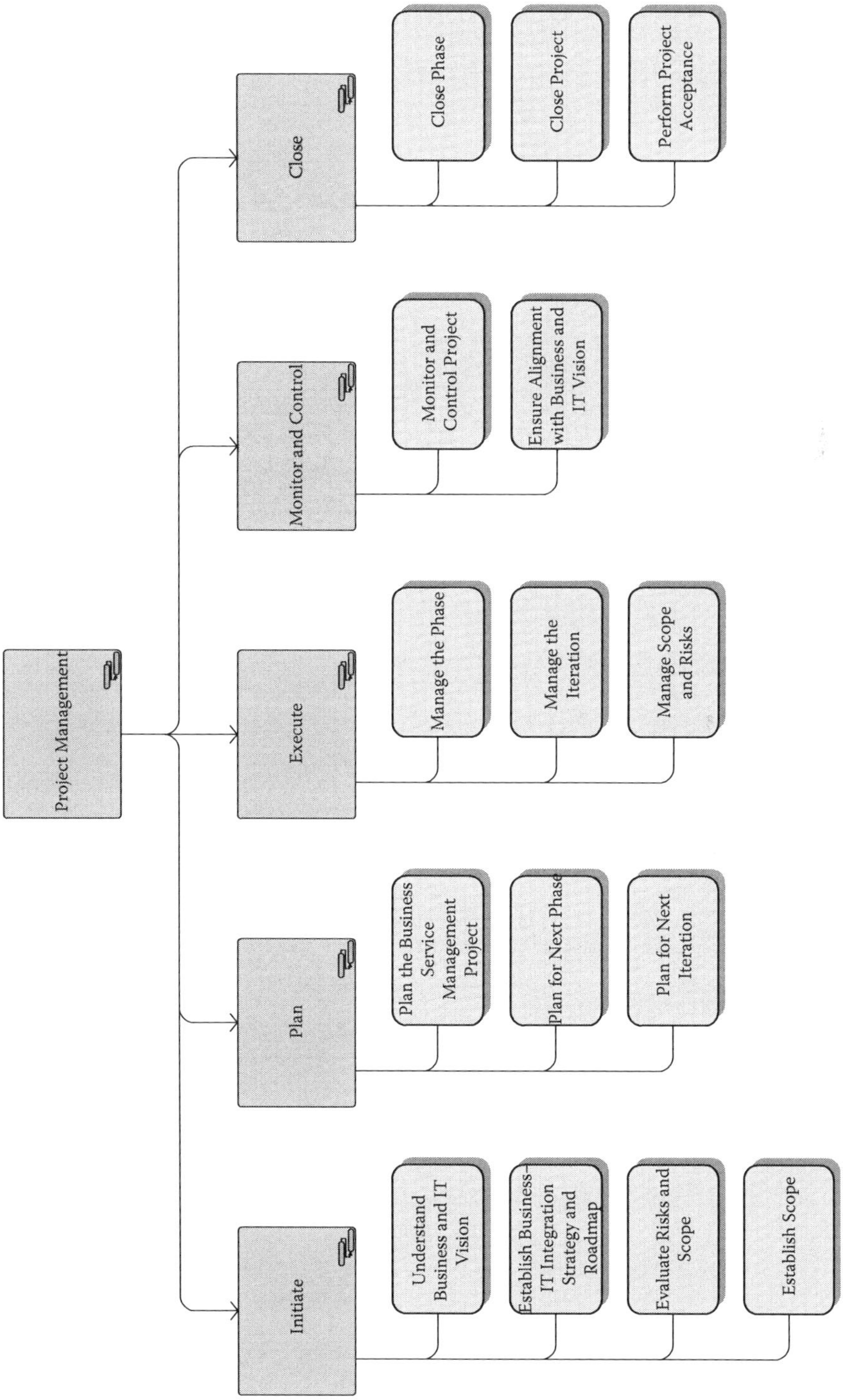

Figure 5.2 Project management work breakdown structure.

Work Breakdown Structure

To ensure that the above-mentioned objectives are realized, there are some core activities that should be performed within project management. Figure 5.2 shows the program management work breakdown structure (WBS).

Project Management Workflow

We have discussed the different activities that need to be performed within the project management discipline. Figure 5.3 provides a recommended sequence in which project management activities may be performed.

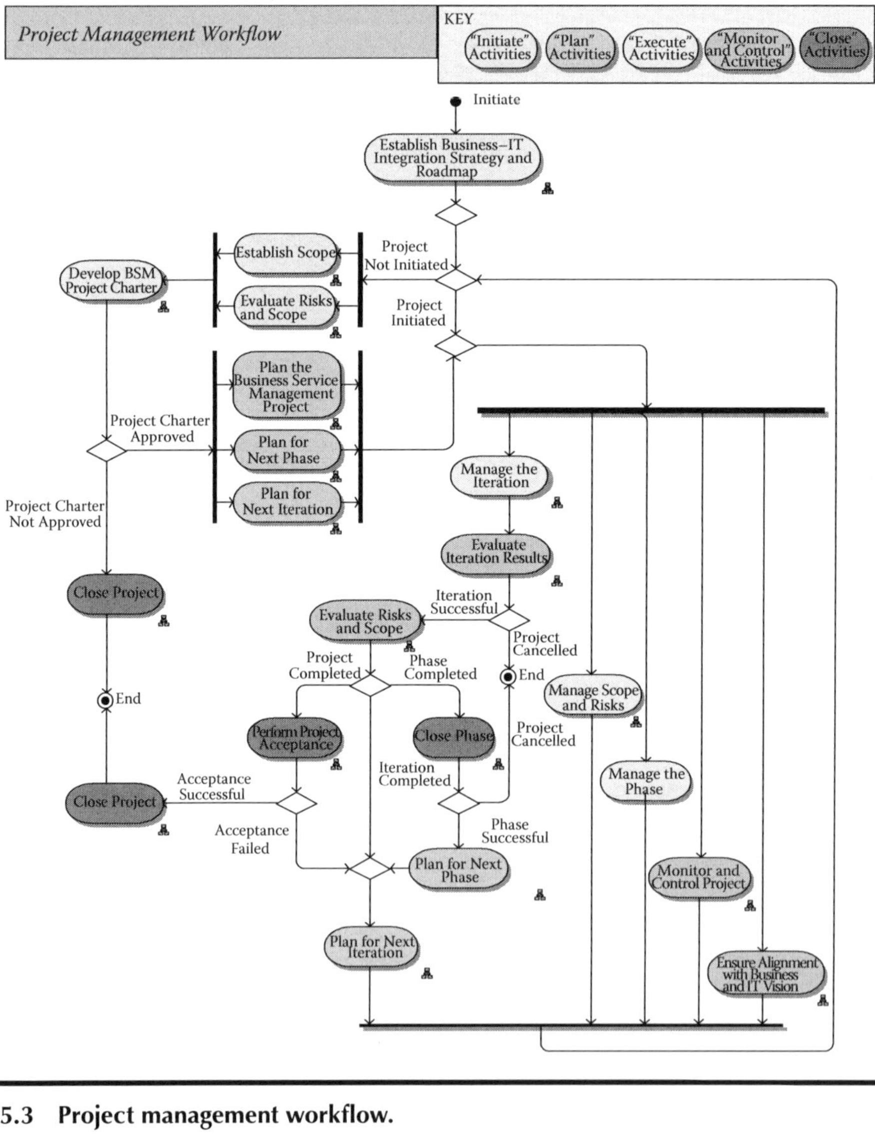

Figure 5.3 Project management workflow.

Please note that this sequence may vary depending on the organization-specific culture and needs. Let us discuss each of the five level 2 WBS elements in detail.

Initiate

This is the commitment from the organization to begin the project. Initial assessments and feasibility studies are performed during this step to ensure that the organization is ready to undertake such a strategic effort and that required agreements and approvals are achieved. There are several key activities involved in this element of WBS.

Understand Business and IT Vision

This activity is performed to analyze the current business and IT vision. This will enable the BSM project team to align the overall effort effectively.

Establish a Business–IT Integration Strategy and Roadmap

Purpose

- To establish a clear understanding of the long-term vision for service management
- To develop a BSM strategy and implementation roadmap
- To review and agree on the overall service management implementation approach

Preconditions

- Senior management support for implementing BSM
- Acquisition of needed ITIL expert resources

Activity Overview

During this activity, an IT strategy is defined that is in line with the overall business vision and a business case is created to embark on the BSM journey. Overall accountability for this activity stays with the executive sponsor, and an ITIL expert consultant contributes to the successful delivery of artifacts (Figure 5.4).

Activity Details

Input Artifacts	*Tasks Performed*	*Output Artifacts*	*Roles (RACI)*
Business Vision Document IT Vision Document	Understand Business and IT Vision	Business and IT Vision Traceability Document	R: ITIL Expert Consultant A/C: Executive Sponsor
Business Vision IT Vision Business and IT Vision Traceability	Develop Business–IT Integration Strategy	IT Strategy Document	R: ITIL Expert Consultant A/C: Executive Sponsor

Input Artifacts	*Tasks Performed*	*Output Artifacts*	*Roles (RACI)*
Business Vision IT Vision IT Strategy	Develop Business Case	BSM Project Charter Document	R: ITIL Expert Consultant A/C: Executive Sponsor
IT Strategy	Create BSM Project Roadmap	BSM Strategy and Roadmap Presentation Deck	R: ITIL Expert Consultant A/C: Executive Sponsor
Program Charter Program Roadmap	Achieve Agreement and Required Approvals	Agreement Achieved and Approval Received	R: Executive Sponsor A/C:
Program Charter Program Roadmap	Acquire Preliminary Resources	Resources Acquired and Assigned	

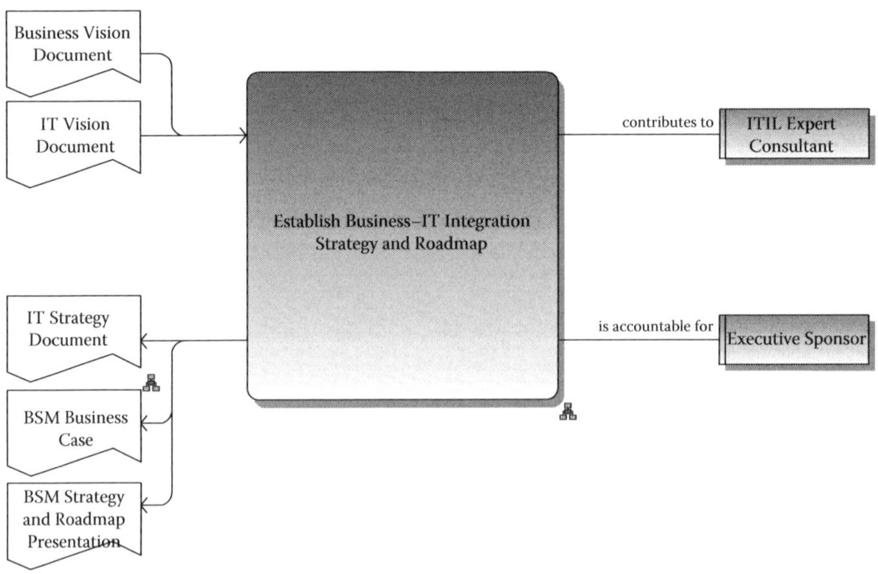

Figure 5.4 Establish business–IT integration strategy and roadmap.

Postconditions

- Agreement on the overall service management implementation roadmap and approach
- Service management program charter reviewed and agreed on
- Resources acquired for initiating the program

Evaluate Risks and Scope

Purpose

- To identify, assess, and prioritize risks
- To determine and agree on appropriate risk management strategy
- To document the risks and related details using the risk list template

Preconditions

- Project charter reviewed and approved
- Project budget reviewed and approved
- Project management resources—project management office (PMO) manager and project manager—assigned

Activity Overview

During this activity, risks to the BSM implementation projects are identified and its scope is defined. Overall accountability for this activity stays with the project manager and the ITIL expert consultant contributes as appropriate (Figure 5.5).

Activity Details

Input Artifacts	*Tasks Performed*	*Output Artifacts*	*Roles (RACI)*
BSM Strategy and Roadmap IT Strategy Document BSM Project Charter	Identify Risks	Risk List	A/R: Project Manager C: ITIL Expert Consultant
BSM Strategy and Roadmap IT Strategy Document BSM Project Charter Risk List	Analyze and Prioritize Risks	Risk List	A/R: Project Manager C: ITIL Expert Consultant
BSM Strategy and Roadmap IT Strategy Document BSM Project Charter Risk List	Establish Risk Management Strategies	Risk Mitigation Approach	A/R: Project Manager C: ITIL Expert Consultant

Input Artifacts	*Tasks Performed*	*Output Artifacts*	*Roles (RACI)*
BSM Strategy and Roadmap IT Strategy Document BSM Project Charter Risk List Risk Mitigation Approach	Develop Risk Management Plan	Risk Management Plan	A/R: Project Manager C: ITIL Expert Consultant I: Executive Sponsor

Postconditions

- Potential risks identified and impact of each understood
- Risk management strategies reviewed and agreed on

Establish Scope

Purpose

- To establish a clear scope statement
- To clearly state the high-level deliverables of the overall program
- To document anything that falls outside the scope statement

Preconditions

- Roadmap and project charter approved
- Project management resources assigned

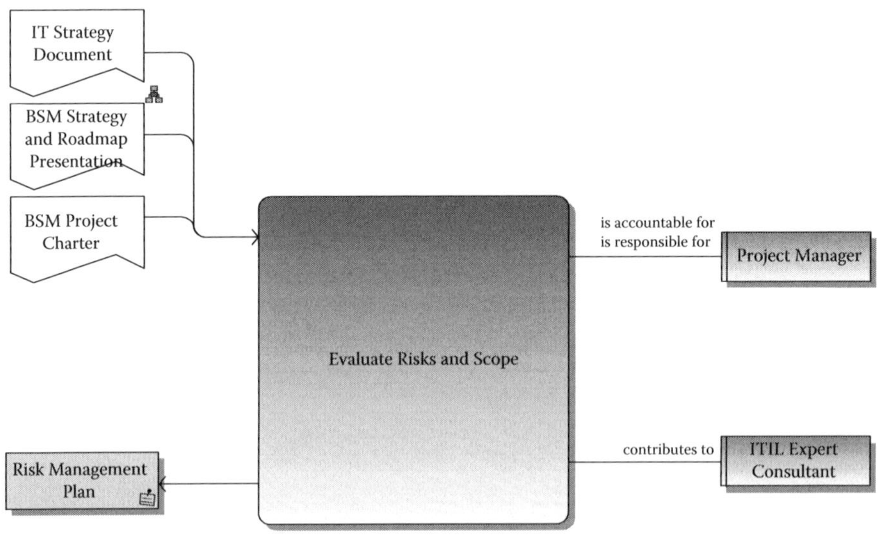

Figure 5.5 Evaluate risks and scope.

Activity Overview

A scope statement is created. The scope statement clearly identifies all deliverables that will be completed as a result of the project (Figure 5.6).

Activity Details

Input Artifacts	*Tasks Performed*	*Output Artifacts*	*Roles (RACI)*
BSM Strategy and Roadmap Presentation BSM Business Case IT Strategy Document	Define Scope Statement	Scope Statement	A/R: Project Manager C: ITIL Expert Consultant
BSM Business Case IT Strategy Document	Identify and Describe Key Deliverables	Key In-Scope Project Deliverables	A/R: Project Manager C: ITIL Expert Consultant
Key In-Scope Project Deliverables	Describe Evaluation Criteria	Success Evaluation Criteria	A/R: Project Manager C: ITIL Expert Consultant
BSM Business Case IT Strategy Document Key In-Scope Project Deliverables	Identify and Document Out-of-Scope Components	Key Out-of-Scope Components	A/R: Project Manager C: ITIL Expert Consultant

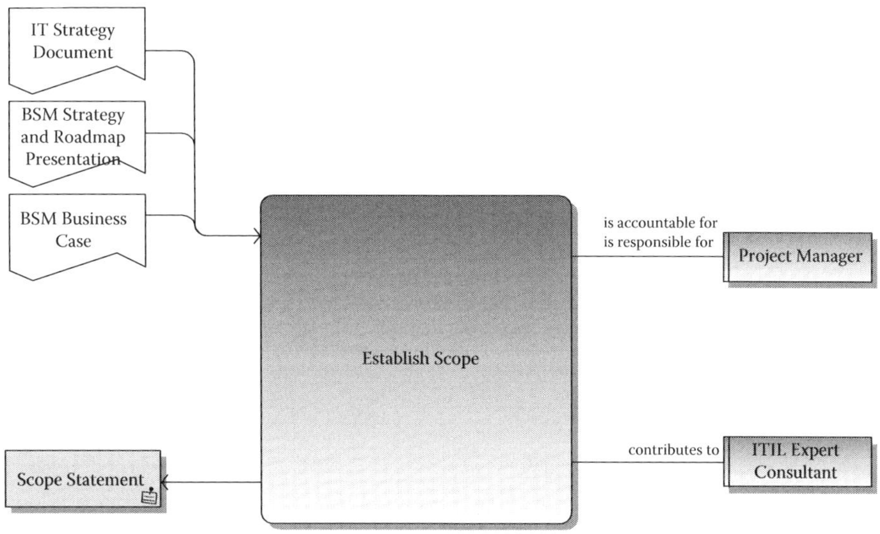

Figure 5.6 Establish scope.

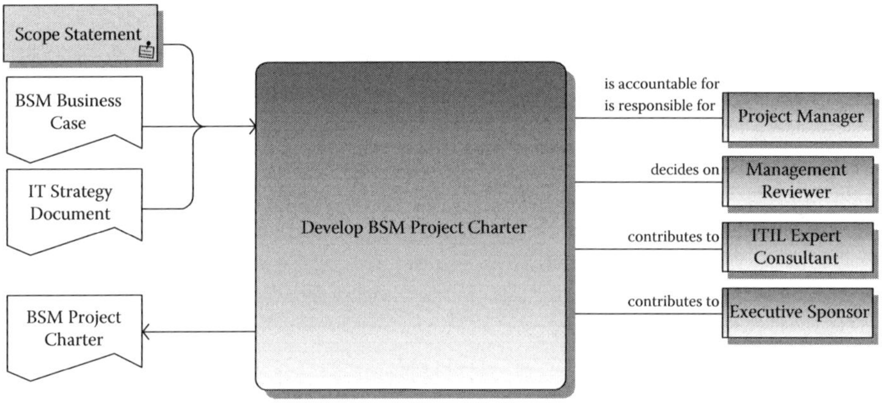

Figure 5.7 Develop BSM project charter.

Postconditions

The program or project scope is clearly understood and agreed on.

Develop BSM Project Charter

Purpose

- To define a clear project charter for BSM implementation
- To review and approve BSM project charter

Preconditions

Risk and scope assessment has been completed.

Activity Overview

Based on the scope statement, BSM business case, and IT strategy document, a BSM project charter is drafted (Figure 5.7).

Activity Details

Input Artifacts	*Tasks Performed*	*Output Artifacts*	*Roles (RACI)*
Scope Statement Key In-Scope Project Deliverables Success Evaluation Criteria Key Out-of-Scope Project Components	Create BSM Project Charter	BSM Project Charter	A/R: Project Manager C: ITIL Expert Consultant

Input Artifacts	*Tasks Performed*	*Output Artifacts*	*Roles (RACI)*
BSM Business Case IT Strategy Document BSM Project Charter	Approve BSM Project Charter	BSM Project Charter	A/R: Management Reviewer C: Executive Sponsor, Project Manager and ITIL Expert Consultant

Postcondition

The program or project scope is clearly understood and agreed on.

Plan

Planning is critical to the overall success of the project. Key deliverables include a service management implementation roadmap, a service management implementation plan, iteration plans, and other supporting plans.

Plan the BSM Project

Purpose

- To develop an overall program plan
- To develop plans for each of the projects prioritized for the immediate next phase
- To build a service management implementation plan and all necessary enclosures

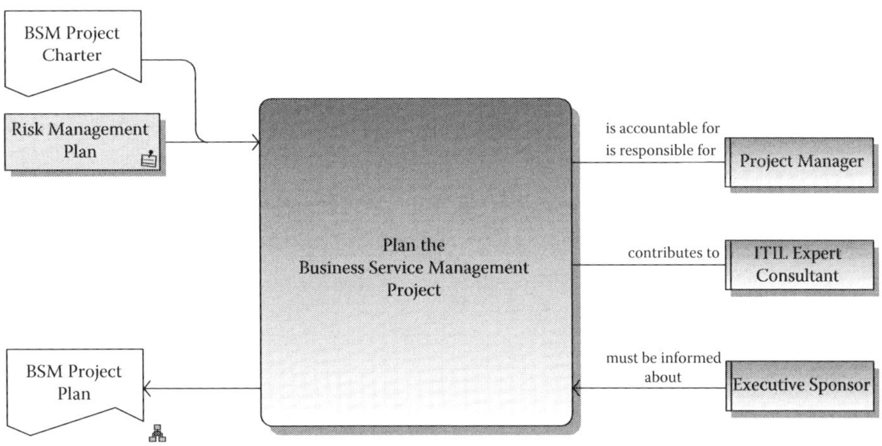

Figure 5.8 Plan the BSM project.

Preconditions

- Program and project charters approved
- Risk list created
- Project management resources acquired and assigned

Activity Overview

This is one of the main activities within the plan phase of project management and the key artifact produced is a BSM project plan. The project manager is responsible for completing this artifact and the ITIL expert consultant also contributes to its creation (Figure 5.8).

Activity Details

Input Artifacts	*Tasks Performed*	*Output Artifacts*	*Roles (RACI)*
BSM Project Charter Risk Management Plan BSM Project Plan Template	Elaborate Scope Statement	Project Scope Definition–Project WBS	A/R: Project Manager C: ITIL Expert Consultant
Project Scope Definition–Project WBS	Assess Resource Requirements	Project Resources	A/R: Project Manager C: ITIL Expert Consultant
Project Scope Definition–Project WBS Project Resources	Identify Key Project Milestones	Project Milestones	A/R: Project Manager C: ITIL Expert Consultant
Project Milestones	Assign Milestones to Project Phases	Time-Boxed BSM Project Phases	A/R: Project Manager C: ITIL Expert Consultant
Project Scope Definition–Project WBS Project Resources Time-Boxed BSM Project Phases Risk List	Create Cost Estimates	Project Cost Estimates	A/R: Project Manager C: ITIL Expert Consultant
Risk List Risk Mitigation Approach Project Scope Definition–Project WBS	Assess Project Monitoring Requirements and Create Related Plans	Project Monitoring and Control Plans	A/R: Project Manager C: ITIL Expert Consultant
Risk List Risk Mitigation Approach	Assign Risk Owner	Risk Response and Management Plan	A/R: Project Manager C: ITIL Expert Consultant

Input Artifacts	*Tasks Performed*	*Output Artifacts*	*Roles (RACI)*
BSM Project Charter Project Scope Time-Boxed BSM Phases Project Resources	Compile Supporting Plans and Create BSM Project Plan	BSM Project Plan	A/R: Project Manager C: ITIL Expert Consultant
BSM Project Plan	Achieve Agreement and Management Approval	Approved BSM Project Plan	A/R: Project Manager C: Management Reviewer, Executive Sponsor, and ITIL Expert Consultant

Postcondition

The BSM project plan is developed, reviewed, and agreed on.

Plan for Next Phase

This activity produces the plan for the next phase.

Purpose

The purpose of this activity is to develop a plan for the next phase of the BSM implementation project.

Preconditions

- BSM project charter approved
- BSM project plan created and agreed on
- Project management and other resources acquired and assigned

Activity Overview

The plan for the next phase, which is part of the overall BSM project plan, is produced here (Figure 5.9).

Activity Details

Input Artifacts	*Tasks Performed*	*Output Artifacts*	*Roles (RACI)*
BSM Project Charter BSM Project Plan	Refine Schedule and Cost Estimates and Agree on Deliverables for the Next Phase	BSM Project Plan (Phase-Related Details are Further Elaborated)	A/R: Project Manager C: ITIL Expert Consultant I: Executive Sponsor

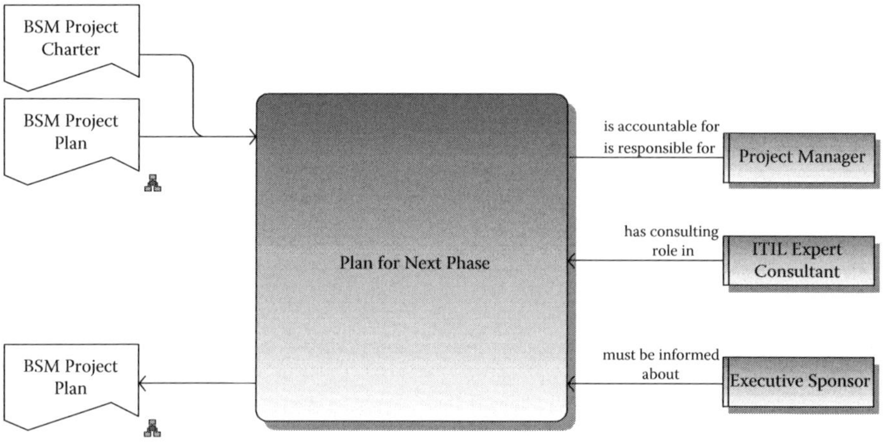

Figure 5.9 Plan for next phase.

Postcondition

A detailed plan for the next phase is developed, reviewed, and agreed on.

Plan for Next Iteration

Purpose

- To develop a detailed iteration plan
- To identify and agree on iteration deliverables
- To develop and agree on iteration evaluation criteria

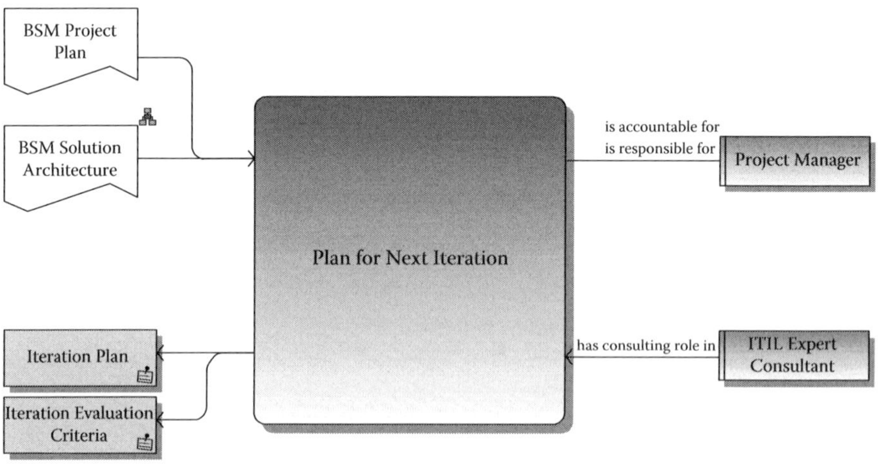

Figure 5.10 Plan for next iteration.

Preconditions

- BSM project plan developed
- Phases time-boxed and deliverables identified

Activity Overview

When a given iteration is approaching its end, one of the main activities that should be performed is to plan for the next iteration. The plan for the next iteration is created as a result. Key deliverables for the next iteration are identified and evaluation criteria are discussed and agreed on. Note that the iteration plan is a component of the overall BSM project plan (Figure 5.10).

Activity Details

Input Artifacts	*Tasks Performed*	*Output Artifacts*	*Roles (RACI)*
	Define Iteration Goals	Iteration Goals	
BSM Project Plan BSM Solution Architecture	Establish Iteration Scope	Iteration Deliverables *(Service Improvement, Service Management Process Improvement, and Quick Wins)*	A/R: Project Manager C: ITIL Expert Consultant
Iteration Deliverables	Define Iteration Evaluation Criteria	Evaluation Criteria	A/R: Project Manager C: ITIL Expert Consultant
Iteration Deliverables	Assess Resource Requirements and Acquire Project Resources	Project Resources	A/R: Project Manager C: ITIL Expert Consultant
Iteration Goals Iteration Deliverables Iteration Evaluation Criteria Time-Boxed BSM Phases	Develop Iteration Plan	Iteration Plan	A/R: Project Manager C: ITIL Expert Consultant

Postconditions

- Detailed iteration plan developed and agreed on
- Resources required for the iteration acquired
- Iteration evaluation criteria documented and agreed on

Execute

Planned activities are executed and desired deliverables are produced. If appropriate planning is performed, the execution runs smoothly and risks are effectively managed.

Manage the Phase

The current phase is appropriately managed.

Manage the Iteration

Purpose

- To initiate the activities of the next iteration according to the iteration plan
- To ensure that required resources are acquired and assigned
- To ensure that iteration is executed as planned
- To ensure that iteration results are evaluated and reviewed
- To ensure that iteration is closed

Preconditions

- Iteration plan developed, agreed on, and approved
- Iteration evaluation criteria documented, reviewed, and approved
- Resources acquired

Activity Overview

This activity ensures that appropriate tasks are carried out to start, review, and finish an iteration. Risks are managed throughout the iteration and the risk list is continually updated. To close an iteration, an iteration assessment is carried out against the predefined and agreed on evaluation criteria (Figure 5.11).

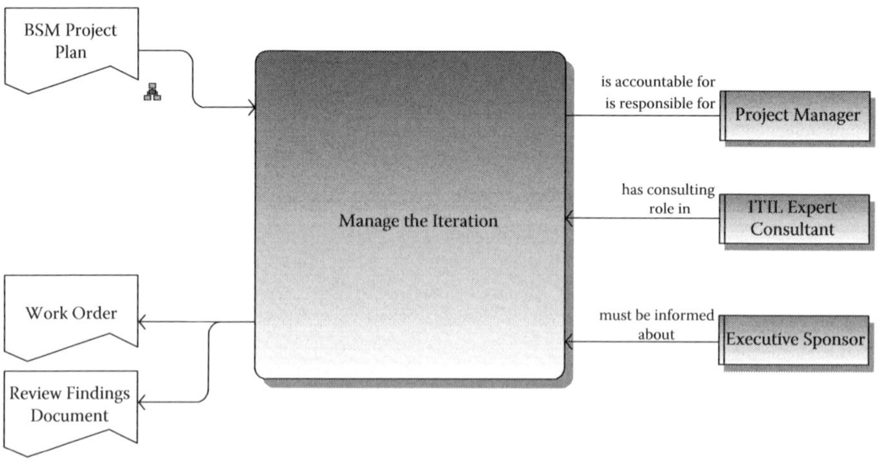

Figure 5.11 Manage the iteration.

Activity Details

Input Artifacts	*Tasks Performed*	*Output Artifacts*	*Roles (RACI)*
BSM Project Plan Iteration Plan	Initiate Iteration	Work Order	A/R: Project Manager
Risk List	Monitor and Update Risk List	Risk List	A/R: Project Manager
Iteration Plan Test Results Summary	Evaluate Iteration Against Predefined and Approved Evaluation Criteria	Iteration Assessment	A/R: Project Manager C: ITIL Expert Consultant
Iteration Evaluation Criteria	Review and Approve Iteration Results	Review Findings Document	A/R: Project Manager C: ITIL Expert Consultant I: Executive Sponsor

Postconditions

- Work assigned to the team members
- Iteration plan tracking initiated
- Iteration completed as planned
- Risk list updated

Manage Scope and Risks

Purpose

The purpose of this activity is to ensure that the risks and scope are effectively and efficiently managed.

Preconditions

- Risk list created
- Risk owner(s) assigned
- Risk response and management plan developed and agreed on
- BSM project plan developed and agreed on

Activity Overview

During this activity, the scope of the project, phase, or iteration is managed based on risks. The risk owner is then responsible for monitoring all assigned risks. If a risk materializes, the associated risk mitigation plan is executed by the risk owner and the risk list is updated (Figure 5.12).

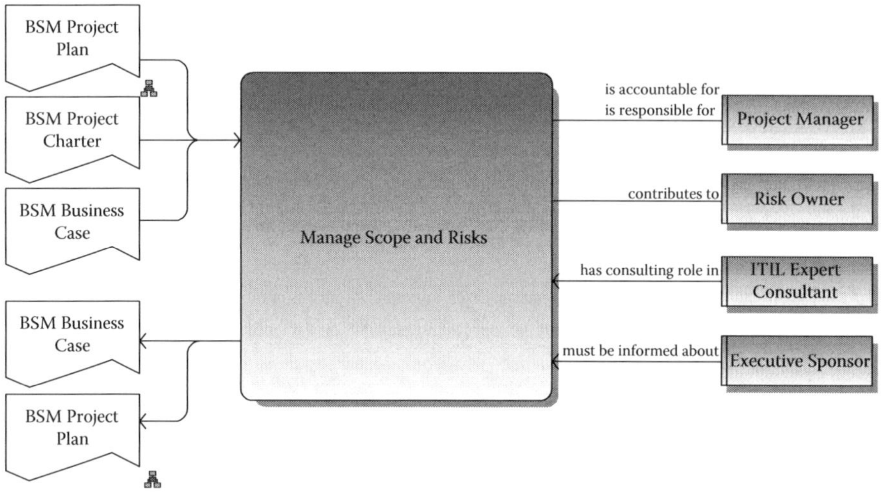

Figure 5.12 Manage scope and risks.

Activity Details

Input Artifacts	*Tasks Performed*	*Output Artifacts*	*Roles (RACI)*
Risk List Business Case BSM Project Charter BSM Project Plan	Evaluate and Manage Project Scope	Risk List Business Case	A/R: Project Manager C: ITIL Expert Consultant I: Executive Sponsor
Risk List	Monitor Risk List	Risk List Monitored	A: Project Manager R: Risk Owner C: ITIL Expert Consultant
Risk Response and Management Plan	Instantiate Risk Mitigation Approach	Risk Mitigation Approach Instituted	A: Project Manager R: Risk Owner C: ITIL Expert Consultant I: Executive Sponsor
Risk List	Update Risk List	Risk List Updated	A / R: Project Manager C: ITIL Expert Consultant I: Executive Sponsor

Postconditions

- Risks managed
- Minimal negative impact of risk materialization

Monitor and Control

This activity ensures that daily project performance is monitored and controlled, variances are identified, and associated status reports are produced in a timely manner. Significant variances that can potentially put the project at risk are closely monitored and preventive actions are taken as needed.

Monitor and Control Project

Purpose

- To monitor and document project progress
- To provide regular reports on project status
- To manage risks and deal with daily project issues

Preconditions

- Program initiated
- Project plan and iteration plan agreed on and approved
- Risk list and issues list created

Activity Overview

Monitoring and controlling the project requires effective management of issues and timely communication to the identified relevant stakeholders (Figure 5.13).

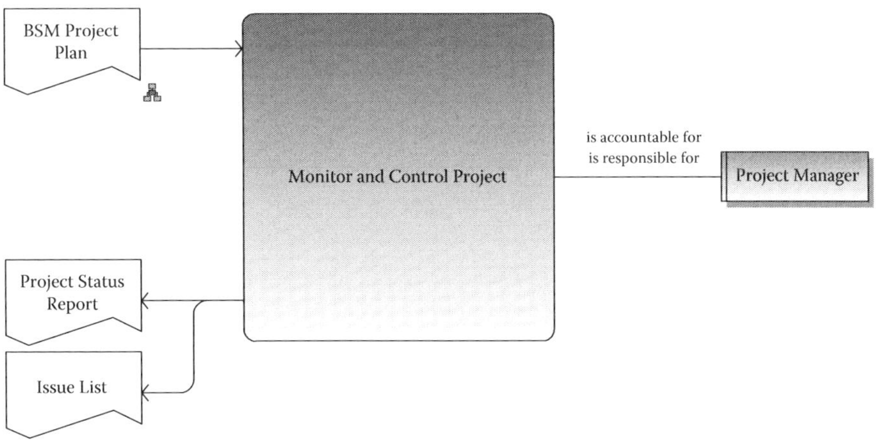

Figure 5.13 Monitor and control project.

Activity Details

Input Artifacts	*Tasks Performed*	*Output Artifacts*	*Roles (RACI)*
BSM Project Plan Iteration Plan Risk List Issues List	Monitor and Report Project Status	Risk List (Updated) Issues List (Updated) Project Status Report	A/R: Project Manager
	Manage Issues	Issues List (Updated) Work Order	A/R: Project Manager
Project Status Report	Organize and Facilitate Periodic Project Reviews	Work Order	A/R: Project Manager C: ITIL Expert Consultant

Postconditions

- Project effectively monitored and controlled
- Issues managed in a timely manner
- Status reports published in a timely manner

Evaluate Iteration Results

Purpose

To ensure that iteration delivered the desired results.

Preconditions

- BSM project plan completed and agreed on
- BSM project initiated
- Iteration evaluation criteria defined and agreed on

Activity Overview

Each iteration must end with an assessment and evaluation of the iteration deliverables. This evaluation is performed during this activity (Figure 5.14).

Activity Details

Input Artifacts	*Tasks Performed*	*Output Artifacts*	*Roles (RACI)*
BSM Project Plan Iteration Evaluation Criteria	Evaluate Iteration Results	Iteration Assessment Report	R/A: Project Manager C: ITIL Expert Consultant I: Executive Sponsor

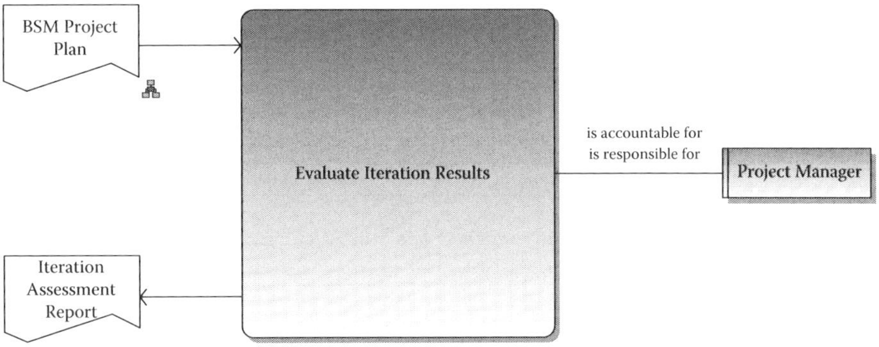

Figure 5.14 Evaluate iteration results.

Postcondition

Iteration assessment performed and improvement opportunities identified.

Ensure Alignment with Business and IT Vision

Purpose

The purpose of this activity is to ensure that project deliverables are planned, prioritized, and implemented so that they contribute to the overall alignment between business and IT.

Preconditions

- BSM project plan completed and agreed on
- BSM project initiated

Activity Overview

One of the key objectives of monitoring and controlling the project is to ensure that IT vision is completely aligned with the business vision. This is one of the key activities performed within the *Monitor and Control* phase of the project life cycle. This activity ensures that continual alignment of business and IT vision and strategy is achieved (Figure 5.15).

Activity Details

Input Artifacts	*Tasks Performed*	*Output Artifacts*	*Roles (RACI)*
BSM Project Plan Review Findings Document BSM Business Case IT Strategy Document	Ensure Alignment of BSM Project Deliverables with Overall Business Vision and IT Strategy	BSM Project Plan	A/R: Project Manager C: ITIL Expert Consultant I: Executive Sponsor

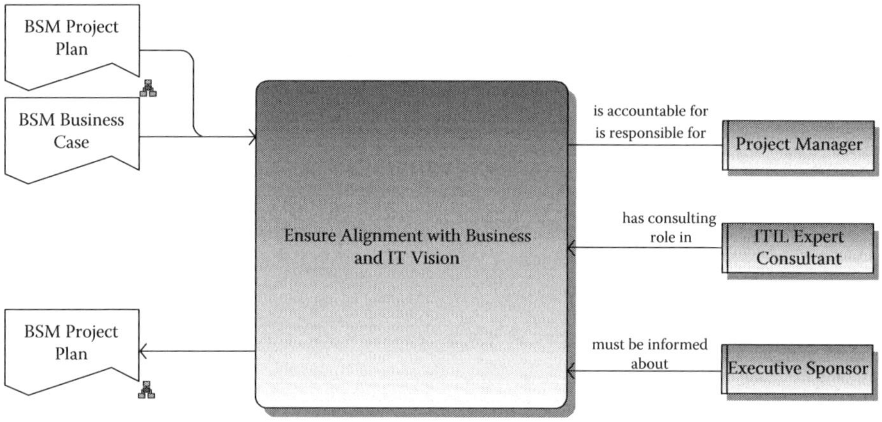

Figure 5.15 Ensure alignment with business and IT vision.

Postcondition

BSM project plan updated.

Close

The project, phase, and iteration are formally closed.

Close Phase

Purpose

The purpose of this activity is to ensure that the project phase is brought to closure and that the phase objectives have been achieved.

Preconditions

- All necessary iteration assessments completed
- Issues list updated

Activity Overview

In this activity, the project manager brings the current project phase to closure. The project manager ensures that all phase objectives have been successfully achieved. During the final iteration (realize iteration) of the given phase, the project manager holds a phase closure review and also plans for the next phase, assuming the project is to continue. This review should aim to achieve concurrence among all stakeholders on the current state of the project. This review should be formally performed and should demonstrate to all key stakeholders that the phase objectives were achieved. The objectives of each phase are discussed in Chapter 12. Figure 5.16 shows the key inputs, outputs, and primary roles that must be engaged during this activity.

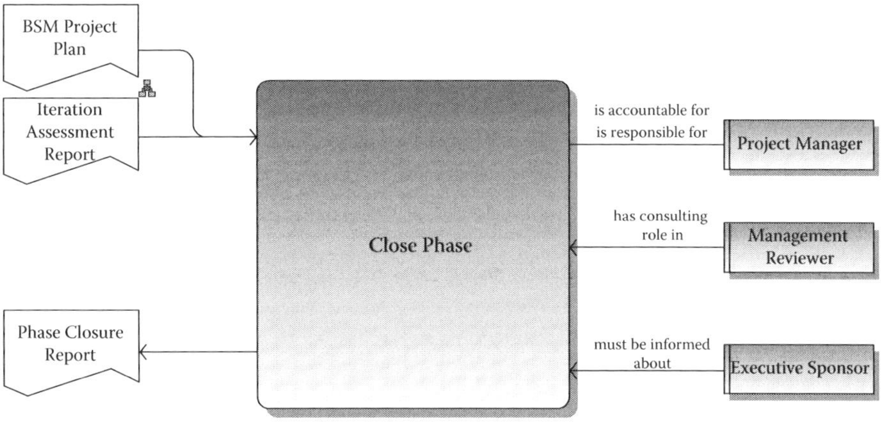

Figure 5.16 Close phase.

Activity Details

Input Artifacts	*Tasks Performed*	*Output Artifacts*	*Roles (RACI)*
BSM Project Plan Iteration Plan Iteration Assessment Report	Review Iteration Assessment Report(s)	BSM Project Plan	A/R: Project Manager I: Executive Sponsor
BSM Project Plan Iteration Assessment Report Phase Closure Report	Perform Phase Closure Review	Phase Closure Report	A/R: Project Manager C: Management Reviewer I: Executive Sponsor

Postcondition

The phase must be effectively and efficiently closed.

Perform Project Acceptance

Purpose

- To ensure that the PMO manager prepares the project for closure
- To perform project acceptance review
- To document any issues to be resolved during project warranty period

Precondition

Last iteration has been assessed and an iteration assessment report has been created.

Activity Overview

Before closing the project, project results must be reviewed and accepted by the relevant stakeholders who are identified as those responsible for reviewing the results and formally accepting the deliverables. As a result of this activity, "Project Acceptance Report" is created, agreed on, and signed. Any outstanding issues that may need to be resolved are documented and appropriate action items documented (Figure 5.17).

Activity Details

Input Artifacts	*Tasks Performed*	*Output Artifacts*	*Roles (RACI)*
BSM Project Plan Iteration Assessment Report	Organize Project Acceptance Review	Project Acceptance Report Issue List	A/R: Project Manager C: ITIL Expert Consultant and Management Reviewer I: Executive Sponsor

Postcondition

The project acceptance report must be created and agreed on.

Close Project

Purpose

- To ensure that the project manager prepares the project for closure
- To close the project

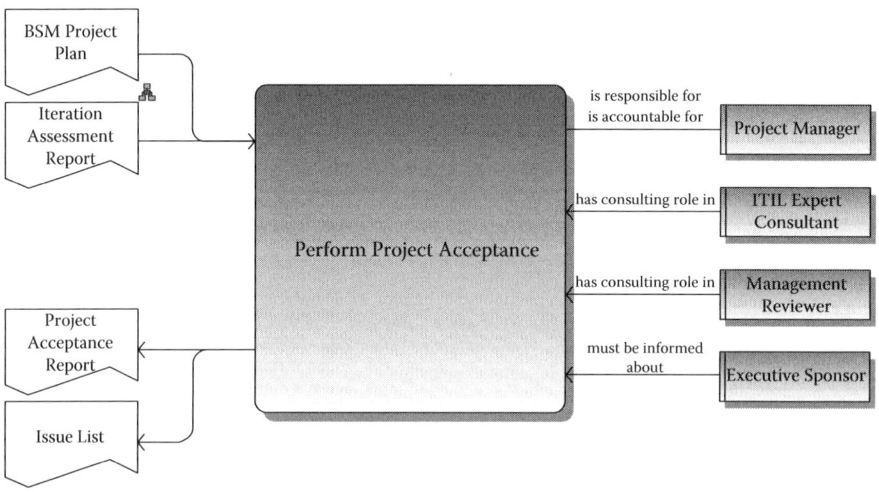

Figure 5.17 Perform project acceptance.

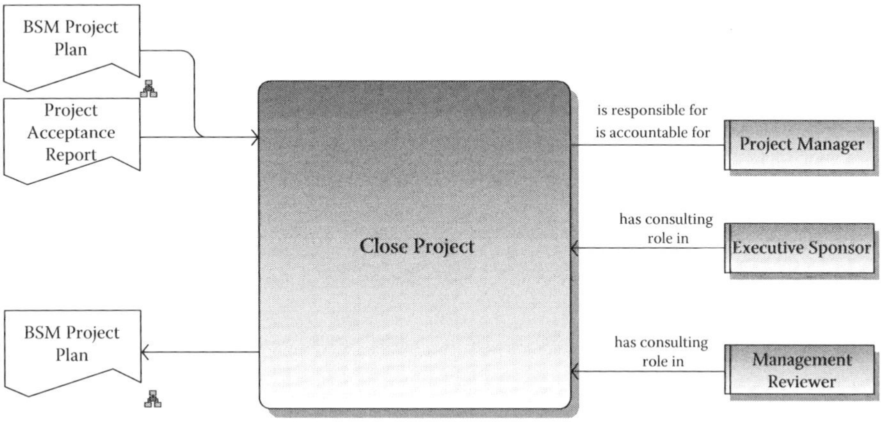

Figure 5.18 Close project.

Precondition

The project acceptance report must be created and agreed on.

Activity Overview

During this activity, the project is formally closed. Project closure takes place once the project deliverables are formally reviewed and accepted (Figure 5.18).

Activity Details

Input Artifacts	*Tasks Performed*	*Output Artifacts*	*Roles (RACI)*
BSM Project Plan Project Acceptance Report	Close Out the Project	BSM Project Plan	A/R: Project Manager C: Executive Sponsor and Management Reviewer

Postcondition

The project is successfully closed.

Primary Roles and Responsibilities

Figure 5.19 shows the primary roles and their responsibilities.

Please note that additional roles may be required depending on the size and complexity of the organization.

Figure 5.19 Primary roles.

Project Manager

- Ensure that regular reviews are conducted
- Ensure that project status reports are consolidated and distributed in a timely manner
- Escalate issues and risks that present significant threats to the success of the overall program
- Ensure that the overall project stays on target and delivers the desired results
- Plan and manage assigned projects
- Prioritize work and allocate resources
- Coordinate interactions with the customer and users
- Keep the project team focused
- Establish a set of practices that ensure the integrity of project artifacts
- Document and appropriately share lessons learned

Executive Sponsor

- Establish the Business–IT Integration vision
- Provide ongoing sponsorship and support
- Review and provide feedback in a timely manner
- Own the BSM

Management Reviewer

- Represent the stakeholders responsible for reviewing the deliverables throughout the project phases
- Represent the organization from the end user or customer perspective

Risk Owner

- Continually monitor assigned risks
- Invoke the risk mitigation plan when and if risk materializes
- Update the risk list as appropriate

ITIL Expert Consultant

This individual provides service management expertise.

Key Artifacts

Key artifacts produced during the BSM project are shown in Figure 5.20.

Business Vision Document

This document explains the overall business vision.

IT Vision Document

The IT vision must be created in support of the business vision. This document contains the IT vision.

IT Strategy Document

This document outlines the approach that the IT organization is going to take to achieve its stated vision.

BSM Business Case

This is the business case that must justify the investment to be made in the BSM implementation.

BSM Project Charter

The project charter provides the authorization to commit resources to a given project. Key contents of a project charter are shown in Figure 5.21.

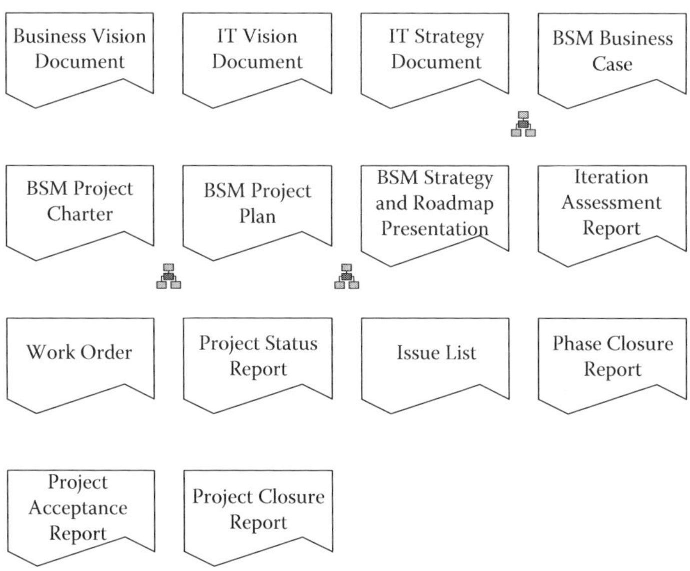

Figure 5.20 Key artifacts.

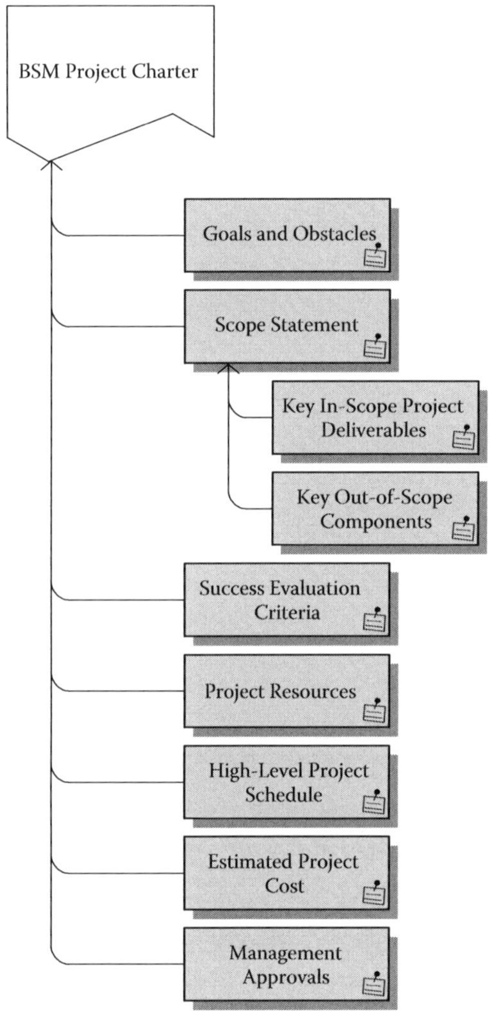

Figure 5.21 BSM project charter.

BSM Project Plan

The BSM project plan guides all the activities that should be performed to achieve BSM. The key contents of this document are shown in Figure 5.22.

BSM Strategy and Roadmap Presentation

The BSM strategy and roadmap presentation provides an overview of the approach that will be adopted to achieve BSM.

Iteration Assessment Report

The iteration assessment report summarizes the result of iteration assessments.

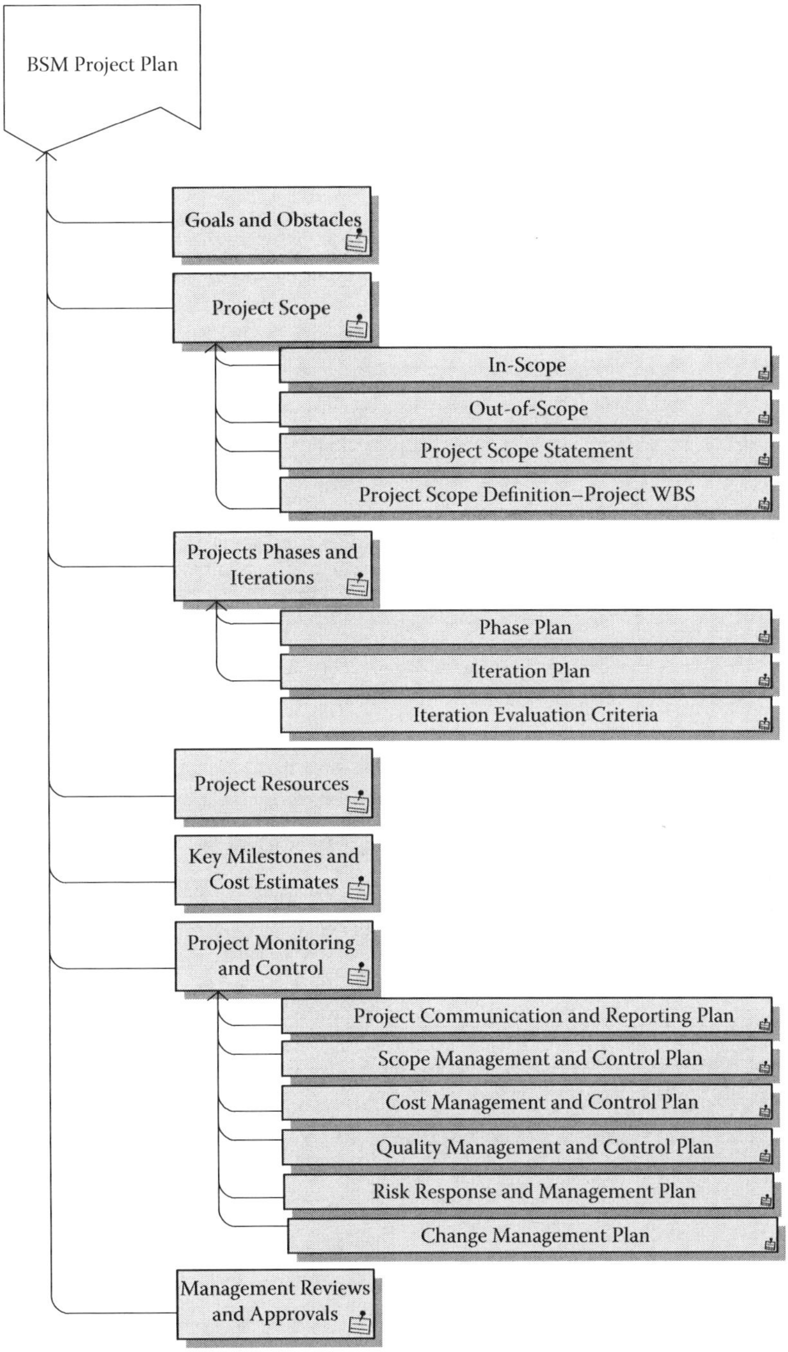

Figure 5.22 BSM project plan.

Work Order

A work order is an authorization by the project manager for the project resources to perform planned project activities.

Project Status Report

This report provides a regular status update to the project stakeholders.

Issue List

This document lists all the project issues and related details.

Summary

BSM is more about organizational change and transformation than any other single factor and project management is one of the most critical components of successfully achieving BSM. In this chapter, we discussed the project management discipline in detail, as well as the WBS, the workflow, key artifacts, and primary roles.

Reference

Shuja, A., and J. Krebs. 2008. *Rational Unified Process: Reference and Certification Guide*. New York: IBM Press.

Chapter 6

Discipline: People and Organization

Introduction

Understanding the complexity of organizations and their environments has been a long-standing concern of organization theory. Organization plays an important role at all levels of a business enterprise: from a single-person enterprise to a global enterprise with thousands of employees. The high-level goals of an organization may remain the same, that is, optimizing enterprise functioning. It seems intuitive to assume that the intensity* of organization varies with the size and complexity of the enterprise. As an enterprise (industry or business) begins to involve greater size, numbers, and complexity, organization becomes necessary simply for direction, control, and handling of affairs, aside from any question of direct economy (Robb, 1910). A virtue has been made of this necessity for division because it becomes possible, by dividing duties and functions, to conserve special skills and abilities and to direct all efforts into definite paths, to which it becomes accustomed and, thus, gains in efficiency. Figure 6.1 gives a pictorial overview of some of the critical factors that affect the organization of an enterprise.

According to Levy (2000), strategy concerns itself with the development and deployment of corporate resources in such a way as to compete more effectively in a particular industry. Business success and failure are outcomes of complex interactions between an organization and its changing environment, without simple cause-and-effect relationships.

Compared to the organizational importance for a business enterprise in the context of its purpose, Levy (2000) presents an interesting discussion of the influence that an enterprise's (or firm's) behavior can have on the organizational structure. Industries evolve in a dynamic, path-dependent manner over time as a result of complex interactions among firms, government, labor, consumers, financial institutions, and other elements of the environment. Not only does industry structure influence firm behavior, but firm behavior can, in turn, alter the structure of an industry and the

* Intensity refers to the level and extent of organization needed. For a smaller business enterprise with a single location, flatter organization structure may be more appropriate compared to a larger global business enterprise.

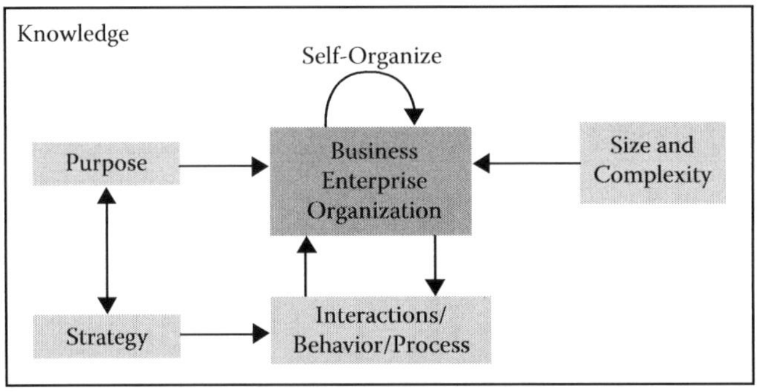

Figure 6.1 Factors impacting organization.

contours of competition. Existing theoretical models, however, tend to assume relatively simple linear relationships without feedback.

As with most aspects of operating a business enterprise, organization comes with its own limitations; it is crucial to have the right organization for the right purpose. *Over*-organization or *under*-organization may not be at all beneficial. In implementing BSM, an IT organization needs to be appropriately structured so that it enables and supports the achievement of business–IT integration. According to Robb (1910, p. 24) a business organization exists for the purpose of accomplishing definite pieces of work and arriving at a definite result with the least possible expenditure of labor and materials and the shortest possible use of the plant's time. If organization does not prevent waste or enable us to get results attainable in no other way, it has no value. In any undertaking, there are many factors that influence the result. We shall make the best use of time, labor, and money if we keep all of these factors in view and if we develop the whole in harmony, with consideration of the impact of each factor, and work for improvement of the factors in proportion to their relative importance—rather than getting pulled in one direction because it interests us, is more visible, or is the path of least resistance. It helps us to appreciate true thoroughness, the value of attention to what is significant, and the elimination of wasted time and effort (Robb, 1910, p. 30).

Purpose

The goal is to effectively envision, plan, and implement the organization required to achieve BSM.

Objectives

Some key *people and organization* objectives are as follows (Figure 6.2):

- To ensure that people with the required competencies and capabilities are identified
- To plan and deliver required training and mentoring
- To plan and design enabling organizational structures
- To define clear roles and responsibilities
- To ensure that people are assigned appropriate roles
- To continually review and align organization to deliver on BSM objectives

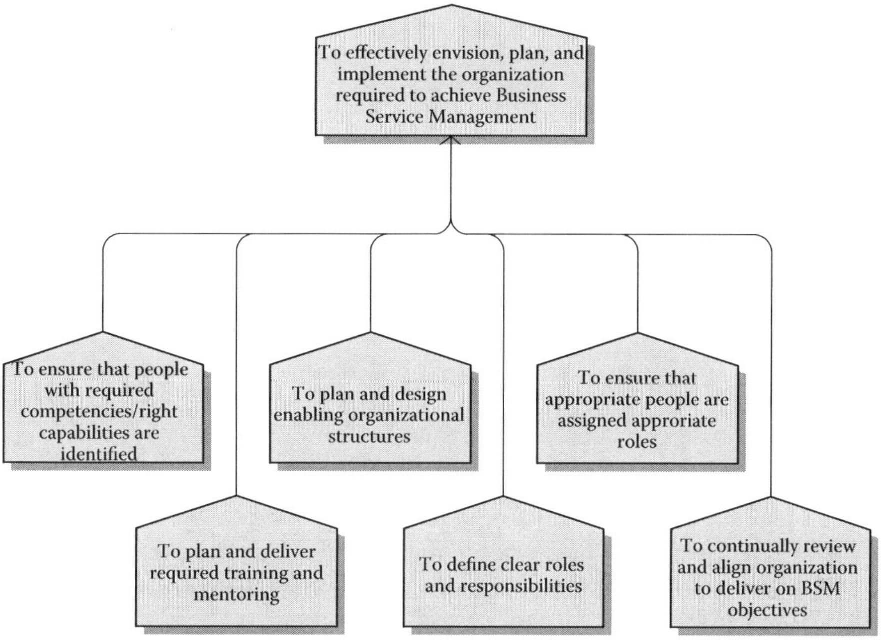

Figure 6.2 People and organization objectives.

Work Breakdown Structure

To ensure that the above-mentioned objectives are realized, there are some core activities that should be performed within the people and organization discipline. Figure 6.3 shows the people and organization work breakdown structure (WBS).

The activities shown in the WBS should be performed to create the appropriate organization required to achieve BSM. We will discuss the sequence in which these activities should be performed and the details of each in the next section.

People and Organization Workflow

Figure 6.4 provides a recommended sequence in which the people and organization activities may be performed. Please note that this sequence can vary depending on an organization's specific culture and needs.

As shown in the workflow, when the need to improve the organization is identified, the most important activity is to clearly understand the direction in which the IT organization plans to go and the core underlying principles. These underlying principles must then drive the organizational mission statement and the overall design. We will discuss some of these principles later in this chapter.

Once organizational principles are defined and a mission statement is established, the AS-IS organization must be assessed to identify and analyze the existing gaps preventing the organization from achieving its intended mission. Accordingly, the TO-BE organization is designed and the organizational change is managed. Let us discuss each of the activities in the workflow in greater detail.

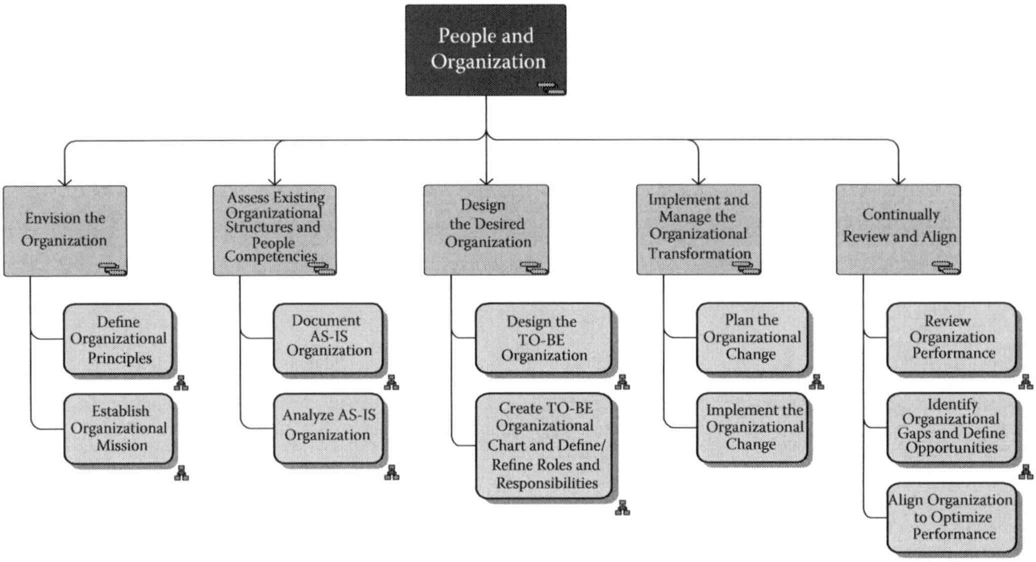

Figure 6.3 People and organization work breakdown structure.

Envision the Organization

Before assessing existing organizational structures, teams, and people, it is important to take a step back and really look at what your customers plan to achieve and what they need from you. It is criti cal to understand how IT management visualizes the future role of IT organization. These factors must define core organizational principles and the mission statement. Note that organizations are business systems and are in constant states of change—they are created, operated, revised, and often eliminated (Johnson et al., 1964). In this regard, the idea of organic structures seems more appealing and effective to me than mechanistic ones in coping with turbulent environments, as is truly supported by Burns and Stalker (1961). Complexity theory suggests that organic networks poised on "the edge of chaos" might give rise to self-organization and emergent order that enable firms to prosper in an era of rapid change (Allen, 1988; Brown and Eisenhardt, 1997). Therefore, to be efficient and effective, approaches to organization design must change as well. Most texts on the subject focus on tasks and structures, with detailed discussions of roles, positions, levels, and reporting relationships (Galbraith, 1977; Schlesinger and Sathe, 1992). They say relatively little about processes or about how the work actually gets done. From these readings, the implicit argument seems to be that organization design is largely a matter of architecture: drawing the right boxes and connecting them appropriately. A "process perspective," discussed earlier, suggests that more attention should be paid to organizational functioning and that design efforts should begin by attending to processes and only later should attention shift to the structures needed to accommodate them. Structuring organizations as decentralized, nonhierarchical networks is an important component of achieving this vision (Nohria and Eccles, 1992; Senge, 1990; Stacey, 1995; Wheatley, 1996). ITIL v3 provides detailed guideline to envision the organization and may be consulted to gain further insights as you perform this activity.

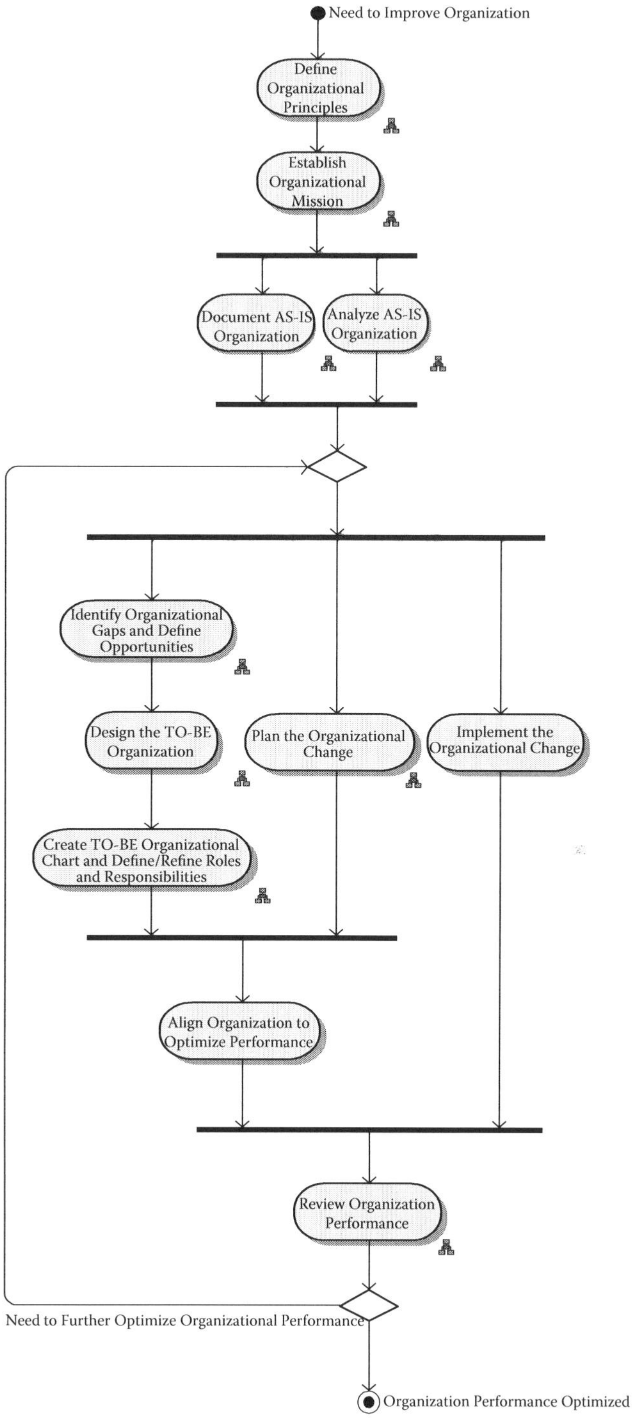

Figure 6.4 People and organization workflow.

Define Organizational Principles

Some of the key questions that the senior management and executives should ask about the future of their organization may be as follows:

- Who are our customers and what do they expect from us?
- What is our business (i.e., business partner and business service provider, back-office IT support, infrastructure, or data center management and support, etc.)?
- Are our customers' expectations in line with the business we are in?
- If we are in the "right" business, are we delivering what our customers expect from us?
- What is the core set of principles that we need to follow to integrate well with our customers?

Based on the responses to the above questions, you may identify the following organizational principles:

- *IT is the business and business is IT (in-house or outsourced).* Businesses that completely rely on IT services to operate their business are the ones where IT is the business and business is the IT. Ideal examples are Google, eBay, and Amazon. These are businesses that have been primarily established based on the capabilities provided by IT and the Internet. In these businesses, IT services are actually business services. For example, browsing and searching products are business processes enabled by business services (the capability of the visitor to search for the products online). In such businesses, IT performance directly impacts the business performance and it is critical that IT be completely integrated with the business to effectively enable the core business processes. In these cases, parts of IT may be outsourced and that should be completely seamless.

The model shown in Figure 6.5 can be used to define an architecture for your specific organization and to support your core organizational principles.

Purpose

The goal is to ensure that core organizational principles, which will drive the organization structure and people development, are defined and in line with business and IT visions.

Preconditions

- BSM project charter is approved.
- BSM project has been initiated.
- Business vision document has been created.
- IT vision document is created.

Activity Overview

During this activity, the human resource manager is accountable for analyzing both business and IT visions and for identifying and documenting organizational principles. The ITIL expert consultant should be consulted. The executive sponsor may influence these principles (Figure 6.6).

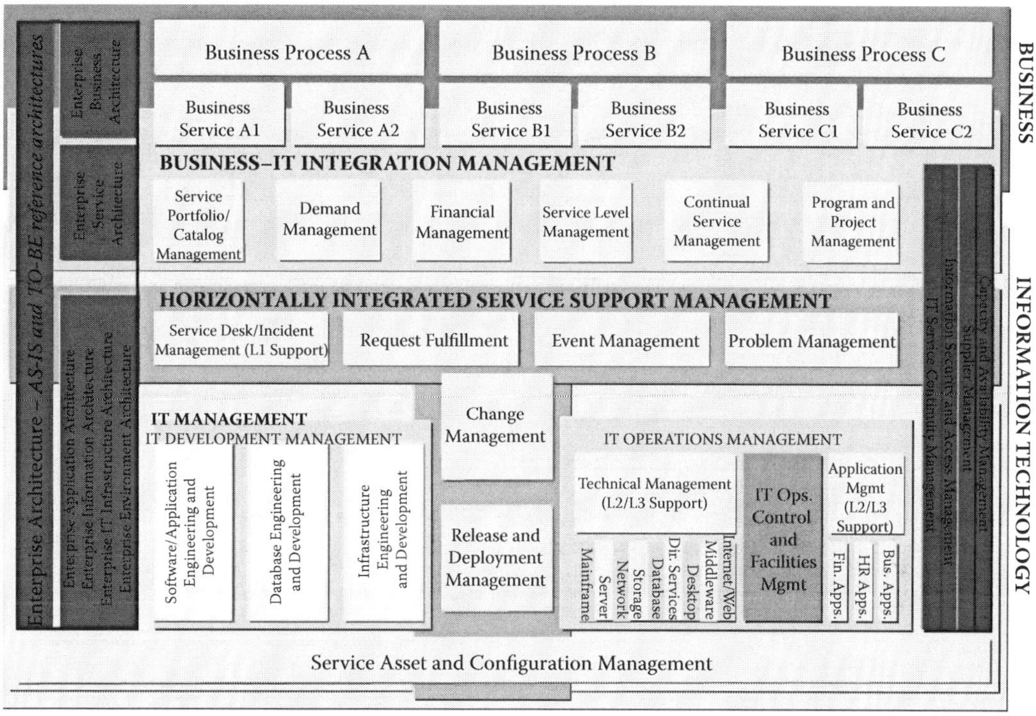

Figure 6.5 Conceptual organizational architecture.

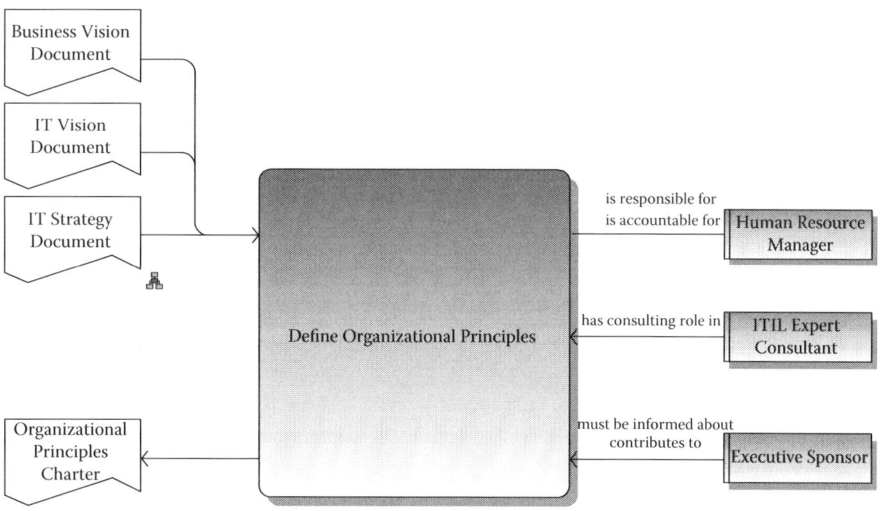

Figure 6.6 Define organizational principles.

Practical Tip: Note that "Conceptual Organizational Architecture" aims to provide a conceptual architecture on how to envision and design the organization in order to ensure that your business enterprise is able to effectively and efficiently manage the production and delivery of its respective products and/or services. The key concept is to design the organizational structure to address the business needs including hierarchical as well as more flatter organizational structures.

Postcondition

Organizational principles are defined and agreed on.

Establish Organizational Mission

Based on the business and IT visions, IT strategy, and organizational principles, mission statement is created for the IT organization. This mission statement will further drive how the future-state organization will be defined.

Purpose

The goal is to define, agree on, and establish an organizational mission statement.

Preconditions

- BSM project charter approved
- BSM project initiated
- Organizational principles charter defined

Activity Overview

An organizational mission statement must come from the senior management and executives. They should take the organizational principles charter and vision documents into consideration when defining the mission statement (Figure 6.7).

Postcondition

The organizational mission statement is defined and agreed on.

Assess Existing Organizational Structures and Peoples' Competencies

Note that the organization was envisioned before performing formal AS-IS assessment. The rationale is that you do not want your mission statement to be impacted by existing organizational limitations. Organizational principles and mission statements are defined independent of how well the organization is prepared to achieve that mission. The key drivers for organizational principles and mission statements should be the business and IT visions.

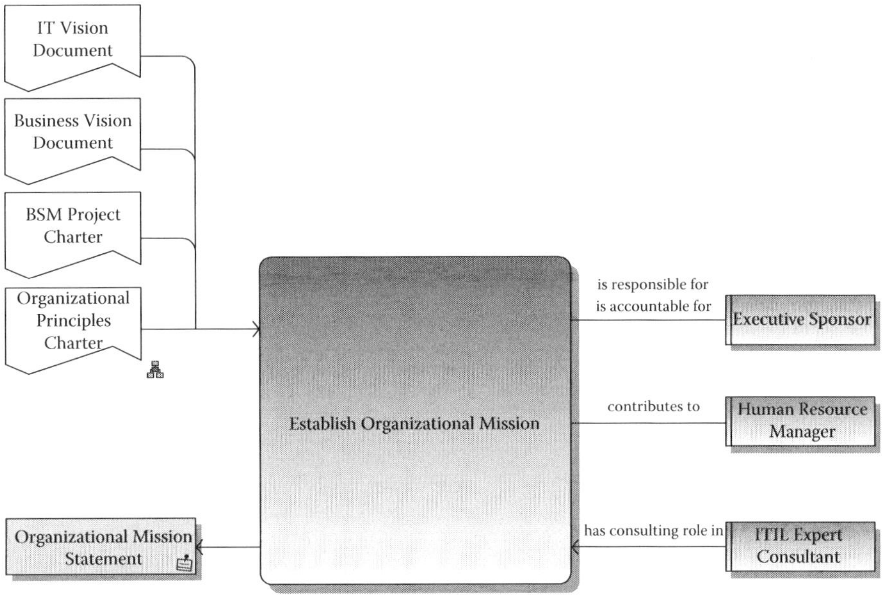

Figure 6.7 Establish organizational mission.

Document AS-IS Organization

Current organization structures are documented as a result of this activity.

Purpose

- To accurately document the current state structure of the IT organization
- To document existing key roles and their responsibilities

Precondition

The future state of organization has been envisioned.

Activity Overview

The key output of this activity is the AS-IS organization chart. The human resource analyst is responsible for completing this activity (Figure 6.8).

Postcondition

The existing organization is completely documented.

Analyze AS-IS Organization

This activity should be aligned with the activity that is carried out to analyze the current-state or AS-IS processes of the organization. Depending on the process strategy, we will need to establish

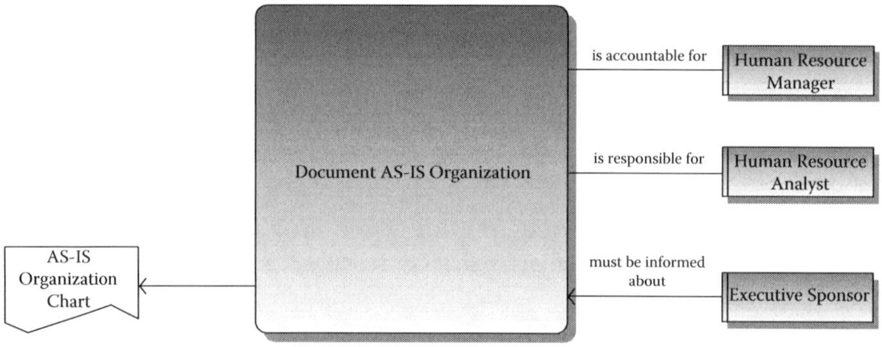

Figure 6.8 Document AS-IS organization.

appropriate targets for the organizational realignments. The existing organization is analyzed in this activity and findings are documented.

Purpose

- To analyze existing organization structures
- To assess the existing competencies of IT staff
- To document the findings

Precondition

The AS-IS organization structure is documented.

Activity Overview

The AS-IS organization chart and related details are analyzed and an assessment report is created (Figure 6.9). This assessment report must provide an accurate as possible picture of existing organizational competencies. The human resource analyst is responsible for completing this activity. The ITIL expert consultant may be consulted to complete this activity.

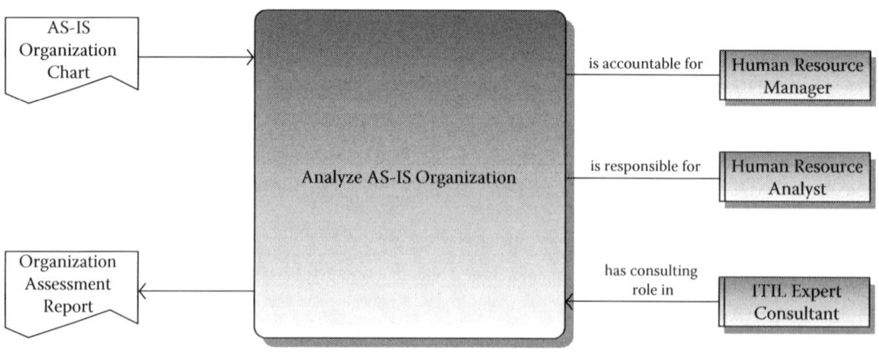

Figure 6.9 Analyze AS-IS organization.

Postcondition

The organization is completely analyzed and findings are documented.

Design the Desired Organization

To enable the organization to execute the processes in an effective and efficient manner, it will be critical to align the organization appropriately. For example, if you are trying to establish service level management at the service level (those defined within the catalog), you will need to have a central team that establishes service targets at that level and brings together underlying delivery teams from across the different functional organizations. At one of my clients, incident management was carried out at a silo level, that is, the application management team had their own incident management, the network organization had their own, and so on. To manage incidents to ensure alignment with overall business needs, we needed to consolidate the varying incident management processes into a single, standard incident management process and establish the global service desk function. Based on the assessment of the existing organization, a design of the organization—based on the organizational principles and driven by the mission statement—is created.

Design the TO-BE Organization

Based on the assessment of the respective service management processes, as well as the organization and process strategies, we should now think about the organization that will be required to most effectively and efficiently execute the processes. Note that in ITIL v3, organization is considered as one of the capabilities (others are management, processes, knowledge, and people) and during this activity, we will lay out the foundation for further establishing this capability in line with the business vision. Design of the desired organization is completed during this activity.

Purpose

The purpose of this activity is to create the design of the future-state organization so that it enables achievement of the organizational mission statement.

Preconditions

- Business vision document created
- IT vision document created
- Organizational principles charter created
- Assessment of existing organization completed
- Service management processes assessed and process vision and strategy established

Activity Overview

The human resource manager is accountable for the creation of the future-state organizational design. The TO-BE organization design may be created based on the *conceptual organizational*

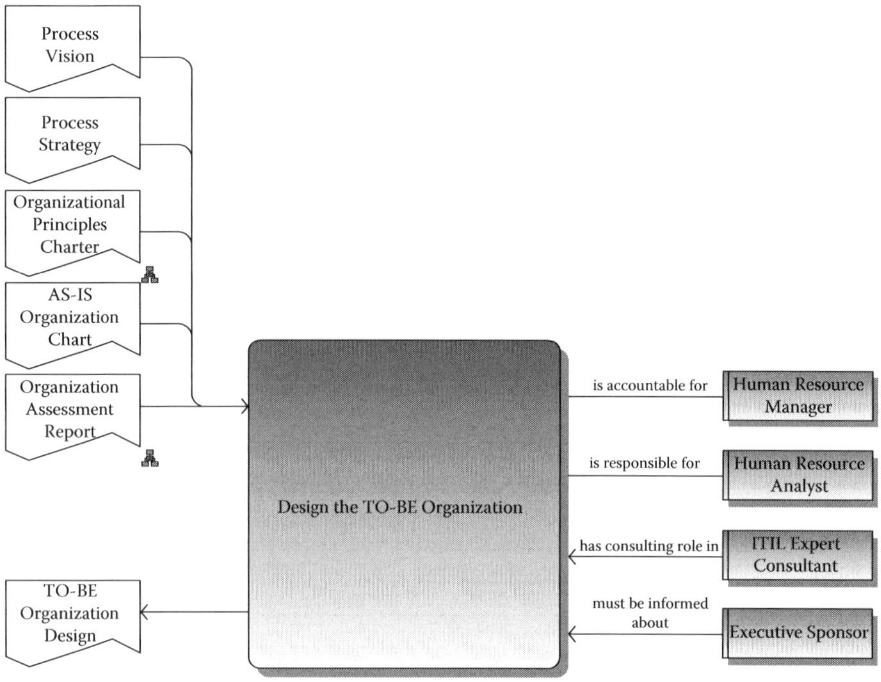

Figure 6.10 Design the TO-BE organization.

architecture discussed earlier in this chapter. This design will drive the actual organization chart (Figure 6.10).

Postcondition

The design of the future-state organization has been created and approved.

Create a TO-BE Organization Chart and Define and Refine Roles and Responsibilities

Roles are identified and responsibilities are defined when a target state or TO-BE processes are defined in the *design TO-BE process* activity. When it comes to designing the right organization, these roles and responsibilities defined during the process design are considered from the organizational perspectives. Note the importance of the alignment of organizational realignments with process design. Therefore, during this activity, desired organization charts are created and roles are defined. If they already existed in the current-state organization, then they are revisited and refined as appropriate.

Purpose

The purpose of this activity is to clearly define and agree on the future-state organization structures, roles, and responsibilities.

Preconditions

- Organizational principles are defined and agreed on
- Design of future-state organization has been completed
- Design of the future-state or relevant TO-BE processes completed

Activity Overview

The human resource manager is accountable for the execution of this activity. As a result of this activity, the TO-BE organization document is created and agreed on (Figure 6.11).

Postconditions

- Future-state organizational chart completely defined
- Roles and responsibilities are clearly described and agreed on

Implement and Manage the Organizational Transformation

During this activity, the changes necessary to achieve the desired organizational state are managed and implemented. Organizational change management is going to be critical to successfully complete this activity. Let us discuss this in detail.

Plan the Organizational Change

Based on the design of the future-state organization and assessment of the current state, a plan is created to achieve the desired state (Figure 6.12).

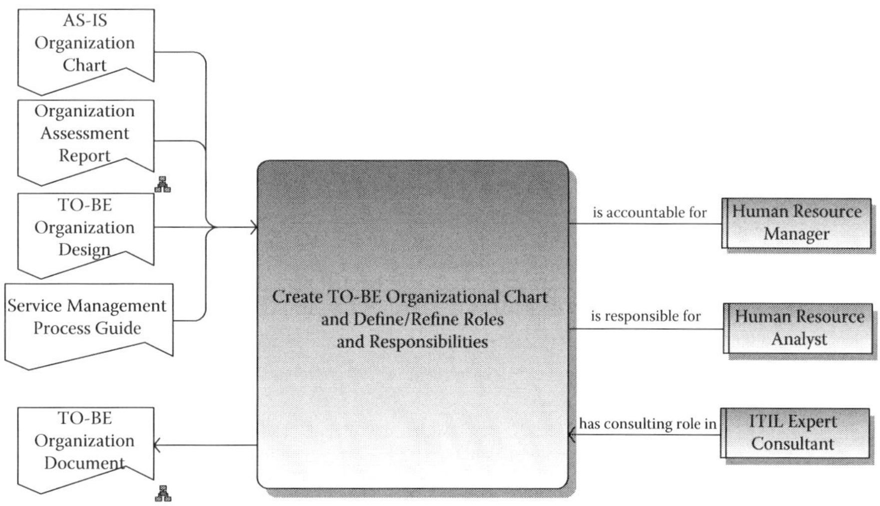

Figure 6.11 Create a TO-BE organizational chart and define and refine roles and responsibilities.

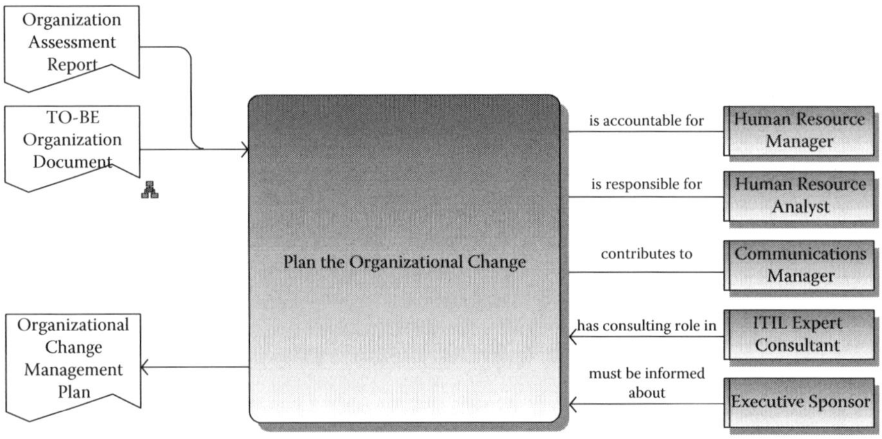

Figure 6.12 Plan the organizational change.

Purpose

The objective is to plan the organizational change so that risks are minimized and the desired state is achieved.

Preconditions

- Clear understanding of existing organizational structures and roles
- Completed design of the future-state organization

Activity Overview

Achieving BSM may have a significant impact on the way an organization is be structured. During this activity, due diligence is performed to ensure that appropriate plans are created to achieve the desired state and that associated risks are appropriately managed. Some of the key aspects of planning an organizational change may include the following:

- Human resource requirements analysis
- Staff acquisition planning
- Training and development planning
- Organizational change implementation schedule and milestones

Postcondition

A clear plan for managing the organizational change is created, agreed on, and approved.

Implement the Organizational Change

During this activity, the organizational change activities are performed according to the plan. The communications manager plays a critical role in ensuring that appropriate communications are managed as per the communication plan. During this activity, we will acquire the right resources (i.e., those that are able to execute the processes designed during the *design TO-BE process* activity). If we already have the right people, then we will need to ensure that they receive appropriate training to be better able to execute the activities.

Continually Review and Align

This is an ongoing activity that is performed to ensure that organizational performance is continually improved. This will be the key measure of how efficient the organization is. One way to achieve this is to measure the number of resources required to keep things going, that is, to perform operational activities. If we are making the right kind of improvements, then the number of resources required to keep things going should reduce over time.

Review Organization Performance

This activity primarily focuses on the overall quality of services provided by the IT organization. This performance review may be conducted with the overall performance assessment of services provided by the IT organization, as well as the performance of the service management processes. For example, if the number of failed changes is increasing and impacting the service targets and delivery timelines, then you will need to assess the performance of the change management organization along with the underpinning processes, tools, etc. It may be that processes are correctly defined and tools are appropriately implemented but gaps exist in the skills of the people who are responsible for executing the processes. In that case, those performance metrics should be reviewed here.

Purpose

The objective is to review performance data and document assessment findings.

Preconditions

- Organizational improvements implemented
- Service and service management process improvements realized for the organization and for the teams responsible for those services and service management processes

Activity Overview

Service performance and service management process performance reports are used to assess how the organizations and teams responsible for delivering and managing those services and processes are performing. Improvement opportunities are identified and achieved (Figure 6.13).

Postcondition

The related metrics is analyzed and findings are documented.

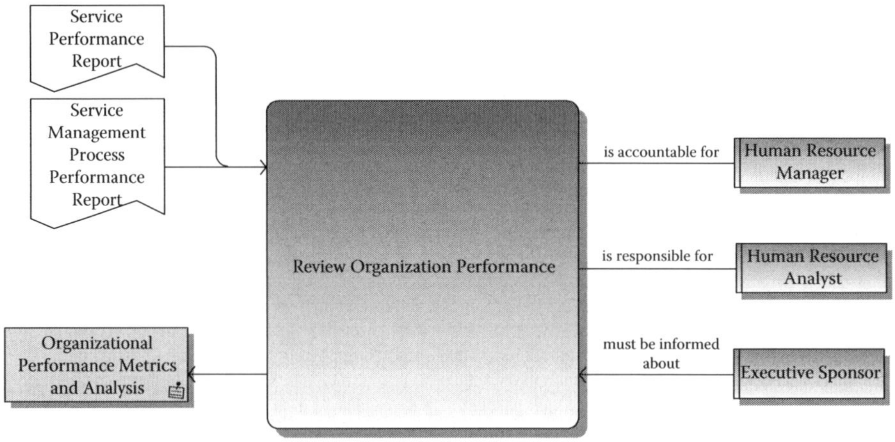

Figure 6.13 Review organization performance.

Identify Organizational Gaps and Define Opportunities

This activity focuses on gaps and opportunities that are specifically related to organizational aspects. We will see in Chapter 12 that this activity is performed in parallel with service management process performance assessment and service performance assessment activities to create a complete picture of where the gaps actually exist.

Purpose

The purpose of this activity is to clearly identify organizational (structures, roles, and competencies) gaps and improvement opportunities (training, staff acquisition, etc.).

Preconditions

- Related metrics completely assessed
- Organization being assessed accurately documented

Activity Overview

This activity primarily focuses on identifying gaps and opportunities as they relate to organizational improvements. Improvement recommendations are made as a result of this activity (Figure 6.14).

Postconditions

- Gaps and improvement opportunities identified and agreed on
- Recommendations made

Align Organization to Optimize Performance

Based on the recommendation made as part of the organization assessment, actions are planned and executed to achieve organizational improvements and optimize performance. Depending on the size of the effort and scale of the impact, this may or may not be managed as a project.

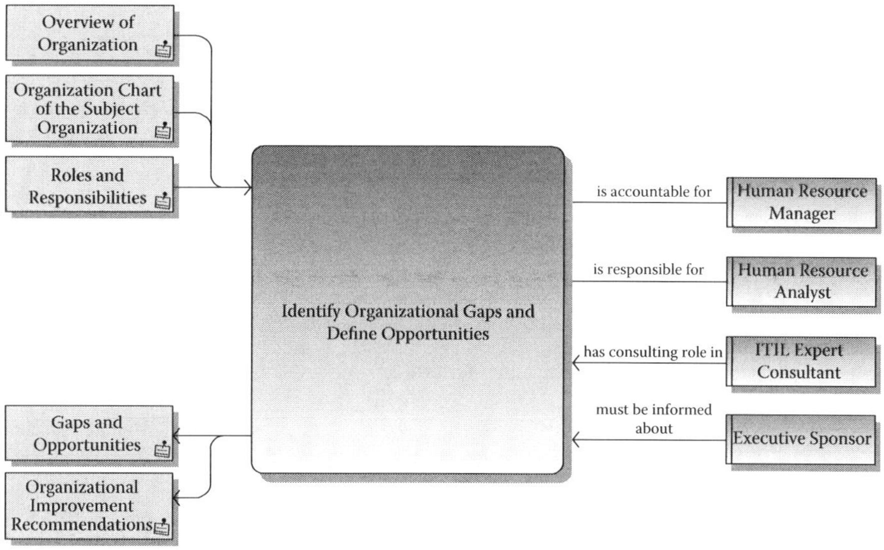

Figure 6.14 Identify organizational gaps and define opportunities.

Primary Roles and Responsibilities

People and organization primary roles and their responsibilities are shown in Figure 6.15.

Human Resources Manager

- Accountable for assessing, planning, and achieving improvements across the organization
- Provides complete sponsorship for achieving the desired improvements

Human Resources Analyst

The human resource analyst performs all the assessment, documentation, and analysis activities related to organizational improvement effort.

Communications Manager

The communications manager is responsible for planning and managing all communications related to organizational changes.

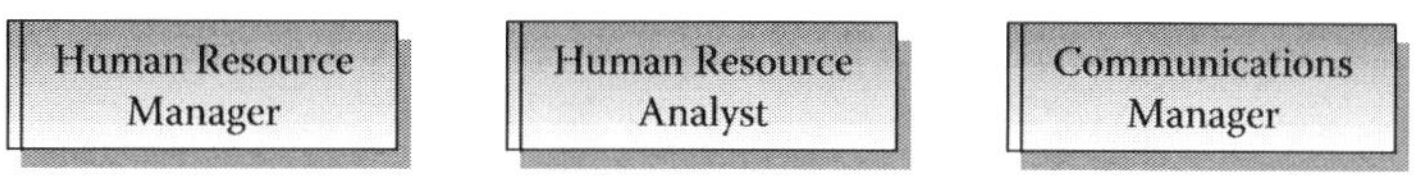

Figure 6.15 Primary roles and responsibilities.

Key Artifacts

Key artifacts related to this discipline are shown in Figure 6.16.

Organizational Principles Charter

This charter documents all the principles that will drive the organization design and structure.

AS-IS Organization Chart

- Provides current-state view of the organization
- Contains details on roles and responsibilities

Organization Assessment Report

- Provides results of the organizational assessment
- Contains descriptions of gaps identified as a result of the assessment and identifies opportunities for improvements
- Provides recommendations for improvements

Figure 6.17 provides an overview of the different sections that may be contained within the organization assessment report.

TO-BE Organization Design

- Derived from the conceptual organization architecture and organization principles charter
- Provides a logical design of how the organization should be structured to achieve its stated objectives

TO-BE Organization Document

- Based on the TO-BE organization design (Figure 6.18)
- Provides the actual organization chart and the related roles and responsibilities

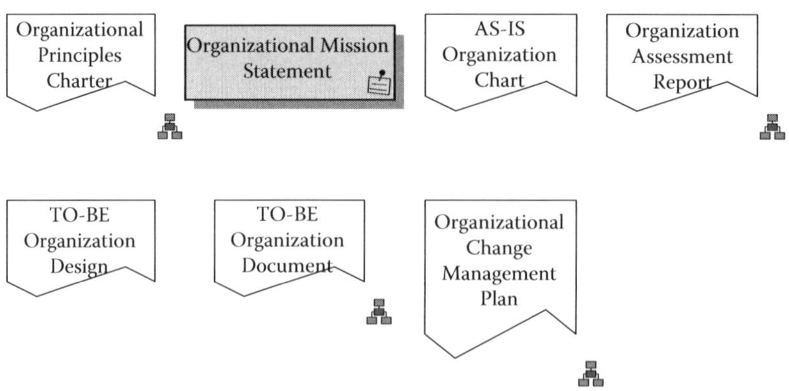

Figure 6.16 Key artifacts.

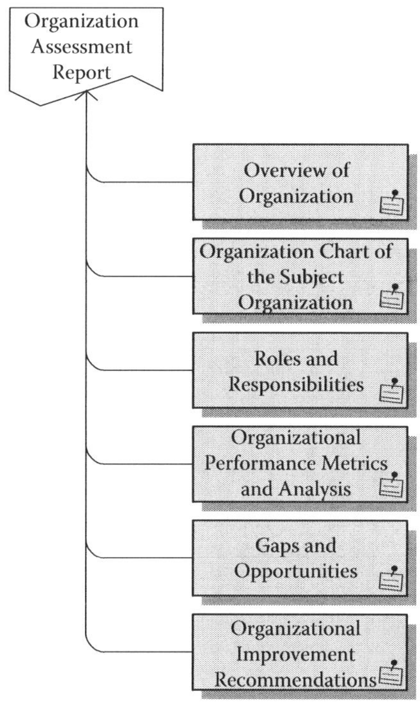

Figure 6.17 Organization assessment report.

Organizational Change Management Plan

- Provides a holistic plan to transition the organization from its current state to the desired future state
- Contains human resource requirements, required staff acquisition plan, training and development plan, and organization change schedule (Figure 6.19)

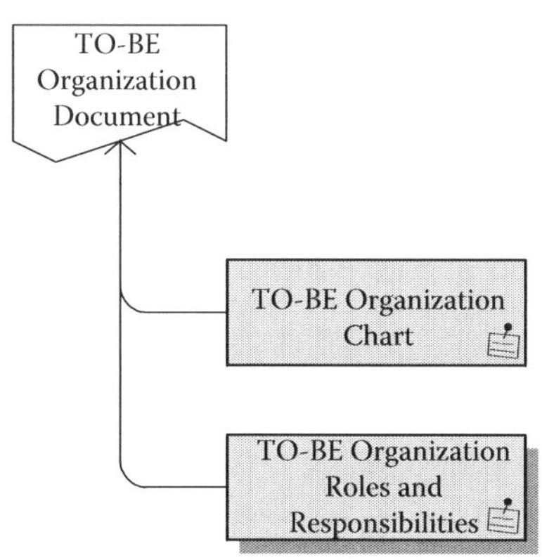

Figure 6.18 TO-BE organization document.

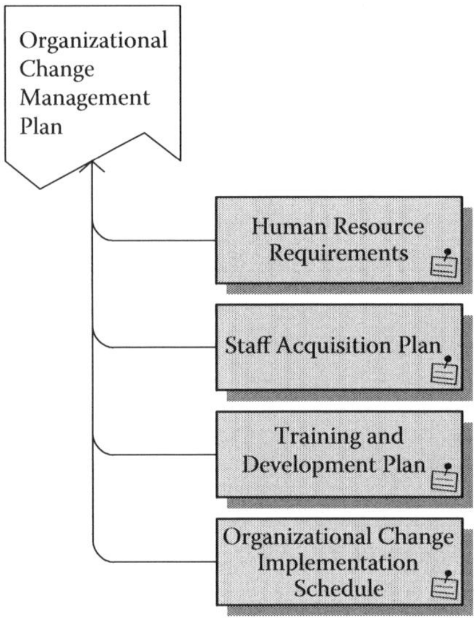

Figure 6.19 Organizational change management plan.

Summary

People and organization are among the most critical factors that will determine whether the BSM implementation effort becomes a success or failure. At the end, it is people who are going to embrace change, execute improved activities, and take pride in the quality of their work. It is critical that organizational related changes are carefully planned and effectively executed.

In this chapter, we have discussed some of the core activities that may need to be performed in order to successfully transform the organization in the one that enables achievement of service-oriented and customer-focused culture.

Note here that all the financial planning and management in order to support activities/deliverables of "People and Organization" discipline should be considered and planned as part of "Project Management". All the budget planning activities should be completed and performed at the project-level and not at discipline level.

References

Allen, P. M. 1988. Dynamic models of evolving systems. *System Dynamics Review* 4: 109–130.

Burns, T., and G. M. Stalker. 1961. *The Management of Innovation*. Tavistock, London.

Brown, S., and K. Eisenhardt. 1997. The art of continuous change: Linking complexity theory and time-paced evolution in relentlessly shifting organizations. *Administrative Science Quarterly* 42: 1–34.

Galbraith, J. 1977. *Organizational Design*. Addison Wesley Publishing Company.

Johnson, R. A., F. E. Kast, and J. E. Rosenzweig. 1964. Systems theory and management. *Management Science* 10(2): 367–384.

Levy, D. L. 2000. Applications and limitations of complexity theory in organization theory and strategy. In *Handbook of Strategic Management, Second Edition*, ed. J. Rabin, G. J. Miller, and W. B. Hildreth. New York: Marcel Dekker.

Nohria, N., and R. G. Eccles. 1992. *Networks and Organizations*. Boston: Harvard Business School Press.

Robb, R. 1910. *Lectures on Organization*. Hive Publishing Company.

Schlesinger, P. F., and V. Sathe. 1992. *Organization: Text, Cases, and Readings on the Management of Organizational Design and Change*. (3rd Ed). Richard D Irwin.

Senge, P. M. 1990. *The Fifth Discipline: The Art and Practice of the Learning Organization*. New York: Doubleday.

Shuja, A., and J. Krebs. 2008. *Rational Unified Process: Reference and Certification Guide*. New York: IBM Press.

Stacey, R. 1995. The science of complexity: An alternative perspective for strategic change processes. *Strategic Management Journal* 16: 477–495.

Weatley, M. 1996. *A Simpler Way*. San Francisco: Berrett-Koehler.

Chapter 7

Discipline: Continual Service Improvement Institutionalization

CSI is at the core of ensuring that momentum stays alive. CSI should be responsible for gathering service and service management process performance data, new and emerging business and regulatory requirements, and other related information. Depending on how the organization implements CSI, it may provide recommendations on improving services and service management processes or implement these improvements to ensure that the desired outcomes are achieved.

Cultural changes do not happen overnight; they take time. In simple terms, cultural change is simply an aggregate of small behavioral changes over a certain period. CSI, at its core, aims to drive these small incremental behavioral changes through continual performance measurements, analytics, and through building awareness across service and service management process teams about how these improvements can enable achievement of the business objectives in a sustainable manner. Operational organizations are continuously working to keep the lights on. It is sometimes difficult for these teams to see the big picture and identify opportunities for improvements. CSI must proactively identify, analyze, and share these gaps and opportunities for improvement with the service and service management process owners, and enable these teams to take ownership of the quality of their work. CSI Institutionalization can be defined as follows:

> CSI Institutionalization is achieved when individuals and teams take complete ownership of the quality of their work and want to be able to proactively make continual improvements in the quality of their work. In other words, when institutionalized, continual service and service management process improvements become part of culture.

CSI is not a new concept. Most organizations have teams that are responsible for driving quality improvements. CSI brings quality into perspective. Its implementation may be central or distributed in nature.

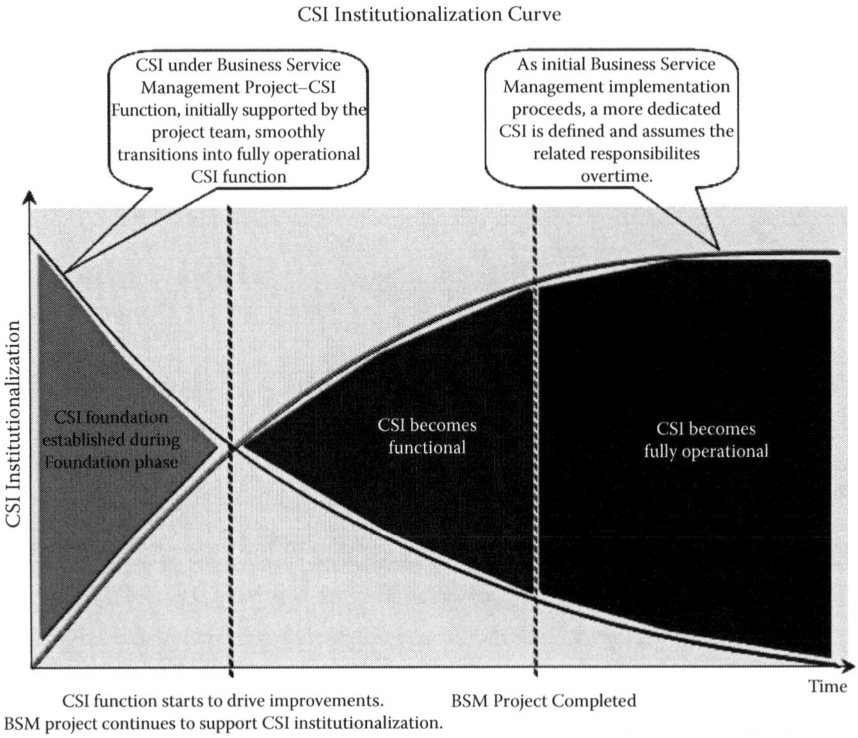

Figure 7.1 CSI institutionalization curve.

Practical Tip: Note that in a real world business enterprise, Business Service Management Implementation Project provides an incubation for the establishment of CSI function. This CSI function must support Service Management Process as well as Service Improvements efforts which are managed as part of Business Service Management Implementation Project.

CSI institutionalization goes through its own evolution, life cycle, and maturity. It is important to note that the BSM implementation project should provide the necessary incubation for the newly established CSI function to mature throughout the organization. The CSI institutionalization curve is shown in Figure 7.1.

There are three distinct phases shown in Figure 7.1. These are as follows:

- **Establishing the CSI Foundation**—During the foundation phase of the i2-SOSMI methodology, the CSI foundation is established. This may include the following:
  - Identifying and assessing existing quality functions
  - Creating and agreeing on a CSI vision and charter
  - Appointing a CSI manager
  - Establishing an appropriate foundation and acquiring required resources to support the envisioned CSI function

- **Functional CSI**—During the remaining three phases of the i2-SOSMI methodology (design, align, and integrate), CSI plays an active role in driving service and service management process related improvements.
- **Operational CSI**—After the BSM project is closed, CSI must become completely operational.

Purpose

The main purpose of the CSI discipline is to provide guidelines on establishing, leveraging, and institutionalizing a CSI function within the organization.

Objectives

- Envision CSI and demonstrate that it is critical to achieving organizational maturity.
- Ensure that CSI is established so that it is able to shape and transform organizational behaviors.
- Integrate CSI within the organization.
- Ensure that CSI is transitioned into a fully functional component and becomes culture.
- Continually contribute to service and service management process improvement.

Figure 7.2 illustrates CSI institutionalization objectives.

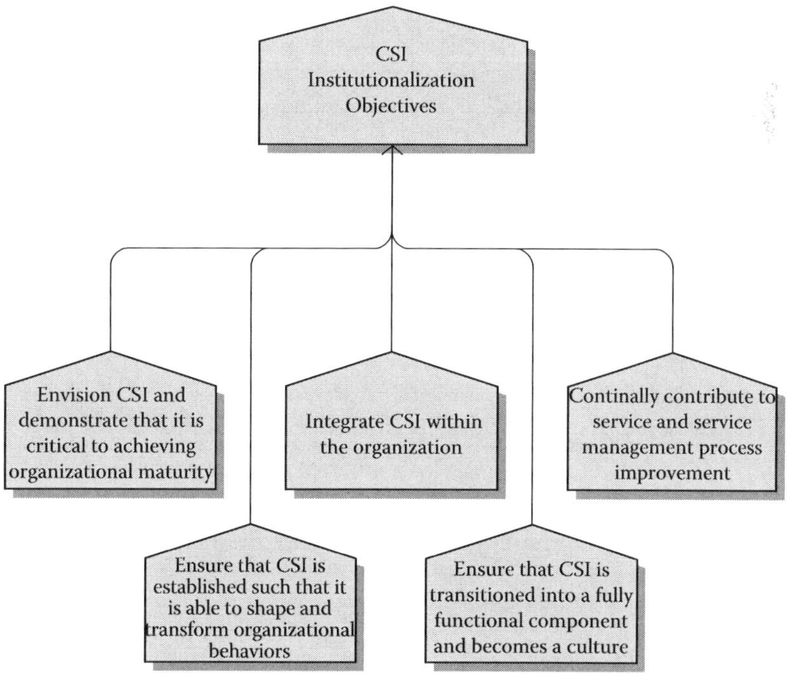

Figure 7.2 CSI institutionalization objectives.

Work Breakdown Structure

CSI work breakdown structure is illustrated in Figure 7.3.

Workflow

Figure 7.4 provides a recommended sequence in which CSI institutionalization activities may be performed. Please note that this sequence can vary depending on the organization's specific culture and needs.

Plan CSI

In the early stages of the BSM project, it is important to start planning how the CSI function will be implemented and established within the organization. In fact, as shown in Figure 7.1, the CSI

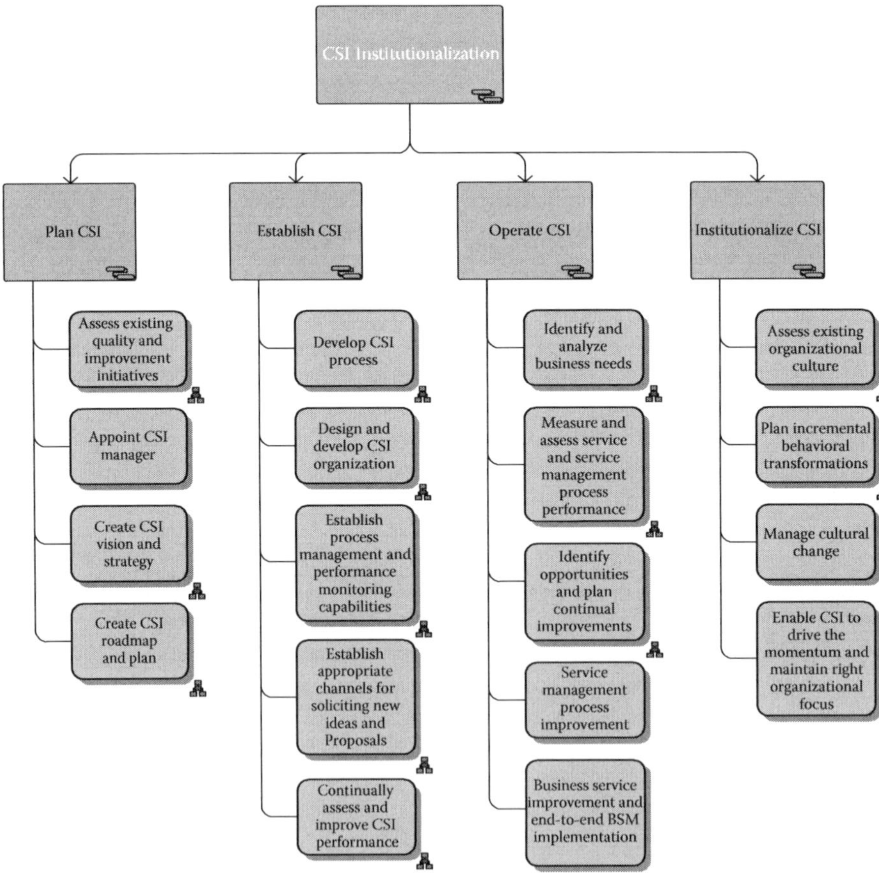

Figure 7.3 CSI institutionalization work breakdown structure.

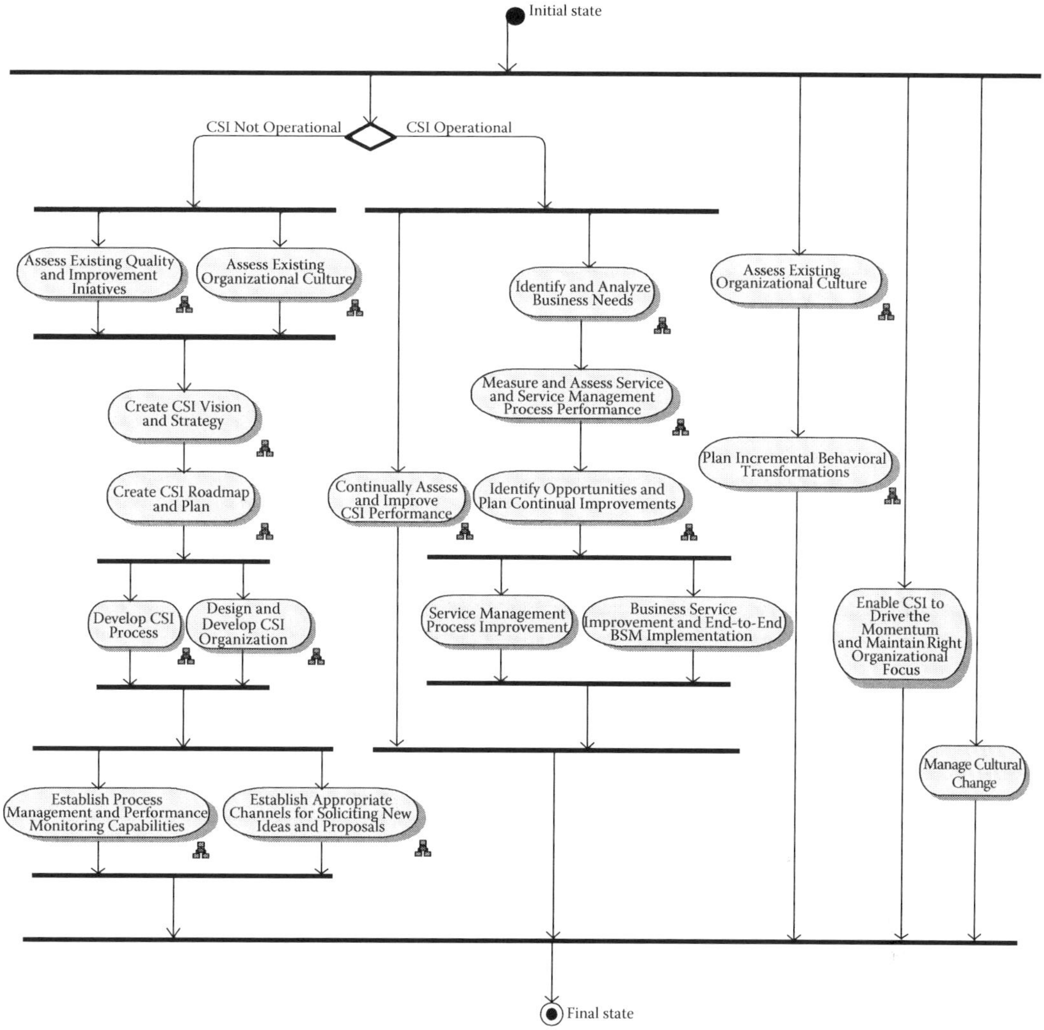

Figure 7.4 Workflow.

foundation should be established during the foundation phase of the BSM project. Some activities that should be performed include the following:

- Identifying and appointing a CSI manager to lead the establishment and be accountable for the operations of the CSI function within the organization.
- Assessing existing quality and related functions to see if they can be evolved or leveraged in institutionalizing the CSI function. Such an assessment will enable the BSM project stakeholders to gain a better understanding of the quality culture within the organization.
- Creating, agreeing on, and communicating CSI vision and strategy.
- Finally, creating the CSI development and institutionalization roadmap and plan.

Let us discuss some of the activities that should be performed to plan for the CSI.

Assess Existing Quality and Improvement Initiatives

Quality initiatives are not new to organizations. In my view, ITIL v3 takes these generalized quality initiatives a step further in maturity by explicitly defining what the CSI function needs to achieve and how it will contribute to keeping the improvement momentum going.

Purpose

The purpose of this activity is to identify and assess existing quality initiatives.

Precondition

The BSM project charter is approved.

Activity Overview

As soon as the BSM project is initiated, one of the first activities that should be performed is assessment of existing quality improvement and related initiatives at the organization. This is done to analyze any existing efforts that can be brought into alignment with the BSM project and if there are existing available resources that can be leveraged. The key output produced as a result of this activity is the quality assessment report (Figure 7.5).

Input Artifacts	*Tasks Performed*	*Output Artifacts*	*Roles (RACI)*
BSM Business Case BSM Project Charter	Identify and Document Existing Quality Initiatives	Quality Initiatives List	A: Executive Sponsor R: ITIL Expert Consultant
Quality Initiatives List	Assess Current State of Organization's Quality and Related Initiatives	Quality Assessment Report	A: Executive Sponsor R: ITIL Expert Consultant

Postconditions

- Major quality initiatives and teams identified
- Key stakeholders engaged in different quality improvement initiatives identified and interviewed
- Commonalities identified across these initiatives and potential leverage points discussed

Appoint CSI Manager

Based on the results of the *assess existing quality and improvement initiatives* activity, a proposal to appoint a CSI manager is drafted. Based on that proposal and approvals from senior management and executive sponsors, the appropriate individual is identified and appointed CSI manager. A

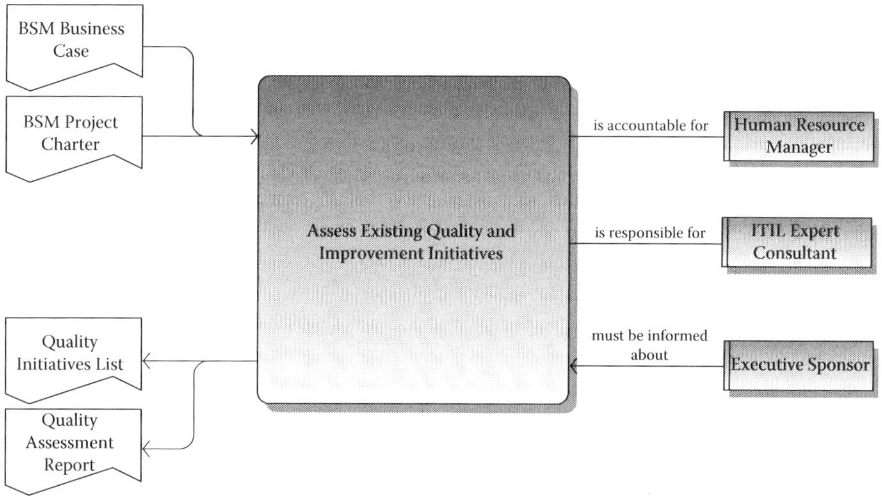

Figure 7.5 Assess existing quality and improvement initiatives.

detailed description of the CSI manager's role and responsibilities can be found in the book *ITIL v3 Continual Service Improvement*. From the perspective of institutionalizing CSI, this individual will have total accountability for setting the vision, implementing, and operating CSI.

Create CSI Vision and Strategy

CSI-related efforts are not new. We have all seen quality assurance and management teams throughout our careers. What is new in CSI is the focus on improving two very clear components: services and service management processes. ITIL v3 views CSI as having a critical role in keeping the momentum going and ensuring that tangible benefits are delivered to the businesses and customers. In my experience in helping my clients implement CSI, I have come across a number of different strategies.

Purpose

- To design a CSI strategy that will ensure that the culture of continual improvements can be achieved in a sustainable manner
- To appoint an appropriate CSI manager early in the project life cycle (critical to the success of CSI within the organization)

Preconditions

- BSM project approved
- Executive sponsorship achieved

Activity Overview

Figure 7.6 illustrates the process of creating a CSI vision and strategy.

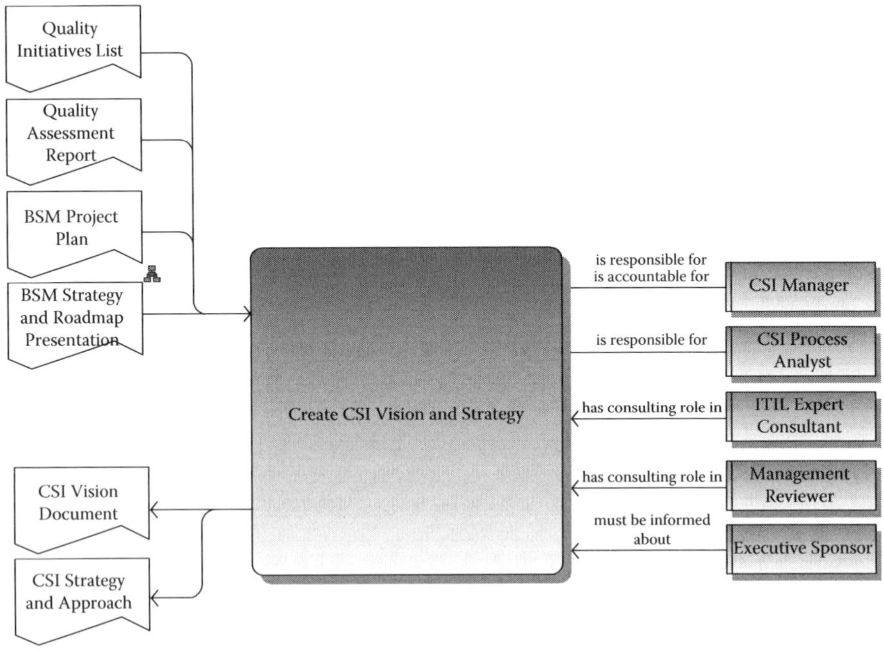

Figure 7.6 Create CSI vision and strategy.

Activity Details

Input Artifacts	*Tasks Performed*	*Output Artifacts*	*Roles (RACI)*
Quality Assessment Report	Establish Organization's CSI Vision and Business Case	CSI Vision Document	A: Executive Sponsor R: ITIL Expert Consultant C: Management Reviewer and Executive Sponsor
Quality Assessment Report CSI Vision Document	Build CSI Strategy to Achieve Stated Vision	CSI Strategy and Approach	A/R: CSI Manager C: ITIL Expert Consultant, Management Reviewer, and Executive Sponsor
CSI Vision Document CSI Strategy and Approach	Review and Agree on CSI Vision and Strategy	CSI Vision Document CSI Strategy and Approach	A/R: CSI Manager C: Management Reviewer I: Executive Sponsor

Postconditions

- Clear understanding of the strategy for implementing CSI
- Identification of existing similar functions that may need to be consolidated
- Required approval to more forward secured
- CSI manager appointed

Create CSI Plan

Based on the CSI vision and strategy, a detailed plan is developed to establish CSI within the larger organization.

Purpose

The purpose of this activity is to create a CSI implementation plan that will ensure smooth and organization-aligned CSI implementation.

Preconditions

- CSI vision and strategy approved
- CSI manager appointed
- Project manager assigned

Activity Overview

During this activity, the CSI manager develops a roadmap and plan that will be executed to achieve the stated BSM vision. Figure 7.7 illustrates the process.

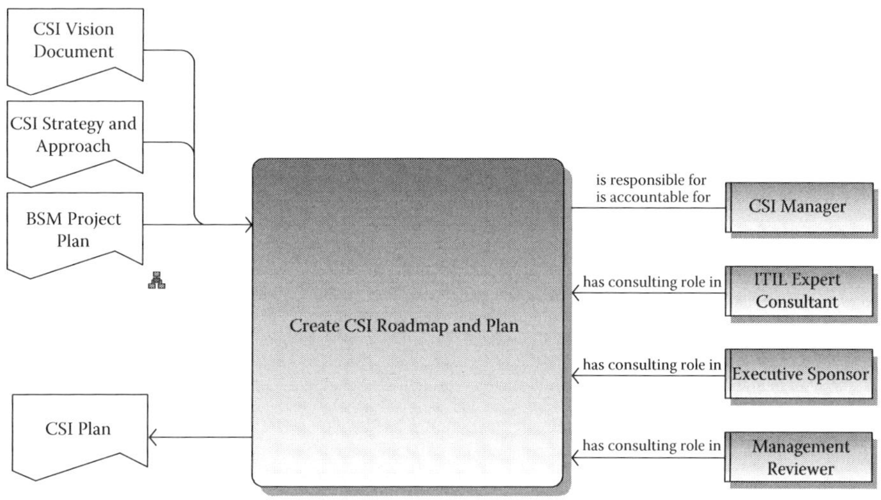

Figure 7.7 Create CSI roadmap and plan.

Activity Details

The following tasks are carried out within this activity:

Input Artifacts	*Tasks Performed*	*Output Artifacts*	*Roles (RACI)*
CSI Vision Document CSI Strategy and Approach BSM Project Plan	Develop CSI Plan	CSI Plan	A/R: CSI Manager C: ITIL Expert Consultant and Executive Sponsor
CSI Plan	Gain Approval on CSI Plan	CSI Plan	A/R: CSI Manager C: Management Reviewer I: Executive Sponsor

Postcondition

The CSI plan is developed, reviewed, approved, and baselined.

Establish CSI

The CSI plan is executed and CSI is established within the organization.

Develop CSI Process

ITIL v3 provides guidelines on the CSI process. This activity ensures that those guidelines are appropriately followed. The ITIL v3 CSI process is reviewed and tailored to meet the specific organizational needs, and the first release of this process is ready for production.

Purpose

The purpose of this activity is to design, develop, and approve the CSI process.

Preconditions

- CSI vision clearly established and agreed on
- CSI strategy designed and approach agreed on

Activity Overview

During this activity, the CSI process is designed, reviewed, and agreed on. *ITIL v3 Continual Service Improvement* provides detailed guidelines on the key steps (also known as the seven-step process) required to successfully achieve CSI objectives. Figure 7.8 illustrates this activity.

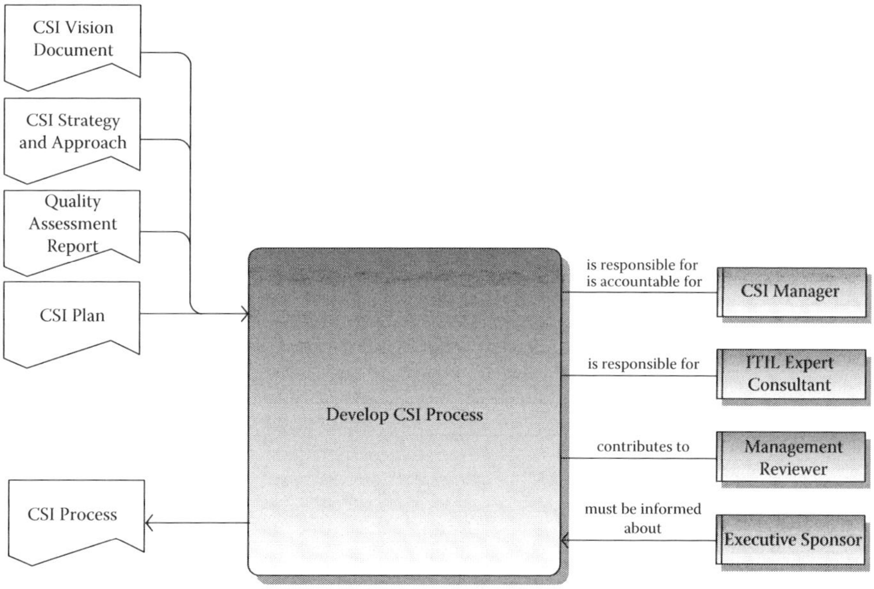

Figure 7.8 Develop CSI process.

Design and Develop CSI Organization

Once a CSI manager is appointed and a CSI process is developed, we have a good base to start planning the acquisition of the right resources for the CSI function.

Purpose

The purpose of this activity is to identify, acquire, and assign responsibilities to CSI resources.

Preconditions

- CSI manager appointed
- CSI plan developed and baselined
- CSI process developed, reviewed, and approved

Activity Overview

Based on the CSI process and plan, a CSI organization is designed and resources are acquired. Key inputs and outputs are shown in Figure 7.9.

Activity Details

The following tasks are performed within this activity:

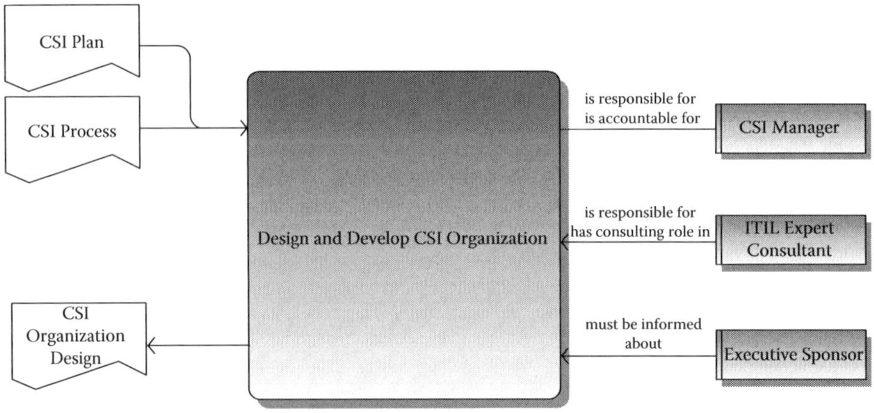

Figure 7.9 Design and develop CSI organization.

Input Artifacts	*Tasks Performed*	*Output Artifacts*	*Roles (RACI)*
CSI Process	Identify CSI Roles and Detail Their Responsibilities	CSI Organization Design	A/R: CSI Manager R/C: ITIL Expert Consultant I/C: Executive Sponsor
CSI Plan CSI Process CSI Organization Design	Acquire CSI Resources and Assign Responsibilities	CSI Resources Acquired	A/R: CSI Manager C: ITIL Expert Consultant I/C: Executive Sponsor

Postcondition

The CSI organization is appropriately staffed.

Establish Process Management and Performance Monitoring Capabilities

As shown in Figure 7.10, service and service management performance data are among the key inputs into the CSI. Manual collection and processing of data creates many potential inefficiencies. ITIL v3 explicitly lists these as critical success factors and stresses the importance of having appropriate technology in place for effective and efficient execution of CSI activities.

Purpose

The purpose of this activity is to enable establishment of appropriate capabilities for monitoring and managing service and service management process improvements.

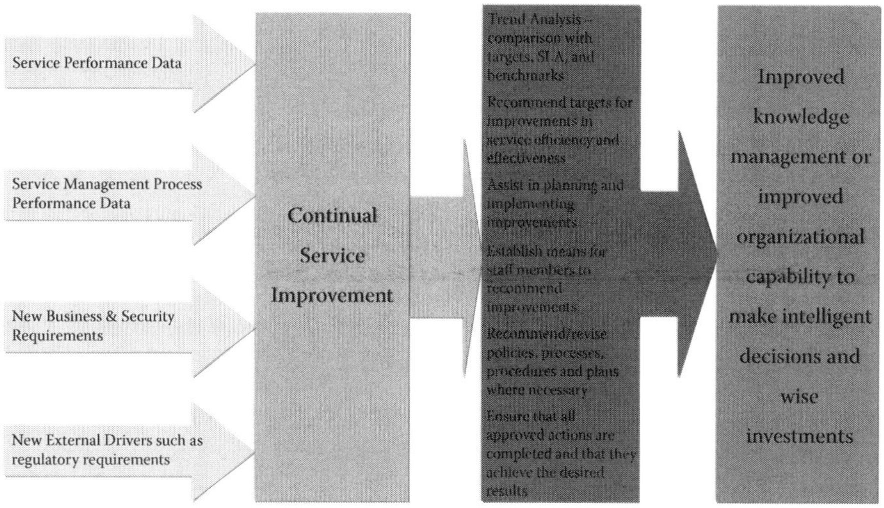

Figure 7.10 Key CSI inputs and outputs.

Preconditions

- CSI vision and strategy are defined and agreed on
- CSI charter created and communicated
- CSI manager acquired and assigned
- CSI process developed

Activity Overview

Members from across different teams work toward establishing an environment where process performance can be monitored and process improvements can be managed. To effectively and efficiently operate CSI and deliver the business value, it is critical to establish appropriate technological capabilities, as shown in Figure 7.11.

Activity Details

The following tasks may be performed within this activity:

Input Artifacts	*Tasks Performed*	*Output Artifacts*	*Roles (RACI)*
CSI Vision Document CSI Strategy and Approach CSI Process	Determine Process Management and Performance Monitoring Needs	Business Process Management Requirements Document	A: CSI Manager R: ITIL Expert Consultant, BSM Technology Architect, Process Owner, Business Service Owner

Business Process Management Requirements Document Business Process Management Solution Architecture	Agree on Process Management and Monitoring Platform Architecture	Business Process Management Solution Architecture Document (Agreed)	A: CSI Manager R: BSM Technology Architect I: Process Owner, Business Service Owner
Business Process Management Requirements Document Business Process Management Solution Architecture Document Business Process Management Solution	Review and Approve Process and Performance Management Solution	Business Process Management Solution (Approved)	A: CSI Manager C: ITIL Expert Consultant, Process Owner, Business Service Owner I: Executive Sponsor

Postcondition

Service and process performance monitoring and management capabilities are established.

Establish Appropriate Channels for Soliciting New Ideas

ITIL v3 recommends that CSI provide appropriate channel(s) for internal and external partners and customers to propose new ideas and suggest improvements. This activity ensures that those channels are developed. This activity is shown in Figure 7.12.

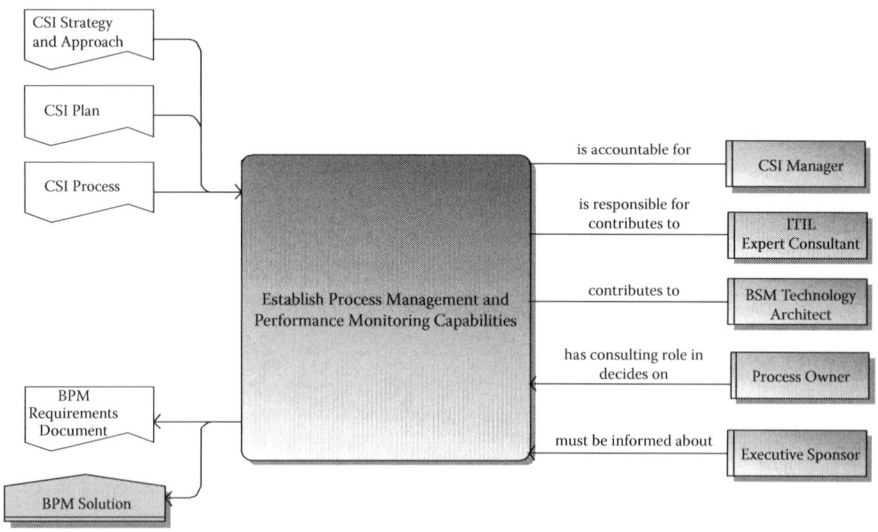

Figure 7.11 Establish process management and performance monitoring capabilities.

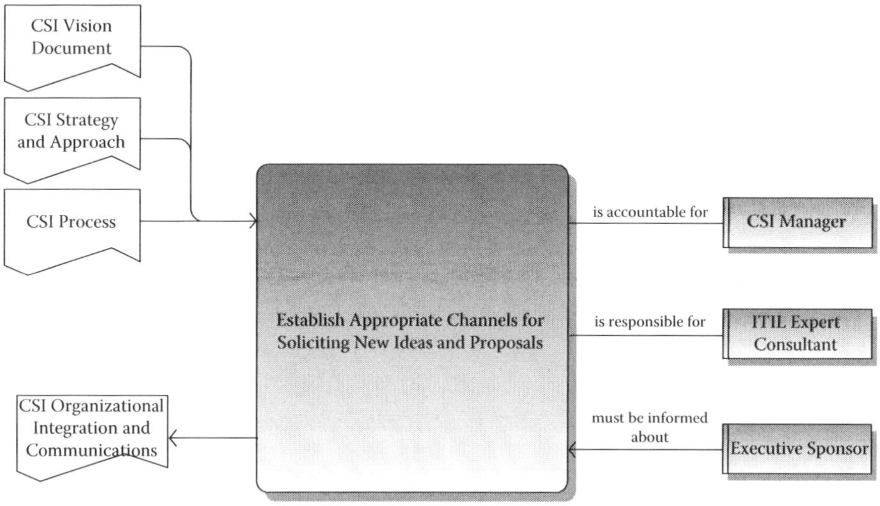

Figure 7.12 Establish appropriate channels for soliciting new ideas and proposals.

Continually Assess and Improve CSI Performance

CSI is continually refined to align with organization-specific needs and to produce optimal business value.

Operate CSI

Once CSI is established, it should be managed to ensure that it meets its stated objectives. As mentioned earlier in this section, a BSM project should provide the incubation platform for the CSI function. Operating CSI means to continually assess business needs and manage service and service management process improvements to address those needs in the most efficient and effective manner. As shown in Figure 7.10, the key inputs into CSI include performance measurements (service as well as service management processes) along with new requirements (business, regulatory and others). CSI would ensure that these are appropriately analyzed and improvement opportunities are identified such that the overall improvement momentum continues. This momentum is what enables organizations to continue to achieve greater maturity levels. Let us discuss some of the key activities performed to ensure this.

Identify and Analyze Business Needs

It is imperative that the CSI organization is able to continually assess changing business needs to ensure that the improvement recommendations it provides align with those needs (see Figure 7.13).

Measure and Assess Service and Service Management Process Performance

All improvements achieved on services should be measured and successes should be appropriately communicated. These measurements should be made to ensure that improvements are strategically aligned, that better design practices are implemented, that utility and warranty aspects are

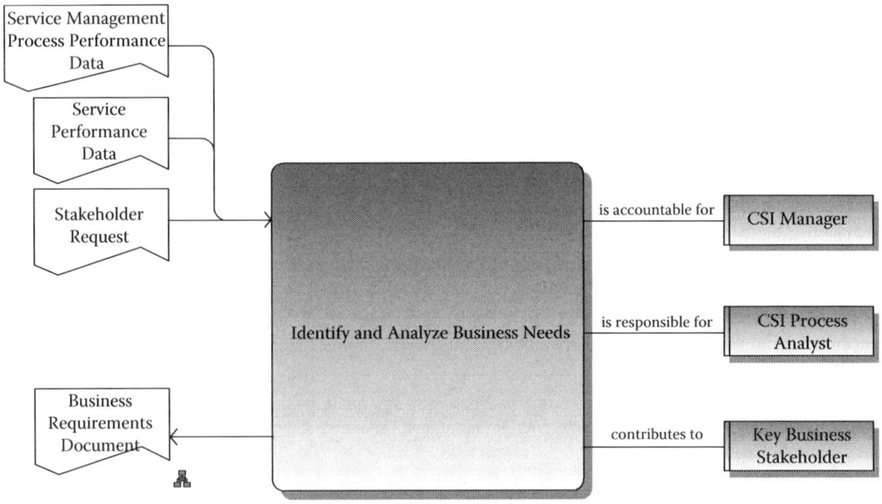

Figure 7.13 Identify and analyze business needs.

addressed, that service is smoothly transitioned into operations, and, once operations, that these services deliver the expected outcome. Some key types of measurements that may be performed on services may include the following:

- *Strategic Alignment Measurement*: Are these improvements made in relation to the services that have the most impact on the business profitability? How are the improvements assessed and prioritized?
- *Service Design Measurement*: Once new services or changes to existing services are designed, does the design follow an established pattern? Does it make use of existing service assets? Is the design scalable?
- *Service Transition Measurement*: In measuring service transition–related improvements, focus will be on the number and quality of change models and standard changes developed for the new or improved services. Other aspects that should be measured may include the following:
  - Data quality of configuration items related to the new or improved service
  - Completion of configuration information
  - Completion of release notes and the quality of the known error record information
  - Scripts and other supporting material provided for service desk to adequately support operational activities
  - Any other measurements related to established and agreed on targets
- *Service Operations Measurement*: Service operations measurements will be primarily driven by targets established and agreed on in service level agreements, operational level agreements, and underpinning contracts.

Purpose

The purpose of this activity is to clearly analyze service and service management process performance.

Preconditions

- Process and service key performance indicators and metrics are defined
- Measurement mechanisms are in place

Activity Overview

As a result of this activity, the CSI process analyst produces reports on service management process performance and service performance, as shown in Figure 7.14.

Postcondition

There is a clear understanding of how different services and service management processes are performing.

Identify Opportunities and Plan Continual Improvements

Based on the results of performance analytics performed within the *measure and assess service and service management process performance* activity, high-value opportunities are identified and continual improvements are planned (see Figure 7.15). This planning should include reviewing those opportunities with the relevant stakeholders and prioritizing them.

The main focus of this activity is to ensure that appropriate improvements are effectively identified and prioritized and efficiently implemented for each service. This process is discussed in detail in Chapter 8.

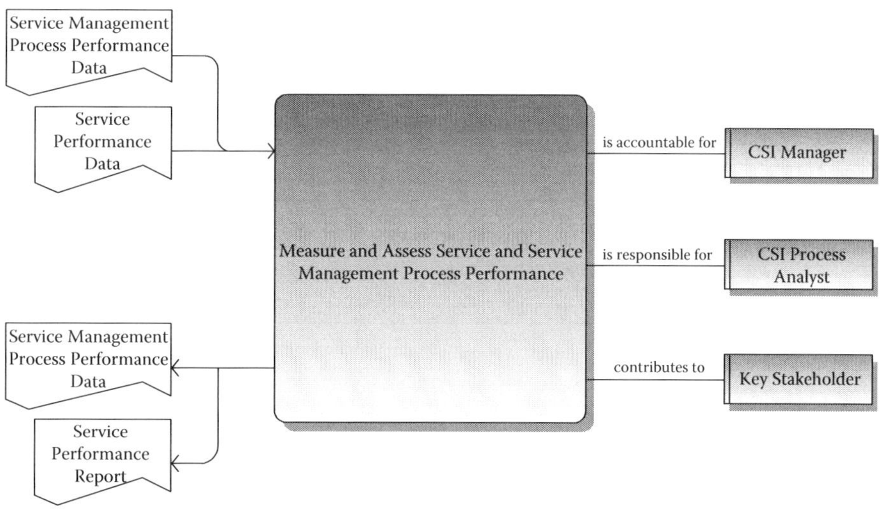

Figure 7.14 Measure and assess service and service management process performance.

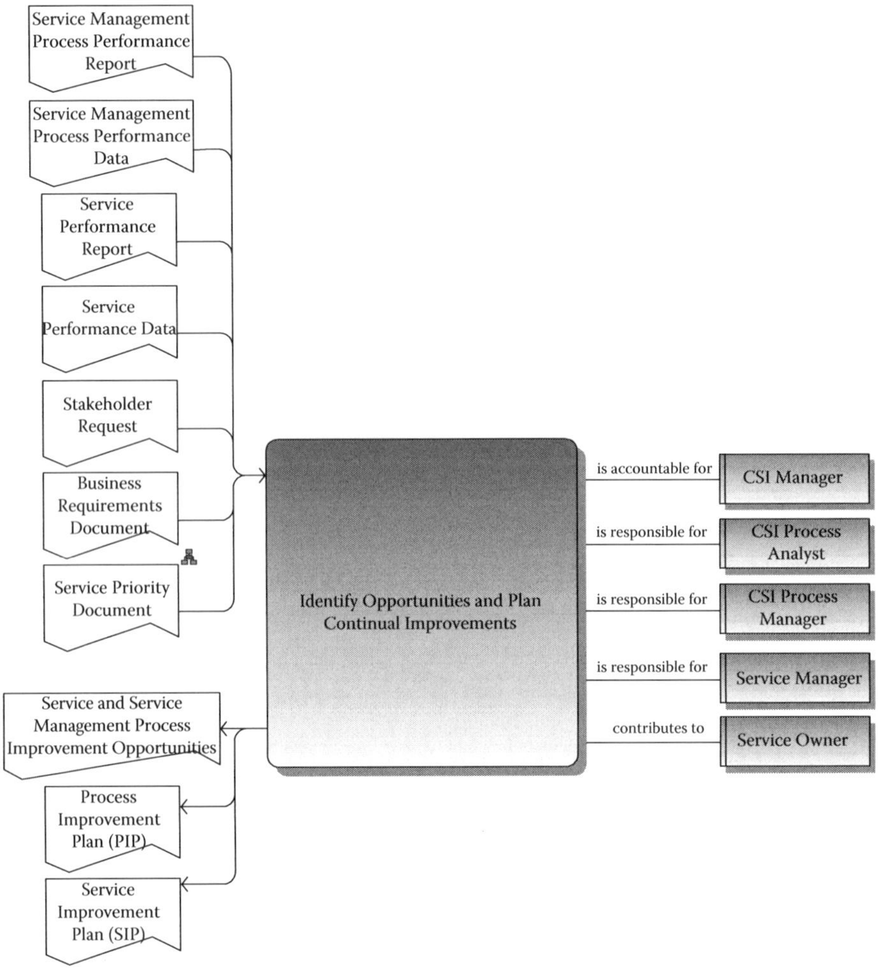

Figure 7.15 Business service improvement and end-to-end BSM implementation.

Service Management Process Improvement

The main focus of this activity is to ensure that appropriate improvements are effectively identified and prioritized and efficiently implemented within the service management processes. We will discuss this process in detail in Chapter 9.

Institutionalize CSI

What does it mean to integrate CSI within an organization? This section will discuss what it really means to integrate CSI within the larger organization and what specific activities and tasks need to be performed to achieve that.

Assess Existing Organizational Culture

Purpose

The purpose of this activity is to gain a clear understanding of the existing organizational culture and how it enables customer-oriented, service-focused, performance-driven behavior (see Figure 7.16).

Preconditions

- BSM project charter approved
- Business vision document understood
- IT vision and strategy understood
- BSM strategy and overall roadmap understood

Activity Overview

CSI culture is one where the organization is continually thriving, not merely surviving. CSI must play a key role in enabling an organization to achieve this culture. It must be positioned so that continual improvements become second nature to the organization. Depending on the current maturity of the organization, this may mean a significant impact on the organizational culture. It is important to appreciate that every organization is different and may implement CSI differently. It is also important to clearly understand and appreciate what CSI implementation is appropriate and what behaviors we are trying to shape within the organization. This must all be driven by the overall BSM vision and strategy.

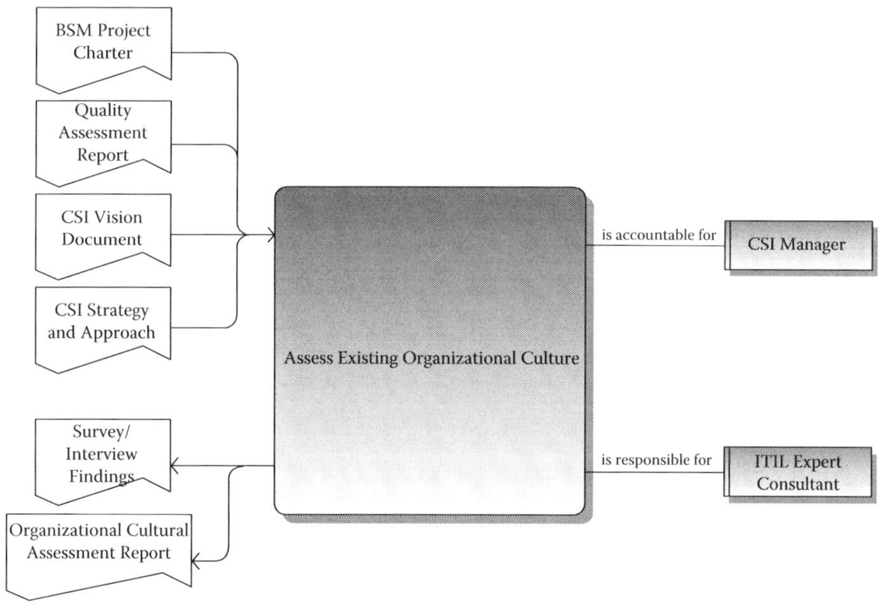

Figure 7.16 Assess existing organizational culture.

Activity Details

The following tasks should be performed within this activity:

Input Artifacts	*Tasks Performed*	*Output Artifacts*	*Roles (RACI)*
BSM Project Charter Quality Assessment Report	Identify and Interview or Survey Key Stakeholders	Survey/Interview Findings	A: CSI Manager R: ITIL Expert Consultant
Survey/Interview Findings CSI Vision Document CSI Strategy and Approach	Analyze Behaviors and Patterns and Document Key Cultural Attributes	Organizational Cultural Assessment Report	A: CSI Manager R: ITIL Expert Consultant

Postcondition

The organizational culture is clearly assessed and analyzed.

Plan Incremental Behavior Transformations

Once we understand what CSI means for an organization, it will be critical for the BSM project team to plan how we achieve CSI objectives. Cultural transformations are difficult and must be planned and managed effectively to achieve the stated objectives. The most critical component of cultural transformation is behavioral change. In this activity, we discuss the tasks that need to be planned and performed to achieve incremental behavioral transformations. Figure 7.17 illustrates this planning.

Manage Cultural Change

Managing cultural change is a key component of implementing BSM. CSI must enable and support the cultural transformation by keeping the momentum going. Value created by CSI through

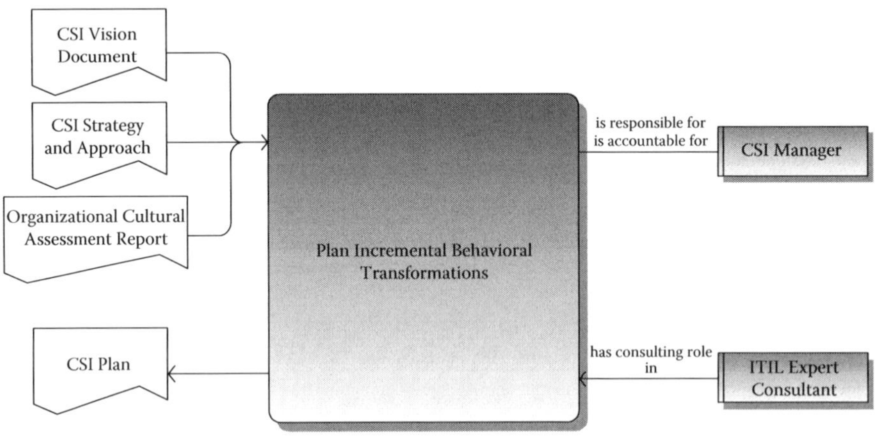

Figure 7.17 Plan incremental behavioral transformations.

performance measurements and continual improvement recommendations and implementations will enable CSI to survive. These improvements will continually generate value and sustained sponsorship.

Enable CSI to Drive the Momentum and Maintain the Right Organizational Focus

A well-integrated CSI should enable IT to continually align and realign the portfolio and performance of its services to enable business processes in the most effective and efficient manner. This activity is also related to the *manage cultural change* activity and aims to ensure that the right organizational focus is maintained on the most critical and high-value improvements.

Primary Roles and Responsibilities

Some of the key CSI roles and their responsibilities are discussed below (also see Figure 7.18).

CSI Manager

Detailed responsibilities of the CSI manager can be found in *ITIL v3 Continual Service Improvement*. From the perspective of implementing CSI, it is enough to understand that the CSI manager is accountable for the establishment and institutionalization of CSI throughout the entire organization.

CSI Process Analyst

The key responsibilities of the CSI process analyst role are:

- Analyzes service management process performance data
- Identifies bottlenecks, gaps, and opportunities for improvements
- Documents the process performance findings and shares the results with respective process owners to enable them to plan further improvements throughout their processes
- Creates and shares dashboards and reports on process performance

CSI Process Manager

This role will be discussed in detail in Chapter 9 (Service Management Process Improvement).

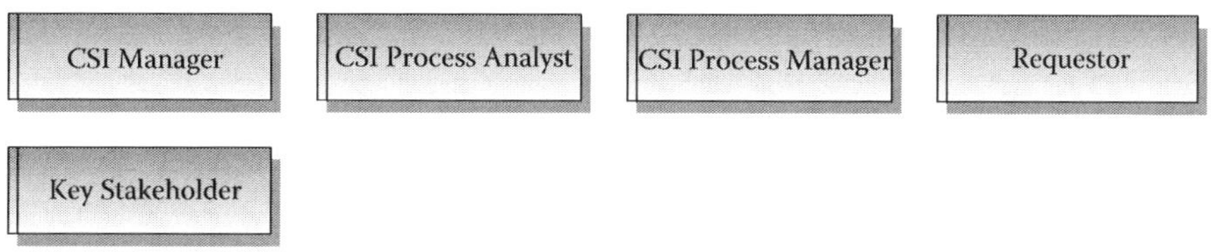

Figure 7.18 Primary roles and responsibilities.

Requestor

A requester is anyone who has submitted a new request for either an improvement to an existing service or process or for a new service.

Key Stakeholder

These are those stakeholders that are key to planning and achieving the service and service management process improvements.

Key Artifacts

The key CSI artifacts are discussed below (see Figure 7.19).

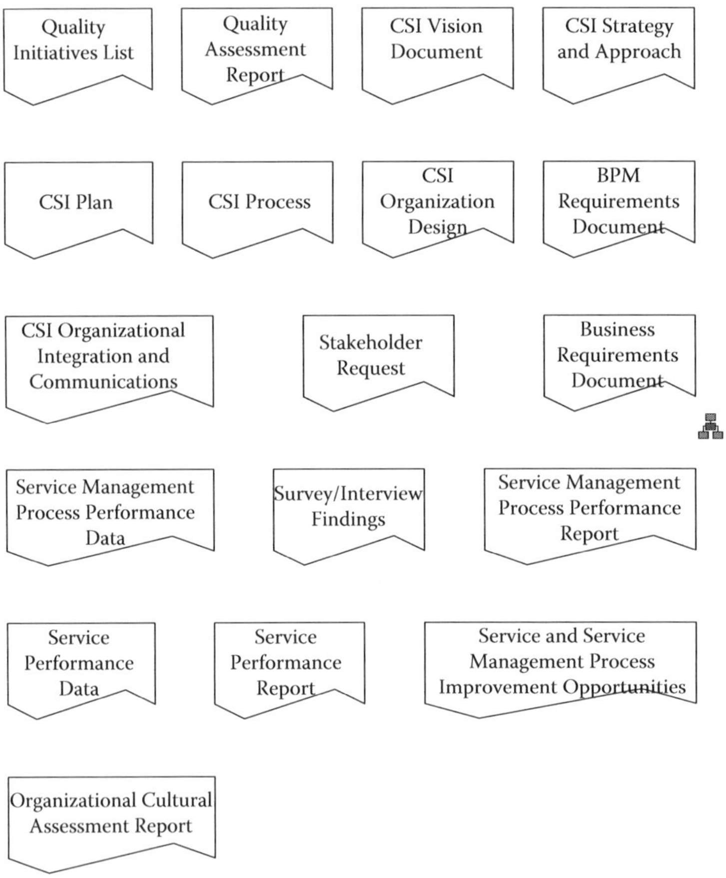

Figure 7.19 Key artifacts.

Quality Initiatives List

This artifact lists all the quality and related initiatives that may be present in the organization. The main purpose is to gain a better understanding of what level of quality awareness already exists within the organization and if the level is sufficient to leverage other related projects and initiatives.

Quality Assessment Report

Based on the quality initiatives identified, this report provides an assessment of those initiatives including their key objectives, their success (or lack of success), the challenges they encountered, any lessons learned, etc. The main purpose here is to assess how historical quality initiatives performed within this organization and if there are any lessons to be learned from them.

CSI Vision Document

This artifact clearly establishes the CSI vision. There are many different ways in which CSI can be implemented and this document should clearly state which type of CSI implementation will be achieved within this organization. CSI may be centralized or decentralized. Centralized CSI indicates that all performance data are analyzed and improvement opportunities prioritized and achieved within or by a central organization. Decentralized CSI, as the name suggests, indicates that such improvements may be achieved locally within each location, department, and team. However, in both cases, there will be a CSI manager who will be responsible for establishing and institutionalizing the CSI and transforming the organizational culture.

CSI Strategy and Approach

Primarily driven by the CSI vision, this artifact clearly lays out the strategy and approach required to achieve the stated vision.

CSI Plan

Based on the CSI vision and CSI strategy and approach, this artifact clearly defines the plan for how that vision will be realized.

CSI Process

The CSI process is the key process that will be followed by the CSI organization to envision, measure, analyze, plan, and achieve improvement.

CSI Organization Design

This artifact defines the design of the CSI organization. CSI organization design will be driven by the CSI vision and CSI strategy and approach.

Business Process Management Requirements Document

Managing processes from their creation, through their life cycle, and to their retirement is one of the key areas where CSI will play a key role. This artifact defines the key requirements that should be realized by the BPM tool. We will discuss this in greater detail in Chapter 9 (Service Management Process Improvement).

CSI Organizational Integration and Communications

This artifact defines all the different relationships that the CSI organization should have with other organizations. For example, CSI must define a channel to solicit requests on service and service management process improvement ideas. CSI may leverage the service desk to channel those requirements and requests. Therefore, this document must clearly identify and define all communications and integrations that may be required between CSI and other departments.

Stakeholder Request

This is any request submitted to CSI by any stakeholder.

Business Requirements Document

As a result of service and service management process performance data analysis, there will be opportunities identified for improvements. This document presents all requirements that must be met to achieve the desired improvements. An example of a high-level table of contents for this type of document is shown in Figure 7.20.

Survey and Interview Findings

This artifact contains the findings of any surveys and interviews conducted as services, processes, and other areas are assessed and analyzed.

Service Management Process Performance Data

This is data about service management process performance and is used by the CSI process analyst to assess the performance of the service management process.

Service Management Process Performance Report

This is a result of analytics performed on service management process performance data. The main purpose is to enable respective process owners, process managers, and other stakeholders to clearly see gaps, bottlenecks, and to understand improvement opportunities.

Service Performance Data

This is data about service performance that is used by the CSI process analyst to assess the performance of the respective service.

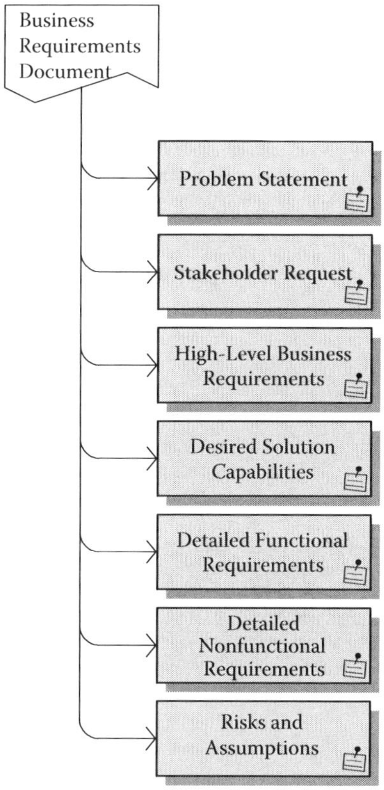

Figure 7.20 Business requirements document.

Service Performance Report

This is a result of the analytics performed on service performance data. The main purpose is to enable service owners, service managers, and other stakeholders to clearly see gaps, bottlenecks, and to understand improvement opportunities.

Service and Service Management Process Improvement Opportunities

This document summarizes the improvement opportunities that may exist within the service management process or service.

Organizational Cultural Assessment Report

This is an assessment report on the organizational culture. The main purpose is to understand, based on the assessment of previous and related quality initiatives, what needs to be done to successfully achieve CSI within the organization. The most important part of this report should be about risk management.

Summary

CSI is critical to achieving BSM within the organization. If implemented correctly, CSI enables the organization to keep its organizational improvement momentum going. CSI must establish the right focus within the organization by ensuring that service and service management performance data are appropriately analyzed and that high-value improvements are correctly identified, prioritized, and achieved. We will discuss two important processes within CSI in Chapters 8 and 9, respectively: *business service improvement and end-to-end BSM implementation* and *service management process improvement.*

Reference

Shuja, A., and J. Krebs. 2008. *Rational Unified Process: Reference and Certification Guide.* New York: IBM Press.

Chapter 8

Discipline: Business Service Improvement and End-to-End Business Service Management Implementation

Introduction

I would like to summarize business expectations for all IT investments made in one sentence: All and any IT investments made must translate into value delivered to our customers. This may sound like an extreme statement, but, if you think about it for a moment, you may begin to realize that it makes perfect sense. Some would argue that this may not apply to all potential situations. One example would be the case of a regulated environment. However, if you think about it, even regulations imposed by regulatory bodies are there to protect the interests of our customers. Another argument may be that we spend money to keep the engine going and these are really maintenance-type expenses. Well, you are performing these maintenance activities to ensure that services continue to deliver business value and meet customer expectations. IT does not and should not exist for IT. According to ITIL v3, "Business is IT. And IT is the business." This integration must exist for IT to become a value-added business partner.

Service is the means of delivering value to our customers and service improvement is the key service management implementation component that enables the businesses and customers to benefit from the investments made in implementing service management (Figure 8.1).

Service improvement or business service improvement is one of the most critical components of BSM implementation. It brings all improvement investments together and enables customers to actually realize tangible service improvement benefits. If managed and organized appropriately, business service improvement actually becomes core to keeping the sponsorships and necessary support alive and thereby enables the organization to keep momentum going. This is the

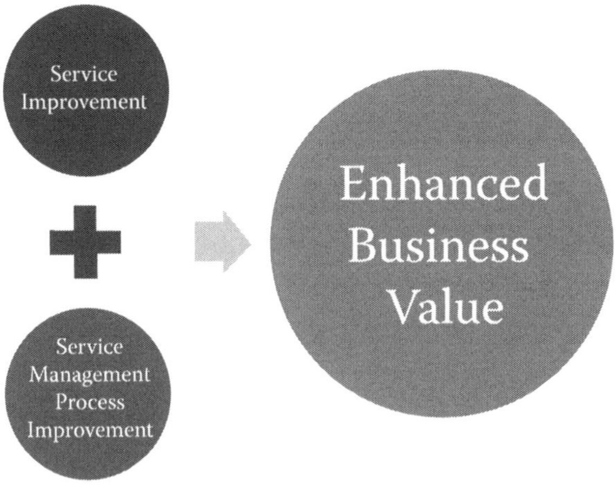

Figure 8.1 Enhanced business value.

component that will iteratively and incrementally create business value. If planned appropriately, the business service improvement component will ensure that all service management process improvements are planned and implemented in a targeted fashion and are optimally leveraged to deliver the expected value.

In this chapter, we will learn about the effort required to implement the business service improvement piece of CSI. Although business service improvement is an integral part of the CSI, we have this as a dedicated discipline to further emphasize the criticality of this discipline.

Before we get into that detailed discussion, let us build greater appreciation of what business service improvement really is. Earlier in this book, we briefly discussed the challenges faced by a traditional siloed organization, shown in Figure 8.2.

In a siloed organization, most technology-focused teams tend to *manage technology for technology*. Lack of appreciation for the business value created by the individual siloed technology components prevents siloed enterprises from managing technology for the business. Each silo may have siloed technology-focused partnerships and may provide technology solutions with a limited cross-technology view of how these various technology components actually create value for our customers and shareholders. In interviewing one of my clients within a large global network operations organization, I asked how they prioritized any improvements to be made and problems to be resolved within their organization. The response was that they had technology-focused teams that specialized in the given technologies and, based on their experiences, they were able to make intelligent "guesstimates" on where to focus their efforts—a guesstimate based on feelings and experiences.

Let us look at the *supply chain management* example in Figure 8.3. *Electronic order intake* service depends on the *global e-commerce exchange* service, which runs on an *e-commerce service* configuration item. As shown in that figure, if multiple configuration items (CIs) are down, how do you prioritize which one is more critical from a business perspective rather than the other?

BSM enables organizations to manage technology for the business. If end-to-end BSM is implemented for services that enable supply chain business processes, we will be able to ensure that the right services are available when they are needed, at the performance levels that are necessary, and that the utility features that are required to enable the business process efficiently perform

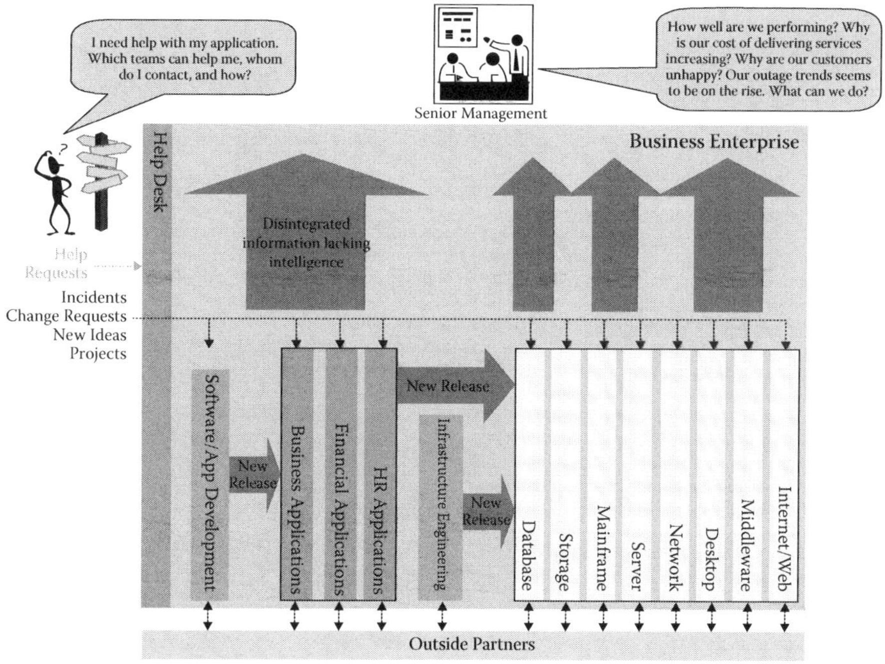

Figure 8.2 Siloed organization.

as needed. In ITIL v3, there are two aspects of a service that ensure that the right services are available at the right time. These are called *utility* and *warranty*. Utility ensures that the managed service is fit for purpose and warranty ensures that the managed service is fit for use.

If the services that enable supply chain business processes are managed appropriately, we will be able to ensure both utility and warranty for those services. In Figure 8.4, there are four of these services—*electronic order intake, customer service order intake, order processing*, and *shipping and handling*—that need to be managed end-to-end to enable the supply chain business process effectively and efficiently.

Figure 8.5 further demonstrates the significance of using an end-to-end service management approach to predictably deliver IT services to our customers. We can make the following important observations:

- If we only make sure that each component is available 99% of the time, it does not really mean that our customers are going to have 99% net availability for their respective business services.
- The example below shows that the electronic order intake business service component may have 99% component availability. However, the net availability is really 94%. Accumulated net availability of the supply chain business process is only 93%.

Such problems are very much visible in organizations where technology components are managed in silos.

BSM requires that all individual technology components that make up a given business service are managed so that the real business needs are met. Each component that enables a given business

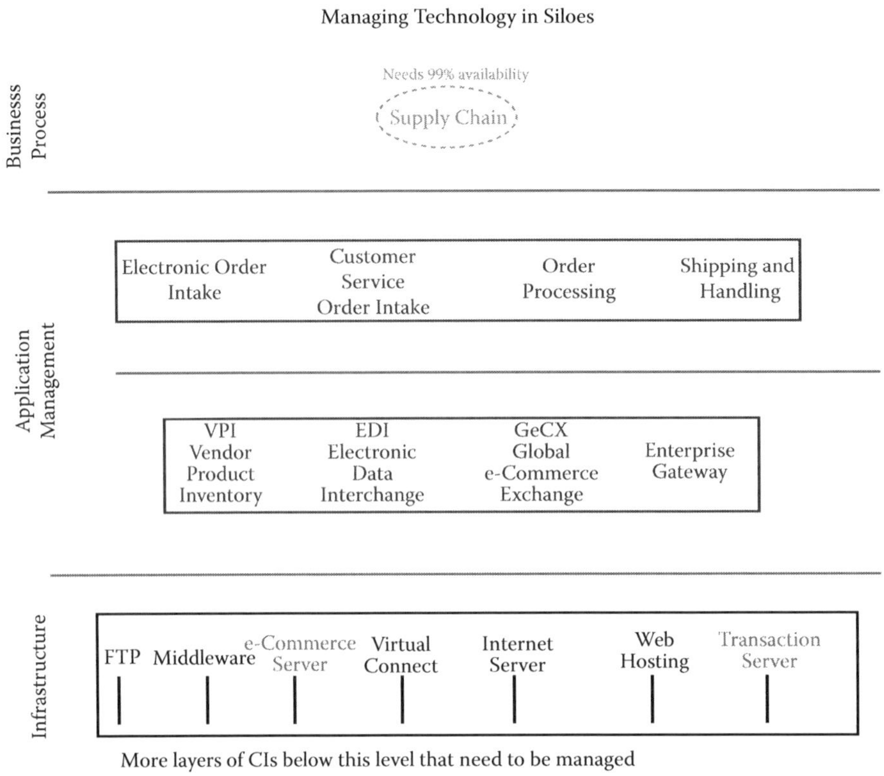

Figure 8.3 Managing in silos.

process needs to be managed to ensure that the business process that they support is appropriately enabled.

Business service improvement in ITIL v3 is primarily discussed in the context of CSI. What about common situations that we face today? Examples of those situations are:

- There has been no concept of CSI in the organization.
- Most times, teams are engaged in "fighting fires" to ensure that the individual components are available at targets that were, perhaps, established in a vacuum.
- In most established (but not necessarily mature organizations), IT services are being provided but not necessarily being managed.

We need to start somewhere. The business value created as a result of service improvements may be one of the most crucial factors in keeping the momentum going.

Imagine IT organizations spending millions of dollars to improve service management processes and not being able to show the immediate returns on investments that are necessary to keep sponsorship alive and to survive the frequent management shuffles. The answer is the ability of an IT organization to deliver an immediate return on investments made to improve service management processes.

Any initiatives targeted to improving service management processes need to plan and implement these improvements so that these improvements are immediately leveraged to create business

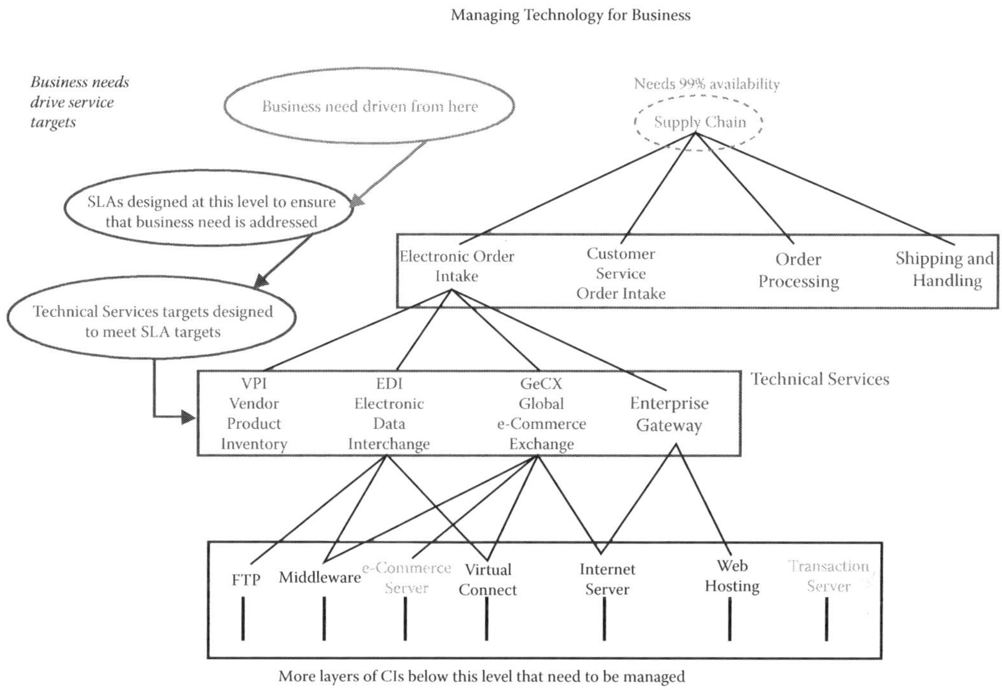

Figure 8.4 Managing technology for the business.

Component	Example	Component Availability	Net Availability
Business Process	Supply Chain	N/A	99% × 99% × 99% × 99% × 99% × 99% × 99% = 93%
Business Service	Electronic Order Intake	99%	99% × 99% × 99% × 99% × 99% × 99% = 94%
Technical Service	Electronic Data Interchange	99%	99% × 99% × 99% × 99% × 99% = 95%
Technology Components	Middleware	99%	99% × 99% × 99% × 99% = 96%
	Database	99%	99% × 99% × 99% = 97%
	Operating System	99%	99% × 99% = 98%
	Network	99%	= 99%

Figure 8.5 High-performing silos and low-performing services.

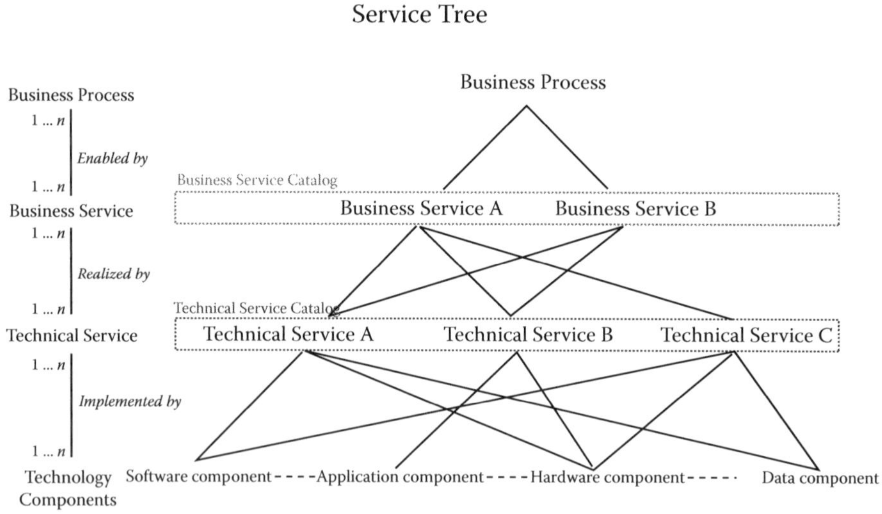

Figure 8.6 The service tree.

value. Iterative service management improvements need to be aligned with incremental business value creation. If we are improving multiple service management processes during any given phase of a larger program, we need to ensure that we also improve on the business services that immediately leverage these service management process improvements in creating immediate business value.

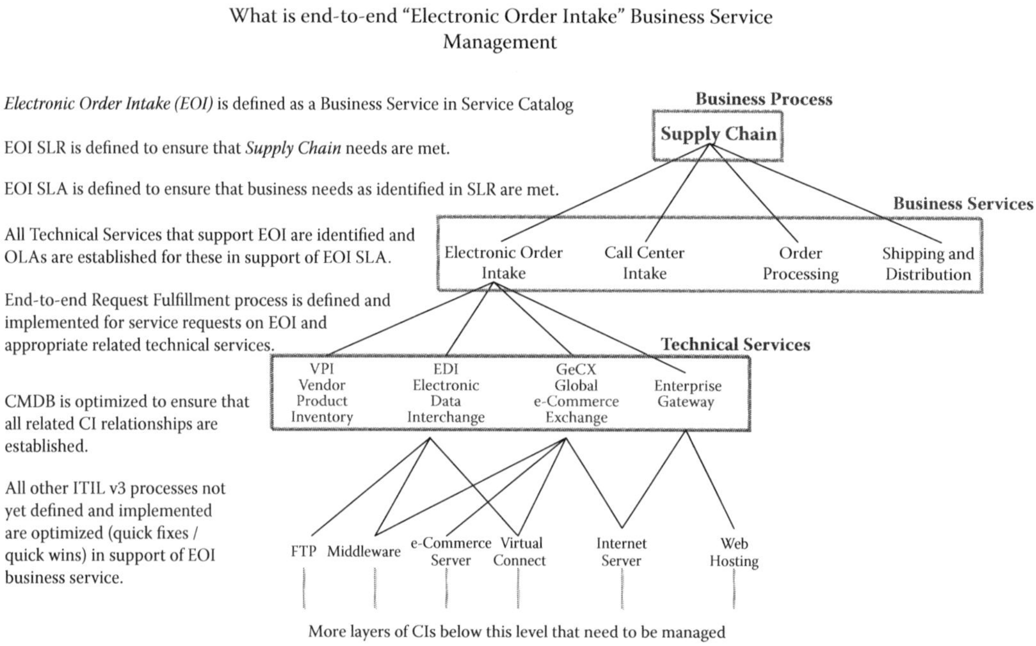

Figure 8.7 End-to-end BSM.

The service tree in Figure 8.6 shows the high-level relationships that exist between business processes, business services, technical services, and other technical components. Figure 8.7 shows how service management process improvements can be aligned to efficiently achieve the desired service improvements.

BSM is all about delivering and managing IT services end-to-end, that is, from the business processes down to IT infrastructure components. BSM drives IT to deliver services that add value to the business and enables performance of IT services to be measured in terms of business performance. Figure 8.8 shows another view of BSM. Note that I have shown that:

- Business services are types of IT services. We discuss this in detail in Chapter 2.
- Business services are divided into core business services and business services. Core business services are shared across businesses, whereas business services may be business-specific or unique to the business.

With this brief service improvement discussion, let us now discuss the business service improvement and end-to-end BSM implementation discipline in greater detail and look into the effort that will be required to ensure that services are improved efficiently and effectively.

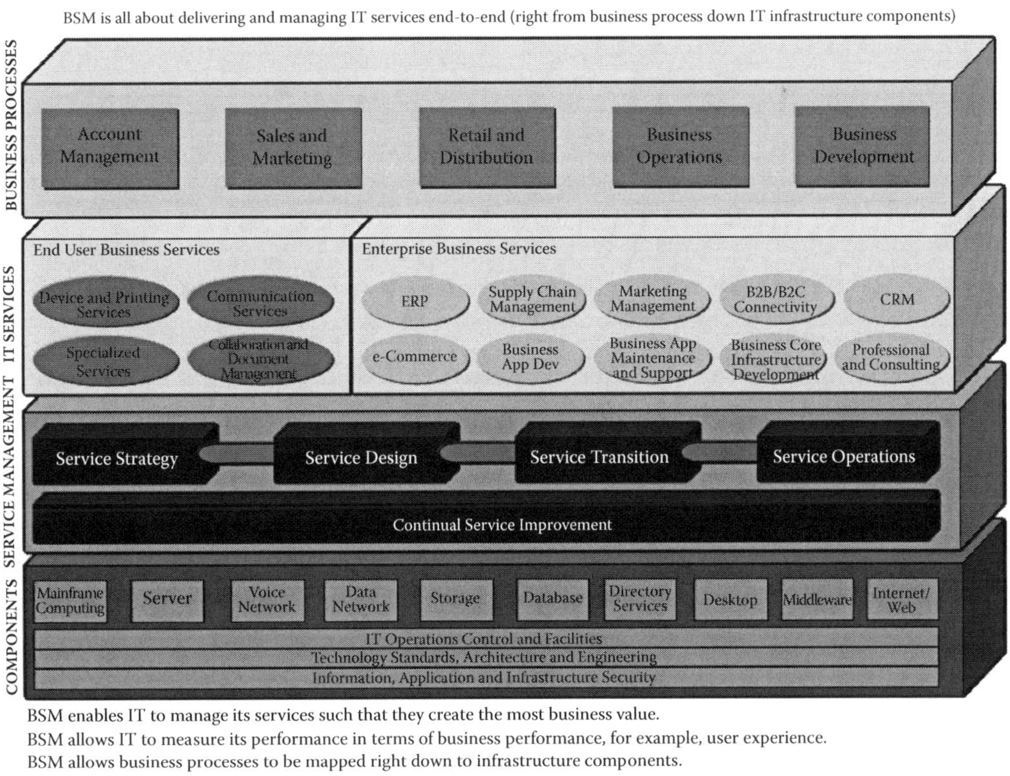

Figure 8.8 Business service management.

Purpose

The goal is to incrementally implement end-to-end BSM for all business services delivered by the IT organization.

Objectives

The service improvement discipline has the following key objectives (Figure 8.9):

- Gain a clear understanding of all services delivered by the IT organization.
- Prioritize services based on the business value and business impact delivered.
- Ensure that prioritized services are effectively managed to deliver desired business value.

Work Breakdown Structure

The service improvement work breakdown structure is shown in Figure 8.10.

Workflow

Business service improvement and end-to-end BSM implementation workflow is shown in Figure 8.11. Please note that a precondition for initiating process is that the service catalog is already developed.

Services defined within the service catalog are prioritized based on the business impact. Performance is then assessed and desired practical target performance levels are agreed. Based on this, a service improvement plan (SIP) is created.

Once SIP is produced and agreed on, end-to-end BSM is implemented. Note that all relevant components of service strategy, service design, service transition, and service operation need to be

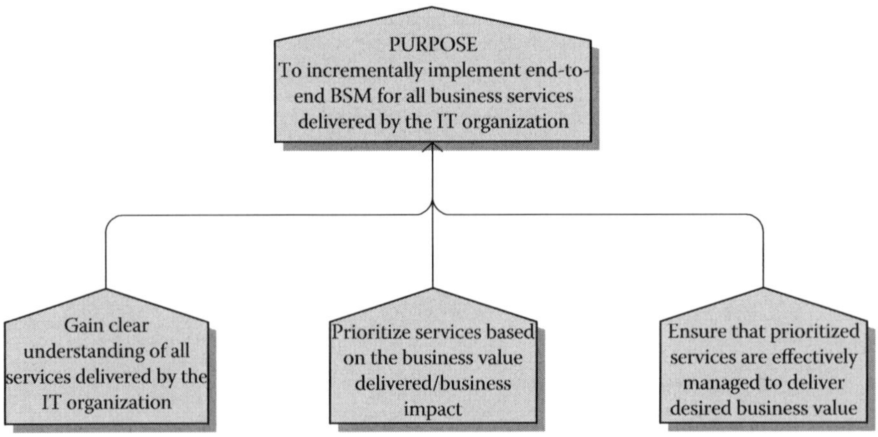

Figure 8.9 Key objectives.

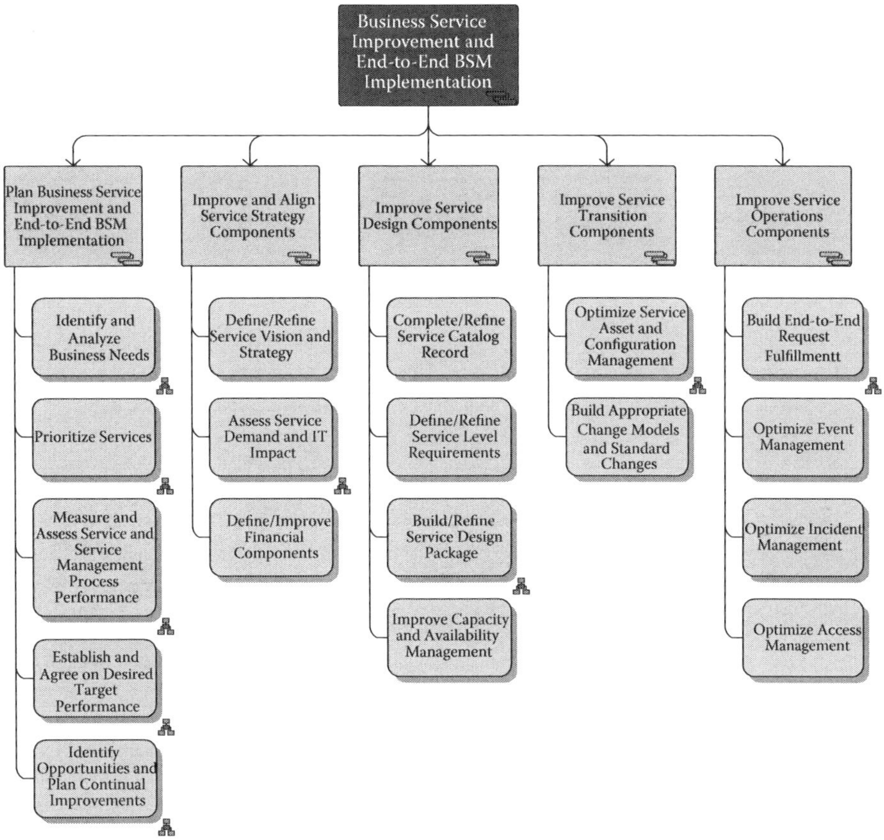

Figure 8.10 Business service improvement and end-to-end BSM implementation work breakdown structure.

improved to achieve the end-to-end BSM for that service. In doing so, all aspects of a given service are improved. These aspects include processes, tools, organization, partnerships, and governance. Let us now discuss these activities in greater detail.

Plan Business Service Improvement and End-to-End BSM Implementation

The following are the key activities that should be performed while planning to implement end-to-end BSM.

Identify and Analyze Business Needs

Business needs are identified and analyzed during this activity. This activity is discussed in detail in Chapter 7.

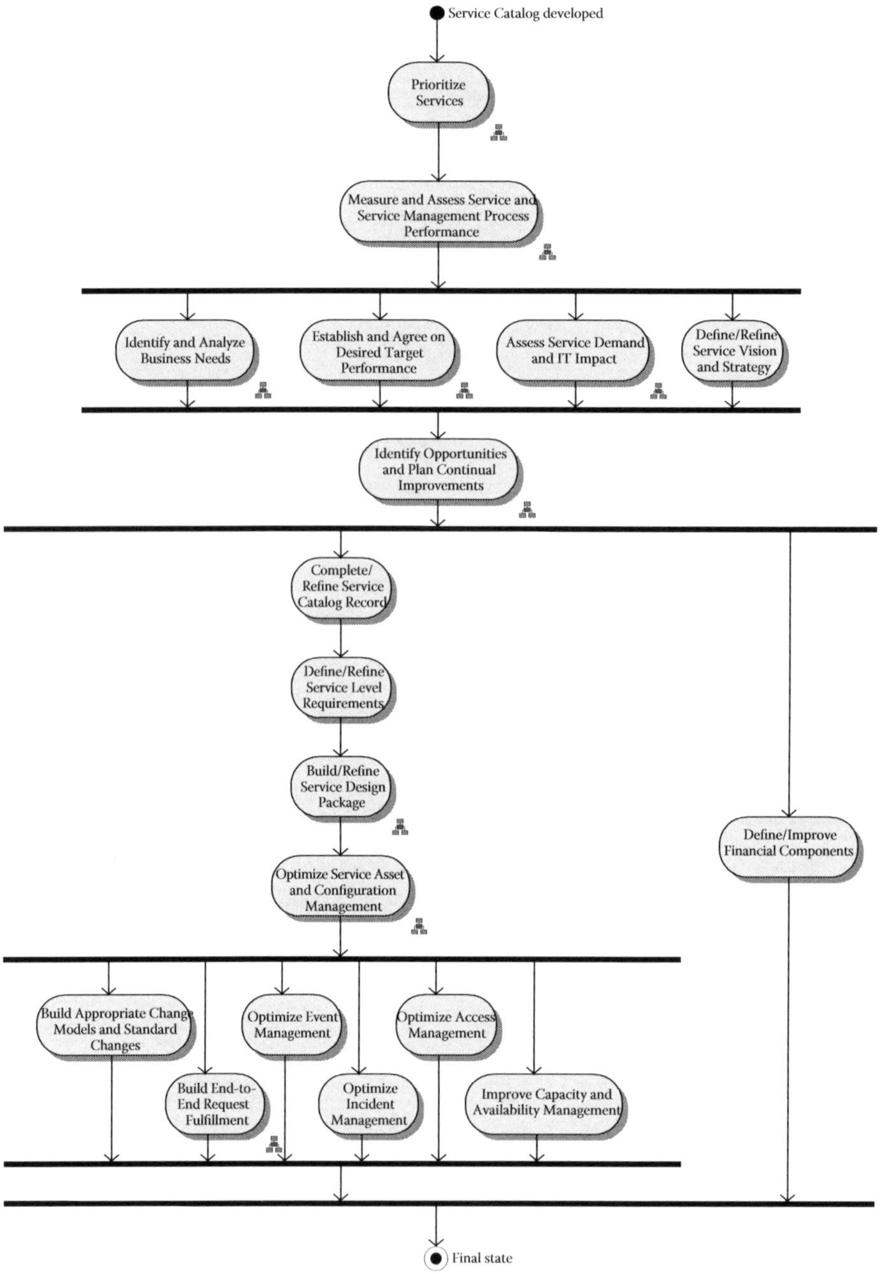

Figure 8.11 Business service improvement and end-to-end BSM implementation.

Prioritize Services

Purpose

The goal is to prioritize services for improvement based on business needs.

Preconditions

- Services offered by the IT organizations are documented and understood.
- Business needs and pain points have been documented and analyzed.

Activity Overview

During this activity, services listed in the service catalog are discussed and prioritized based on business needs and impact (Figure 8.12).

Postcondition

The services provided by the IT organization have been prioritized for improvements.

Measure and Assess Service and Service Management Process Performance

As a result of this activity, the CSI process analyst produces reports on service management process performance as well as service performance. This is discussed in detail in Chapter 7.

Establish and Agree on Desired Target Performance

During this activity, desired and achievable target performance levels are agreed on (Figure 8.13).

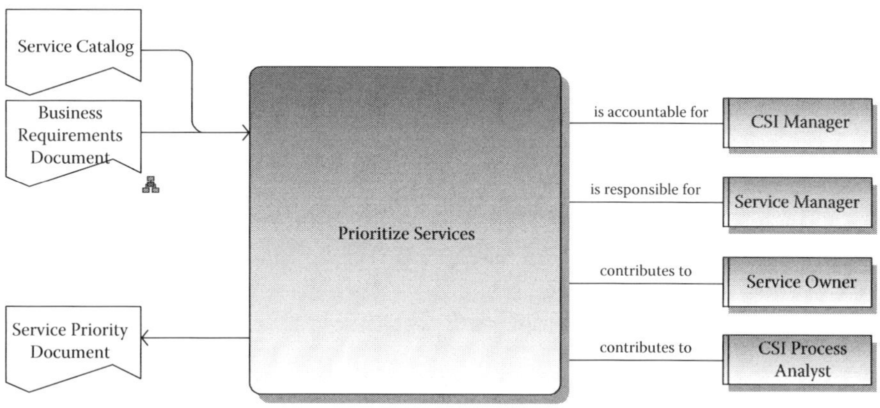

Figure 8.12 Prioritize services.

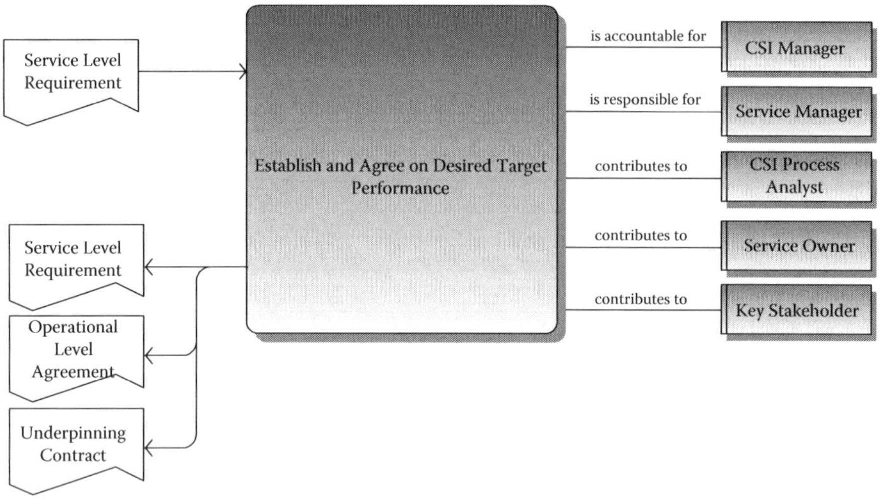

Figure 8.13 Establish and agree on desired target performance.

Purpose

The goal is to clearly define service targets that are acceptable to the customers and businesses and that are achievable for the IT organization.

Precondition

Business and service requirements are clearly documented, understood, and agreed on.

Activity Overview

During this activity, the service manager discusses the business requirements and achievable service targets with stakeholders from both the IT organization and the business and agrees on realistic targets to be achieved.

Postcondition

Clear agreements have been achieved between IT and business and customer organizations.

Identify Opportunities and Plan Continual Improvements

Improvement opportunities for both services and service management processes are identified and respective improvement plans are created. Key outputs include the process improvement plan (PIP) and SIP. This activity is discussed in detail in Chapter 7.

Improve and Align Service Strategy Components

Regardless of which industry we talk about, it is not a profitable business proposition to offer something that your customers really do not care about or perceive as nonvalue-added. Imagine establishing a business enterprise without clearly understanding why anybody would pay for whatever products and services that enterprise is going to produce. *Managing IT as a business* requires a clear and comprehensive understanding of the market, customer needs, and how the services that are created and delivered by IT address and fulfill those needs (Figure 8.14). In most low-maturity IT organizations, it is no surprise to see a lack of clear understanding on any of the following:

- Services delivered by the IT organization.
- Services consumed by the customers and businesses: You will come across cases where customers are using IT services, but IT has not realized that the services were delivered or needed.
- Whether the services that are delivered by the IT organization are actually needed.

Business needs should drive what IT services are offered. In case of new technologies and innovations, it may be that emerging IT services drive business process reengineering leading to new ways of doing business. One example is the emergence of the Internet and how it completely redefined some businesses and significantly impacted others. One of the industries completely redefined by the Internet is the bidding industry and eBay is a prime example.

If you do not understand what you do for your customer, it will become more difficult to understand why you are doing what you are doing. In low-maturity organizations, where technology teams normally operate in silos and specialize in technology areas, you will likely see new technological gizmos being introduced simply because they are new. Having said all this, we still see that IT teams work hard to provide services that their respective businesses and customers actually need. So, the key question to ask here is "Where is the disconnect?"

When customers engage IT to address their needs, in the absence of a standard set of services, IT will go about creating custom services to address the business needs. It is like running a restaurant without a menu: every customer gets a custom-made meal. This will result in increased costs, reduced predictability, and inconsistent quality.

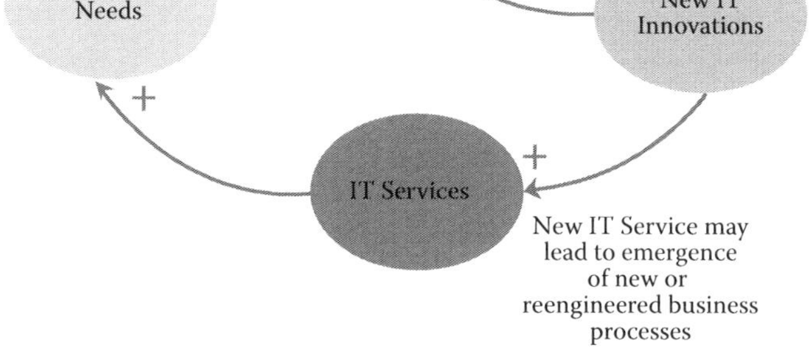

Figure 8.14 The relationship between business needs and IT services.

One of my clients hosted applications for its business customers. In the request initiation process, the IT organization would ask the customer to provide detailed specification of the server that the customer would need to host their respective applications. What is wrong with this process and what is the impact on overall IT operations? Do customers really want to order a box? Or do they want to host their applications so that their specific business needs are satisfied? The main focus should always be on understanding the business needs. The IT teams should decide what technology will meet those needs.

In the case discussed above, the IT organization should be offering an "Application Hosting" service. Depending on the service level requirements (SLRs) and service level agreements (SLAs), the IT organization should ensure that there is enough IT (network, server, etc.) capacity to meet those needs. In this particular case, since customers build their own respective applications, the IT organization must play a critical role in ensuring the *warranty* side of the services. The absence of "right" IT services may lead to the following challenges, in addition to others:

- Greater cost of delivering IT services
- Inconsistent service delivery
- Poor knowledge management
- Unpredictable service performance

How should business services be managed to ensure that service delivery is aligned with overall business vision and strategy and to business and customer needs? Overall BSM strategy and approach are defined and this will further drive the service management process improvement effort that we will discuss in Chapter 9. For example, if your business or customer depends heavily on IT to deliver its products and services to the end customer (business customer who pays the business) and IT is the key business enabler, then it will be more effective for IT to own the improvement and ongoing management of business processes. For example, the financial services industry is one that is always growing in the ways in which IT is enabling business processes. If the business process behind the loan approval service is broken or ineffective and IT gets engaged at automation level and not at the business process level, then IT may only enable a broken process. It is critical to clearly define how service management applies to a given organization. This will further drive the level at which service needs to be managed. BSM strategy and approach should be aligned with the overall business–IT integration strategy. While ensuring alignment with the overall business–IT integration strategy, BSM for our organization is defined.

Improving and aligning service strategy will involve both top-down and bottom-up approaches. This is graphically represented in Figure 8.15.

There are some businesses that are completely driven by IT and IT is completely driven by the business. Companies such as Amazon, eBay, and Google are perfect examples where "Business is IT and IT is the business." In these companies, business processes are tightly integrated with service processes. Business managers and IT managers are one team. Outages in IT directly impact the business revenues. These are the companies where business–IT integration is not optional, but necessary for survival. Business visions and strategies drive IT visions and strategies. Business changes cannot be realized without changes in IT services. Let us now discuss some of the key activities that should be performed to achieve this strategic alignment.

Assess Service Demand and IT Impact

What is the demand for the product or service that we offer? What is the size of the market and how does our service impact the customer?

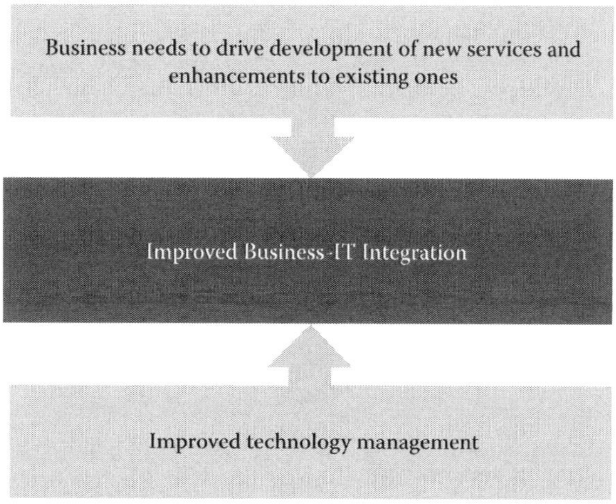

Figure 8.15 Business–IT integration requires top-down and bottom-up approaches.

Purpose

The goal is to clearly and accurately assess, document, and agree on the demand for services provided by the IT organization and analyze the impact on IT infrastructure.

Preconditions

- Clear understanding of all services provided by the IT organization
- Complete assessment of business requirements

Activity Overview

The service manager and the service owner (these roles are discussed in detail later in this chapter) work together to assess demands on various services and analyze the impact on IT infrastructure. The main purpose is to effectively identify opportunities for improvement and achieve agreement between the IT and the business and customers. This process is shown in Figure 8.16.

Postconditions

- Service demands clearly understood and documented
- IT impact assessed

Define and Refine Service Vision and Strategy

With a concrete understanding of the market for our particular service, we will need to define the vision and strategy of that service and how it will address the need of the identified market. In defining the service strategy, we must consider the financial impact and how much it will cost to produce or improve and manage that service.

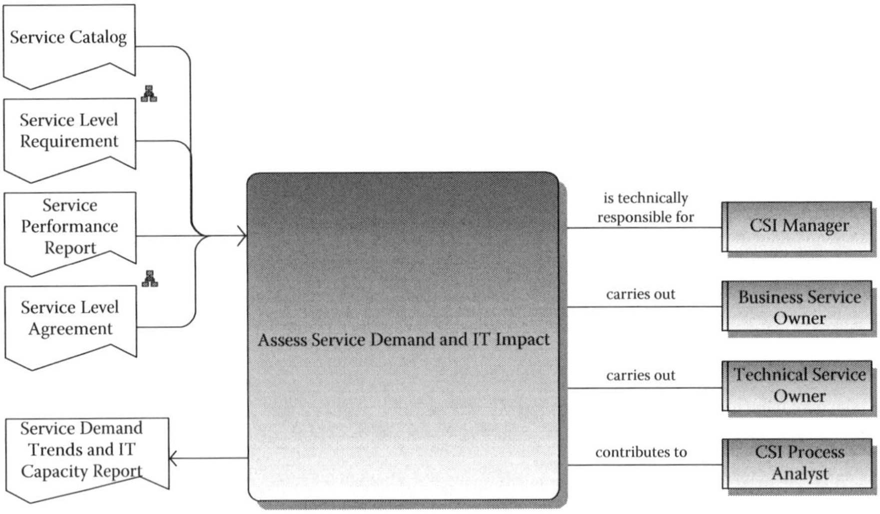

Figure 8.16 Assess service demand and IT impact.

Improve Service Design Components

After we have achieved an accurate understanding of the market for a given service and have defined the vision and strategy for how that service addresses that need, we will now look at how that service should be designed to ensure that we are able to effectively and efficiently address that need. In this section, we will see what we will need to do to improve an existing service or to build a new one.

Complete and Refine Service Catalog Record

The first step in designing a new service is to clearly define that service. By the end of this activity, we will have completed a draft definition of the service as it will appear in the catalog. In defining that service, the goals identified in the strategy must be considered. One of the techniques that ITIL v3 recommends to enable better definition of a service is called SLR. Appropriate discussions need to happen between IT and the customer or business representatives so that all understand, document, and agree on service requirements. In some of my engagements, we also discussed specific targets and related requirements and designed preliminary pricing models.

Define and Refine Service Level Requirements

If it has not been done already during the *complete and refine service definition* activity, we will need to define the SLR during this activity. If preliminary work has already been done during the earlier activity, then we will further refine SLR during this activity as follows:

- Align with availability needs
- Align with capacity and manage demand
- Define IT service continuity management requirements
- Analyze risks and define information security requirements

Build and Refine Service Design Package

One of the key challenges that the IT industry faces today is related to siloed approaches to managing IT and also to developing IT. Most IT organizations today operate in three key silos when it comes to designing and building new IT services. These include application and software, infrastructure, and data center. Applications are largely designed within the application development organization by application experts and when these are ready for deployment, they are handed off to operations teams (infrastructure and data center) for deployment. In most cases, infrastructure and data center teams are not appropriately engaged earlier in the process. The impact is lack of appropriate infrastructure and data center planning to ensure that the overall service performance will meet utility and warranty requirements. Under such conditions, when applications are put into production, for the first couple of weeks or months, related incidents and call volume to the service desk increases and most of the development and operations teams find themselves in extensive firefighting activities.

ITIL v3 takes a holistic approach to designing IT services. The service design package (SDP) allows IT teams to design a holistic service that considers all aspects, which may include application, software, hardware, infrastructure, network, data center, and others.

Purpose

The goal is to achieve a holistic understanding of what needs to be designed to satisfy the utility and warranty requirements in the most cost-effective and technologically sound manner.

Precondition

There should be a comprehensive understanding of what is required by the customers and businesses.

Activity Overview

During this activity, a complete service architecture and design is produced. This process is illustrated in Figure 8.17.

Activity Details

Creating an SDP is an intensive activity that consumes time and resources. It requires the following activities to be completed successfully:

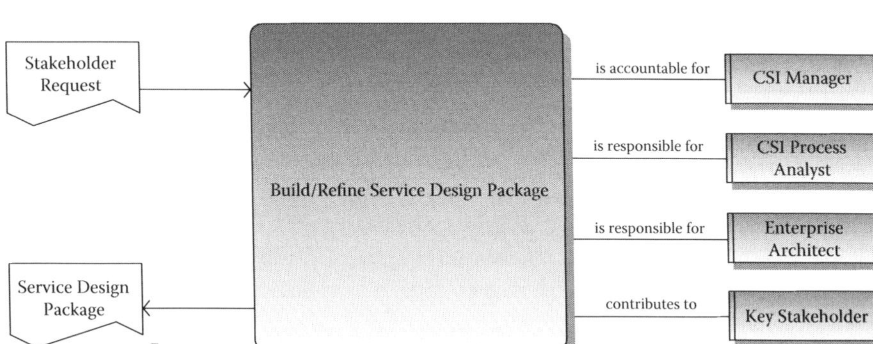

Figure 8.17 Build and refine the service design package.

- Analyze business needs and document service requirements
- Architect and design the service
- Assess organizational readiness
- Develop service life cycle plan

Let us discuss the above-mentioned activities in greater detail.

Activity *Analyze Business Needs and Document Service Requirements*			
Input Artifacts	*Tasks Performed*	*Output Artifacts*	*Roles (RACI)*
Stakeholder Request	Perform Service Stakeholder Analysis	Stakeholder list	A: CSI Manager R: CSI Process Analyst C: Business Service Owner and Technical Service Owner
Stakeholder Request	Identify and Analyze Business Needs	Business Requirements Document (BRD – Initial draft created)	A: CSI Manager R: CSI Process Analyst C: Key Stakeholders including Business Service Owner and Technical Service Owner
Business Requirements Document	Assess and Establish Service Applicability	Service Catalog (Service Definition completed)	A: CSI Manager R: CSI Process Analyst C: Key Stakeholders including Business Service Owner and Technical Service Owner

Activity *Architect and Design the Service*			
Input Artifacts	*Tasks Performed*	*Output Artifacts*	*Roles (RACI)*
Stakeholder Request Stakeholder List	Define Service Functional Requirements	Business Requirements Document (updated with functional requirements)	A: CSI Manager R: CSI Process Analyst C: Key Stakeholders including Business Service Owner and Technical Service Owner
Stakeholder Request Stakeholder List	Build Service Level Requirements	Service Level Requirements	A: CSI Manager R: CSI Process Analyst C: Key Stakeholders including Business Service Owner and Technical Service Owner

Activity *Architect and Design the Service*			
Service Level Requirement (SLR)	Design and agree on SLA(s) and OLA(s)	SLA and / or OLA (draft agreements crafted)	A: CSI Manager R: CSI Process Analyst C: Key Stakeholders including Business Service Owner and Technical Service Owner
SLR, SLA, OLA and UC	Define Service and Operational Management Requirements	Business Requirements Document (BRD – Updated with more information)	A: CSI Manager R: CSI Process Analyst C: Key Stakeholders including Business Service Owner and Technical Service Owner
Business Requirements Document	Build Service Architecture	Service Architecture Document	A: CSI Manager R: CSI Process Analyst R: Enterprise Architect C: Key Stakeholders including Business Service Owner and Technical Service Owner
Service Architecture Document	Build Service Design	Service Design Document	A: CSI Manager R: CSI Process Analyst R: Enterprise Architect C: Key Stakeholders including Business Service Owner and Technical Service Owner

Activity *Assess Organizational Readiness*			
Input Artifacts	*Tasks Performed*	*Output Artifacts*	*Roles (RACI)*
AS-IS Organization Chart	Analyze AS-IS Organization	Organization Assessment Report	A: Human Resource Manager R: Human Resource Analyst C: Business Service Owner and Technical Service Owner

Activity *Develop Service Lifecycle Plan*			
Input Artifacts	*Tasks Performed*	*Output Artifacts*	*Roles (RACI)*
Service Architecture Document Service Design Document	Define Service Development and Transition Plan	Service Development and Transition Plan	A: CSI Manager R: Project Manager R: CSI Process Analyst R: Enterprise Architect C: Key Stakeholders including Business Service Owner and Technical Service Owner
Service Architecture Document Service Design Document	Build Service Operational Acceptance Plan	Service Operational Acceptance Plan	A: CSI Manager R: Project Manager R: CSI Process Analyst R: Enterprise Architect C: Key Stakeholders including Business Service Owner and Technical Service Owner
Service Architecture Document Service Design Document	Establish Service Acceptance Criteria	Service Acceptance Criteria (SAC)	A: CSI Manager R: Project Manager R: CSI Process Analyst R: Enterprise Architect C: Key Stakeholders including Business Service Owner and Technical Service Owner

Postcondition

The SDP is delivered.

Improve Capacity and Availability Management

During this activity, capacity and availability capabilities are assessed based on the requirements documented in SLRs. As a result, necessary improvements are implemented to ensure that targets agreed on in SLAs are achieved.

Improve Service Transition Components

Most service outages are caused by lack of proper service transition and related management activities. Improving service transition will bring the following benefits for a given service:

- Reduction in number of failed changes
- Reduction in service outages
- Efficient and effective management and implementation of changes
- Reduced disruption to services due to better management of new releases
- Higher configuration management database (CMDB) integrity
- Improved quality of configuration data

Let us now discuss some of the key activities that will be performed in improving service transition.

Optimize Service Asset and Configuration Management

Accurate configuration information is critical to not only effectively and efficiently transition services into production but also to the management of these services during operations. Optimizing service asset and configuration management for a given service will involve the following:

- Identifying all configuration items (CIs) that make up the given service
- Improving quality of CI data
- Identifying and establishing relationships among those service CIs

Always keep this rule of thumb in mind:

> The 80/20 rule applies. Not every configuration item is important in your IT infrastructure. Some are more important than others because they contribute to delivering services that are more important to the business and customers than others.

Optimizing service asset and configuration management must be driven by business needs and business impact. CMDB and related processes are improved for those services that make the most.

Technology architectures combined with CMDB must represent the logical structure of IT infrastructure. Here is what it means:

- All technology components (hardware, software, and application components—also known as configuration items or CIs) are clearly and accurately identified and inventoried.
- Interrelationships among these CIs are documented and managed.
- CI-specific details are captured and managed at justifiable levels to manage the services that they implement.

Figure 8.18 shows a scenario where a logical view of the IT infrastructure does not represent the actual view. When service asset and configuration management is optimized for a given service, such discrepancies are removed and a complete list of all CIs that make up that service is compiled. We will discuss later in this book (Chapter 17—Business Service Management, Enterprise Architecture and Service-Oriented Architecture). Let us discuss this activity in detail.

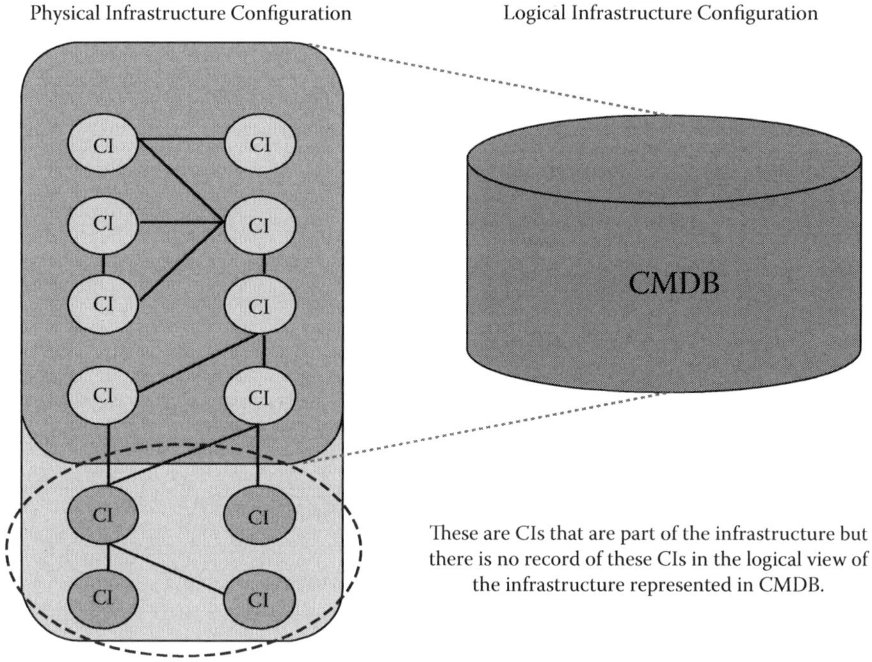

Figure 8.18 Configuration management database quality measurement and improvement.

Purpose

The goal is to establish a clear and precise understanding of all components of a service so that service delivery can be effectively and efficiently managed.

Preconditions

- Service catalog defined
- Services assessed and prioritized

Activity Overview

Key outputs of this activity include an optimized configuration management system for the prioritized services (Figure 8.19).

Postcondition

All CIs that enable the prioritized service have been successfully brought under BSM.

Build Appropriate Change Models and Standard Changes

To ensure that change requests submitted in relation to a given service are managed effectively and efficiently, it is critical to build the appropriate change models and standard changes.

Change models for a given change will include a predefined set of activities that will be performed to implement that particular change effectively and efficiently. Let us consider a simple example of

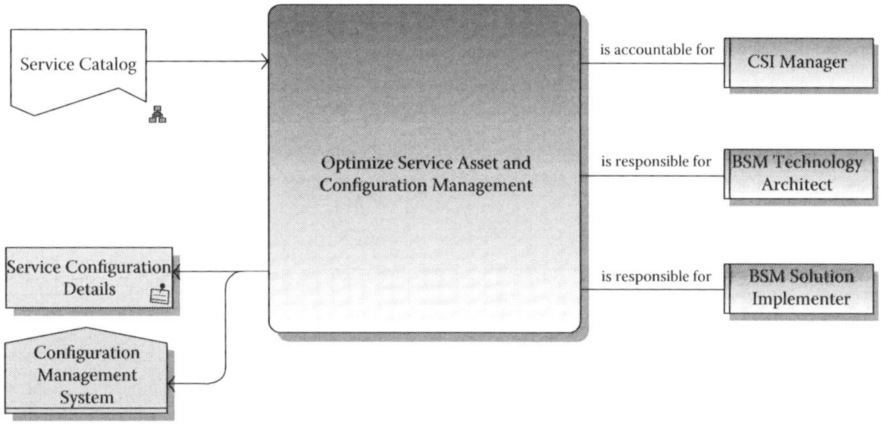

Figure 8.19 Optimize service asset and configuration management.

an e-mail service. One of the change requests may be a request for additional e-mail storage. Such a request may need financial and other approvals. However, there are a standard set of activities that will be performed to implement this change. The change model for this request will consist of a standard, predefined set of activities that will be executed each time such a change request is submitted.

Standard changes, on the other hand, not only consist of a predefined set of activities that are performed but are also preauthorized and preapproved. We will discuss standard changes in relation to service requests in the next section.

Improving Change Management in support of service improvement will certainly help realize some of the benefits discussed earlier in this section. In order to minimize potential service outages due to planned maintenance activities, Release and Deployment Management should be optimized for selected services. In other words, when you have achieved a certain level of maturity across other Service Transition processes, it will be truly a value-add for the business enterprise to institutionalize Release and Deployment Management to further achieve greater degree of service quality. The i2-SOSMI methodology recommends that Release and Deployment Management should be improved during the "Align" phase (see Figure 4.14) when you already have established a solid Service Transition foundation.

Improve Service Operations Components

All phases of a service life cycle offer value. However, service operations is where the value is created and delivered to customers and businesses. All service strategy and service design activities are carried out to ensure that services deliver the desired business value. Improving service operations includes activities that ensure that, once in operation, services continue to deliver business value at the agreed levels of performance. Let us see what activities need to be carried out to ensure that services keep operating at desired levels:

- Customers and businesses should be able to understand what value is delivered by the service. Services should be described clearly in the service catalog. A service catalog and related materials are shown in Appendix A.
- Customers and businesses should be able to order services using the information provided in the service catalog.

- The IT organization and teams should have a clear understanding of what activities need to be performed to fulfill customer and business requests.
- The IT organization and teams should be able to manage and resolve issues and problems associated with the service.
- Customers and businesses should be able to submit requests for new services and communicate new ideas.

Some of the core activities performed in order to improve service operations are discussed in the following subsections.

Build End-to-End Request Fulfillment

Request fulfillment is one of those processes that has been newly added to ITIL v3 and, if implemented properly, can generate enormous returns for the business (Figure 8.20). We are making an assumption here that the organization has already implemented some form of service catalog and identified the services that it offers to its customers and businesses. If those services have been defined, then we can begin to identify the standard types of requests that can be placed against those services. As shown in Figure 8.18, we have electronic order intake as one of the services available to our customers. Some of the common requests that can be initiated for that service include:

- I want to open a new account
- I want to change my plan

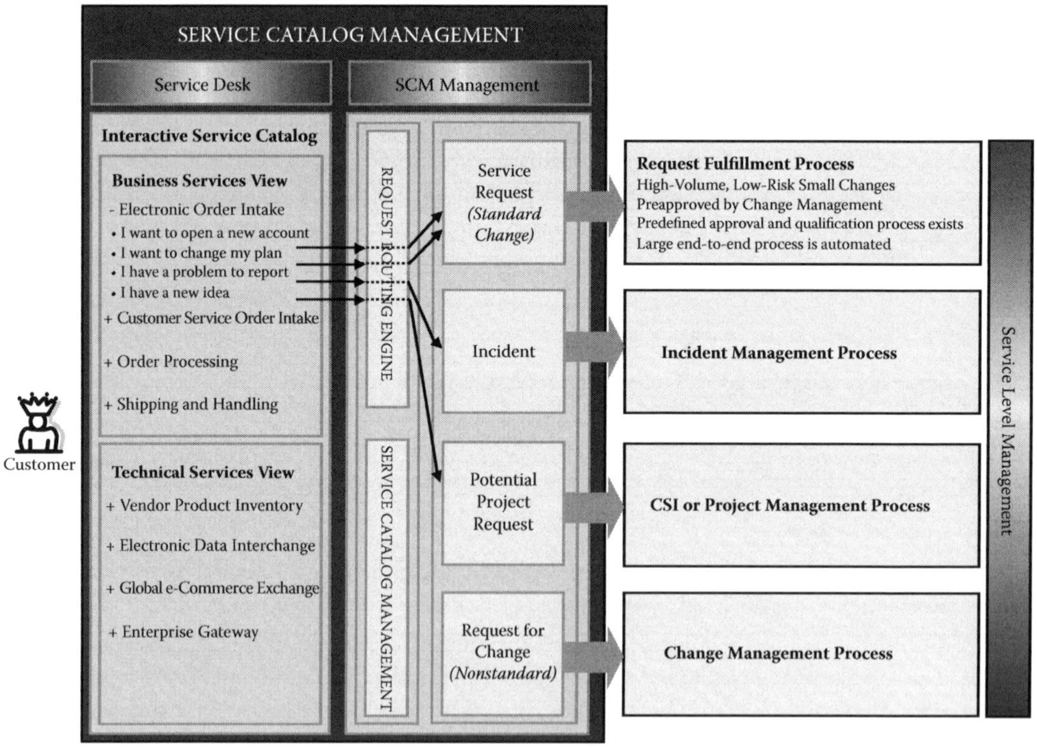

Figure 8.20 Request fulfillment.

- I have a problem to report
- I have a new idea

Of the above mentioned requests, the first two ("I want to open new account" and "I want to change my plan") can be treated as service requests. The request fulfillment process for those requests will include the standard set of activities that must be performed to successfully fulfill them. Such requests are sometimes called "standard changes." These are most commonly high-volume and low-risk changes.

Again, applying the 80/20 rule means that 80% of the total service request volume will most likely be for 20% of the types of service requests. Streamlining fulfillment processes for these high-volume requests will result in large returns for your IT organization.

Purpose

The goal is to streamline the end-to-end request fulfillment process for high-volume service requests.

Preconditions

- Service catalog completed
- Service asset and configuration management optimized for the service
- High-volume service requests identified and prioritized

Activity Overview

The end-to-end request fulfillment process is automated as a result of this activity (Figure 8.21).

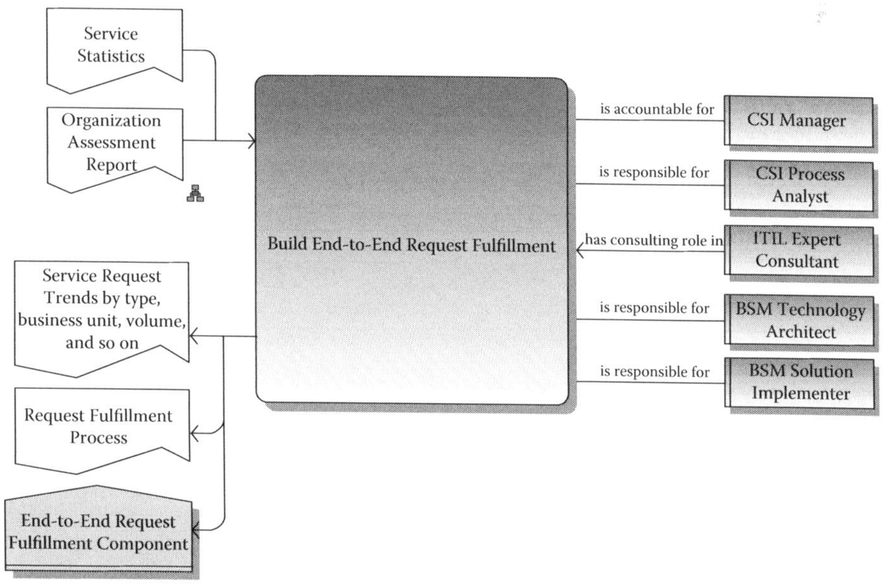

Figure 8.21 Build end-to-end request fulfillment.

Activity Details

Input Artifacts	*Tasks Performed*	*Output Artifacts*	*Roles (RACI)*
Service Statistics	Identify and Define Potential High-Volume Requests	Service Request Trends	A: CSI Manager R: CSI Process Analyst
ITIL v3 Guidelines Organization Assessment Report	Define Request Fulfillment Process	Request Fulfillment Process	A: CSI Manager R: CSI Process Analyst C: ITIL Expert Consultant
Request Fulfillment Process	Automate Request Fulfillment	Request Fulfillment Component (of BSM tool)	A: CSI Manager R: BSM Technology Architect, BSM Solution Implementer C: CSI Process Analyst C: ITIL Expert Consultant

Postcondition

Request fulfillment is streamlined for the service.

Optimize Event Management

Optimizing event management will ensure that:

- Event monitoring capabilities are implemented for all CIs that make up a given service. Strictly speaking, this particular activity is not part of the event management process scope. However, it is critical to ensure that required monitoring capabilities are in place as one of the preconditions for this activity.
- Appropriate event detection, filtering, correlation, responses, and other activities are designed and implemented to ensure proactive management of events and thereby reducing incident volume.

Optimize Incident Management

Optimizing incident management will ensure that appropriate incident models and other scripts exist to ensure effective and efficient management of incidents related to that service.

Optimize Access Management

Depending on the service, it may be critical to ensure that only the right resources have the right level of access to the right resources. Optimizing access management will ensure that access to a given service is managed effectively and efficiently.

Primary Roles and Responsibilities

Primary roles and responsibilities related to this discipline are discussed below (also see Figure 8.22).

Business Service Owner

- May own one or more business service(s) as defined in Service Catalog
- Represents these business service(s) to the entire organization
- Accountable for ensuring that business service(s) meet agreed targets (SLA targets)
- Represents IT to the Business and Business to IT
- Participates on Change Advisory Board and represents his/her business services
- Possesses required IT expertise and is business savvy
- Manages business demand to optimize business value
- Performs business service performance reviews on a periodic basis
- Develops Service Improvement Plan(s) and ensures continual service improvement
- Collaborates with technical service owner(s) to understand warranty and utility service attributes including capacity management
- Manages business/customer expectations

Technical Service Owner

- May own one or more technical service(s) as defined in Service Catalog
- Represents these technical services to Business Service Owner(s) and other IT stakeholders
- Thorough understanding of technical services that make up business services
- Accountable for ensuring that technical services meet agreed targets (OLA targets)
- Participates on Change Advisory Board and represents his/her technical services.
- Possess technical expertise related to technical services s/he owns
- Advises on business demand and service/component capacity management to optimize business value
- Performs technical service performance reviews on periodic basis
- Develops technical Service Improvement Plan(s) in support of business service needs.
- Accountable for ensuring that technical service capacity is inline with business demand
- Represents business needs to Technology Owners and technology capabilities to Business Service Owner(s) (Figure 8.23)

Enterprise Architect

The enterprise architect is a role that is completely accountable and responsible for architecting and designing the total BSM solution. We will discuss this role in detail in Chapter 17.

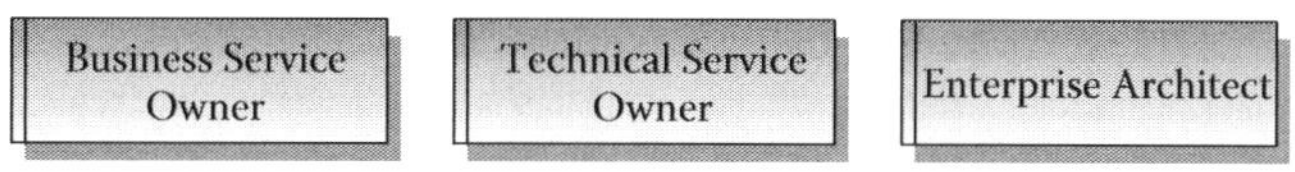

Figure 8.22 Business service improvement and end-to-end BSM implementation primary roles.

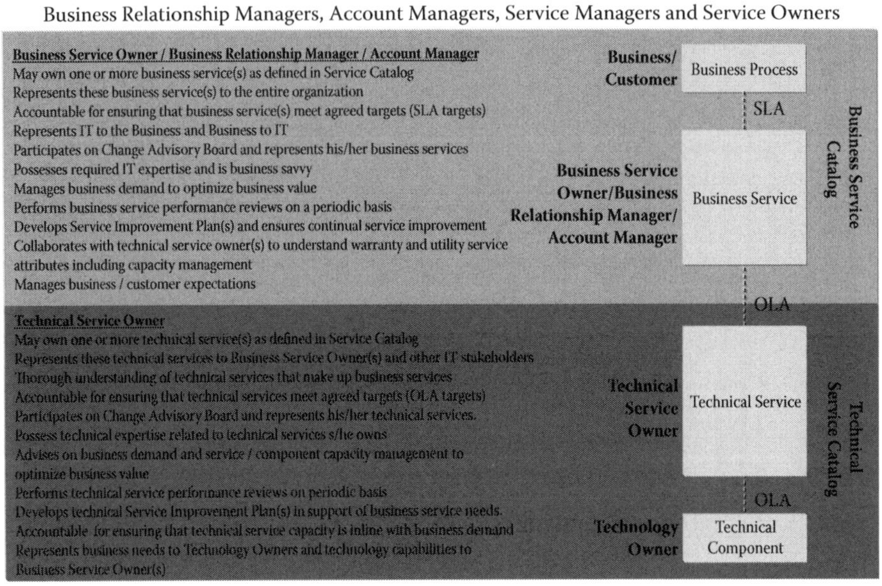

Figure 8.23 Business relationship managers, account managers, service managers, and service owners.

Key Artifacts

Key artifacts related to BSM are shown in Figure 8.24.

Service Catalog

The service catalog lists and describes all services that are offered by the IT organization. It also contains other service information that may include the following:

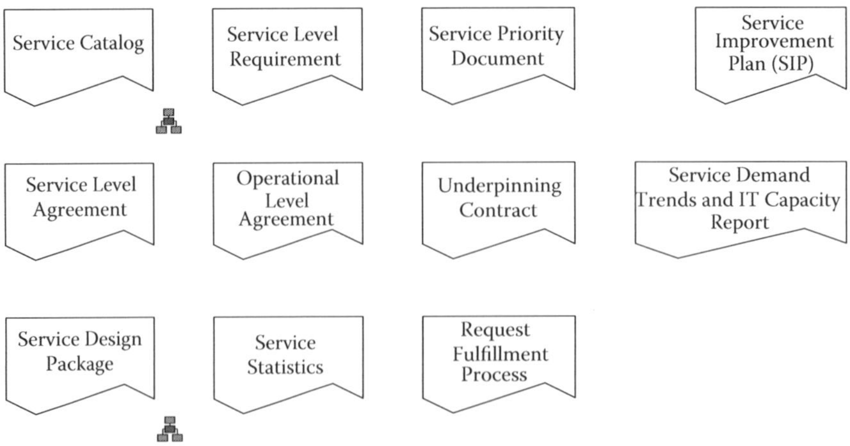

Figure 8.24 Key artifacts related to implementing end-to-end BSM.

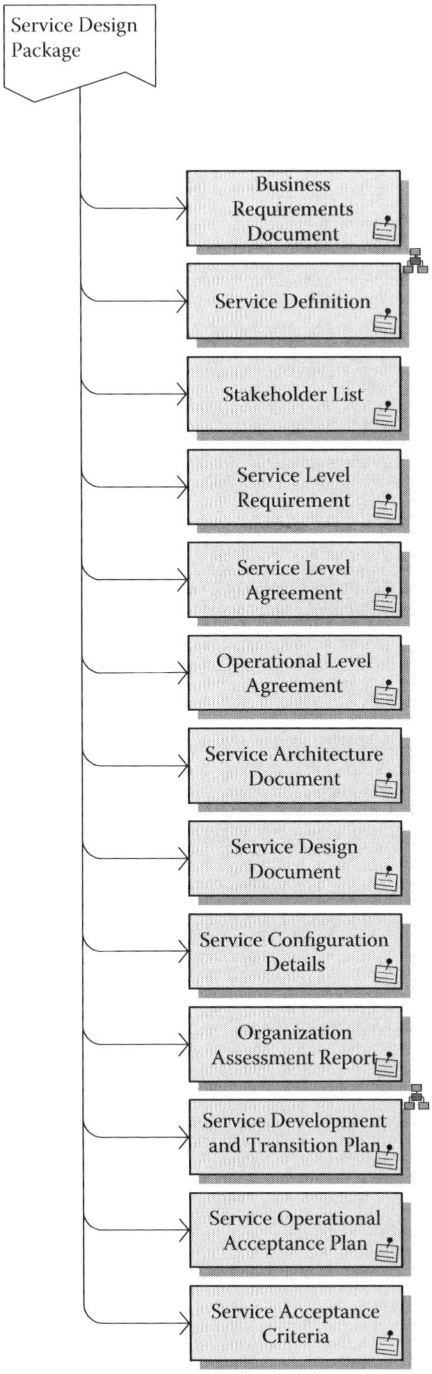

Figure 8.25 Service design package.

- Introduction
- Description
- Service packages
- Pricing and chargeback
- Service commitments and targets
- Security and privacy
- Complementary and prerequisite services
- Requesting services
- Placing an order for service
- Service level metrics and targets

Service Level Requirement

This states the service requirements. This should include both functional and nonfunctional requirements.

Service Priority Document

This lists all services in the order of priority. This is performed to prioritize the services in the order in which those will be improved.

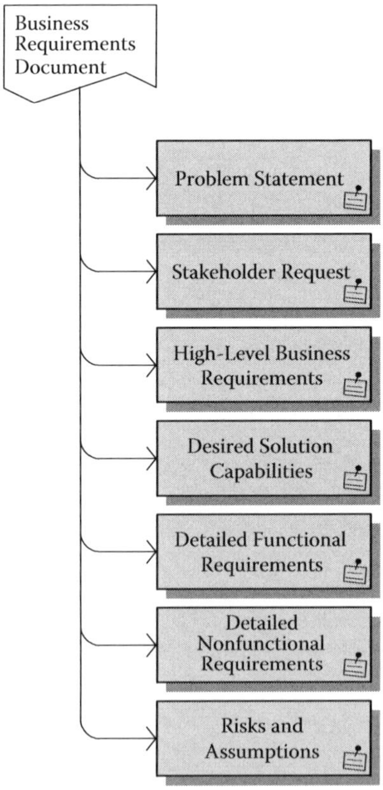

Figure 8.26 Business requirements document.

Service Improvement Plan

The service improvement schedule, efforts, and resources are documented in the SIP. This document is commonly used to plan service improvements in a continual manner.

Service Level Agreement

This lists all the target goals that should be achieved. This is primarily used to ensure that customer expectations are agreed on and service delivery is managed and measured to those targets.

Service Demand Trends and IT Capacity Report

This report provides a clear and accurate picture of demand trends for a given service. In addition, it contains information on the IT capacity to meet those demands. This report feeds into managing demands from businesses and customers and the IT capacity to meet those demands. For example, if there is unused capacity available within the IT, then it may be a wise decision to reduce the prices of the related services to optimize utilization.

Service Design Package

The SDP is one of the key artifacts within ITIL v3. It captures holistic architectures and designs of services. Key components of the SDP are shown in Figure 8.25.

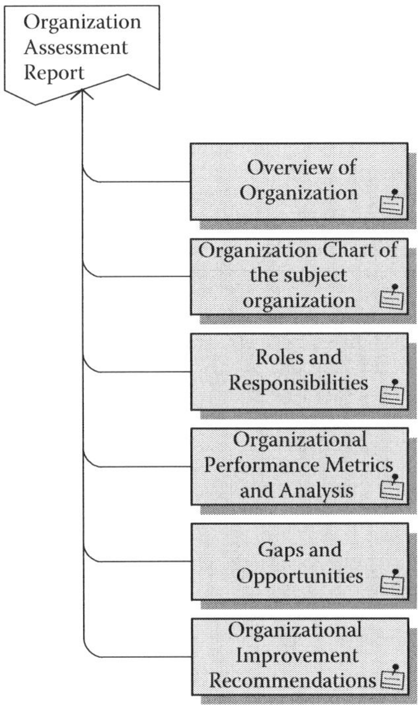

Figure 8.27 Organization assessment report.

Business Requirements Document

The business requirements document (BRD) contains the requirements that need to be fulfilled to satisfy customers' and businesses' needs. Key components of the BRD are shown in Figure 8.26.

Organization Assessment Report

This report provides insights into the organization and its readiness to undergo improvements (see Figure 8.27).

Service Statistics

This artifact contains statistical information on services such as incident volume and trends, service request volume and trends, number of outages, capacity utilization trends, and so on.

Key Concepts

In this section, we will discuss some of the key concepts that are related to BSM implementation.

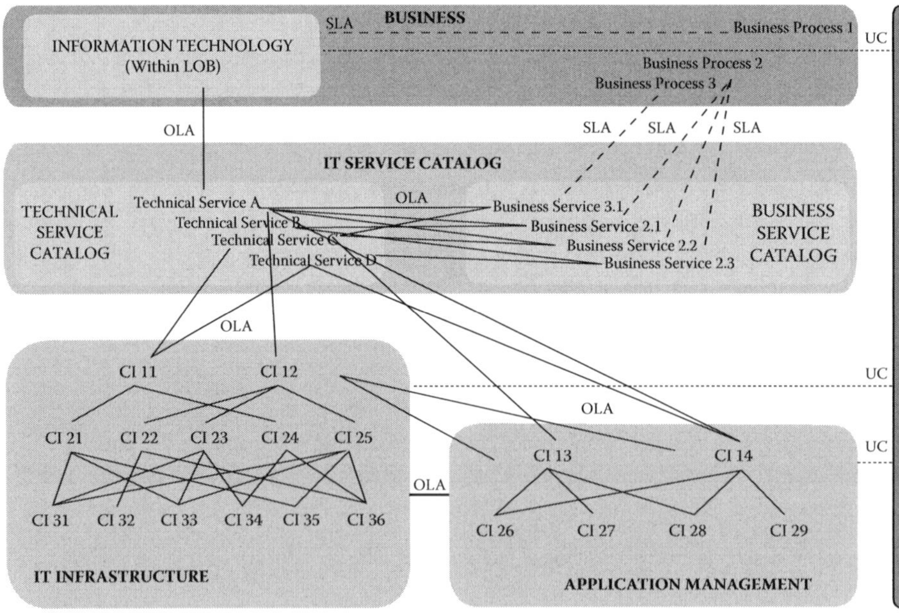

Service Level Agreements (SLAs):

- Provide the basis for managing the relationship between the service provider and the customer.
- Is a written agreement between an IT service provider and the IT customer(s), defining the key service targets and responsibilities of both parties.

Operational Level Agreements (OLAs):

- Is an agreement between an IT service provider and another part of the same organization that assists with the provision of services.

Figure 8.28 SLAs, OLAs, and UCs in the context of organization structure.

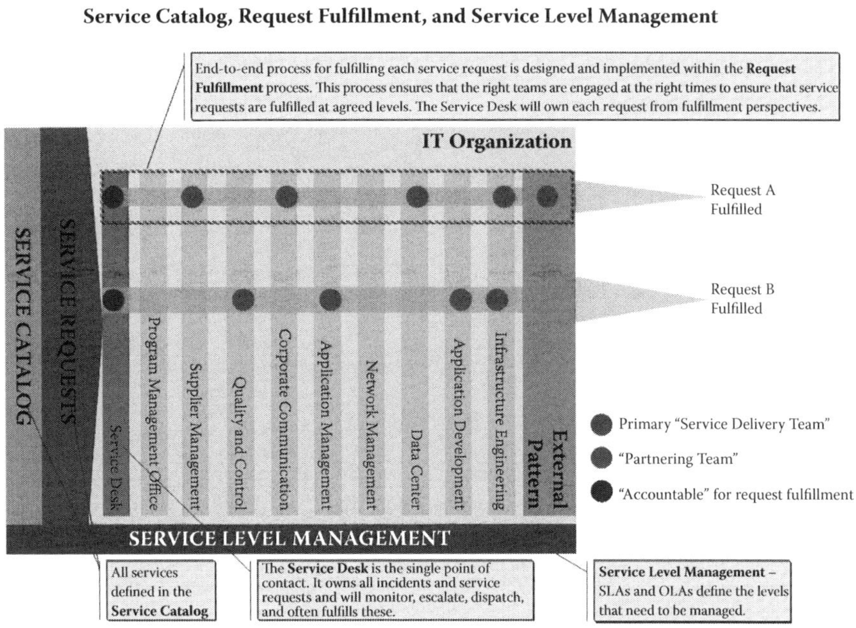

Figure 8.29 Service catalog, request fulfillment, and service level management.

Service Level Agreements, Operational Level Agreements, and Underpinning Contracts

Figure 8.28 shows SLAs, operational level agreements (OLAs), and underpinning contracts (UCs) in the context of the service catalog and organizational structures. Note that SLAs only exist between IT and its customers and businesses. OLAs exist between teams and departments within the IT organization.

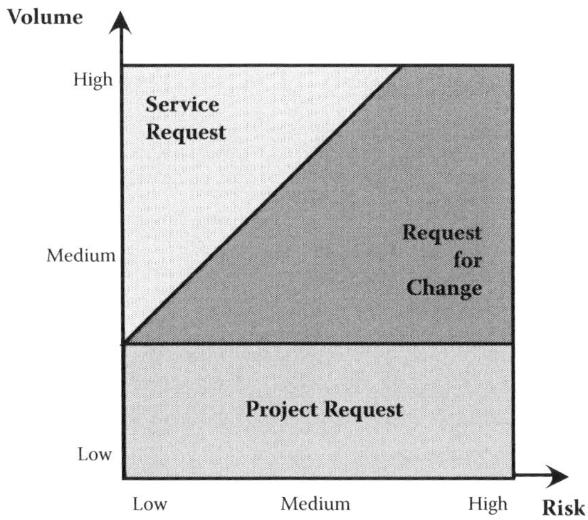

Figure 8.30 Request volume and risk.

Table 8.1 IT Request Classification Matrix

IT Request Classification Matrix				
Terms		*Service Request*	*Service Request Leading to RFC*	*Project Request*
Definition	ITIL v3/ PMBOK Definitions	"Request from a user for information, for access to an IT service, or for a Standard Change." (ITIL v3)	"Addition, modification, or removal of anything that could have an effect on IT services." (ITIL v3)	"A temporary endeavor undertaken to create a unique product, service, or result." (PMBOK)
Characteristics	Request initiator	Any authorized user	Business relationship manager or authorized IT manager	Business relationship manager or authorized IT manager
	Complexity	Simple/Low	High/complex	Unique
	In service catalog	Yes	Yes	No
	Service targets	Standard/ published in service catalog	Estimate provided by "service transition" team	Formal estimate prepared/ provided by PMO/project manager
	Annual volume	High	Medium	Low
	Risk	Low/medium	Medium/high	High
	Size/scale	Minor	Major	Major/significant
	Impact	Low (<5 users)	Medium (5–200 users)	High (public facing or 200+ users)
	Pricing	Standard/ published in service catalog	Depends/varies	High
	FTE/Labor	Up to 40 hours	Up to 120 hours	120+ hours
	Time to close/ deliver	1–10 business days	Depends/varies	1–18 months
	Prioritization criteria	Agreed/ published service targets	Depends/varies	Depends/varies

(continued)

Table 8.1 IT Request Classification Matrix (Continued)

IT Request Classification Matrix				
Terms		*Service Request*	*Service Request Leading to RFC*	*Project Request*
	Change Management	Standard/ Preapproved Changes	Formal RFC/Not Preapproved	Formal PMO Life Cycle
	CMDB Update Required	No	Yes	Yes
Examples		Install PC Install Phone VPN Access Blackberry Request Password Reset	Add PBX/Other Component Set up new B2B or B2C connectivity Deploy Web site Add storage to a DB DNS change	Develop new business application Acquire and integrate new solution (application, hardware, and software) Add new DB

Service Catalog, Request Fulfillment, and Service Level Management

We have discussed these concepts thoroughly. Let us see how the three are related to end-to-end BSM.

Here are the key points that we need to remember:

- All services are defined in the service catalog.
- The service desk is the single point of contact. It owns all incidents and service requests and will monitor, escalate, dispatch, and, often, fulfill these.
- Service level management—SLAs and OLAs define the levels that need to be managed.
- The end-to-end process for fulfilling each service request is designed and implemented within the request fulfillment process. This process ensures that the right teams are engaged at the right times to ensure that service requests are fulfilled at agreed levels. The service desk will own each request from fulfillment perspectives (Figure 8.29).

IT Request Classification

IT organizations are normally service delivery organizations. IT organizations create services and enable their businesses and customers to receive those services. To ensure streamlined delivery of these services, an IT organization defines what requests can be made against each of the services defined in the service catalog. To effectively manage these requests, it is critical to categorize, classify, and prioritize these requests so that they can be fulfilled within the agreed targets.

Figure 8.30 shows the three most common requests received by the IT organization (except incidents). Table 8.1 shows how these requests can be classified.

Summary

Improving business services and achieving end-to-end BSM must be achieved to ensure that business services can be delivered to businesses and customers at agreed levels. In this chapter, we have learned about the key activities that should be performed to achieve end-to-end BSM.

Reference

Shuja, A., and J. Krebs. 2008. *Rational Unified Process: Reference and Certification Guide*. New York: IBM Press.

Chapter 9

Discipline: Service Management Process Improvement

Introduction

It would be truly difficult to achieve cost-effective service improvements without improving the underpinning service management processes. Figure 9.1 shows that all underlying service management processes enable the delivery of high-quality services that ultimately impact the business profitability.

Let us consider a simple example. In the case of most services, there may be more than one configuration item (CI) that makes up a given service. These CIs may include software, hardware, application, and other infrastructure components (switches, routers, firewalls, and so on). Degradation at one of those CIs can impact the bottom-line performance of a given service. The chain is as strong as the weakest link. One of the most common CIs will be a server that hosts the application CIs that make up a given service. One of the service level targets that is common for almost any service is availability. To guarantee a certain level of availability, you will have the following options:

- If our event and incident management processes are not mature enough, then we will need to add resiliency at each CI level (by adding duplicate CIs) to ensure that availability targets can be achieved. This is not the most cost-efficient means of achieving these availability targets.
- If we improve our event and incident management processes to allow us to do proactive event and incident management, we will be able to detect potential incidents before they have occurred. This way, we will be able to guarantee that we achieve the availability targets in the most cost-effective manner.

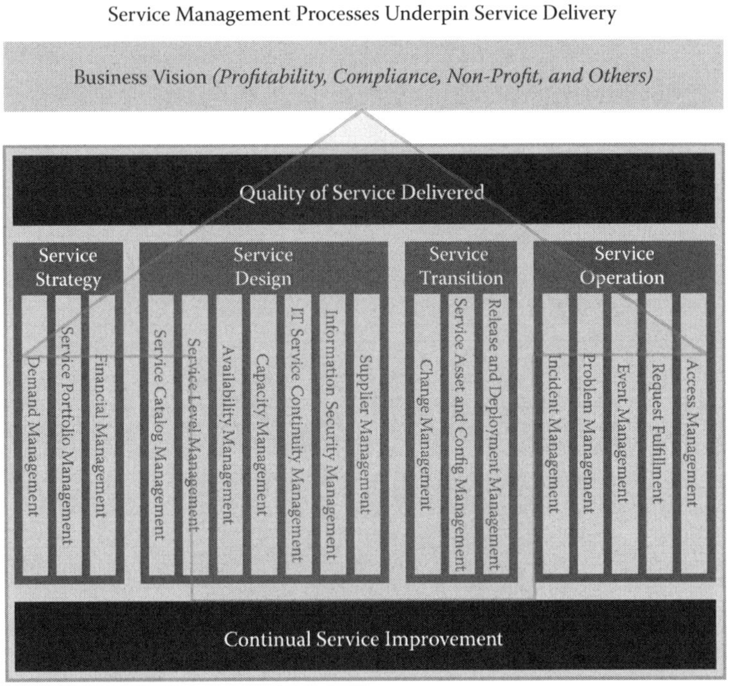

Figure 9.1 Service management processes underpin quality of service delivered.

Service management process improvement (SMPI) is critical to the overall improvement of the quality of services delivered. Let us discuss this in further detail.

Purpose

The purpose of SMPI is to achieve targeted improvements across all service management processes so that high-value services perform at the desired levels.

Objectives

Some of the core objectives of SMPI are as follows (see also Figure 9.2):

- Establish or improve BSM processes (service strategy, service design, service operation, and service transition processes) over the course of the project
- Establish the foundation for necessary organizational realignments
- Plan and build organizational capabilities to effectively support BSM
- Continually improve and manage BSM processes

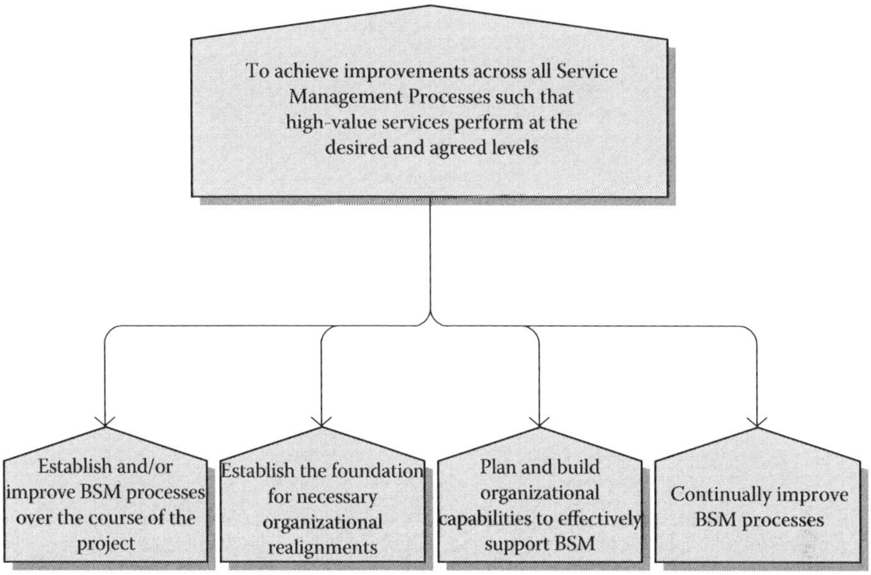

Figure 9.2 SMPI objectives.

Work Breakdown Structure

The SMPI work breakdown structure is shown in Figure 9.3. There are six key SMPI areas within the work breakdown structure. We will discuss each of these in greater detail in the next section.

Figure 9.4 shows the service management process improvement workflow. Note that it is critical that the process owner is identified and appointed for each process. After the appointment

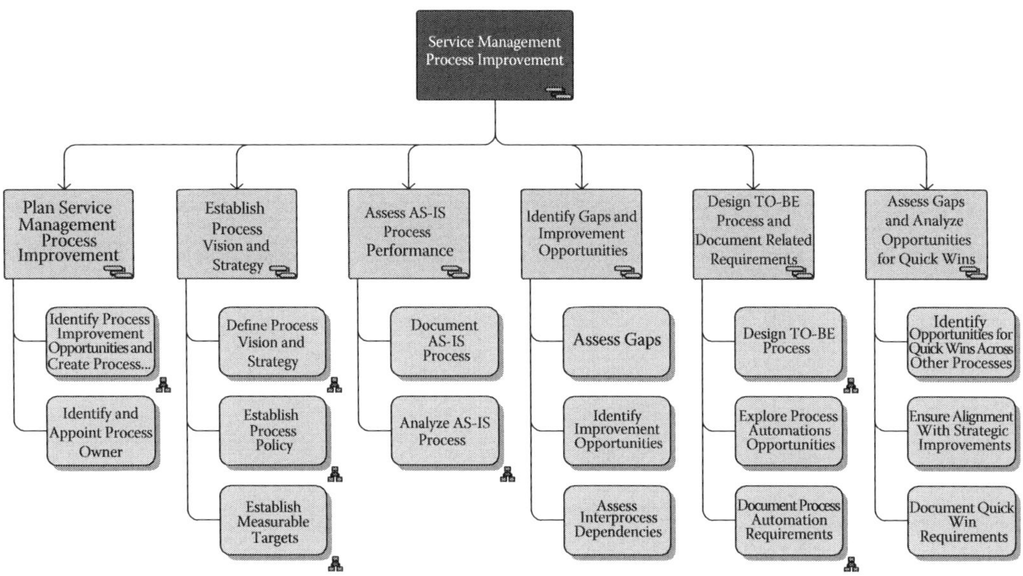

Figure 9.3 SMPI work breakdown structure and SMPI workflow.

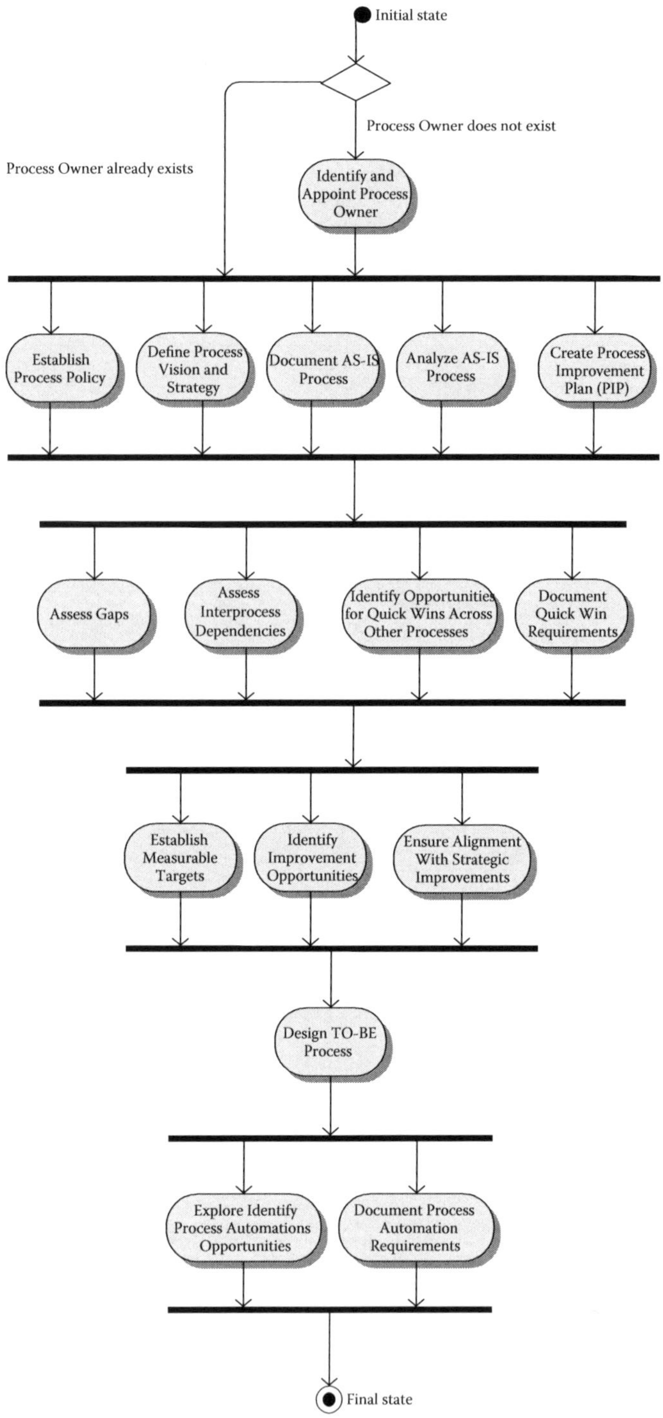

Figure 9.4 SMPI workflow.

of the process owner, process vision and strategy are defined and assessment of the current-state, or AS-IS process, is performed. Based on the process vision and the current-state, process policy is defined and an improvement plan, called a process improvement plan (PIP), is created. Gaps are assessed and improvement opportunities are identified. We know that almost every process depends on outputs created by other processes. If inefficiencies exist in other processes, these will definitely impact downstream processes. For example, if incident management or request fulfillment processes are not appropriately defined, they may result in routing requests that are not really change requests to the change management process, thereby congesting the process. Therefore, it is important to clearly identify interprocess dependencies and make appropriate improvements (also referred to as "quick wins" or "quick fixes") to maximize returns on process improvement investments. Based on the assessment of the current-state process and identification of opportunities, the future state, or TO-BE process, is defined. Finally, process automation opportunities are identified and requirements are documented in the business requirements document (BRD).

Plan Service Management Process Improvement

During this activity, a process improvement plan is created to achieve the agreed on process vision.

Create PIP

The PIP lays out the overall plan to achieve the desired improvements in the process. The process owner is accountable for creating the PIP and the project manager is responsible (see Figure 9.5). This plan drives the process improvement to be achieved.

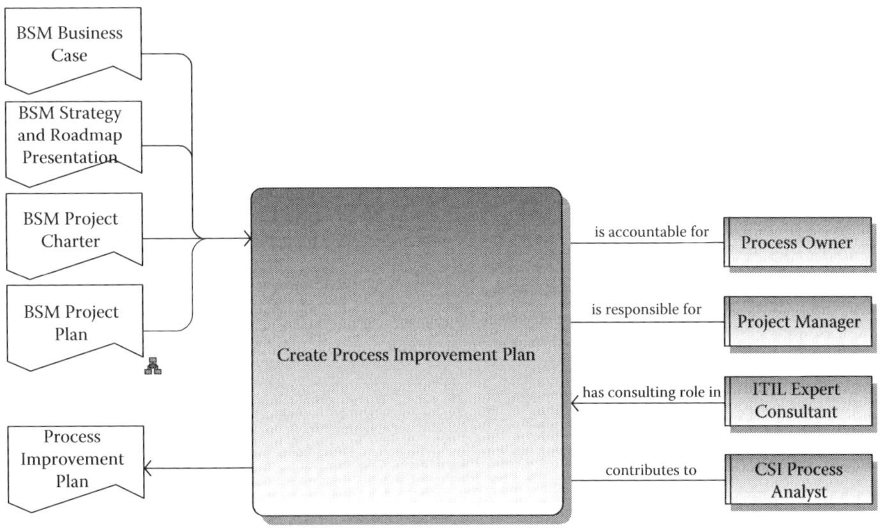

Figure 9.5 Create PIP.

Purpose

The purpose of this activity is to clearly define the plan to improve service management processes so that it supports the overall BSM vision and strategy.

Preconditions

- BSM appropriately and clearly envisioned
- BSM strategy laid out for the organization

Activity Overview

The process owner is accountable for ensuring that process improvements are clearly identified and continually improved. The project manager is responsible for creating the PIP to help realize the BSM vision.

Postcondition

PIP is created.

Identify and Appoint Process Owner

If processes are to be managed like other assets, then it is critical to identify and appoint a process owner for each process who will be responsible for effective management and ongoing continual improvements related to the process.

Establish Process Vision and Strategy

Processes also need their visions, and the strategies to achieve those visions, defined. Policies define the mandate from senior management regarding execution and compliance with those processes and aid in the institutionalization or establishment of those processes. Let us discuss these activities in detail.

Define Process Vision and Strategy

Once overall BSM strategy and approach have been defined, we start to define individual service management process strategy. One question should be considered: Why should these two—overall BSM strategy and individual process strategy—be aligned? Let us consider an example.

If the overall BSM strategy aims to enable businesses and customers to see performance of a given service on a real-time basis and to report any issues with the service online, then the respective process strategies need to address these strategic BSM objectives. In this case, these objectives will be addressed by appropriate service level management and incident management process designing and automations. From the IT perspective, it is critical for us to gain an in-depth understanding of our businesses' and customers' real needs and then to strategize on how we will address those needs through BSM. Let us discuss the core activities that should be performed to define process strategy and to reengineer processes.

When we have identified a given service management process for improvement, our first step is to define the process strategy. Process strategy may be addressed by the following questions:

- How does this process relate to the overall BSM strategy?
- At a high level, what does this process enable the IT organization to do for the business?
- What is the business case for investing in this process?
- How will this process look in five years? In other words, what does the target state look like?

Purpose

This activity is performed to create a process vision and strategy.

Precondition

BSM vision and strategy clearly understood by the process owner.

Activity Overview

Each process owner is responsible for defining process vision and strategy.

Postcondition

Vision and strategy for the service management process completely and clearly defined and agreed on (see Figure 9.6).

Establish Process Policy

Process policy is necessary to drive organizational behavior. Policies must be endorsed and approved by executive management or corporate board and compliance must be ensured. Control

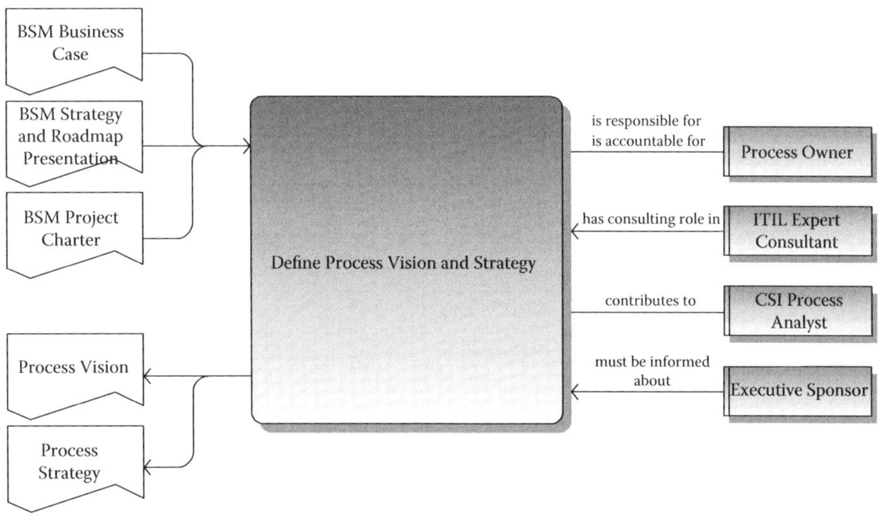

Figure 9.6 Define process vision and strategy.

Objectives for Information and Related Technology (COBIT) defines some of the control objectives for IT and provides a good starting point for defining process policies. Process policies must be driven by process vision and strategy.

Purpose

To establish clear and concise process policy to further drive organizational behavior.

Preconditions

- BSM strategy documented and agreed on
- Process vision and strategy defined
- Senior management sponsorship and support

Activity Overview

The process owner is responsible for defining, reviewing, and achieving senior management support and agreement on the process policy. Figure 9.7 illustrates this activity.

Postcondition

Process policy defined, reviewed, agreed on, and approved.

Establish Measurable Targets

Following the current-state, or AS-IS, process assessment and the identification of gaps and opportunities, we will define our targets and improvement objectives in a quantifiable manner. You must establish achievable objectives that can be measured. This will help plan the incremental improvements necessary to achieve the longer term objectives and be able to measure our achievements.

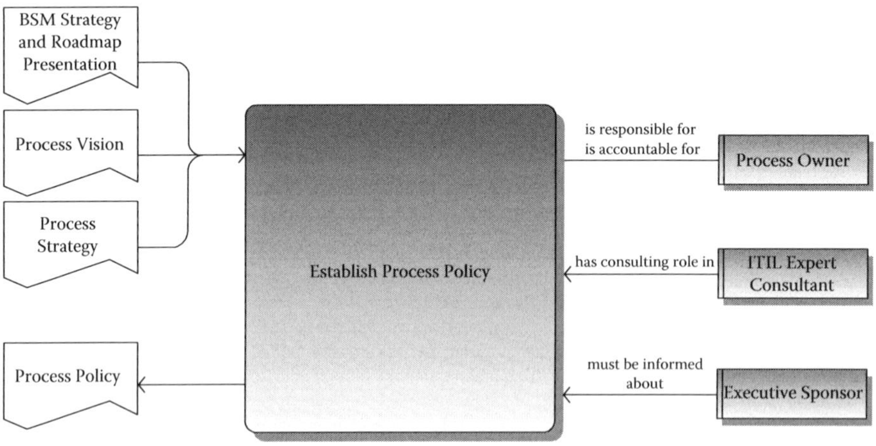

Figure 9.7 Establish process policy.

Preconditions

- BSM vision and strategy clearly established and agreed on
- Current-state, or AS-IS, process assessment completed and reviewed

Activity Overview

Current-state assessment helps us understand where we are at the present time and business and IT vision and strategy establish where we are heading as an organization (see Figure 9.8). With this information at hand, we will now establish such objectives that can be measured to demonstrate achievements.

Postcondition

Measurable targets are defined and agreed on.

Assess AS-IS Process Performance

Process performance should be assessed so that achievable targets can be defined.

Document AS-IS Process

To do process assessment, it is important that the current-state or AS-IS processes are appropriately defined. You will encounter situations where there are no existing processes defined and there are so many gaps in the process that there is need for a clean start (also known as process reengineering). Therefore, it is very important to use your own experience and professional judgment to decide the level of details that you should document as the AS-IS processes. If processes are already working and need incremental improvements (simplifying processes or removing redundant or

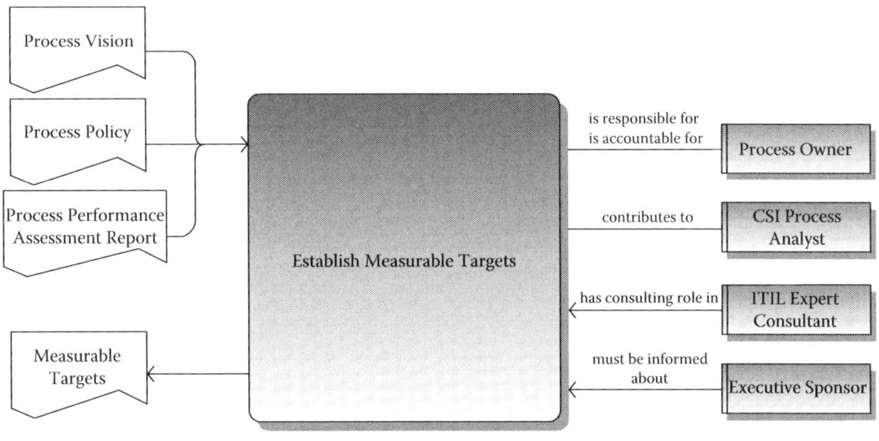

Figure 9.8 Establish measurable targets.

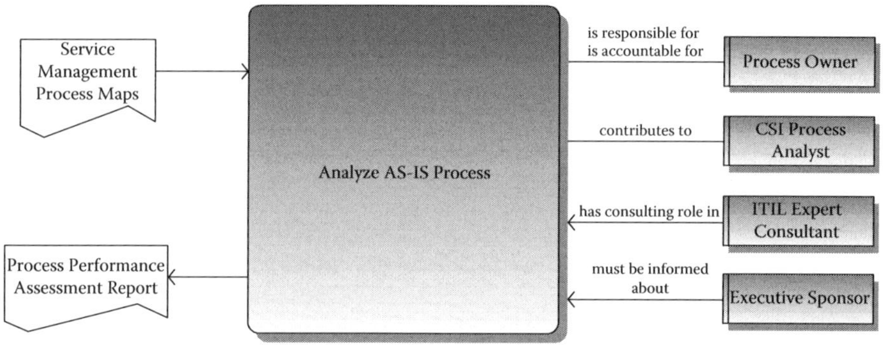

Figure 9.9 Analyze the AS-IS process.

nonvalue-added components, filling gaps, and removing disconnects), then it is important to have the AS-IS processes documented.

Analyze AS-IS Process

Once the AS-IS processes are documented, the process owner will analyze those processes and put together a process performance assessment report.

Precondition

The service management process is documented with all relevant details.

Activity Overview

Assessment of current-state or AS-IS process is performed during this activity and assessment report is created as a result. This is shown in Figure 9.9.

Postcondition

Process performance assessment report has been created.

Identify Gaps and Opportunities

Based on the process performance assessment, gaps are analyzed and process improvement opportunities are identified.

Assess Gaps

Gaps should be assessed for their impact on the realization of the overall BSM vision and should be prioritized accordingly. Always keep the 80/20 rule in mind (80% of problems can be fixed by solving 20%).

Identify Improvement Opportunities

Based on the process vision and the assessment of the process gaps, appropriate improvement opportunities are identified.

Design TO-BE Process and Document-Related Requirements

Based on the identified improvement opportunities, appropriate changes need to be made in the AS-IS processes. During this activity, such changes are designed and related requirements are documented.

Design TO-BE Process

Based on the assessment of the AS-IS process and driven by the process vision and strategy, TO-BE or target-state process is defined (see Figure 9.10).

Purpose

The purpose of this activity is to design the target-state or TO-BE process based on the challenges, gaps, and opportunities identified during the assessment of the current-state or AS-IS process performance.

Preconditions

- Business process management environment (notation, tools, etc.) established
- Process owner identified and trained in the business process management environment
- Process owner acquired practitioner-level training in the assigned process area

Activity Overview

A service management process guide is created as a result of this activity.

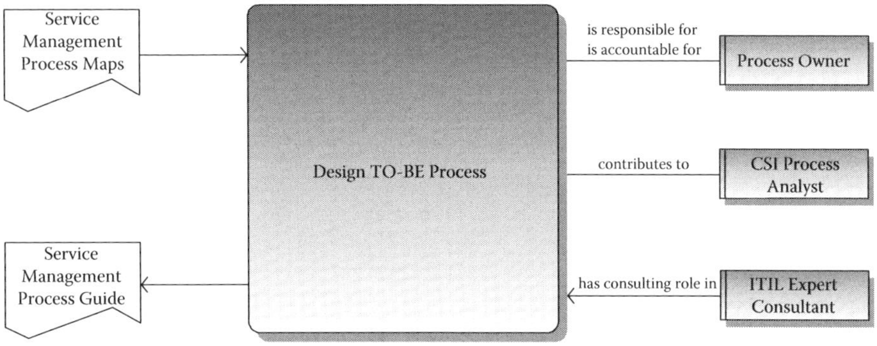

Figure 9.10 Design TO-BE process.

Activity Details

Input Artifacts	*Tasks Performed*	*Output Artifacts*	*Roles (RACI)*
ITIL v3 Literature	Build Initial Process Based on ITIL v3 Guidelines	Service Management Process Maps	A/R: Process Owner C: CSI Process Analyst
Service Management Process Maps	Design Target State or TO-BE Process	Service Management Process Maps	
	Create Process Input and Output Artifact Templates		
	Design Process Key Performance Indicators		
	Define or Refine Roles and Responsibilities		
	Compile Process Guide	Service Management Process Guide	

Postcondition

Comprehensive understanding of TO-BE process has been achieved.

> Practical Tip: It is important to appreciate that business services underpin business processes. Business Processes are composed of a structured set of activities that must be performed in order to contribute towards the realization of the value generated by the business process. Some activities within the business process may be better candidates for automation compared to others. For example, within a "Loan Origination Process", it may be a good idea to automate the application initiation activities. However, in order to decide which application is approved and/or denied, there may be a need for human intervention based on a set of pre-defined business rules.

Explore Process Automation Opportunities

Remember that not everything that can be automated should be automated. Following a comprehensive understanding of how the overall process should look, we will now need to analyze which components of that process should be automated. This activity contributes to the creation of a requirements document for the potential process automations.

Document Process Automation Requirements

Based on the process automation opportunities identified in the *explore process automation* activities, requirements are documented during this activity. This activity is shown in Figure 9.11.

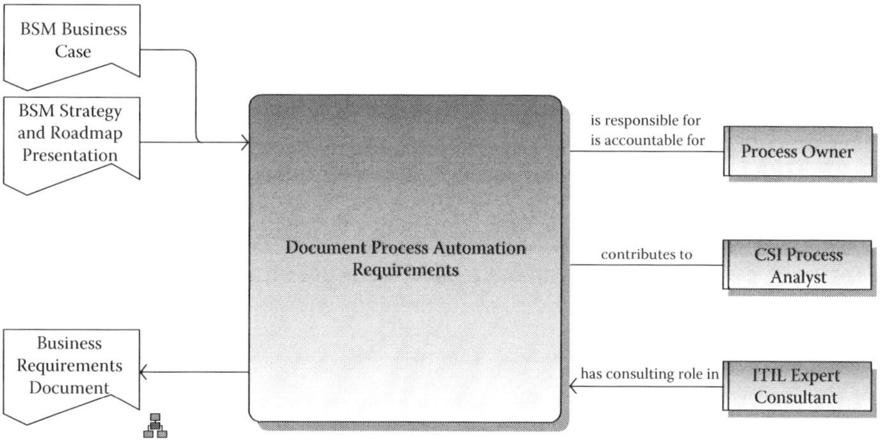

Figure 9.11 Document process automation requirements.

Purpose

The purpose of this activity is to identify process components that can and should be automated and to document related requirements.

Precondition

There should be a clear understanding of automation opportunities.

Activity Overview

As a result of this activity, a BRD is created.

Activity Details

Input Artifacts	*Tasks Performed*	*Output Artifacts*	*Roles (RACI)*
BSM Business Case BSM Strategy and Roadmap Presentation Service Management Process Guide	Identify Actors and Use Cases	BRD (Actors and Use Cases)	A/R: Process Owner C: CSI Process Analyst C: ITIL Expert Consultant
BRD (Actors and Use Cases)	Detail Use Cases and Build Use-Case Model	BRD (Actors and Use Cases detailed and Use-Case Model developed)	

Achieve Quick Wins or Quick Fixes

Almost all ITIL v3 and service management processes depend on others to provide mandatory inputs so that those inputs can be processed and desired outputs produced. If you try to mature service asset and configuration management in isolation, you may be able to achieve some level of process maturity but not without limitations. Two challenges that you will likely face include:

- In the absence of a service catalog, you will focus your efforts on trying to improve everything in the configuration management database (CMDB) and that is going to result in much wasted effort and many unwise improvement investments.
- In the absence of a working change management process, your CMDB will become outdated as soon as it goes into production because of uncontrolled changes to the IT infrastructure.

To maximize returns on process improvement investments, you should identify and make quick improvements across other processes. In doing so, it is critical to ensure that these improvement opportunities are identified and implemented so that these do not conflict with the strategic direction. For example, in the case of CMDB, the quick improvement that you must make in the change management process is to ensure that all change information is communicated to the configuration manager so that those changes are reflected in the CMDB.

Therefore, achieving quick wins is a critical part of service and service management process improvement efforts. However, these need to be carefully planned and executed to ensure that they align with the larger improvement effort. This will ensure that improvements are not "throw-away" improvements and are leveraged effectively. As shown in Figure 9.12, at any given point in time throughout the life cycle (with likely exceptions in the early and later stages of the life cycle), the following five categories of improvements take place:

- Quick wins/quick fixes
- Business service improvements
- Service management process improvements
- Continual service improvements
- Continual service management process improvements

It is important to note that as you perform planned service and service management process improvements, you will need to identify quick wins that may be across numerous service management processes and must be achieved in order to maximize return on improvement investments. These quick wins can continue to be implemented in support of other planned service as well as service management process improvements. Note here that these quick wins must always support other planned improvements. This will also enable us to continue to demonstrate incremental business value that is at the core of ensuring continual senior management sponsorship. Proper governance is going to be crucial in identifying, assessing and prioritizing the quick wins that will generate most value by maximizing return on improvement investments and in ensuring that only those quick wins are implemented that allow us to move the overall organizational maturity in the desired direction.

Quick wins and quick fixes are normally implemented for services and service management processes that, if not improved, can undermine the overall service and service management process improvements planned for that given phase or iteration. Another way to look at these

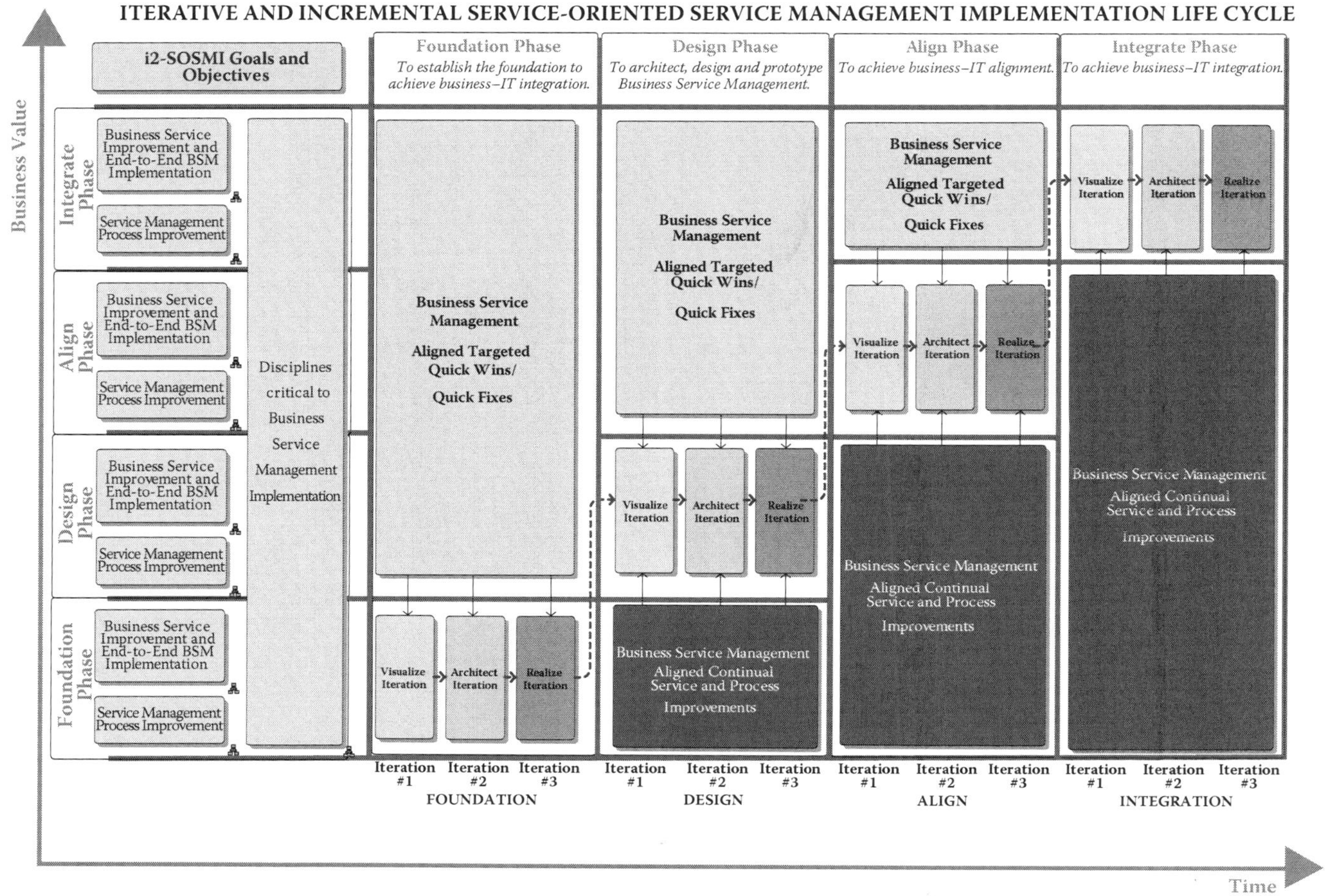

Figure 9.12 The i2-SOSMI life cycle.

improvements is that these quick wins and quick fixes further enhance the business value delivered as a result of service and service management process improvement efforts. Quick wins and quick fixes may also be aligned with remediating pain points.

Let us now discuss some of the key activities that should be carried out to achieve the desired quick wins.

Assess Interprocess Dependencies

Based on the process details captured in the service management process guide, assessment is performed on dependencies across other process management processes. Based on these dependencies, potential gaps are identified and analyzed.

Identify Opportunities for Quick Wins across Other Processes

During this activity, opportunities for quick wins and quick fixes across all other related processes are identified.

Ensure Alignment with Strategic Improvements

As discussed earlier, to optimize the returns achieved as a result of quick wins and quick fixes, it is critical to ensure that these are aligned with strategic improvements.

Document Quick Win Requirements

During this activity, all requirements that should be met to achieve the identified quick wins are documented. It is recommended that these quick wins–related requirements are documented as part of the BRD so that they can be managed effectively.

Primary Roles and Responsibilities

The key role within this discipline is process owner.

The process owner (see Figure 9.13) is the primary role within this discipline and has the following responsibilities:

- Owns the overall process from an end-to-end process management perspective
- Responsible for continual process measurements and improvements

Key Artifacts

The following are key artifacts related to service management process improvement. They are also illustrated in Figure 9.14.

Figure 9.13 Process owner.

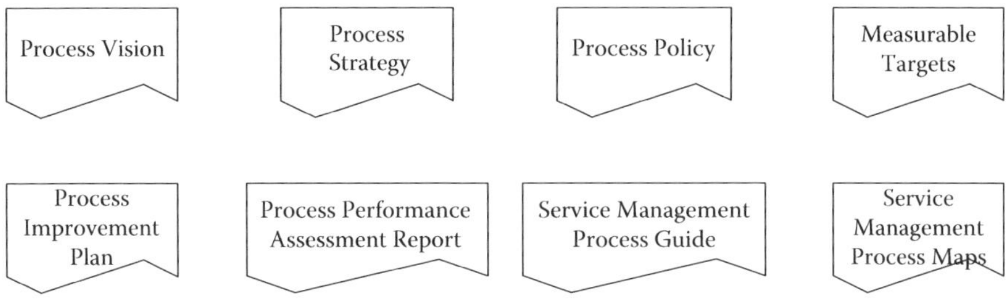

Figure 9.14 Service management process improvement key artifacts.

Process Vision

This artifact provides the process vision. This vision must lay out a clear picture of how the process is going to look longer term. It is important to document this vision in terms of the capabilities that need to be delivered, for example, all customers will be able to request new services through an online service portal.

Process Strategy

This document lays out the roadmap and strategy for how the stated and agreed on vision will be realized.

Process Policy

Process policy is one of the control mechanisms and plays an important role in shaping desired organizational behavior. Each policy statement must be well planned to ensure that compliance can be objectively measured.

Measurable Targets

Measurable targets must be established to objectively measure progress. Key performance indicators (KPIs) aim to provide performance in terms of achievement of the agreed on targets. KPIs must be grouped into efficiency measurements and compliance measurements. Compliance measurements are performed to measure compliance with control objectives.

Process Improvement Plan

PIP contains a detailed plan on how the agreed improvements will be achieved. It should contain schedule, cost, and other related plans as appropriate.

Process Performance Assessment Report

This report highlights the results of process assessment and allows identification of gaps and prioritization of opportunities.

Key Concepts

In this section, we will discuss the key concepts related to SMPI.

Process Maturity

Service management process maturity is measured using the Capability Maturity Model Integration (CMMI) model. CMMI defines five different levels of process maturity as shown in Figure 9.15. When performing process assessment, it considers the following aspects:

- Vision and steering
- Process
- People
- Technology
- Culture

Service Management Process Development Boot Camp

Process analysis, documentation, and socialization require dedicated workshop-style efforts. Figure 9.16 shows a typical boot camp workshop format.

Prerequisites

- Process development and management environment established
- Process owners trained in their processes and in process development techniques
- ITIL v3–compliant baseline processes already developed and related details included

Steps

Build Individual Processes

- Key objective: to achieve deeper understanding of particular business needs and build tailored and customized versions of service management processes based on guidelines provided by ITIL v3 literature

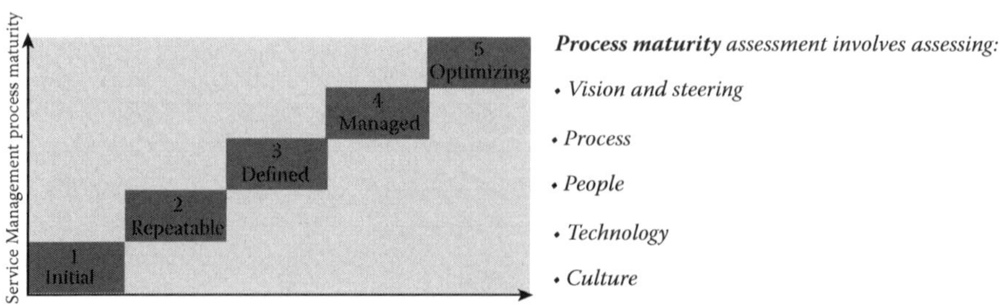

Figure 9.15 Process maturity.

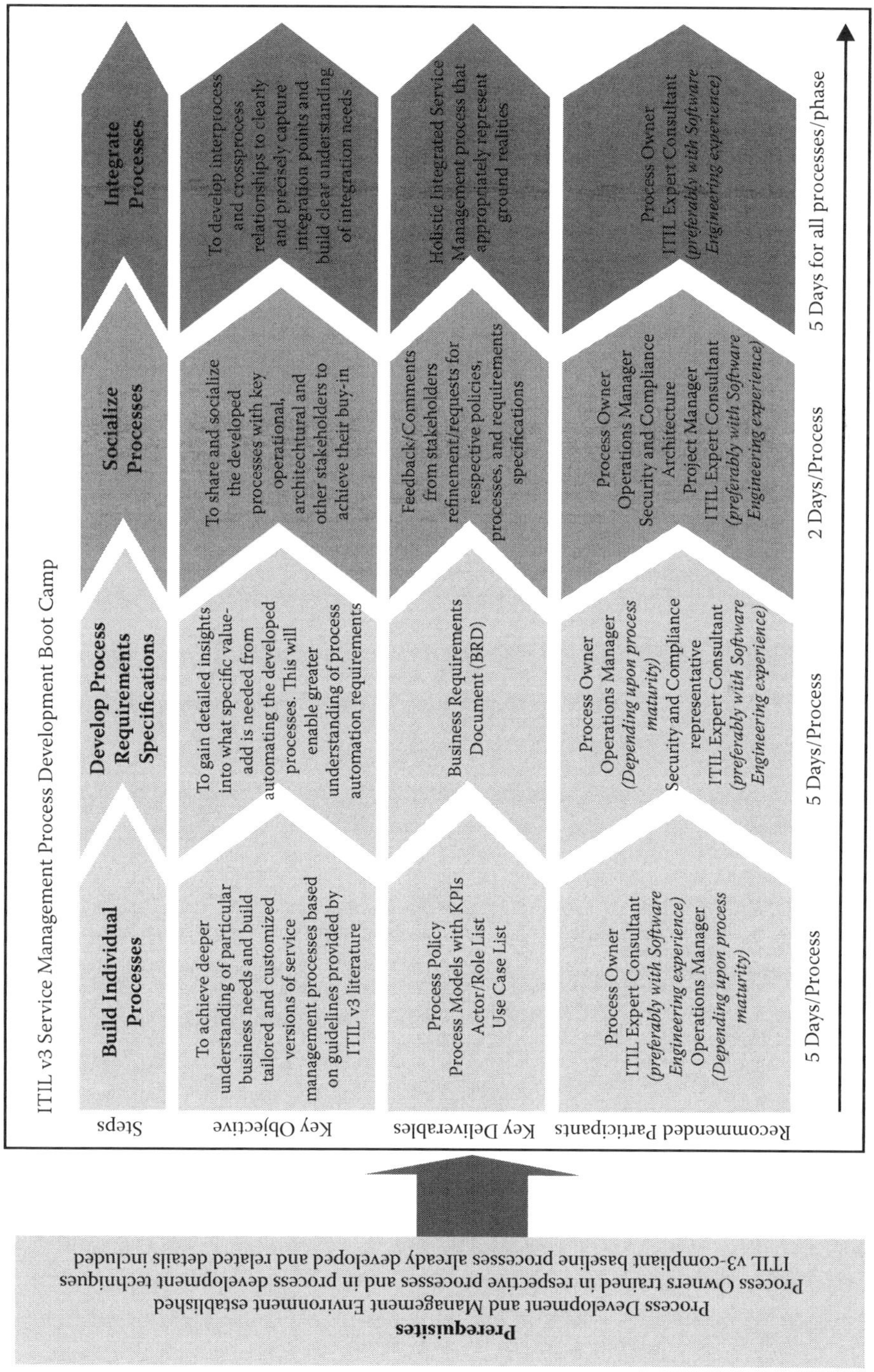

Figure 9.16 Service management process development boot camp.

- Key deliverables
  - Process policy
  - Process models (service management process guide) with KPIs
  - Actor and role list
  - Use case list
- Recommended participants
  - Process owner
  - ITIL expert consultant (preferably with software engineering experience)
  - Operations manager (depending on process maturity)

Develop Process Requirements Specification

- Key objective: to gain detailed insights into what specific value-add is needed from automating the developed processes (this will enable greater understanding of process automation requirements)
- Key deliverable: BRD
- Recommended participants
  - Process owner
  - Operations manager (depending on process maturity)
  - Security and compliance representative
  - ITIL expert consultant (preferably with software engineering experience)

Socialize Processes

- Key objective: to share and socialize the developed processes with key operational, architectural, and other stakeholders to achieve their buy-in
- Key deliverables
  - Feedback and comments from stakeholders
  - Refinements or refinement requests for respective policies, processes, and requirements specifications (BRD)
- Recommended participants
  - Process owner
  - Operations manager
  - Security and compliance representative
  - Architecture representative
  - Project manager
  - ITIL expert consultant (preferably with software engineering experience)

Integrate Processes

- Key objective: to develop interprocess and crossprocess relationships to clearly and precisely capture integration points and build clear understanding of integration needs
- Key deliverables: service management process guide (holistic, integrated service management process that appropriately represents ground realities)
- Recommended participants
  - Process owner
  - ITIL expert consultant (preferably with software engineering experience)

Summary

One of the most critical and time-consuming activities that is performed in implementing BSM is actually assessing and improving the service management processes. Process institutionalization will require organizational transformations to happen in support of the improved service management processes. In this chapter, we discussed the key activities that must be performed to improve service management processes.

Reference

Shuja, A., and J. Krebs. 2008. *Rational Unified Process: Reference and Certification Guide.* New York: IBM Press.

Chapter 10

Discipline: Business Service Management Technology Architecture and Integration

Introduction

Technology is a crucial component of successful implementation of BSM. This discipline's aim is to enable us to visualize, strategize, architect, and integrate the right technological capabilities that are required to achieve the envisioned level of business–IT integration (see Figure 10.1).

Purpose

The main purpose of the BSM technology architecture and integration discipline is to deliver a well-architected and integrated BSM solution so that the desired technological capabilities are cost-effectively delivered and that are necessary to achieve the envisioned business–IT integration.

Objectives

The key objectives of BSM technology architecture and integration disciplines are as follows:

- To clearly define the BSM technology strategy that is aligned with business strategy
- To maximize reuse of existing assets
- To ensure that all nonfunctional and functional requirements are cost-effectively and efficiently met
- To architect, design, and prototype the BSM solution
- To ensure that architected solutions get implemented

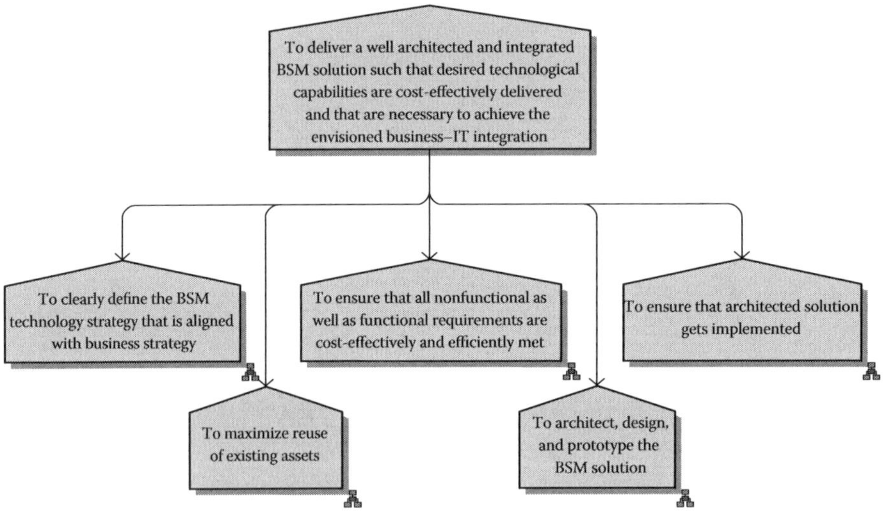

Figure 10.1 BSM technology architecture and integration objectives.

Work Breakdown Structure

The BSM technology architecture and integration work breakdown structure is shown in Figure 10.2.

Workflow

Figure 10.3 shows the BSM technology architecture and integration workflow. The first activity that must be performed before we start architecting the solution is to clearly define the BSM technology strategy and ensure that it is aligned with the overall business strategy, BSM strategy, and IT strategy. After that, the existing architectures (enterprise architecture) are reviewed, actual BSM requirements are analyzed, automation requirements are assessed, and a high-level BSM architecture roadmap is created. This roadmap must show how the overall BSM solution is going to be architected, implemented, and delivered. After the roadmap is established, different BSM solution components are architected, designed, and delivered based on the overall BSM project plan. The BSM architecture and roadmap must align with the overall BSM Project Plan.

If risks are high or if new components or technologies are introduced, proof-of-concept (PoC) should be implemented to assess the risks and find mitigation measures.

Define BSM Technology Strategy and Architecture

As we did for processes, we need to define the overall technology strategy for BSM. This technology strategy may focus on two aspects: the actual service delivery and the underlying service management processes. For example, to enable cost-effective reusability of appropriate services, we may decide that we should leverage service-oriented architecture (SOA). To manage service management processes effectively, we will standardize our platforms on a particular enterprise solution

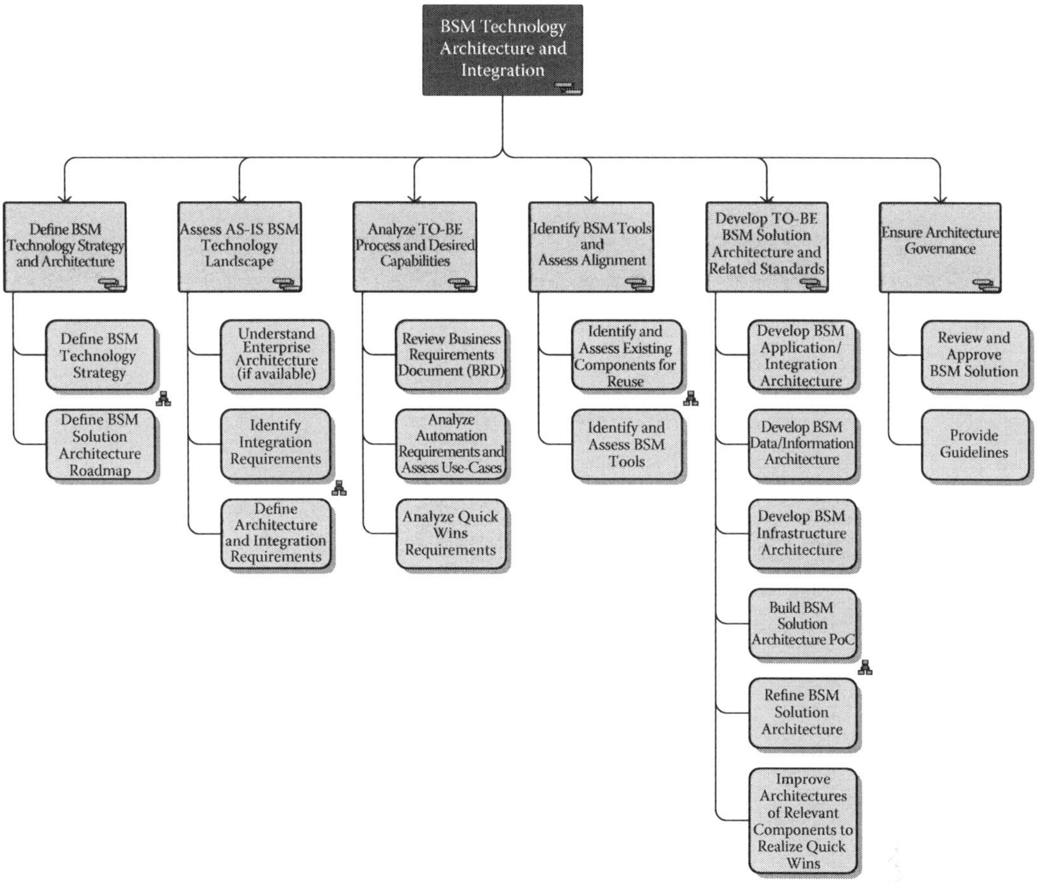

Figure 10.2 BSM technology architecture and integration work breakdown structure.

provided by the specific vendor. These and other related visions and technology strategies must be established during the activities discussed in this section.

Define BSM Technology Strategy

When implementing BSM, we need to consider technologies at the following levels:

- At the service level: How do we enable the improvement, refinement, and development of new or enhanced services in the most effective and efficient manner?
- At the service management process level: How do we ensure that the various service management processes are appropriately automated so that the desired efficiency outcomes are achieved?

BSM strategy should consider both of these aspects.

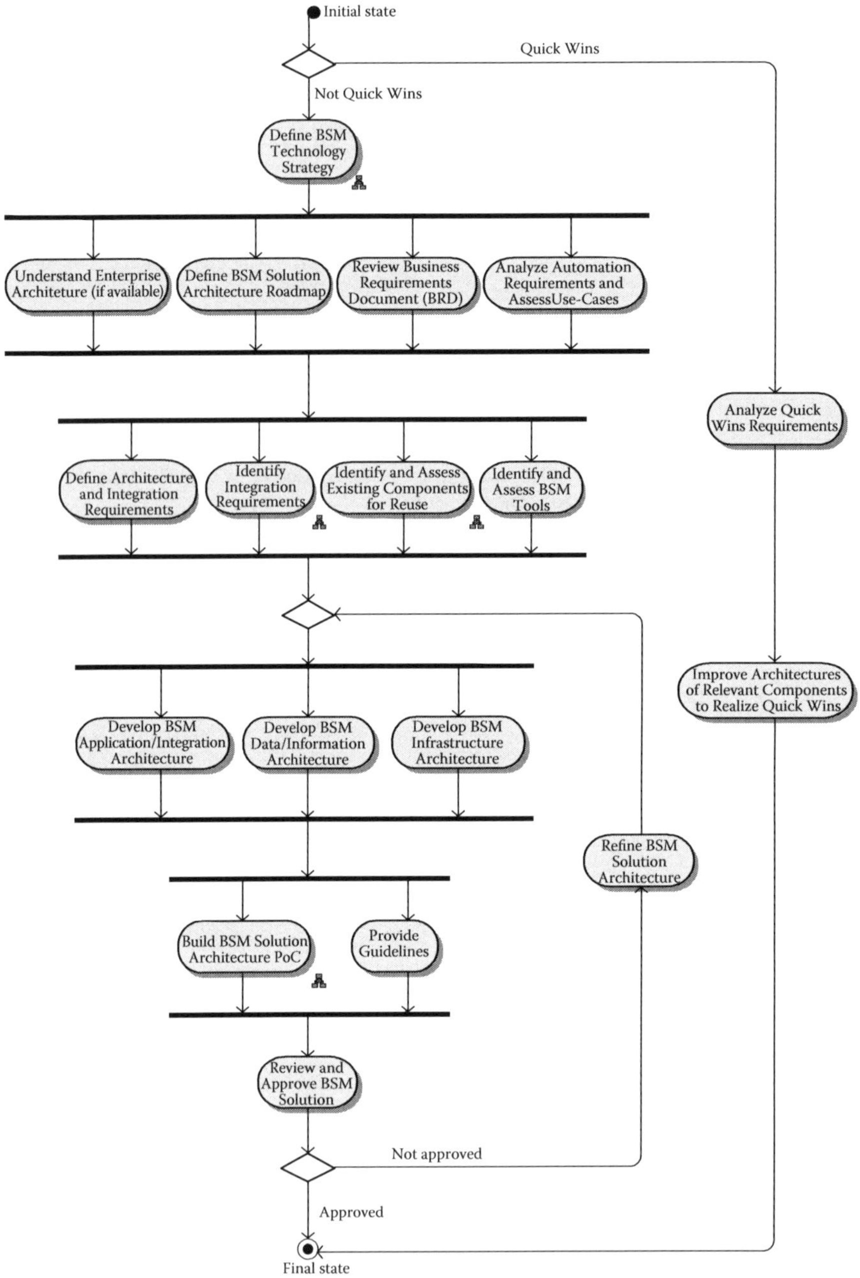

Figure 10.3 BSM technology architecture and integration workflow.

Purpose

The purpose of this activity is to establish a clear BSM technology strategy.

Preconditions

BSM business case, strategy, and roadmap are defined and agreed on.

Activity Overview

The BSM technology architect is responsible for assessing the business and technology needs and for defining the BSM technology strategy (see Figure 10.4).

Define the BSM Solution Architecture Roadmap

The BSM solution architecture roadmap provides a high-level milestone plan to implement the BSM solution. It may be combined with the overall project roadmap.

Assess the AS-IS BSM Technology Landscape

The AS-IS technology landscape is assessed to better understand the impact of implementing a BSM solution on the IT infrastructure and to identify any components that can potentially be reused. Let us discuss the activities in detail.

Understand Enterprise Architecture (If Applicable)

If an enterprise architecture exists, then we will need to gain a thorough understanding of that architecture to ensure that we align our BSM technology architecture with the overall architecture to minimize any potential conflicts. Enterprise architecture and related topics are further discussed in Chapter 17.

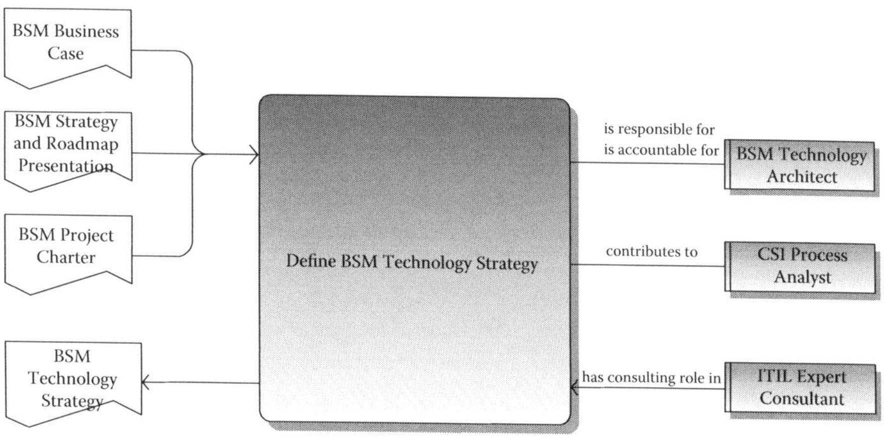

Figure 10.4 Define BSM technology strategy.

Input Artifacts	*Tasks*	*Output Artifacts*	*Roles (RACI)*
Business Requirements Document (BRD) BSM Solution Architecture Document (for the current solution, if available)	Perform Architectural Analysis	BSM Architecture Assessment Report	BSM Technology Architect

Identify Integration Requirements

It is rare to find an environment where you will not be required to integrate with existing legacy systems. To ensure the right level of thinking at the system integration level, we need to understand and identify integration requirements.

Purpose

The purpose of this activity is to clearly identify and understand integration requirements for the BSM solution with other existing (upstream systems) or potential future (downstream systems) systems.

Preconditions

- Business requirements clearly documented
- Service management processes appropriately documented with all relevant details

Activity Overview

These integration requirements are identified and documented in the BSM solution architecture document. Figure 10.5 illustrates this process. Note that this architecture document goes through incremental elaborations and that more details are added as required.

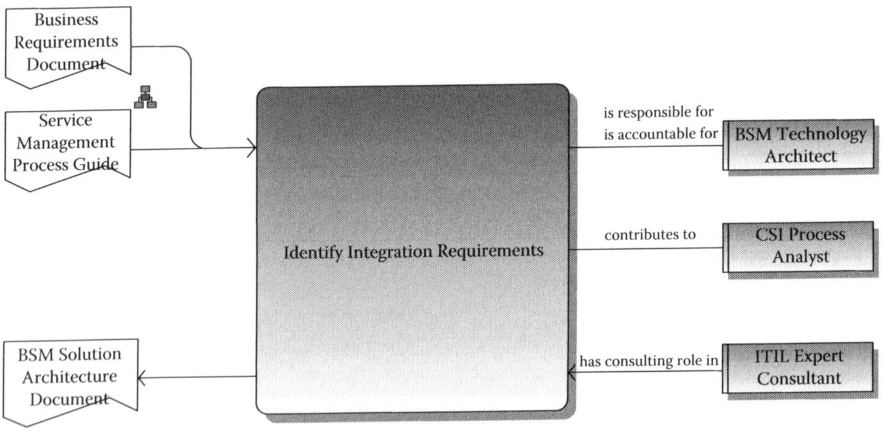

Figure 10.5 Identify integration requirements.

Postcondition

Integration requirements are clearly identified and documented.

Define Architecture and Integration Requirements

Integration requirements are documented during this activity. Note that these integration requirements are defined at the high-level architecture.

Analyze TO-BE Process and Desired Capabilities

During this activity, the TO-BE processes are analyzed and the capabilities (or use-cases) to be delivered by the tool are identified. This is normally performed when the BRD is completed.

Review Business Requirements Document

The BRD is reviewed to identify and assess the use-cases that need to be realized.

Analyze Automation Requirements and Assess Use-Cases

It is a software development good practice to keep the process design and requirements separate from technology design and development. The main rationale behind this thinking is to not let the true requirements get impacted by potential technological limitation or challenges. Once automation requirements are documented in the BRD, they are now assessed from a technology and capabilities development perspective. Use-cases play a critical role during this assessment. Use-cases and use-case models are used to assess the capabilities required from the technological solution.

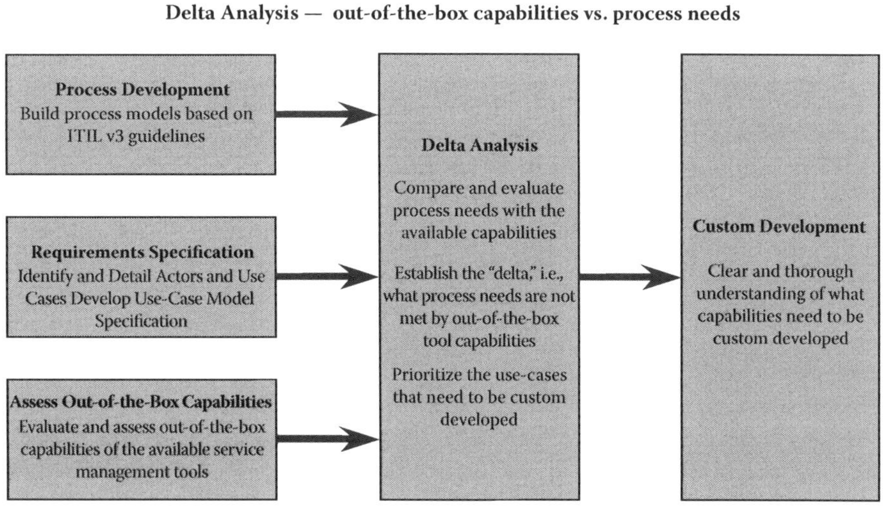

Figure 10.6 Identify and assess existing components for reuse.

Identify BSM Tools and Assess Alignment

When it comes to automating the service management processes, you will find many different tools in the marketplace. However, it is critical to select the right tool for the right process and for the right organization.

The blunder that many companies make is to first find the tool before understanding the problem or even the process. That is the biggest mistake that you can commit during any project and specifically during the BSM implementation project or any project that has an enterprise-wide impact. In enterprise projects, there are many other risks, such as organizational change–related risks, that need to be managed. What you do not want is to further expand those risks by not managing the technology implementation correctly and by not making the correct platform or solution choices.

Once you have gained a reasonable understanding of the process and have identified and detailed key use-cases, it will then be time for you to identify any existing or new tools that can be used to fulfill those requirements. The capabilities offered by off-the-shelf tools need to be objectively assessed and informed decisions should be made as to what are the best options for technology platforms and solutions.

Identify and Assess Existing Components for Reuse

During this activity, BSM technology architect identifies and assesses existing components that may be used to deliver the desired capabilities (see Figure 10.6).

Identify and Assess BSM Tools

Based on the capabilities needed to automate the service management process(es), a delta analysis (see Figure 10.7) is performed and off-the-shelf BSM tools are assessed.

Develop TO-BE BSM Solution Architecture and Related Standards

Based on the BSM technology strategy, we will now define the architecture that will enable us to achieve the stated strategic goals. During this activity, we will build all layers of BSM solution

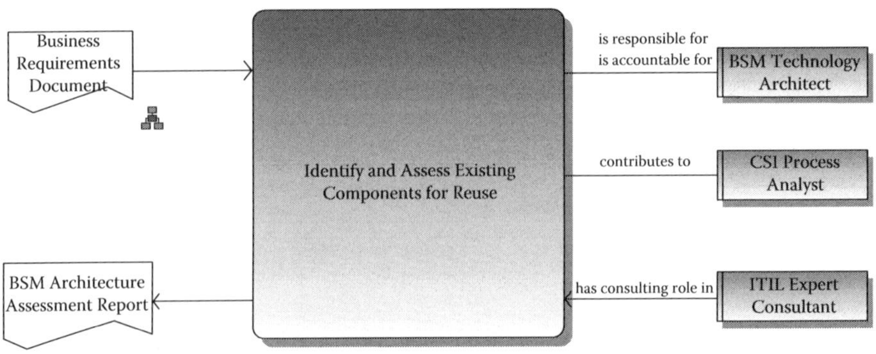

Figure 10.7 Delta analysis.

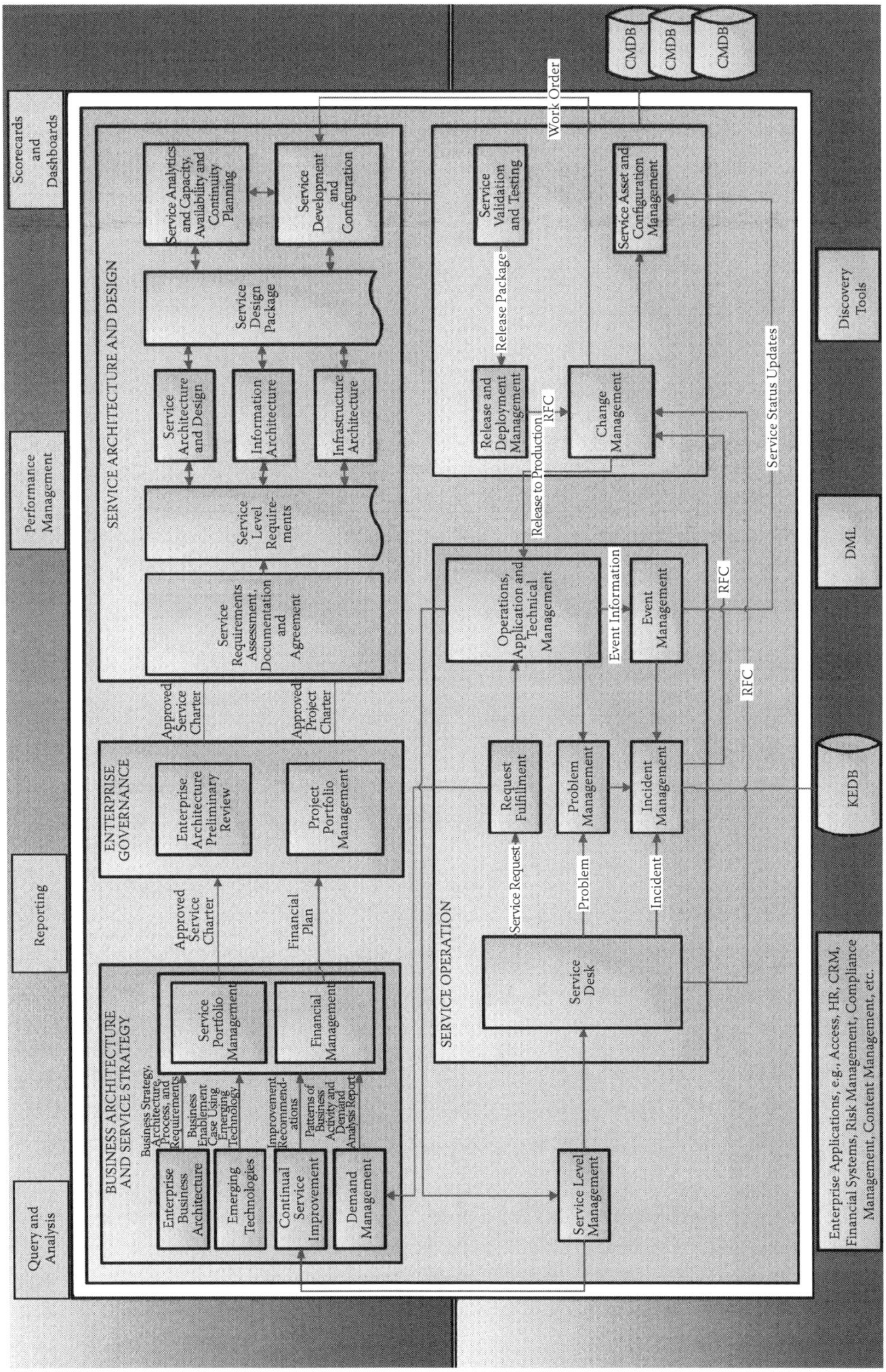

Figure 10.8 BSM conceptual solution architecture.

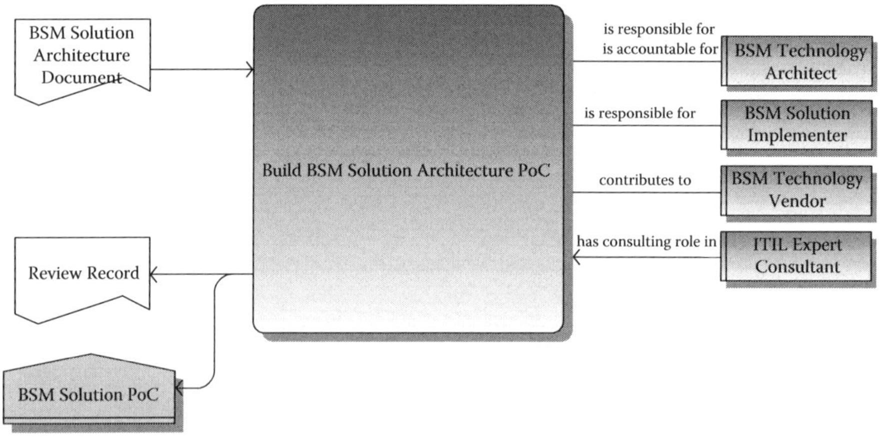

Figure 10.9 Build BSM solution architecture PoC.

architecture. BSM conceptual architecture is shown in Figure 10.8. You will notice that it integrates the enterprise architecture with ITIL v3 BSM. We will discuss this in greater detail in Chapter 17.

Develop BSM Application and Integration Architecture

Application and integration architecture is developed during this activity. Detailed discussions of different architectural domains and layers are provided in Chapter 17.

Develop BSM Data and Information Architecture

Data and information architecture is developed during this activity.

Develop BSM Infrastructure Architecture

Infrastructure architecture is developed during this activity.

Build BSM Solution Architecture PoC

Based on technology architectures, PoC may need to be developed (see Figure 10.9).

A detailed list of activities required to complete this activity is as follows:

Figure 10.10 BSM technology architecture and integration primary roles.

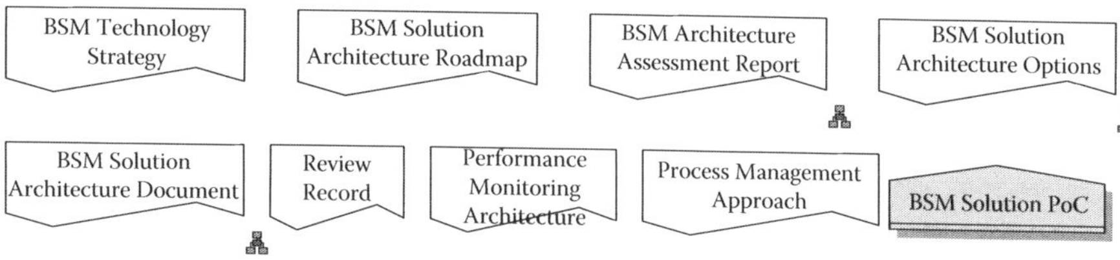

Figure 10.11 BSM technology architecture and integration key artifacts.

Input Artifacts	*Tasks*	*Output Artifacts*	*Roles (RACI)*
BSM Solution Architecture Document	Assess Viability of PoC	Review Record	A/R: BSM Technology Architect C: ITIL Expert Consultant C: Executive Sponsor
BSM Solution Architecture Document	Construct Architectural Proof-of-Concept	BSM Solution PoC	A/R: BSM Technology Architect

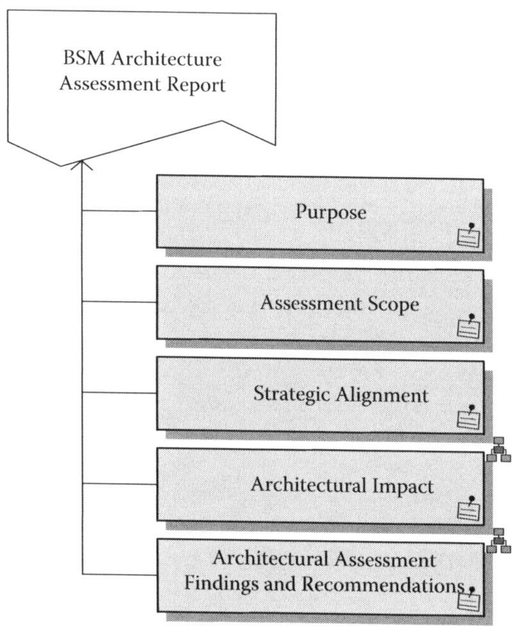

Figure 10.12 BSM architecture assessment report.

Refine BSM Solution Architecture

As we progress through the phases of the BSM implementation project, we must fine-tune the BSM architecture based on our detailed understanding of the organizational needs. However, note that the overall architecture is baselined by the time the project is 50% complete. We discussed the life cycle aspects of the project in Chapter 6.

Primary Roles and Responsibilities

Primary roles are as follows:

- BSM technology architect
- BSM technology vendor

Theses roles are shown in Figure 10.10.

BSM Technology Architect

The BSM technology architect is responsible for the following:

- Defining the BSM technology strategy
- Identifying and assessing existing components and assets for potential reuse
- Identifying integration requirements
- Establishing process management and performance monitoring architecture
- Building architectural recommendations to improve or optimize service management processes

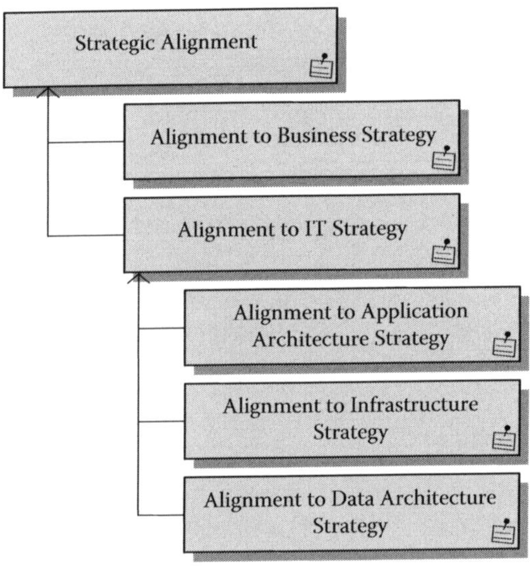

Figure 10.13 Strategic alignment.

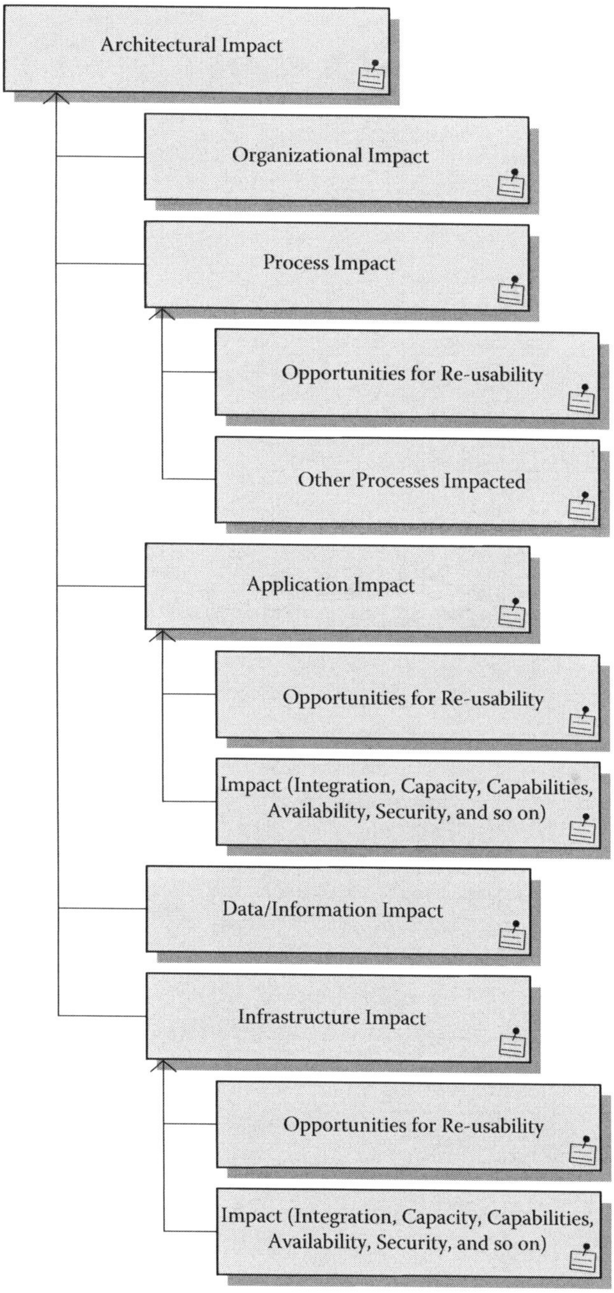

Figure 10.14 Architectural impact.

BSM Technology Vendor

There are many available off-the-shelf solutions that can support BSM. This role applies to any vendor that provides BSM solutions.

Key Artifacts

Key artifacts within the BSM technology architecture and integration discipline are given in this section. The information is also presented in Figure 10.11.

BSM Technology Strategy

BSM technology strategy artifacts detail the longer vision for the technology required to support an organization's BSM vision and objectives.

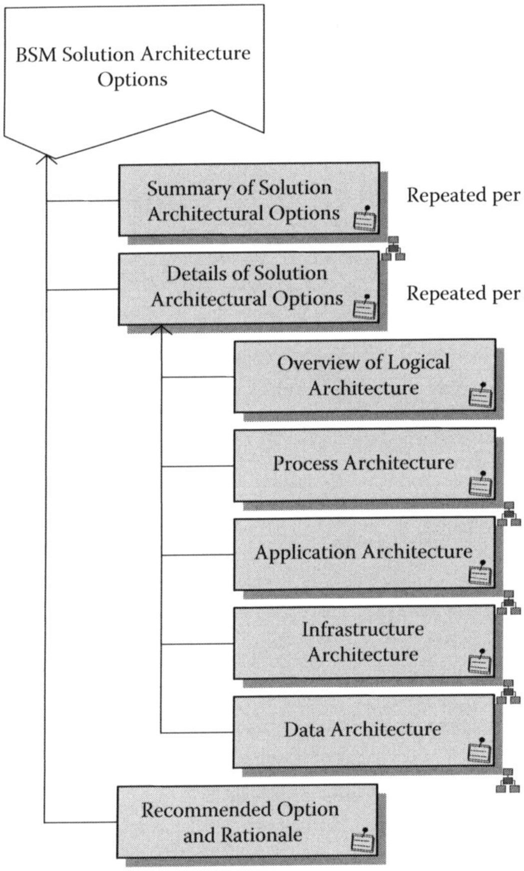

Figure 10.15 BSM solution architecture options.

BSM Solution Architecture Roadmap

This artifact lays out the roadmap with key milestones. It must support the overall BSM technology strategy.

BSM Architecture Assessment Report

The BSM architecture assessment report presents the analysis of the impact of introducing the potential BSM solution into the IT landscape of the organization (see Figure 10.12). Strategic alignment and architectural impact are key sections of this report.

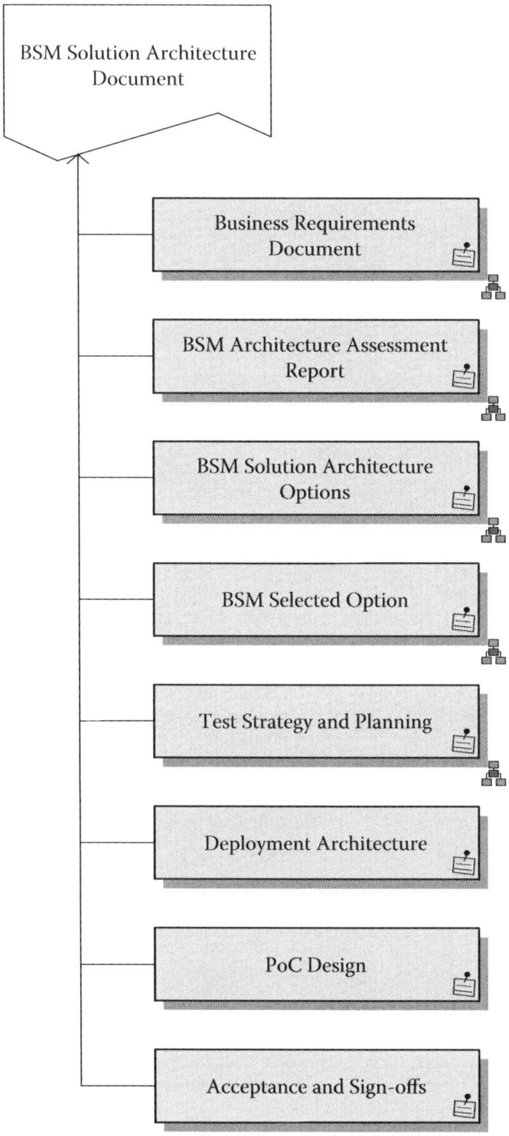

Figure 10.16 BSM solution architecture document.

Strategic alignment assesses the alignment with the overall business strategy as well as with the IT strategy. This is illustrated in Figure 10.13.

Architecting an overall solution that supports an organization's BSM objectives will require thoughtful analysis and integration with other upstream (those that already exist in the environment) as well as downstream (those that will probably be introduced in future) solutions. Architectural impact should provide insights into what it really means to introduce the BSM solution. This impact assessment should include organizational, process, application, data, and infrastructure impact at the very least. An example is given in Figure 10.14.

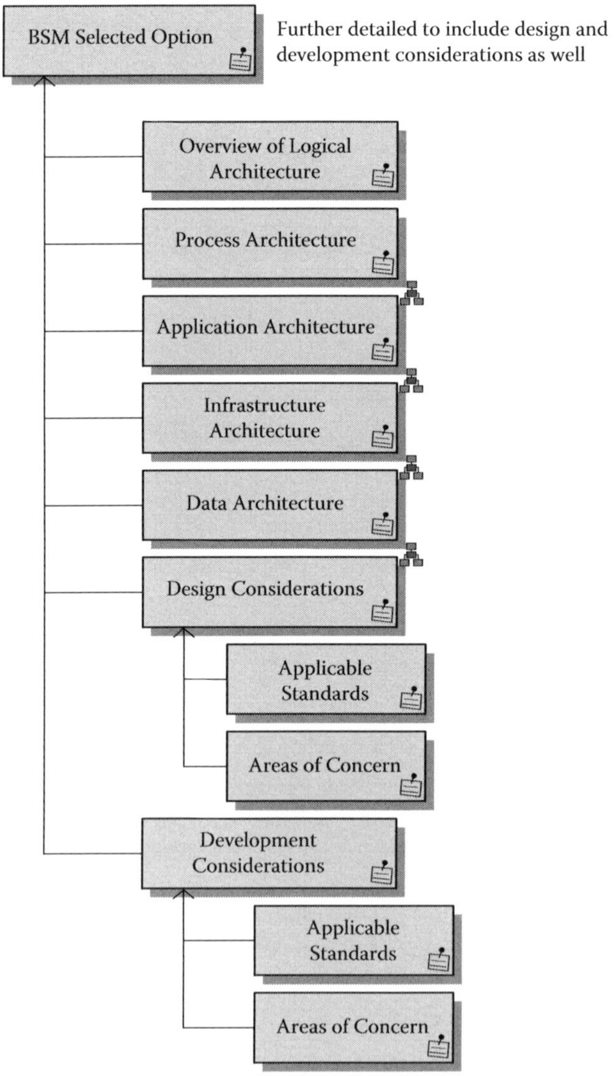

Figure 10.17 Elaboration of selected BSM solution options.

BSM Solution Architecture Options

Based on the requirements for the BSM solution and the potential impact of introducing an off-the-shelf or custom solution into the environment, multiple architectural options should be provided (Figure 10.15).

Each respective architectural domain (process, application, data, and infrastructure) will be discussed in detail later in this book (Chapter 17).

BSM Solution Architecture Document

The BSM solution architecture document must combine various artifacts and present an overall architecture of the BSM solution (see Figure 10.16).

For the option that is selected, the architectures are further elaborated. This elaboration includes design considerations and development considerations (see Figure 10.17).

Review Record

This artifact captures the review results of a given artifact or deliverable.

Summary

BSM implementation involves integrating processes as well as the underlying tools. Architecture and integration play a key role in ensuring that appropriate integrations are identified, planned, and implemented. In this chapter, we have discussed the key activities that should be performed to deliver BSM solution architecture and executable PoC.

Reference

Shuja, A., and J. Krebs. 2008. *Rational Unified Process: Reference and Certification Guide.* New York: IBM Press.

Chapter 11

Discipline: Business Service Management Technology Delivery

Introduction

Technology is a crucial component of successful implementation of BSM. The aim of this discipline is to allow us to visualize, strategize, architect, design, and implement the right technological capabilities required to achieve the envisioned level of business–IT integration.

Purpose

The main purpose of BSM technology delivery discipline is to deliver the architected solution to achieve the envisioned business–IT integration. This is also represented in Figure 11.1.

Work Breakdown Structure

The BSM technology development work breakdown structure is shown in Figure 11.2.

BSM Technology Delivery Workflow

Technology delivery can deliver complete end-to-end BSM solutions and achieve some quick wins by minor technology modifications. If we are aiming to deliver a key component of the BSM technology, we will need to develop the detailed design; build, integrate, and test the component; and then deploy the BSM solution. In case it is a quick win, minor refinements are made and a new release is deployed. This is illustrated in Figure 11.3.

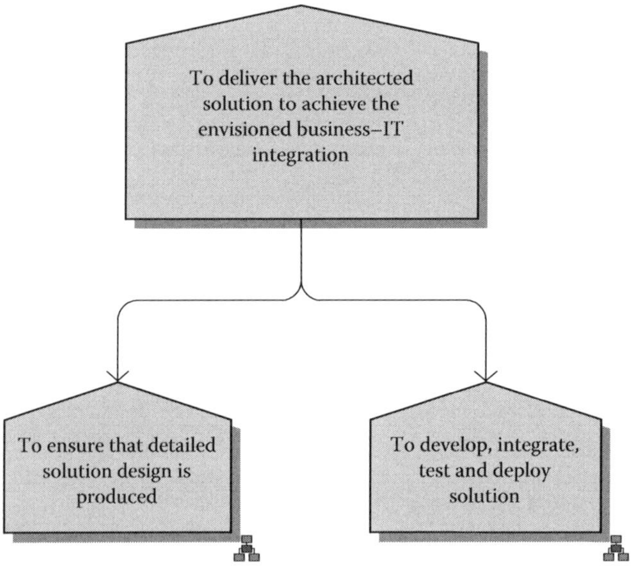

Figure 11.1 BSM technology delivery objectives.

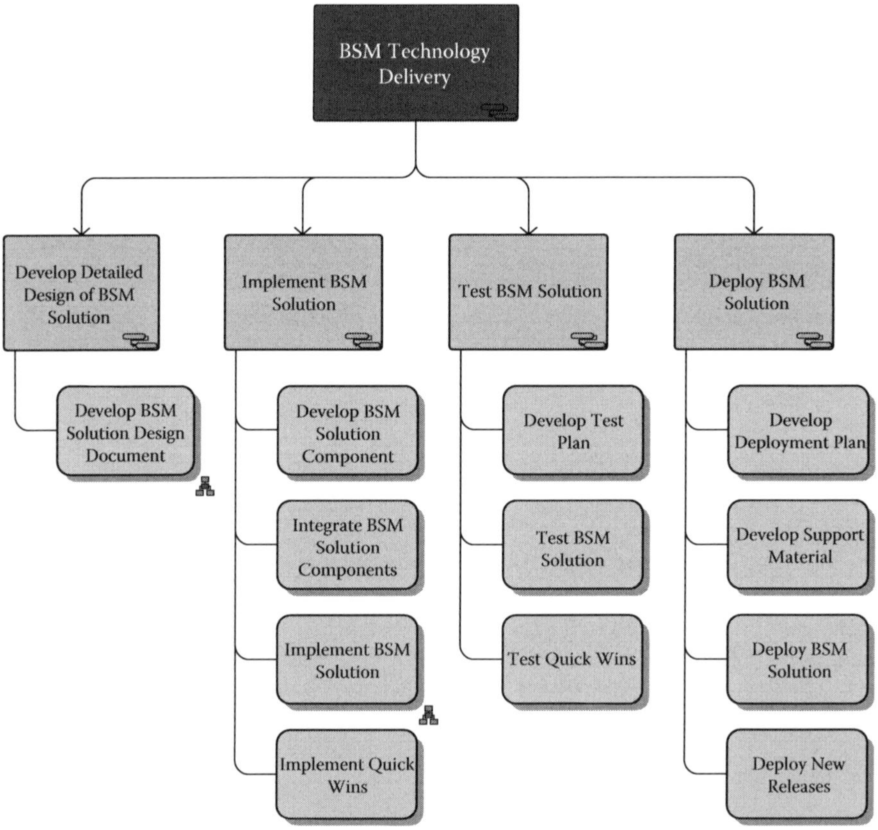

Figure 11.2 BSM technology delivery work breakdown structure.

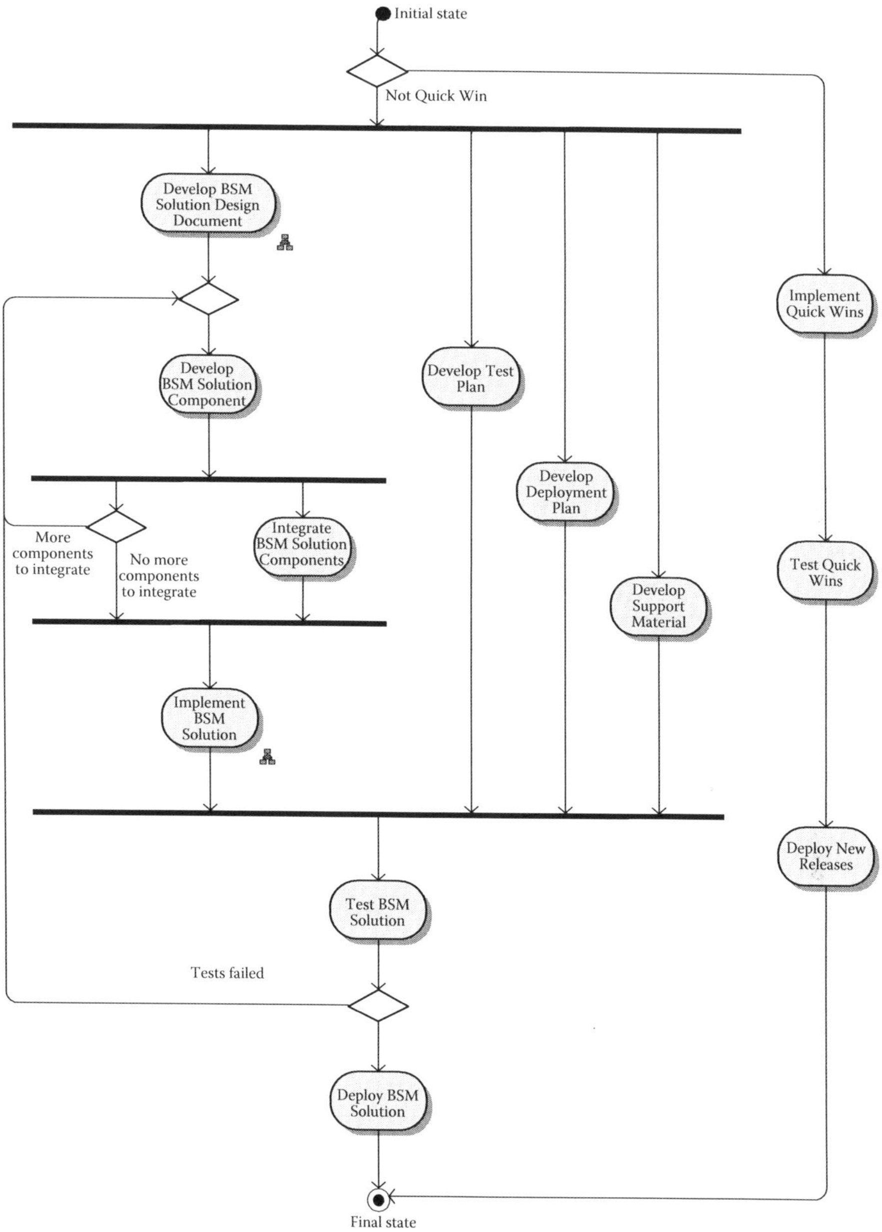

Figure 11.3 BSM technology delivery workflow.

Develop Detailed Design of BSM Solution

This activity creates the detailed design for the BSM solution.

Develop BSM Solution Design Document

Based on the BSM solution architecture, the BSM solution design document is developed by the BSM solution designer (see Figure 11.4). If it is an off-the-shelf solution, then the respective BSM technology vendor will develop the BSM solution design document. Such a design document will largely present the specific configuration details required to make the solution usable for the organization.

Implement BSM Solution

This activity focuses on the development, organization, unit testing, and integration of the BSM solution components based on the BSM solution design document.

Develop BSM Solution Components

Individual BSM solution components are developed. Each component may enable a specific service management process. For example, there may be change management component for enabling the change management processes, and so on. Most of the off-the-shelf solutions offer these components.

Integrate BSM Solution Components

During this activity, different BSM solution components are integrated into a solution.

Implement BSM Solution

During this activity, the desired solution, with all components, is implemented. This activity produces the BSM solution (Figure 11.5).

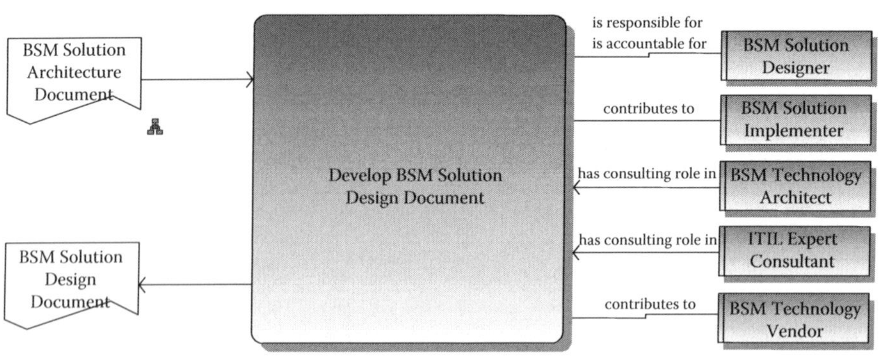

Figure 11.4 Develop BSM solution design document.

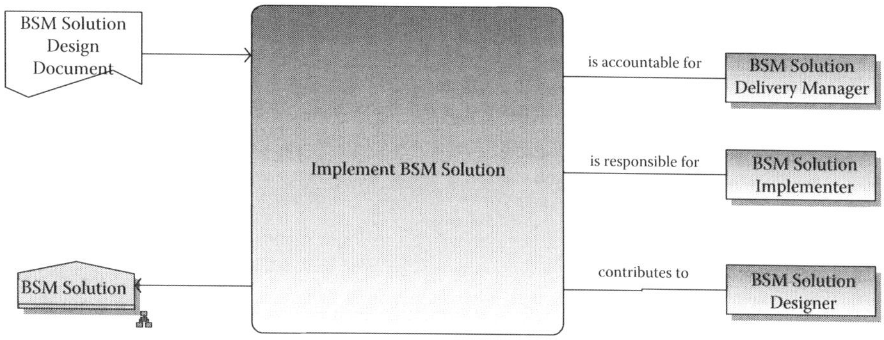

Figure 11.5 Implement BSM solution.

Implement Quick Wins

During this activity, quick wins are implemented. These quick wins represent small modifications or configurations that may be required in existing solutions. For example, there may be performance monitoring tools already deployed within the organization. However, they may not be configured properly to monitor the critical components of a given service. Such configurations will deliver rapid value through small improvements.

Test BSM Solution

During this activity, a BSM solution is evaluated and assessed for both warranty and utility.

Develop Test Plan

This activity defines the test plan that established the objectives of the tests, lists the resources required to perform these tests, establishes the timeline, and gains agreement with the relevant stakeholders on the test plan.

Test BSM Solution

Appropriate breadth and depth of tests are performed on the BSM solution as defined and agreed on in the test plan.

Test Quick Wins

Quick wins and configuration are tested during this activity.

Deploy BSM Solution

This activity ensures that the BSM solution is made available for use.

Develop Deployment Plan

During this activity, a plan is developed that lays out the details on how and when the BSM solution will be made available to the user community. The deployment plan includes packaging details, installation of the BSM solution, migration from the old solution if required, as well as training of the end users.

Develop Support Material

During this activity, user support materials are developed.

Deploy BSM Solution

A BSM solution is deployed during this activity (i.e., is made available to the user community).

Deploy New Releases

New releases are deployed as necessary.

Primary Roles and Responsibilities

Primary roles and responsibilities within the BSM technology delivery discipline are as follows (also see Figure 11.6):

BSM Solution Delivery Manager

The BSM solution delivery manager is overall accountable for the delivery of the architected and designed BSM solution.

BSM Solution Designer

The BSM solution designer is accountable and responsible for developing the BSM solution design document.

BSM Solution Implementer

- Responsible for developing and testing BSM solution components
- Integrates solutions into larger systems and performs integration testing

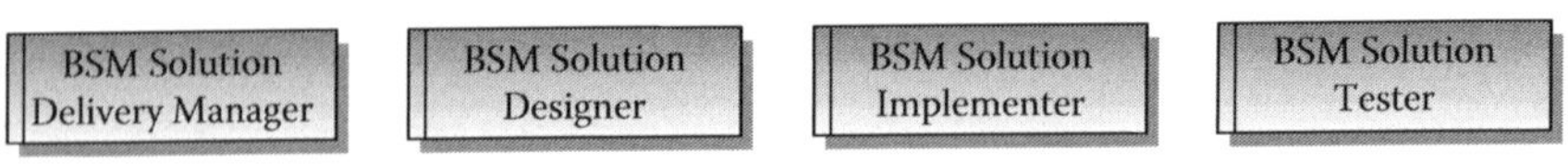

Figure 11.6 BSM technology delivery primary roles and responsibilities.

Figure 11.7 BSM technology delivery key artifacts.

BSM Solution Tester

The BSM solution tester is responsible for planning and executing the BSM solution tests.

Key Artifacts

The following are key artifacts for the BSM technology delivery discipline. They are also shown in Figure 11.7.

BSM Solution Design Document

This is further elaboration of the BSM solution architecture document and provides details required to configure, tailor (in the case of off-the-shelf solution), or implement the BSM solution.

BSM Solution

This is the actual BSM solution.

Summary

Developing, integrating, and testing solutions is an established discipline. There is a tremendous body of literature available (e.g., *Rational Unified Process*) to guide the development and delivery of the solution. In this chapter, we have briefly discussed the high-level activities that must be performed to deliver the BSM solution.

Reference

Shuja, A., and J. Krebs. 2008. *Rational Unified Process: Reference and Certification Guide*. New York: IBM Press.

Chapter 12

Iterative and Incremental Service-Oriented Service Management Implementation Life Cycle: Phases and Iterations

In Chapters 5 through 11, we discussed the various disciplines in detail. We learned about discipline-specific objectives and activities that should be performed in order to meet those objectives. In this chapter, we will discuss the life cycle view/aspect of business service management (BSM) implementation. As the name suggests, in this chapter, we will learn about which related/depending activities should be performed at what time/which phase during the project life cycle to ensure that various BSM implementation deliverables are successfully produced. At the end of this chapter, we will be able to answer the following related questions:

- How can we leverage industry standards and software engineering–related practices to implement BSM in an iterative and incremental fashion?
- What are the different phases of the BSM implementation life cycle? What is the purpose of each of those phases?
- What is the relationship between phases and iterations?

This chapter lays out the foundation for planning to implement BSM.

Introduction

Depending on the role that IT plays in enabling the core business processes, the rate of IT evolution may be critical to the overall business success and profitability. For some organizations, implementing BSM may be transformational, and embarking on such a journey may sometimes be more about cultural transformation than any other single factor. It may need a major shift in how people think about and manage IT. These shifts may include:

- IT is for the business and IT is not for IT.
- Think of IT as the business and run IT as a business.
- Targeted technology capabilities development investments are made to maximize business profitability.
- Firefighting is not rewarded; proactive fire prevention is rewarded.
- We will thrive, not just survive.

Cultural transformation, an aggregate of small behavioral transformations over time, is achieved through:

- Well-aligned business and IT vision and strategies
- Clear definition of enterprise architecture standards and governance policies and procedures
- Thoughtful management of changes in people's attitudes and ways of thinking through clearly defining and effectively enforcing the service management processes
- Careful planning, management, and incremental implementations of a range of continual service and service management process improvements
- Business–IT organizational realignments

These critical aspects of implementing BSM are graphically represented in Figure 12.1. Cultural transformation is easier said than done. Organizations have been struggling to leverage IT Infrastructure Library (ITIL) guidelines to achieve such transformations as necessary to realize the highly anticipated effectiveness and efficiency as business–IT integration benefits. Transformation does not happen overnight and requires consistent, steady, incremental, and ongoing step-by-step improvements. Service management implementation, especially in the case of less mature organizations, is no exception. What makes such transformations even riskier is the lack of organizational knowledge about all that is necessary to make these efforts successful.

It is absolutely critical to realize that ITIL v3 is more than just infrastructure and that service management sometimes means a major shift in the way IT has been managed and operated and

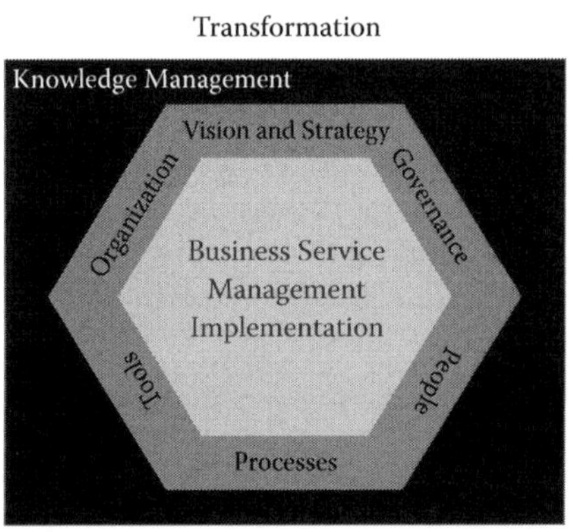

Figure 12.1 Aspects of implementing BSM.

in the manner in which it has been delivering its services to the customers. ITIL v3 and BSM are about integrating IT with the business and ensuring traceability and management right from business processes, business services to technical services, and all the way down to individual technology (infrastructure, application, software, hardware, databases, middleware, and others) components.

Implementing BSM will very likely impact each and every aspect of the organization. In fact, depending on organizational baseline maturity level, implementing BSM may be revolutionary and may take longer than anticipated before the realization of potential benefits. To make matters worse, organizational tolerances to sit tight and wait for these transformational benefits to come through have been declining. Some of the questions that IT managers have asked me over the years mostly pertain to approaches to implementing IT service management and demonstrating the added value before the next management shuffle. To keep the senior management sponsorship alive, create an "excitement" across the larger organization to embrace this transformational change, and generate the business- as well as customer-driven need for higher quality IT services:

> We must demonstrate the business value of implementing IT service management as early in the project life cycle as possible and help the senior management and the larger organization see a small 'slice' of our business service management vision at a time.

Faster turnaround coupled with effective and efficient management of continual improvement efforts is essential. I have often come across situations where there is clear vision at the senior IT executive/management level. The middle management gets under pressure, especially in difficult economic environments, to deliver results, and with that drive starts to make progress at high speeds. If these efforts are not properly coordinated, planned, and executed, the results can be devastating. It is like,

> *. . . you have motivated teams who want to deliver*
> *with this drive to deliver, they all try to show results as soon as possible*
> *with lack of coordination among their team-specific activities*
> *the risk of duplicate and potentially conflicting efforts can result in*
> *significant risks to the project*
> or
> *High speed—low coordination—high risks*

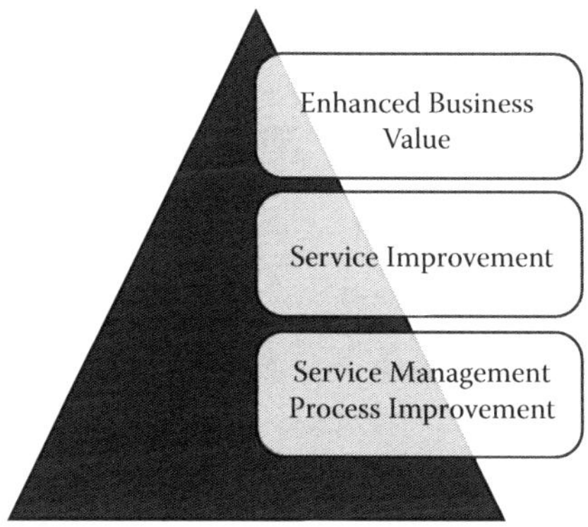

Figure 12.2 Service management process improvements underpin service improvement.

Before we get into the business value creation discussions, let us understand how the three key terms—business value creation, service improvement, and service management process improvement—are related. As shown in Figure 12.2, service management process improvements underpin the business service improvements, which underpin the business value. For example, if your change management process—one of the service management processes in ITIL v3—is not effective, it will cause a majority of changes to fail leading to potential outages. These outages are caused on services that are used by our customers, thereby negatively impacting the business value created by IT.

In this chapter, we will discuss how IT organizations can go about delivering incremental improvements and iterative, measurable, and visible value to business customers through steady and ongoing improvements in an agile fashion.

The i2-SOSMI Life Cycle

As we discussed earlier in this book, the iterative and incremental service-oriented service management implementation (i2-SOSMI) provides a set of comprehensive guidelines that the subject organization will need to successfully implement BSM using ITIL v3 guidelines. The i2-SOSMI consists of seven disciplines and four phases. Content is represented in disciplines and life cycle is represented in phases. Each phase consists of three iterations: Visualize, Architect, and Realize. We will discuss each of these iterations in greater detail.

Practical Tip: After investing almost 6 months and a couple of million dollars, we were able to reduce the failed changes from 18% to 13% at one of the largest global organizations. This resulted in reduced number of incidents as well as lesser infrastructure outages. However, business stakeholders/customers were not able to feel any change in their experience. That is why, it is imperative that any service management process improvements that are undertaken are targeted to achieving desired service improvements that create value. Remember, *process improvements are as important as the quality of services that they underpin*. This is the main objective of i2-SOSMI i.e., to ensure targeted process improvements that deliver real service improvements in the shortest possible time.

In summary, the key i2-SOSMI architectural components comprise:

- Disciplines
- Phases
- Iterations

Figure 12.3 graphically shows the i2-SOSMI architecture with all these key components.

The i2-SOSMI life cycle progresses from left to right. As shown in Figure 12.3, there are four phases: foundation, design, align, and integrate. Note that as the project progresses through the phases and organizational maturity improves, the planned, targeted, and proactive IT improvements become greater and greater and are managed under continual process improvements. On the other hand, quick wins/quick fixes type of reactive unplanned improvements become fewer and fewer.

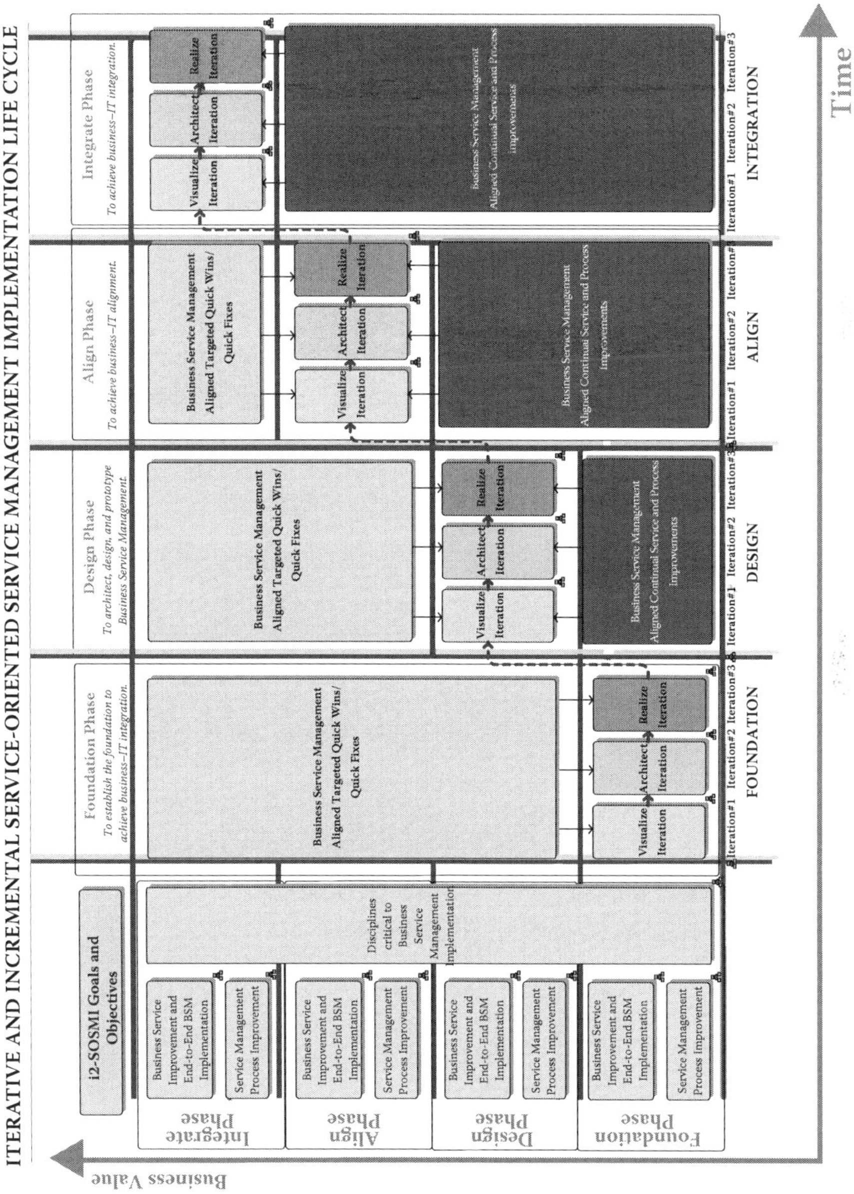

Figure 12.3 The i2-SOSMI architecture.

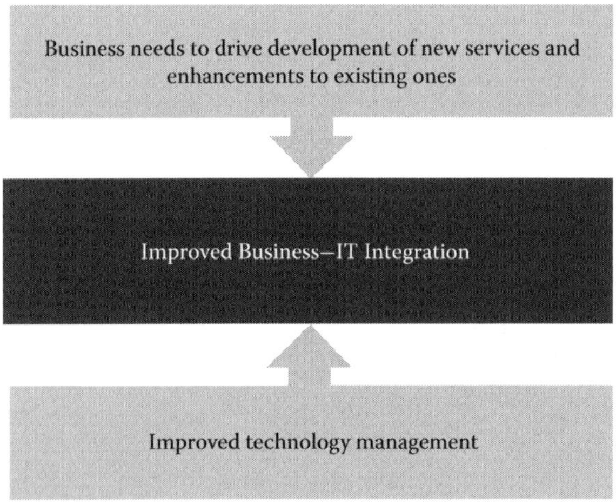

Figure 12.4 Business–IT integration.

You will notice phases named across the vertical axis as well. Each phase is designated as either "service management process improvement" or "service improvement/end-to-end BSM implementation." It shows that within each phase, both service management processes as well as business services are improved. In other words, you are ensuring that you are able to immediately leverage the service management improvements implemented to deliver business value by improving the business services. *Service management process improvement* and *business service improvement and end-to-end BSM implementation* are two of the five disciplines and will be discussed in detail in this chapter. Please note that, as we progress through the life cycle, the *quick wins/quick fixes* are replaced with *continual service improvements* (CSIs) and *continual process improvements*. As organizations mature, these improvements become more aligned and better organized resulting in greater creation of business value. Let us now discuss the different components of the life cycle in greater detail.

Note that ITIL v3 is about achieving business-IT integration; something that is achieved by identifying and statisfying business needs through new services as well as enhancements to existing services and by optimizing technology management (Figure 12.4).

Life Cycle Phases and Objectives

Let us start by looking at the recommended phases and disciplines within the i2-SOSMI approach and their respective objectives (Figure 12.3).

Figure 12.5 shows i2-SOSMI disciplines—project management, people and organization, CSI institutionalization, business service improvement and end-to-end BSM implementation (BSI), service management process improvement, BSM technology architecture and integration, and BSM technology delivery.

We have already discussed these disciplines in detail earlier in this book. In this chapter, we will focus on the activities from across each of these phases and where those should be performed within the project life cycle. Figure 12.6 shows the four phases of the i2-SOSMI methodology—foundation, architect, align, and integrate—along with their respective goals. Figure 12.6 also

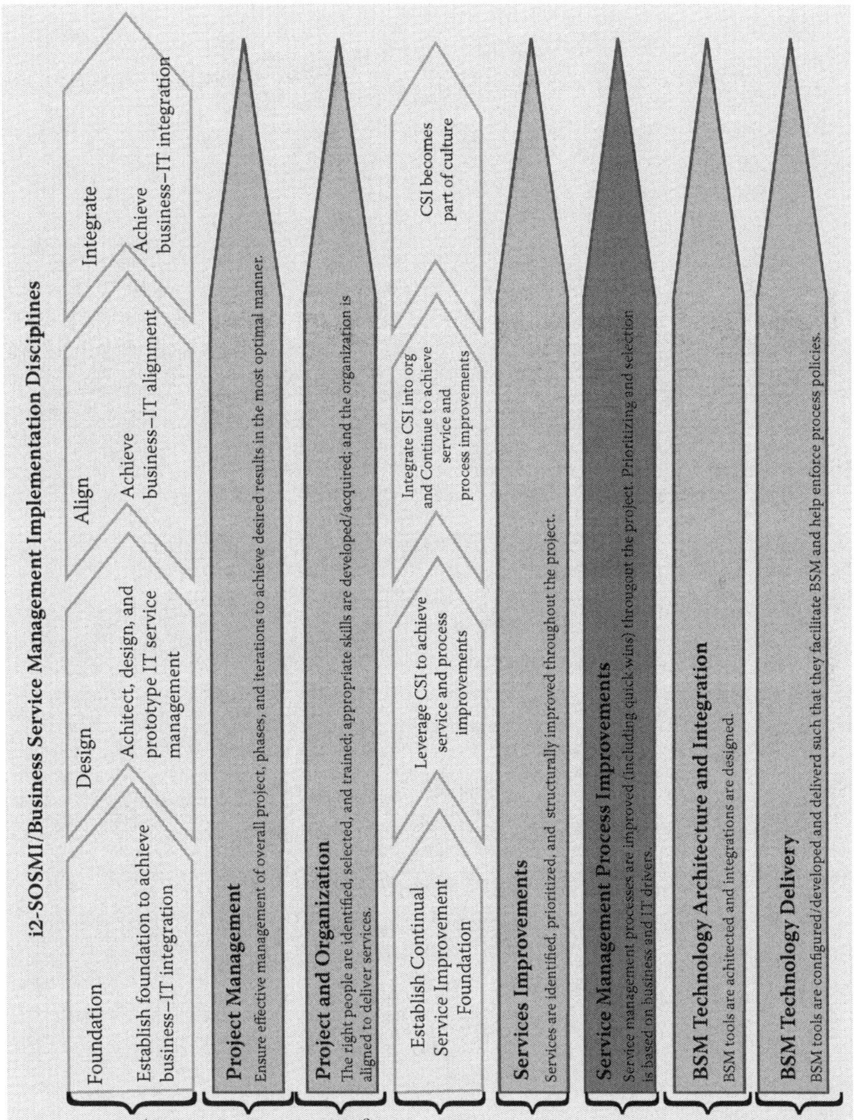

Figure 12.5 i2-SOSMI disciplines.

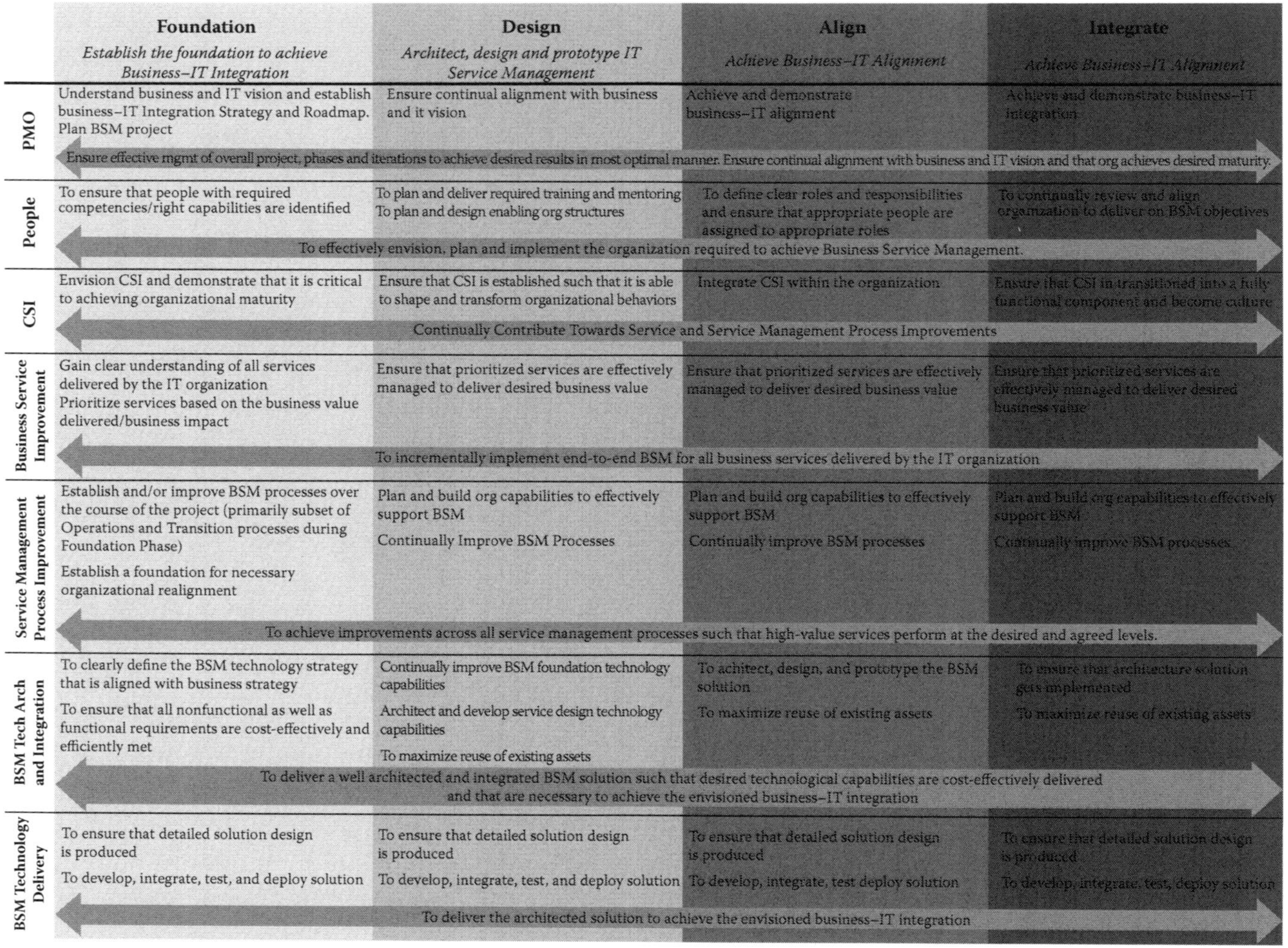

Figure 12.6 The i2-SOSMI phase objectives.

shows the various disciplines and their respective goals and objectives and how those objectives contribute toward achieving the phase goals. Aligned with these discipline objectives are the activities performed to realize those objectives. We will discuss each phase, how the various discipline objectives support the overall phase goal, and which activities are performed within that phase from across various disciplines.

Rapid Service Improvement Framework

Before we get into the details of each phase and iteration, I would like to introduce a framework that I call the *rapid service improvement* (RSI) framework. It leverages the seven-step ITIL v3 CSI (discussed in the book *ITIL v3 Continual Service Improvement*) process in an innovative manner. The RSI framework is specifically designed to help plan out the BSM implementation project. It helps reduce the turnaround time and accelerates the overall service improvement effort.

As shown in Figure 12.7, there are five key steps that need to be performed at all levels: at a project level, at each phase level, and at each iteration level. The difference will be that, at the project level, you will focus on the business and IT strategy, at a phase level, you will be focusing on individual business service and/or service management process area, and at each iteration level, you will focus on specific components of a service or a service management process area.

Foundation

As the name suggests, the foundation phase of the i2-SOSMI methodology is about establishing the service management foundation that is necessary to ensure end-to-end management of IT services.

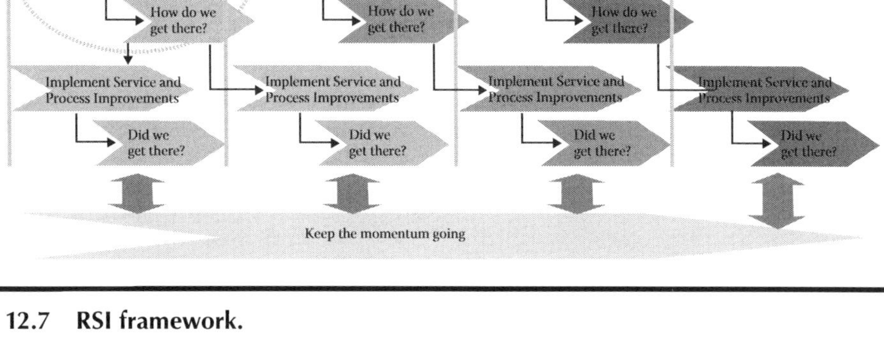

Figure 12.7 RSI framework.

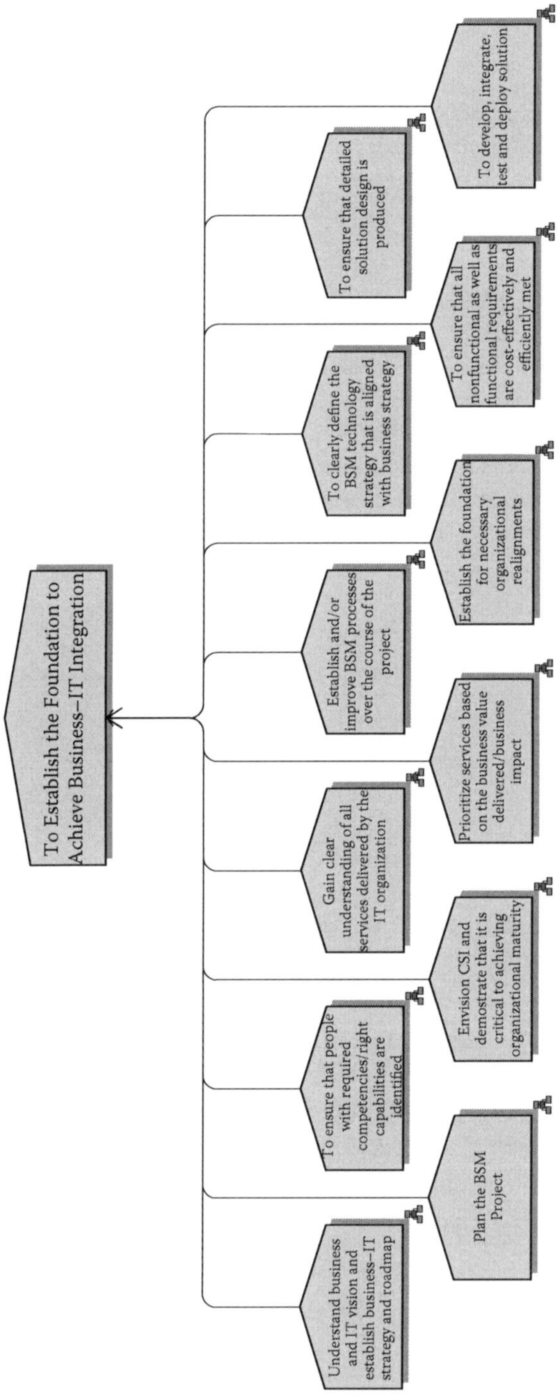

Figure 12.8 Foundation phase objectives.

Purpose

The main purpose of the foundation phase is to establish the foundation for achieving business–IT integration. This phase is about ensuring that the right foundation exists to achieve the strategic objective of BSM. It is somewhat tactical planning with strategic objectives.

Objectives

The key recommended objectives (Figure 12.8) that should be achieved during the Foundation Phase are as follows:

- *Understand business and IT vision and establish business–IT integration strategy and roadmap.* ITIL v3 is about business–IT integration. We want to make sure that we have established the right foundation early on to enable us to realize this vision. Depending on the role that IT plays or is expected to play in the profitability of the business enterprise, the level of business–IT integration will vary. For certain businesses, such as financial services, IT is truly the business enabler and, if managed effectively, can transform the business. Business–IT integration strategy and roadmap should be established with the business vision in view. Strategy will drive the roadmap. The roadmap needs to be continually assessed for alignment with strategy and necessary adjustments should be made throughout the course of this project (Figure 12.9).
- *Plan the IT service management project.*
  The overall project plan is developed during the first iteration of the foundation phase. This plan consists of three main plans and other supporting plans as appropriate. The three main plans include the project plan itself, the phase plan, and the iteration plan. Each one is time-boxed early in the first iteration of the foundation phase. The iteration plan for the next iteration is detailed and the remaining phase and project plans are kept high-level. More details are added and refinements are made throughout the foundation phase. This is similar to the progressive elaboration concept within the Project Management Institute/Project Management Body of Knowledge (PMI/PMBOK). For more details on iterative and incremental project management, please refer to industry practices such as rational unified process (RUP) and SCRUM (Figure 12.10).

  Once the plans are developed, it will be critical to manage those plans to deliver the desired outcomes. We will not discuss this in great detail in this book because enough

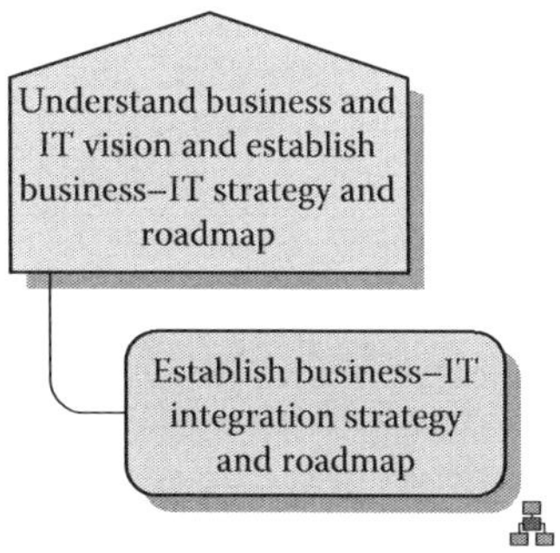

Figure 12.9 Supporting activities: Understand business and IT vision and establish business–IT strategy and roadmap.

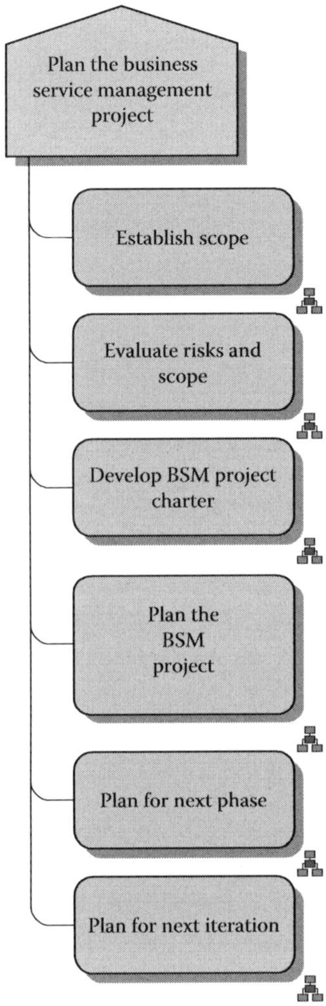

Figure 12.10 Supporting activities: Plan the BSM project.

project management literature already exists. For more information, please refer to PMI/PMBOK, RUP, and SCRUM practices.

- *To ensure that people with the required competencies and the right capabilities are identified.* People are some of the most important capabilities and resources of any organization. Earlier in the project, it is critical to understand and assess the current state or AS-IS organization and based on the organizational changes that are necessary, envision the target state or TO-BE organization (Figure 12.11). It is important to appreciate that documentation and analysis of AS-IS organization (including analysis of existing competencies) is performed during the Foundation phase. You will notice that this organizational analysis and design activities continue during the Design phase as well. Associated activities are presented in Figures 12.11, 12.23 and 12.24.
- *Envision CSI and demonstrate that it is critical to achieving organizational maturity.* If implemented correctly, CSI becomes the engine of cultural transformation. CSI is at the core of keeping the momentum going and it is therefore critical for the overall success of CSI

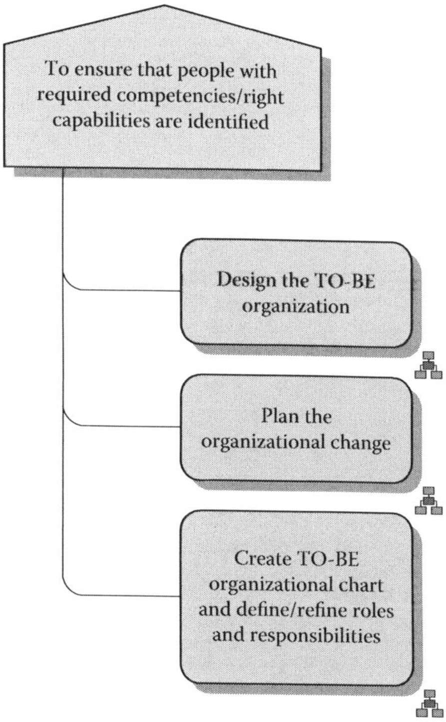

Figure 12.11 Supporting activities: Ensure that people with the required competencies/right capabilities are identified.

that tangible value-added results are demonstrated as early as possible. In i2-SOSMI, we will see the activities that are recommended to effectively establish the base CSI function within the organization. In later phases, CSI should really be driving most of the service and service management process improvements (Figure 12.12).

- *Gain clear understanding of all services delivered by the IT organization.* The service catalog is going to play a critical role throughout the project and after it has been completed. The service catalog is the source of all services that are operational or provided and those that are soon to be operational or provided. Depending on the organizational maturity levels, it is understandable not to have a complete service catalog early in the project and that is fine. However, the goal should be to capture all the known operational services in the catalog and then to continue to optimize and complete it throughout the course of this project. Remember when you first embarked on the service management implementation project and you did not have a service catalog before this project. It will take a couple of iterations before you start to complete your catalog; you don't know what you don't know. From the requests that you receive at your service desk, you will be able to identify what requests are related to which service and what requests do not have any associated service defined. The reality is that if there are known critical "things" that our customers expect us to do and that we should do, then these will, in most cases, be defined as the first set of services. Exceptions are always there when your customers are in the habit of receiving something that they should not have been receiving in the first place and that will require a complete behavioral change, which is something that is expected to be realized as part of

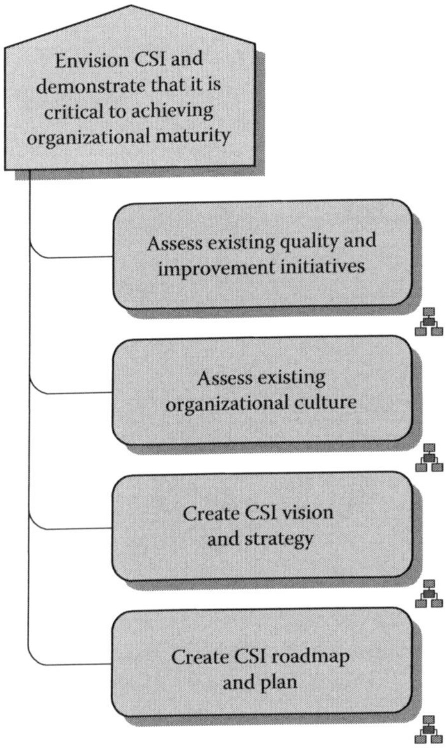

Figure 12.12 Supporting activities: Envision CSI and demonstrate that it is critical to achieving organizational maturity.

this project; for example, if you provide application hosting services and your customers are used to ordering for servers. This behavior results, most likely, in access unutilized capacity, increased costs of delivering services, wasted resources, and more. In short, if we are able to identify some of the critical services that we provide to our customers, we are in a good shape to move forward to the design phase. If we missed something, it is most likely not critical. In fact, an argument can be made that if there is something that we do and it is not captured in the first release of the catalog, then it may not be worth doing. The first release of the catalog should enable the project team to agree on the high-priority services that need to be improved (Figure 12.13).

This activity assumes that the service catalog is already in place. We will discuss later in this chapter which activities will need to be performed to create the service catalog.

- *Prioritize services based on the business value delivered/business impact.*
  Operational services listed in the service catalog are assessed and prioritized based on the business value that they deliver to the businesses and customers so that appropriate improvements can be envisioned and appropriately managed (Figure 12.14).
- *Establish and/or improve BSM processes over the course of the project.*
  Depending on the size and maturity of an organization, business and IT visions, and any specific pain points, the processes that need to be improved in the foundation phase may vary. However, there are certain core elements that are critical to effectively managing services. In

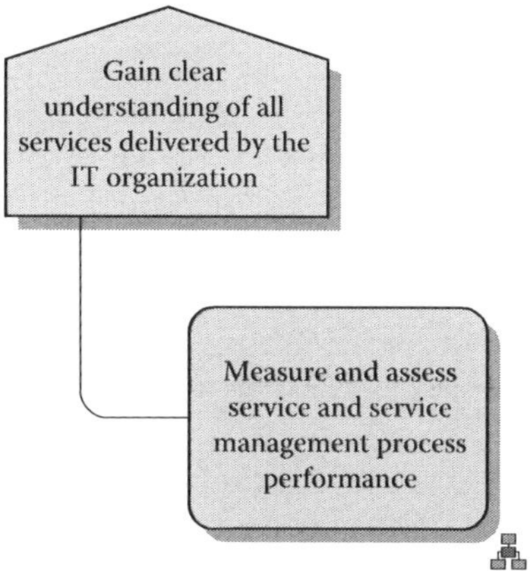

Figure 12.13 Supporting activities: Measure and assess service and service management process performance.

most cases, a common platform and right level of automation will be essential to effective and efficient implementation of service management. Having said this, in most cases, I have seen organizations assess and improve upon four processes to ensure that the right foundation is established for service management. These are incident management, problem management, change management, and service asset and configuration management. With ITIL v3, an additional process that I strongly recommend my clients to improve upon is service catalog management. It will be difficult to make real value-added service improvements without clearly understanding what services our customers really need and which ones really need improvements. Establishing service catalog management during the foundation phase will enable organizations to start to prioritize services that need to be immediately improved. Remember, the service catalog is our menu for our customers. Customers know about what

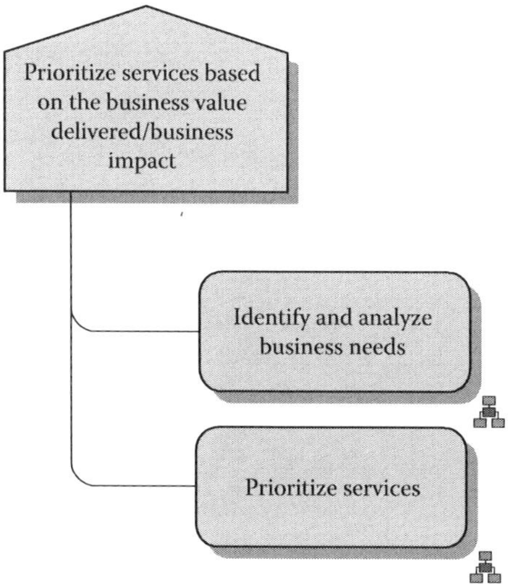

Figure 12.14 Supporting activities: Prioritize services based on the business value delivered and business impact.

we do through our service catalog. If we do not have a service catalog, discussions with our customers and improvement decisions will be difficult (Figure 12.15).

Note that all ITIL v3 processes are largely interdependent and, to maximize return on investments made, any major issues related to relevant processes need to be improved. Therefore, at any point in time during the life cycle of the BSM project, the following improvements are made:

- Comprehensive service management process improvements, which may involve total process reengineering, tooling architecture design and development, organizational realignments, and more. For example, if you are reducing the number of outages that happen for a given service to achieve higher availability targets, you will most likely need to improve the overall change management process. To ensure that these improvements make the most impact on the quality of the service that is under improvement, you will need to achieve some quick wins across other processes. For example,
    - You will need to identify and document details and configurations of all CIs that implement that service.
    - In doing so, you will be refining your configuration management database and improving the quality of data associated with those CIs in support of effective change impact assessment.

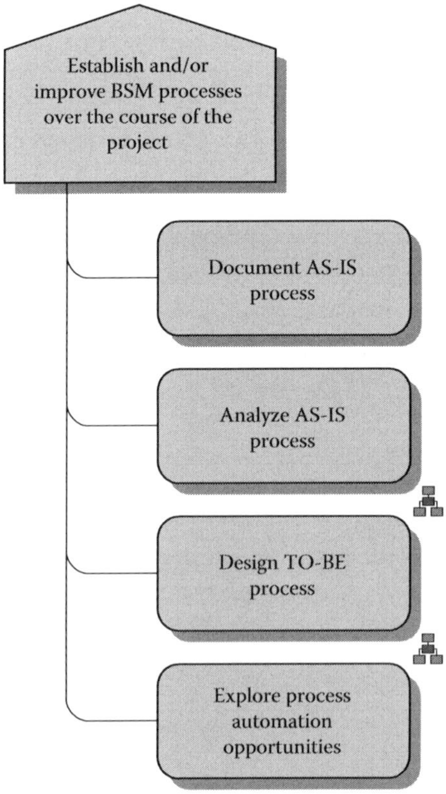

Figure 12.15 Supporting activities: Establish and improve BSM processes over the course of the project.

- Quick wins/quick fixes, which may include minor adjustments, as discussed in the example above, in the identified/related processes that will: (1) further improve the results of making comprehensive improvements to the prioritized service management process; (2) enable the project team to further their understanding on the potential challenges that need to be addressed in this process area; and (3) make incremental small high-value improvements. It is critical to manage these quick wins so that they take the process closer to its desired maturity level.

  We will discuss these in detail during our iteration discussions later in this chapter.

- *Establish the foundation for necessary organizational realignments.*

  Organizational changes are difficult and impact peoples' jobs. If these changes are not managed carefully, they not only impact organizational morale but also its capabilities to perform core operational activities. In most low-maturity level organizations, I have seen a lot of consistent reorganizations without much process thinking. I had clients that did organizational realignments in a well-planned and organized manner, and those that constantly kept on doing trial-and-error reorganizations. The latter cases are largely damaging to the overall organization. Process development provides a sound foundation to think about and design the organization so that it is able to execute the processes in the most efficient manner. As we continue to improve service management processes, we will explore opportunities for organizational realignments (Figure 12.16).

- *Clearly define the BSM technology strategy that is aligned with business strategy.*

  To achieve this objective, BSM technology strategy is defined based on the current enterprise architectures (infrastructure and application capabilities and any relevant standards).

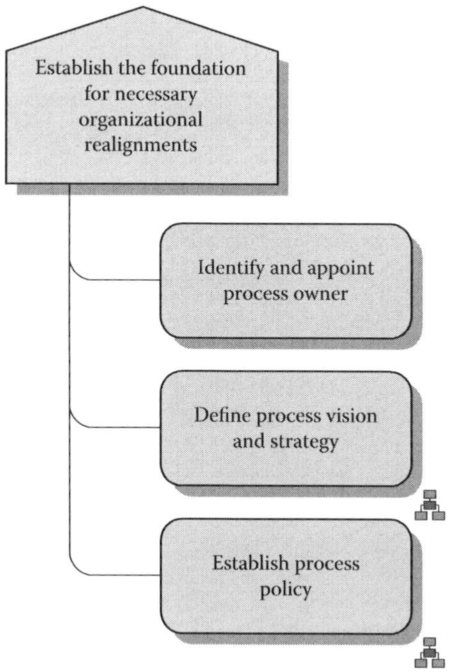

Figure 12.16 Supporting activities: Establish the foundation for necessary organizational realignments.

A roadmap for building the technological capabilities to support the BSM is developed (Figure 12.17).

Depending on organizational maturity level, there may be an existing enterprise architecture practice in place. If there is one, it is a good idea to align BSM-related architectures with enterprise architecture. We will discuss ITIL v3 and enterprise architecture in greater detail in Chapter 17. In most cases, implementing BSM will have cross-organizational impact in a number of ways. As discussed, organizational, technological, process-specific, and other changes will need to take place and need to be managed carefully.

- *Ensure that all nonfunctional and functional requirements are cost-effectively and efficiently met.*
  Organizations largely focus on getting the functional requirements right. However, most of them forget that if the system is slow or is not available, then it will not matter whether it satisfies all the functional requirements. I have intentionally mentioned the nonfunctional requirements (NFRs) first in this objective. It is critical for the system to have reasonable performance capabilities if it is to be successfully adopted by the organization (Figure 12.18).
- *Ensure that a detailed solution design is produced.*
  Detailed solution design will be critical to the correct implementation of the solution. This design must take a holistic view of the solution (i.e., both warranty and utility) (Figure 12.19).
- *Develop, integrate, test, and deploy solution.*
  It focuses on ensuring that the right solution is developed and deployed (Figure 12.20).

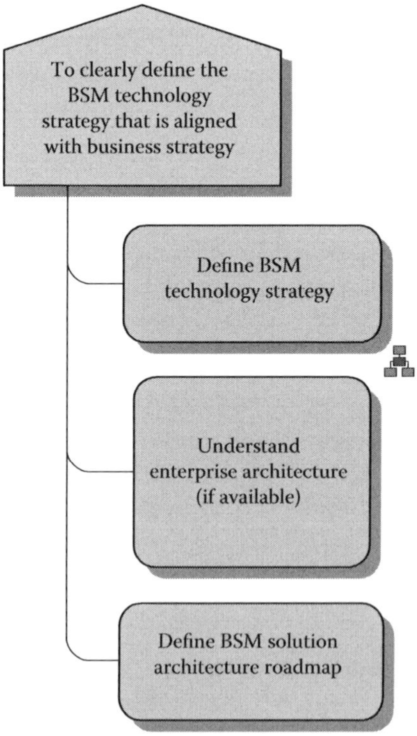

Figure 12.17 Supporting activities: Clearly define the BSM technology strategy that is aligned with business strategy.

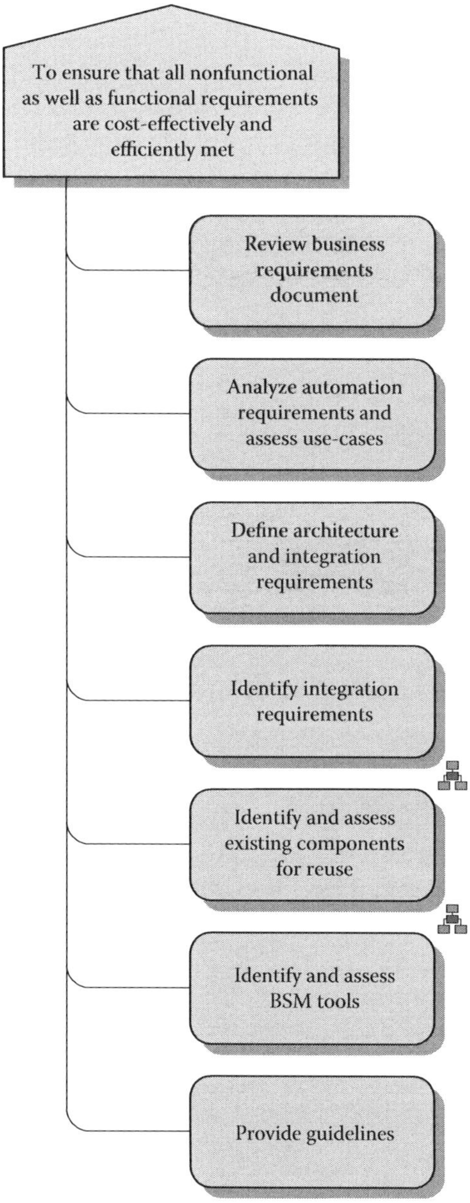

Figure 12.18 Supporting activities: Ensure that all nonfunctional and functional requirements are cost-effectively met.

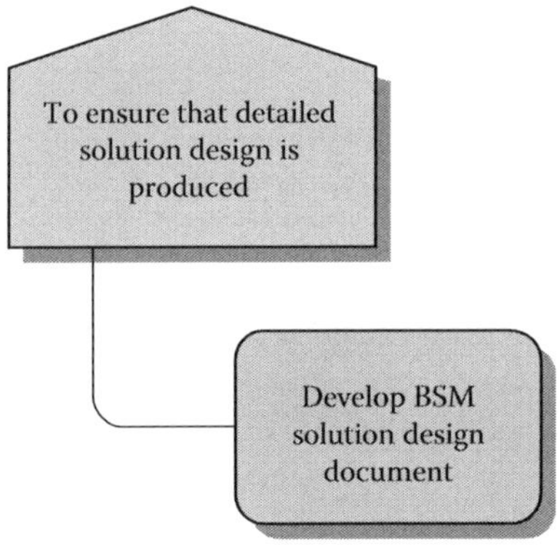

Figure 12.19 Supporting activities: Ensure that a detailed solution design is produced.

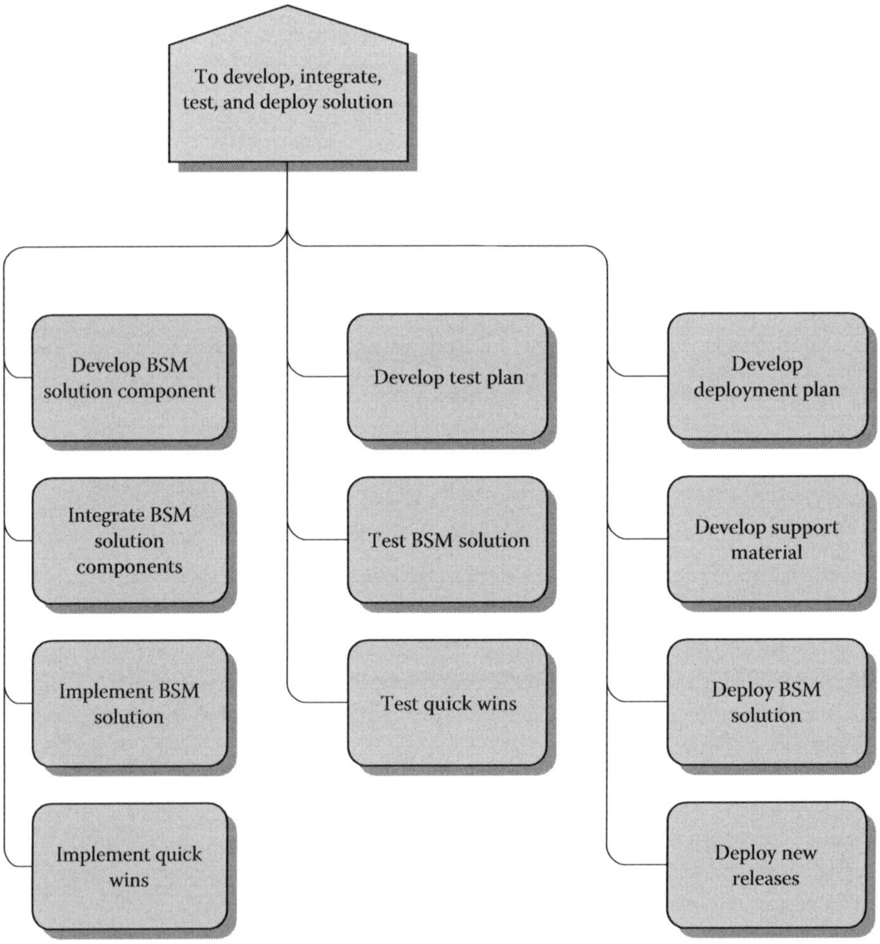

Figure 12.20 Supporting activities: Develop, integrate, test, and deploy solution.

Depending on the organizational maturity, size, and complexity, the foundation phase may take from 3 to 12 months to complete. The BSM processes comprising this foundation include incident management, problem management, change management, service asset and configuration management, and service catalog management. Although possible, it will be difficult for organizations aspiring to achieve BSM to achieve their goals without having these foundation processes in place. As we improve business and technical services, we will not only be introducing changes to the environment, but will also be establishing new foundations for our relationships with our customers. It is, therefore, essential that we manage these changes in a controlled environment and have the foundation in place to ensure that any incidents and problems along the way are effectively and efficiently managed. The service catalog will enable us to gain a better understanding of what business services we offer to our customers and will serve as the foundation to implementing BSM.

Design

The design phase is critical to the success of the overall IT service management project. To effectively and efficiently implement IT service management, it is strongly recommended to develop IT service management proof-of-concept and prototype the IT organization (process, people, partners/suppliers, and products/tools—the four P's of Service Design) during the design phase. Note that we are talking about prototyping the organization and not just the tooling aspect. This will enable senior IT management to rapidly see how all aspects of service management including people, organization, processes, services, technologies/tooling, and CSI will need to be aligned and implemented to achieve the desired results.

Purpose

The purpose of this phase is to architect, design, and prototype IT Service Management.

Objectives

Design phase objectives are shown in Figure 12.21.

Let us discuss these key objectives in detail.

- *Ensure continual alignment with business and IT vision.*
  During the foundation phase, we gained comprehensive understanding of business and IT visions and, based on that, we established business–IT integration strategy and roadmaps. As we go through the project, gain a deeper and clearer understanding of the organization, and progressively elaborate on the project plan, it is critical to continue to ensure that an appropriate alignment is maintained between the business and the IT vision and the business–IT integration strategy and roadmaps as well as BSM project plans (Figure 12.22).

  Once the plans are developed, it will be critical to manage those plans to deliver the desired outcomes. We will not discuss this in great detail in this book because enough project management literature already exists. For more information, please refer to PMI/PMBOK, RUP, and SCRUM practices.

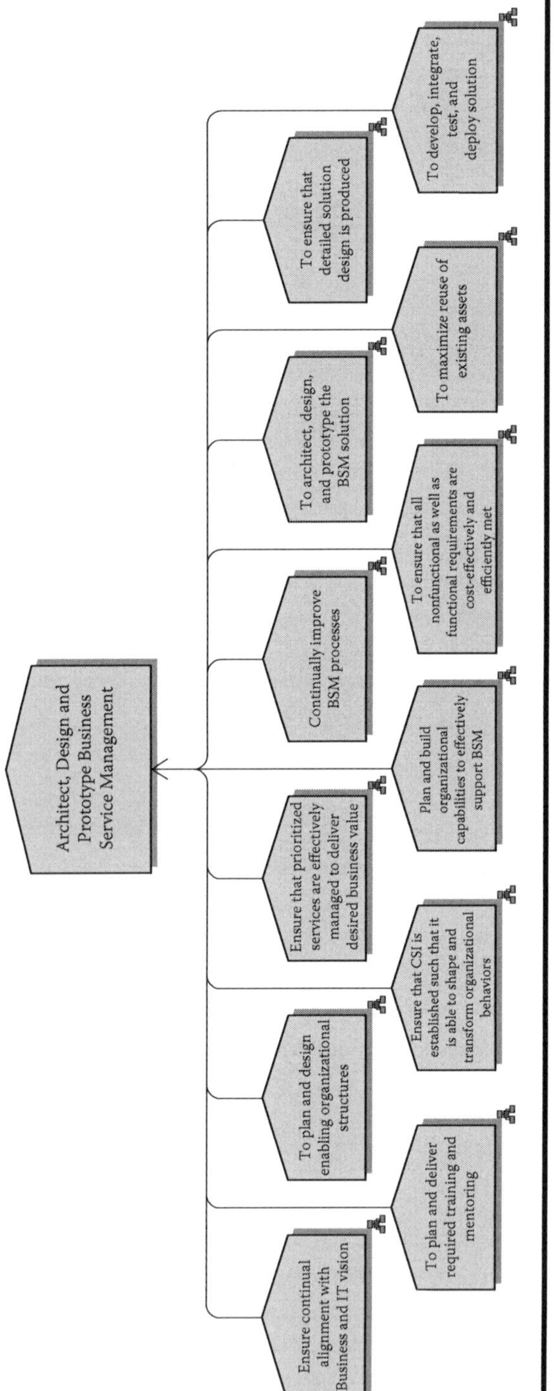

Figure 12.21 Design phase objectives.

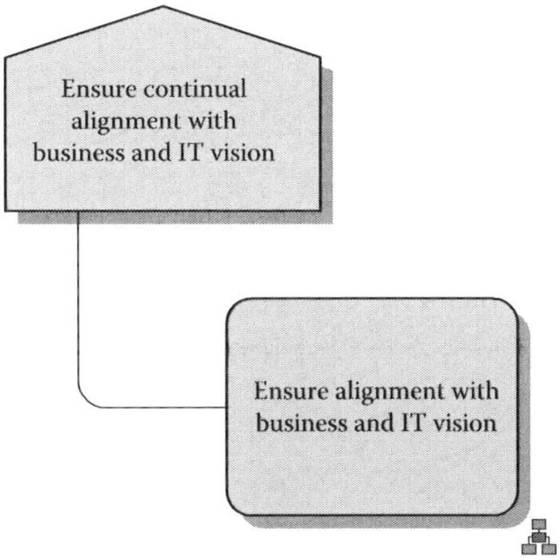

Figure 12.22 Supporting activities: Ensure continual alignment with business and IT vision.

- *Plan and deliver required training and mentoring.*
  Training needs are addressed and required mentoring efforts are planned and executed (Figure 12.23).
- *Plan and design enabling organization structures.*
  It does not matter how good your process is if the organization is not positioned to effectively and efficiently execute those processes. To institutionalize a given process, it is critical to ensure that you have the right policies, people, tools, partnerships, and other resources and metrics in place to enable the organization to embrace that process. Organizational alignments should be aligned with process improvement efforts to ensure that the two are in sync (Figure 12.24).

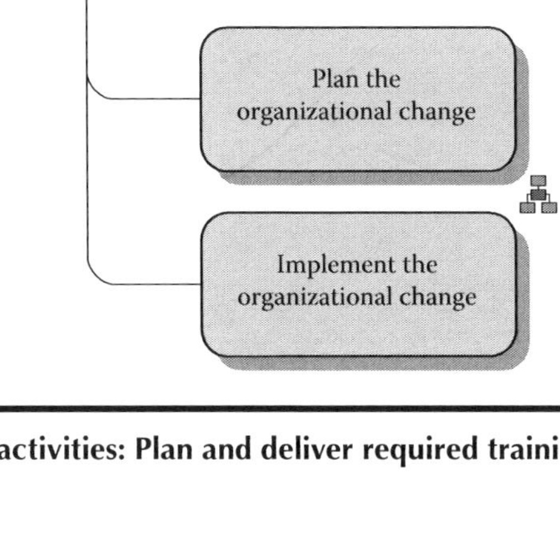

Figure 12.23 Supporting activities: Plan and deliver required training and mentoring.

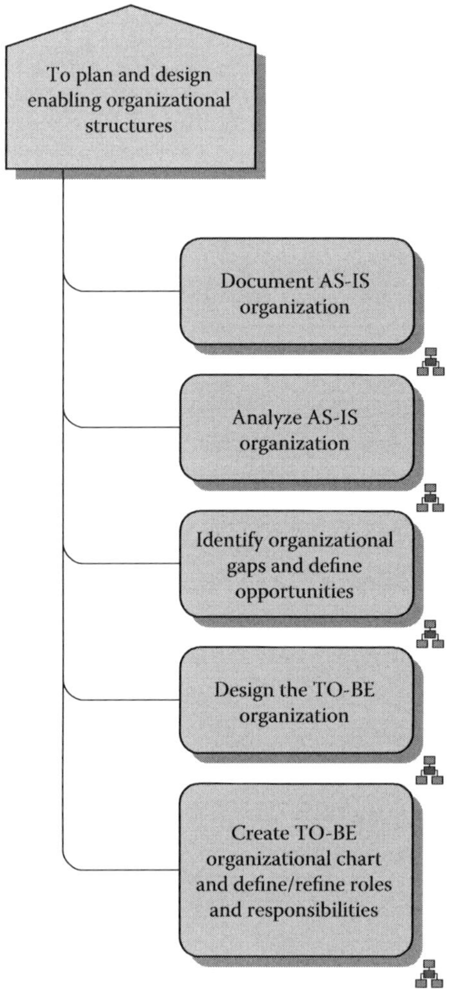

Figure 12.24 Supporting activities: Plan and design enabling organizational structures.

- *Ensure that CSI is established so that it is able to shape and transform organizational behaviors.* As discussed, CSI is absolutely critical for the overall organizational transformation and for ensuring that the momentum is kept alive. In the foundation phase, we focused on creating a vision for CSI and demonstrated on how the CSI can provide true business value through: (1) understanding business needs; (2) performing current state assessments; (3) identifying improvement opportunities; (4) developing CSI processes and approaches; (5) prioritizing opportunities and making wise recommendations; and so on. If these activities are executed appropriately, we will have a very good foundation to further establish the CSI organization. In the design phase, the key objective is to establish CSI so that it is able to mature, as a function, throughout the remaining project while delivering tangible value through continual improvements. What specific responsibilities a given CSI organization will have really depends on the organization. CSI may be engaged from setting the improvement vision, performing the current state assessments, setting achievable and measurable targets, and implementing those improvements to only performing part of these functions. Therefore, with regard to the design phase, we need to ensure that CSI is appropriately established to be able to ensure that momentum is kept alive and the organization is able to make wise investments in improvement opportunities (Figure 12.25).

- *Ensure that prioritized services are effectively managed to deliver desired business value.* One of the key objectives of implementing service management is to be better able to manage and deliver services that our customers expect from IT and that we have committed to. Service management implementation is not something that can be achieved in one "big bang" fashion. As discussed in Chapter 4, we need to appreciate the importance of incrementally and iteratively implementing service management primarily to: (1) create tangible business value incrementally; (2) manage risks related to service management implementation effectively; (3) demonstrate the returns that the organization should expect to receive as a result of service management implementation; and (4) ensure that service management implementation efforts and the cultural transformation survives management shuffles. To that end, during the design phase, early builds of service management prototypes are developed. This service management

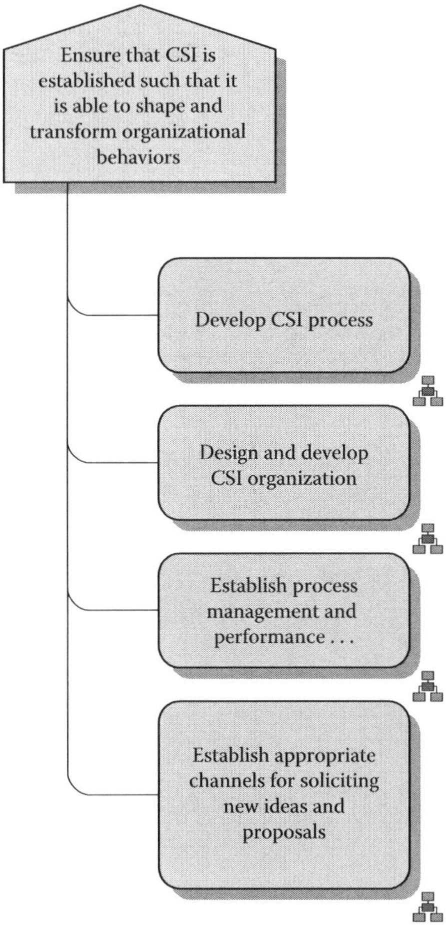

Figure 12.25 Supporting activities: Ensure that CSI is established so that it is able to shape and transform organizational behaviors.

prototype needs to be aligned with a subset of services—prioritized services are improved and complete end-to-end service management is implemented for these services (Figure 12.26).

As discussed, the service catalog contains all the operational services, in addition to those that may become operational soon. The first version of the service catalog is developed during the foundation phase. However, as we go through phases and iterations, we will most likely discover services that we do deliver but that are not yet captured in the service catalog.

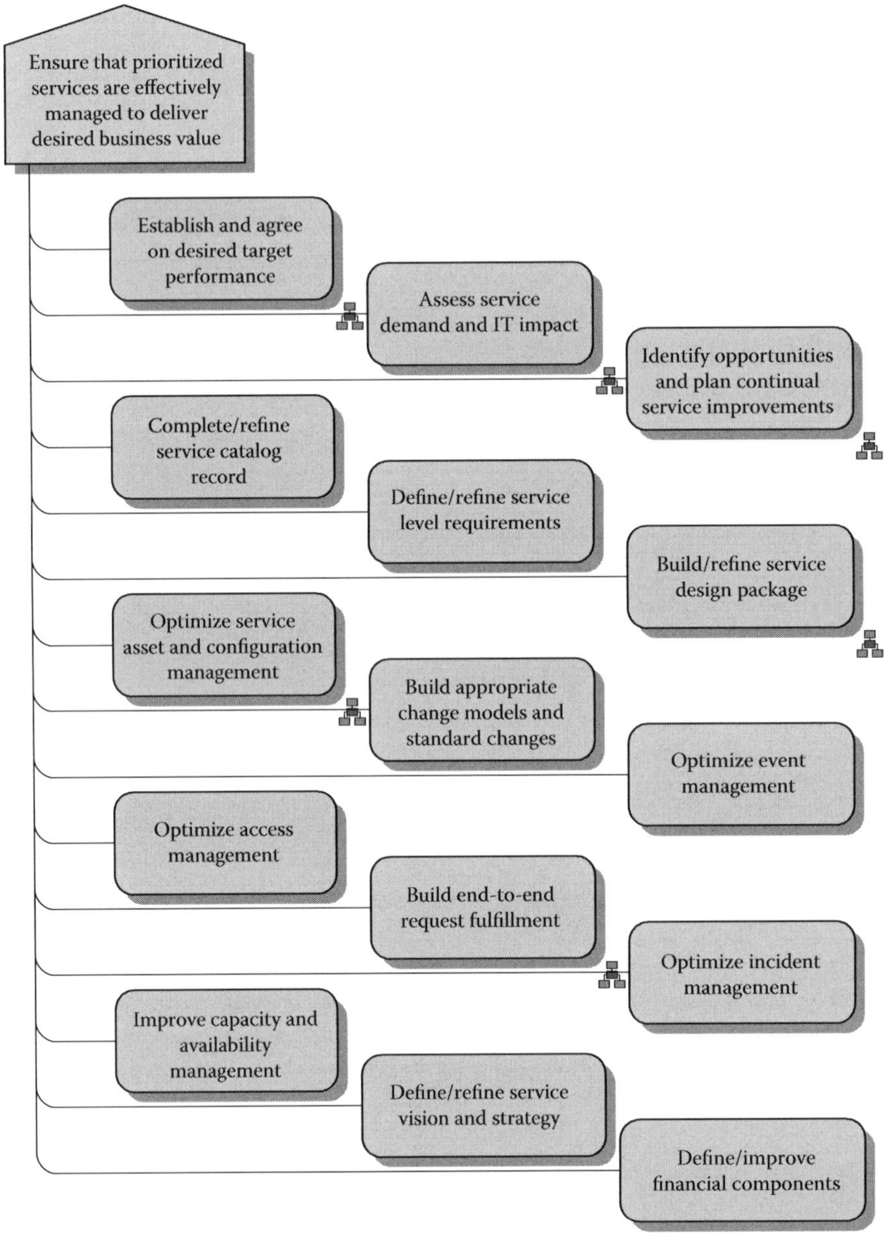

Figure 12.26 Supporting activities: Ensure that prioritized services are effectively managed to deliver desired business value.

It is critical to ensure that the service catalog is continually refined to reflect all newly discovered services.

- *Plan and build organizational capabilities to effectively support BSM.*
  In relation to end-to-end BSM, it is critical to build organizational capabilities to be able to support service management. Building organizational capabilities will involve improving processes, building people and talent, realigning organizational structures, refining or defining relationships with partners and other suppliers, and so on (Figure 12.27).
- *Continually improve BSM processes.*
  At the core of ITIL v3 is the notion of continual improvement. Therefore, improvements do not just end with the phase or the project. These improvements should continue and become more targeted and better aligned to maximize the return on investments made. The service management foundation established during the foundation phase is continually improved (Figure 12.28).

  As we have already discussed, foundation processes, such as incident, problem, change, service asset and configuration, and service catalog management processes have been improved during the foundation phase. These processes come from service design, service

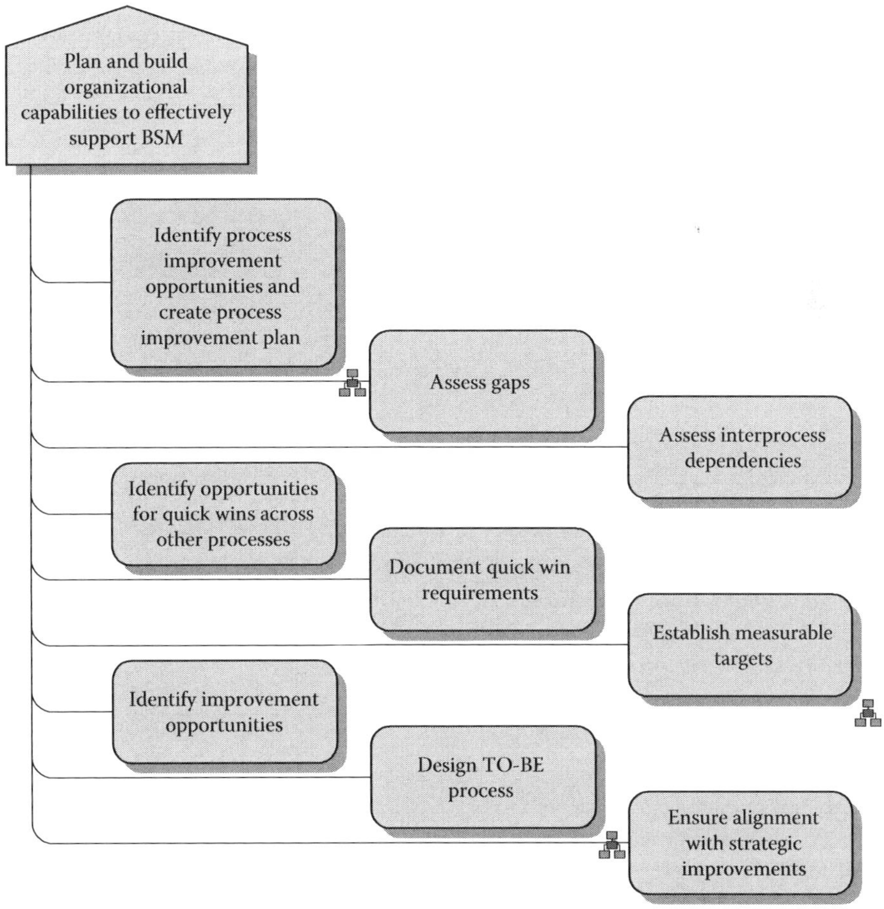

Figure 12.27 Supporting activities: Plan and build organizational capabilities to effectively support BSM.

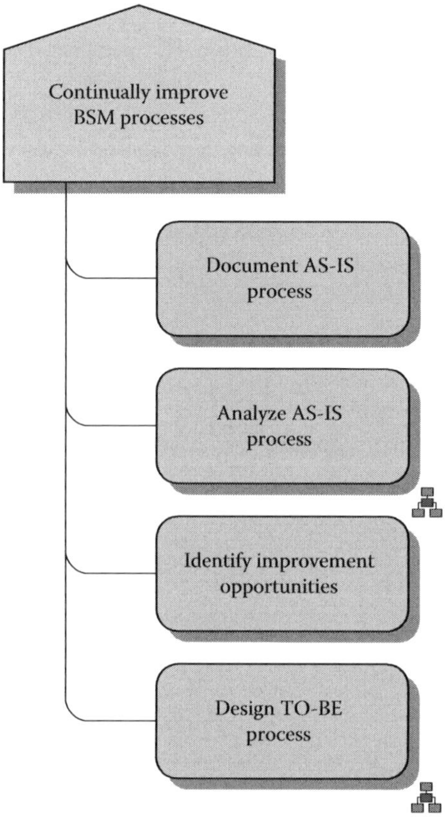

Figure 12.28 Supporting activities: Continually improve BSM processes.

transition, and service operations phases of the ITIL v3 service life cycle and are improved during the foundation phase. Note that all ITIL v3 processes are interrelated and largely depend on each other to be effective and efficient. To maximize the return on improvement-related investments, we will need to make necessary improvements across other closely related processes. This is something that will be a consistent focus throughout the life of service management implementation efforts. A good example is an effort to improve service asset and configuration management in the absence of an appropriate change management process. Therefore, it is critical to plan improvements across individual processes and also to carefully identify opportunities and achieve quick wins across other related process areas as well.

- *Ensure that all nonfunctional and functional requirements are cost-effectively and efficiently met.* This objective has been discussed earlier.
- *Architect, design, and prototype the BSM solution.* By the end of the design phase, we should plan to have an executable BSM target state architecture. One of the most valuable outcomes of the BSM implementation is to achieve a horizontal organizational integration across all relevant vertical silos in the organization and to enable those to work in harmony to deliver the services listed in the service catalog. Baselining the BSM target state architecture will enable us to see: (1) how BSM implementation will fit into the larger enterprise architecture; (2) what existing assets can be reused; (3) what integrations need to be implemented; (4) how

technology will be able to support BSM implementation; and (5) what key tooling capabilities the organization will need to have in place to achieve BSM (Figure 12.29).

BSM architecture is reviewed and feedback is provided. Based on those factors, appropriate refinements are made and recommendations that are more strategic and/or major are recorded and planned to be implemented during the remaining phases. BSM architecture is approved. In most cases, implementing IT service management will have cross-organizational impact in a number of ways. As discussed, organizational, technological, process-specific, and other changes will need to take place and need to be managed carefully.

- *Maximize reuse of existing assets.*
  Existing assets must be reused in order to gain possible efficiencies and reduce costs (Figure 12.30).

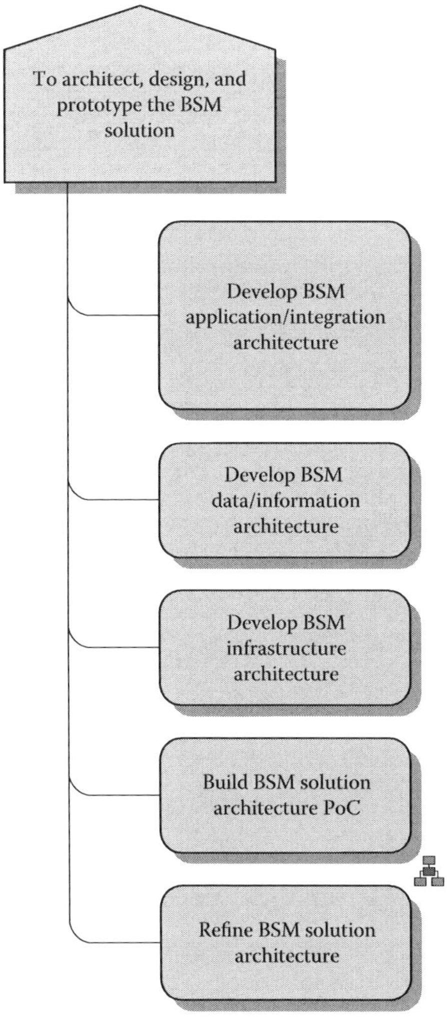

Figure 12.29 Supporting activities: Architect, design, and prototype the BSM solution.

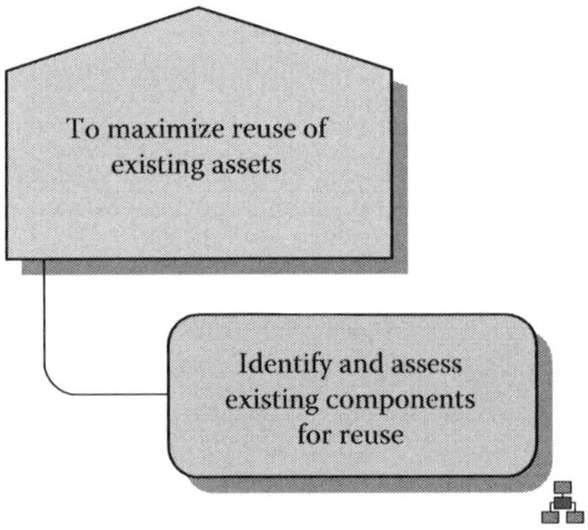

Figure 12.30 Supporting activities: Maximize reuse of existing assets.

- *Ensure that a detailed solution design is produced.*
  This objective has been discussed earlier.
- *Develop, integrate, test, and deploy solution.*
  This objective has been discussed earlier.

One of the key deliverables of the design phase is BSM architecture and to validate that architecture, end-to-end BSM is implemented for the prioritized or selected business services from the service catalog. The BSM architectural prototype should provide the foundation to build further alignment and, finally, the desired integration between the business and IT.

In addition, organizational capabilities are built to support the BSM culture. This involves a combination of communication, marketing, training, and awareness. CSI is now established. Although still part of an ITIL implementation program, it starts to own the organizational maturity baselines, the feeds from range of sources including customer, internal and external IT partners, regulatory bodies, business needs, and others, and is able to provide recommendations on what specific improvements should be pursued.

Align

By the time the service management implementation effort gets into the align phase, we will have achieved the following:

- Of the services listed in the service catalog, 70% will have end-to-end service management implemented.
- Service management foundation processes (e.g., incident management, problem management, change management, service asset and configuration management, and service catalog management, and others as appropriate) will have gone through a second round of improvements.
- The service catalog will have gone through another round of improvements, hopefully now reflecting a more complete set of services offered by your organization.
- Service design capabilities will have been improved.

If we have achieved the above, we will have established a good foundation to create and ensure alignment between the business and IT.

Purpose

The purpose of the align phase is to achieve business–IT alignment.

Objectives

The key objectives of this phase are shown in Figure 12.31.

The key objectives of this phase are as follows:

- *Achieve and demonstrate business–IT alignment.*
  One of the key objectives of the align phase is to achieve and demonstrate that IT is aligned with the business. Alignment can be demonstrated by: (1) having a majority of IT services in the catalog under end-to-end service management; (2) showing improved trends of customer satisfaction; and (3) improving the quality of services that are brought under service management (Figure 12.32).
- *Define clear roles and responsibilities and ensure that appropriate people are assigned to appropriate roles.*
  Make necessary organizational improvements to encourage creation of BSM culture. In low-maturity organizations, technologies are normally managed for the sake of managing technology. Technology excites our technologists, and that is fine. However, there should be a broader appreciation across the IT organization in general, and for the technology manager responsible for an important specific technology component in particular, of the relative importance of that component to the business and what the impact will be if it fails or the performance deteriorates. Service management culture requires service thinking and an organization that is aligned to effectively execute service management processes and deliver the needed services at the right levels (Figure 12.33).
- *Integrate CSI within the organization.*
  CSI is not only an established function with a number of success stories under its belt, but is also beginning to integrate within the larger organization (Figure 12.34).
- *Ensure that prioritized services are effectively managed to deliver the desired business value.*
  At this point in implementing end-to-end BSM for prioritized business services, approximately 70% of the catalog should be under service management by this time. The majority of the services listed in the service catalog are brought under end-to-end service management by the end of this phase. The service catalog is continually improved—that is, existing service definitions, associated targets, and other details are further refined and those services that might not have been captured earlier are now included in the service catalog.
- *Plan and build organizational capabilities to effectively support BSM.*
  This objective has been discussed earlier.
- *Continually improve BSM processes.*
  Refine BSM foundation and service design processes. The service management foundation established during the foundation phase and service design processes developed during the design phase are further refined as part of continual process and service improvement efforts. Establish and/or improve service strategy processes. With service management foundation

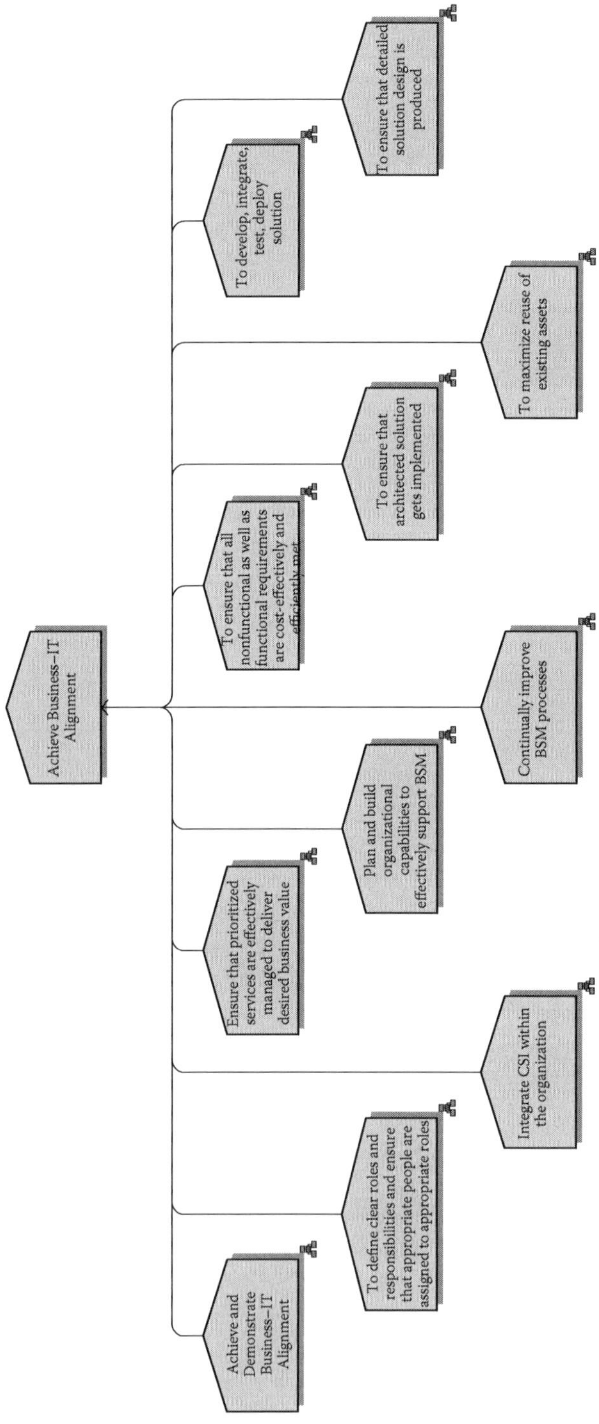

Figure 12.31 Align phase objectives.

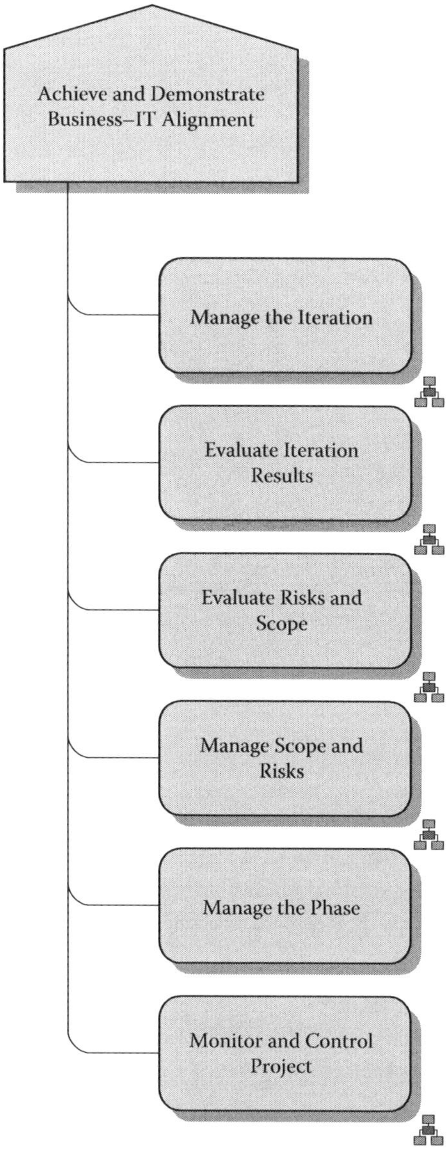

Figure 12.32 Supporting activities: Achieve and demonstrate business–IT alignment.

and design processes in place, we now have the right foundation to start maturing our service strategy processes. These specifically include maturing parts of demand, financial, and/or service portfolio management processes. To maximize returns on improvement investments, it will be critical to continually identify and achieve quick wins across all other relevant ITIL v3 processes to maximize value. All ITIL v3 processes are interrelated and largely depend on each other to be effective and efficient. To maximize returns on improvement-related investments, we will need to make necessary improvements across other closely related processes. This is something that will be a consistent focus throughout the life of service management implementation effort. A good example is an effort to improve service

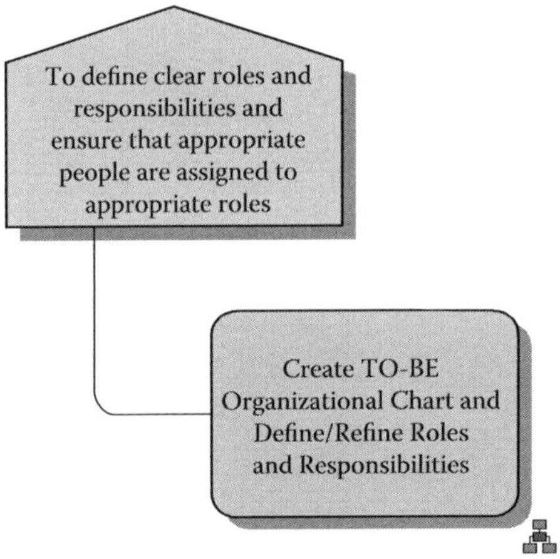

Figure 12.33 Supporting activities: Define clear roles and responsibilities and ensure that appropriate people are assigned to appropriate roles.

asset and configuration management in the absence of an appropriate change management process. Therefore, it is critical to not only plan improvements across individual processes but also carefully identify opportunities and achieve quick wins across other related process areas as well.

- *Ensure that all nonfunctional and functional requirements are cost-effectively and efficiently met.* This objective has been discussed earlier.
- *Ensure that the architected solution gets implemented.* The following needs to be achieved:
  - Fine-tune BSM target state architecture—The BSM target state architecture baselined at the end of the design phase is further validated and refined if required. These refine-

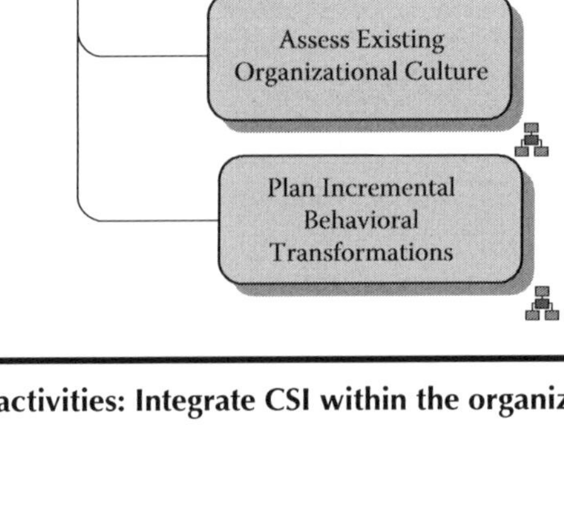

Figure 12.34 Supporting activities: Integrate CSI within the organization.

ments, however, should be minimal and should not impact the fundamental BSM architecture.
  - Review BSM architecture and provide feedback—The BSM architecture should be reviewed toward the end of each phase and feedback provided. As discussed, refinements to this architecture should be minimal and should continue to reduce over the course of this project.
  - Review architectural risks and ensure that they are managed effectively—With the review of the BSM architecture and evaluation of the beta solution, potential risks are identified and necessary action items are identified to mitigate those risks.
- *Ensure that detailed solution design is produced.*
  This is discussed in the previous phase.
- *Develop, integrate, test, and deploy the solution.*
  There may be point solutions to support a subset of BSM processes. However, there is also a total and integrated BSM solution. It is critical that by the end of the align phase, the beta BSM solution is released. This is the overall integrated solution that will support end-to-end BSM. The executable prototype that helped baseline the architecture in the design phase is further evolved into a beta release. This will be done along with realignment across the IT organization, redefinition of partner relationships, and reengineering processes.

Integrate

This is the last phase of BSM project implementation. If we have made it to this phase in our organization, it is evidence of the fact that we have been able to create value for our businesses and customers and we have been able to continue to sustain the sponsorship and support required for transformation efforts like ours. This is a huge success for the team that has been engaged in managing and implementing BSM and for the organization that has been able to mature to the level from where it will be able to partner with their businesses and customers and create value for them. By now, we are now mature enough to move further down the path of becoming a value-add partner for our businesses and customers. We have achieved a comprehensive understanding of what we do and why our customers and businesses pay for our services. By the end of this phase, we will have achieved improvements across all of the service management processes and 100% of the services in the service catalog.

Purpose

The main purpose of the integrate phase is to achieve business–IT integration.

Objectives

Integrate phase objectives are shown in Figure 12.35.

Key objectives of this phase are as follows:

- *Achieve and demonstrate business–IT integration.*
  Ensure that organization achieves the desired maturity levels. This is the final phase of BSM implementation project and we need to ensure that we achieve the planned maturity levels. Integration between business and IT is the key objective of the integrate phase (Figure 12.36).

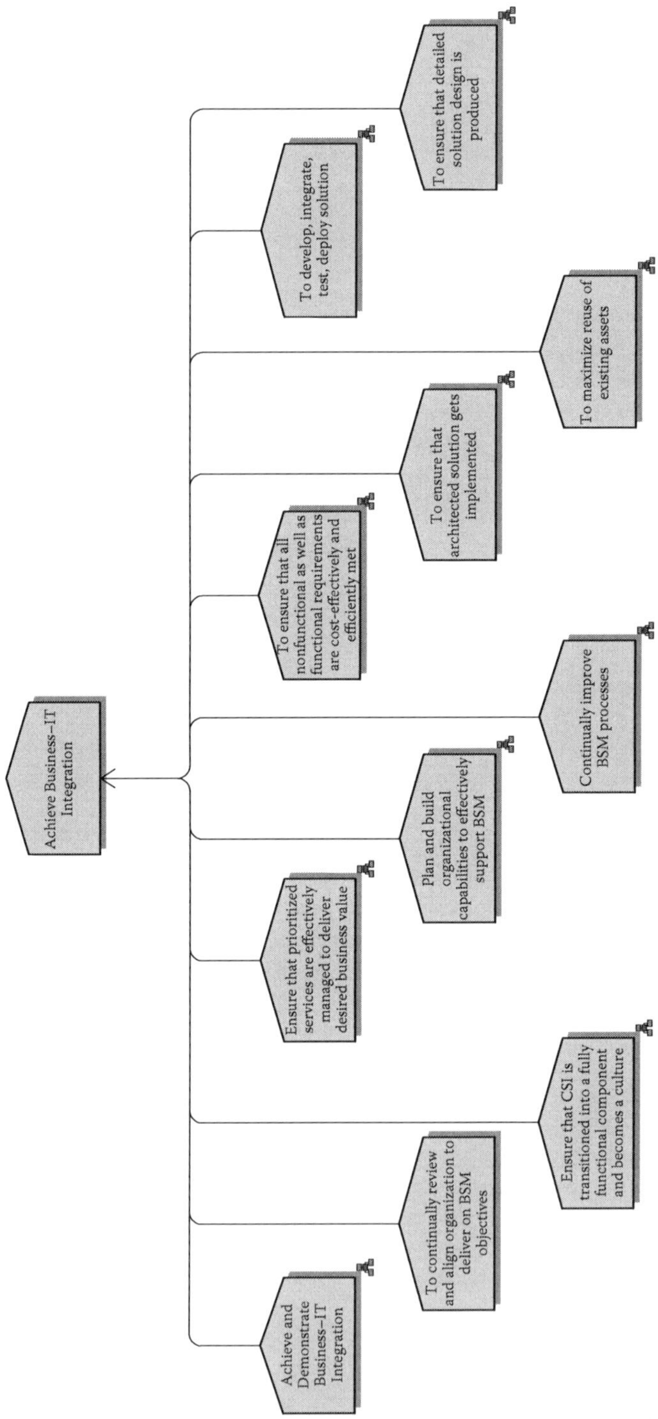

Figure 12.35 Integrate phase objectives.

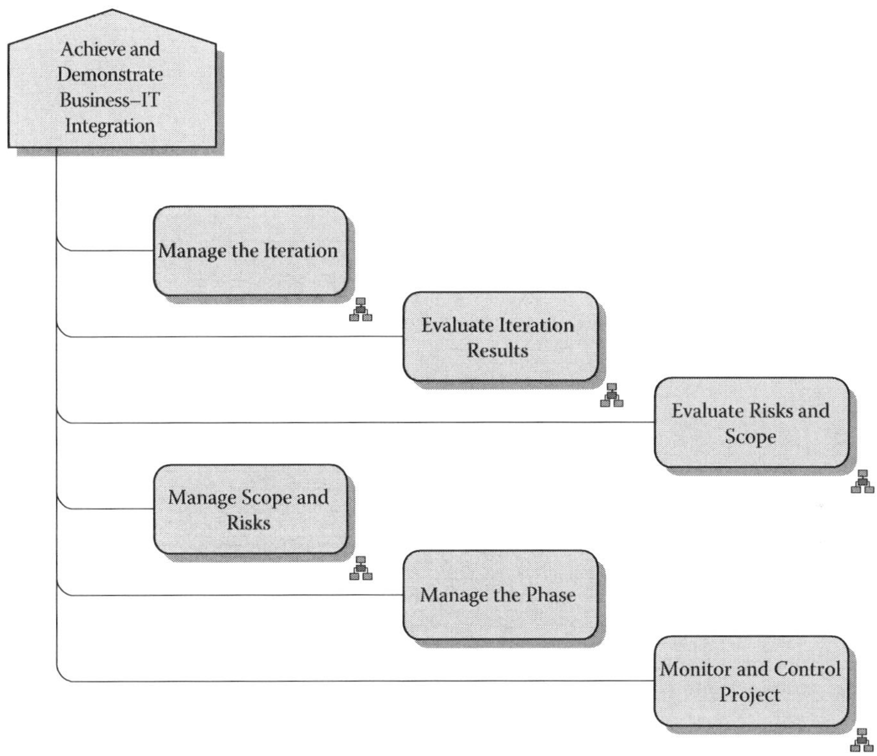

Figure 12.36 Supporting activities: Achieve and demonstrate business–IT integration.

- *Continually review and align the organization to deliver on BSM objectives.*
  This ensures that organizational performance is continually reviewed and necessary organizational improvements are realized to encourage the creation of service management culture (Figure 12.37).
- *Ensure that CSI is transitioned into a fully functional component and becomes culture.*
  Over the course of the first three phases of this project, we have been maturing our CSI function and team. In other words, we have been incubating the CSI and helping it grow both in terms of its influence and impact on the overall success of this project and in terms of its own maturity. By now, if we have managed this project right, CSI should have demonstrated the value it offers to the organization and should be ready to spin off into an independent function or organizational unit (Figure 12.38).
- *Ensure that prioritized services are effectively managed to deliver the desired business value.*
  Implement end-to-end service management for prioritized business services. Of the services listed in the service catalog, 100% brought under service management by the end of this phase. This has been discussed previously.
- *Plan and build organizational capabilities to effectively support BSM.*
  This was discussed in the previous phase.
- *Continually improve BSM processes.*
  This has been discussed in the previous phase; however, there are some core activities that must be ensured during the integrate phase. These include:

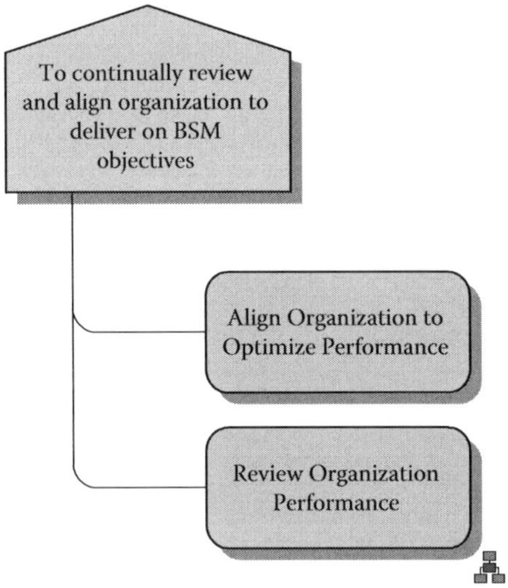

Figure 12.37 Supporting activities: Continually review and align organization to deliver on BSM objectives.

- Ensure continual refinement of the service catalog—The service catalog is continually improved. This means that existing service definitions, associated targets, and other details are further refined, and those services that might not have been captured earlier are now included in the service catalog.
- Identify and achieve quick wins across all other relevant ITIL v3 processes to maximize value—All ITIL v3 processes are interrelated and largely depend on each other to be effective

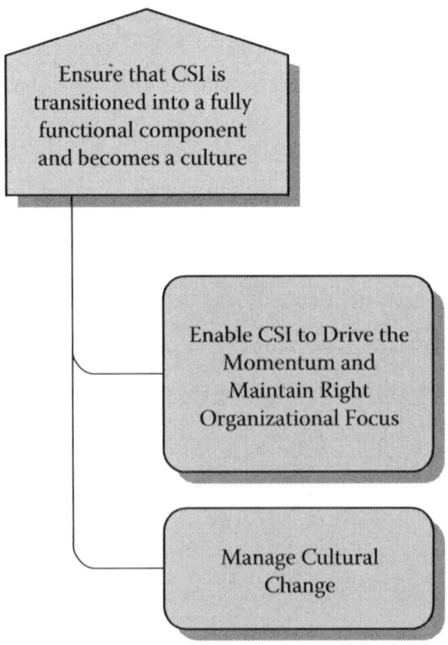

Figure 12.38 Supporting activities: Ensure that CSI is transitioned into a fully functional component and becomes culture.

and efficient. To maximize returns on improvement-related investments, we will need to make necessary improvements across other closely related processes. This is something that will be a consistent focus throughout the life of service management implementation efforts. A good example is an effort to improve service asset and configuration management in the absence of an appropriate change management process. Therefore, it is critical to not only plan improvements across individual processes, but to also carefully identify opportunities and achieve quick wins across other related process areas.

- *Ensure that all nonfunctional and functional requirements are cost-effectively and efficiently met.*
  This was discussed in the previous phase.
- *Ensure that the architected solution gets implemented.*
  This was discussed in the previous phase.
- *Maximize reuse of existing assets.*
  This was discussed in the previous phase.
- *Ensure that detailed solution design is produced.*
  This was discussed in the previous phase.
- *Develop, integrate, test, and deploy the solution.*
  This was discussed in the previous phase.

Overview of a Typical Iteration

In this chapter, we have discussed the four phases within the i2-SOSMI methodology. Now, we will review the key constituent components of each phase (i.e., iteration). Each phase comprises three well-defined iterations. Each iteration results in the creation of tangible business value (improvement in services delivered by the IT organization through improvements in underpinning service management processes). Each iteration may be between 4 to 12 weeks in duration. Each iteration increases the business value delivered by IT in a measurable fashion. Depending on the size, complexity, and maturity of the organization, the overall duration of the BSM implementation program may range from 1 to 4 years. This section delves into some greater phase and iteration level details.

Let us see, at a very high level, what all is performed within each iteration. Note the importance of alignment with the business and IT vision and strategy at the top and development of the foundation at the base. We will also briefly discuss some of the common key components of this figure.

Align with Vision and Strategy

Each iteration ensures the continual alignment of IT vision and strategy with the overall business vision and strategy. Ideally, each iteration should begin by revisiting and ensuring that a continual alignment between the deliverable of the given iteration and the business and IT strategy exists. If executed appropriately, the IT service management strategy should further refine the larger IT strategy.

Establish BSM Foundation

As the name suggests, this foundation is absolutely critical to effective and efficient implementation and management of BSM. In most cases, the processes included should be enough to establish this foundation. The service catalog plays an important role in providing the foundation for implementation of service management. The service catalog provides a single source of all operational (and soon-to-be operational) services provided by the IT organization. More details on what the service catalog contains can be found within the ITIL v3 service design literature.

The Pattern

Each iteration focuses on specific business needs. To ensure that needs are understood and addressed objectively, key associated business processes are prioritized and enabling business services are identified. Note that the service catalog needs to be established as part of the service management foundation. This service catalog is then used to identify and prioritize the business services and technical services that need to be improved. To maximize business benefits, it is recommended that prioritization should be carried out at the business services level and technical services should be improved to improve the selected business services. In almost all cases, there may be one or more technical services required to realize a given business service and each technical service may be shared by one or more business services. These business service and technical service relationships are shown at a high level in the service tree discussed earlier in this book. To improve a given business service, improvements will be implemented within the underpinning technical services.

Quantifiable improvement opportunities are identified that will be delivered by the end of that iteration at business processes as well as business service levels. Service level requirements (SLRs) are understood and associated service level agreements (SLAs) are established and agreed on.

As per the SLRs and SLAs, business services and technical services are improved to ensure that agreed targets are met. To improve the quality of business and technical services, IT service management processes will need to be improved.

Each iteration will result in service and service management process improvements. With this generic overview of an iteration, let us discuss each type of iteration in greater detail.

Visualize Iteration

The visualize iteration is intended to achieve the following:

- During the foundation phase, visualize iteration aims to
  - Analyze and envision IT organization
  - Envision and create service catalog management process improvement plan
  - Envision, design, and establish CSI
  - Define BSM technology strategy
  - Develop BSM architecture roadmap
  - Plan the BSM project
- For all other phases, other than the foundation phase:
  - Plan continual improvements and cultural change
  - Prioritize and plan business service improvements
  - Prioritize and plan service management process improvements
  - Analyze business services and service management process automation requirements
  - Identify, analyze, architect, and realize quick wins

As shown in Figure 12.39, during visualize iteration, a given service(s) or service management process(es) is analyzed and potential improvements are envisioned and service improvement plans

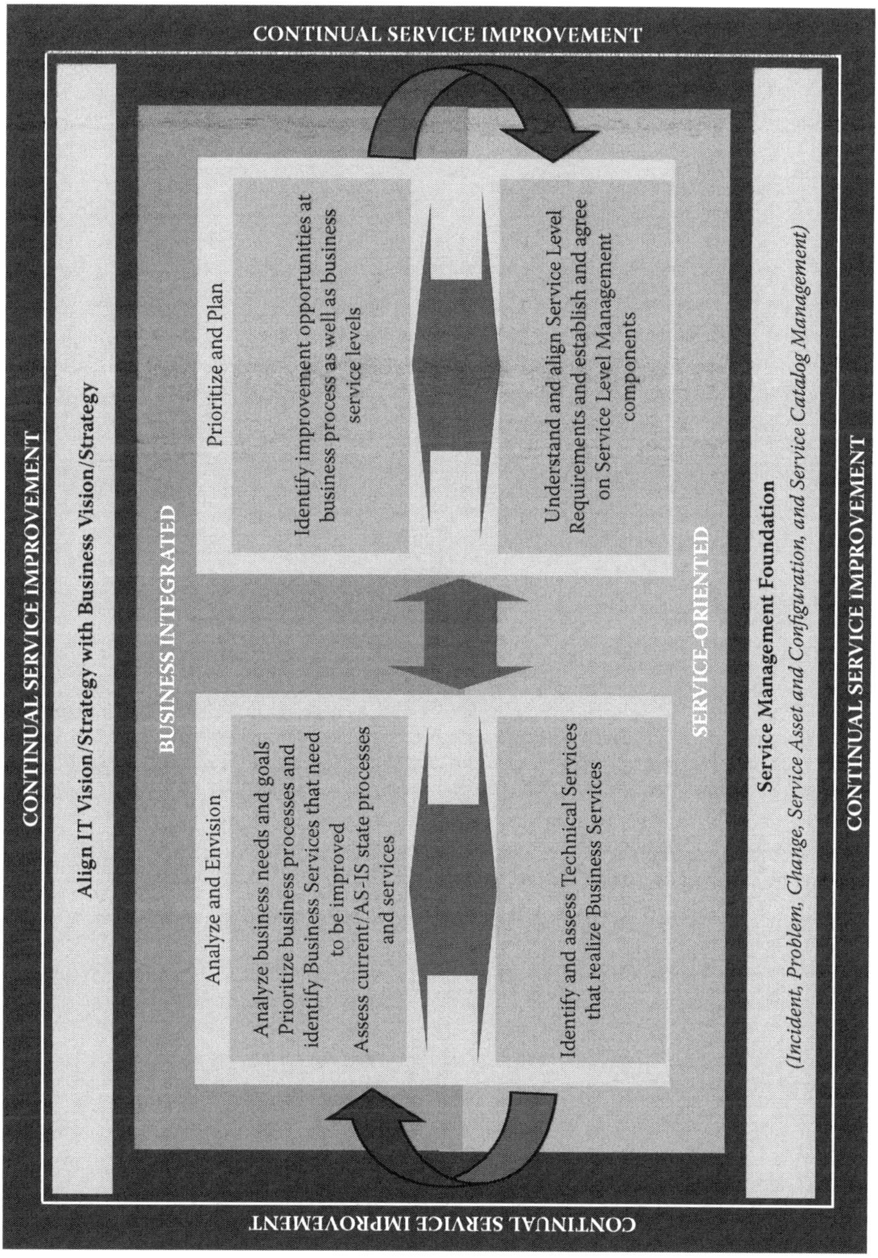

Figure 12.39 Overview of visualize iteration.

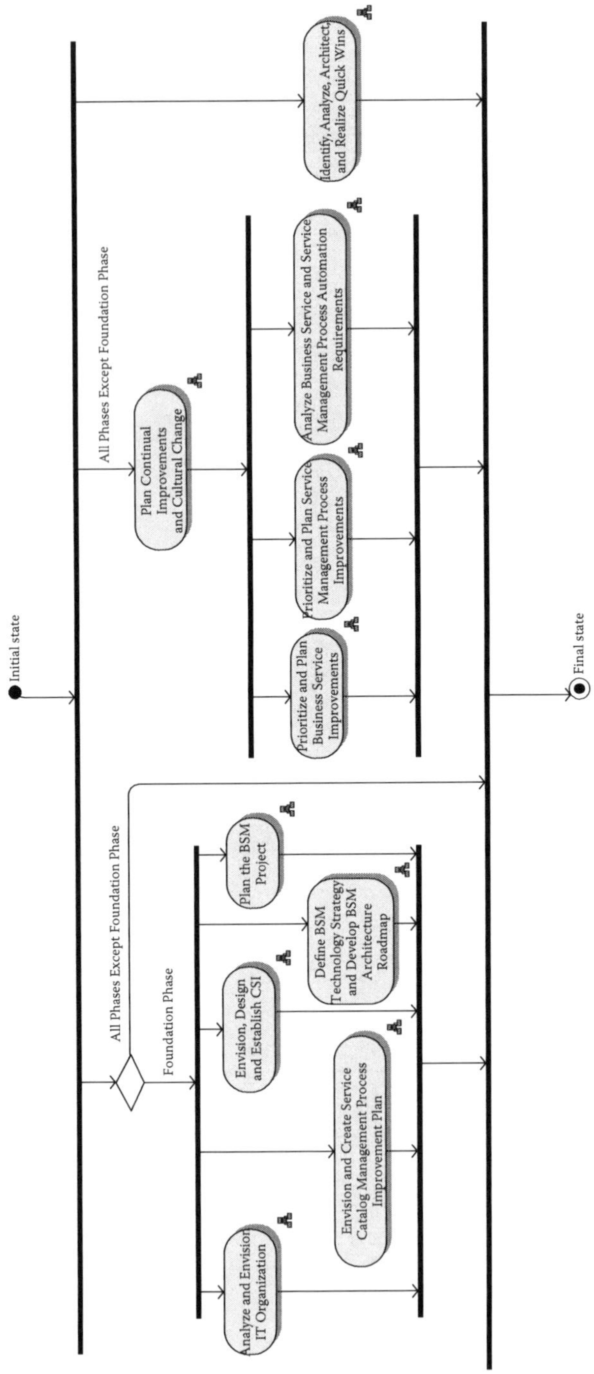

Figure 12.40 Visualize iteration workflow.

are developed. The visualize iteration workflow is shown in Figure 12.40. Let us discuss each of the activities within the workflow in detail.

Analyze and Envision IT Organization

The IT organization is analyzed and its TO-BE organization is envisioned (Figure 12.41). It is critical to define the organizational principles and establish an organization mission statement. Is the organization an internal service provider and what is the organization aspiring to achieve?

Envision and Create Service Catalog Management Process Improvement Plan

As discussed earlier, the service catalog must be at the core of BSM implementation. Service catalog management is one of the ITIL v3 processes and must be developed during the foundation phase.

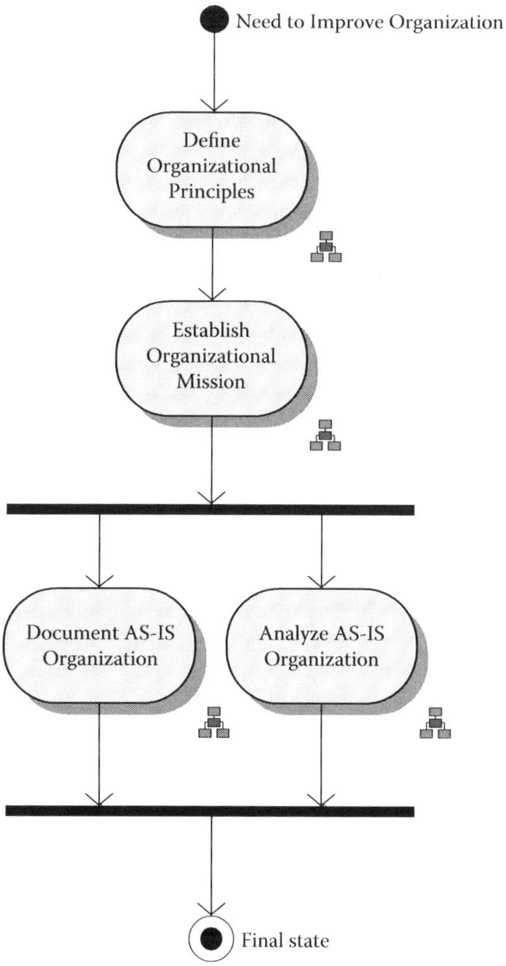

Figure 12.41 Analyze and envision the IT organization.

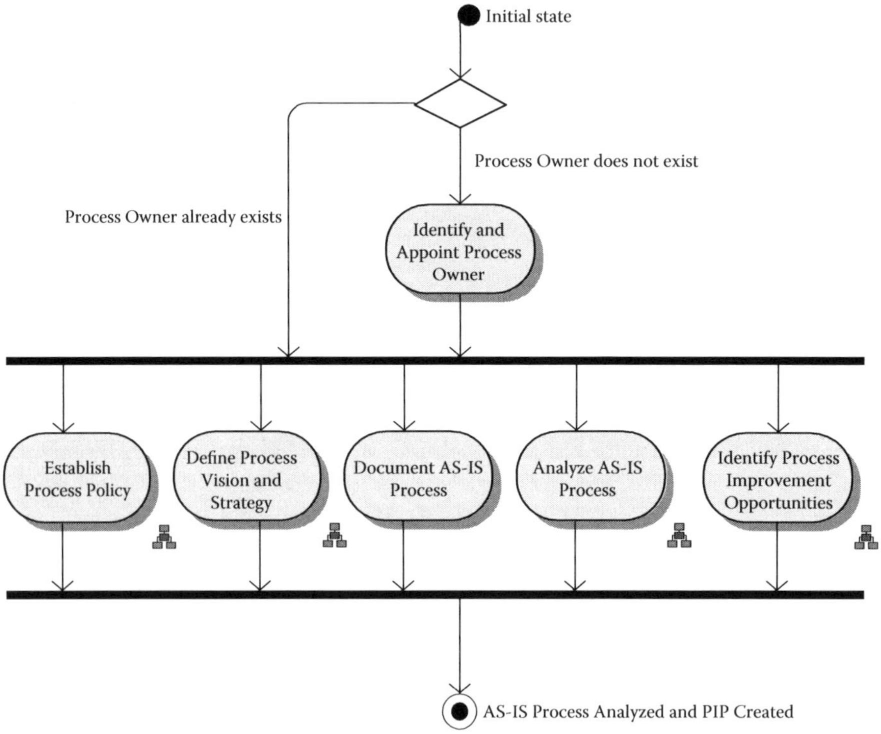

Figure 12.42 Improving or developing service catalog management.

Figure 12.42 shows a generic set of activities that should be performed to improve or develop the service management process. These activities should be performed to analyze and define the service catalog management process.

Envision, Design, and Establish CSI

As discussed, CSI is an engine to achieve the culture of continual improvements. CSI is the most critical component to keep the momentum going. The foundation required for establishing CSI must be established during the first iteration of the foundation phase.

Figure 12.43 shows the activities that should be performed to envision, design, and establish CSI. Key outputs include the CSI vision and strategy and the CSI roadmap and plan.

Define the BSM Technology Strategy and Develop a BSM Architecture Roadmap

It is critical to define the enabling BSM technologies strategy and envision the architecture during the foundation phase (Figure 12.44).

Plan the BSM Project

The BSM project is planned during the first iteration of the foundation phase. The key activities performed are shown in Figure 12.45.

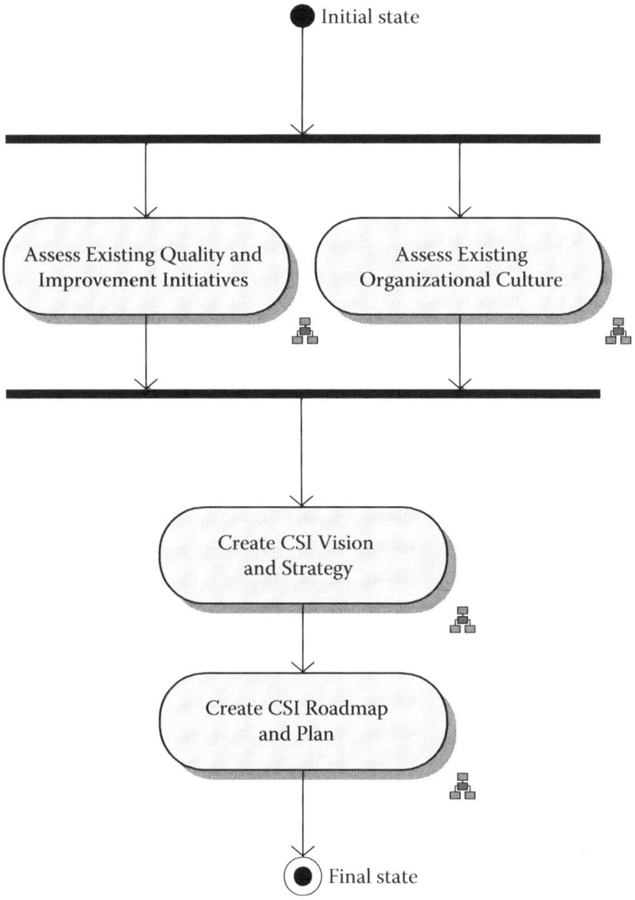

Figure 12.43 Envision, design, and establish CSI.

Plan Continual Improvements and Cultural Change

Note that during the foundation phase, CSI must be established. In the remaining three phases (i.e., design, align, and integrate), CSI should drive the improvements. Therefore, for all phases except the foundation phase, CSI must assess IT performance and identify opportunities for improvement. These opportunities are prioritized and related plans are developed (Figure 12.46).

Prioritize and Plan Business Service Improvements

Business service improvements are prioritized and planned during this activity. Details are shown in Figure 12.47.

Prioritize and Plan Service Management Process Improvements

Service management process improvements are prioritized and planned. Details are shown in Figure 12.48.

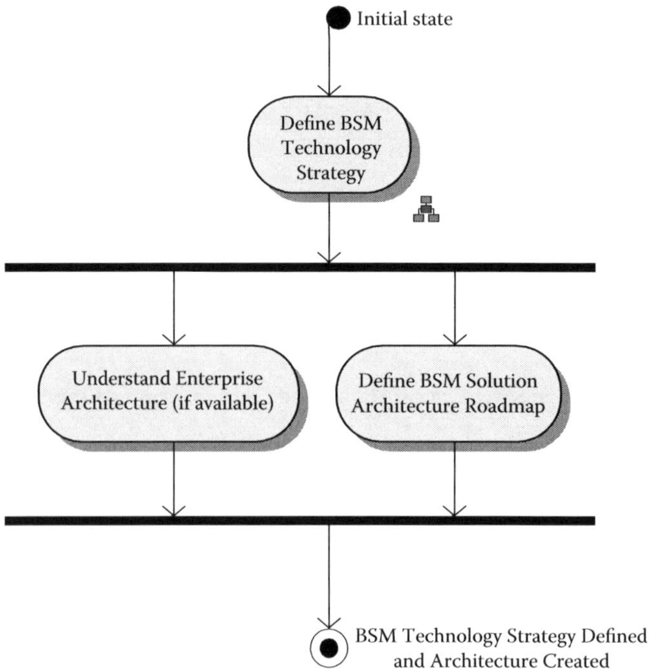

Figure 12.44 Define a BSM technology strategy and develop a BSM architecture roadmap.

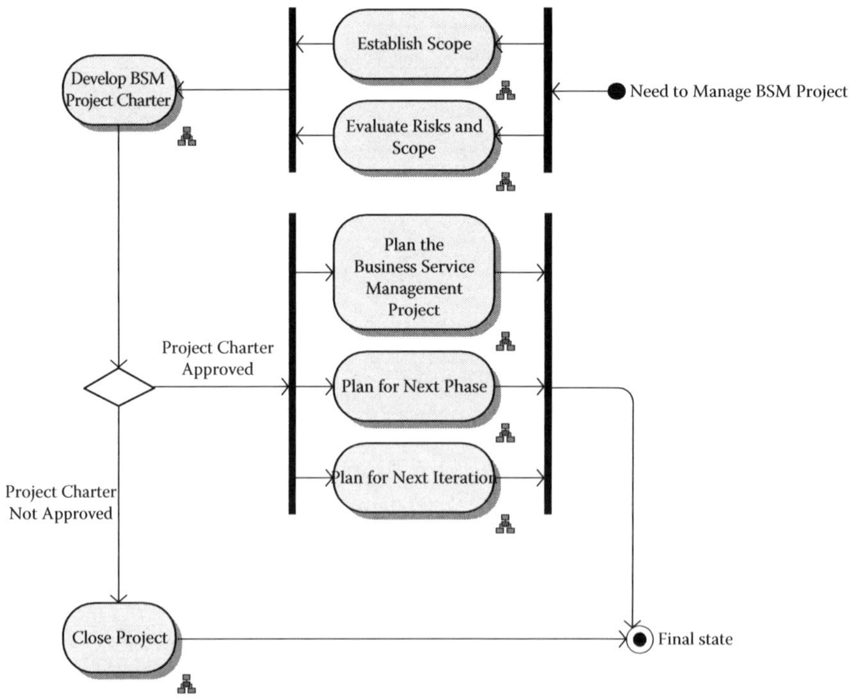

Figure 12.45 Plan the BSM project.

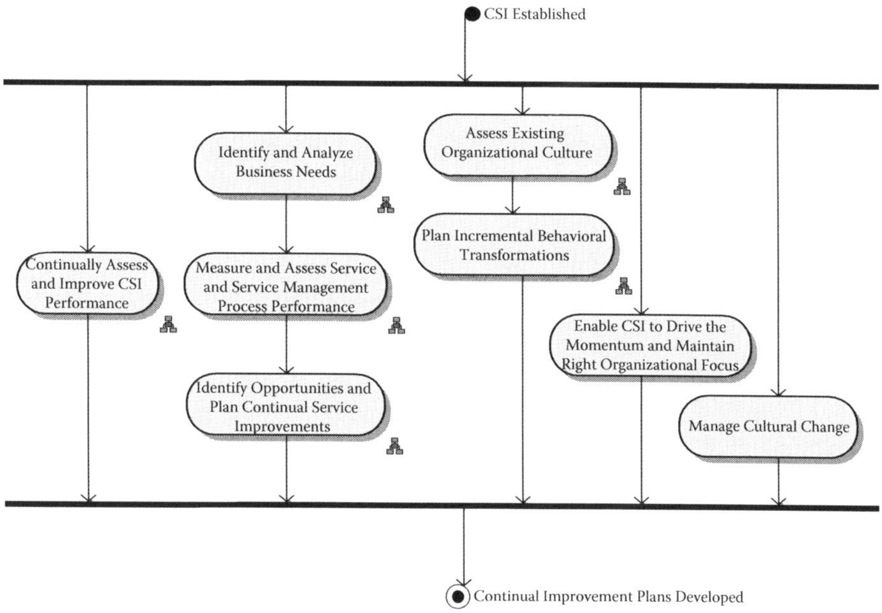

Figure 12.46 Plan continual improvements and cultural change.

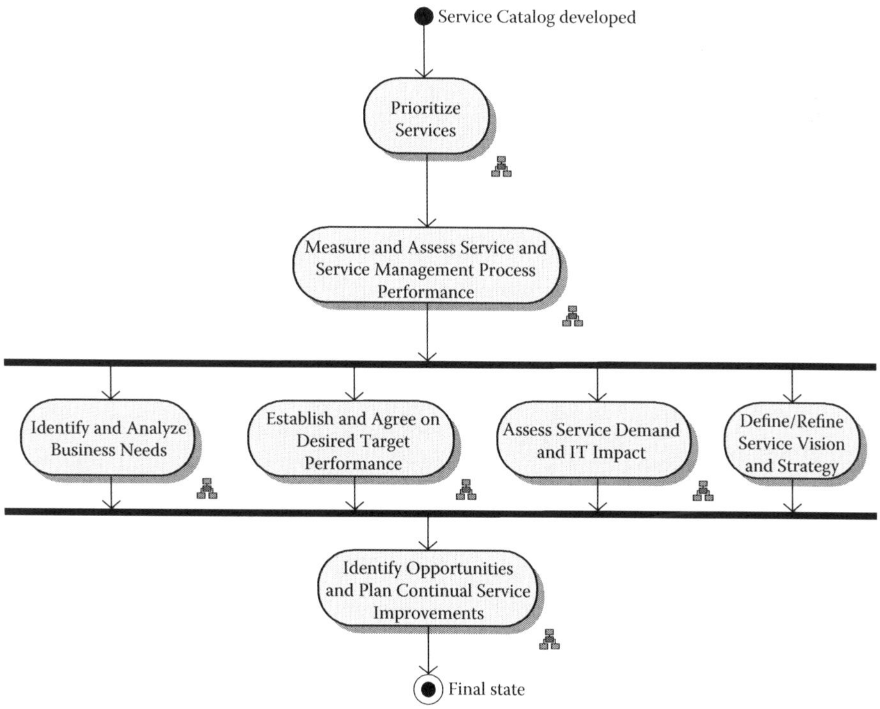

Figure 12.47 Prioritize and plan business service improvements.

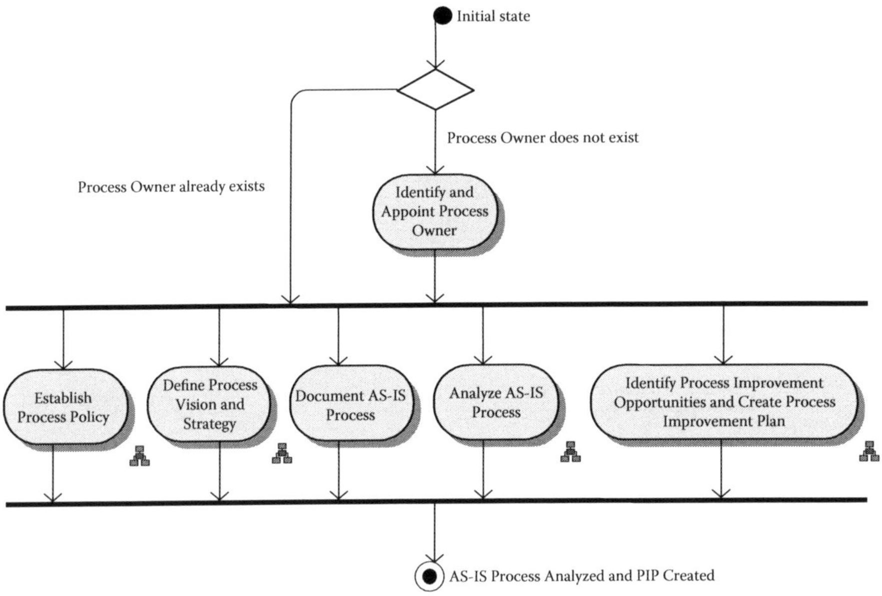

Figure 12.48 Prioritize and plan service management improvements.

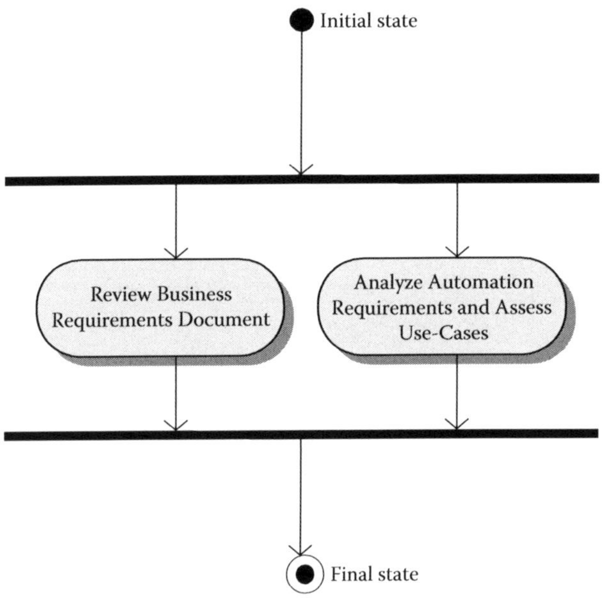

Figure 12.49 Analyze business service and service management process automation requirements.

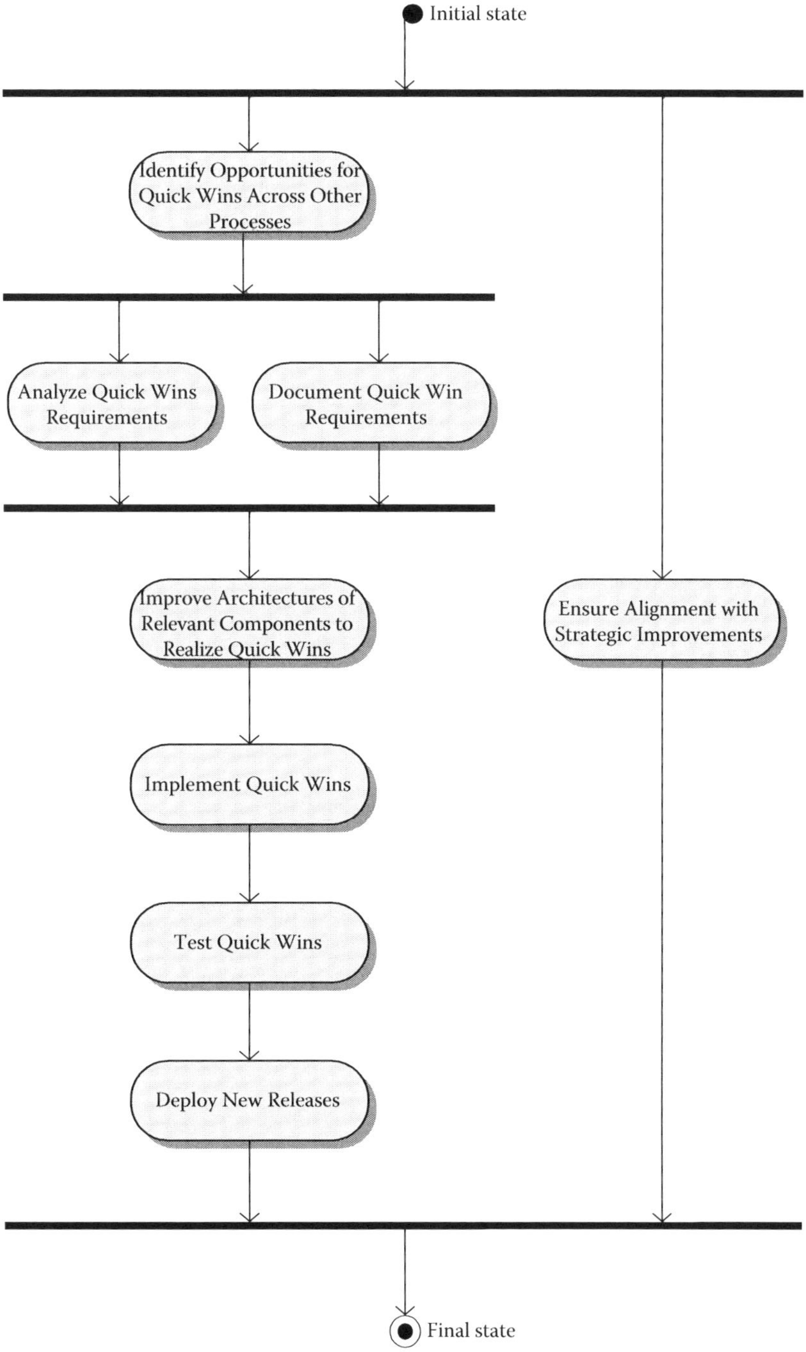

Figure 12.50 Identify, analyze, architect, and realize quick wins.

Analyze Business Service and Service Management Process Automation Requirements

As AS-IS business services and service management processes are analyzed, potential automation requirements are identified and documented. Note that process analysis and automation requirement analysis are performed in parallel (Figure 12.49).

Identify, Analyze, Architect, and Realize Quick Wins

Quick wins are critical to maximize returns on improvement and related investments. Quick wins must be carefully planned, prioritized, and implemented to minimize downstream rework or wasted effort and to maximize returns. Quick wins must be considered integral to each iteration (Figure 12.50).

Architect Iteration

During this iteration, prioritized improvements across business services as well as service management processes are architected, designed, and, if necessary, the desired solution and other BSM capabilities are prototyped. Figure 12.51 shows a high-level overview of the architect iteration.

There are two main activities performed during this iteration:

- Architect and design
- Implement and prototype

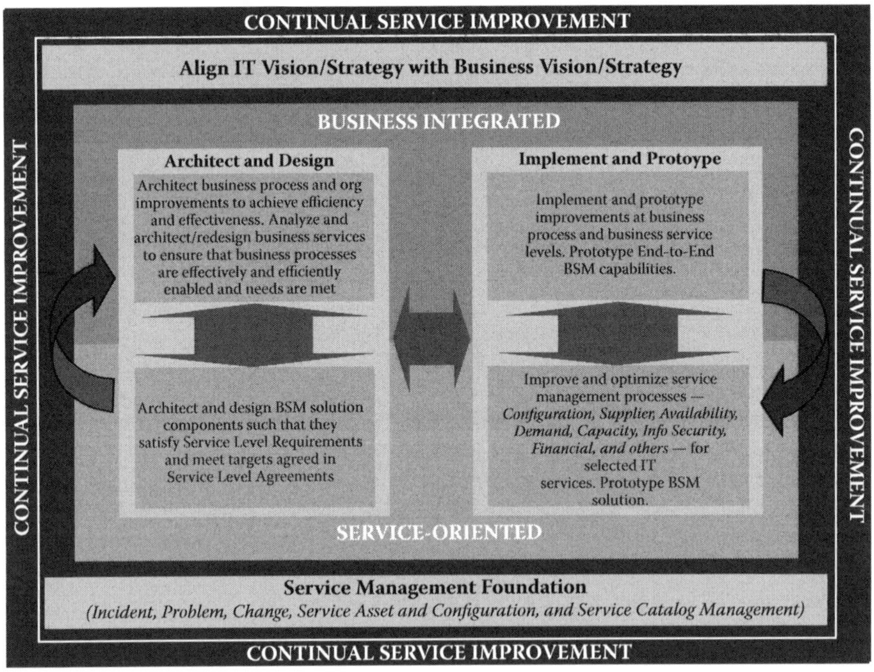

Figure 12.51 Overview of architect iteration.

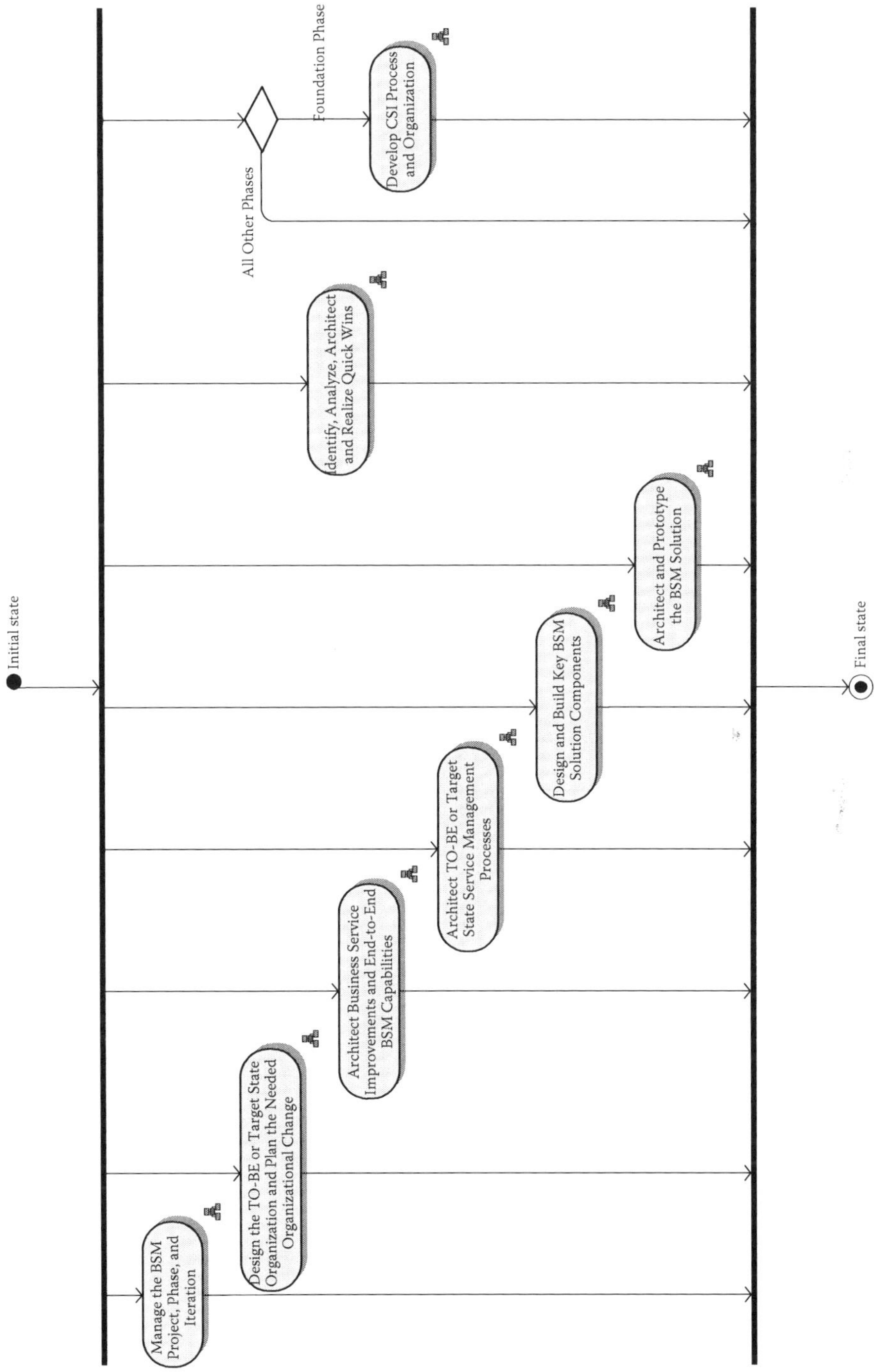

Figure 12.52 Architect iteration workflow.

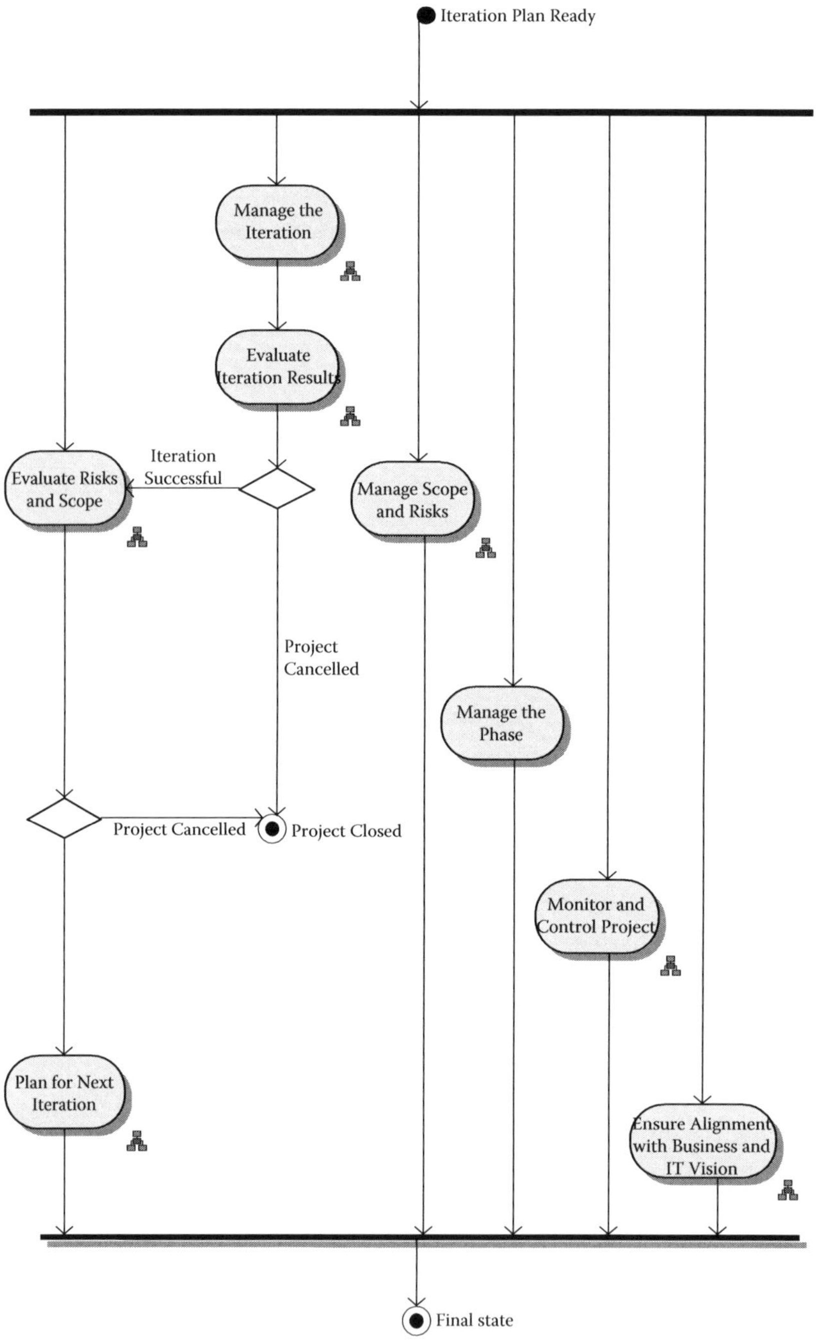

Figure 12.53 Manage the BSM project, phase, and iteration.

Details are shown in the architect iteration workflow in Figure 12.52. During the architect iteration, the following is achieved. If it is architect iteration for the foundation phase, then the CSI process and the organization are developed. In addition, during this iteration:

- The BSM project, phase, and iteration are managed to ensure that desired results are achieved.
- The TO-BE organization is designed and the needed organizational change is planned.
- Business service improvements and end-to-end BSM capabilities are architected.
- The TO-BE service management processes are architected.
- Key BSM solution components are designed and built.

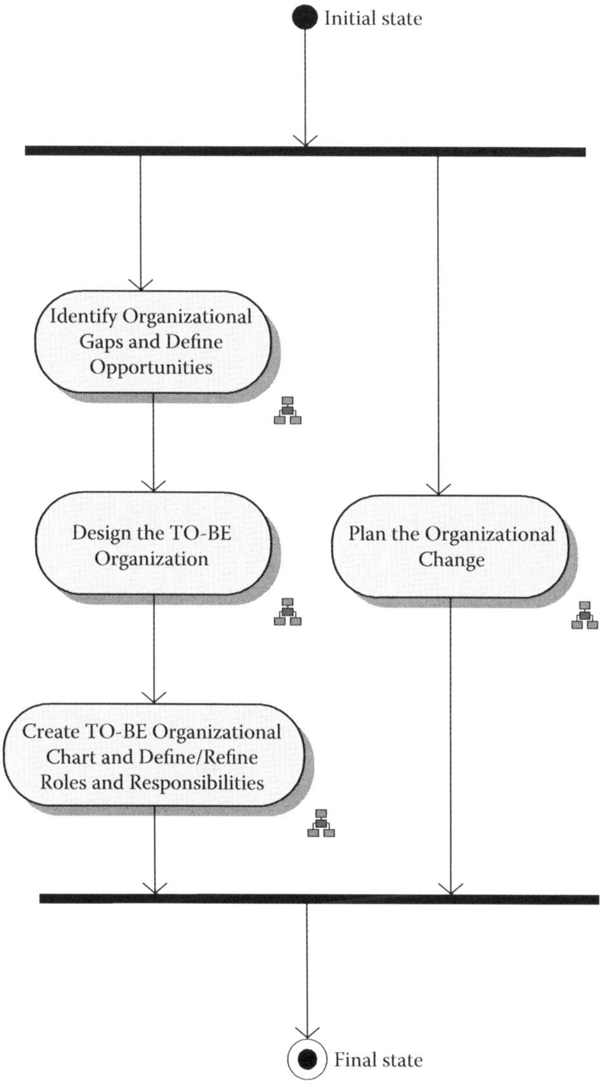

Figure 12.54 Design the TO-BE organization and plan the needed organization change.

- A BSM solution is prototyped.
- Quick wins are identified, analyzed, architected, and realized.

Let us discuss each of the activities. Note that each of these activities represent logical groupings of activities performed within i2-SOSMI disciplines. These discipline activities have already been discussed earlier in this book.

Let us discuss these activities in detail.

Manage the BSM Project, Phase, and Iteration

The project as well as respective phase and iteration are managed to ensure that risks are effectively managed and the desired results are efficiently delivered within cost and schedule (Figure 12.53).

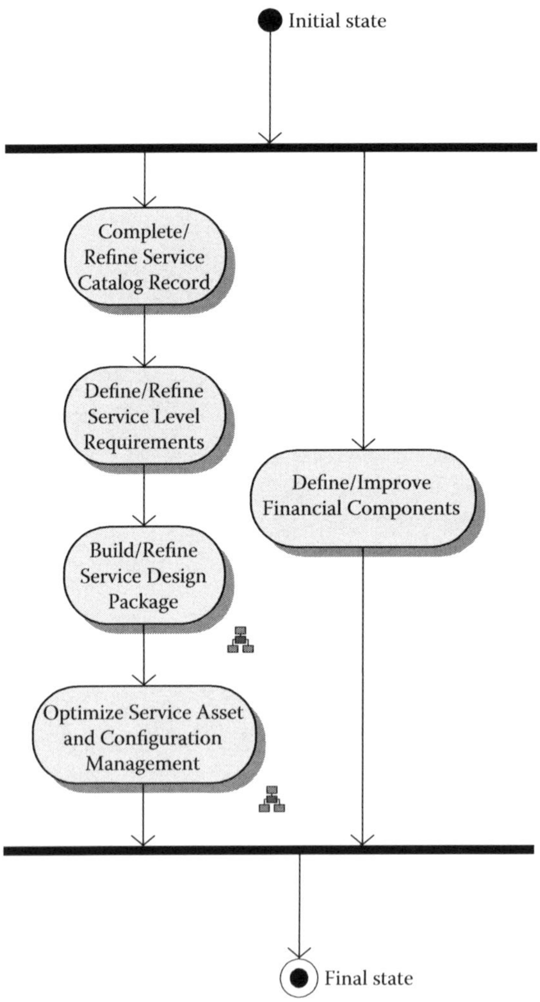

Figure 12.55 Architect business service improvements and end-to-end BSM capabilities.

Design the TO-BE Organization and Plan the Needed Organizational Change

The following activities are performed to design the target state organization and develop the plans for the necessary organizational changes (Figure 12.54).

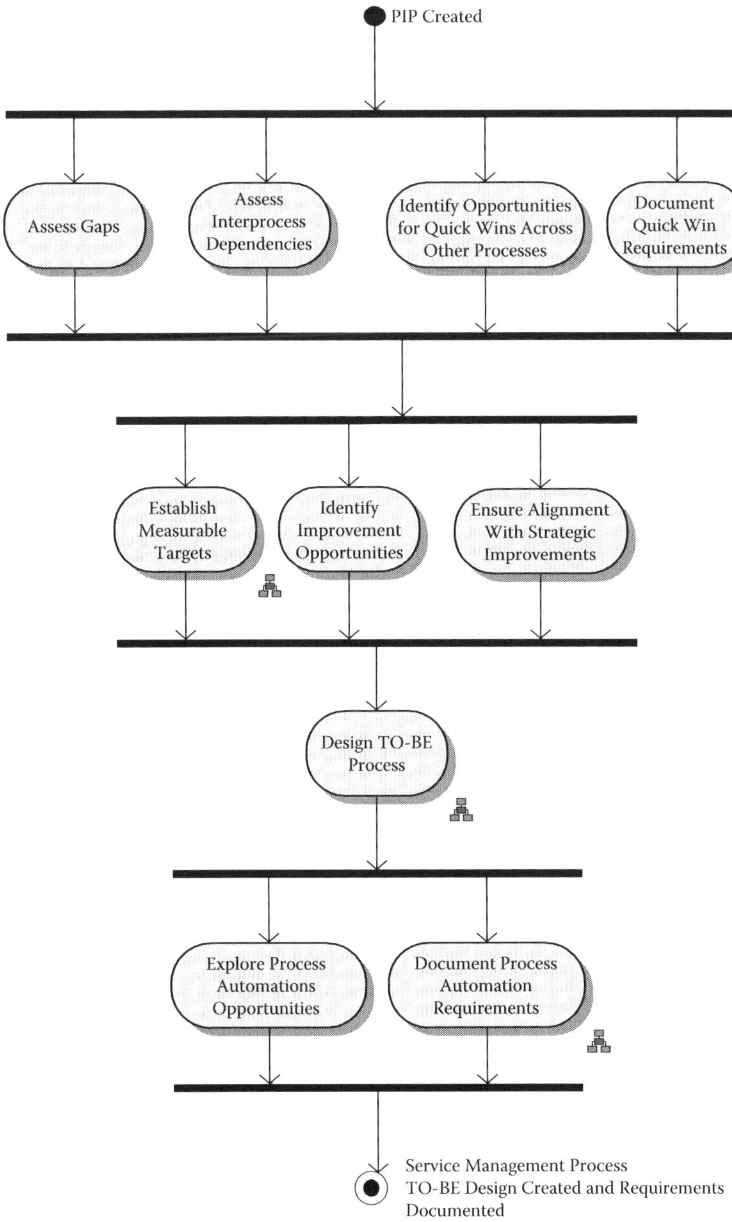

Figure 12.56 Architect TO-BE service management processes.

Architect Business Service Improvements and End-to-End BSM Capabilities

Business service improvement starts with a clear understanding of what it exactly stands for. The service catalog record for this business service is completed or refined, SLR is completed, a service design package (SDP) is developed, and a service asset and configuration management process is optimized in support of this service (Figure 12.55).

Architect TO-BE Service Management Processes

The activities shown in Figure 12.56 are performed to architect the target state processes.

Design and Build Key BSM Solution Components

Based on the requirements captured in the SLR document and design build in SDP, BSM solution components are now designed and developed so that the business service delivers the desired value (see Figure 12.57).

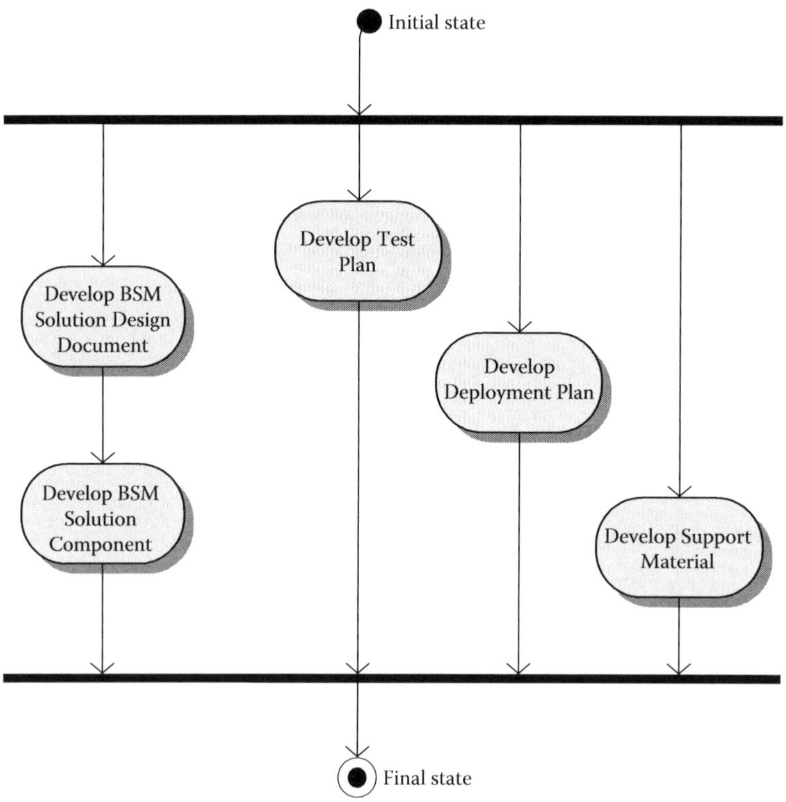

Figure 12.57 Design and build key BSM solution components.

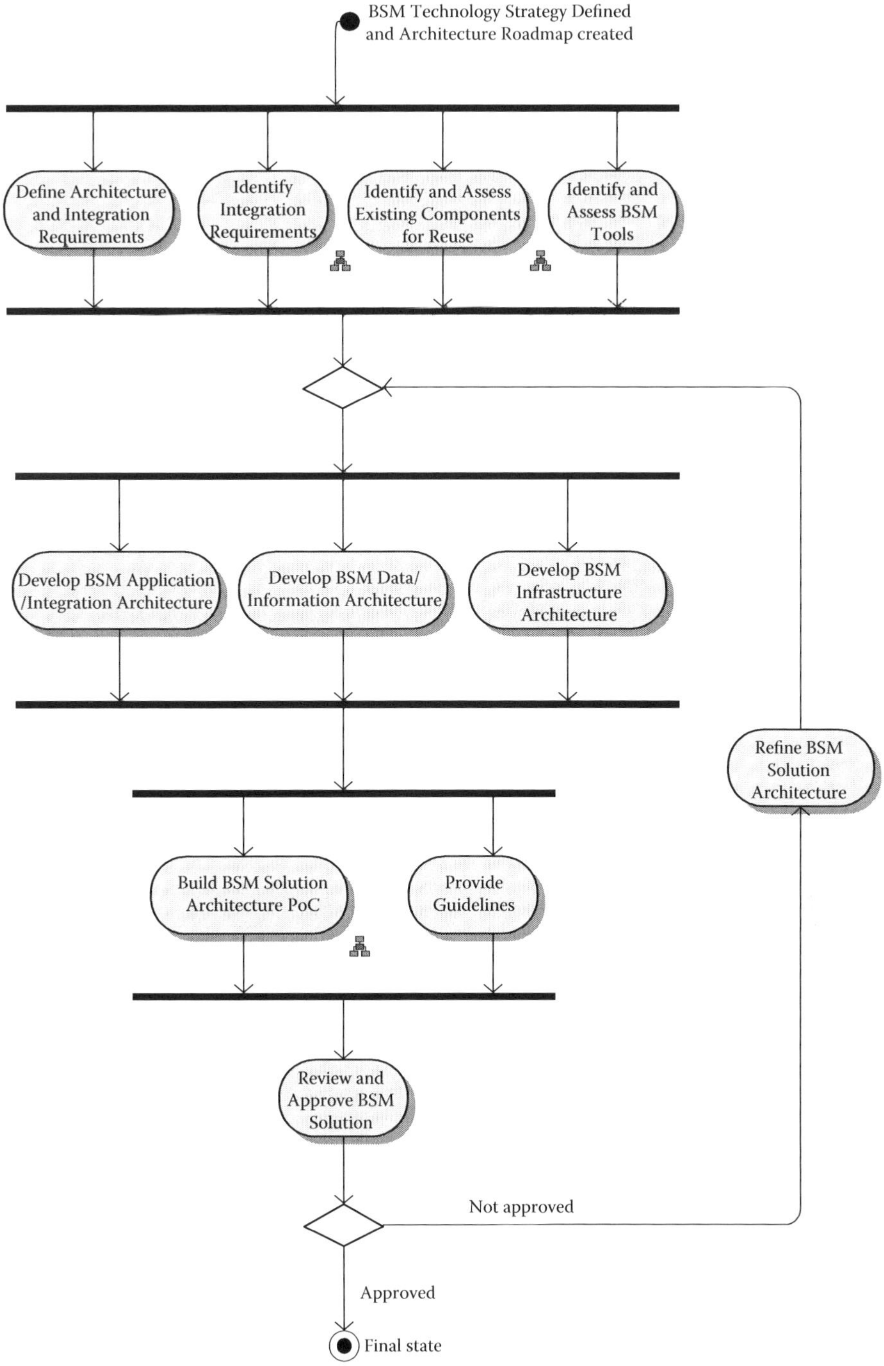

Figure 12.58 Architect and prototype the BSM solution.

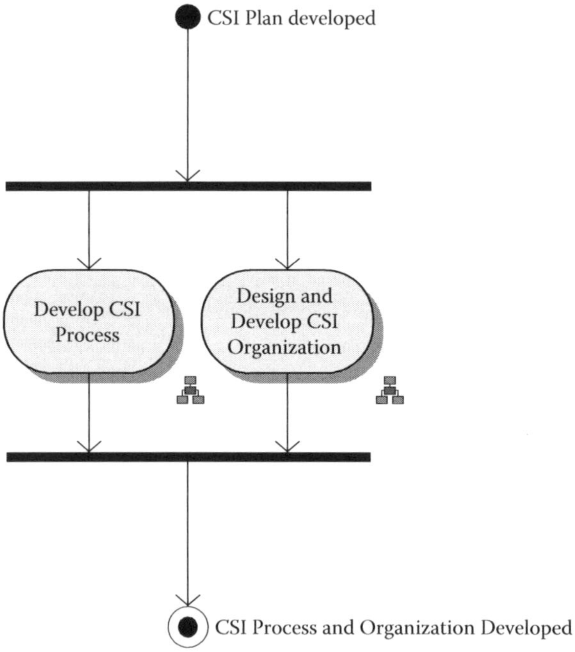

Figure 12.59 Develop CSI process and organization.

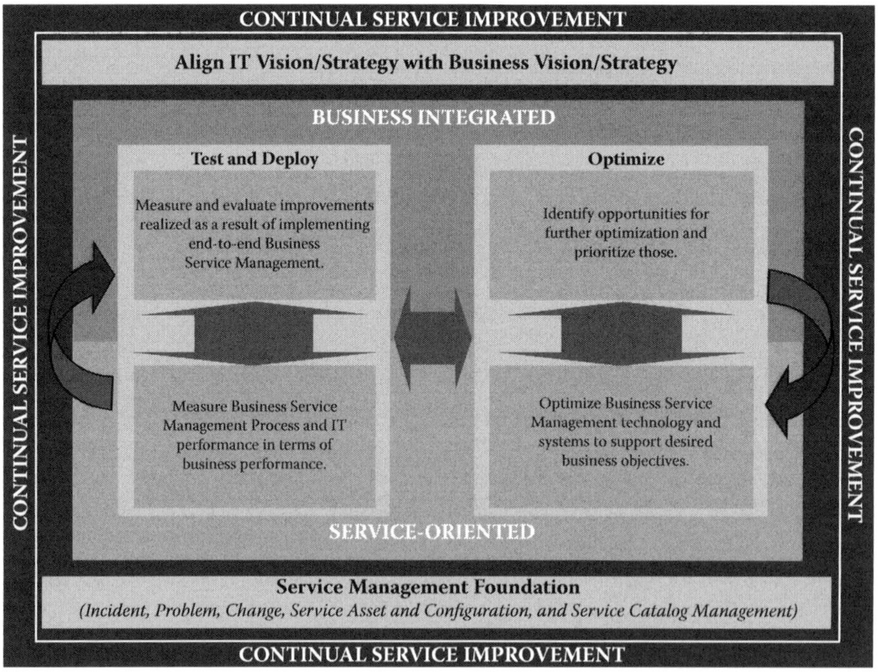

Figure 12.60 Realize iteration overview.

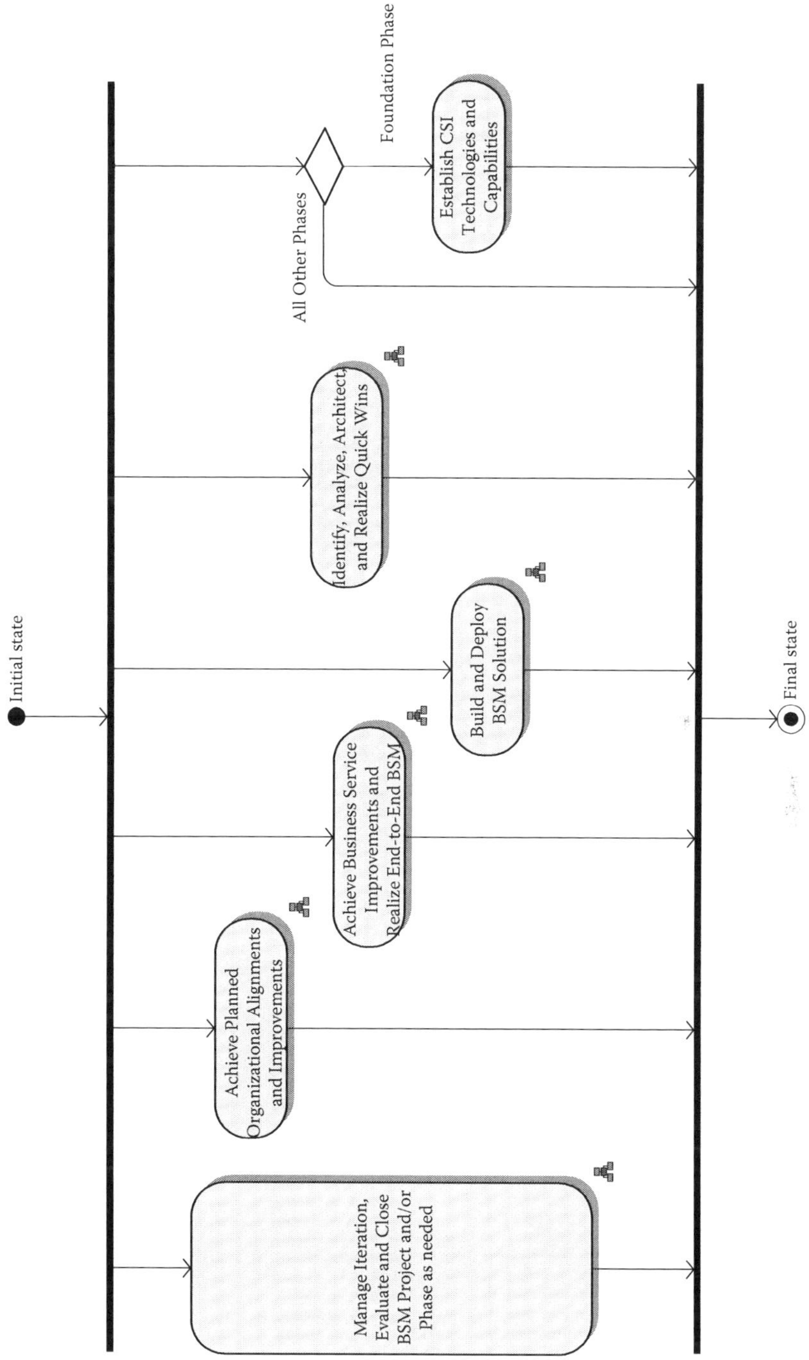

Figure 12.61 Realize iteration workflow.

Architect and Prototype the BSM Solution

Prototyping helps to reduce risk. The activities shown in Figure 12.58 should be performed to architect and prototype the BSM solution.

Develop CSI Process and Organization

This activity is performed only during the foundation phase. In the visualize iteration of the foundation phase, the CSI plan and roadmap are developed. Based on those plans, the CSI process is developed and the CSI team and organization is designed and developed (Figure 12.59).

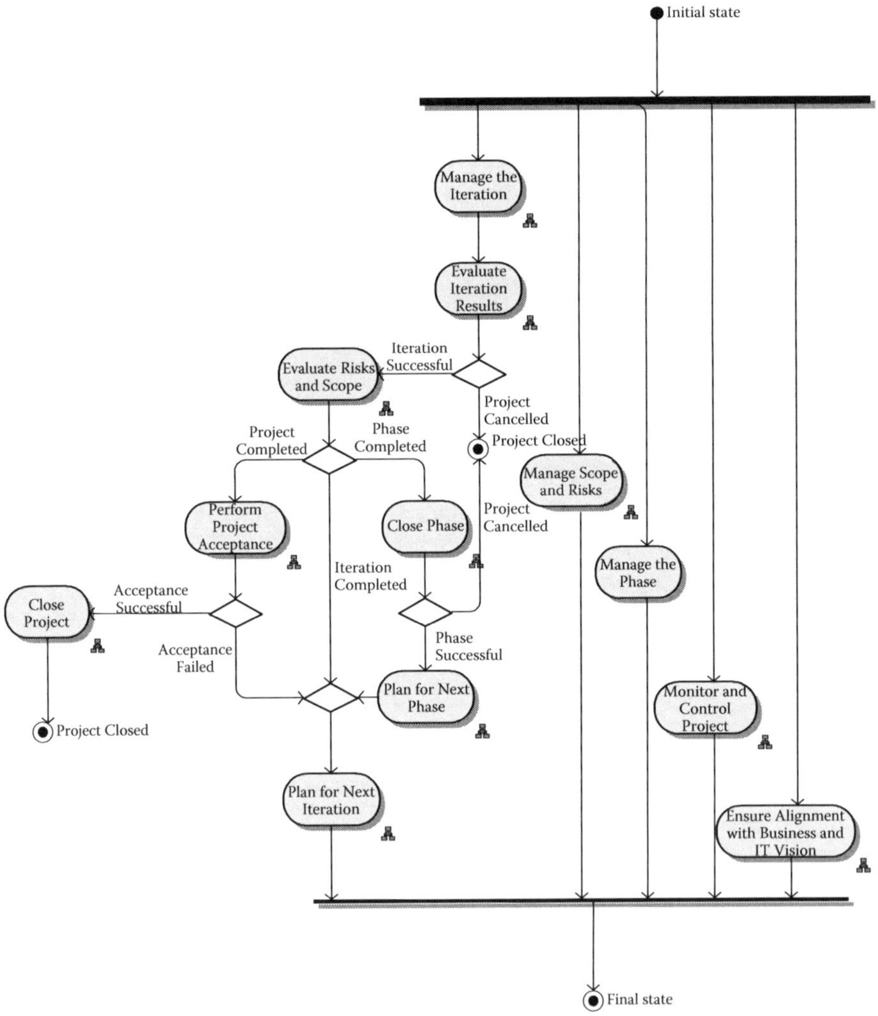

Figure 12.62 Manage iteration, evaluate, and close the BSM project and/or phase as needed.

Realize Iteration

During this iteration, the architected and prototyped improvements and related solutions are achieved or implemented, tested, and deployed (Figure 12.60). Focus is maintained on the following two activities:

- Testing and deploying
- Optimizing

Note that this is the third and final iteration of a given phase and it must enable the organization to realize the envisioned value. By the time you enter into this iteration, the prioritized improvements should already have been architected and designed and the enabling BSM solution should have been prototyped. The success of this iteration depends heavily on the successes of previous iterations. There should be no surprises during this iteration and expectations should be very clear on all sides.

The realize iteration workflow is shown in Figure 12.61. Let us discuss the activities in detail.

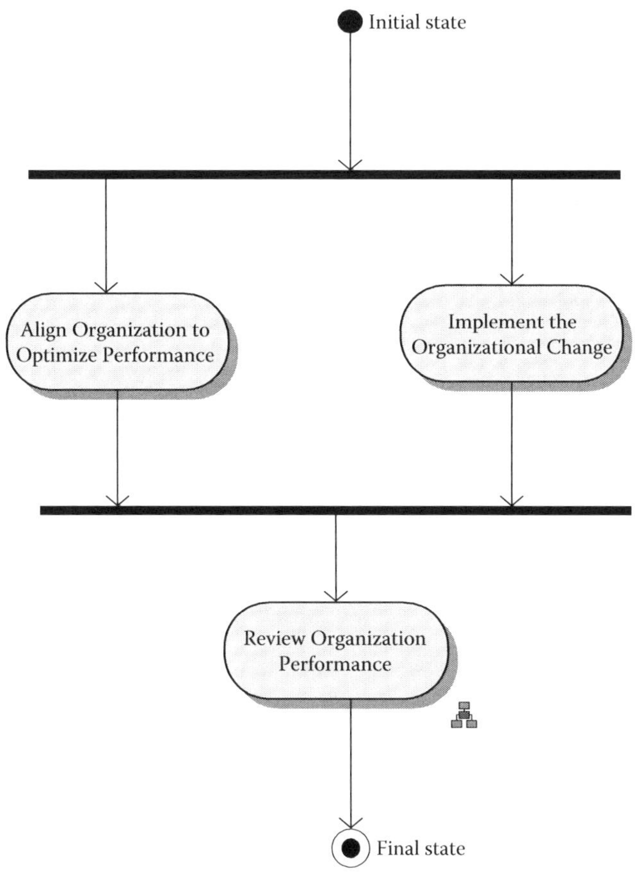

Figure 12.63 Achieve planned organizational alignments and improvements.

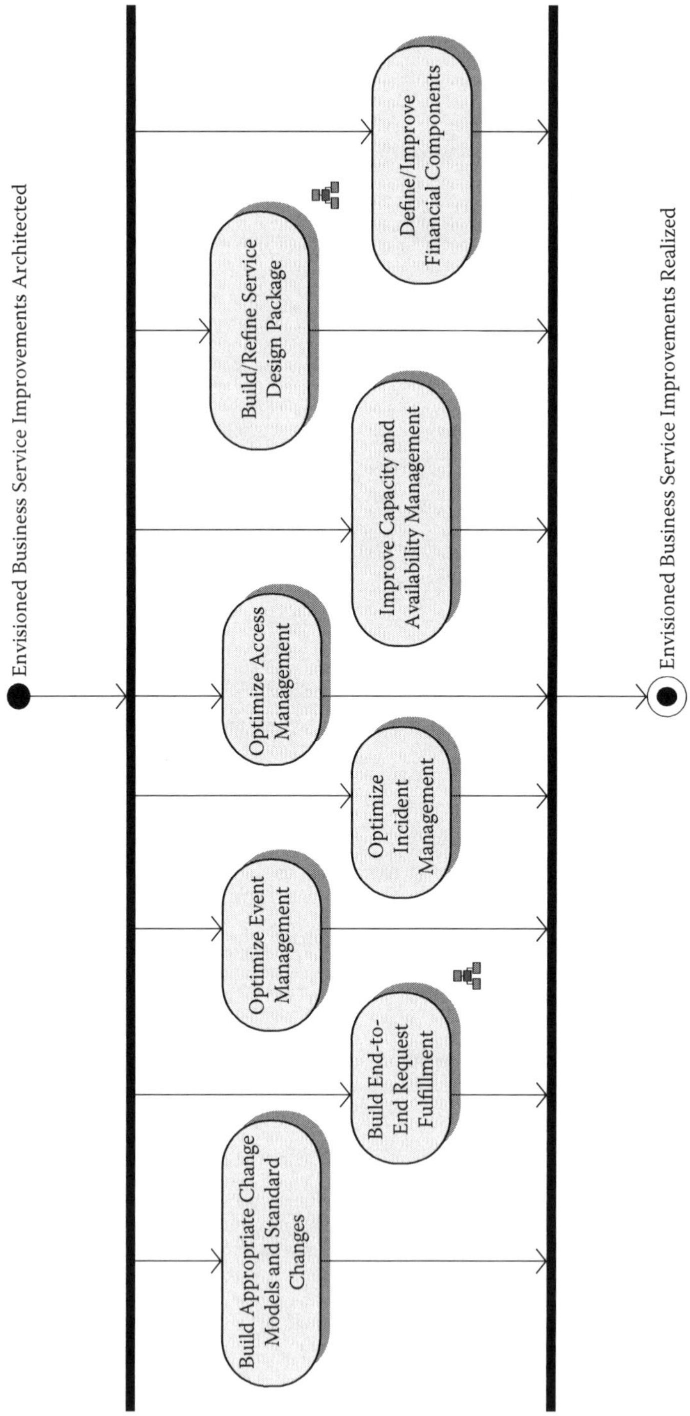

Figure 12.64 Achieve business service improvements and realize end-to-end BSM.

Manage Iteration, Evaluate, and Close BSM Project or Phase as Needed

Iteration is managed and the project or phase is evaluated and closed as appropriate. Iteration results are evaluated and project acceptance tests are conducted in order to close the project. It is important to note that continual alignment with the overall business and IT vision must be maintained throughout the project (Figure 12.62).

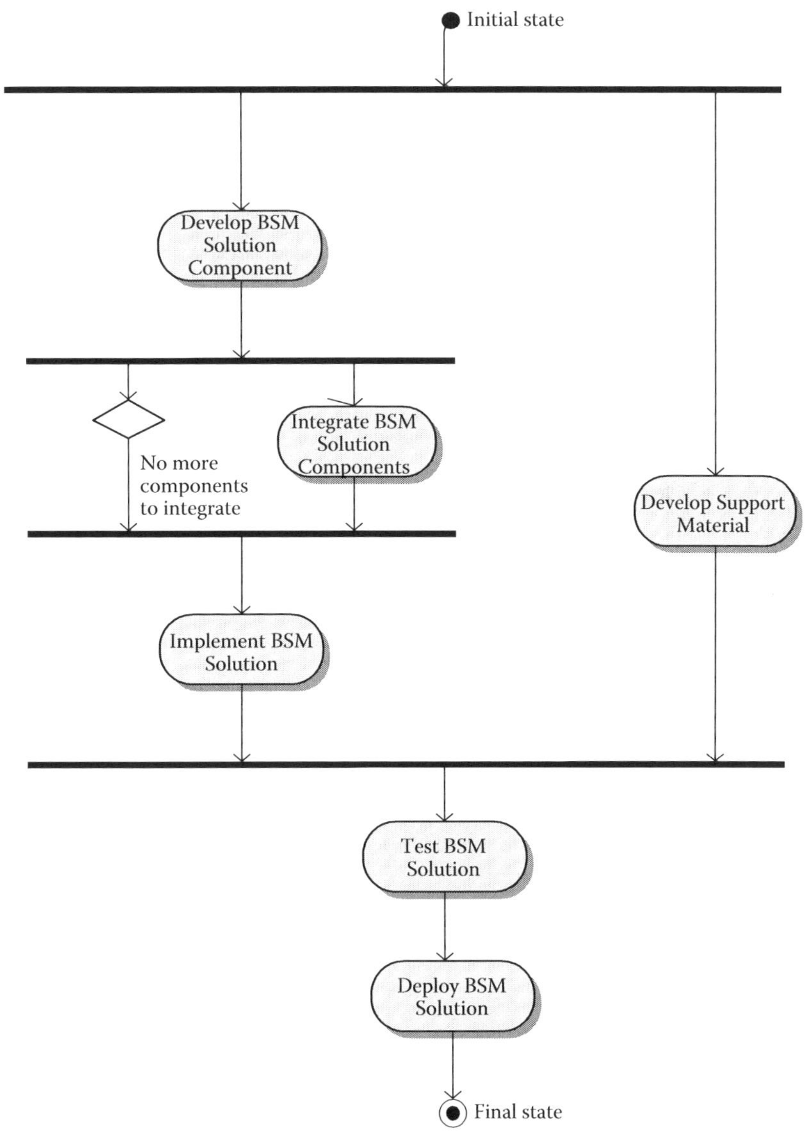

Figure 12.65 Build and deploy BSM solution.

Achieve Planned Organizational Alignments and Improvements

Planned organizational changes are implemented and organizational alignments are achieved to optimize performance (Figure 12.63).

Achieve Business Service Improvements and Realize End-to-End BSM

Envisioned business service improvements are achieved and end-to-end BSM is realized during this iteration. Figure 12.64 shows that the improvements are made across all high-value service management processes during this iteration.

Build and Deploy BSM Solution

This activity ensures that the designed BSM solution components are developed, integrated, and implemented. Note that there are many off-the-shelf service management tools available in the marketplace. For these tools, the core activities will focus on configuring (instead of developing) and integrating with other tools. BSM solution is tested and deployed and support materials are delivered (Figure 12.65).

Establish CSI Technologies and Capabilities

By the end of the foundation phase, CSI must be established with all technical capabilities to support the envisioned improvements throughout the project and beyond (Figure 12.66).

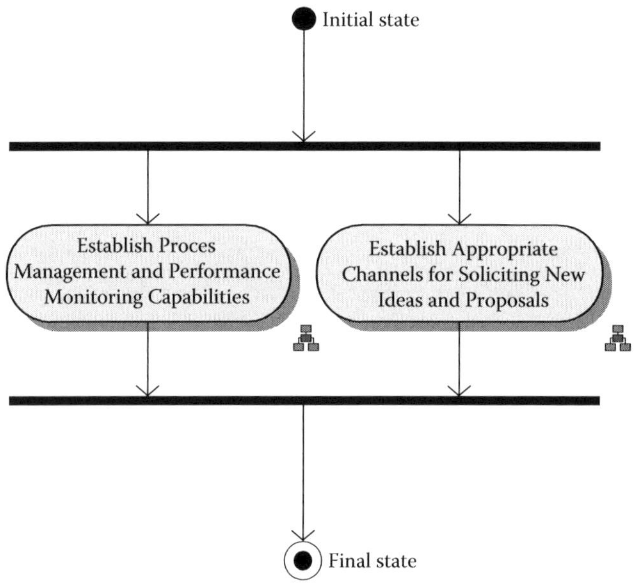

Figure 12.66 Establish CSI technologies and capabilities.

Conclusion

The i2-SOSMI life cycle uses the activities defined within each of the disciplines in a specific sequence to maximize the probability of successfully achieving the desired objectives. All these sequences are based on my experience and none are mandatory. Based on organizations' specific situations, business drivers, complexities, and other factors, these may need to be further tailored to deliver the desired value.

PLANNING AND IMPLEMENTING BUSINESS SERVICE MANAGEMENT

III

Chapter 13

Business Service Management Implementation Roadmap

In Part I of this book, we learned about *Information Technology Infrastructure Library version 3* (ITIL v3), business service management (BSM), and how these are related to organizational transformation. We also discussed that organizational transformations do not happen overnight and must be very carefully planned and implemented. In Part II, we discussed one possible approach to achieving higher organizational maturity through incrementally and iteratively implementing BSM, thereby optimizing risks and opportunities.

In Part III, we will discuss how an organization can approach planning and implementation of BSM within an organization. By the end of this chapter, you will be able to:

- Clearly understand how to layout the overall BSM implementation.
- Identify service management processes within your respective organization that need to be improved first.
- Create a roadmap to incrementally and iteratively implement BSM.
- Clearly identify and understand the critical success factors as they relate to implementing BSM.

Introduction

Implementing BSM is a journey and not an end in itself. ITIL v3 provides guidelines on what BSM is and how the IT organization that manages its customers' business services looks. ITIL v3 IT Service Management (ITSM) processes provide the foundation required to achieve BSM.

Traditionally, ITIL-based service management implementations have been process-centric. Within a process-centric approach, you have the option to implement one single process at a time, multiple processes at a time, or all the processes at once. I have rarely seen companies implement all processes concurrently since it is heavy on resource requirements and impacts IT management and operations functions significantly. Whichever approach—single, multiple, or all processes—that you adopt to implement ITIL processes, if you are unable to demonstrate quick value and return on investments in improving IT processes to your business customers, you will be facing a risk of running out of business sponsorship. Initiatives such as ITIL and ITSM require relatively large investments and, depending on IT organizational maturity, longer time commitments. Without being able to demonstrate business value, it will become challenging for you to maintain the support and sponsorship that are required to sustain the ITIL program.

Those IT organizations that are able to keep the business value in the forefront and make investments in improving IT to deliver greater business value are the ones that are able to successfully achieve greater returns on IT improvement investments. As shown in Figure 13.1, a value-centric approach is one that combines the following to maximize the creation of business value early in the project life cycle:

- Service management process improvements
- Business service improvements and end-to-end BSM implementation

Business service improvements enable IT organizations to show real benefits of improving the underlying ITIL processes.

The roadmap that we are going to discuss here will make use of the "value-centric" approach. Before we discuss how we can build our BSM roadmap, let us briefly discuss some of the critical aspects of successful BSM implementation.

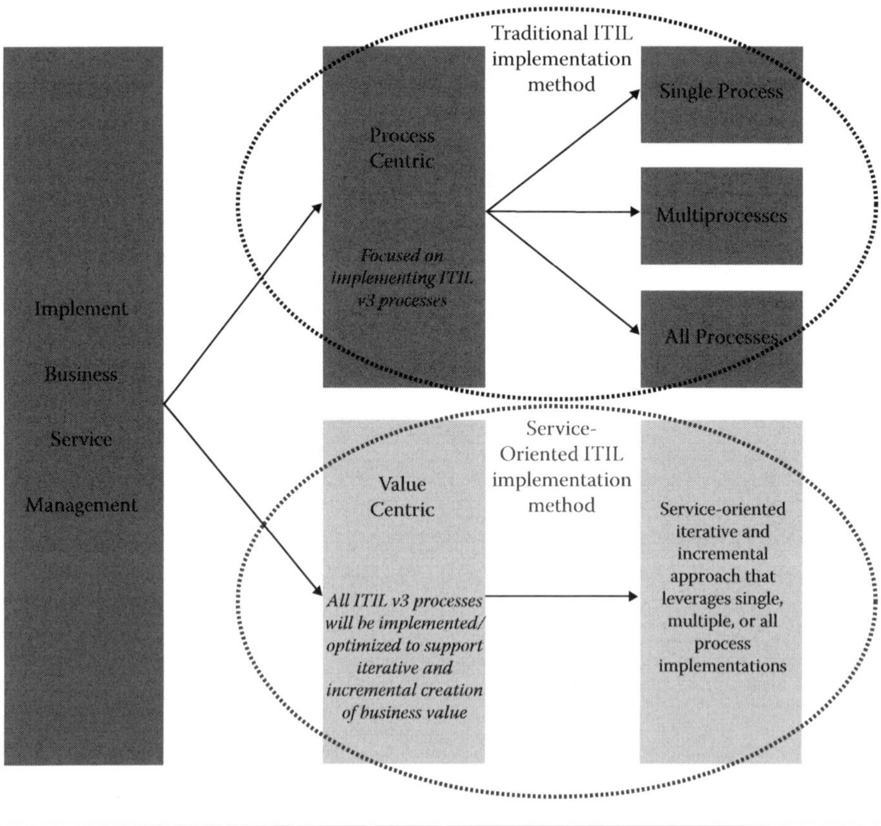

Figure 13.1 Key BSM implementation approaches.

Critical Aspects of BSM Implementation

What are those aspects that will not only need to be defined but also properly managed and supported? They are some of the core aspects that make the difference between success and failure in organizational transformation. We will discuss each of these in greater detail here. They are also shown in Figure 13.2.

Vision and Strategy

Embarking on a BSM journey is a significant endeavor. A clear vision and concrete strategy will be the cornerstone to creating a BSM culture within the organization. Employees, partners, suppliers, and business stakeholders all need to be familiar with the BSM vision and strategy.

Governance

Since the BSM is largely a new concept to most organizations, the IT operations department normally ends up running the program. Almost all of my clients that started off with BSM in operations ended up with the project either failing or needing to be revamped.

It is not recommended for the IT operations department to run the BSM project. If a service management organization does not already exist, it is recommended that the BSM implementation project be treated as any other large project and IT operations teams be the key stakeholders of the project.

Governance will ensure whether the organization is taking the right steps at the right time in the right direction to maximize the probability of achieving its vision. Governance, in most cases, is achieved by having a dedicated project office for the BSM project. The project office will be accountable and responsible for ensuring that the following items are properly defined:

- Defining project goal and scope
- Establishing project timelines
- Identifying and prioritizing deliverables
- Managing risks
- Continual monitoring and control
- Ensuring that overall vision is realized

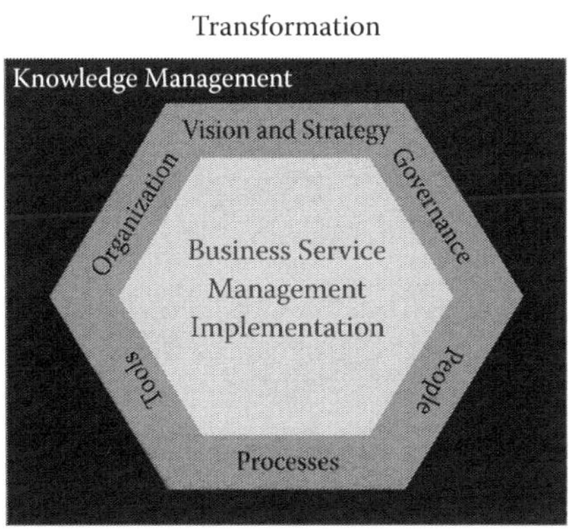

Figure 13.2 BSM implementation critical aspects.

According to the Institute on Governance (IOG), the central purpose of governance is to provide a process through which a group of people make decisions that direct their collective efforts. The purpose of governance is summarized by the IOG as, "Good governance is about both achieving desired results and achieving them in the right way" (http://www.iog.ca).

The right way is then qualified by explaining the organizational values that would be evident in best practice governance. These values include:

- Participation—involvement of all stakeholders
- Transparency—based on the free flow of information
- Responsiveness—timely and relevant decisions
- Equity—opportunities to be involved
- Consensus oriented—decisions and actions supported by broad agreement
- Effectiveness and efficiency—meeting needs with the best use of resources
- Accountability—of decision-makers to stakeholders
- Strategic vision—taking the long-term view

People

People are critical from all perspectives (i.e., project, organization, enablers, risks, adopters, etc.). People will deliver the project, people will need to change behaviors as a result of this project, people will support this project, and people will resist this project. In short, people will need to be managed throughout the life cycle of this project.

Processes

Processes comprise one of the critical aspects since they are what bring most of the other aspects together. For example, processes will define or impact what specific activities people perform, how organizations realign to enable efficient execution of processes, the way tools automate parts or all of processes, and so on. When implementing BSM, it is common to assess and prioritize which service management processes will make the most impact on the effectiveness and efficiencies of the IT organization. Accordingly, the respective roadmap is defined for the BSM project.

Tools

Tools are used to enforce the process in an efficient and effective manner. Tools must underpin the process and not the other way around. As IT professionals, tools excite us. Most ITSM tools require significant investments and must be well planned. There is no such thing as an ITIL v3–compliant tool. These tools may claim that they have implemented the process as per the ITIL v3 recommendations. However, as it is most frequently written in the ITIL v3 literature, how a given organization adopts ITIL v3 recommendations totally depends on the organization. Therefore, there is no single way that is the right way. If you see that tools are taking the front stage, you must raise this as a risk and rethink and reassess the overall approach.

Organization

How can the IT team can be organized to effectively deliver IT services and manage the customers' business services? Teams need to be organized in a manner that enables efficient execution of defined processes. As part of the BSM project, organizational alignments and definitions will take place. When organizational changes take place, they impact people's day-to-day jobs and therefore need to be very well planned and well managed. Let us discuss the key organizational components of the conceptual organization architecture shown in Figure 13.3.

Business–IT Integration Management

Different organizations refer to this function differently. Some call it "business relationship management" and others call it "account management." This function primarily ensures that business and IT are integrated and that IT investments are made so that they create the most value for the businesses and customers. Key areas that must be managed by this function are as follows:

- What services do we offer? This includes all services including services offered in the past, existing services, and the services to be offered in the future. In terms of ITIL v3 processes, service portfolio and service catalog management should be owned and managed within this function.
- Having known the services that the IT organization offers, the next question that needs to be answered is about the demand on those services. Do we want to invest in building or improving services that are not in high demand? Does it make business sense to offer services for which there is an insufficient market to justify the investment?
- Financial management must be considered along with the demand. Service pricing will further enable us to analyze if the demand can be met in a cost-effective manner.
- What are the levels that we can guarantee on the services that we offer?
- How can we improve these services to create more value and make them cost-effective?

Figure 13.4 shows the key roles that should exist from the perspective of managing services. Let us discuss these in detail.

- Business Service Owner/Business Relationship Manager/Account Manager
  - May own one or more business service(s) as defined in Service Catalog
  - Represents these business service(s) to the entire organization
  - Accountable for ensuring that business service(s) meet agreed targets (SLA targets)
  - Represents IT to the Business and Business to IT
  - Participates on Change Advisory Board and represents his/her business services
  - Possesses required IT expertise and is business savvy
  - Manages business demand to optimize business value
  - Performs business service performance reviews on a periodic basis
  - Develops Service Improvement Plan(s) and ensures continual service improvement
  - Collaborates with technical service owner(s) to understand warranty and utility service attributes including capacity management
  - Manages business/customer expectations
- Technical Service Owner
  - May own one or more technical service(s) as defined in Service Catalog
  - Represents these technical services to Business Service Owner(s) and other IT stakeholders
  - Thorough understanding of technical services that make up business services

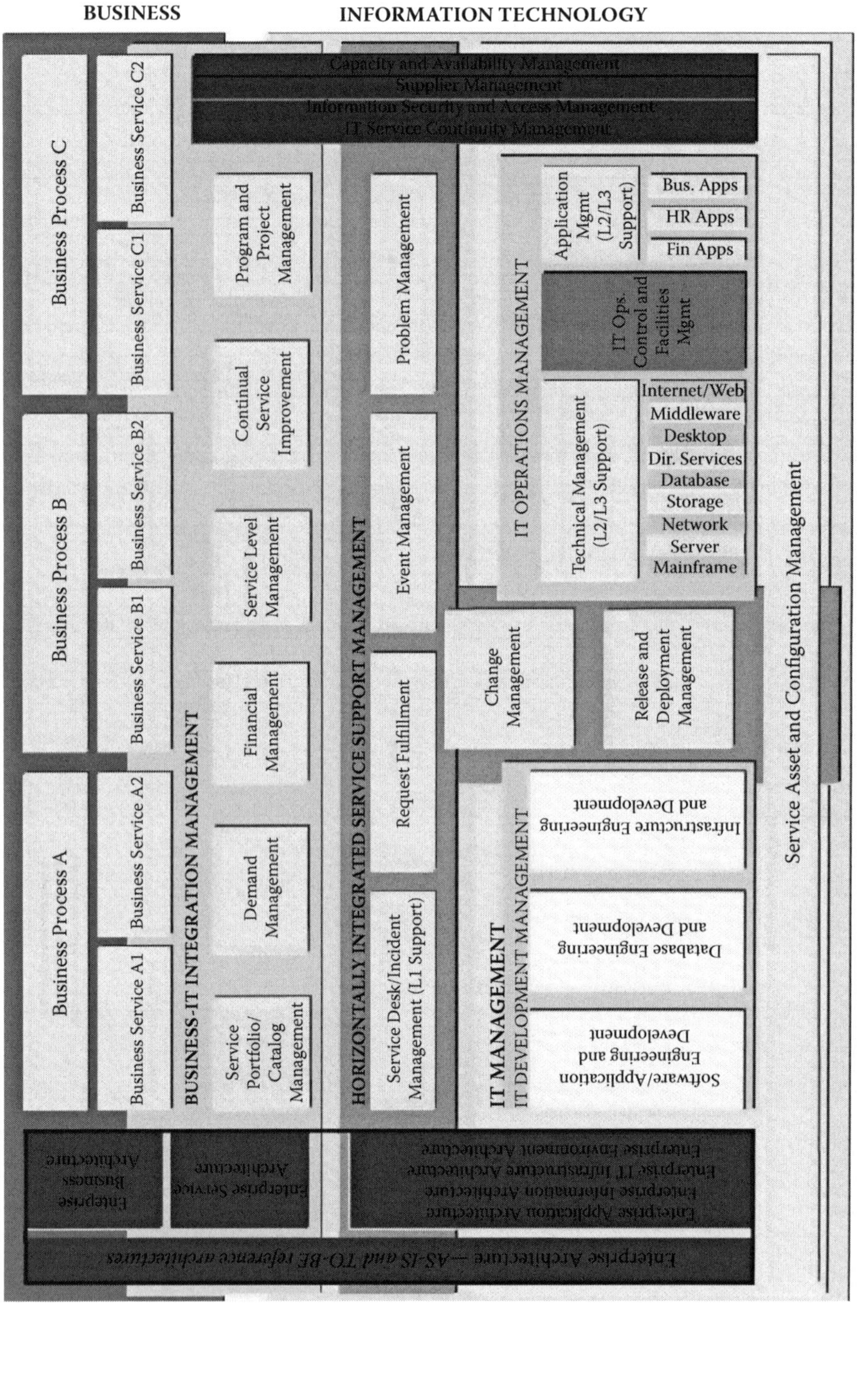

Figure 13.3 BSM conceptual organization architecture.

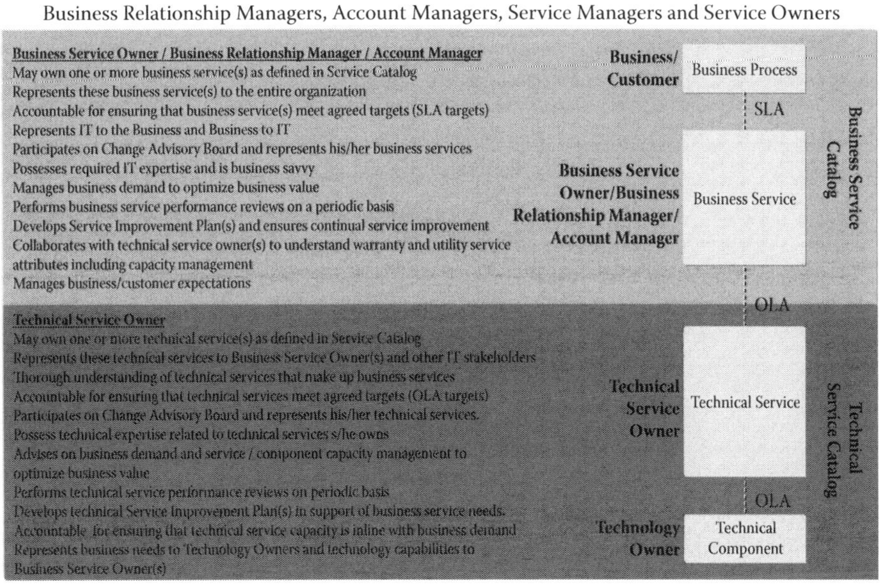

Figure 13.4 Business relationship managers, account managers, service managers, and service owners.

- Accountable for ensuring that technical services meet agreed targets (OLA targets)
- Participates on Change Advisory Board and represents his/her technical services
- Possess technical expertise related to technical services s/he owns
- Advises on business demand and service/component capacity management to optimize business value
- Performs technical service performance reviews on periodic basis
- Develops technical Service Improvement Plan(s) in support of business service needs.
- Accountable for ensuring that technical service capacity is inline with business demand
- Represents business needs to Technology Owners and technology capabilities to Business Service Owner(s)

Horizontally Integrated Service Support Management

The emphasis here is on "horizontally integrated." There should be a single service desk for customers and businesses to reach out to for all their service-related needs. These include the following:

- *Request Fulfillment.* The service desk must be the single point of contact for customers to make requests for services. Request fulfillment is the back-end process executed to fulfill those requests.
- *Incident Management.* I have seen organizations where network-focused teams have their own service desk, data center teams have their own service desk, and so on. This creates many inefficiencies. There should be one single point of contact for customers to call and register incidents related to their services.

- *Problem Management.* There should be a centralized problem management process to identify, prioritize, and invest in problems needing resolution. Known errors must be documented and workarounds must be managed centrally.
- *Change Requests.* A request for changes is another form of service request and must be received centrally by the service desk.
- *Project Requests.* A request for projects should also be received by the service desk. It may have other channels as well. However, the service desk should be able to provide status and other related information on projects.

IT Management

IT management combines the two key components of IT (i.e., development and operations). Note that there is a change and release management between development and operations functions. These Service Transition capabilities may also be considered as part of IT Management.

Enterprise Architecture Management

Enterprise architecture provides the overall governance, defines related technology and process standards, manages the overall current-state and target-state architectures, and makes improvement recommendations. This is further discussed in Chapter 17.

BSM Implementation Roadmap

Having discussed the critical aspects of BSM implementation, let us now see how you can actually approach the definition of the BSM implementation roadmap.

Establishing the BSM Vision

Ask yourself this question. Why BSM? Is it important that you are able to manage and deliver services that actually impact your customers' profitability? Is your customer asking for it? Will your customer need it? BSM is about managing the business services that are delivered to the end customers and measuring IT performance in terms of business performance. BSM provides the foundation to effectively manage the business services. Look longer-term and establish a clear and concrete vision for your IT organization. Do not think about all the challenges that you are going to encounter along your journey. Think about what you will be able to achieve when you get where you aim to go. Thinking "big" is not out of bounds here. We, in IT, need to think "big" and think "business." That is the key to our successfully becoming business partners. One of the sample BSM vision statements can be:

> *We will become a high-quality, cost-efficient, preferred IT service provider enabling the business growth of our customers.*
>
> *Transform the IT organization into a business-integrated, high-quality, cost-efficient IT service organization through incremental improvements in organizational culture and service management capabilities.*

Think hard where you would like your IT organization to be. If you are an internal service provider, this vision becomes even more critical for you. Being an internal service provider does not mean that your customer cannot value you as a partner.

Factors to Consider When Building a BSM Roadmap

There are key factors that need to be considered when building the BSM roadmap. We will discuss them in this section.

Organizational Culture

Organizational culture is the single most important factor when planning to embark on the BSM journey. Some of the questions to be considered are:

- Is IT considered a back-office function or is it viewed as a business enabler?
- Is IT's focus on the customer or business or on technology?
- Is there a common understanding among IT teams that IT exists to enable greater business growth and profitability?
- Is it about thriving or just surviving?

Organizational cultural assessment should be performed to establish if the organization is actually ready to embrace change and what key factors should be considered to optimize the probability of success.

Creating, Measuring, and Communicating Success

BSM implementation must lead to success stories. These successes must be measured in business terms and appropriate communications must be managed to ensure that the right environment is created to further develop awareness and, subsequently, support.

Foundation Maturity

There are some foundational processes that are essential to enable BSM. These include incident, problem, change, and configuration management. If these processes are weak, you will see the following symptoms in your organization:

- Increasing number of unplanned service outages
- Increasing costs of delivering IT services
- Increasing focus on keeping the lights on
- Reducing number of new developments
- Increasing number of staff members working overtime
- Increasing customer dissatisfaction

Prioritizing Processes and Services

Business and IT drivers will greatly influence the processes and services that should be improved first. In addition, the current state of organizational culture and foundation process maturity will contribute to process prioritization.

High-Level BSM Roadmap

There should be four logical phases of a BSM implementation roadmap (see Figure 13.5). Depending on organizational and process maturity, complexity, distribution, size, and other factors, each phase may be anywhere from 4 to 12 months.

Figure 13.6 shows a detailed view of the high-level roadmap. Note that processes are identified, prioritized, and time-boxed.

Key BSM Implementation Work Streams

The key BSM work streams are the same as the iterative and incremental service-oriented service management implementation (i2-SOSMI) disciplines already discussed (Figure 13.7). These are discussed here.

Project Management

BSM implementation must not be managed by technology management or development organizations. IT operations, like others, are key stakeholders in the project. However, BSM implementation must be managed like a project to ensure that the desired objectives are effectively achieved. If a BSM organization already exists, then they should be the sponsor of this project.

People and Organization

People are the most important resources as well as capabilities. People make transformations successful and prevent them from being successful. Comprehensive steps must be taken to enable people to develop, grow, and contribute the most.

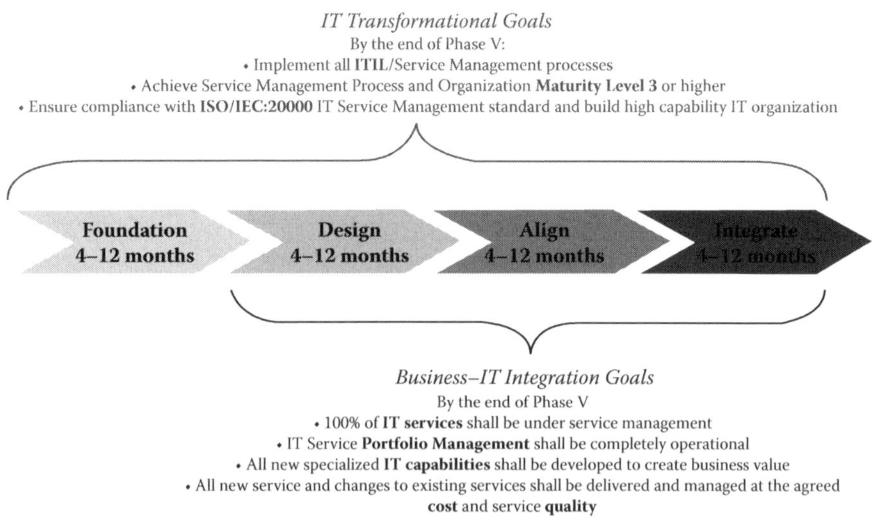

Figure 13.5 Sample BSM high-level roadmap.

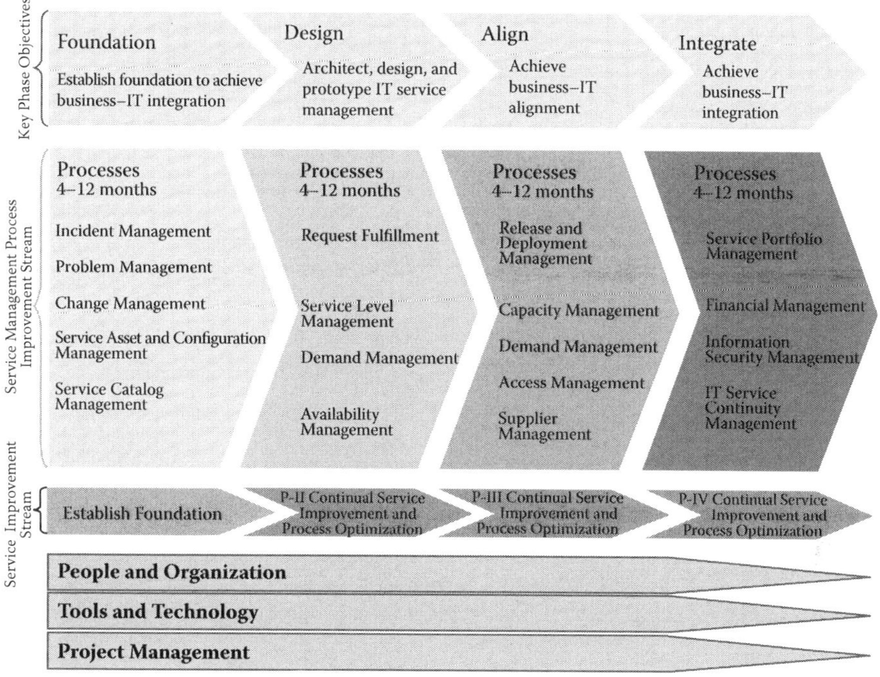

Figure 13.6 BSM implementation roadmap.

Continual Service Improvement Institutionalization

Continual service improvement (CSI) ensures that process and service improvements are continually made. CSI must aim to function as a catalyst for cultural transformation. Key CSI objectives include measurements, analysis, and enabling a wise decision-making process.

Business Service Improvement

Service management process improvements help create the foundation to support service delivery. However, if these improvements are not made in a targeted manner, it will take longer than necessary for businesses to realize the benefits of the process improvements. Remember that:

Not everything is important.

There are few IT components that are more important than others because they support critical business processes and, if they break down, it will lead to significant business impact. Focus process improvements and improve management on those IT components that create the most business impact.

Service Management Process Improvement

In this work stream, service management process improvements are planned and implemented. It is critical that baseline measurements are made and quantitative improvements are achieved.

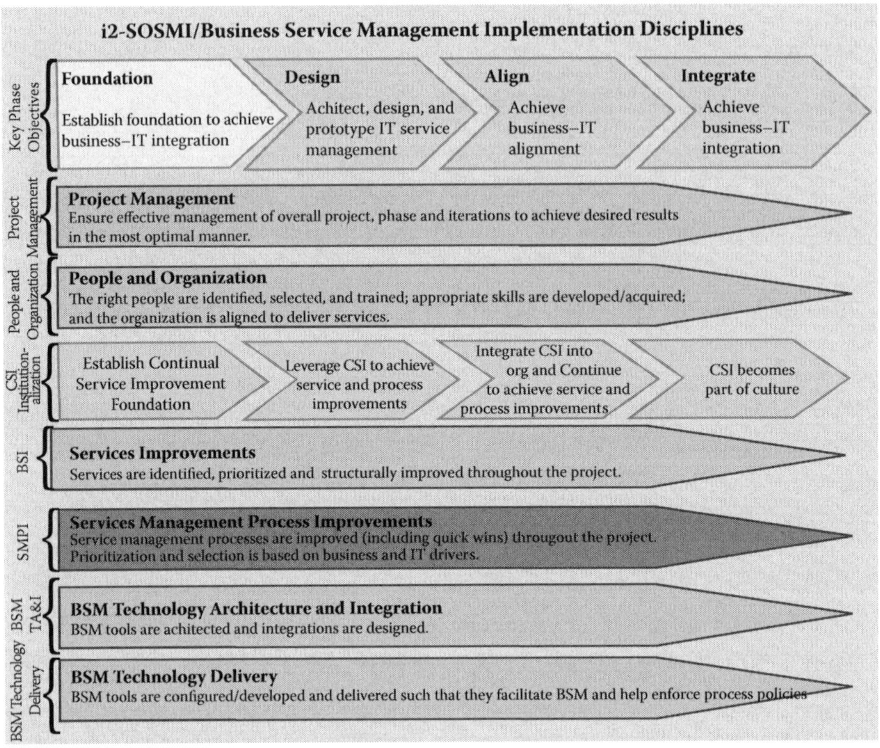

Figure 13.7 Key BSM project work streams.

BSM Technology Architecture and Integration

BSM technology must be integrated across other tools to ensure that business services can be effectively and efficiently managed end-to-end.

BSM Technology Delivery

BSM tools must support, automate, and enable process enforcement. Tools can sometimes be both tricky and risky and, therefore, must be well planned. I have seen major BSM initiatives fail due to tools being brought in too early in the project. Tools do not automatically transform organizations. Tools need organizations to utilize them and achieve desired efficiencies.

Critical Success Factors

Every day spent in planning the BSM implementation is time well spent. It is one of the most critical investments that you will make in ensuring that the overall program is a success. To maximize the chances of successfully implementing BSM across the organization, it is critical that you consider these key points.

- The service management organization must be accountable for implementing service management. If the service management organization does not already exist, then the first step is to appoint the head of the service management organization.

- Why BSM? Achieving BSM will mean that all ITSM processes (ITIL process) will need to be improved, respective roles and responsibilities will need to be redefined, new human resource competencies will need to be developed, and organizational and departmental boundaries will need to be redrawn. Some who are able to think objectively and question intelligently will be on-board for embarking on the BSM journey. Others, who are comfortable in their current ways of working, may see the value in BSM, but do not want to change from what they have been doing for many years now. You will hear a long list of excuses like:

  "I don't think that business service management applies to us."
  "Business service management is another buzzword and is really nothing new."
  "It seems like an overhead cost."
  "It is just another theory and another academic practice."

  To ensure that all relevant parties have a common understanding of why we are embarking on the BSM journey, you will need to have a clear communication strategy and plan in place. In fact, communication has been identified as one of the critical success factors by O'Neill et al. (2007).
- Not everything is important. This is one of the most critical realities that will help you throughout your BSM journey. The goal is to maximize the business value with minimal investment and to ensure that all IT investments are targeted to improving or creating business value. Most IT professionals will agree with these and similar statements. However, their agreement will, in most cases, follow with an assertion that such claims sound good in theory, but none of them are practical. Well, the good news is that it is very possible and that mature firms have achieved greater benefits from making wise IT investments. "It all comes down to the fact that IT is an integral part of supporting the business," said Morton Cohen, manager of global service management at Procter & Gamble. "When IT processes are done by 5000 people consistently across one company, service management can deliver tremendous savings." Cohen said Procter & Gamble's IT group avoided spending $125 million by implementing the service management processes outlined by ITIL (Dubie, 2002). There are many ways to achieving BSM. How efficiently you are able to get there depends on the approach and your organizational readiness. Organizational readiness, which also includes factors such as organizational and process baseline maturity and culture, may not be under your control. However, the approach that you adopt to achieve BSM is definitely something that you can control. A great deal of thought should be put into adopting a particular approach because an inappropriate approach can actually cost you the entire initiative. The approach that will be the core focus of our discussion in this book is based on a couple of key principles. These are:
  - Proactive risk management
  - Incremental cultural transformation
  - Iterative process improvement
  - Business-aligned improvement investments
  - Rapid business value realization
- Business processes are prioritized and business-critical improvements are achieved.
- Do not skip critical improvement steps. ITIL v3 lays steps for achieving CSI. These are based on years of collective industry experience. At a high level, the following key questions should be answered:
  - What is the vision? Knowing the overall business and IT vision.
  - Where are we now? Clearly understanding the current maturity.

- Where do we want to be? Defining a target state in a measurable manner.
- How do we get there? Planning and implementing necessary improvements.
- Did we get there? Measuring success.

- Demonstrate measurable improvements. Making fuzzy claims of improving efficiencies and reducing costs will not take you far. Measurements must be designed in the BSM implementation approach so that achievements can be quantified as much as possible. There are some areas, such as customer satisfaction, that will need to stay subjective. However, attempts must be made to minimize subjectivity to reduce skepticism.
- Are your various BSM-related projects coordinated (O'Neill et al., 2007)?

Summary

In this chapter, we discussed the key considerations that should be made in the creation of a BSM roadmap. It is critical to clearly define the BSM vision and ensure that the organization clearly understands and embraces it. BSM implementation requires efforts across a range of work streams and, therefore, the effort must be thoughtfully envisioned and carefully planned.

References

Dubie, D. Procter & Gamble touts IT services model, saves $500 million. *ComputerWorld* October 1, 2002. http://www.computerworld.com/s/article/74762/Procter_Gamble_touts_IT_services_model_saves_500_million (accessed April 15, 2009).

O'Neill, P., T. Mendel, and R. Iqbal. 2007. *Business Service Management: Early Birds Are Catching the Worm, But IT Still Doesn't Get It.* http://www.forrester.com/rb/Research/business_service_management_early_birds_are_catching/q/id/41458/t/2 (accessed March 2007).

Chapter 14

Business Service Management Implementation Planning

The business service management (BSM) journey will be unique for each organization. The path that an organization takes will depend on many factors such as organizational culture, baseline process maturity, technical and environmental complexity (distributed vs. centralized, global vs. local, etc.), organization, governance, and so on. It is highly unlikely that any two organizations will go through exactly the same steps in the same sequence and will encounter the same challenges when trying to achieve BSM. However, it is very possible to learn from other companies' experiences, create key BSM implementation patterns as appropriate, and identify the core set of activities that every organization will need to go through to achieve BSM. There is no silver bullet to implementing service management and realizing BSM. However, it is very possible to discuss what successful implementations look like and how to make these successes visible to your customers and businesses. The goal is to achieve a level of maturity where your IT department emerges as a "Value Partner" and to remove any perceptions about IT being technology-focused and not business-focused.

In Part II, we discussed the activities that should be carried out to iteratively and incrementally achieve business value through BSM. In this chapter, we will discuss in detail the key factors that should be considered when planning to implement BSM and the most common implementation patterns (i.e., the possible sequences in which processes can be improved and activities may be performed). We will also discuss some of the factors that may drive the order in which processes are improved.

BSM is about building a culture of continuous organizational learning that adapts to ever-challenging and ever-changing business needs and competitive landscapes. BSM is about identifying, designing, developing, and delivering IT services so that business enablement is at the forefront of the creation and management of these services. Accordingly, there will be a great deal of emphasis on the people and culture part of the equation, as well as on processes, tools, and organization because it is people who perform defined activities and use available tools. By the end of this chapter, you will be able to achieve the following:

- Clearly state the problems that will be addressed by implementing BSM.
- Create a scope statement.
- Identify key deliverables that will be produced as a result of this project.
- Document the most common assumptions and constraints.
- Identify key milestones and establish timelines for completing the deliverables.
- Plan for the resources required for the project.
- Develop a realistic plan while being able to demonstrate real value to the business stakeholders.

Introduction

Achieving BSM is more about cultural transformation than any other single factor. Process, tools, training, and awareness are all planned and implemented to enable people to shift from inward technology-focused thinking to customer service-oriented thinking. There is no single plan for achieving this. There are many that will influence how you take the guidelines and the process defined in this book and tailor it to your specific organization's needs. Some of the factors that are likely to influence any organization's approach to make process-related improvements are discussed below.

Organizational Complexity

In most cases, the more complex the organization, the greater the complexity of service management implementation. This complexity emerges from the scale of impact on the organization and the level of care and management required to ensure success. More complex organizations may have hundreds of locations across the globe, following different aspects of the same processes. To make it more complex, these organizations may have different levels of process maturity across locations. Figure 14.1 shows a graphical depiction of an organization with multiple lines of businesses and multiple IT departments that may be spread across multiple locations.

In the situation presented in Figure 8.1, the overall service management project will require greater planning and discipline as compared to an organization with one line of business and one IT department. According to Shuja and Krebs (2008), the greater the complexity, the greater the formality and control required to ensure successful completion of a given project. The term formality normally involves greater plan-driven development and more discipline.

Organizational Maturity

Organizational maturity refers to the maturity level necessary to understand the need, to identify opportunities for improvement, to learn from experiences, and to successfully align the IT organization to ensure business–IT integration. Therefore, less mature organizations will likely require more discipline and formality than the more mature ones.

Process Maturity

The term "process maturity" is taken from Capability Maturity Model Integrated (CMMI). It is usually easier to improve a low-maturity process than a high-maturity process.

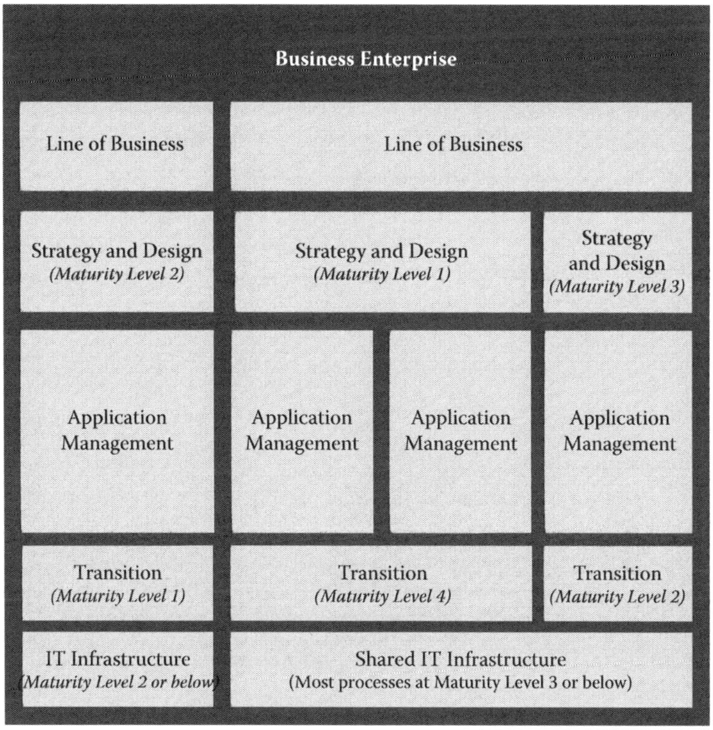

Figure 14.1 Varying levels of maturity across the organization.

Organizational Culture

Culture plays an important role in the successful adaptation and adoption of the processes described throughout *Information Technology Infrastructure Library version 3* (ITIL v3) literature (across the five books). Process development and improvement must be planned and designed carefully to achieve the optimal balance between efficiency and bureaucracy.

Regulatory, Compliance, and Policy Requirements

Some industries, especially financial and healthcare, might be driven to achieve compliance with Control Objectives for Information and Related Technology (COBIT), ISO20000, ISO17799, and other regulatory and related standards. Accordingly, organizations within such industries will need to plan their BSM implementations so that those processes that enable realization of control objectives are implemented first. We will discuss this in greater detail later in the "BSM Implementation Patterns" section.

Organization Size

The size of the organization determines how to tailor the proposed approach to enable successful implementation of service management.

Factors to Consider When Building a Detail Plan

Every organization is different and will need a somewhat customized approach to service management implementation. However, there are components that are common, there are challenges that most organizations encounter, and there are common opportunities that can be realized. In this section, we will discuss the various factors that are critical and should be considered when planning to achieve BSM.

Who Is Asking for It?

Who is asking for this cultural shift, for this change in the way IT is managed and services are delivered, and all this effort necessary to improve? Depending on who is asking for it, the plan will be different. In most cases, such large transformational efforts are undertaken because senior management sees the value. In other cases, there are real challenges with IT's capability to deliver its services and, if things are not improved, IT may be outsourced. In yet another case, improvements take place at grass-roots levels where individual teams take this initiative and decide that they need to improve the quality of their work and personal lives. Let us discuss each of these cases in greater detail.

Senior Management

The senior management sponsor is one of the most important sponsors. Depending on organizational maturity, implementing service management may mean a fundamental shift in ways in which IT is managed and IT services are delivered. Change initiatives of such magnitude require time, effort, dedication, visibility, and funds, and most of these will be difficult to get without full senior management sponsorship and support. Note that the mere provision of financial support is not enough. I have seen a case where a chief information officer (CIO) provided all the financial support required but did not ensure that the right teams were established and the right accountabilities were defined and assigned. When she followed up after about a year to check on the progress, what she got was a powerful service management tool and no organization around it to use and benefit from it. The entire initiative had to be revamped. Some of the lessons learned from that implementation that are critical include:

- When initiating a service management project, an appropriate management and governance structure and framework must be established to ensure that clear expectations are established and the right investments are made to deliver on those commitments.
- Service management implementation programs must never be left with IT development or operations teams on their own to lead. Formal project management is essential. The project manager must have clear understanding of and, preferably, experience with implementing service management.
- Regular updates must be provided to all relevant stakeholders and appropriate communications must be managed.
- The focus must be on creating business value and not on just improving processes. In other words, all service management process improvements must create a visible service improvement.

Needed for Survival

In cases where it is difficult for the IT organization to demonstrate its value to the business or is finding it difficult to consistently deliver the services at levels agreed on and promised, improving service management processes is largely the only realistic option available to IT to prevent any potential outsourcing possibilities. One of the largest global financial institutions was facing the following challenges:

- Due to ongoing mergers and acquisitions, the IT environment at this institution became more complex than it really had to be and looked something like Figure 8.1. There was no concept of IT services and IT was largely technology-focused. There were multiple lines of businesses and each of those spanned over a large number of global locations. IT management and delivery was divided into regions. Regional IT departments were at different levels of maturity and largely operated in silos.
- Because each of the regional IT departments operated in silos, there was a lack of standard hardware and software. The result was greater cost and effort to manage the environment.
- Uncontrolled changes and low-maturity event management led to a rising number of outages. Events were generated by devices, but a lack of appropriate information, inefficient and ineffective routing, and a large volume of false alerts made it difficult for the respective teams to take appropriate actions in a timely manner to prevent outages. Regional change management processes and associated regional change approval boards (CABs) that largely operated in silos were unable to do effective prioritizations, impact assessments, and manage change implementations.
- The overall impact of the above factors was that the cost of delivering IT services was continually on the rise and was getting beyond control.
- The weak state of the IT organization at this institution encouraged IT outsourcing companies to reach out to the business management and make less expensive proposals for the bank to consider outsourcing IT. Business leadership and senior management started looking at these options very seriously.
- To make matters even worse, there were increasing pressures from the regulators to bring the IT environment under control. In case of noncompliance, the bank's future acquisitions were at risk of being banned.

Under the above-mentioned and other related pressures, the IT leadership and IT management at this institution did not have any choice but to invest in improving the overall IT and demonstrate these improvements rapidly. It was a question of survival. The CIO, therefore, decided to achieve compliance with ISO20000 and COBIT while ensuring that IT services were properly managed. As a result, a complete ITIL project was established with a goal addressing the challenges listed above.

Don't Want to Fight Fires Anymore

In a few cases, I have seen individual teams take an initiative to improve their respective processes. Such improvements normally take place at team levels and bring about limited benefits. These improvements are not usually institutionalized and are normally lost if the team lead or other core team members leave the team.

Business and IT Drivers

It is important to understand the drivers for implementing service management. Some of the drivers may include:

- Business
  - Need more value-added services
  - Greater performance
  - Reduced costs
  - Greater reliability
- IT
  - Need to put greater focus on new value-added developments
  - Increasing need to minimize the costs for keeping the lights on
  - Drive to reduce service delivery costs
  - Need to become more proactive and less reactive

Organizational Culture

Organizational culture should be one of the most important factors to be considered when implementing service management. Organizational culture must drive the approach that is adopted to implement service management. Let us discuss some of the important cultural factors.

People's Attitudes (Service-Focused Thinking and Customer-Oriented Approach)

People make up organizational cultures. Processes can be defined and tools can be implemented. If people are not motivated to collaborate, to go an extra mile to deliver superior services, to consider how their actions will impact the customers, and to take ownership of their actions, no process or tool can help. Therefore, people's attitudes are critical to the overall success of BSM implementation. It is important for the project management and sponsors to identify ways to influence peoples' behaviors. Management policies provide the right tools to drive the desired behaviors. In planning to influence people's behavior, consider asking the following questions:

- What are peoples' attitudes toward IT services and, most importantly, toward customers?
- Do people understand service management and think of IT organization as a service delivering organization?
- Are customers the primary focus? Or are customers viewed as overdemanding and non-appreciating?
- Do people make up one team or are they trying to step on each other?
- What behaviors are rewarded? Do we have heroes here?

Surviving vs. Thriving

Is it a culture of surviving or thriving? Do people want to go an extra step to provide better service to customers?

Ad hoc vs. Planned and Reactive vs. Proactive

Is it a culture of heroes or one where planning and proactive approaches are encouraged?

Middle Management Challenge

I have seen cases in which even a strong senior management sponsorship did not yield the expected successes. Believe it or not, there are still companies out there where the size of the team that you manage is perceived to make a bigger impact than how efficiently your team operates. In the presence of incompetent middle management, service management and other process improvement programs are at greater risk. Keep the following in mind:

- Process improvements mean greater team efficiencies
- Greater team efficiencies mean a smaller headcount
- A smaller headcount means reduced responsibilities
- Reduced responsibilities mean smaller bonuses

Incompetent middle management will not let the above happen.

Cultural Transformation Cannot Be a "Big Bang"

As discussed, cultural transformations require behavioral changes and such changes should not be expected to be implemented as a "big bang" in one step. Instead, smaller, more targeted, and well-planned steps are likely to yield greater benefits sooner.

Changing cultures means changing people's behaviors. Behaviors do not change overnight and require a consistent approach, strong leadership, clear vision, and demonstrable incremental improvements. Healthy cultures are the ones where people are motivated to perform superior jobs and are aligned with the strategic business objectives. In planning to embark on the BSM journey, a dedicated focus must be placed on how best to transform and improve organizational cultures. In fact, this factor should drive the overall BSM implementation approach. Two key aspects that must be planned in the overall service management process and service improvement plans are as follows:

- Acquiring and developing the right people who are able to completely embrace the performance-driven culture for the right work.
- Carefully define key performance indicators and associated measures that reinforce the desired behavioral changes required for cultural transformations. If you are embarking on the BSM journey, your metrics and measurements must reflect this (i.e., IT measurements must measure business impact, not just IT activities).

Size and Complexity

The size and complexity of the organization will impact how you approach service management implementation. Complexity should take into account some of the following factors:

- Central vs. distributed
- Organization
- Services delivered
- Political environment

Service Management Process Maturity

Depending on the baseline service management process maturity, you will likely take different approaches. As one of the first steps in any service management implementation project, the current maturity of service management processes is assessed and baselined. This assessment, coupled with business and IT drivers, will determine how service management is implemented.

Service Management Technological Enablement

As a result of baseline assessment, service management automation and tooling is also assessed. Technological enablement is an important component of service management implementation and the current state of technology must be taken into account as you embark on planning for a service management implementation project.

In one large global organization, we had a range of in-house and vendor-based service management tools and components in place. For example, while one region was using a in-house change management tool, others had BMC, HP, and IBM tools. The decision was made to integrate these tools. Integration became one of the most critical components of technological enablement and service-oriented architectures (SOA)-based middleware was assessed as a potential integration solution. In another, equally complex organization, a strategic decision was made to standardize one platform instead of going through all the integrations and assessments.

Building on the BSM Roadmap

With the above-mentioned factors and the roadmap in place, let us now continue to build a comprehensive plan.

Figure 14.2 shows the iterative and incremental service-oriented approach to implementing service management. We have discussed this approach in great detail in Part II of this book. In this chapter, we will use that content to build a service management implementation plan. This implementation plan will consist of the following key components:

- A BSM project plan document
- A project schedule planning template for each iteration (within each phase)

Before we get into the details of an actual project, let us review some of the service management implementation patterns that may be useful in situations that we commonly encounter.

BSM Implementation Patterns

In this section, we will discuss the three key patterns that I have come across. A specific combination of factors discussed above may lead to selecting a given pattern. Let us first discuss briefly what each of these patterns means. After that, we will look at the selection matrix to identify which one is probably right for your particular situation. I am going to make the following assumptions that will be true for each of the patterns:

- Baseline service management process maturity remains the same.
- Management sponsorship exists in all cases.
- Technology enablement will be available for all cases.

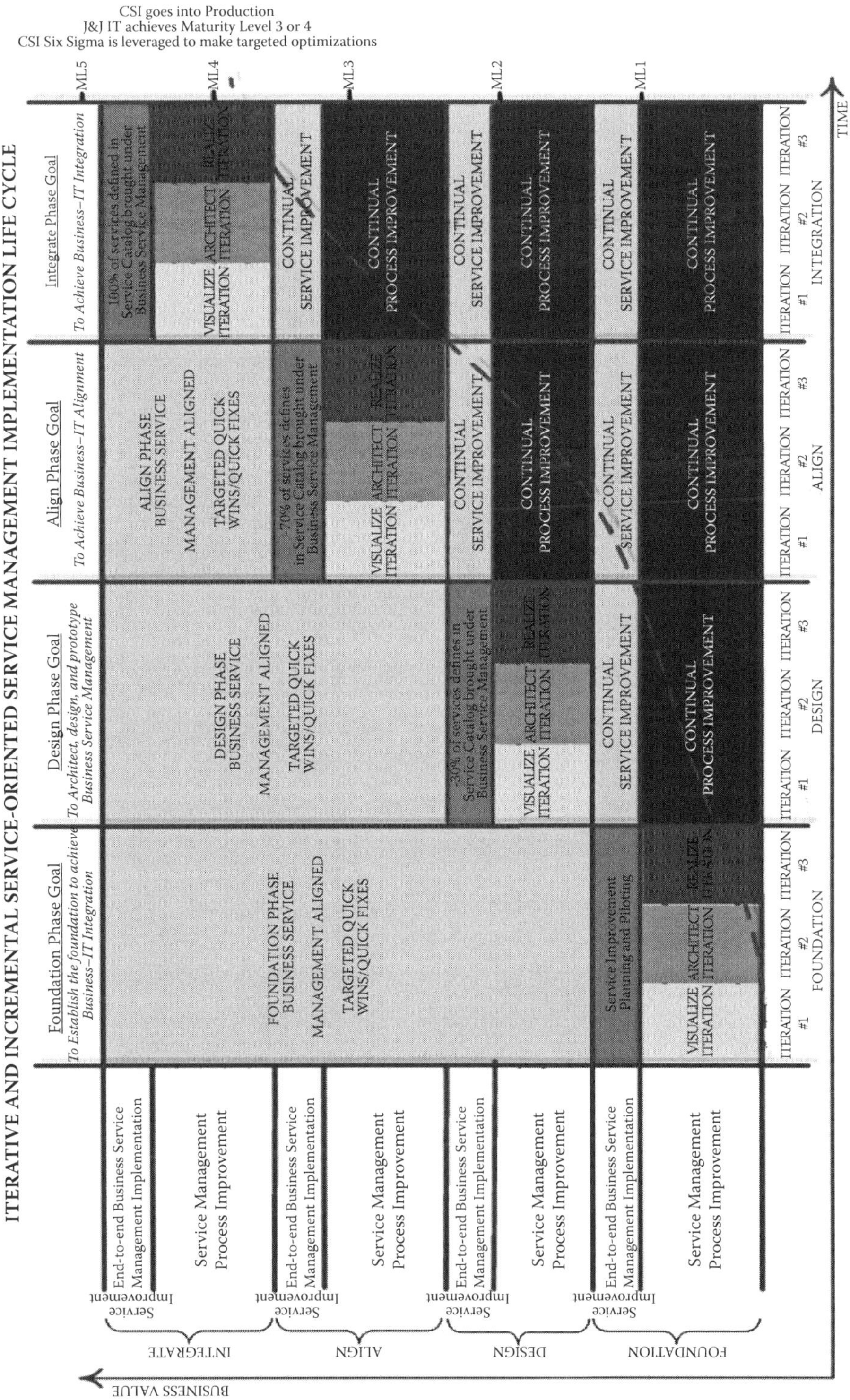

Figure 14.2 Service management implementation approach overview.

Note that these patterns are just patterns and are based on experience and interprocess dependencies. This sequence should be further refined and adjusted based on an organization's unique needs and situation.

Business Value Creation

Let us discuss this pattern in detail.

Purpose

The purpose of this pattern is to make all IT improvements achieved as a result of investing in service management visible to businesses, customers, and executive sponsors.

Description

This pattern is recommended when the main driver for embarking on the BSM journey is to be able to offer greater value to your businesses and customers as soon as possible. This pattern ensures that all service management process-related improvements actually result and impact in service improvement.

We know that processes underpin the delivery of services and process improvements are not cheap. If IT management is under pressure to demonstrate how it is using the funds to improve its services, this pattern will enable the IT team to make the impact of process improvements highly visible. It will result in a greater degree of business–IT integration, greater efficiencies, and reduced costs.

Service Management Process Improvements

Processes are improved in the following sequence in each i2-SOSMI phase.

Foundation Phase

The service management processes to be improved during the *foundation phase* are selected to enable the IT organization to achieve the following:

- Clearly understand what services are offered by the IT organization and who uses those services.
- Identify those services that contribute the most business revenue and prioritize them.
- Ensure that the IT environment is quickly brought under control and that all future changes are governed to minimize potential impact on service delivery.
- Ensure that all customer complaints and requests are handled in a professional, effective, and efficient manner.
- Establish the foundation upon which service and service management process improvements can be achieved in a consistent, measurable, and controlled manner.

To achieve the above-mentioned objectives, it is recommended that the following processes are improved during the foundation phase:

- Service catalog management
- Change management
- Incident management
- Problem management
- Continual service improvement (CSI)

Design

Service management processes to be improved during the *design phase* are selected to enable the IT organization to achieve the following:

- Identify IT components (applications, hardware, and software) that contribute to the delivery of identified or prioritized services. Ensure that information about these components is accurate and complete. Establish clear relationships (configurations) between the above-mentioned identified components. This will result in the creation or targeted refinement of your configuration management database (CMDB) in support of the most critical services. If you already have a CMDB, remember that not everything in your CMDB is important. Always keep the "80/20 Rule" in mind.
- Identify strengths, weaknesses, and capabilities to establish realistic service targets.
- Start to streamline the service fulfillment processes for the most important services.
- Establish the foundation to enable effective monitoring of events, creation of intelligent information, and accurate and timely routing of this information so that potential outages can be avoided.

To achieve the above-mentioned objectives, it is recommended that the following processes are improved during the design phase:

- Service asset and configuration management
- Service level management
- Request fulfillment
- Event management

Align

Service management processes to be improved during the *align phase* are selected to enable the IT organization to achieve the following:

- Ensure that appropriate processes are defined to manage availability of services.
- Achieve a balance between capacity and demand.
- Start to refine processes to manage the costs of delivery of the desired services.
- Ensure that new releases are deployed in an effective and efficient manner.

To achieve the above-mentioned objectives, it is recommended that the following processes are improved during the align phase:

- Availability management
- Release and deployment management

- Demand management
- Capacity management
- Financial management

Integrate

Service management processes to be improved during the *integrate phase* are selected to enable the IT organization to:

- Achieve appropriate information security and access management.
- Ensure that IT is able to plan its continuity to support businesses in the event of a disaster.
- Effective management of suppliers and service portfolio.

To achieve the above-mentioned objectives, it is recommended that the following processes are improved during the integrate phase:

- Information security management
- Access management
- IT service continuity management
- Supplier management
- Service portfolio management

A business value creation service management implementation pattern is shown in Figure 14.3.

Compliance and Regulation

Those organizations that are under strict pressures from government agencies and regulators to implement and demonstrate appropriate controls may want to base their project design on the "compliance and regulation" service management implementation pattern (see Figure 14.4). The processes may be implemented in the following sequence:

- Foundation
  - Service asset and configuration management
  - Change management
  - Incident management
  - Problem management
  - Continual service improvement
- Design
  - Access management
  - Release and deployment management
  - Information security management
  - Financial management
- Align
  - IT service continuity management
  - Supplier management
  - Service catalog management

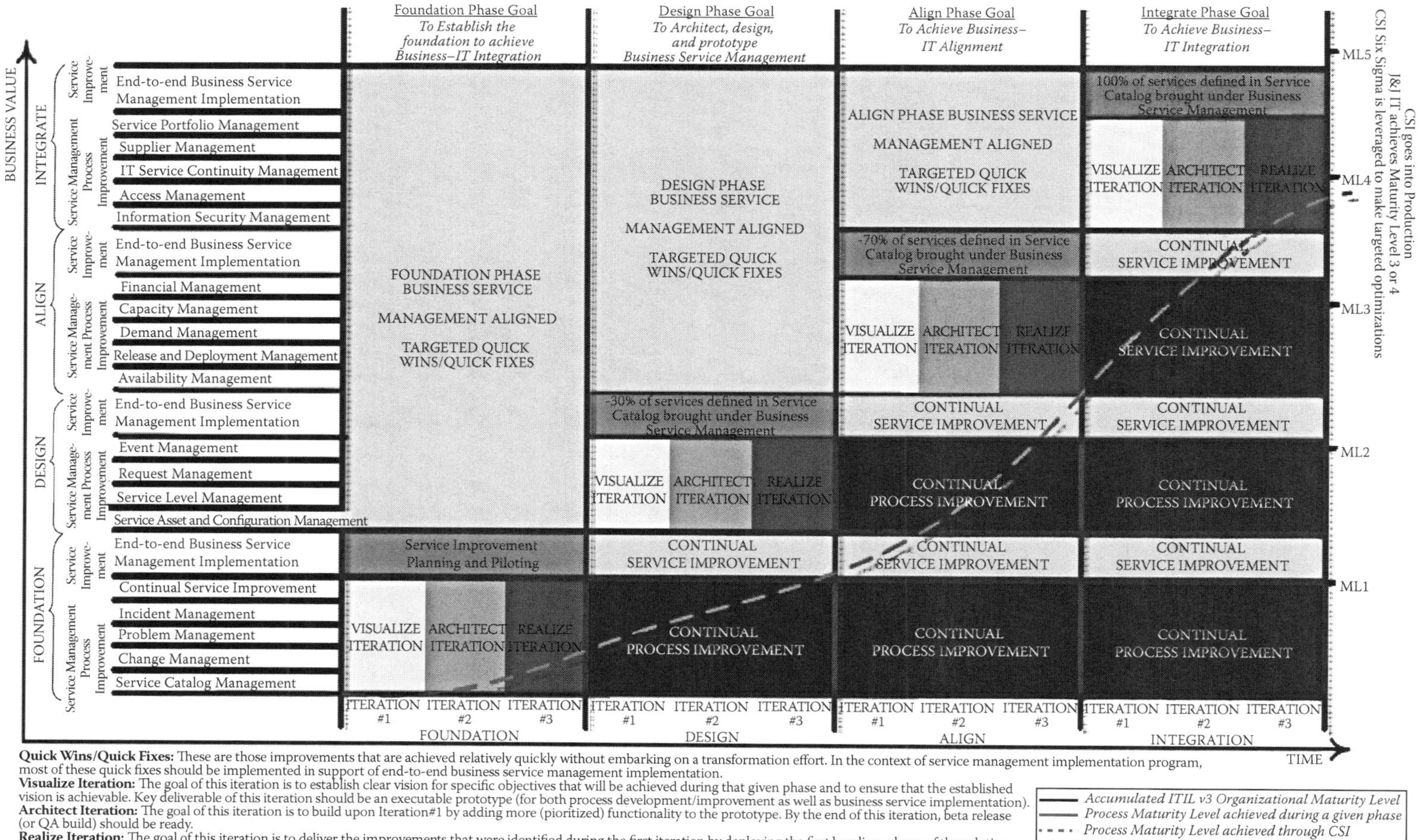

Quick Wins/Quick Fixes: These are those improvements that are achieved relatively quickly without embarking on a transformation effort. In the context of service management implementation program, most of these quick fixes should be implemented in support of end-to-end business service management implementation.
Visualize Iteration: The goal of this iteration is to establish clear vision for specific objectives that will be achieved during that given phase and to ensure that the established vision is achievable. Key deliverable of this iteration should be an executable prototype (for both process development/improvement as well as business service implementation).
Architect Iteration: The goal of this iteration is to build upon Iteration#1 by adding more (pioritized) functionality to the prototype. By the end of this iteration, beta release (or QA build) should be ready.
Realize Iteration: The goal of this iteration is to deliver the improvements that were identified during the first iteration by deploying the first baseline release of the solution.
End-to-end Business Service Management Implementation: For selected services, end-to-end BSM (process, tooling/integration, people, and partners) is implemented to realize an incremental "slice" of our vision
Continual Process/Service Improvement: This consists of the ongoing continual process/service improvements based on the analysis of process KPIs and business needs.

Figure 14.3 Business value creation service management implementation pattern.

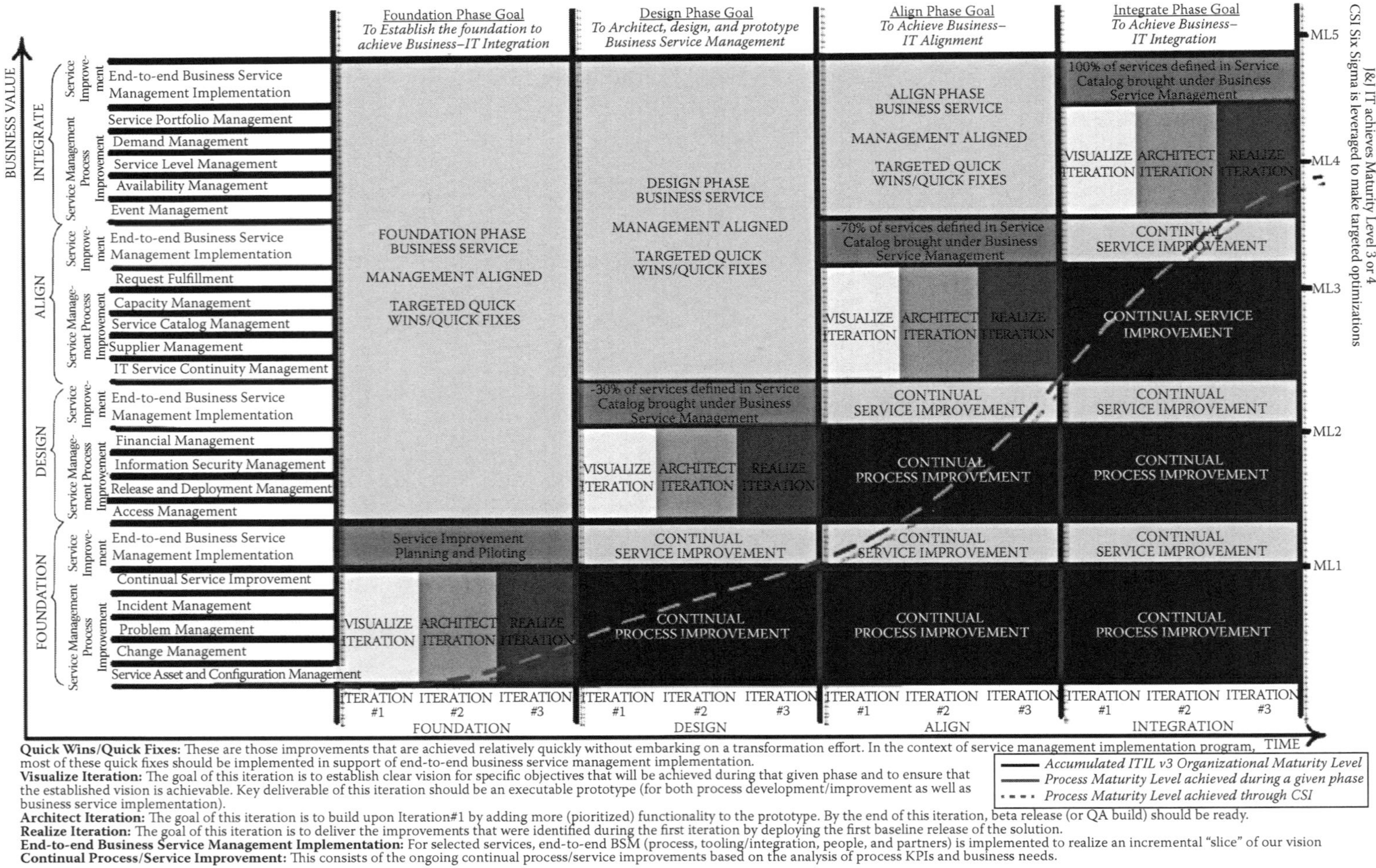

Figure 14.4 Compliance and regulation service management implementation pattern.

  - Capacity management
  - Request fulfillment
- Integrate
  - Event management
  - Availability management
  - Service level management
  - Demand management
  - Service portfolio management

Hybrid

Hybrid, as the name suggests, enables organizations to achieve both compliance- and efficiencies-related improvements. This is illustrated in Figure 14.5. Processes are improved in the following order.

- Foundation
  - Service asset and configuration management
  - Change management
  - Incident management
  - Problem management
  - Continual service improvement
- Design
  - Request fulfillment
  - Release and deployment management
  - Information security management
  - Service catalog management
- Align
  - Event management
  - IT service continuity management
  - Access management
  - Capacity management
  - Service level management
- Integrate
  - Supplier management
  - Availability management
  - Financial management
  - Demand management
  - Service portfolio management

Irrespective of the implementation pattern, please note that all these process improvements are primarily achieved in support of service improvements. Services to be improved are prioritized based on the impact that they have on the businesses and customers.

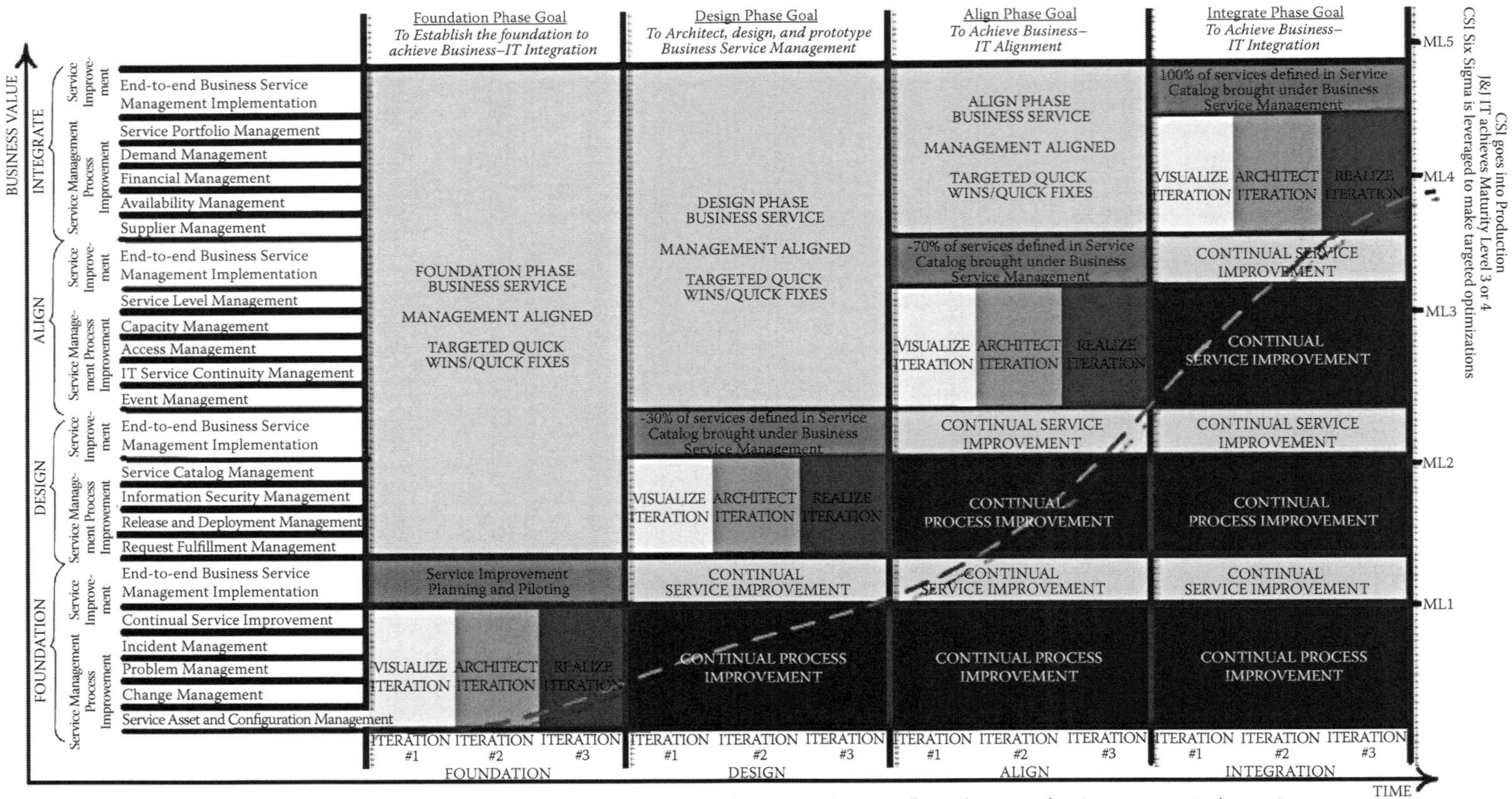

Quick Wins/Quick Fixes: These are those improvements that are achieved relatively quickly without embarking on a transformation effort. In the context of service management implementation program, most of these quick fixes should be implemented in support of end-to-end business service management implementation.

Visualize Iteration: The goal of this iteration is to establish clear vision for specific objectives that will be achieved during that given phase and to ensure that the established vision is achievable. Key deliverable of this iteration should be an executable prototype (for both process development/improvement as well as business service implementation).

Architect Iteration: The goal of this iteration is to build upon Iteration#1 by adding more (pioritized) functionality to the prototype. By the end of this iteration, beta release (or QA build) should be ready.

Realize Iteration: The goal of this iteration is to deliver the improvements that were identified during the first iteration by deploying the first baseline release of the solution.

End-to-end Business Service Management Implementation: For selected services, end-to-end BSM (process, tooling/integration, people, and partners) is implemented to realize an incremental "slice" of our vision

Continual Process/Service Improvement: This consists of the ongoing continual process/service improvements based on the analysis of process KPIs and business needs.

——— *Accumulated ITIL v3 Organizational Maturity Level*
——— *Process Maturity Level achieved during a given phase*
- - - *Process Maturity Level achieved through CSI*

Figure 14.5 Hybrid service management implementation pattern.

BSM Project Work Streams

The BSM project must address, plan, and manage the following key work streams to ensure optimal results:

- Project management
- People and organization
- CSI institutionalization
- Business service improvement
- Service management process improvement
- BSM technology architecture and integration
- BSM technology delivery

These streams and their respective objectives are shown in Figure 14.6.

Common Challenges or Opportunities

Challenges and opportunities will be discussed at the same time. If managed appropriately, the very aspects that can lead to potential challenges can be transformed into opportunities. There are, however, some challenges that must be managed before embarking on the BSM journey as they pose significant risks to the success of this effort.

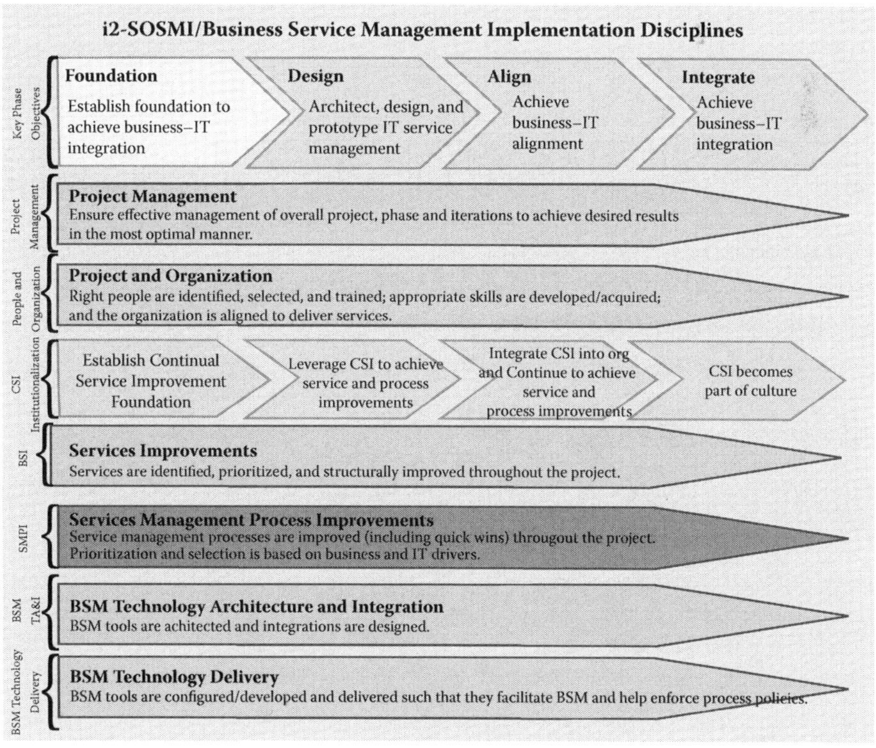

Figure 14.6 Key BSM project work streams and i2-SOSMI disciplines.

People

People, people, people. People are the most significant organizational capabilities and resources. People must be kept in the forefront as you initiate the service management implementation effort. The right people must be identified, acquired, and trained.

Senior Management

It is highly unlikely that service management effort is successful without strong, dedicated, ongoing, steady, and clear support from the senior management.

Organization

Appropriate expectations must be established on organizational realignments. In almost all service management implementation projects, organizational changes will need to take place. Ideally, this should be done in parallel with process improvement efforts. However, that may become very complicated. Therefore, it is recommended that appropriate teams and related structures are put in place before formally kicking off the effort. An argument can be made about how those organizations can be made in the absence and/or in situations where improvements and changes are going to be made across the service management processes.

If there is an agreement on why service management is being implemented, then certain organizational principles will need to be established. These principles should guide the organizational design. Organizational architecture is shown in Figure 14.7.

Technology and Tools

Technology is one of the key enablers of service management processes and should be carefully architected and implemented. Technology and tooling will not help achieve organizational maturity. Technology enables processes and not the other way round. In cases where service management projects are led by IT development or operations organizations, tools actually "highjack" the core purpose of embarking on the service management journey. There are many vendors including BMC, HP, and IBM that may claim that their respective tools are ITIL v3 compliant. It does not mean that acquiring any of these tools is going to take care of everything by itself.

Critical Success Factors

Some of the factors that will be most critical to the success of this project are listed here.

People, People, People

People must be kept in the forefront. As discussed, people are the most critical capabilities and resources of any organization.

Communication

Communication is one of the most critical factors to achieving cultural transformation.

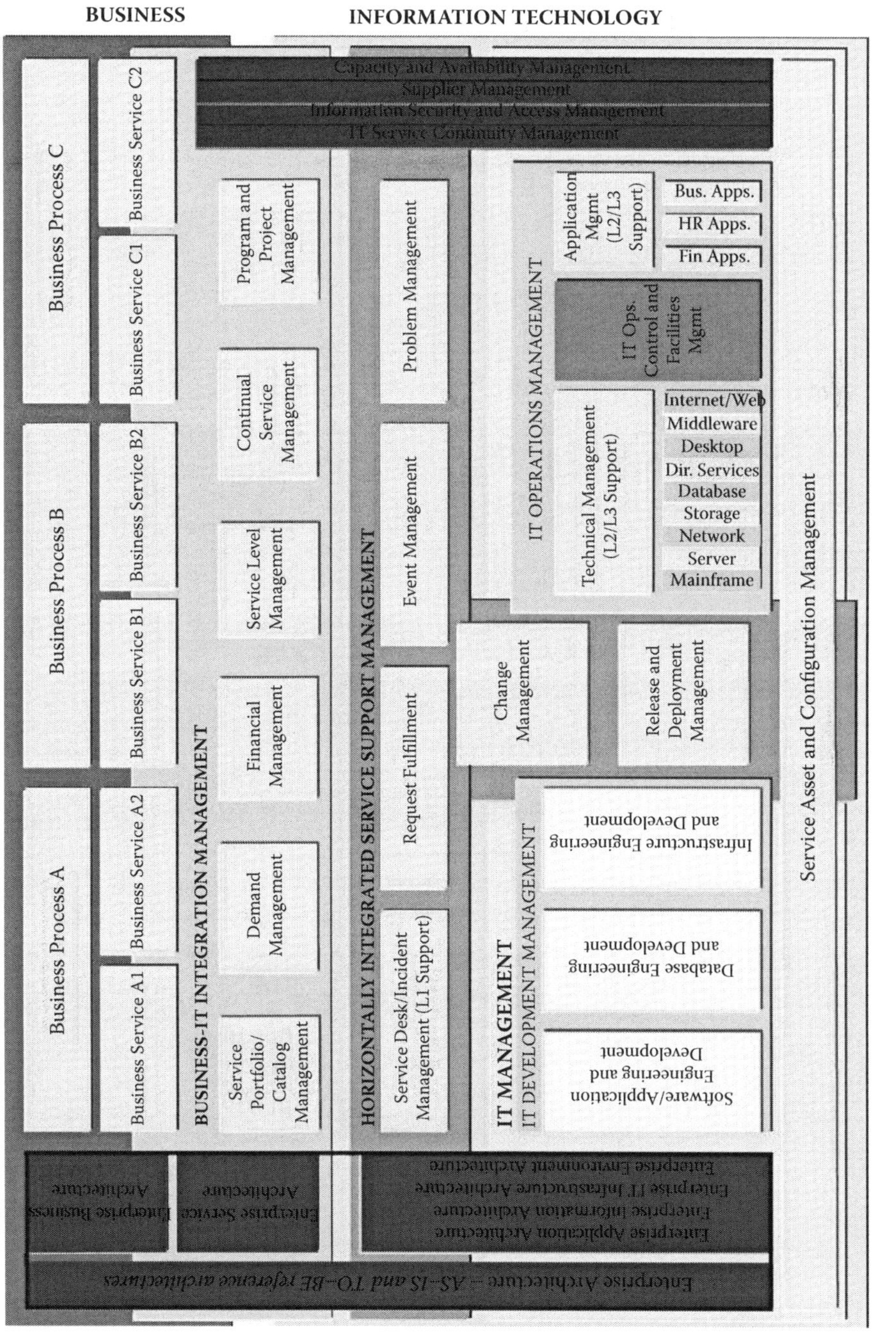

Figure 14.7 Organizational architecture.

Communicating Value to the Business

To ensure that businesses and customers clearly understand how IT is using the funds allocated for service management implementation, it is critical to ensure that service improvement initiatives are appropriately communicated and measurable improvements are shared in a timely manner. This will be critical to enabling continual business sponsorship.

Communication Value to the IT

It takes hard work to achieve service improvements. IT teams need to be appreciated when they do achieve such improvements.

Organizational Change Management

Organizational change management needs to be well planned and well implemented. Key steps that should be taken to achieve this are as follows:

- Establish a clear organizational vision and BSM project goals.
  Without a clear vision for the IT organization, it will become more difficult to achieve a service-oriented culture. A goal for the BSM project must be aligned with the overall vision for the IT organization. The organizational vision and BSM goal must clearly state why there is a strong need for the IT organization to transform to deliver what it needs to deliver. People must be able to buy into this vision and clearly visualize the future state.
- Ensure complete and dedicated senior management sponsorship.
  Organizational changes will not happen without dedicated and complete sponsorship by someone who is powerful in the organization. This sponsorship must be clear and visible and must enable IT leadership to achieve IT transformational goals.
- Create an urgent case for change.
  The case for change must be clear, precise, and concise. You may want to consider these questions. Why now? Why not later? Why transform? What if we do not change? What will be the impact? These are the questions that people will ask. Change is difficult and it will become more difficult if people do not buy into the underlying reasons for change.
- Maintain consistent communication to reinforce the IT vision, BSM goal, and success stories.
  Communication is one of the most effective and critical tools to drive successful organizational changes. Constant and consistent communication is absolutely critical to ensure achievement of a service-oriented culture. It sometimes takes the same message to be communicated over and over again for it to be understood and bought into. However, it is critical that the same message is communicated in a consistent, clear, and constant manner.
- Align people, process, organization, culture, and tools.
  For the organizational transformation and BSM to be successful, people, processes, organization, culture, and tools must be aligned. BSM requires teams across IT functions to collaborate together to deliver the desired business services at expected levels. Siloed processes, organizations, or tools will hurt the change effort and therefore need to be carefully designed.
- Measure change.
  Ensure that appropriate measurements are in place that enable you to measure the successful achievement of service-oriented, customer-focused cultures.

Process Change Management

There are many best practices available on process improvement. These include Six Sigma, CMMI IDEAL, CSI 7-step process, and so on. There are a great deal of similarities between these methodologies. Discussion of their similarities is not within the scope of our discussion here. What I want to share with you is the organization and planning part of process improvement activities. Regardless of which approach you select to achieve your process improvements, required activities must be coordinated and planned to achieve the following key objectives for each of the service management processes:

- Achieve deeper understanding of particular business needs and build tailored and customized versions of service management processes based on guidelines provided by ITIL v3 literature.
- Gain detailed insights into what specific value-add is needed from automating the developed processes. This will enable greater understanding of process automation requirements.
- Share and socialize the developed processes with key operational, architectural, and other stakeholders to achieve their buy-in.
- Develop interprocess and cross-process relationships to clearly and precisely capture integration points and build a clear understanding of integration needs.

Process Automation and Tool Development

After the process analysis and development, the next step (which may happen in parallel with the process development and improvement effort) is to understand how best to enforce the process in an efficient, high-throughput (e.g., the number of changes processed per year), and effective, high accuracy (e.g., number of changes where impact assessment was not accurate) manner. Automating the process is one of the most important means of enforcing the process. This requires development and customization of software tools. There are many off-the-shelf tools available on the market and most of them require configuration and some of them even support customization. It becomes critical to assess the suitability of the tool and the requirements of the process. A clear understanding of needs is always critical to appropriate implementation of the right tool.

Understanding the "Big Picture": BSM Architecture

To ensure smooth and effective implementation and to optimize the benefits to be realized as a result of implementing BSM, it is critical to understand the overall service management architecture and how it will impact the organization (see Figure 14.8). My advice to my clients is always to establish and communicate this service management architecture picture as early as possible during the service management journey. Debate and discussions between the senior and middle management is expected and the architecture team plays an important role. Let me share with you a service management architecture picture that combines ITIL v3 as well as enterprise architecture (EA) concepts. ITIL v3, EA, SOA, and service management architecture are further discussed in detail in Chapter 17.

Business Architecture and Service Strategy

Business architecture and service strategy aims to achieve the following key objectives:

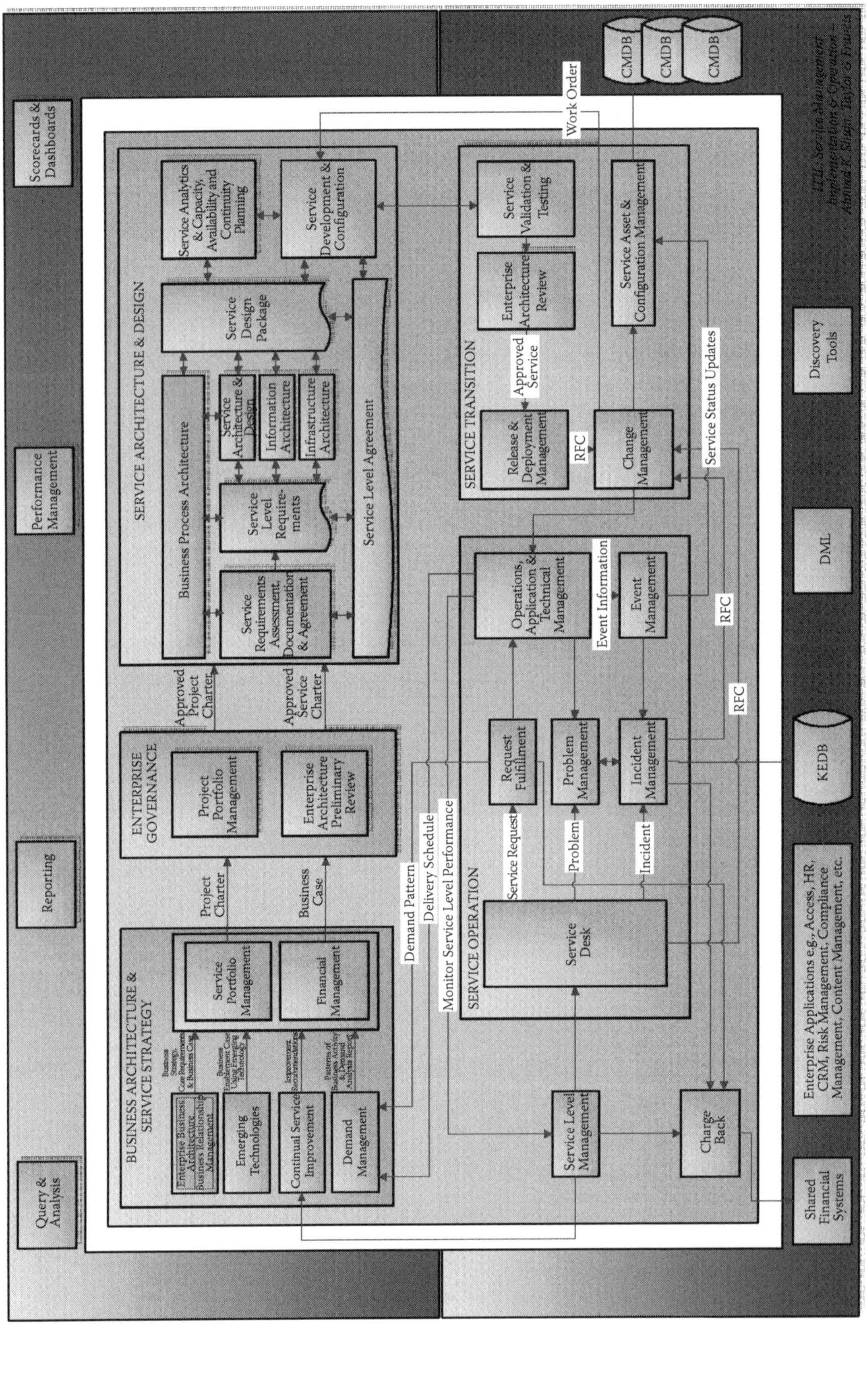

Figure 14.8 BSM architecture.

- Gain a clear understanding of business strategy and identify core emerging business requirements.
- Identify patterns of business activity and forecast demand.
- Create a business case for building new IT services or improve existing services so that these IT investments are aligned with customers' business priorities.

Enterprise Governance

Enterprise governance ensures that the right projects are selected to ensure continual business–IT alignment.

Service Architecture and Design

Selected services are architected and designed during this process. The service architecture and design stage combines ITIL v3 guidelines with the IT architecture practices (service, integration, application data and information, and infrastructure architectures) to ensure that the right IT services are architected and designed.

Service Transition

Service transition encompasses development, testing, and deployment of new services. It is based on ITIL v3 guidelines.

Service Operation

The service operation stage here is based on ITIL v3 guidelines and provides an overview of high-level activities.

Understanding and Planning for CSI

In my opinion, CSI is one of the strongest concepts introduced in ITIL v3. Let us understand what is at the core of CSI. CSI aims to achieve improved organizational capability to make intelligent decisions and wise investments.

To achieve the above-mentioned objectives, CSI requires the following inputs:

- Service performance data
- Service management process performance data
- New business and security requirements
- New external drivers such as regulatory requirements

A CSI organization or team will process the above-mentioned data and produce the following outputs:

- Trend analysis—comparison with targets, service level agreements, and benchmarks
- Recommended targets for improvements in service efficiency and effectiveness
- Assistance in planning and implementing improvements

- Establishment of a means for staff members to recommend improvements
- Recommendation or revision of policies, processes, procedures, and plans where necessary
- Ensure that all approved actions are completed and that they achieve the desired results

These inputs and outputs are graphically shown in Figure 14.9.

A CSI manager should be identified and appointed to ensure that the above-mentioned objectives are achieved. Depending on the organization, CSI may be comprised of process analysts and engineers.

BSM Implementation Project Plan Template

Recommended content includes the following:

- Introduction
- Goals and obstacles
  - Stakeholders and their goals
  - Project constraints
  - Project assumptions
- Project scope
  - In-scope
    - Outside of the boundary
    - Inside of the boundary
    - Life cycle coverage
    - Geographical
  - Out-of-scope
    - Outside the boundary
    - Inside the boundary

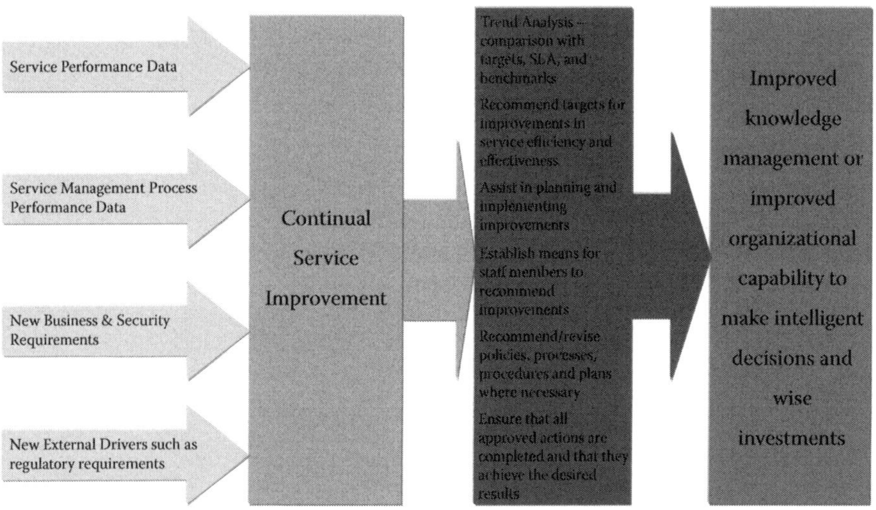

Figure 14.9 CSI inputs and outputs.

    - Life cycle coverage
    - Geographical
- Project scope statement
  - Project objectives
  - Deliverables
- Project scope definition
  - WBS outline
  - Detailed WBS template
- Phases and iterations
  - Foundation phase
  - Design phase
  - Align phase
  - Integrate phase
- Project resources
  - Project organization chart
  - Governance architecture
  - Roles and responsibilities
  - Project resource and effort requirements
    - Human resource requirements
    - Computing requirements
    - Storage requirements
    - Shelf and space requirements
    - Other requirements
- Major milestones and cost estimates
- Senior management approval

BSM Project Charter and Plan

This is discussed in detail in Appendix C.

Summary

In this chapter, we discussed in detail the key aspects that should be considered to plan a BSM implementation project. We discussed some of the critical success factors among which *people* are of significant importance. It is people who will need to follow processes, utilize tools, and deliver services to the customers. It is, therefore, important that people are given due importance. In the next chapter, we discuss how implementation can be managed by the plan to ensure success.

References

Dubie, D. Procter & Gamble touts IT services model, saves $500 million. *ComputerWorld* October 1, 2002. http://www.computerworld.com/s/article/74762/Procter_Gamble_touts_IT_services_model_saves_-500_million.

O'Neill, P., T. Mendel, and R. Iqbal. 2007. Business Service Management: Early Birds Are Catching the Worm, But IT Still Doesn't Get It. http://www.forrester.com/rb/Research/business_service_management_early_birds_are_catching/q/id/41458/t/2 (accessed March, 2007).

Shuja, A., and J. Krebs. 2008. *Rational Unified Process: Reference and Certification Guide*. New York: IBM Press.

Chapter 15

Implementing Business Service Management

We have discussed in detail what should be considered in planning the business service management (BSM) implementation. We discussed the key activities that should be performed during the project. In this chapter, we will learn about the key aspects of implementing BSM. These aspects will enable us to maintain our focus in the right direction during the implementation phase.

Iterative and Incremental BSM Implementation

We have discussed in great detail what it means to implement BSM in an iterative and incremental manner. The iterative and incremental service-oriented service management implementation (i2-SOSMI) life cycle processes provide a comprehensive set of guidelines on planning the BSM implementation. After the planning step, the next is to execute the plans and ensure that desired results are achieved. Projects in Controlled Environments (PRINCE2) and Project Management Body of Knowledge (PMBOK) provide detailed guidelines on executing and monitoring project plans.

Measuring and Communicating Improvements

BSM implementation is, in most cases, not a low-risk, low-impact effort. There are returns, but there are associated risks as well. As discussed earlier in this book, the single largest aspect that is impacted as a result of implementing BSM is the organizational culture. The impact of BSM implementation should measure the following key areas:

- Customer satisfaction
- Business performance
- Service performance

- Organization and people performance
- Service management process performance
- Technology performance

Transforming an organizational culture will need improvements across all aspects of the organization. This includes processes, people, and technology. Performance across each of these factors will need to be measured and appropriately communicated to all stakeholders including sponsors and those that are getting impacted. The *communicate strategy and plan* template is attached in Appendix C.

Let us discuss different types of performance measurements that will be critical to continually keep the sponsorship alive and to keep the momentum going. Note that as you go through the project, you must define ways and means to measure across the following categories and communicate the results in a timely and appropriate manner. This will go a long way toward keeping the momentum.

Customer Satisfaction

Customer satisfaction is one of the key objectives of implementing BSM and measuring it is critical. When customers are satisfied, it means that they were able to realize the anticipated business benefits as a consequence of using the service.

Business Performance

A cornerstone of BSM is the ability to measure IT performance in terms of business performance. Business performance must be measured in terms of the impact as a result of services provided by the IT organization. Business–IT alignment and integration must be measured to ensure that IT improvements do actually contribute to business performance. For example, if the supply chain management process is appropriately enabled by IT services (which were available at agreed levels and performed as committed), then there should be visible results in terms of manufacturing plans and inventory levels.

Service Performance

You must be able to relate the performance of your services to the performance of your customers' businesses. Service performance must be measured to demonstrate that agreed service levels were met. As shown in Figure 15.1, service performance is impacted by the performance of people and the organization, performance of the underpinning service management processes, and performance of underlying technology components.

Organization and People Performance

As an organization, how much time and resources do you spend "keeping the lights on" and how much on development? This is an important indicator. If you are dedicating most of your resources to keeping the lights on, then it is very likely that you are operating in the firefighting or crisis management mode most of the time. In my experience, high-performing IT organizations should spend no more that 35% of their time and effort in keeping the lights on and more than 65% on development.

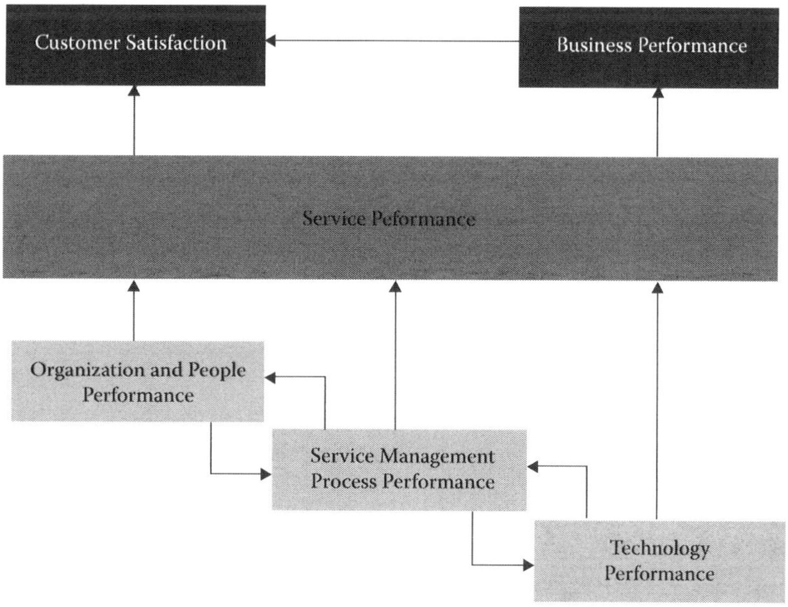

Figure 15.1 Performance measurements.

Service Management Process Performance

As service management processes are improved, they will contribute to improving the service performance. For example, if the change management process is well institutionalized within the organization, there will most likely be fewer emergency changes and fewer failed changes. Another example is the performance of the incident management process and the metric can be "incident closure time." This will contribute to improving the service reliability and availability. Service management process key performance indicators and metrics must be baselined beforehand. Target improvements must be clearly defined and agreed on. As processes are improved, the improvements must be measured against the baselines and targets.

Technology Performance

If technology components are maintained (patched, secured, updated, and controlled) properly, they will last longer and provide higher performance. At a technology component level, performance should be measured in the same way that process performance is measured (i.e., performance measurements are baselined and targets are established).

Service Catalog—The Foundation for BSM Implementation

As discussed earlier in this book, one of the key and most critical components upon which the entire BSM implementation depends and that must be developed early in the project life cycle is the service catalog. Designing and building the service catalog early means that the organization will have a better understanding of the services that are offered by the IT service provider early in the project. Keep in mind that if the catalog never existed in the organization before this project, then you should not expect the catalog to be complete at this stage. It will be a continual process whereby unknown services will be discovered and the service catalog will be continually updated. Calls to the service desk that are related to services not captured in the service catalog are one source. There is a sample catalog along with detailed questionnaires and other supporting materials provided in Appendix A.

Service Principles

When embarking on a BSM journey, it is always helpful to define and agree on the core set of principles that apply to services and the service catalog for a given organization. Some of these principles may include the following:

- *How many service catalog views will you have for your customers?*
  This will depend on the type of customers that you are catering to. If you have nontechnical business customers and technical customers, then there may be multiple views of the catalog. Such a situation happens if there are shared infrastructure services and businesses have their own application development teams (Figure 15.2). One of the core principles may read, "There shall be one customer-facing service catalog."
- *Does the IT service provider provide anything other than services?*
  For example, does the IT service provider organization sell "Blackberry" as a hardware device or does it sell "Blackberry Service"? A hardware device only means no data or voice communication with the hardware. Or does it provide complete service with the hardware? In most cases, IT service providers are not in the business of selling hardware. Accordingly, one of the service principles may read, "IT service provider organization shall deliver services (i.e., assets plus life cycle of services around those assets) and not stand-alone products (e.g., handheld devices, servers, routers, etc.)."
- *How will the overall quality of service be managed?*
  Server ownership is critical to ensuring that services continue to deliver the desired value to its customers. In most organizations, you will see network teams, server teams, and so on. You will not see many service teams. In such cases, whenever there is an outage of a given service, each silo owner comes back and says that their component is working fine (Figure 15.3). There is nobody who owns the delivery of end-to-end service, which is the only aspect that the customers see. Therefore, it is absolutely critical to appoint owners for each service that is offered by the service provider (Figure 15.2). Accordingly, one of the core principles may read, "Each service shall have an owner who shall be accountable for the overall quality of that service, associated SLA, and performance targets."

Service Catalog

Communication Services	**Data Centre Services**	**ERP Services**
Email Service	Business Application Hosting	Financial Management
Internet Service	Server Management	Project Management
Blackberry Service	Rack-space Leasing	Human Resource Management
Knowledge Service		

Figure 15.2 Service catalog example.

Infrastructure Component	Component Availability	Net Service Availability
Network	99%	99%
Operating System	99%	99% × 99% = 98%
Database	99%	99% × 99% × 99% = 97%
Middleware	99%	99% × 99% × 99% × 99% = 96%
ERP System	99%	99% × 99% × 99% × 99% × 99% = 95%
Advanced Planning	99%	99% × 99% × 99% × 99% × 99% × 99% = 94%

Figure 15.3 Service availability vs. component availability.

- *How are the services priced?*
  In the case of an internal IT service provider, profitability is not the goal. Instead, it is about cost recovery. In case you are providing services to external customers, then profitability is an important factor. Accordingly, one of the core principles must lay out whether it is going to be a cost-recovery model or a profitability model. In the case of cost recovery, the principle may read, "Each service shall be priced for cost recovery, not profitability."
- *How are new services going to be identified and how will those that are not in demand any more be retired?*
  New services will be needed and those that are not needed any more will need to be retired.
  How are related decisions made?
  As shown in Figure 15.4, the service portfolio includes all services—new ones to be offered, existing operational ones, and those that need to be retired. It is important to define a single working group, with representatives from across businesses and customers, as well as from IT, to review new services and decide on retiring old services.
- *What factors will drive the identification and selection of new services?*
  It is critical to clearly define the criteria that will be used to identify and select new services to be offered. Is it going to be determined by the potential revenue that can be generated with the introduction of this new service, or is it going to be determined by efficiency? Will a single business or customer have more influence or is it going to be determined by the potential demand for the service and cost of developing and managing the delivery of the potential new service? Developing new services should take into account demand patterns across both the IT service provider organization and its businesses and customers. More information on related topics can be found in the book *ITIL v3 Service Strategy*. On a related topic, it is important to define related policies and processes to manage the exceptions, that is, how will the requests for services that are not currently offered by the IT service provider be handled? This becomes a serious issue where the IT service provider is an internal one. In such cases, it becomes critical to define an exception process for approving services that are not part of the service catalog.

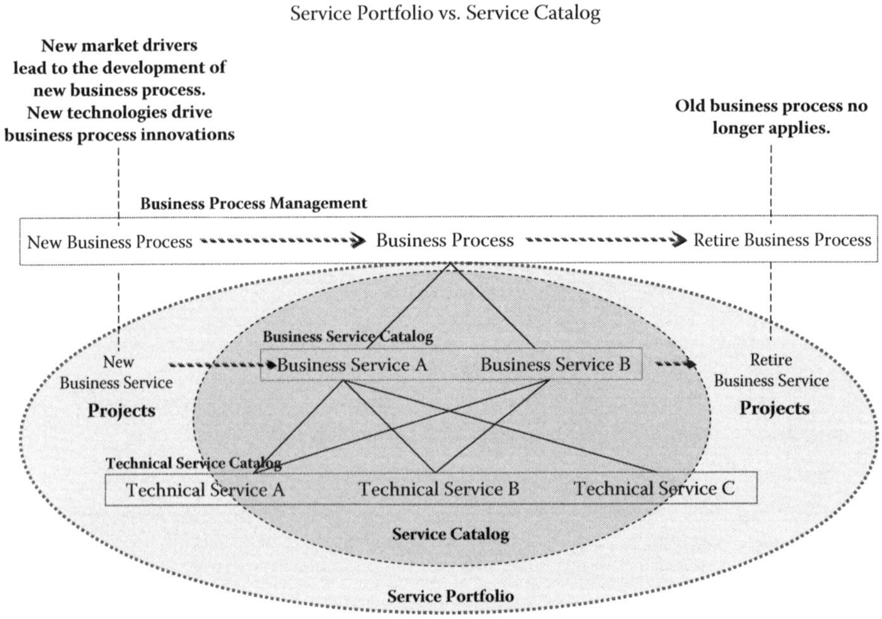

Figure 15.4 Service portfolio vs. service catalog.

Defining the Service Catalog

In this section, we will discuss some of the key steps, as shown in Figure 15.5, that should be taken to identify services and define the service catalog.

Preparing for the Definition of the Service Catalog

If a given organization does not have a service catalog in place, it does not mean that it does not offer services. It may be that the IT service organization does not clearly know what services are offered and the customer may just make ad hoc requests to people they know within back-end IT operations. This is a perfect situation where IT teams work hardest but not wisely. There are many leaks within the IT teams, that is, multiple requests for the same service (e.g., new e-mail account creation) may be fulfilled by multiple individuals following different sets of steps and completing within different timelines. Defining the service catalog is the first step toward gaining clarity on the services that are offered by the IT organization or consumed by the customers and businesses.

In preparing for the definition of the service catalog, there are some prerequisites that are needed. These are as follows:

- Service name or the name by which customers recognize it.
- Screen shots (in the case of Web-based forms) or service request forms that are used by the customers to request a given service. Sometimes e-mails are also used to request services. It will be useful to gather sample e-mails that are submitted by the requestors.
- Process flow diagrams that define how requests for services are fulfilled. These can be in electronic form or hand-drawn diagrams.

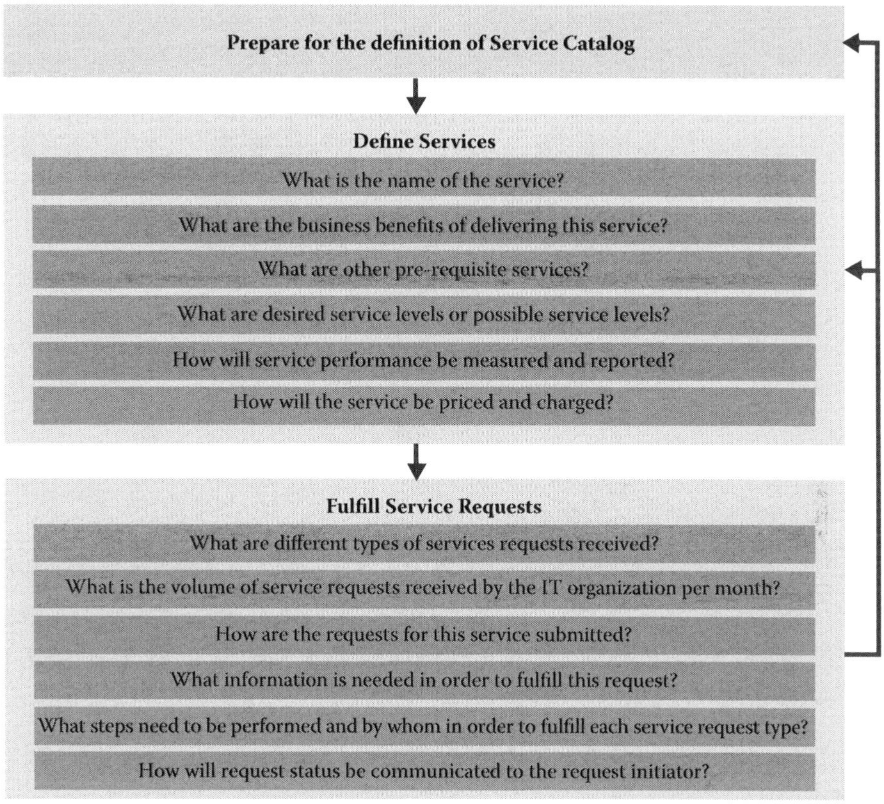

Figure 15.5 Bringing the service catalog to life.

Defining Services

The first and most important step is to identify and clearly define the services that are provided by the IT organization. The goal of clearly and concisely defining services that are provided by the IT organization is to ensure that the customer of the given service clearly understands what should be expected as a result of receiving that service. In other words, it is important to ensure that the value expected as a result of successfully delivering the service to the customer is completely understood by the customer. This is best achieved by first preparing and gathering key information about the services. Once that is done, some of the key questions that should be asked are as follows:

- *What is the name of the service?*
  What potential category does this service belong to? Is it somehow related to collaboration and communication and is it going to support planning activities? Do your customers or businesses refer to this service by another name? What are some of the key words that can be used for the service? For example, mobile communication may be used to define the Blackberry service.
- *What are the business benefits of delivering this service?*
  It is important to explain the benefits that are expected to be realized as a result of using any given service.

- *What are other prerequisite services?*
  Are there other services required to request for this service? For example, to be able to request an e-mail service, you will need to have Internet service.
- *What are the desired service levels or possible service levels?*
  Depending on the situation, it is critical to understand what levels of service levels are needed and can be committed. These will drive the architecture and design of different service components. For example, for *Platinum* members:
  - More than 80% of the service requests will be fulfilled within 24 hours.
  - Service availability will be more than 98%.

  These targets can be defined across a range of categories. For example, availability, delivery, response time, mean time between failures, and so on.
- *How will service performance be measured and reported?*
  Will customers be informed through electronic communication (SMS, e-mail, etc.) or written reports?
- *How will the service be priced and charged?*
  It is important to communicate to the customer how the charge back is going to work.

Fulfilling Service Requests

Once services are defined, the next step is to clearly understand the kind of requests that can be placed on each of those services. For example, if your company is in the business of mobile communication, then one of the requests that can be placed is a request for a new mobile communication account. It is important to clearly identify and define the requests that can be placed for each service defined in the service catalog. To maximize returns, it is critical that those requests be considered during these discussions that are high-volume and low-risk. For such requests, investments in defining processes to efficiently fulfill these requests will bring the most return on those investments.

- *What are different types of service requests received?*
  If you look through the request log, you should be able to identify some common and recurring requests that are received by the IT organization. For example, you may find requests for services such as new e-mail accounts, computer repair, external party connections, and so on. The goal is to identify a small subset of requests that make up the most volume. Improving and streamlining the fulfillment process for these high-volume, low-risk recurring requests will result in achieving high efficiencies.
- *What is the volume of service requests received by the IT organization per month?*
  The volume of requests received for a given service will help us identify those requests that can be automated. This volume will be key to identifying the right group of requests for which the fulfillment process should be streamlined and appropriately automated.
- *How are requests for this service submitted?*
  Services can be requested by a number of means such as completing and submitting an online form, calling the service desk, printing, completing, signing, and faxing the form. It is important to define how the service-related requests are submitted. Once a service request is submitted, is it possible and is there a way to make any changes to the request?
- *What information is needed to fulfill this request?*
  Answering this question correctly is critical to the definition of the fulfillment process. Does the request fulfillment require any financial approvals or any additional security clearance? It is important to document the needed information.

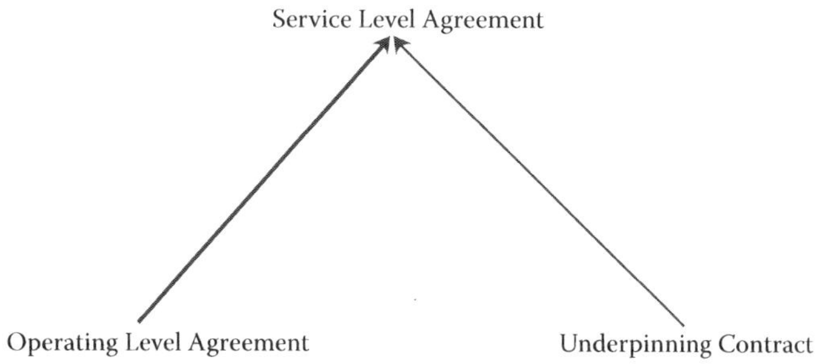

Figure 15.6 OLAs and UCs underpin SLAs.

- *What steps should be performed, and by whom, to fulfill each service request type?*
  In answering this question, you will need to interview relevant fulfillment teams from across the IT organization. It will be important to identify exceptions such as:
  - Will there be an expedited process when a certain VIP or senior executive requests a service?
  - What will happen if a customized service is requested?
  - Will such requests be fulfilled? If yes, how will these impact the pricing and chargeback?

  In identifying the relevant teams that will be required to fulfill the service request, you will need to identify if there are any third parties or suppliers involved. Note that this activity, along with the service levels defined or identified earlier, will drive the definition of potential operating level agreements (OLAs) with internal teams and underpinning contracts (UCs) with external suppliers. These will be defined to support the service level agreement (SLA) (Figure 15.6).
- *How will request statuses be communicated to the request initiator?*
  Customers must be kept informed on the status of their requests. Status updates can be "pushed" out to the customer or status requests can be "pushed" in by the customer. If customers receive regular updates regarding the status of their respective requests, it will reduce the potential volume of calls received from the customer inquiring about the request status. These updates can be pushed out to the customer via e-mails, automated phone calls, SMS, and online status tracking.

Common Challenges and Risks

BSM implementation will often result in organizational changes. These changes will most likely include changes to job descriptions and team structures. As such, the key challenges that must be managed effectively are related to organizational change management. If organizational changes are not managed well, it will result in the following key risks:

- Losing high-performing staff members and colleagues
- Creating an environment of mistrust leading to undesired performance problems
- Keeping more control than necessary

Team building events can be of great help during the implementation of BSM.

Summary

BSM implementation involves risks that span across a range of areas including organizational, people, cultural, and technological. Managing projects in ways that ensure that these risks are appropriately managed and mitigated will be key to the successful implementation of BSM. Measuring and communicating success stories will play a key role in ensuring that sponsorship stays alive and momentum is maintained.

OPERATING BUSINESS SERVICE MANAGEMENT

IV

Chapter 16

Operating Business Service Management

Business service management (BSM) operation is what creates value for the customers and businesses. If implemented appropriately, BSM should enable the IT organization to effectively manage its processes, people, and technologies to deliver the needed services in the most cost-effective and predictable manner. By the end of this chapter, you will be able to answer the following key questions as they relate to operating BSM:

- How can strategy, design, transition, and operation be unified into a holistic approach to ensure that the desired business value is delivered by IT services?
- How can operational success be measured?
- What are some of the key options for outsourcing IT?
- What are the key aspects required to run effective operations?

Business and IT: Integration and Traceability

To deliver the desired business value through IT services, a unified approach is mandatory. Networks, servers, databases, business applications, storage technologies, and other factors need to be managed in a unified manner to ensure that businesses and customers receive the promised services. We have discussed Figure 16.1 in the context of organizational architecture. Let us now see how it applies to ensuring that business and IT are integrated.

Service Strategy and Planning

Service Strategy and Planning (SSP) is about understanding the entire portfolio (retired, operational, and future) of services, understanding and managing demand for services, establishing appropriate financial management, managing service levels, and achieving continual improvements.

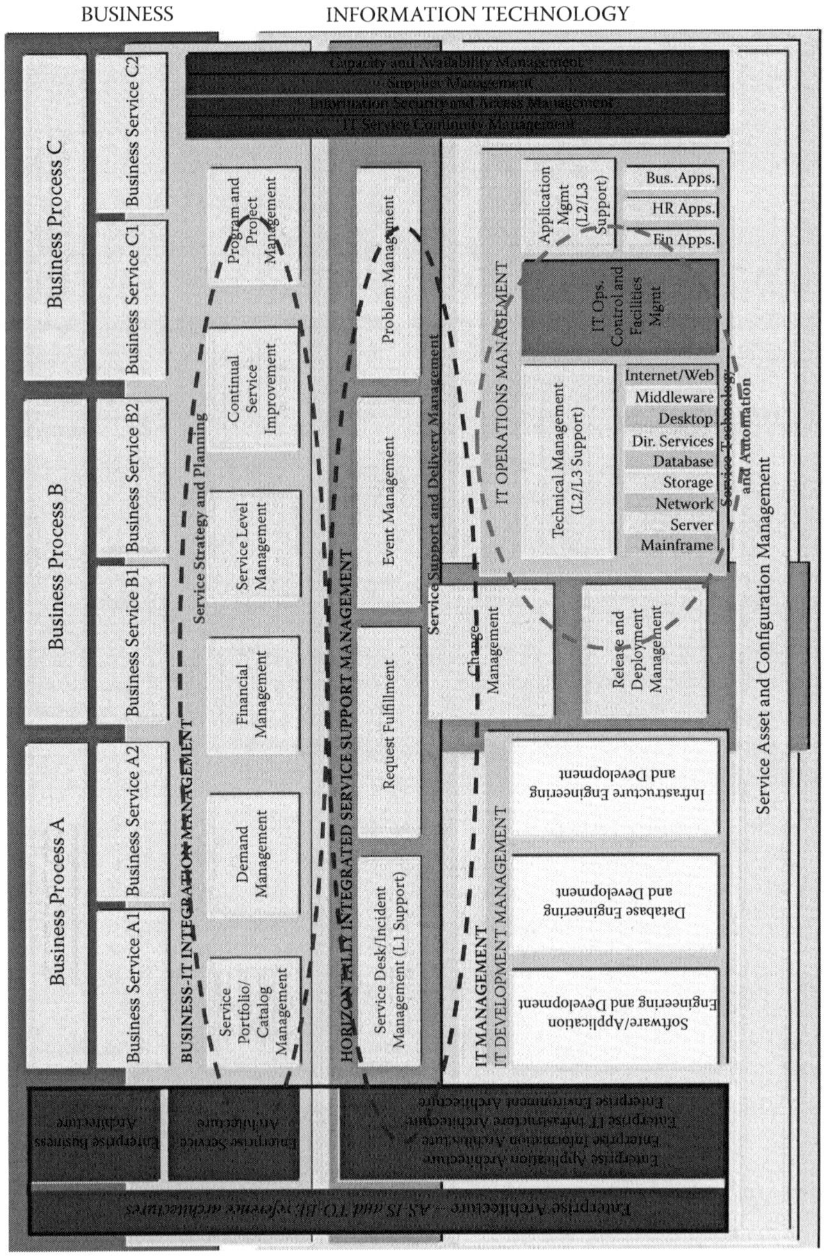

Figure 16.1 Unified IT service and operations management.

SSP ensures that business and IT are integrated, that is, IT capabilities are developed based on business needs.

Service Support and Delivery Management

Service Support and Delivery Management (SSDM) is about ensuring that incidents are resolved as soon as possible and that requests are fulfilled in a timely manner that meets commitments. Incidents may be generated as a result of a customer call to the service desk or may be a result of automated events and alerts. SSDM must identify, prioritize, and orchestrate management of problems. These problems may be identified as a result of recurring incident and historical trends. SSDM does not provide deep technical expertise in any given vertical.

Service Technology and Automation

Service Technology and Automation (STA) includes:

- *Enabling technologies*
  These include networks, servers, business applications, databases, middleware, and so on. These technologies contribute directly to implementing a given business service and enabling business processes.
- *Automation tools*
  These primarily include tools that are used to automate and support service management processes (e.g., service catalog management, request fulfillment, change management, etc.). These also include other tools to support project management activities. Either configuration management system or configuration management database (CMDB) tools are critical to effectively managing the architecture, design, development, and management of a service throughout its life cycle.
- *Diagnostics and monitoring tools*
  These include tools that are primarily used to support problem management activities (i.e., root cause analysis and problem resolution) and service and service component performance monitoring.
- *Technology management tools*
  These include those tools that are used to manage technology components. These management activities may include patch management, upgrades, capacity management, security management, and so on. Technology management tools also include those that are used to create reports and dashboards.

Measures of Operational Performance

Measuring operational performance of IT is critical to ensuring that customers and businesses are satisfied and that their expectations are being managed as well to continue to plan and make improvements across IT. For example, one of the measures may be the administrator-to-server ratio. In a mature IT organization, this ratio should be greater than 1:100. Such maturity is realized by implementing and utilizing automation and management tools. For example, with the right tools, you can automate patch management and task monitoring. Some key categories that help measure organizational improvements include:

- *Planned vs. unplanned work*
  If your IT organization spends more time in performing planned activities, you should know that you are most likely not firefighting. This is good news, indicating that you have reduced the number of unforeseen events and can plan your activities. In most low-maturity organizations, this is not the case. If you perform an initial assessment of the ratio of planned vs. unplanned work, you will be able to see how mature your IT teams really are. As shown in Figure 16.2, as you move through the BSM implementation project life cycle, you will see a shift in the ratio between planned vs. unplanned work.
- *Routine maintenance vs. new development*
  Routine maintenance includes all those activities that are required to be performed to keep the systems up-to-date and running. If you own a car, you know what you should do to ensure that it is well maintained with timely services. With systems monitoring and management tools, these routine maintenance activities can be performed much more efficiently. For example, patch updates can be automated, problem root cause analysis can be more efficient, system security can be made more proactive, capacity can be managed, and so on. If you make the right investments in building the right system monitoring and management capabilities, you will see a shift whereby you will be spending less time and effort in maintaining your systems and will have more resources available to invest in innovation and new development. At this maturity, you will see that your organization is getting away from "trial and error" culture and moving toward "cause and effect" culture, that is, you will be able to become more predictable and proactive.

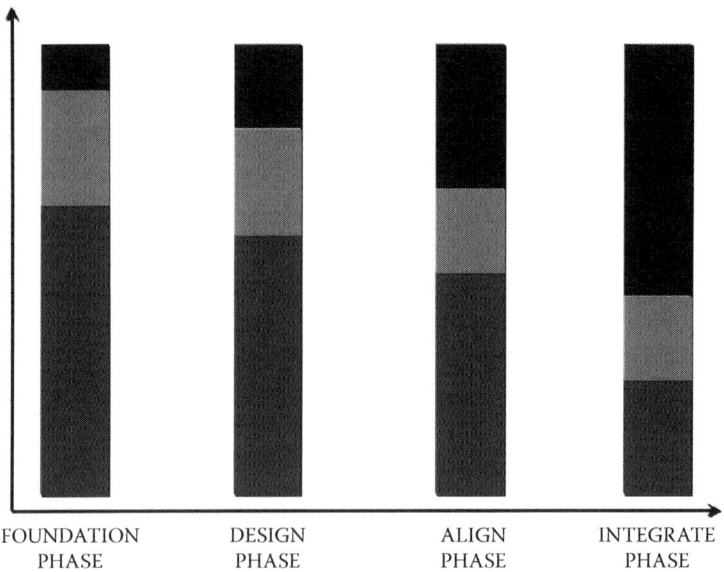

Key
Planned work: Project Support, Change Implementation, and Problem Management activities
Routine work: OS support, component security management, capacity and performance, standard builds, patch management, and so on
Unplanned work: Incident Management and Emergency Changes.

Figure 16.2 Measuring operational performance.

- *Iterative Service Development*
  It is always more cost-effective to identify and fix problems before moving the service into the production environment. There will be reduced impact on the business and fewer outages as a result of development errors. There are well-known methodologies that enable you to detect risks and issues in services earlier so that those can be resolved sooner. Some of the methodologies include Rational Unified Process (RUP), SCRUM, and XP (eXtreme Programming).

Key Aspects of Effective Operations

Service operations are where all investments in building new services and capabilities produce returns on those investments. BSM must enable an IT organization to manage the services that it provides from a business perspective, that is, IT performance must be measured in terms of business performance. The BSM framework shown in Figure 16.3 aims to enable:

- Management of IT services so that the desired business value is delivered
- Measurement of an IT organizations performance in terms of business performance
- End-to-end traceability (i.e., from business processes down to technology components)
- Monitoring of performance and controls
- Creation of the basis for continuous improvement

Let us discuss the key aspects across the service life cycle as they relate to impact on operations.

Service Strategy

The following key aspects must be considered during strategizing and planning IT services:

- Business needs
- Demand for IT service
- Cost and pricing

Service Design

The service design phase is where desired and approved services are architected and designed to ensure that they deliver the agreed and needed capabilities to its users (customers or businesses). In my opinion, service design is, by far, the most important phase in the service life cycle. Errors introduced at this stage will not only impact the reliability, usability, and performance of the service but they will also impact the image of IT. It is during this phase that the services and other components must be architected correctly to achieve the agreed *warranty* and *utility* of the service. The following key aspects must be considered during the service design phase of the service life cycle:

- Service definition
- Service requirements
  - Functional requirements
  - Nonfunctional requirements

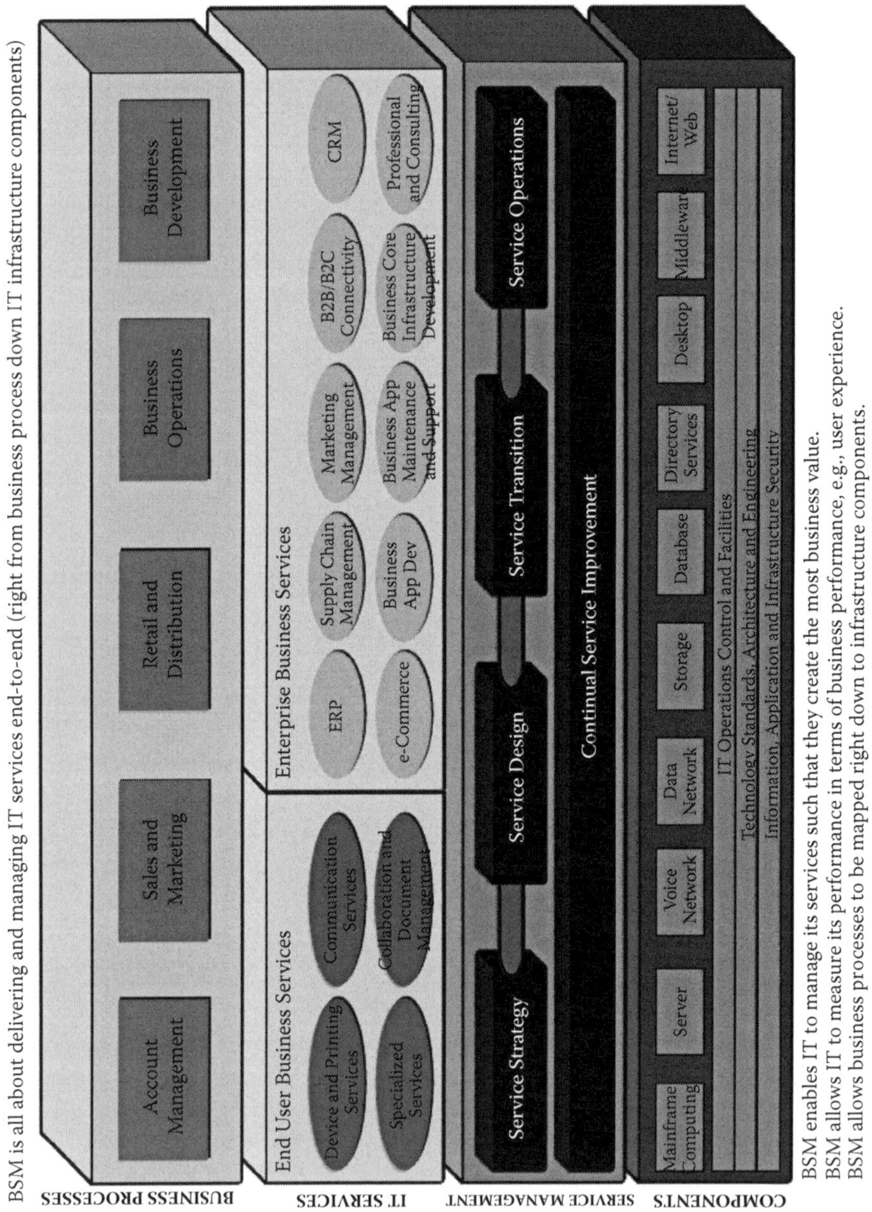

Figure 16.3 BSM-driven operations.

- Operational requirements
- Capacity requirements
- Security requirements
- Availability requirements
- IT service continuity requirements

■ Desired service targets
■ Existing assets that can be reused

Service Transition

Some of the key aspects that must be considered during the service transition are discussed below.

Testing and Validation

Service transition processes offer the last opportunity to identify and fix issues before a given service goes into production. If there are issues and they are not caught during the transition phase, they will impact the quality of service and, ultimately, business profitability.

Controlling Changes

Figure 16.4 shows some of the key components of ensuring that appropriate controls are in place to protect the production environment. Note that projects as well as requests for change (RFCs) ultimately mean that something in the production environment is going to be changed. Impact

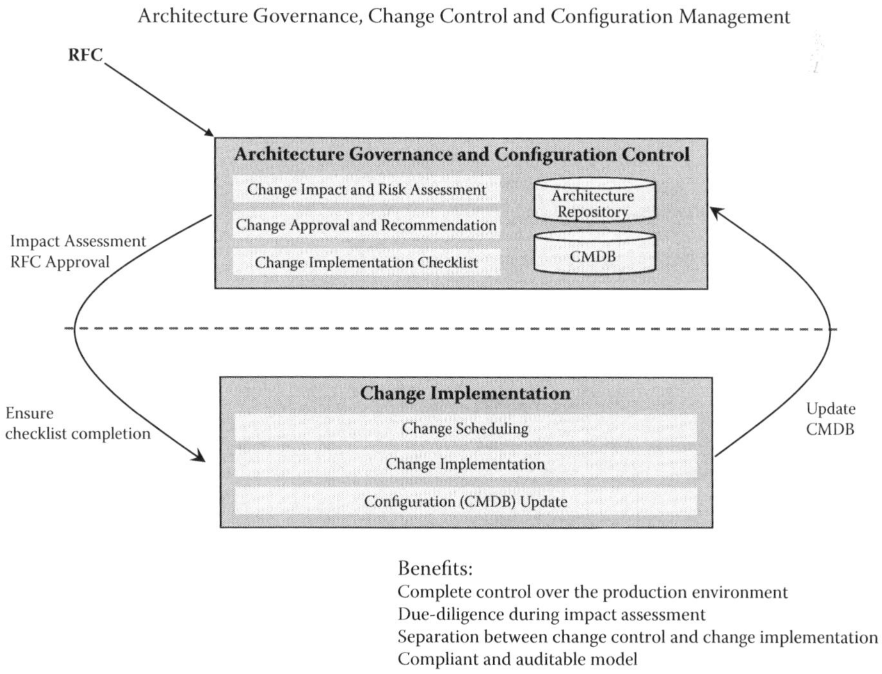

Figure 16.4 Controlling changes.

assessment is one of the key steps that must be performed during the change management process to assess the impact on other components that depend on the components that need to be changed, the services that will be impacted, the users who will need to plan around this scheduled outage, and so on. There needs to be a way to assess this impact. There are two important components that enable this impact assessment to be performed. One is enterprise architecture and the other is configuration management. Combined together, they represent the logical picture of IT infrastructure. The more accurate this picture, the more accurate the impact assessment.

Figure 16.4 presents the process. Here are the key steps:

- Once an RFC is preliminarily approved, perform impact and risk assessment using architecture repository and CMDB.
- If the impact is acceptable, approve the RFC.
- The change implementation team must ensure that they have all the needed information before implementing the change. The information can be in the form of a checklist. Commonly in this checklist, you have the implementation plan, roll-back plan, communication plan, impact assessment report, approval from the change approval board, and test results.
- Once the change is implemented, appropriate updates must be made to the CMDB as well as to the architecture repository.

We will discuss the architecture repository and related topics in detail in the next chapter. The above-mentioned process will ensure that you have an auditable environment that has appropriate control measures.

Service Operation

Service operation is where the rubber meets the road; all planning, architecture, design, development, transition, and management efforts will finally generate value for the businesses or customers when the given service goes into production. There are some key aspects that must be managed during the service operation phase of the service life cycle. These aspects are discussed below.

Configuration Item Ownership

Ownership is the key to ensuring that each configuration item (CI) is appropriately managed. Owning a CI means that the owner is responsible for the following:

- Overall CI performance
  - Availability: Is it available to ensure that agreed targets are met?
  - Response time.
  - Utilization: Is the component optimally utilized?
- CI management
  - Is the CI kept up-to-date?
  - Is it being serviced in a timely manner?
  - Are all the patches applied in a timely manner?
  - Are the routine backups taken in a timely manner?
  - Are backup and restoration tests conducted?
  - Is the access to the CI appropriately controlled and access control lists appropriately managed?

- CI changes
  Before making any changes to the CI, the owner has to ensure that the required assessment has been completed, the RFC has been approved, the appropriate roll-back plan has been developed, and so on.
- Incident and problem management support
  - Are there any incident trends that are impacting the overall performance?
  - Are the problems related to the CI appropriately managed?

CI ownership is essential to ensure that there is overall accountability for a given CI and that every CI is appropriately managed to deliver the optimal value (Figure 16.5).

Service Request Management or Request Fulfillment

We have discussed service requests earlier in this book. Managing service requests is critical to ensuring that your service desk continues to provide the greatest value while ensuring that these requests get fulfilled in the most efficient manner possible.

Without an appropriate request fulfillment and management process, requests (that are not incidents) will be mismanaged (Figure 16.6). Customers reaching out to individuals at the service desk without having their tickets logged in the central service desk system is a *disaster.* I call these "leaks in the system" because:

- Requests are received by individuals through personal relationships.
- Resources are committed to fulfill these valid business requests.
- Time and effort spent in fulfilling these requests that are not recorded is never accounted for.
- The above impacts the overall perception that IT is not doing as much as they should.

All requests must be received and logged by the service desk (Figure 16.7). Depending on the nature and type of the request, these may be fulfilled by the service desk or by other teams in partnership with the service desk (Figure 16.8).

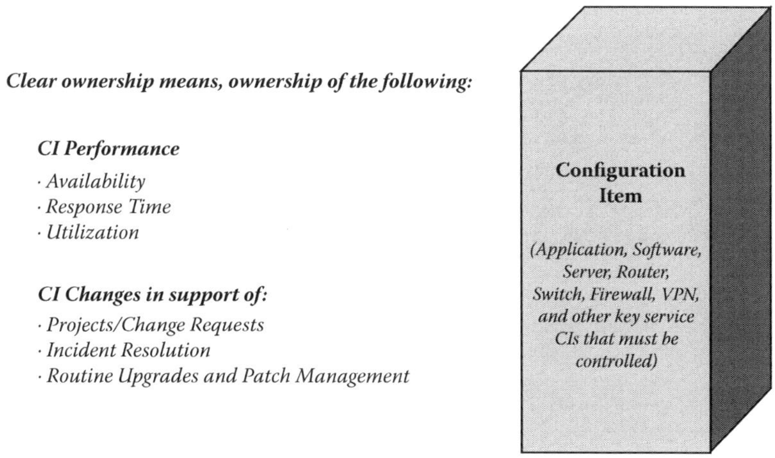

Figure 16.5 CI ownership.

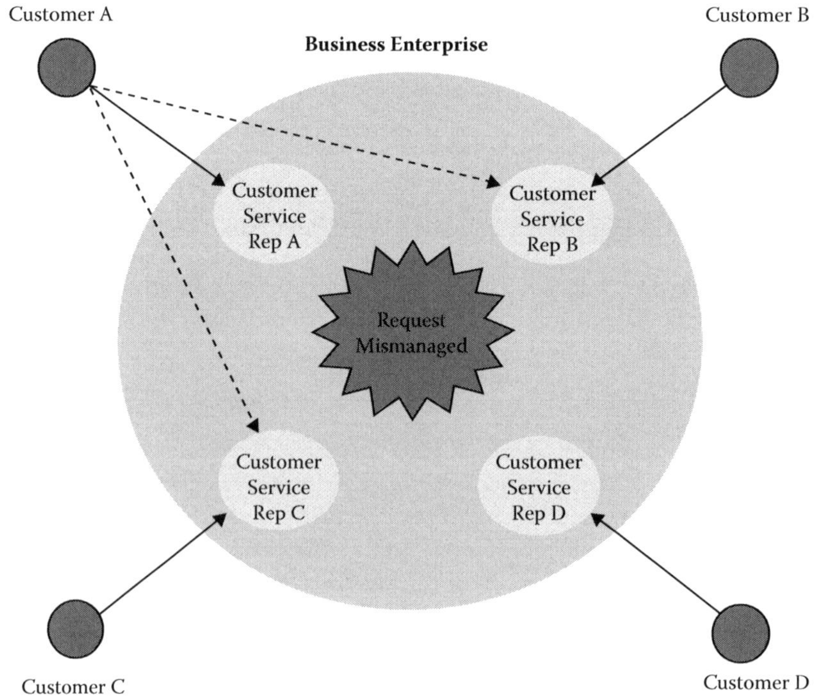

Figure 16.6 Mismanagement of a service request.

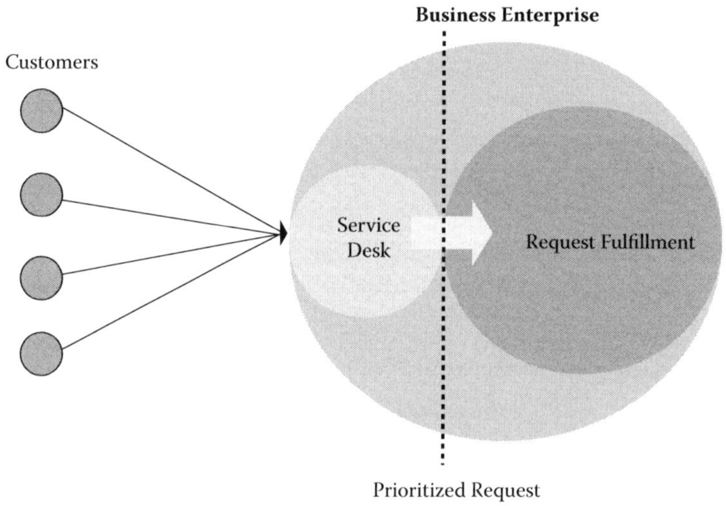

Figure 16.7 Management of service requests.

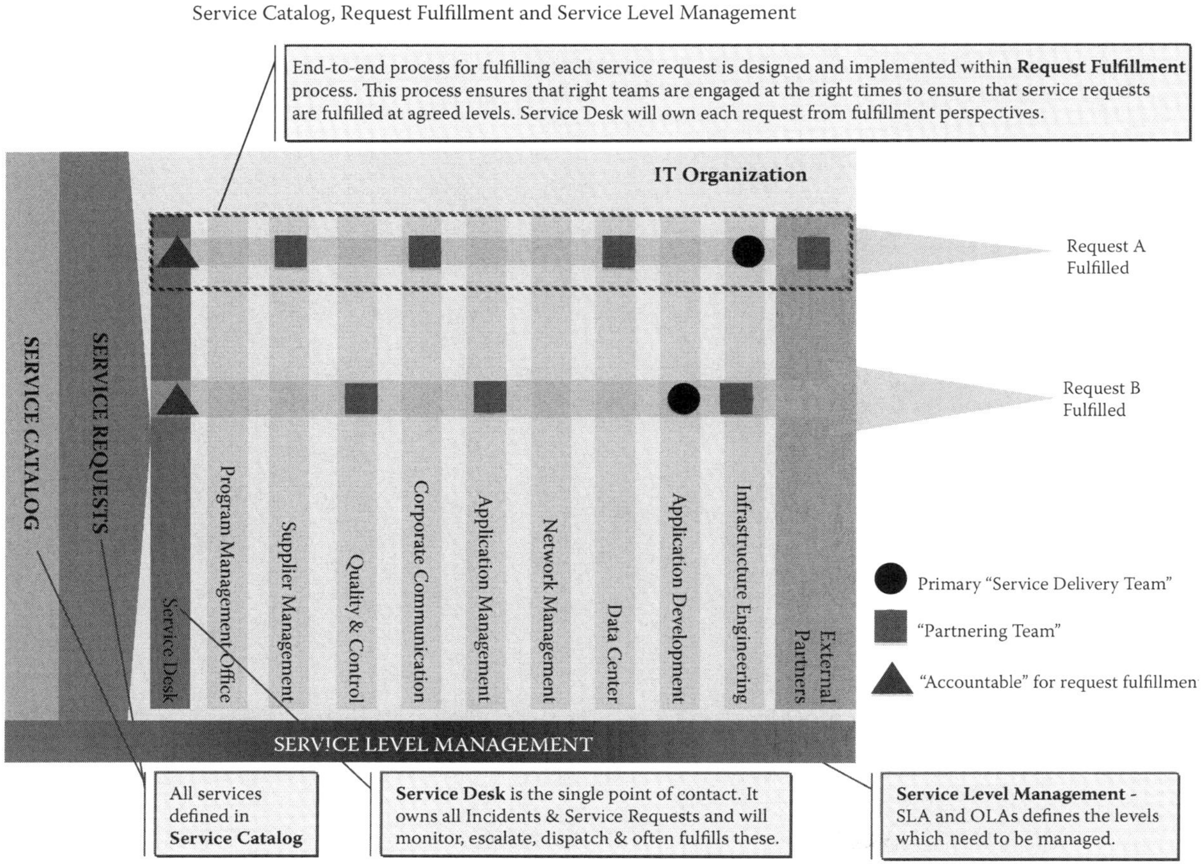

Figure 16.8 Fulfilling service requests.

Achieving operational efficiencies requires reducing custom solutions and defining a standard set of services. Just like any fast-food chain, you need to define the standard set of services that you will provide to your customer and the standard set of requests for each of those services. As shown in Figure 16.9, for each service, you will need to define the type of requests that can be initiated by your customers. For each service request, you will then need to define the overall fulfillment steps that need to be executed and by whom. This will be done as part of Request Fulfilment process. If your goals are to reduce cost and provide predictable quality of service, you must define and execute the following:

- All services must be defined in your service catalog.
- Each service must have an associated service request that can be fulfilled. For example, if you provide e-mail service, then one of the requests can be related to opening a new account.
- Each service request must have an associated fulfillment process. In the case of opening a new e-mail account, there are a number of steps that will be performed. The better those steps and associated roles are defined, the more efficiently this request will be fulfilled.
- Service request fulfillment targets must be defined, measured, and managed within the service level management process. For example, it will take up to 2 hours to create a new e-mail account.

Service Performance Monitoring and Management

End-to-end service performance monitoring and management capabilities must be established. This will enable you to measure your performance as it is experienced by your customers. There are many monitoring tools available in the market; however, the most important part is not the

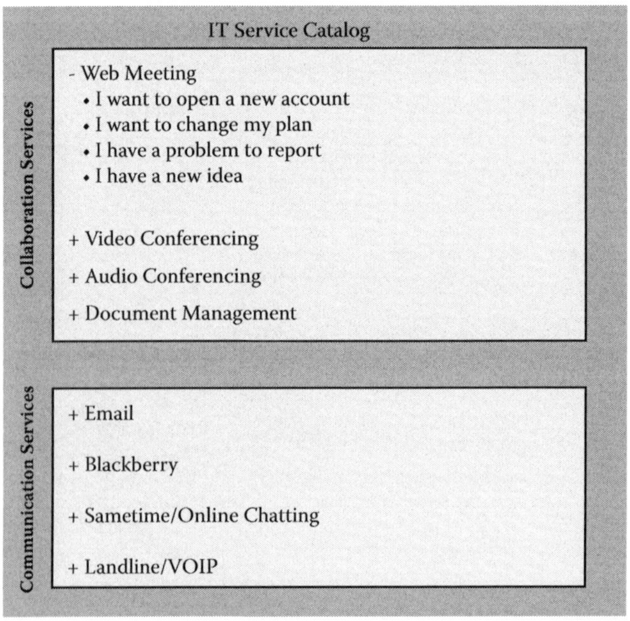

Figure 16.9 Services and service requests.

purchase but the actual configuration and implementation of these tools. I have many organizations with very powerful tools that generate millions of events everyday. But, to make sense of these events, appropriate filtering, correlation, and routing need to be done.

Other Common Aspects

Some of the other aspects that are common across the service life cycle phases are discussed in the following subsections.

Not Everything Is Important

Always remember that not every component in your IT infrastructure carries the same importance. The same can be said about the processes (service management as well as other development and operations processes). You should always be asking this question, "Why is this important?" The importance of any component (technology, process, organizational, etc.) must be driven by and based on what it does for the customers or businesses. The greater the business impact of the failure of a given component, the more important it is. Always remember the 80/20 rule.

Measure and Communicate

We have discussed this earlier in this chapter. I would like to highlight again that measurement is the key to achieving a culture of continual improvements. A top-down approach must be adopted when planning and designing measurements. The important metrics are those that have a direct impact on and enable better measurement of IT performance based on the business performance. Top-down means that:

> All measurements must be driven by a top-level need. This top level need must be driven by business need. There is no IT improvement or activity that cannot be related to business or customer value. If you are improving management of IT components, that will ultimately contribute towards reduction in the overall cost of management of respective IT component which will in turn mean lower cost for the business.

Realizing Vision through Process Ownership

Let us consider the following IT organization vision statement:

> To be a business-aligned, service-oriented, performance-driven and transparent IT service provider that will deliver cost-effective, high-quality and measurable services in a controlled and compliant manner.

In most cases, these vision statements end up getting printed on mouse pads or charts and that is, in almost all cases, all that happens to the vision statement. The organization itself continues to be the same old place that it used to be and rarely sees the stated vision or mission statement realized. It is important to establish a clear vision. However, I believe that it is equally, if not more, important to establish the means to realize the stated vision.

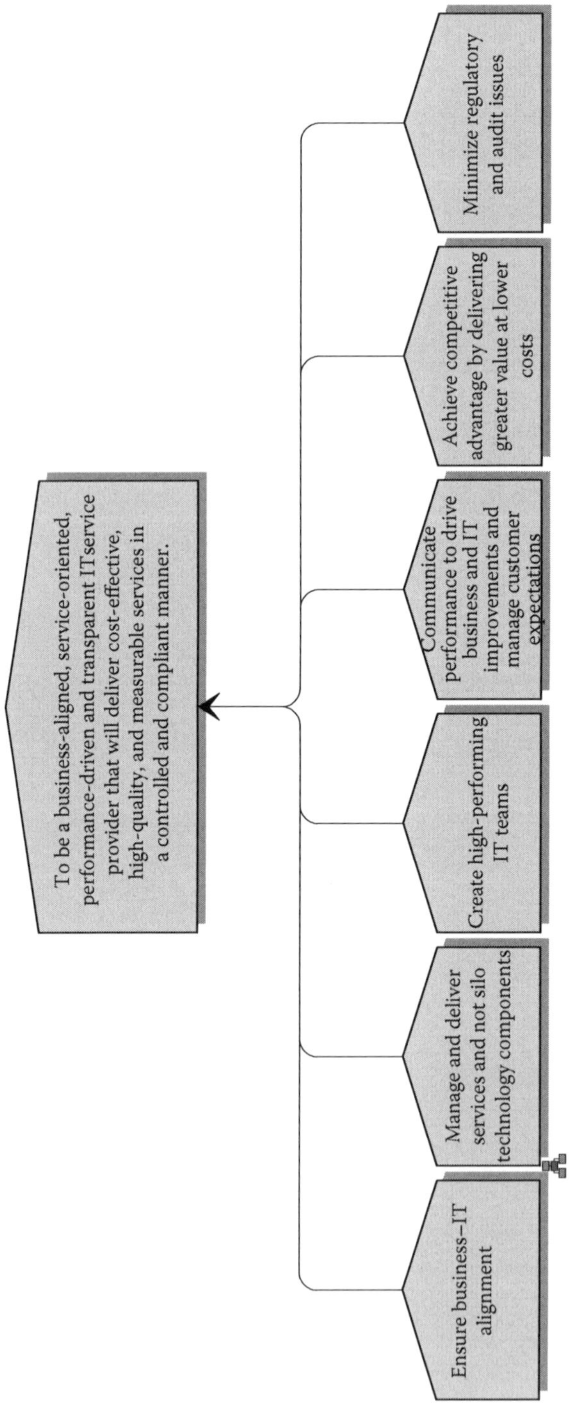

Figure 16.10 From vision to goals.

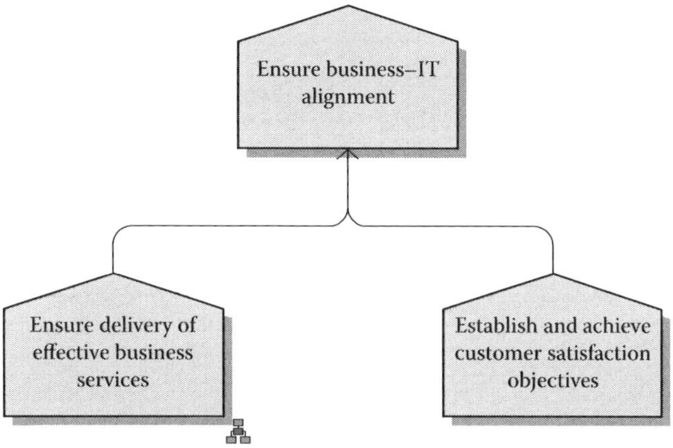

Figure 16.11 From goals to subgoals.

Figure 16.10 shows the goals that are needed to be met to achieve the stated vision. For the sake of our discussion, let us consider one dimension within the vision statement: business-aligned. When translated into an actionable goal, it may read "Ensure business–IT alignment." What needs to be done to ensure that an IT organization is planning, designing, and delivering services that are business-aligned? You may need to achieve the following goals:

- Ensure delivery of effective business services.
- Establish and achieve customer satisfaction objectives.

Let us drill down even further. Ask yourself what objectives need to be achieved to realize the *ensure delivery of effective business solutions* goal? Some of the supporting objectives may include the following (Figure 16.11):

- Build and maintain architectural standards.
- Build and manage enterprise business architecture.
- Build and manage enterprise technology architectures.
- Architect and design services to achieve *warranty* and *utility* goals.
- Support service planning, implementation, and change management.

So far, we have been largely discussing the "what" part of the vision and associated goals. Respective processes must be defined that will support the lowest level of the goal (Figure 16.12). Looking at the big picture, all the processes combined will contribute to the achievement of the larger vision. As an example, Figure 16.13 shows the *technology standards management process.*

It is important to perform the above-mentioned analysis and traceability to ensure that organizational resources and capabilities are being applied to the realization of the established vision and mission. Note that it is in the *service operation* phase of the service life cycle that all the defined processes and efforts put in by all the teams come together and result in the creation and delivery of service.

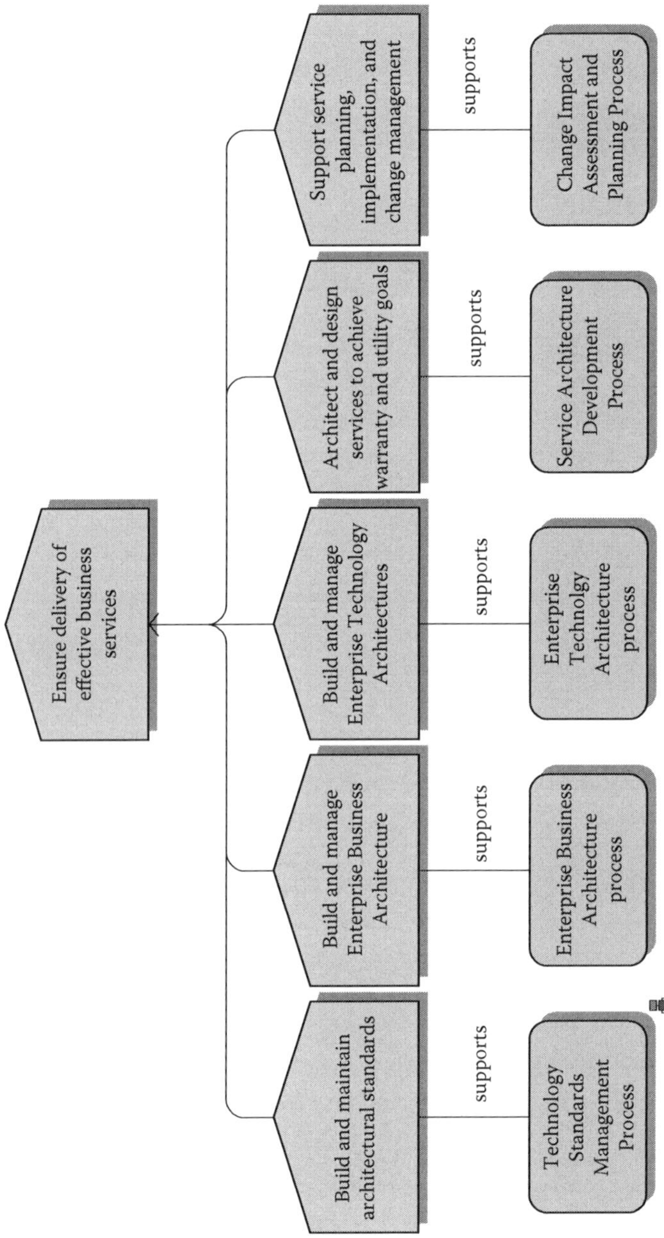

Figure 16.12 From subgoals to processes.

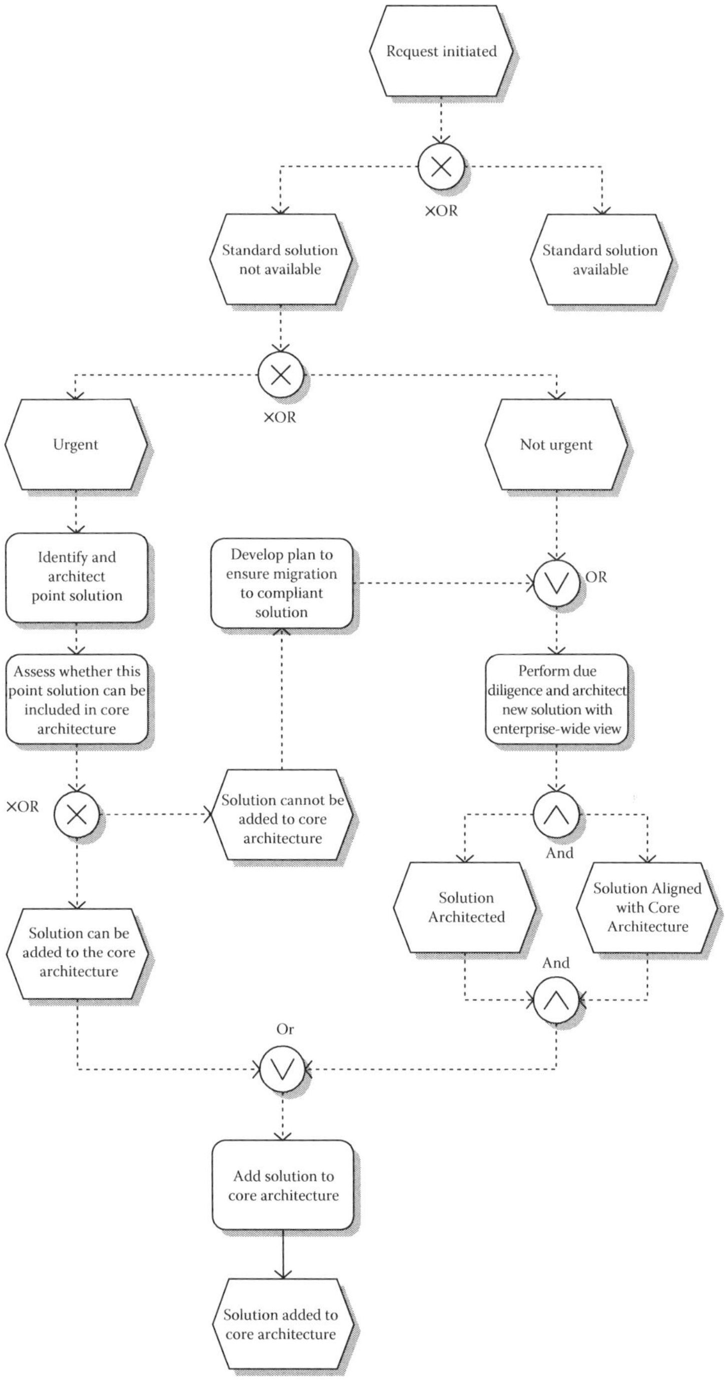

Figure 16.13 The process.

Manage Processes

Processes are organizational assets just like any other asset (e.g., servers, desktops, etc.). Processes go through their respective life cycle phases as follows:

- *Envisioned*—Process is envisioned.
- *Ownership*—Each process has an owner.
- *Developed*—Each process has to be designed and developed.
- *Production*—Processes are put into production to be executed.
- *Managed*—During production, processes need to be managed. This management includes measuring process performance, identifying areas of improvement, and further optimizing based on targets.
- *Retired*—Processes are retired when the service or product that they are producing is no longer necessary. For example, if you sell part of your business, say PC manufacturing, will you still need to manage the processes that are needed to manufacture PCs?

The above sounds like common sense. However, you will be surprised at how many organizations actually do not believe that processes need to be managed.

Formal Problem Management Is Important

In most low-level maturity organizations, problem management is largely confused with incident management. Formal problem management means that problems needing to be managed should be identified, prioritized, and managed just like any other efforts (e.g., changes, projects, etc.). Root cause analysis may lead to a request for change or a request to undertake a project. Root cause analysis will enable you to identify what led to the respective errors. If you are managing your processes appropriately, you will be able to identify process components that need to be fixed to remove the respective issues from the process itself. For example, if you identify problems with IT infrastructure capacity, you will need to fix the application and infrastructure sizing processes as appropriate. If your particular organization has a large number of emergency changes, then the change management process needs to be institutionalized (i.e., brought into practice). Remember, it is the process that results in the development and management of services and products. Quality issues with products almost always point to issues in the underlying processes.

Leadership and Management Are the Foundation

It cannot be said enough how critical the appointment of the right leaders and managers is to the overall success of BSM and to the achievement of a high-performing IT organization. Leaders need to establish clear vision, delegate responsibilities, have trust in their teams, provide needed resources and capabilities, and continually measure and stay on course. There is a large amount of literature available on leadership and management and it is not in the scope of our discussion here. However, it is important that the right individuals are appointed to lead IT organizations through this cultural transformation.

Shape the Right Behavior

BSM implementation is largely about cultural transformation (i.e., from technology-driven to business-driven, from reactive to proactive, from silo-based to service-oriented, and so on). This cultural transformation will not take place overnight; it will require small behavioral changes over time and an aggregate of these behavioral changes will enable the organization to achieve the desired culture. Key performance indicators (KPIs) must be carefully selected and targets thoughtfully agreed on. Having a KPI to close to 100% of tickets within 5 business days may result in shaping an undesired behavior. Continual service improvement is about achieving a culture of continual improvements.

IT Outsourcing and BSM

IT outsourcing is not a new topic. It may make sense for some businesses and may be disastrous for others. I would like to briefly discuss what IT outsourcing options are available in relation to BSM. I will use the conceptual organization architecture to discuss these.

Complete IT Outsourcing

In this option, most components of IT are outsourced (Figure 16.14). The following are outsourced if this option is selected:

- Service desk (incident management and request fulfillment)
- Event management
- Problem management
- Change management
- Release and deployment management
- Service asset and configuration management
- IT development management and IT operations management

This option is mostly adopted when an IT organization is providing service to in-house businesses and customers. The most important processes that will have to be kept in-house and be managed well will include:

- *Service portfolio management and service catalog management*
  It will be very critical for the organization to define the strategy and identify the services that will be required in order to meet the business needs. The service catalog must enable customers to clearly understand the services that are offered.
- *Service level management*
  Service level management will become more important in any form of outsourcing. Underpinning contracts will need to be carefully designed, agreed on, and managed to ensure that suppliers are providing services at the desired and agreed on performance levels.
- *Financial management*
  Financial management will enable services to be priced while taking into account the overall cost of outsourcing and how charge-back is going to be managed.
- *Supplier management*
  Supplier management will be a critical process whenever there is any form of outsourcing.

Service Desk Outsourcing Option

This is another common outsourcing option. In my professional opinion, for those IT organizations that aim to achieve greater customer satisfaction and provide customer-oriented services,

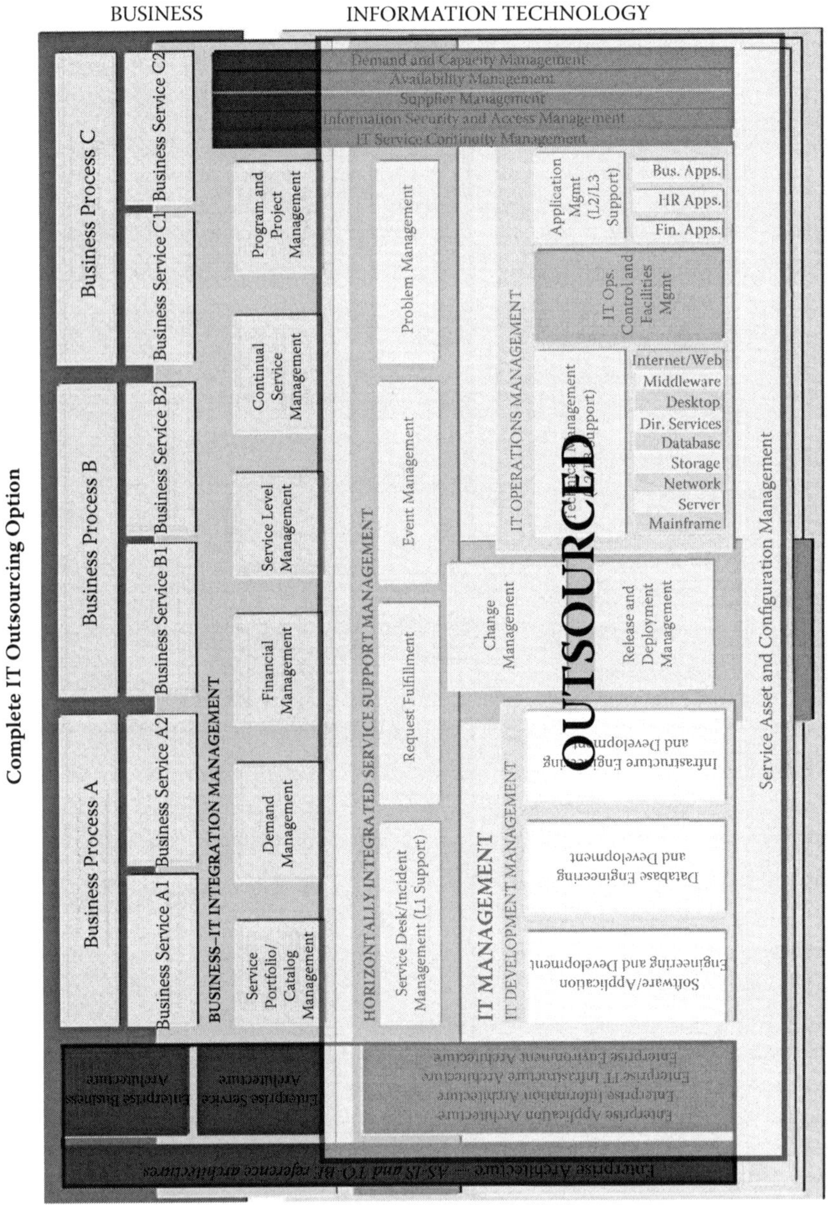

Figure 16.14 Complete IT outsourcing option.

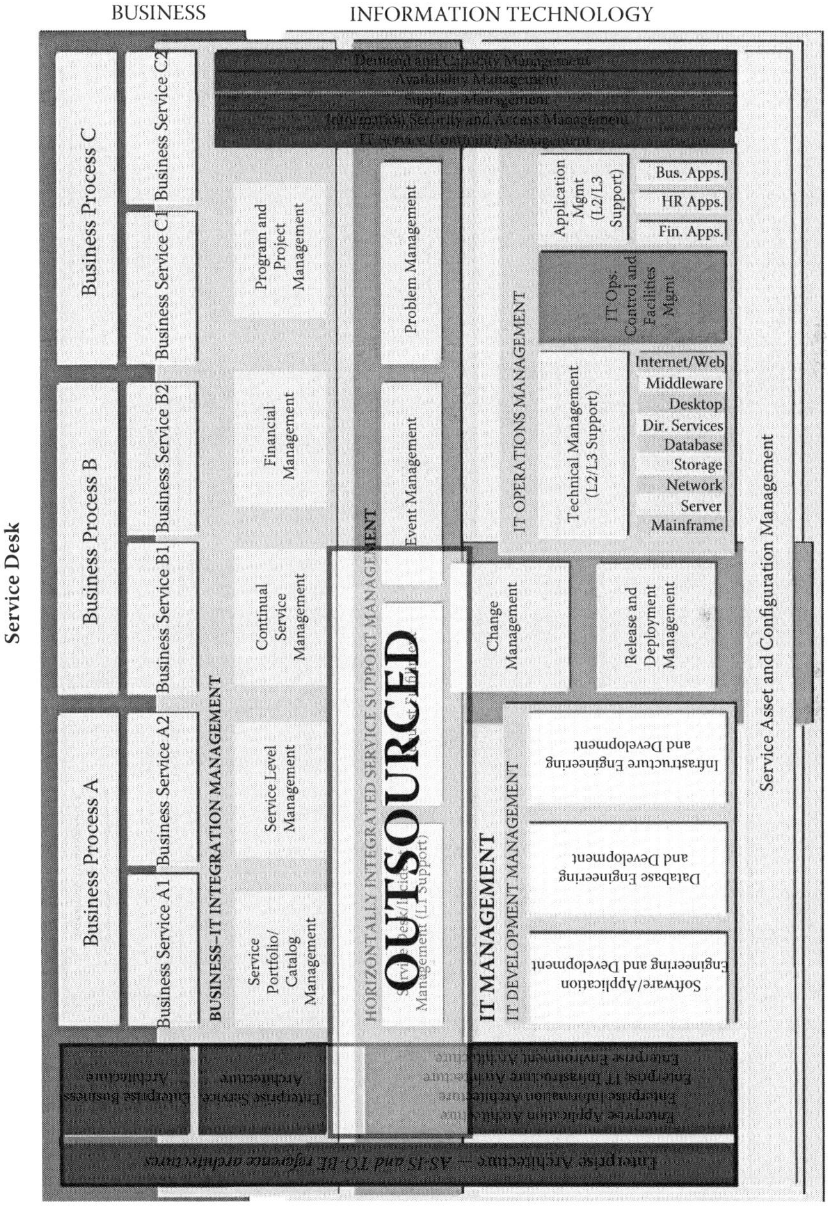

Figure 16.15 Service desk outsourcing option.

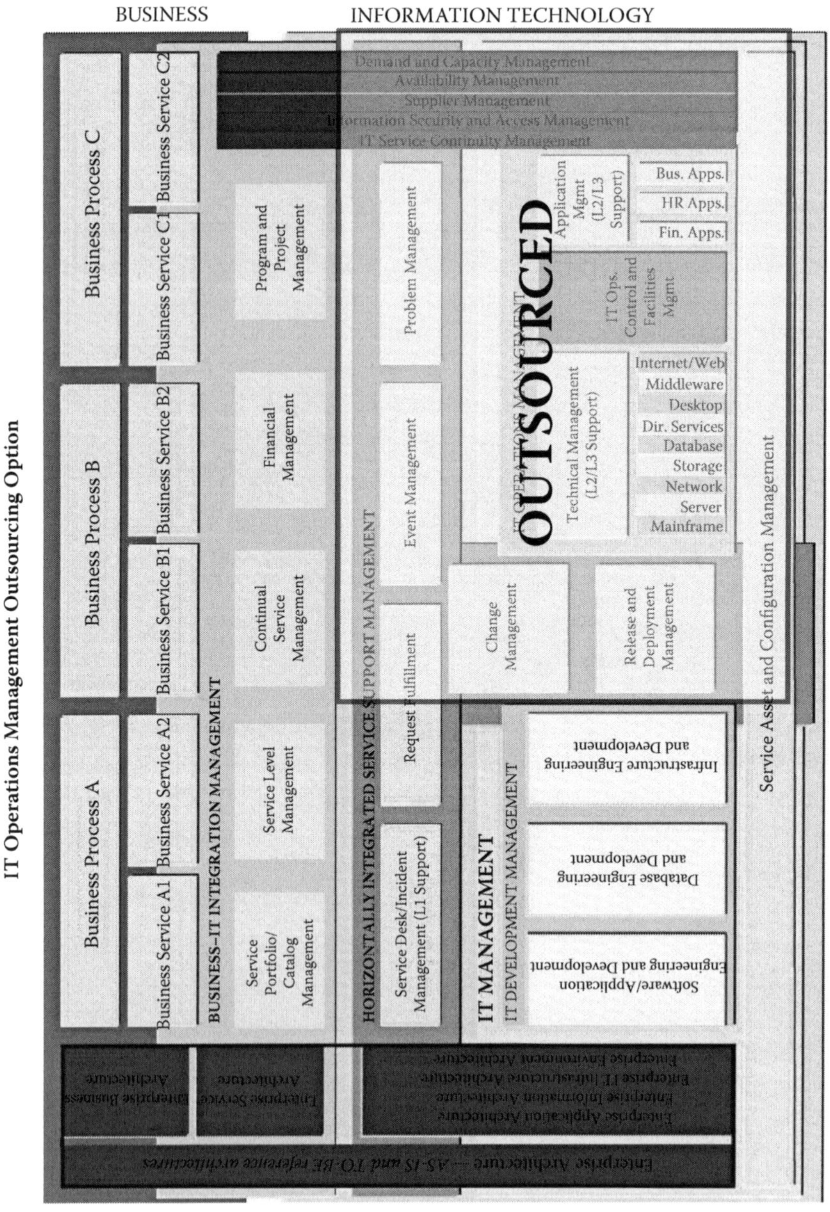

Figure 16.16 IT operations management outsourcing option.

outsourcing the service desk should not be an option. The service desk is the face of the IT organization and is a source of very valuable information and insights. Outsourcing the service desk may provide short-term benefits, but it will not be valuable in the long term (Figure 16.15). Having said this, the service desk itself may choose to further outsource certain services and that is fine. However, for immediate customers, the first point of contact should be an in-house service desk. In this way, you will still be able to provide direct support to your customers, while still benefiting from outsourcing those services that may make financial sense.

IT Operational Management Outsourcing Option

In this option, your data center and everything in it, along with network infrastructure, is outsourced (Figure 16.16). In this case, you will still own the design and development of your business-specific applications. These applications will be hosted at the outsourced data center. Note that the service desk should still be in-house. As discussed earlier, the service strategy will still be kept in-house and the new services will need to be identified. Those services that are no longer required will need to be retired. Supplier management and service level management will be critical.

Summary

Operations is where all organizational resources and capabilities create value for the business and customers. There are some key components to ensuring smooth and optimal utilization of resources. The service catalog must drive how an IT organization uses its resources and capabilities to create business value. Ownership is critical to ensuring that each IT infrastructure component is appropriately managed to deliver the most value over a longer life. Effective event-monitoring and management capabilities will enable operations to be more proactive in their management of incidents. Clarity in roles and responsibilities of key operational teams (server management and support, network management, data center management, and others) will play an important role in further optimizing the teams' performance.

Reference

Dubie, D. Procter & Gamble touts IT services model, saves $500 million. *ComputerWorld* October 1, 2002. http://www.computerworld.com/s/article/74762/Procter_Gamble_touts_IT_services_model_saves_500_million.

Chapter 17

IT Service Management, Enterprise Architecture, and Service-Oriented Architecture—Effective Enablement of Business Service Management

In this chapter, we will gain insight into enterprise architecture (EA) and service-oriented architecture (SOA) and how they relate and do not relate to *Information Technology Infrastructure Library version 3* (ITIL v3). We will see how service management and EA can be positioned to create greater business value for the business enterprise. We will specifically discuss in detail the areas where there is or should be potential overlap between ITIL v3 and EA practices and these can be combined to create a more business-integrated, service-oriented, customer-focused, and efficient IT organizations.

When discussing EA and business service management (BSM), it will be very difficult to leave SOA out. While EA and ITIL v3 may provide the guidelines and framework, respectively, for the business enterprises that are trying to align business and IT, SOA provides the technological capabilities and the technical architecture framework to implement service-oriented business enterprises. This chapter is not intended to provide an exhaustive discussion of EA and SOA; a separate book can be written on the subject.

Introduction

Before we discuss and establish the relationship between BSM, EA, and SOA, it is important to clearly understand what each of these disciplines really means. We have already had detailed discussions on BSM throughout this book. We will focus on EA and SOA in this section. After this discussion, we will relate the three into a comprehensive life cycle—extended service life cycle (ESL).

The Business–IT Gap Problem

Having an efficiently running IT operations function does not necessarily mean that you are running the right capabilities (i.e., ensuring warranty and utility). Imagine your customers or businesses need video conferencing capabilities, but you are offering audio conferencing and you keep this audio conferencing up and running. Well-oiled and well-managed IT operations are critical, but alignment between what IT operations is delivering and what customers need is equally, if not more, important. This *needs-capability* gap (between business needs and IT capabilities) is most common in business enterprises where IT is considered a back-office function. In these cases, you will find that there are always gaps between what businesses are trying to achieve and how IT organizations enable their respective businesses. Most businesses do have some form of vision document and a strategic plan that lays out how the stated vision is going to be realized. Similarly, most IT organizations have their vision document, along with plans on how to realize that vision. So far, there seems to be no problem. Problems, however, will start to surface if IT vision and strategy is internally focused or IT-driven, that is, if IT capabilities are developed because IT teams feel that it is a better technology and not necessarily needed by the business. Since IT is viewed by the businesses as a back-office function, they do not feel that it is important to engage IT during business strategy and planning

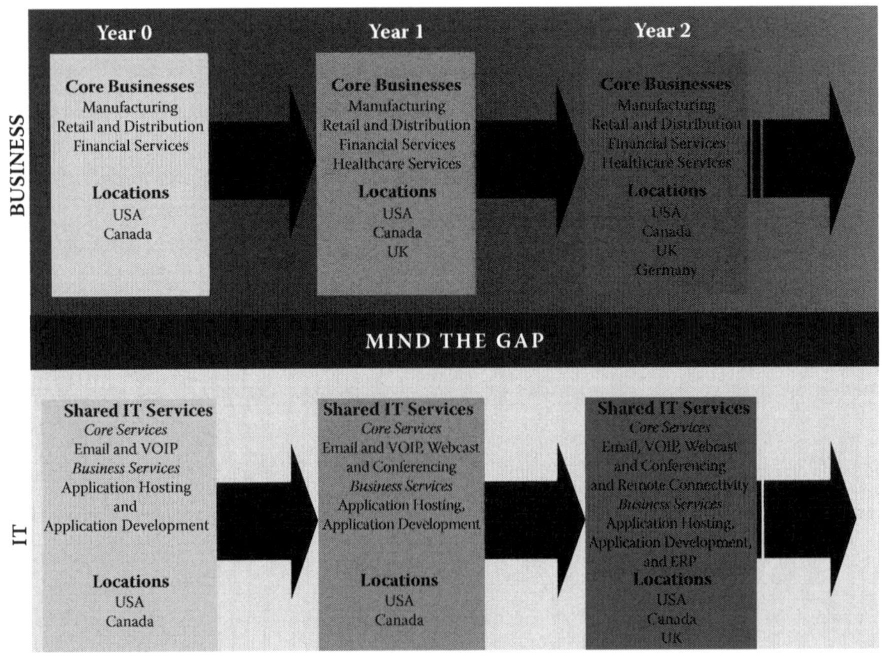

Figure 17.1 The gap between business needs and IT capabilities.

discussions. These internally focused IT functions create a gap between what business actually needs from IT and what IT actually provides. The end result is bad news for both.

> *Businesses feel that IT is not doing what it is supposed to be doing. This further confirms business perception of IT being a back-office function.*
>
> *IT does not have a clear understanding of what capabilities to build and builds those that they feel are best for IT. This does not satisfy what businesses need and IT continues losing the sponsorship and support.*

The *needs-capability* gap issues discussed above are further illustrated in Figure 17.1.

Businesses may establish their visions and strategies to realize those visions. A strategic plan is mostly multiyear (commonly referred to as a 3-year plan or 5-year plan). IT develops its own vision, strategy, and yearly plan. If the respective business vision and strategy plans and IT vision and strategy plans are not aligned, they lead to the gap between the two. The larger the gap, the greater the impact on planned business growth. Whenever this gap exists, it will lead to IT organizations not having much understanding about the business plans of their customers. And that may be fine if the goal is just to provide basic services (e.g., e-mail, Internet, desktop support, etc.). However, if the goal is to truly enable businesses and customers to achieve their long-term business goals, then business and IT goals need to be completely aligned and IT capabilities and resources appropriately planned and developed (Figure 17.2).

"Bridging the gap" means that businesses engage IT during the business planning discussions and IT plans to build new IT capabilities are primarily driven by the business needs. EA can provide insights into business strategies and plans and ITIL v3 service strategies can ensure that the service portfolio is managed based on business needs. IT architectures (application, service,

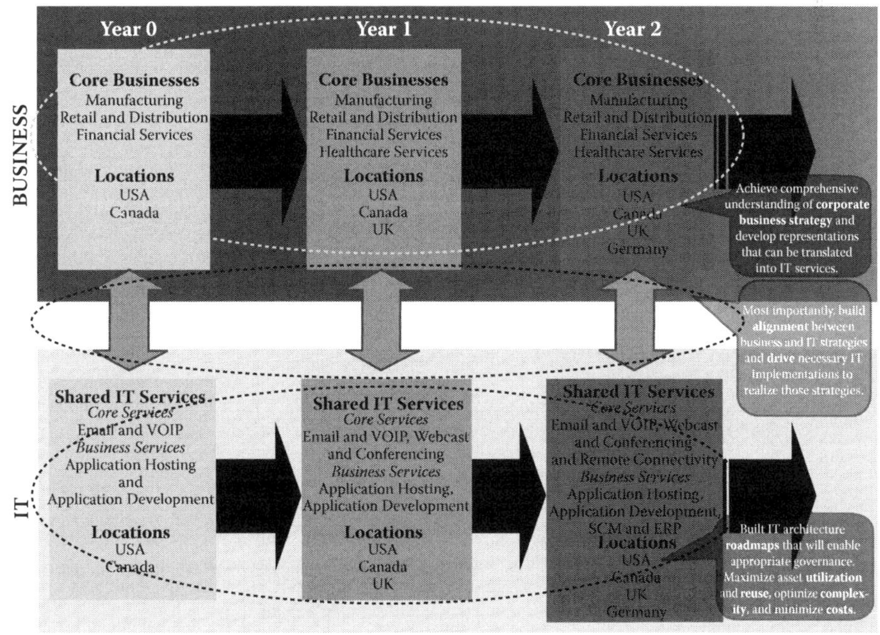

Figure 17.2 Business–IT integration.

integration, and infrastructure) can provide AS-IS and TO-BE architectures that can enable efficient design and development of new technological capabilities and IT services.

Business–IT Integration Solution

Achieving business–IT integration means that:

> All IT strategies, plans, and investments are completely aligned with the business strategies and plans and result in the creation and delivery of the IT services that exactly deliver the desired capabilities at the desired levels.

BSM enables an IT organization to manage its IT services from business perspectives and measure its performance in terms of business performance. EA enables an IT organization to achieve alignment with the businesses' and/or customers' needs. It is now imperative to see how these different disciplines can complement each other to enable business enterprises to make the most of its potential through optimal utilization of its IT capabilities.

Before we get into detailed discussions on Unified Business Service Management, let us briefly discuss the key disciplines that make up this unified architecture. These include BSM, EA, and SOA.

Business Service Management

BSM ensures that IT services are appropriately managed to meet business needs and that IT performance is measured in terms of business performance. Throughout this book, we have been discussing BSM. Later in this chapter, we will see how the ITIL v3 service life cycle needs to be extended to benefit from EA and related practices.

Enterprise Architecture

With the introduction of ITIL v3 and BSM, EA and related discussions have become even more interesting and concepts more valuable. EA, if positioned and implemented appropriately, will strongly complement the BSM implementation and operation. Before we go into a detailed discussion of ITIL v3 and EA, let us first see what EA is really all about.

EA Goals

Let us briefly discuss the goals of EA based on some very well known industry standards and frameworks. These are as follows:

- To *align* more effectively the strategies of enterprises together with their processes and their resources (business and IT) (Wegmann, 2002).
- To *support* the business by providing the fundamental technology and process structure for an IT strategy. This, in turn, makes IT a responsive asset for a successful modern business strategy (TOGAF: http://www.opengroup.org/architecture/togaf8-doc/arch/).
- To ensure that business strategy and IT investments are *aligned*. As such, EA allows *traceability* from the business strategy down to the underlying technology (Agile Enterprise Architecture: http://process.agileea.com/AgileEA/index.htm).

From the above few statements, we can appreciate that EA is perhaps a broader discipline and probably has a range of definitions. The EA goals are shown graphically in Figure 17.3.

EA Definitions

Each IT professional that you speak to will likely have a different perspective on EA. There are a variety of closely related terms such as Enterprise Software Architecture, Business Architecture, IT Infrastructure Architecture, Application Architecture, Solution Architecture, Technical Architecture, and so on. We will see how these relate to EA. Let us first see what these terms, that is, "enterprise" and "architecture," really mean.

- Enterprise—A project or undertaking that is especially difficult, complicated, or risky. A systematic or purposeful activity (*Merriam-Webster Dictionary*).
- Architecture—The art or practice of designing and building structures and especially habitable ones. Formation or construction as a result of a conscious act. A unifying or coherent form or structure (*Merriam-Webster Dictionary*).

Deriving from the above dictionary definitions, it seems like we can define EA as follows:

> An enterprise architecture is a discipline that enables construction of unifying, coherent, and habitable structures to guarantee the successful implementation of a complicated and difficult project or undertaking or activity.

EA must provide the holistic view of the business enterprise. As organizations mature in BSM and evolve as service-oriented enterprises, EA will become more and more critical to providing the necessary reference architecture models (business and technology) and governance to ensure that:

- IT is always aligned with the business's goals.
- Assets are optimally utilized and reused to achieve these business goals.
- New technologies are introduced in a controlled manner to maximize business benefits and resource utilization and minimize unnecessary overall complexity.

Figure 17.3 Goals of EA.

It is important to note that EA is not intended to provide complete implementation details on functional, data, user, and other requirements for a particular solution. Most architectures, however, are intended to provide an architectural foundation that enable us to answer the following:

- What are the business aspirations and goals? What are the boundaries? What are the rationale, impact, and priority? This information enables us to answer the question, "Why are we pursuing this opportunity?" It enables us to balance and manage often conflicting business stakeholder requirements. In Zachman, as well as Integrated Architecture Frameworks (IAFs), this is normally referred to as the "why" of the architecture.
- What is the solution required to enable the business or customer to achieve its business goals? Goals are decomposed into objectives and high-level critical requirements. Scope is defined and risks are exposed. This often attempts to answer the "what" of the architecture.
- How can the right solution be implemented?
- How will the new solution fit into the overall EA? Does the new solution comply with relevant standards and policies? Figure 17.4 shows a possible process for managing the core architecture and associated standards.
- Are there any existing components or services that can be reused?

Architectural Perspective

There are two common architectural perspectives. One provides a more holistic view and the other provides a specific view (i.e., software, technology, project, etc.). Let us discuss them briefly.

- Enterprise, or holistic, perspective
  - The management and definition of the architecture of the enterprise (business or set of businesses) that includes everything from the business strategy down to the business

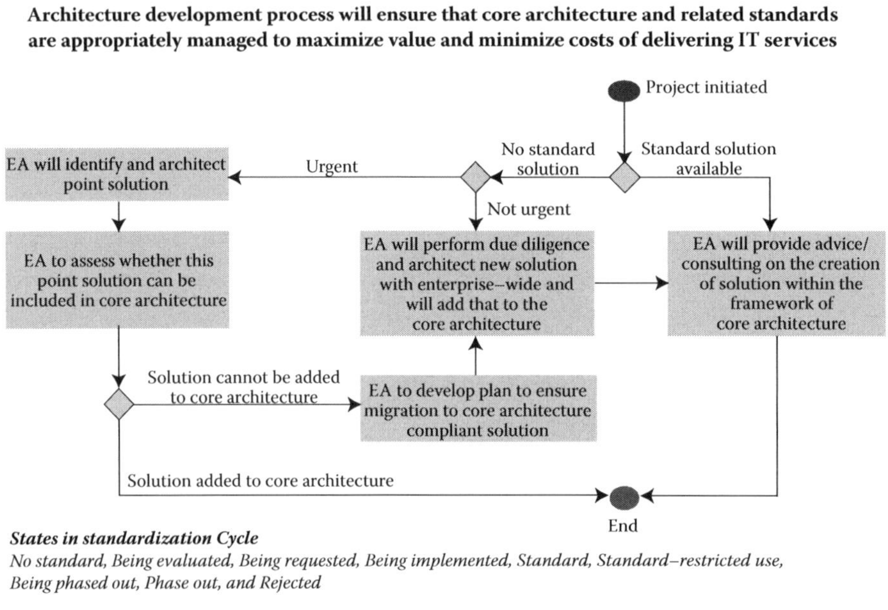

Figure 17.4 Managing architectural standards.

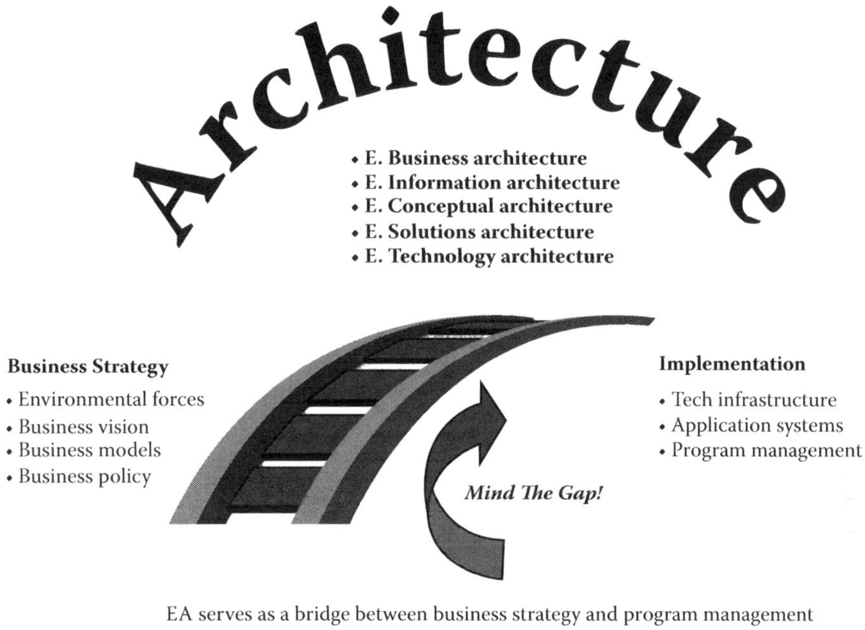

Figure 17.5 Meta Group's view of enterprise architecture.

operation architecture (static and dynamic) for the purposes of optimizing the enterprise; the information systems (made up of applications, services, and data) and the technology and infrastructure that this runs on. It also includes aspects such as security, data, people, and performance.*

- According to Gartner, EA is the process of translating business vision and strategy into effective enterprise change by creating, communicating, and improving key principles and models that describe the enterprise's future states and enable its evolution.
- A strategic information asset base, which defines the agency's mission and business activities supporting the mission, the information necessary for agency operations, the technologies necessary to support operations, and the transitional processes necessary for implementing new technologies in response to changing business needs. According to Treasury Enterprise Architecture Framework, an EA is an integrated model or representation.
- For Meta Group, EA represents a process, not a thing. The process will result in the creation and iterative refinement of many artifacts that collectively define a future EA, and it will identify the gaps between the current state and this future architecture. The EA, in effect, describes the logical linkages between the enterprise business, information and technical architectures, and the enterprise solutions architectures (Buchanan and Soley, 2002) (Figure 17.5). Buchanan and Soley (2002) continue, "The traditional notion of an Enterprise Architecture is extended so that the hierarchy or architectures extends from the business strategy level and links to the IT investment plans, and facilitates communication and decision-making between business strategy and IT management groups."

* For more information, see Agile Enterprise Architecture, http://process.agileea.com/AgileEA/index.htm.

- Software, technology, or project perspective
  - IEEE 1471-2000 standard defines software architecture as the fundamental organization of a system, embodied in its components, their relationships to each other, and the principles governing its design and evolution. "System," in this definition, is used in the most general, not necessarily IT, sense. A system is a collection of components organized to accomplish a specific function or set of functions.
  - The development of a coherent set of application architectures for an enterprise-level system or set of application systems. In some cases, this might also involve the definition of business processes and other business domain modeling specifically for the application. Typically carried out by a solutions architect who knows about databases, messaging, portals, application and Web servers, etc. This would also typically be implemented in a program or a project of work.*
  - Tarabanis et al. (2001) view EA more at a data-modeling level and use the concept to create an integrated process and data repository for public administration that could serve as a knowledge base for all parties, and to structure these processes and data in a generic process and data model.

Business Drivers

EA promises to deliver the following business value:

- Effective risk management as it relates to investing in building new capabilities.
- Definition of future state EA necessary to meet business needs.
- Identification of gaps between current and future EA states.
- Ensuring clear traceability between business strategy and IT strategy.
- EA shows how different components of an enterprise collaborate and integrate to achieve current and future business goals.
- Deliver effective IT governance that is aligned with corporate governance.
- Bridge the divide between Business and IT.
- Maximize reuse of existing assets.
- Lower costs of building new capabilities.
- Lower overall costs of supporting and maintaining IT components (software, hardware, network, etc.).

Key EA Standards and Frameworks

Let us now discuss the most popular EA standards and frameworks and other related terms:

- *The Zachman Framework*
  The Zachman Framework, as it applies to enterprise, is simply a logical structure for classifying and organizing the descriptive representations of an enterprise that are significant to the management of the enterprise as well as to the development of the enterprise's systems (Popkin, 2003). The framework (Zachman, 1987) is a matrix that describes the various ways

* Agile Enterprise Architecture, http://process.agileea.com/AgileEA/index.htm.

the stakeholders of an enterprise view the business and its systems. It characterizes architecture in terms of the perspectives of the different stakeholders (represented by rows) and focuses on the different aspects of architecture (represented by columns) (ZIFA, 2003). The framework is claimed to have been derived from the analogous structures that are found in the older disciplines of architecture, construction, engineering, and manufacturing that classify and organize the design artifacts created over the process of designing and producing complex physical products (e.g., buildings or airplanes). Figure 17.6 illustrates this framework.

- *The Open Group Architecture Framework (TOGAF)*
  As an increasingly popular framework, TOGAF provides robust advice on architecture governance and is well aligned with contemporary EA concepts.
- *SAP Enterprise Architecture Framework (SAP EAF)*
  SAP EAF is an extension of TOGAF designed to support the effective adoption of packaged solutions in a service-oriented enterprise.
- *Architecture of Integrated Information Systems (ARIS) Framework*
  Business–IT alignment and integration are at the core of ITIL v3 and are the key objectives of most EA frameworks and methodologies. Achieving alignment with business goals requires comprehensive understanding of business processes and how those processes are enabled by IT. Business process reengineering serves as the key enabler for enterprises to sustain competitiveness. The ARIS approach provides a generic framework and well-documented methodology to effectively and efficiently manage and reengineer business processes. To implement this methodology, ARIS also offers a business process reengineering and management toolset.
- *Gartner's EA Framework (EAF)*
  Gartner EAF explicitly derives architecture from business strategy and supports governance within both the framework and the process.
- *Extended Enterprise Architecture Framework (E2AF)*
  Created by the Institute for Enterprise Architecture Development, E2AF was influenced by several other frameworks (e.g., the Zachman Framework).
- *Technical Architecture Framework Information Management (TAFIM)*
  The TAFIM reference model was developed by the Defense Information Systems Agency to guide the evolution of Department of Defense (DoD) systems, including sustaining base, strategic, and tactical systems, as well as interfaces to weapon systems. TAFIM is a set of services, standards, design components, and configurations that are used in design, implementation, and enhancement of information management system architectures. The intent is that the DoD infrastructure will have a common architecture that will, over time, be a fully flexible and interoperable enterprise (SEI, 2000). TAFIM addresses the following six software components:
  - Application software: mission area and support applications.
  - Application platform: hardware and software services (O/S, real-time monitoring, and peripheral drivers).
  - Application platform cross-area services: those that have a direct effect on the operation of one or more of the functional areas (e.g., security, system administration, etc.).
  - External environment: supports system-application interoperability and user and data portability, including information services, communication capabilities, etc.
  - TAFIM application program interface: interface between an application and a service that resides on a platform and specifies how a service is invoked.

	The Zachman Framework	Data *What*	Function *How*	Network *Where*	People *Who*	Time *When*	Motivation *Why*
Business Managers	**SCOPE** *(Contextual)* *Planner*	List of Things Important to the Business	List of Processes the Business Performs	List of Locations in which the Business Operates	List of Organizations Important to the Business	List of Events Significant to the Business	List of Business Goals/Strategies
	Interprise Model *(Conceptual)* *Owner*	Semantic Model	Business Process Model	Business Logistics System	Work Flow Model	Master Schedule	Business Plan
IT Managers and Developers	**System Model** *(Logical)* *Designer*	Logical Data Model	Application Architecture	Distributed System Architecture	Human Interface Architecture	Processing Structure	Business Rule Model
	Technological Model *(Physical)* *Builder*	Physical Data Model	System Design	Technology Architecture	Presentation Architecture	Control Structure	Rule Design
	Detailed Representations *(Out-of-Context)* *Subcontractor*	Data Definition	Program	Network Architecture	Security Architecture	Timing Definition	Rule Specification
	Functioning Enterprise	Actual Business Data	Actual Application Code	Actual Physical Networks	Actual Business Organization	Actual Business Schedule	Actual Business Strategy

Figure 17.6 The Zachman Framework.

- TAFIM external environment interface: This interface is between the application platform and the external environment.

- *Generalized Enterprise Reference Architecture and Methodology (GERAM)*
GERAM provides a description of all the elements recommended in enterprise engineering and integration and, thereby, sets the standard for the collection of tools and methods from which any enterprise would benefit. Tools and methods designed to tackle more successfully the initial integration design, and the change processes that may occur during the enterprise operational lifetime.
- *Integrated Architecture Framework*
IAF reflects Cap Gemini's architecture approach. IAF focuses on business, information, information systems, technology infrastructure, security, governance, and solution architecture. The IAF is used to structure and define the architecture content. The framework provides a model for architecture development and usage, describes the format and content of elements of the architecture, and specifies the way in which these elements relate to each other.

Service-Oriented Architecture

In this section, we discuss how SOA can provide a truly transformational platform to implement ITIL v3 BSM. Web services provide the perfect platform for implementing SOA. Let us first briefly understand SOA, then discuss how we can leverage its capabilities to effectively implement BSM.

Introduction

SOA offers a fundamental paradigm shift in the way we view and manage information technology solutions.* It offers technology managers and leaders the opportunity to address technology-related challenges in a business-focused manner.

This shift means that we design our technical services (technical service view of the service catalog) from business and reusability perspectives. In Figure 17.7, the services that may be good candidates for SOA-based services are those that are largely shared (i.e., economies of scale). The migration to SOA-based IT is a fundamental shift and needs to be carefully planned. It will leverage existing applications that deliver business value. As shown in the "service-oriented" tier in Figure 17.7, those business or technical services that are largely shared across other services or business processes may make good candidates for the SOA architecture. To make it a successful one, this migration to SOA should be an incremental one and should be largely driven by the service catalog, as discussed in ITIL v3 service design literature. SOA will enable the best possible enhancement to establishing focus on technological innovation while seamlessly delivering business value to customers across multiple platforms.

---

* There is a pervasive view among most of the senior enterprise architects with whom I am in touch that SOA presents a fundamental paradigm shift. An excellent presentation of this view is found in the minutes of a teleconference by the Meta Group: Sholler, Gall, and Hill, *Disruptive Service-Oriented Architecture Trends: Integration & Development Strategies, Server Infrastructure Strategies*, August 2003. Meta Group.

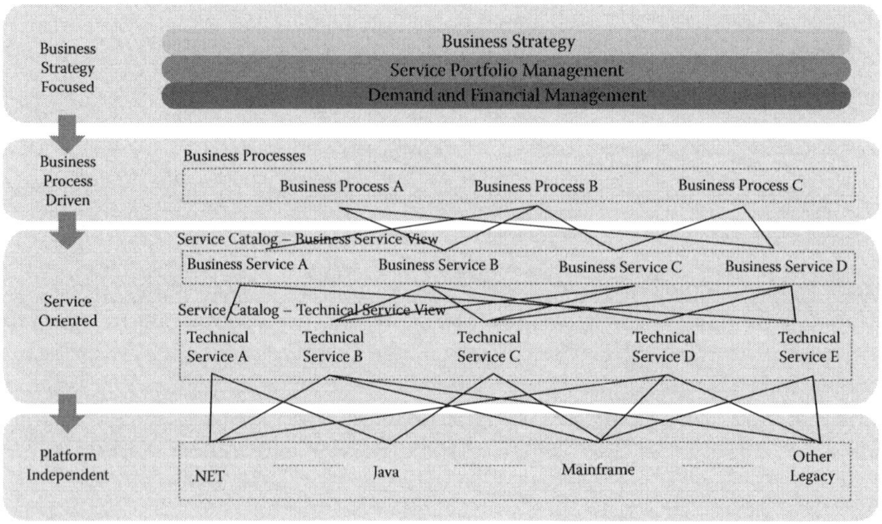

Figure 17.7 SOA and ITIL v3 services.

The Service-Oriented Model

SOA views automation as a set of coarse-grained business components and offers a brokered means for the consumers of that service to communicate with providers of that service. A Web service SOA (WS SOA) implementation is one that uses the standards-based Internet protocols. Thus, a WS SOA has two constituent parts: a general SOA part and a Web service part that it is built upon. According to W3 Architecture,* the service-oriented model can be represented as in Figure 17.8.

The key components as shown in the figure are:

- Message: A service contains a message that is the actual content inherent to the exchange of information and transactions the service will conduct.
- Metadata: The metadata is the machine-readable description of the service that uses the message. The advantage of this metadata is that the services exist in a catalog and are discoverable by technology strategists in the enterprise who need to aggregate these services to solve their problems.
- Person or Organization: A person or organization that owns or controls the service.
- Agent: An agent helps realize the service.

Another useful diagram to express the architecture is illustrated in Figure 17.9.†

In general, SOA and Web services are most appropriate for applications:

- That must operate over the Internet, where reliability and speed cannot be guaranteed

* http://www.w3.org/TR/2004/NOTE-ws-arch-20040211/#concepts.

† There, the metadata is represented and used by the producer and consumer of a service in order to create a brokerage layer wherein the binary representation of the agreement between consumer and producer may be enforced.

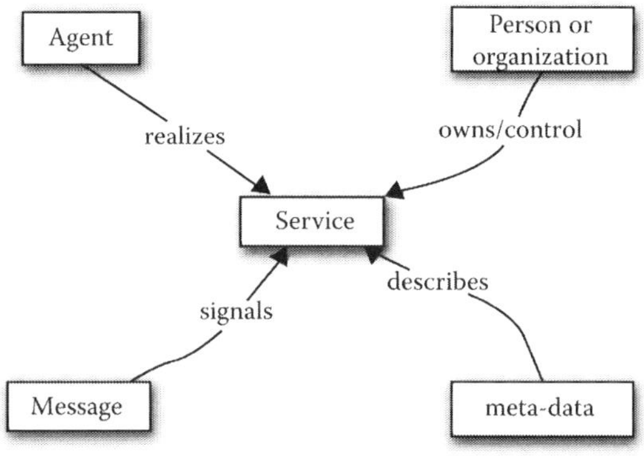

Figure 17.8 Service-oriented model.

- Where there is no ability to manage deployment so that all requesters and providers are upgraded at once
- Where components of the distributed system run on different platforms and vendor products
- Where an existing application needs to be exposed for use over a network, and can be wrapped as a Web service

SOA Benefits

There are the following key business benefits driving SOA adoptions:

- *Effectiveness*
  - Agility to continually align with changing business needs
  - Improved end-to-end business process visibility and control

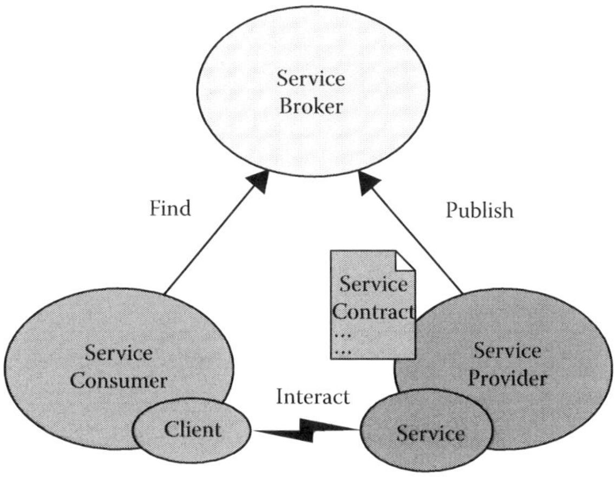

Figure 17.9 SOA architecture.

- *Efficiency*
  - Maximize utilization and eliminate redundancy.
  - Increased development return on investment (ROI): Operations within a service are reusable throughout the enterprise. Because all details of code are well encapsulated, no particular technology expertise is required for participation. Thus, services will be more reusable. They can be aggregated together to create complex business scenarios. For example, to execute the account opening function, several core services will be utilized. Services such as *gather customer information*, *authenticate identity*, *record and agree on contracts*, *mail paper statements*, and others will be utilized in a business process. As organizations mature, more and more of these services will have a global service-oriented implementation. IT investments will have longer lives and greater ROI because legacy and current production systems can be easily wrapped and a service interface can be exposed.
  - Lower IT costs: The cost of performing these operations overtime will decline as more and more business units will be able to simply assemble these services together with operational or system interventions in accordance with their maturity in this process.
  - Reduced integration costs.
  - Reduced complexity through industry standards.
  - Ubiquitous interoperability.
- *Speed to market (i.e., faster delivery through service reusability and sharing)*
  One of the key long-term wins delivered by SOA is an enterprise consisting of a set of well-known services that can be reused across business processes. All existing major vendors are enabling their products for web services SOA.
- *Better security*
  Security in SOA is network-centric instead of application-centric. The traditional elements of security authentication, authorization, encryption, and auditability are consistently implemented through infrastructure. This means that application development becomes more focused on solving core business challenges.
- *Better maintainability*
  Encapsulated implementation details make change management and maintenance efforts simpler.

SOA Critical Success Factors

In enterprises new to SOA, successful implementation will require:

- Quick wins: By implementing showcase SOA solutions for selected projects.
- Targeted investments: Build SOA for those technical services that will maximize returns (i.e., applying 80/20 rule—20% of technical services are probably shared by 80% of consumers).
- Heterogeneous and interoperable environment: Build a management infrastructure for Web services to ensure efficient creation of the envisioned heterogeneous and interoperable environment. Web services use standard protocols and no implementation details need be understood by the consumer or producer of the service. This allows for widely diverse software cultures to communicate with almost no learning curves about the way in which the other cultures work. IBM Mainframe, Oracle, SAP, PeopleSoft/Siebel, Microsoft, Linux,

and other shops can all participate in the SOA without having to understand how the other parties work. Unlike other integration middleware technologies such as RMI, CORBA, and others, SOA does not have specific learning requirements enabling faster implementation.

- Business integration: SOA enables diverse businesses to achieve integration so that cross-business opportunities can be exploited to deliver value-added unique business products and services. Citigroup, Inc., leveraged SOA to grow through cross-marketing to deliver a broad range of services in practically any location throughout the world.

Unifying EA, ITIL v3, and BSM

ITIL v3 is about business–IT integration. One of the core objectives of EA is to enable effective alignment between business and IT and to help bridge the gap between the two. Combined, EA and ITIL v3 can provide a very powerful framework to any business enterprise trying to achieve BSM.

From our discussions above, EA and ITIL v3 share the following common drivers:

- Achieve business–IT alignment and integration.
  - Establish high-level relationships between business and IT.
  - Understand business strategy.
  - Business needs and IT service alignment—ensure that IT services underpin business needs.
  - Align business–IT visions, strategies, goals, objectives, and plans.
- Provide enterprise governance.
- Maximize ROIs.
- Make the right changes (i.e., make those changes that result in the most returns).
- Achieve continual improvements.

Let us discuss how these common drivers can be realized. We will discuss how EA, ITIL v3, and BSM can be integrated into a stronger and much more comprehensive framework to achieve business–IT integration.

Extended Service Life Cycle

The ITIL v3 business service life cycle represents the complete life cycle: service strategy, service design, service transition, service operation and continual service improvement (CSI)—that each service goes through over the course of its life cycle. The service life cycle, however, does not incorporate, for instance, activities carried out to manage innovations and introduce new technologies to implement business strategies. The ITIL v3 service life cycle does present a life cycle view of each service. However, it does not show how the architectural governance, required to manage complexity and ensure reusability, should be implemented.

The ESL is an attempt to position ITIL v3 and EA so that greater business value is realized. To achieve this, the following aspects are addressed:

- Business process innovation and emerging technologies
- Project and portfolio management
- Enterprise architecture

Let us discuss this in greater detail.

The ESL Model

The ESL model addresses some of the most critical elements of managing services as they relate to EA, BSM, and SOA.

The additional components added to the ITIL v3 service life cycle include the following:

- Business process innovation and emerging technologies
- Project and portfolio management
- Enterprise architecture
- Service-oriented architecture

The ESL model is shown in Figure 17.10. Let us discuss each of the new components in detail.

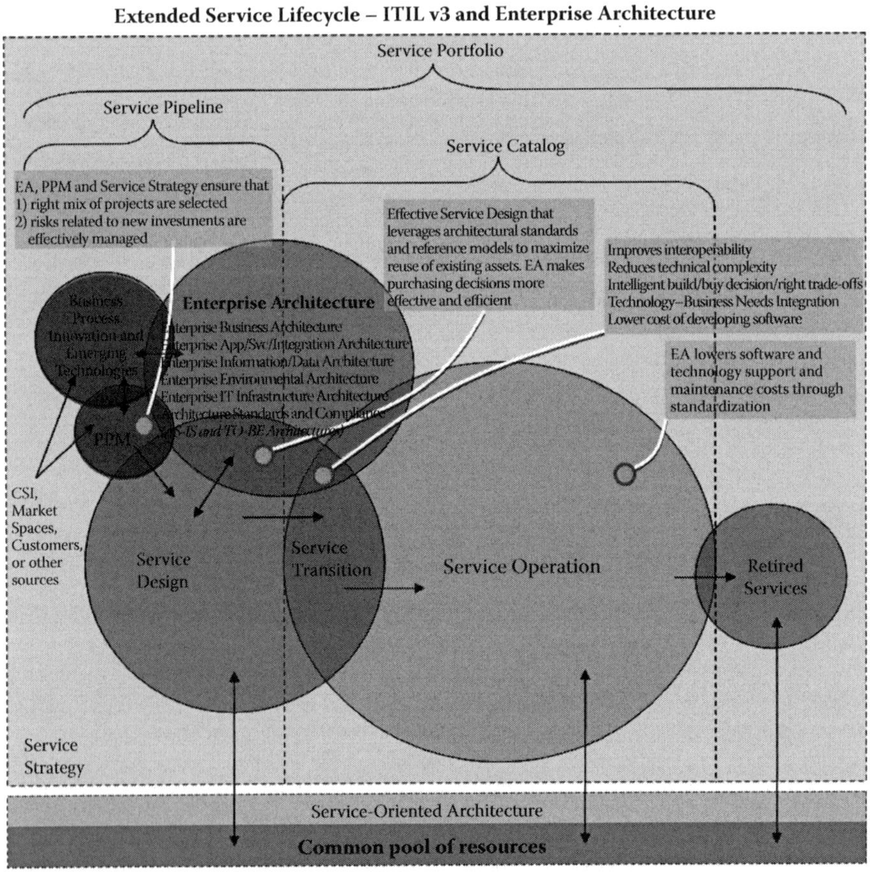

Figure 17.10 ESL model.

Business Process Innovation and Emerging Technologies

Innovation is what keeps businesses alive and fuels the competitive advantages necessary to compete in today's global markets. John Reed's "Citi Never Sleeps" vision from the 1970s, which led to the emergence of ATMs, is once again Citi's slogan. Citi's new CEO, Vikram Pandit, clearly views innovation as the cornerstone of Citi's revival and the foundation for further growth. In an attempt to reestablish foundations for innovation at Citi, the new position of "Chief Innovation Officer" has been created to drive innovation throughout the enterprise (Figure 17.11).

Innovation is something that is larger than the incremental improvements that CSI aims to deliver. CSI may contribute to analyzing, prioritizing, and implementing innovation and related efforts; however, the main focus of CSI is primarily operational improvements and not emerging technologies and major innovations. This is the reason why a separate component, *business process innovation and emerging technologies*, has been added to the traditional ITIL v3 service life cycle. Innovation needs to be managed as part of the service life cycle to ensure that innovations are aligned with the business drivers. Let us discuss innovations in detail.

Adoption, Diffusion, and Habitation of New Innovations

Adoption, diffusion, and habitation are critical to ensuring that new innovations survive. How is EA related to, or not related, to innovation and emerging technologies? EA provides the foundation upon which to innovate and the governance necessary to enable new innovations to be adopted, diffused, and inhabited throughout the enterprise. This can be achieved in a number

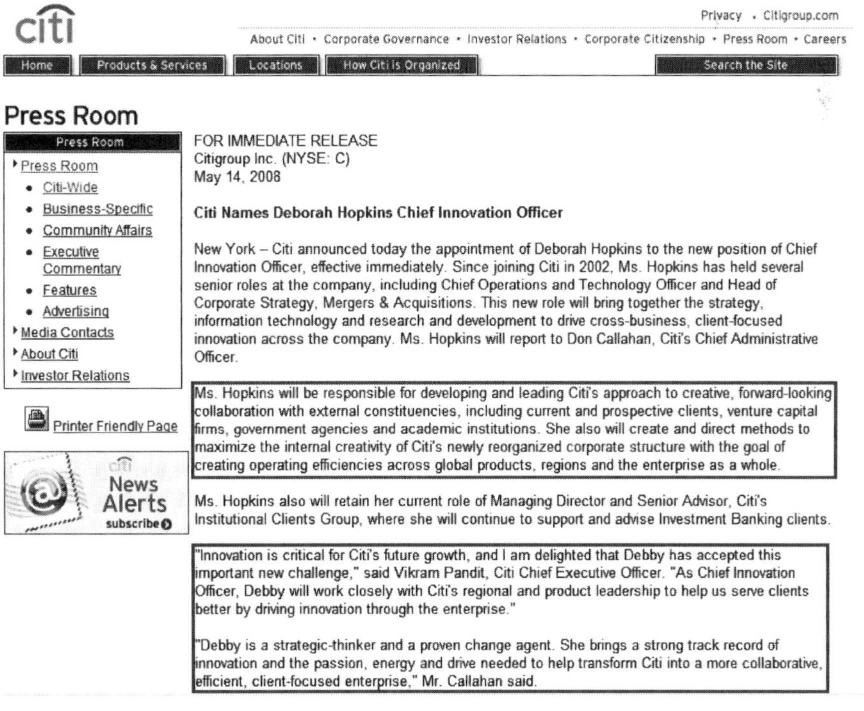
citi

Privacy • Citigroup.com

About Citi • Corporate Governance • Investor Relations • Corporate Citizenship • Press Room • Careers

Home | Products & Services | Locations | How Citi is Organized | Search the Site

Press Room

Press Room
- Press Room
  - Citi-Wide
  - Business-Specific
  - Community Affairs
  - Executive Commentary
  - Features
  - Advertising
- Media Contacts
- About Citi
- Investor Relations

Printer Friendly Page

citi News Alerts subscribe

FOR IMMEDIATE RELEASE
Citigroup Inc. (NYSE: C)
May 14, 2008

Citi Names Deborah Hopkins Chief Innovation Officer

New York – Citi announced today the appointment of Deborah Hopkins to the new position of Chief Innovation Officer, effective immediately. Since joining Citi in 2002, Ms. Hopkins has held several senior roles at the company, including Chief Operations and Technology Officer and Head of Corporate Strategy, Mergers & Acquisitions. This new role will bring together the strategy, information technology and research and development to drive cross-business, client-focused innovation across the company. Ms. Hopkins will report to Don Callahan, Citi's Chief Administrative Officer.

Ms. Hopkins will be responsible for developing and leading Citi's approach to creative, forward-looking collaboration with external constituencies, including current and prospective clients, venture capital firms, government agencies and academic institutions. She also will create and direct methods to maximize the internal creativity of Citi's newly reorganized corporate structure with the goal of creating operating efficiencies across global products, regions and the enterprise as a whole.

Ms. Hopkins also will retain her current role of Managing Director and Senior Advisor, Citi's Institutional Clients Group, where she will continue to support and advise Investment Banking clients.

"Innovation is critical for Citi's future growth, and I am delighted that Debby has accepted this important new challenge," said Vikram Pandit, Citi Chief Executive Officer. "As Chief Innovation Officer, Debby will work closely with Citi's regional and product leadership to help us serve clients better by driving innovation through the enterprise."

"Debby is a strategic-thinker and a proven change agent. She brings a strong track record of innovation and the passion, energy and drive needed to help transform Citi into a more collaborative, efficient, client-focused enterprise," Mr. Callahan said.

Figure 17.11 Citi's press release on reestablishing innovation focus.

of ways and those will be discussed later in this chapter. For now, let us discuss and build an appreciation for these terms.

Defining the Terms

First, we will look at what these terms mean. According to *Merriam-Webster Online Dictionary*:

- *Adopt* is defined as (1) to take by choice into a relationship; especially, to take voluntarily (a child of other parents) as one's own child; (2) to take up and practice or use; (3) to accept formally and put into effect.
- *Diffusion* is defined as the spread of cultural elements from one area or group of people to others by contact.
- *Habitat* is defined as (1) the place or environment where a plant or animal naturally or normally lives and grows; (2) the typical place of residence of a person or a group; (3) a housing for a controlled physical environment in which people can live under surrounding inhospitable conditions (as under the sea); (4) the place where something is commonly found.

Relating the Terms to Technology Innovation

Here is how I believe these terms relate to technology. A new technology is adopted because an adopter perceives a certain value to be realized as a result of adoption. The term "adopt" here does not take into account the extent and life of the relationship after adoption (i.e., you may adopt a certain technology and abandon it, maybe after realizing costs involved in deploying it). In the context of a business enterprise, if new technologies are adopted in a siloed, uncoordinated fashion, they will add to the overall complexity of the IT portfolio, thereby increasing the costs of delivering IT services. I will also illustrate that "adopt" has always been used limitedly to refer to the fact that a company or an individual has invested some resources in acquiring the new technology. What happens after that is neither considered nor analyzed.

As more and more people adopt the new technology, it starts spreading from one group of people to others by contact leading to a wide diffusion and, thus, saturation. After adoption, to realize the value, the technology must be deployed. After deployment, appropriate technology advancements and proper technology management is required to ensure that the technology lives and grows overtime. The goal for any technology should not be to be "adopted" or just "deployed" by masses, but in fact, "inhabited" (Figure 17.12).

Utilization of New Innovations

EA combined with ITIL v3 service strategy and service design provides the required architectural and technological governance, which ensures that any new technology is appropriately adopted and deployed so that it is inhabited across the business enterprise. Many observers in the past have pointed to the fact that when the number of users of a new product or invention is plotted versus time, the resulting curve is typically an S-shaped distribution (Mansfield, 1961). It seems natural (and is a common view) to imagine adoption proceeding slowly at first, accelerating as it spreads throughout the potential adopters, and then slowing down as the relevant population becomes saturated. For innovations in IT to have a positive impact on quality and productivity, however, they must actually be deployed (Fichman and Kemerer, 1999) and then inhabited (defined later).

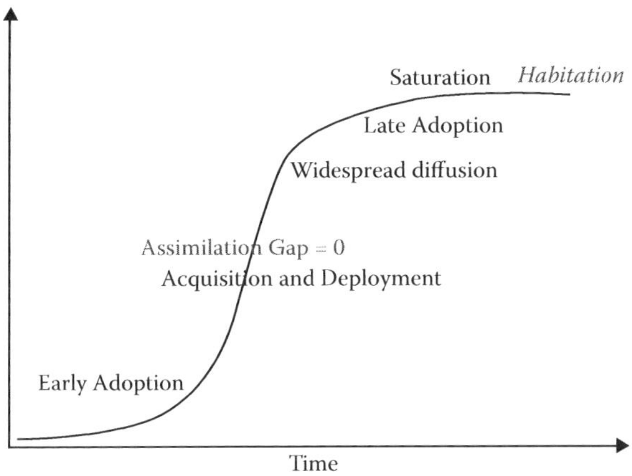

Figure 17.12 Adoption life cycle.

A new technology may be introduced amid great enthusiasm and enjoy widespread initial acquisition, but nevertheless still fail to be thoroughly deployed among many acquiring firms (Fichman and Kemerer, 1999). To address this challenge, EA and ITIL v3 can jointly offer the enterprise governance, discussed later in this chapter, needed to ensure that: (1) targeted and business-driven innovations are encouraged and (2) the emerging technologies are adopted driven by the business need and not for the sake of new technology.

Liker et al. (1992) report that computer-aided design (CAD) technologies had achieved unusually rapid market penetration in the 1980s, yet, as late as 1992, "true CAD/CAM [utilization was] still quite rare."

Assimilation Gap

Let us now look at the impact of these implications on the process of diffusion. According to Hall and Khan (2002), diffusion can be seen as the cumulative or aggregate result of a series of individual calculations that weigh the incremental benefits of adopting a new technology against the costs of change, often in an environment characterized by uncertainty and by limited information. Roger (1995) defines diffusion as a process whereby an innovation spreads across a population of potential adopters over time. A typical approach is to define adoption as "the purchase or physical acquisition of the innovation," and then to fit a times series of observed cumulative adoption counts or percentages to some functional form, such as the logistic distribution (Mahajan and Peterson, 1985). Some compare multiple innovations, seeking to explain why some innovations diffuse more rapidly and widely than others (Mansfield, 1993). Still others have a more applied focus and seek to make predictions about the future course of innovation for a technology (Mahajan et al., 1990). Assimilation gap can be defined as the difference between the pattern of cumulative acquisitions and cumulative deployments of an innovation across a population of potential adopters (Figure 17.13). When a substantial assimilation gap exists for an innovation, the use of cumulative acquisition as the basis for diffusion modeling can present an illusory picture of the diffusion process—leading to potentially erroneous judgments about the robustness of the diffusion process already observed, and about the technology's future prospects (Fichman and Kermerer, 1999). Practitioners may commit to a technology based on a mistaken belief that pervasive adoption is

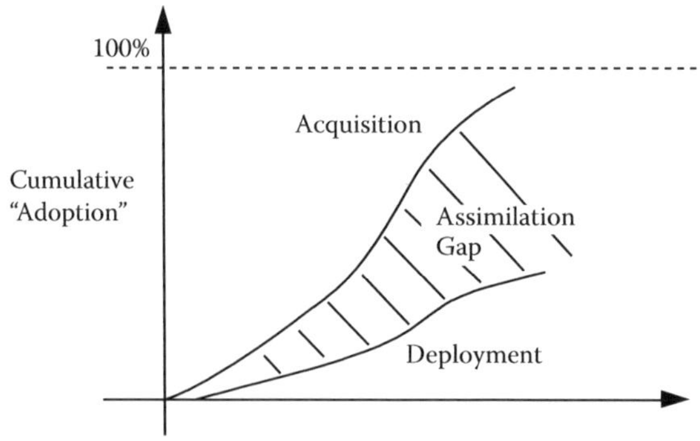

Figure 17.13 Assimilation gap.

inevitable, when it is not. From an information technology perspective, appropriate enterprise governance is needed to ensure that investments are made in a wise manner. ITIL v3 service strategy addresses demand management, that is, if a given service starts to achieve diffusion, how this increasing demand should be managed in line with capacity and to ensure the overall profitability.

EA—A Component of ESL

EA provides the current-state and envisioned target-state views of the enterprise. With that, EA aligns business needs with technological capabilities and provides the enterprise governance necessary to ensure that the right changes are identified and selected to maximize ROI. Earlier in this chapter, we briefly discussed the different EA standards and frameworks. An organization that is planning on embarking on the EA journey will initially need to invest some time and effort in identifying the framework(s) that will be most applicable and then in tailoring that framework to meet organizational needs.

Regardless of which framework is selected for the EA effort, there are certain core and somewhat common deliverables that will be required. These may include (but are not limited to) the following:

- *Architectural views*
  Depending on the organizational maturity and needs, some or all of the following architectural views may be required. These views should be developed for both current and target states. These may include:
  - Enterprise business architecture
  - Enterprise service architecture
  - Enterprise application architecture
  - Enterprise information and data architecture
  - Enterprise IT infrastructure architecture
  - Enterprise environment architecture
- *Reference architectures (technical, infrastructure, and so on)*
  Reference architecture normally provides an architecture of generic services and functions. Reference architecture serves as a generic foundation upon which more specific architectures and architectural components can be designed and built. EA provides different reference

models for planning, architecting, designing, building, deploying, and retiring services and solutions.

- *Project-specific or solution architectures (for large projects)*
  EA may get engaged in building project-specific architectures (also known as solution architectures) for projects that may have cross-organization impact.
- *Mentoring and training*
  The EA organization may provide architecture-specific training and mentoring services to the larger organization.
- *EA governance*
  One of the most important functions of the EA group is to ensure that the right changes are identified, selected, and approved. As shown in Figure 17.14 (end-to-end enterprise governance), achieving end-to-end enterprise governance requires the following:
  - EA governance
    This governance ensures that the right changes are selected, approved, and implemented. In establishing which changes are right for the organization, EA governance considers the following:
    - Current state of AS-IS business architectures
      - Business vision and strategy
      - Business needs
      - IT vision and strategy
    - Current-state and target-state architectures
    - Reference architectures
    - EA principles, policies and standards
    - Technological capabilities
    - Other relevant factors

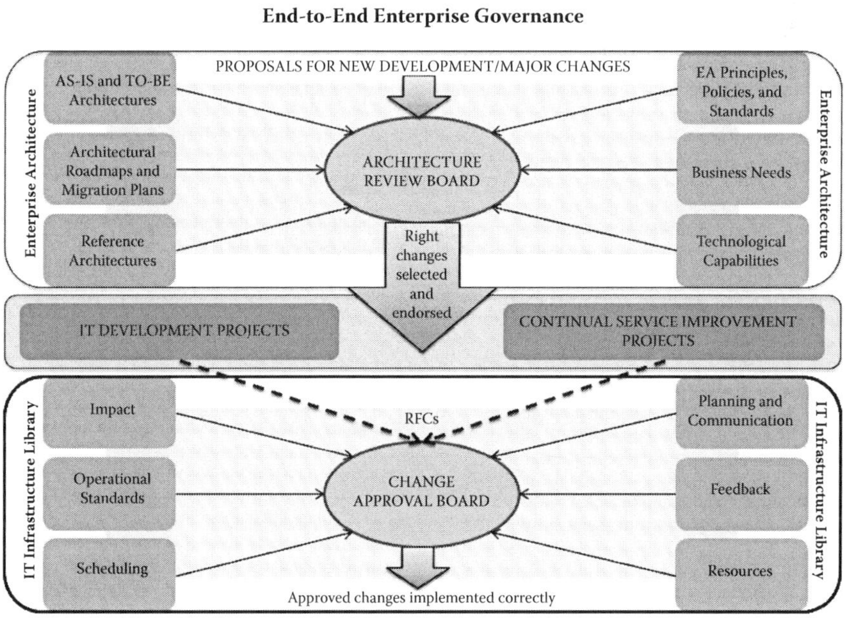

Figure 17.14 End-to-end enterprise governance.

The ultimate goal of EA governance is to ensure that the right change proposals are selected.
  - ITIL/Operational governance
    After the proposals are reviewed and endorsed by the architecture review board (ARB), these most commonly translate into projects. These projects mostly include new development/major enhancement as well as other improvement efforts initiated by CSI. As shown in Figure 17.14, the ARB considers a range of perspectives to identify, prioritize, select, and endorse the right changes (i.e., those changes that are right for the business). These perspectives include business strategy and needs, AS-IS and TO-BE EAs, architectural roadmaps and migration plans (to migrate the business enterprise from its current state to future states), standards and policies, and reference architectures. After the changes are approved from the architectural perspective, these are taken through the change approval board for implementation.

EA Interfaces with All Components of the Service Life Cycle

EA plays a key role in effectively enabling business–IT alignment. To achieve such an alignment, EA interfaces with all components of the ESL discussed earlier. These are as follows:

- Business process innovation and emerging technologies
  EA may interface with the business process innovation and emerging technologies to create real business value. The goal is to ensure that new technologies and capabilities are established driven by the business needs. The primary architectural domain that enables to appropriately govern and guide these innovations is the enterprise business architecture.
- Project and portfolio management
  This enables effective portfolio planning from investment perspective. EA, project, and portfolio management, and ITIL v3 service strategy ensure that:
  - The right mix of projects is selected.
  - The risks related to new investments are effectively managed.
- Service design
  EA interfaces with service design to enable achievement of the following:
  - Improved interoperability
  - Reduced technical complexity
  - Intelligent build and buy decisions and the right trade-offs
  - Technology–business needs integration
  - Lower cost of developing software

Role of EA to Ensure Habitation

It is diffusion rather than invention or adoption that ultimately determines the pace of economic growth and the rate of change of productivity. Until many users adopt a new technology, it may contribute little to our well-being. As Nathan Rosenberg (1972) said, ". . . in the history of diffusion of many innovations, one cannot help being struck by two characteristics of the diffusion process: its apparent overall slowness on the one hand, and the wide variations in the rate of acceptance of different inventions, on the other." With regard to information technology, EA should provide the effective, up-front governance process and the appropriate architectural views and reference architectures to ensure that new IT services and products are successfully inhibited.

ESL Workflow

This work is supposed to provide a high-level overview of activities that need to be performed in order to achieve the Business–IT alignment and eventually integration (Figure 17.15).

First, the need is identified and investment justified. If all goes well and the new proposal or idea gets approved, the following activities are carried out in parallel:

- The solution's proof-of-concept is developed to demonstrate that the solution does indeed address the business needs.
- While architecting and developing the prototype, a dedicated effort should be made to leverage existing assets as much as possible.
- Lastly, the architected solution must ensure alignment with the larger EA target-state vision, principles, and standards.

After those activities, the ARB will review the solution architecture and the architectural proof-of-concept. If all is approved, the new or enhanced solution is designed, developed, and transitioned into production.

EA and ITIL v3–Driven Conceptual Organizational Architecture

We have already discussed conceptual organizational architecture. However, we will discuss the EA component and its relationship with the conceptual, organizational architecture in greater detail.

EA looks across the enterprise, from the business processes to IT operations. This is graphically represented in Figure 17.16.

Enterprise Business Architecture and ITIL v3 Service Strategy

Some of the main components of the enterprise business architecture domain are as follows:

- Business vision and strategy.
- Business processes that will be required to produce envisioned products and/or services to realize the stated vision and strategy.
- Organization and structure that will enable support and enable efficient execution of business processes. Roles or positions defined within the organizational structure are related to activities performed within the business processes. A given role or position can be responsible for an activity, can be accountable for an activity, can be consulted during an activity, or can be informed on an activity. There can be many roles or positions responsible for an activity. However, there has to be only one accountable for the overall success of an activity. This is also known as the responsible-accountable-consulted-informed (RACI) model.

Enterprise business architecture will drive IT strategy and the Service Portfolio. As businesses plan to introduce new products or services, they will need to define new business processes to manufacture or develop and deliver those products or services to the end customer. This knowledge is captured within the enterprise business architecture and will drive the identification and definition of IT services that may need to be retired or new ones that may need to be envisioned.

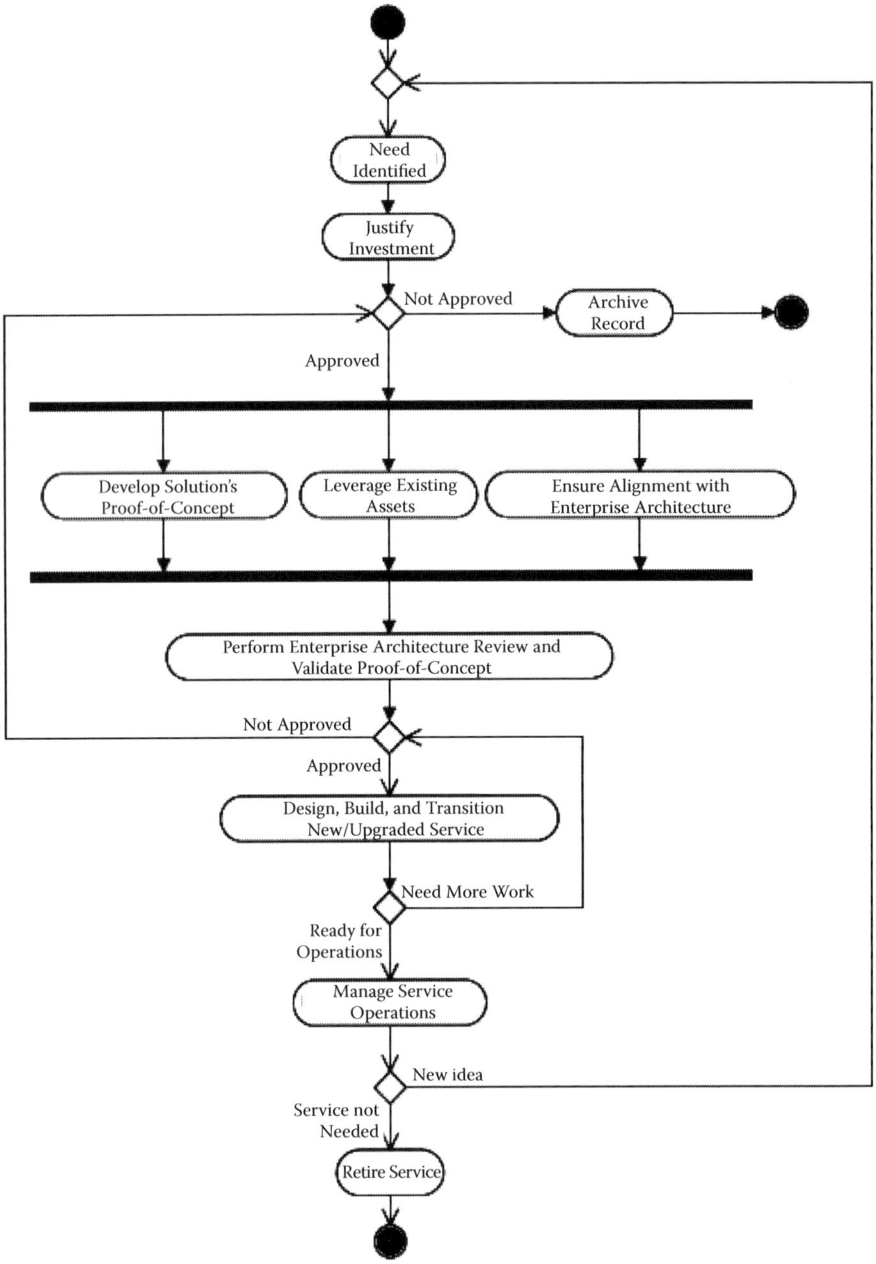

Figure 17.15 ESL: high-level workflow.

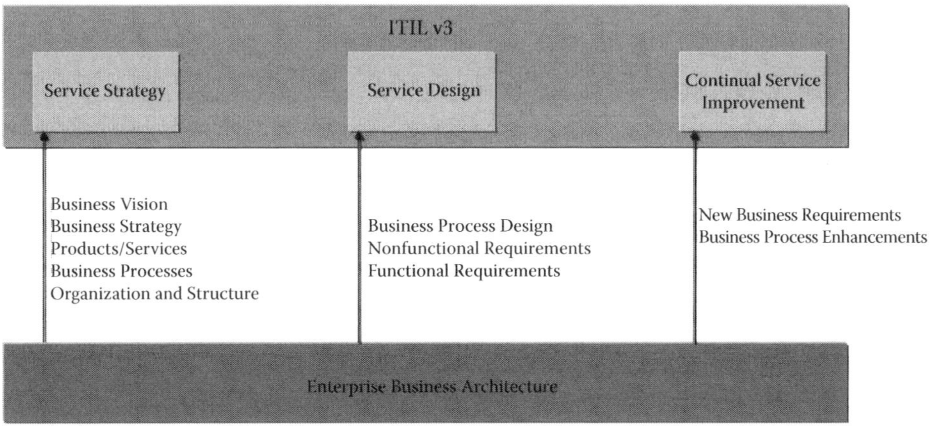

Figure 17.16 Enterprise business architecture and ITIL v3.

As shown in Figure 17.16, enterprise business architecture plays the following role:

- *Service strategy*
  Enterprise business architecture provides the following information that will help drive the service strategy:
  - Business vision
  - Business strategy
  - Products or services
  - Business processes
  - Organization and structure
- *Service Design*
  Enterprise business architecture provides the following information that will help drive the right design for the service:
  - Business process design
  - Nonfunctional requirements
  - Functional requirements
- *Continual Service Improvement*
  Enterprise business architecture provides the following information that will enable business-driven identification of improvement opportunities:
  - New business requirements
  - Business process enhancements

Enterprise Service, Application, Integration and Infrastructure Architectures, and ITIL v3

As shown in Figure 17.17, enterprise service, application, and integration and infrastructure architectures (IT architectures) provide the key pieces of architectural information that will ensure that the requirements captured in the enterprise business architecture are appropriately met, thereby

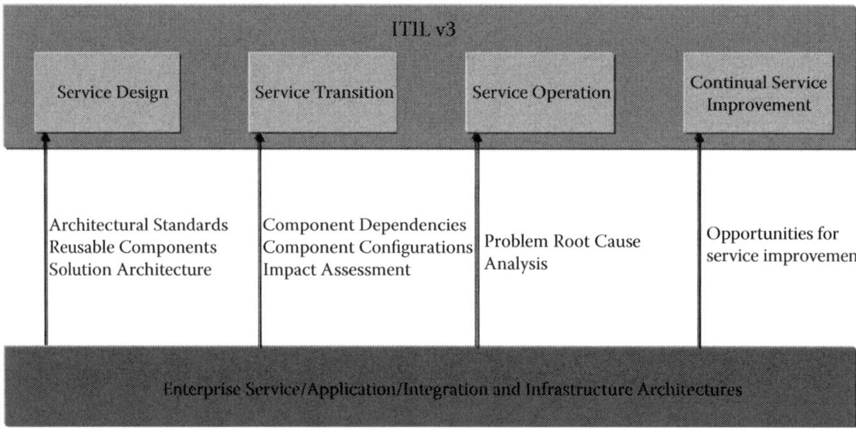

Figure 17.17 Enterprise service, application, integration and infrastructure architectures, and ITIL v3.

supporting the overall realization of business goals. Specifically, these IT architectures provide the following key information:

- *Service design*
  IT architectures provide the following information during the service design phase:
  - Any architectural standards that should be followed.
  - Components that can be reused.
  - In some organization, this will drive the overall architecture of the service or solution.
- *Service transition*
  IT architectures provide the following information during the service transition phase:
  - Any dependencies between components that may need to be considered when planning changes.
  - The impact of making changes to a given component. Although this may also be supported by configuration management databases, high-level component relationships are also captured within respective architectures.
- *Service operation*
  IT architectures will, in most cases, support problem root-cause analysis activities.
- *Continual service improvement*
  IT architectures will enable identification of service improvement opportunities.

Business process and business service–specific architectures may be represented and influenced by the enterprise business architecture and enterprise service architecture views, respectively. There are application-, information-, infrastructure-, and environment-specific views that represent more technical views. Please note that these views do not exist in isolation. In fact, for the EA practice to generate the business value that it is intended to, all these views must be traceable. For example, components within the enterprise business architecture view should be traceable from the appropriate enterprise service architecture components to the application, information, and infrastructure components. Figure 17.19 shows the various roles that can exist within Enterprise Architecture function. Note that solution architecture is cross-domain and solution specific.

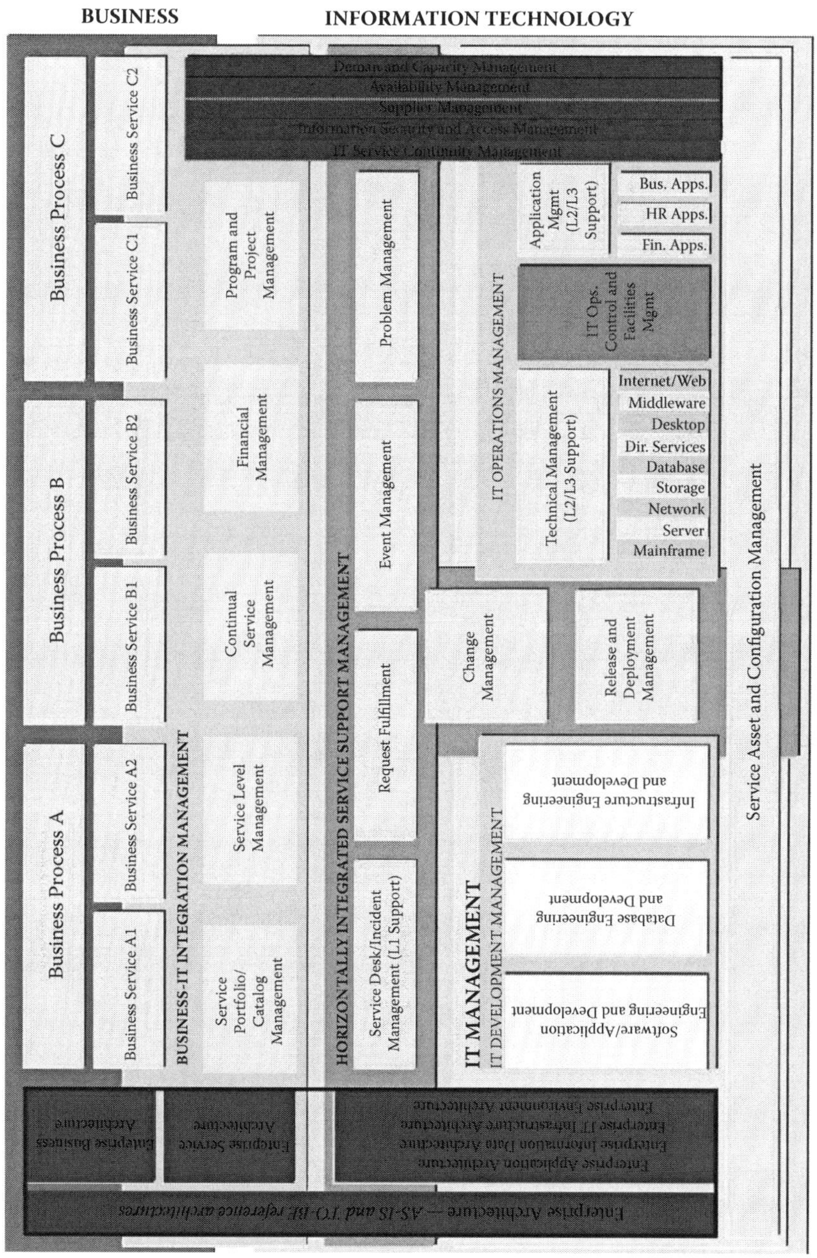

Figure 17.18 Enterprise architecture and ITIL v3-driven organizational principles.

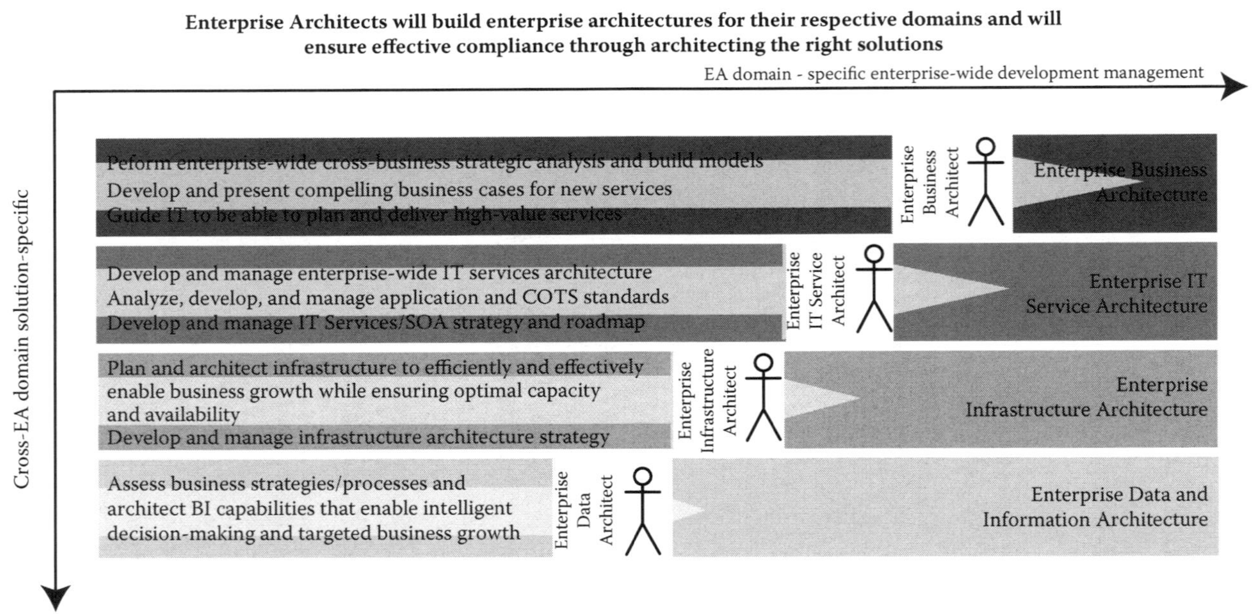

Figure 17.19 Enterprise architecture roles.

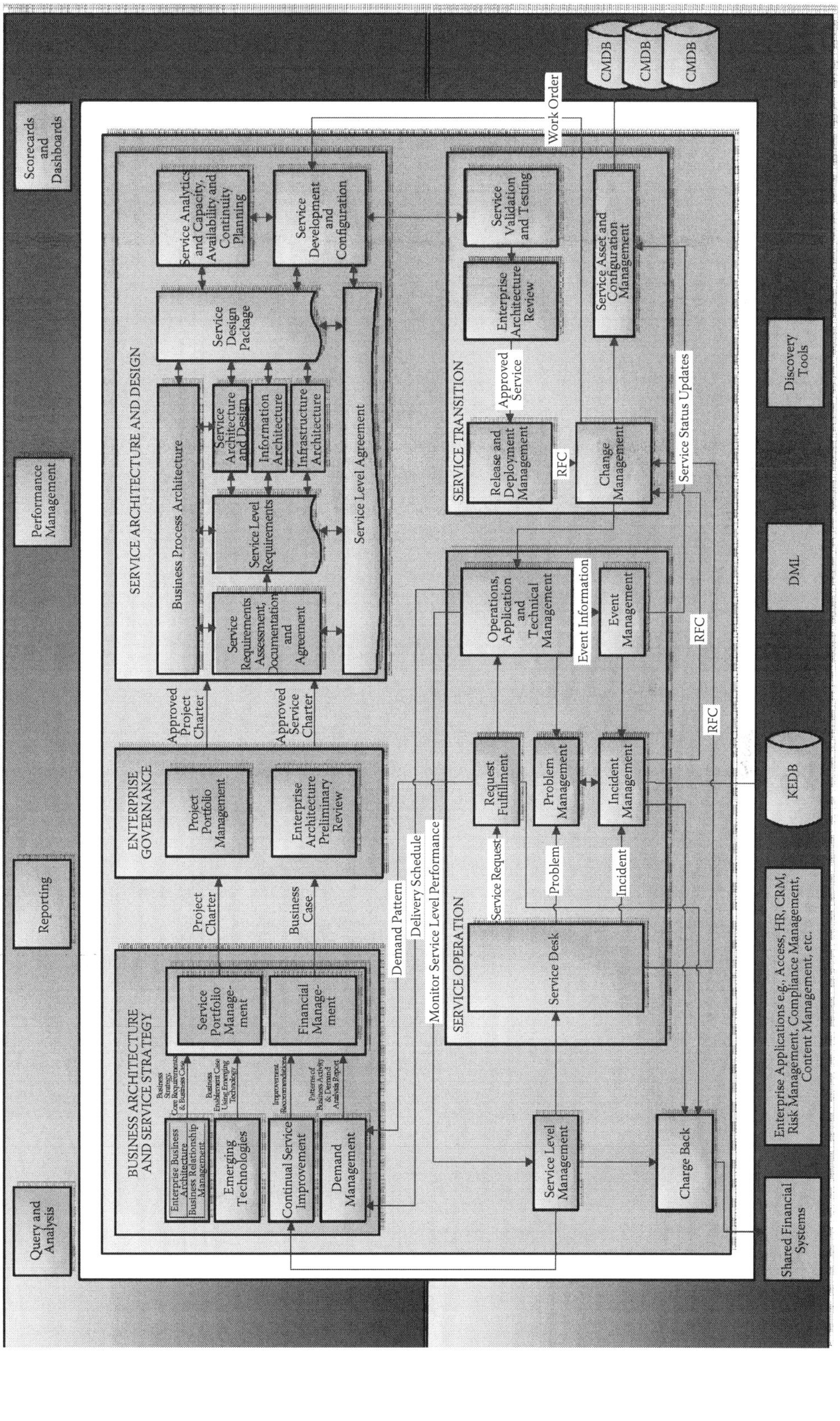

Figure 17.20 Enterprise architecture and ITIL v3-driven end-to-end BSM.

Bringing EA and BSM Together—Unified BSM

We have already discussed EA, ITIL v3, and BSM earlier in the chapter. In this section, we will see how EA, ITIL v3, and BSM will operate in a streamlined manner. Figure 17.20 shows the end-to-end architecture of EA-driven BSM. Figures 17.18 and 17.20 show the high-level architecture and process of end-to-end BSM that is integrated with and driven by EA.

Business Architecture and Service Strategy

Business architecture and service strategy aims to achieve the following key objectives:

- Gain a clear understanding of business strategy and identify core emerging business requirements.
- Identify patterns of business activity and forecast demand.
- Create a business case for building new IT services or improving existing services so that these IT investments are aligned with customers' business priorities.
- Create business cases on how new and emerging technologies can be utilized to enhance business profitability and reduce operating costs.
- Create and manage the service portfolio that will ensure that requests for IT services (retired, operational, and future) and needed infrastructure capabilities are assessed and prioritized.
- Create business cases and project charters are created for review and approval.

These project charters and business cases are then forwarded to enterprise governance for review and approval.

Enterprise Governance

Enterprise governance is about reviewing all business cases and project charters and approving those that can bring the most returns. In assessing these business cases and project charters, project portfolio management and an EA preliminary review may consider the following questions:

- How does this project impact the overall strategy? Does it support business and IT strategy or not? If it does support them, to what extent?
- How does the new service impact the overall EA? Is it doable? What are the estimated efforts required? Are the estimates presented in the project charter realistic? What existing components can be utilized or reused?

After the project charter is approved, it goes into the architecture and design phase.

Service Architecture and Design

Although ITIL v3 calls it the "service design" phase of the service life cycle, I prefer to call it "service architecture and design." Business process architecture will drive the service requirements and service level agreements. Service level requirements will drive the service architecture and design, the information architecture, and the infrastructure architecture. Combined together, these different views of architecture contribute to the development of the service design package—a holistic design that considers all aspects of service design (i.e., business requirements, process design, technology architecture, and measurements). After the service is architected and designed, it moves into service transition. Service transition and service operation have been discussed in detail in ITIL v3 literature.

Summary

EA, ITIL v3, and BSM can jointly offer a much more comprehensive platform to an organization that is planning on achieving business–IT integration. EA functions may already exist within organizations. In such cases, it makes complete sense to take a big-picture view and try to align EA function with the BSM implementation effort. At the same time, SOA offers a tremendous platform to actually implement the underlying technologies to optimize the benefits of BSM.

References

Buchanan, R., and R. Soley. 2002. Aligning Enterprise Architectures and IT Investments with Corporate Goals. Retrieved on November 26, 2004 from: http://user.cs.tu-berlin.de/~hochnade/mda/align.pdf

Fichman, R., and C. Kemerer. 1999. The illusory diffusion of innovation: an examination of assimilation gaps. *Inf Syst Res* 10(3):255–275.

Hall, B., and B. Khan. 2002. Adoption of New Technology. Retrieved on November 28, 2004 from http://elsa.berkeley.edu/~bhhall/Hall_Khan_diffusionJan03.pdf

Liker, K., M. Fleischer, and D. Arnsdorf. 1992. Fulfilling the promises of CAD. *Sloan Manag Rev* 33:74–86.

Mahajan, V., E. Muller, and F. Bass. 1990. New product diffusion models in marketing: a review and directions for research. *J Mark* 54:1–26.

Mahajan, V., and R. Peterson. 1985. *Models for Innovation Diffusion*. Beverly Hills, CA: Sage Publications.

Mahajan, V., E. Muller, and F. Bass. 1990. New product diffusion models in marketing: A review and directions for research. *J Mark* 54(January):1–26.

Mansfied, E. 1961. Technical change and the rate of imitation. *Econometrica* 29(4):741–766.

Mansfield, E. 1993. The diffusion of flexible manufacturing systems in Japan, Europe and the United States. *Manage Sci* 39(2):149–159.

Popkin Software. 2003. Building an Enterprise Architecture: The Popkin Process. Retrieved on November 27, 2004 from: http://www.popkin.com/government/frameworks/zachman%5Fframework.htm

Rogers, E. M. 1995. *Diffusion of Innovations*. New York: The Free Press.

Rosenberg, N. 1972. Factors affecting the diffusion of technology. *Explorations in Economic History*, Vol. 10(1): 3–33. Reprinted in Rosenberg, N. 1976. *Perspectives on Technology*: Cambridge: Cambridge University Press.

Tarabanis, K., V. Peristeras, and G. Fragidis. 2001. Building an enterprise architecture for public administration: a high-level data model for strategic planning. Global Co-operation in the New Millennium. The 9th European Conference on Information Systems, Bled, Slovenia, June 27–29, 2001.

Wegmann, A. 2002. *The Systemic Enterprise Architecture Methodology* (SEAM). Technical Report EPFL/I & C, No. 200265.

Zachman, J. 1987. A framework for information systems architecture. *IBM Syst J* 26(3):590–616.

Zachman Institute for Framework Advancement (ZIFA). 2003. The Framework for Enterprise Architecture (The Zachman Framework) and the Search for the Owner's View of Business Rules. Retrieved on November 27, 2004 from: www.zifa.com.

Appendix A: Sample IT Service Catalog

This is a sample IT service catalog that lists and describes the most common services provided by IT organizations. Some services are completely described and others are only listed. Those that are listed and not entirely described may either be dependent on how different businesses and IT organizations define them or are very common across IT organizations. This sample catalog should serve as a starting point for defining your organization's specific IT service catalog.

Please visit www.xceedure.com to download softcopies of templates, a full version of the service catalog, and further guidelines to support ITIL and business service management implementations.

Table of Contents

Introduction to IT Service Catalog

<<Name of IT organization>> delivers a full range of IT services to all business units and end users. This Service Catalog provides descriptions of all the services that <<Name of IT organization>> offers to its customers, both end users and other IT professionals and partners.

Purpose of IT Service Catalog

To provide accurate information on all the operational services and those that are soon to be introduced.

Service List

The IT service catalog is a living document and will be updated on a regular basis. Reviews and updates are expected twice a year. This schedule might change based on the needs of customers as well as IT.

In its current form, the IT service catalog contains the following key services:

Service Name	*Service Point of Contact*
Communication and Collaboration Services	
E-mail and Calendaring Service	Service Desk
Telephone and VOIP Service	Service Desk
Mobile Data, Voice, and Video Communication Service	Service Desk
Internet Service	Service Desk
Document and Knowledge Management	Service Desk
File Storage and Sharing Service	Service Desk
Third-Party or B2B Connectivity Service	Service Desk
Employee Remote Access Service	Service Desk
Conferencing Service	Service Desk
Standard Desktop Applications, Hardware and Support Services	
Desktops and Laptops	Service Desk
Printing Service	Service Desk
Standard End-User Applications	Service Desk
Technology Development Services	
Custom Application and Service Development	Service Desk or Business Relationship Manager (Account Manager)
Infrastructure and Network Development	Service Desk Business Relationship Manager (Account Manager)

Service Name	*Service Point of Contact*
Web site Development	Service Desk or (Business Relationship Manager (Account Manager)
Technology Management Services	
Business Application Hosting Service	Service Desk
Business Application Management Service	Service Desk
Database Administration and Management Service	Service Desk
Server Management and Support Service	Service Desk
Rack Space Leasing Service	Service Desk
Enterprise Resource Planning Services	
Financial Management	Service Desk
Supply Chain Management	Service Desk
Human Resource Management	Service Desk
Project Management	Service Desk
Professional and Consulting Services	
Business Process Reengineering Service	Service Desk or Business Relationship Manager (Account Manager)
Business Process Management Service	Service Desk or Business Relationship Manager (Account Manager)
Enterprise Architecture Management Service	Service Desk Business Relationship Manager (Account Manager)
Technology Strategy and Planning Service	Service Desk or Business Relationship Manager (Account Manager)
IT Project Management	Service Desk or Business Relationship Manager (Account Manager)
Information Security Management Service	Service Desk or Business Relationship Manager (Account Manager)
Value-Pack Service Bundles	
End-User Service Bundles	Service Desk
Business Unit Service Bundles	Service Desk

General Customer Responsibilities

Customers have certain general responsibilities related to requesting and obtaining IT services. These general responsibilities are listed below. Service-specific responsibilities are documented under each service in this catalog.

- All service requests and incidents must be reported to the IT service desk. There are multiple ways to do that (i.e., e-mail, phone call, or online portal).
- Appropriate customer resources must be available to work with IT as needed and be able to respond to IT questions to resolve issues in a timely manner.
- Customer must actively participate in periodic service performance reviews.
- Customers must actively participate in service improvement efforts.
- Customers must provide feedback through IT service desk surveys and participate in customer focus groups as requested.
- Business strategies and plans must be shared appropriately to ensure that <<Name of IT organization>> plan and build appropriate capabilities needed to support your business plans.
- Communicate as far in advance as possible (and no less than 2 months before) any major business initiatives that may have an impact on services provided by <<Name of IT organization>>. These may include mergers and acquisitions, new locations, new products or services, business growth, or downsizing.
- <<Name of IT organization>> will be provided access to customer sites and business offices as needed to ensure optimal and timely service support.
- No third party will be provided any access to those customer sites and business offices that are under the responsibility of <<Name of IT organization>> without prior IT approval.

Communication and Collaboration Services

Communication and collaboration services aim to enable our customers and businesses to effectively communicate and collaborate with teams and stakeholders, both inside and outside the company.

Communication and collaboration services include the following:

1. E-mail and calendaring service
2. Telephone and VOIP service
3. Mobile data, voice and video communication service
4. Internet service
5. Document and knowledge management service
6. File storage and sharing service
7. Third-party or business-to-business connectivity
8. Employee remote access service
9. Conferencing service

E-mail and Calendaring Service

Introduction	E-mail service provides end users with the capability to send and receive e-mails using their desktops and laptops with MS Outlook. The end users will be able to manage their meetings and calendars. There are some add-ons available, described below, that can enable large file exchange and over the Web access.

<table>
<tr>
<td>Description</td>
<td>
Features
<ul>
<li>Receive e-mail</li>
<li>Send e-mail (with or without attachments up to XX MB)</li>
<li>Manage meetings and calendar</li>
</ul>
Alternatives, Limitations, and Restrictions
<ul>
<li>There is a limitation on the size of file that can be attached in an e-mail. However, there is an additional feature that allows larger files to be sent using secure file transfer mechanisms.</li>
</ul>
</td>
</tr>
<tr>
<td>Services and Rates</td>
<td>
All unit prices are subject to market values and prorated for service on hourly bases.
<table>
<tr><th>Service</th><th>Unit Price and Service</th></tr>
<tr><td>Desktop E-Mail and Calendaring</td><td>Price per unit</td></tr>
<tr><td>Web Access to E-Mail</td><td>Price per unit</td></tr>
<tr><td>File Transfer Capability (SFTP)</td><td>Price per unit</td></tr>
</table>
Tips for Reducing Costs
<ul>
<li>Use SFTP for e-mailing large files</li>
</ul>
</td>
</tr>
<tr>
<td>Service Requests and Fulfillment Targets</td>
<td>
<table>
<tr><th>Service Request</th><th>Description</th><th>Target Resolution Time</th></tr>
<tr><td>Request for new service</td><td>New e-mail account is needed</td><td>Within x hours, y% of the time</td></tr>
<tr><td>Request for change to existing service</td><td>Changes are needed in existing e-mail account</td><td>Within x hours, y% of the time</td></tr>
<tr><td>Request to cancel the e-mail service</td><td>E-mail service is no longer needed and should be cancelled</td><td>Within x hours, y% of the time</td></tr>
<tr><td>Request for new features</td><td>Request any new features that you need to efficiently run your business</td><td>Within x hours, y% of the time</td></tr>
</table>
</td>
</tr>
</table>

	Prerequisites You must have: • User account **How to Request Service:** Request online: <<Portal Address>> Contact the service desk at <<Telephone Number>> E-mail <<E-mail Address>> **How to Get Support:** Request online: <<Portal Address>> Contact the service desk at <<Telephone Number>> E-mail <<E-mail Address>>
Responsibilities of Parties	**IT Responsibilities** IT will be responsible for the following: • Creating e-mail account • Managing spam control and antivirus software • Managing of the overall service including availability and capacity • Resolving incidents related to e-mail service • Processing and fulfilling e-mail-related service requests **Customer Responsibilities** Customer will be responsible for the following: • Managing mailbox space • Ensuring that e-mail is used for sending and receiving messages and not for storing files • Backing up and archiving messages to your local hard drive • Reporting incidents and problems • Submitting service requests through the online portal or IT service desk
More Information	**Training:** List and describe available training options. **Glossary:** List and describe any specific terms related to this service. **FAQs and Tips:** List and describe any frequently asked questions.

Telephone and VOIP Service

Introduction	IP telephony service provides you with a lower cost means of voice communications and messaging. You are assigned your dedicated number and are able to make and receive calls. You also get other features like voice mail and call forwarding.

<table>
<tr>
<td>Description</td>
<td>Features
<ul>
<li>Make and receive calls</li>
<li>Voice mail</li>
<li>Call forwarding to internal extensions</li>
<li>Multiline conferencing</li>
<li>Caller ID display</li>
<li>Internal, local, long-distance, and international calls</li>
</ul>
Alternatives, Limitations, and Restrictions
<ul>
<li>IP telephony service uses the Internet. In some countries, it may be illegal.</li>
<li>Alternatives include regular phone line and mobile devices.</li>
<li>Telephone installations, moves, adds, or change (IMACs) requests involving more than 10 telephones must be requested at least x weeks in advance.</li>
<li>External (outside of the company) call forwarding will not be allowed.</li>
<li>IP telephony service may not be available at all locations.</li>
</ul>
</td>
</tr>
<tr>
<td>Services and Rates</td>
<td>All unit prices are subject to market values and prorated for service on an hourly basis.
<table>
<tr><th>Service</th><th>Unit Price and Service</th></tr>
<tr><td>Telephone and voicemail service</td><td>Price per unit</td></tr>
<tr><td>New site development and other projects (request for more than 25 lines)</td><td>Project-specific</td></tr>
</table>
Tips for Reducing Costs
<ul>
<li>Users should direct dial and utilize the conference feature for telephone conversations involving only three parties; audio conferencing should be used for telephone conversations involving four or more parties.</li>
<li>Users should consider less-expensive methods for messages such as e-mail.</li>
</ul>
</td>
</tr>
</table>

<table>
<tr>
<td>Service Requests and Fulfillment Targets</td>
<td>
<table>
<tr><th>Service Request</th><th>Description</th><th>Target Resolution Time</th></tr>
<tr><td>Request for New Telephone Account</td><td>This is a request for new telephone service</td><td>Within x hours, y% of the time</td></tr>
<tr><td>Request to move existing account</td><td>This is a request for moving existing telephone service</td><td>Within x hours, y% of the time</td></tr>
<tr><td>Request to cancel existing account</td><td>This is a request to cancel any existing account</td><td>Within x hours, y% of the time</td></tr>
<tr><td>Request for new features</td><td>This is a request for a new feature that currently does not exist</td><td>Within x hours, y% of the time</td></tr>
</table>
Prerequisites
• You must already have a user account.
How to Request Service:
Request online: <<Portal Address>>
Contact the service desk at <<Telephone Number>>
E-mail <<E-mail Address>>
How to Get Support:
Request online: <<Portal Address>>
Contact the service desk at <<Telephone Number>>
E-mail <<E-mail Address>>
</td>
</tr>
<tr>
<td>Responsibilities of Parties</td>
<td>
IT Responsibilities
IT will be responsible for the following:
• Providing IP office phones (including soft-phones), extension setup, and support for end users
• Providing access to and support for the following features: call forwarding, call waiting, ad-hoc three-way conferencing, distribution list creation and usage, and call routing
</td>
</tr>
</table>

	• Procuring and managing devices and related software • Incident management and problem troubleshooting and resolution of IP phone issues • Performing asset disposal at the end of useful life • Data protection via regular backups of voice messages • Ensuring virus protection **Customer Responsibilities** Customer will be responsible for the following: • Timely payment and reporting of usage and related charges • Timely reporting of incidents and problems
More Information	**Training:** List and describe available training options. **Glossary:** List and describe any specific terms related to this service. **FAQs and Tips:** List and describe any frequently asked questions. **Training** • User guides are issued when a new IP telephone account is created. **Glossary** • External forwarding. • Extension is defined as an internal telephone line attached to a private branch exchange (PBX). **FAQs and Tips** **<<Define FAQs and Tips>>**

Mobile Data, Voice, and Video Communication Service

Introduction	This service provides mobile communication capabilities via cellular technology and handheld devices. Communication includes data, voice, and video.
Description	**Features** • Make calls using a mobile phone • Send and receive text messages (data) automatically or manually • Send and receive e-mails • Participate in mobile video conferencing

<table>
<tr><td></td><td>

Alternatives, Limitations, and Restrictions

<ul>
<li>May not be available in all international locations.</li>
<li>In most cases, there will be extra charges for international roaming.</li>
<li>International dialing and roaming will be provisioned at extra fees based on business needs.</li>
<li>Ability to make cellular data connections is based on the wireless service provider's data coverage at a given location.</li>
</ul>
</td></tr>
<tr><td>Services and Rates</td><td>

All unit prices are subject to market values and prorated for service on hourly bases.

<table>
<tr><th>Service</th><th>Unit Price and Service</th></tr>
<tr><td>Handheld Device (should be included from corporate standard handheld device list)</td><td>Price per unit</td></tr>
<tr><td>Voice Service</td><td>Price per unit</td></tr>
<tr><td>Data Service</td><td>Price per unit</td></tr>
<tr><td>Video Service</td><td>Price per unit</td></tr>
</table>

Tips for Reducing Costs

<ul>
<li>Make cell phone calls only when absolutely necessary.</li>
<li>Use landlines wherever possible.</li>
</ul>
</td></tr>
<tr><td>Service Requests and Fulfillment Targets</td><td>
<table>
<tr><th>Service Request</th><th>Description</th><th>Target Resolution Time</th></tr>
<tr><td>Request for new service</td><td>Describe the request</td><td>Within x hours, y% of the time</td></tr>
<tr><td>Request for change to existing service</td><td>Describe the request</td><td>Within x hours, y% of the time</td></tr>
<tr><td>Request to cancel service</td><td>Describe the request</td><td>Within x hours, y% of the time</td></tr>
<tr><td>Request for new features</td><td>Describe the request</td><td>Within x hours, y% of the time</td></tr>
</table>
</td></tr>
</table>

	Prerequisites You must have: • User account • Corporate e-mail account (for e-mail service) **How to Request Service:** Request online: <<Portal Address>> Contact the service desk at <<Telephone Number>> E-mail <<E-mail Address>> **How to Get Support:** Request online: <<Portal Address>> Contact the service desk at <<Telephone Number>> E-mail <<E-mail Address>>
Responsibilities of Parties	**IT Responsibilities** IT will be responsible for the following: • Service desk support for incident and problem resolution for company-provided handheld devices • Asset disposal at the end of useful life **Customer Responsibilities** Customer will be responsible for the following: • Usage charges, which will be charged to the user account according to corporate mobile communication policy • Timely reporting of incidents and problems
More Information	**Training:** List and describe available training options. **Glossary:** List and describe any specific terms related to this service. **FAQs and Tips:** List and describe any frequently asked questions.

Internet Service

Introduction	This service provides access to the Internet.
Description	**Features** • High-speed Internet access **Alternatives, Limitations, and Restrictions** • None at this time.

<table>
<tr>
<td>Services and Rates</td>
<td>All unit prices are subject to market values and prorated for service on an hourly basis.
<table>
<tr><th>Service</th><th>Unit Price and Service</th></tr>
<tr><td>Internet Service</td><td>Price per unit</td></tr>
</table>
Tips for Reducing Costs
• Value-Pack End-User Bundles</td>
</tr>
<tr>
<td>Service Requests and Fulfillment Targets</td>
<td><table>
<tr><th>Service Request</th><th>Description</th><th>Target Resolution Time</th></tr>
<tr><td>Request for new service</td><td>Describe the request</td><td>Within x hours, y% of the time</td></tr>
<tr><td>Request for change to existing service</td><td>Describe the request</td><td>Within x hours, y% of the time</td></tr>
<tr><td>Request to cancel service</td><td>Describe the request</td><td>Within x hours, y% of the time</td></tr>
<tr><td>Request for new features</td><td>Describe the request</td><td>Within x hours, y% of the time</td></tr>
</table>
Prerequisites
You must have:
• User account
How to Request Service:
Request online: <<Portal Address>>
Contact the service desk at <<Telephone Number>>
E-mail <<E-mail Address>>
How to Get Support:
Request online: <<Portal Address>>
Contact the service desk at <<Telephone Number>>
E-mail <<E-mail Address>></td>
</tr>
<tr>
<td>Responsibilities of Parties</td>
<td>IT Responsibilities
IT will be responsible for the following:
• Delivery and support of Internet service
• Incident and problem management
• Chargeback where needed</td>
</tr>
</table>

	Customer Responsibilities Customer will be responsible for the following: • Making timely payments
More Information	**Training:** List and describe available training options. **Glossary:** List and describe any specific terms related to this service. **FAQs and Tips:** List and describe any frequently asked questions.

Document and Knowledge Management Service

Introduction	Knowledge management enables an organization to identify, create, represent, and share knowledge. Knowledge is something that combines information, expertise, and experiences captured in the form of documents and databases. Knowledge management provides the foundation for the creation of a learning organization. It helps achieve greater focus on the management of knowledge as a strategic asset and on encouraging the sharing of knowledge. Knowledge management efforts can help individuals and groups share valuable organizational insights to reduce redundant work, avoid "reinventing the wheel," reduce training time for new employees, retain intellectual capital as employees turnover in an organization, and adapt to changing environments and markets.[a] The document and knowledge management service enables organizations to achieve greater performance, competitive advantage, innovation, and wise continual improvements.
Description	**Features** • Storage, sharing, and searching of knowledge artifacts. These include documents, processes, procedures, and, in some cases, data as well. **Alternatives, Limitations, and Restrictions** • If you simply want to store and share files, you may want to consider a file storage and sharing service.
Services and Rates	All unit prices are subject to market values and prorated for service on an hourly basis. *Service*: Document and Knowledge Management Service — *Unit Price and Service*: Price per unit **Tips for Reducing Costs** • Tips

Service	*Unit Price and Service*
Document and Knowledge Management Service	Price per unit

<table>
<tr>
<td>Service Requests and Fulfillment Targets</td>
<td>
<table>
<tr><th>Service Request</th><th>Description</th><th>Target Resolution Time</th></tr>
<tr><td>Request for new service</td><td>Describe the request</td><td>Within x hours, y% of the time</td></tr>
<tr><td>Request for change to existing service</td><td>Describe the request</td><td>Within x hours, y% of the time</td></tr>
<tr><td>Request to cancel service</td><td>Describe the request</td><td>Within x hours, y% of the time</td></tr>
<tr><td>Request for new features</td><td>Describe the request</td><td>Within x hours, y% of the time</td></tr>
</table>
How to Request Service:
Request online: <<Portal Address>>
Contact the service desk at <<Telephone Number>>
E-mail <<E-mail Address>>
How to Get Support:
Request online: <<Portal Address>>
Contact the service desk at <<Telephone Number>>
E-mail <<E-mail Address>>
</td>
</tr>
<tr>
<td>Responsibilities of Parties</td>
<td>
IT Responsibilities
IT will be responsible for the following:
• Support:
– Service desk support will be provided as agreed
– Incident and problem management
Customer Responsibilities
Customer will be responsible for the following:
• Reporting incidents in a timely manner
• Providing all necessary information required to fulfill the service request in an effective manner
</td>
</tr>
<tr>
<td>More Information</td>
<td>
Training: List and describe available training options.
Glossary: List and describe any specific terms related to this service.
FAQs and Tips: List and describe any frequently asked questions.
</td>
</tr>
</table>

[a] McAdam, Rodney and Sandra McCreedy (2000), "A Critique of Knowledge Management: Using A Social Constructionist Model," *New Technology, Work and Employment.*

File Storage and Sharing Service

<table>
<tr><td>Introduction</td><td><<Name of IT organization>> provides centralized storage space for files to allow customers and end users to store files centrally in one location, which can then, in turn, be accessed by others according to their predetermined and predefined security and access permissions.</td></tr>
<tr><td>Description</td><td>Features
<ul>
<li>Central storage—One place, not several versions of data, in several locations, which may go missing.</li>
<li>Backups—Each file server is backed up every night.</li>
<li>Space—More space available than in local machines.</li>
<li>Sharing capabilities
<ul>
<li>In the case of some applications, this is extremely vital—for example, Estate Master uses files as its database storage, stored on the file server, and accessible by several MAF properties staff.</li>
<li>Some shared applications sit on the file server itself, MAF Properties' leasing program, for example, so they can be used by anyone.</li>
</ul></li>
<li>Security and Virus Scanning
<ul>
<li>Access: Secured access is provided through permissions.</li>
</ul></li>
<li>Files: Files are safely secured.</li>
</ul>
Alternatives, Limitations, and Restrictions
<ul>
<li>There is a standard cost of XX resource hours to set up and configure each shared file.</li>
<li>This service provides file storage, sharing, and management capabilities.</li>
</ul></td></tr>
<tr><td>Services and Rates</td><td>All unit prices are subject to market values and prorated for service on an hourly basis.
<table>
<tr><th>Service</th><th>Unit Price and Service</th></tr>
<tr><td>Departmental sharing and storage service</td><td>Price per unit</td></tr>
<tr><td>End-user sharing and storage service</td><td>Price per unit</td></tr>
</table>
Tips for Reducing Costs
<ul>
<li>Nonbusiness media files should not be stored on shared folders.</li>
</ul></td></tr>
</table>

<table>
<tr>
<td>Service Requests and Fulfillment Targets</td>
<td>
<table>
<tr><th>Service Request</th><th>Description</th><th>Target Resolution Time</th></tr>
<tr><td>Create new folder</td><td>New folder is requested</td><td>Within x hours, y% of the time</td></tr>
<tr><td>Change access rights and permissions</td><td>Request to change permissions and access rights to a given folder</td><td>Within x hours, y% of the time</td></tr>
<tr><td>Restore folder</td><td>Restore existing folder</td><td>Within x hours, y% of the time</td></tr>
<tr><td>Request for new features</td><td>Describe the request</td><td>Within x hours, y% of the time</td></tr>
</table>
Prerequisites
You must have:
<ul>
<li>The necessary agreements need to be in place for departmental file storage and sharing services.</li>
<li>The user account must be in place for end user.</li>
</ul>
How to Request Service:
Request online: <<Portal Address>>
Contact the service desk at <<Telephone Number>>
E-mail <<E-mail Address>>
How to Get Support:
Request online: <<Portal Address>>
Contact the service desk at <<Telephone Number>>
E-mail <<E-mail Address>>
</td>
</tr>
<tr>
<td>Responsibilities of Parties</td>
<td>
IT Responsibilities
IT will be responsible for the following:
<ul>
<li>Support:
<ul>
<li>Service desk support as agreed</li>
<li>Incident and problem management</li>
</ul>
</li>
</ul>
</td>
</tr>
</table>

	• **Access:** – Network access in business facilities – Remote access for end users **Customer Responsibilities** Customer will be responsible for the following: • Reporting incidents in a timely manner • Providing all necessary information required to fulfill the service request in an effective manner
More Information	**Training:** List and describe available training options. **Glossary:** List and describe any specific terms related to this service. **FAQs and Tips:** List and describe any frequently asked questions.

Third-Party or B2B Connectivity Service

Introduction	Third-party or business-to-business connectivity service enables our customers to connect with their partners. This service provides secure reliable remote connectivity for authorized third parties using the Virtual Private Network (VPN) technology. The service provides: • Secure access to the enterprise network through proper authentication and verification processes • Access to applications and resources on the enterprise network with restrictions based on authentication and role (business-partner level)
Description	**Features** • Secure network connectivity to the enterprise network • Authenticated access to business, enterprise, and other shared applications **Alternatives, Limitations, and Restrictions** • There is a standard cost of **XX** resource hours to set up and configure each connectivity request. • Recommended for short- to long-term contracts that require our partners to remotely access our corporate networks and resources. • This service is not recommended for those partners who do not require regular continual access to our corporate network and resources. These partners should instead work offline on documents and artifacts and synchronize when onsite. • There is a limitation of X.X Mb on bandwidth usage per account for this service.

<table>
<tr>
<td>Services and Rates</td>
<td>
All unit prices are subject to market values and prorated for service on an hourly basis.
<table>
<tr><th>Service</th><th>Unit Price and Service</th></tr>
<tr><td>Third-Party or B2B Connectivity Service</td><td>Price per unit</td></tr>
</table>
Tips for Reducing Costs
<ul><li>None at this time.</li></ul>
</td>
</tr>
<tr>
<td>Service Requests and Fulfillment Targets</td>
<td>
<table>
<tr><th>Service Request</th><th>Description</th><th>Target Resolution Time</th></tr>
<tr><td>Request for new connectivity</td><td>This is a request for new connectivity</td><td>Within x hours, y% of the time</td></tr>
<tr><td>Changes to existing connectivity</td><td>This is a request to make changes to existing service</td><td>Within x hours, y% of the time</td></tr>
<tr><td>Request to cancel existing connectivity</td><td>This is a request to cancel existing service</td><td>Within x hours, y% of the time</td></tr>
<tr><td>Request for new features</td><td>This is a request for new connectivity type (e.g., satellite connectivity)</td><td>Within x hours, y% of the time</td></tr>
</table>
Prerequisites
You must have:
<ul>
<li>Partner account created</li>
<li>Secure ID or other secure access mechanism</li>
<li>Internet access connection</li>
</ul>
How to Request Service:
Request online: <<Portal Address>>
Contact the service desk at <<Telephone Number>>
E-mail <<E-mail Address>>
How to Get Support:
Request online: <<Portal Address>>
Contact the service desk at <<Telephone Number>>
E-mail <<E-mail Address>>
</td>
</tr>
</table>

Responsibilities of Parties	**IT Responsibilities** IT will be responsible for the following: • **Support:** – Service desk support • **Hardware and Software** – VPN client software – Security token or secure ID for accessing network and resources • **Access:** – Secure network access – Encrypted network connection **Partner Responsibilities** Partners will be responsible for the following: • Providing relevant requirements as appropriate • Providing all relevant and required approvals according to the information security policy
More Information	**Training:** List and describe available training options. **Glossary:** List and describe any specific terms related to this service. **FAQs and Tips:** List and describe any frequently asked questions.

Employee Remote Access Service

Introduction	Employee remote access service enables our customers' end users to connect with the corporate network and applications. This service provides secure, reliable remote connectivity for authorized users.
Description	**Features** • Single user remote connectivity to the corporate network for employees and other approved users • Secure access to the corporate network through proper authentication and verification prior to access • Access to business and other applications and IT resources on the corporate network **Alternatives, Limitations, and Restrictions** • There is a standard cost of **XX** resource hours to set up and configure each connectivity request. • There is a limitation of X.X Mb on bandwidth usage per account for this service.

<table>
<tr>
<td>Services and Rates</td>
<td>
All unit prices are subject to market values and prorated for service on an hourly basis.
<table>
<tr><th>Service</th><th>Unit Price and Service</th></tr>
<tr><td>Employee Remote Access Service</td><td>Price per unit</td></tr>
</table>
Tips for Reducing Costs
• None at this time
</td>
</tr>
<tr>
<td>Service Requests and Fulfillment Targets</td>
<td>
<table>
<tr><th>Service Request</th><th>Description</th><th>Target Resolution Time</th></tr>
<tr><td>Request for new connectivity</td><td>This is a request for new connectivity</td><td>Within x hours, y% of the time</td></tr>
<tr><td>Changes to existing connectivity</td><td>This is a request to make changes to existing service</td><td>Within x hours, y% of the time</td></tr>
<tr><td>Request to cancel existing connectivity</td><td>This is a request to cancel existing service</td><td>Within x hours, y% of the time</td></tr>
<tr><td>Request for new features</td><td>This is a request for new connectivity type (e.g., satellite connectivity)</td><td>Within x hours, y% of the time</td></tr>
</table>
Prerequisites
You must have:
• Employee account created
• Secure ID or other secure access mechanism
• Internet access connection
How to Request Service:
Request online: <<Portal Address>>
Contact the service desk at <<Telephone Number>>
E-mail <<E-mail Address>>
How to Get Support:
Request online: <<Portal Address>>
Contact the service desk at <<Telephone Number>>
E-mail <<E-mail Address>>
</td>
</tr>
</table>

Responsibilities of Parties	**IT Responsibilities** IT will be responsible for the following: • **Support:** – Service desk support – Diagnosing and resolving incidents and problems reported to the service desk • **Hardware and Software** – VPN client software – Security token or secure ID for accessing network and resources • **Access** – Secure network access – Encrypted network connection **Customer Responsibilities** Customers will be responsible for the following: • Providing all relevant and required approvals according to the information security policy
More Information	**Training:** List and describe available training options. **Glossary:** List and describe any specific terms related to this service. **FAQs and Tips:** List and describe any frequently asked questions.

Conferencing Service

Introduction	Conferencing service includes a range of audio and video conferencing options. This service is provided by a conferencing service provider and managed by the <<Name of IT organization>>. This service has three components: • Audio conferencing • Video conferencing • Webcast (online presentation) These capabilities are provided using the Internet and IP telephony technologies. Webcast utilizes streaming media technology to take a single-content source and distribute it to many simultaneous participants (both internal as well as external). IT provides video conferencing services for specific long-distance meetings. Video conferencing is a cost-efficient way of communicating with geographically dispersed groups of people inside and outside MAF. Video conferencing allows you to share your PC screen and applications with your long distance counterparts.

<table>
<tr><td>Description</td><td>Features
<ul>
<li>Audio conferencing
<ul><li>Instant meeting</li><li>Operator assistance available</li><li>Regional and local access numbers</li><li>Recording, archiving, and playback</li></ul></li>
<li>Video Conferencing
<ul><li>Instant meeting</li><li>Operator assistance available</li><li>International conferencing capabilities</li></ul></li>
<li>Webcast
<ul><li>Presentations, audio and video capabilities</li><li>Online chat features</li></ul></li>
</ul>
Alternatives, Limitations, and Restrictions
<ul>
<li>Video conferencing requires all sites to have the needed capabilities.</li>
<li>Certain types of conference calls may require special handling and prior arrangement.</li>
</ul></td></tr>
<tr><td>Services and Rates</td><td>All unit prices are subject to market values and prorated for service on an hourly basis.
<table>
<tr><th>Service</th><th>Unit Price and Service</th></tr>
<tr><td>Audio Conferencing</td><td>$XX.XX/minute/participant</td></tr>
<tr><td>Audio and Video Conferencing</td><td>$XX.XX/minute/participant</td></tr>
<tr><td>Webcast Service</td><td>$XX.XX/minute/participant</td></tr>
</table>
Tips for Reducing Costs
<ul><li>Tips</li></ul></td></tr>
</table>

<table>
<tr>
<td>Service Requests and Fulfillment Targets</td>
<td>
<table>
<tr><th>Service Request</th><th>Description</th><th>Target Resolution Time</th></tr>
<tr><td>Request for audio conferencing service</td><td>This is a request for new audio conferencing</td><td>Within x hours, y% of the time</td></tr>
<tr><td>Request for change to existing service</td><td>This is a request to make changes to existing reservation</td><td>Within x hours, y% of the time</td></tr>
<tr><td>Request for canceling the service</td><td>This is a request to cancel existing reservation</td><td>Within x hours, y% of the time</td></tr>
<tr><td>Request for new features</td><td>This is a request for new capabilities</td><td>Within x hours, y% of the time</td></tr>
</table>
Prerequisites
You must have:
• User account
• Desktop or laptop with Internet connection
How to Request Service:
Request online: <<Portal Address>>
Contact the service desk at <<Telephone Number>>
E-mail <<E-mail Address>>
How to Get Support:
Request online: <<Portal Address>>
Contact the service desk at <<Telephone Number>>
E-mail <<E-mail Address>>
</td>
</tr>
<tr>
<td>Responsibilities of Parties</td>
<td>
IT Responsibilities
IT will be responsible for the following:
• Making, changing, and canceling reservations
• Incident management and problem resolution
Customer Responsibilities
Customer will be responsible for the following:
• Making reservations in a timely manner
• Preparing for and running meetings.
</td>
</tr>
</table>

More Information	**Training:** List and describe available training options. **Glossary:** List and describe any specific terms related to this service. **FAQs and Tips:** List and describe any frequently asked questions.

For a softcopy of a complete IT service catalog and development guidelines, please visit www.xceedure.com

Appendix B: <<Organization Name>> Business Service Management Project Charter Template

Please visit www.xceedure.com to download softcopies of templates, a full version of the service catalog, and further guidelines to support ITIL and Business Service Management implementations.

Author: <<Name of author>>
Creation date: <<Date of creation>>

Table of Contents

Introduction

In this section, you should provide a brief background of what led to this initiative. The purpose of providing this background information is for the reader to understand the origin of the proposed product and what led to the decision to embark on the business service management journey.

Project Charter

This project charter must establish the foundation for the establishment of business service management (BSM). It provides the summary of the overall project plan. Each section of this charter is progressively elaborated on to develop a detailed BSM project plan.

Goals and Obstacles

Problem Statement

In this section, you are required to state the problems (obstacles) that are being experienced due to lack of a service management culture. It will be useful if you are able to identify some of the key business and IT goals that the stated problems are affecting.

Note that the problem statement should create awareness of a need for change and an urgency to take action.

One way to state the problem is as follows:

> The problem of <describe the problem> affects <the stakeholders affected by the problem>. The impact of which is <state the goal that it is negatively impacting (i.e., obstacle)>.

A sample problem statement for a BSM project is as follows:

The lack of business service management affects our organizational capability to make the most use of our existing IT assets in ways that optimize our business growth and profitability. The impact of this is missed business opportunities.

Project Goal(s)

In this section, summarize the goal(s) that the BSM project will meet to resolve the obstacles defined in the problem statement.

The goal(s) will form the desired end state of the project. There may be a number of means to this end but those means do not change the end itself. The end is clearly established in the project charter. The specific means are further elaborated in the project plan. The goals that establish the end state need to be accomplished to resolve the problem identified and overcome the obstacle discussed earlier.

These goals must be precise, must be shared effectively, and must remain unchanged throughout the process.

Project Prioritization

To establish the priority of a BSM project, you may want to consider ranking the following based on the level of impact on achieving the established goals as a result of not pursuing this project.

Risk Category	*Severity of Impact*
Operational Risk	IT has increasingly evolved into one of the core business enablers. Most businesses rely heavily on IT services and, in the event of IT service outages, their respective business processes are impacted. If these IT services are not managed to meet specific business needs, then business is operationally at risk.
Regulatory Risk	To protect the rights and interests of the public, different countries require companies to comply with regulatory requirements and policies. For example, the financial services industry is regulated to ensure appropriate monetary protection, the auto industry is regulated to ensure that automobiles provide the required minimum safety, the pharmaceutical industry is regulated to ensure that public health is always kept first, and so on. Companies across these industries and other industries use a variety of IT services to support their business operations and enable their core business processes. Confidential data and sensitive information are largely generated through information systems, processed by information systems, transferred via information systems, and stored in information systems. Therefore, regulatory compliance is critical. In the absence of appropriate IT service management processes, companies find themselves at risk of noncompliance and may be subjected to heavy fines and other reputation risks.
Information Security Risk	Information is an asset and when it is in electronic form, it is at a higher risk of being exploited and causing monetary and reputation damages to companies.

Reputation Risk	Reputation enables investors to trust the company and make investment decisions, enables customers to buy products and do business, and enables partners to enter into joint ventures.
Financial Risk	If certain parts of the business operations and core business processes fail, what will be the financial impact on the business?

These and other factors should enable you to make a strong case for embarking on the business service management journey. In summary, all the above-mentioned risks point to risks to the survival of the company. All risks should be calculated based on their impact on the business.

Overview of Scope of Project's Product

In this section, you should provide an overview of the key features of the product that is believed to contribute to achieving the identified project goals.

In this section, you should briefly describe what the product (i.e., in our case, BSM) should do. This is supposed to be an overview and should not go into details. This should ensure that the project team and other stakeholders clearly understand the overall vision of this project and the key deliverables without losing sight of what is being built.

In our case, it is an organizational transformation involving the service culture, a combination of process, people, and technology.

Specific deliverables should include:

IT operating model
: This model must ensure that IT operational processes are designed and teams are organized in a manner that ensures increased integration with business processes and customers' needs.

Documented service management processes
: Depending on business and IT drivers, you will identify, prioritize, and select processes out of the following ITIL v3 service life cycle phases:
  - Service Strategy
  - Service Design
  - Service Transition
  - Service Operation
  - Continual Service Improvements

Service catalog
: Defines all services that the IT organization delivers, how much each service costs per unit, what support is provided, and other related details.

Quantifiable service management process improvements
: Process improvement investments must yield measurable business improvements.

Measurable service improvements
: As a result of improving service management processes, what specific measurable service improvements should be expected? These improvements may include reduced cost, efficient delivery, greater transparency, and customer-driven control.

Increased customer satisfaction
: As a result of this effort, customer satisfaction must improve. It is critical to engage appropriate customer focus groups to ensure that customer needs are put in the forefront of this effort.

Cost-efficient and transparent service delivery
Improved management of services provided by the IT organization will lead to reduced cost and greater transparency.

Project Resources

Project Manager Responsibilities

Identifying the project manager in the project charter accomplishes the following:

Someone is explicitly held responsible to ensure further exploration.
The project manager is provided with the authority to apply organizational resources to project activities (PMBOK, 2000).

Core Team

The project team for the BSM project must include stakeholders from the following organizations:

Change sponsor: Someone powerful within the organization who is able to drive the change process and is able to completely support the CIO or Head of IT
Business representatives and customer representatives
IT operations
Data centers
IT development
Business relationship management or account management
Service management or similar organization (if it exists)
Quality assurance and compliance

Potential Owner(s)

Potential Business Owner(s)	*Reasoning*	*Have the problem(s) and potential solution(s) been discussed? If yes, with whom? What was the reaction?*
IT Operations		
Service Management		

Level 0 Estimates (–25% to +75%)

Project Schedule Estimates

Identify major milestones and duration in weeks.

Milestone	*Duration (in weeks)*
BSM Foundation Established	*# of weeks*
BSM Design Completed	*# of weeks*
Business–IT Alignment Achieved	*# of weeks*
Business–IT Integration Achieved	*# of weeks*

Project Cost Estimates

You need to do the following for producing L0 cost estimates.

Senior Management Review and Approval

Name
Formal Title appears here

Name
Formal Title appears here

Business Service Management Project Management Plan Template

Author: <<Name of author>>
Creation date: <<Date of creation>>

Table of Contents

Introduction

In this section, you should provide a brief background of what led to this initiative. The purpose of providing this background information is for the reader to understand the origin of the proposed product and what led to the decision to embark on business service management journey.

Goals and Obstacles

This section further elaborates on the "Goals and Obstacles" section of the Project Charter.

Stakeholders and Their Goals

Identify stakeholders and their individual goals that must be satisfied for the project to be successful.

This Stakeholder . . .	*Has these goals of this effort . . .*
Project Sponsor	
Senior Management	
Project Manager	
Business or Customer	
IT Operations	

IT Development	
Data Center Management	
Potential Owner	
Vendors	

Project Constraints

Constraint is defined as an applicable restriction that will affect the performance of the project. Any factor that affects when an activity can be scheduled (PMBPOK, 2000).

There can be the following common categories of constraints that you may want to brainstorm.

Resource Constraints • *Key staff resources will be available only on a part-time basis.* • *Computer resources will be available on a limited basis.* • *Key customer resources will be available on a restricted basis.* • *A significant percentage of the project staff will not be experienced with the development environment.* • *The customer has limited staff capable of adequately describing in detail the functional requirements of the system.* • *The customer has limited staff capable of adequately describing in detail the operational requirements of the system.*
Delivery Constraints • *Deliverables submitted for approval will require at least n working days for review.* • *There is no limit to review and approve cycles.* • *Equipment order lead times cannot be specified with accuracy.*
Environment Constraints • *The development or operating environment is new and no project staff members are familiar with it.* • *An overtime ban is in effect, which restricts all work to normal working hours.* • *Key decision-makers are based out of town and are difficult to contact when issues arise.* • *The project does not have a customer project manager (or executive sponsor).* • *The methodology [name it] is new and not familiar to development team.* • *The project environment is new and the components have not been successfully integrated.* • *The project depends on the successful and timely completion of associated projects.*

Budgetary Constraints
• *Statistics used in preparing the estimates are unreliable.* • *Travel and living expenses cannot be accurately estimated.* • *Outside consulting requirements cannot be accurately estimated.*
Functionality Constraints
• *The scope of the project is unclear.* • *The project depends on receiving data from other, external applications.*

Project Assumptions

Assumptions are factors that, for planning purposes, are considered true, real, or certain. Assumptions affect all aspects of project planning, and are part of the progressive elaboration of the project. Project teams frequently identify, document, and validate assumptions as part of their planning process. Assumptions generally involve a degree of risk (PMBOK, 2000).

There can be the following common categories of constraints that you may want to brainstorm.

Resource Assumptions
• *Project staff resources will be available when and as they are needed.* • *Required computer resources will be available when and as they are needed.* • *Required customer resources will be available when and as they are needed.* • *A significant percentage of the project staff will be experienced with the development environment.* • *A significant percentage of the project staff will be experienced with the operating environment.* • *The customer will provide staff capable of adequately describing in detail the functional requirements of the system.* • *The customer will provide staff capable of describing in detail the operational requirements of the system.* • *Access to industry experts and specialized skills will occur as needed.* • *A "full-time" resource implies at least 35 hours productive work per week.*
Delivery Assumptions
• *Deliverables submitted for approval will be reviewed and returned within n working days.* • *Deliverables will be subject to no more than a specific number of review cycles.* • *Equipment order lead times are known and can be expected to be met.*

Environmental Assumptions
• *No industrial action will be taken that will affect the project.* • *Issues will be resolved in a timely manner.* • *The project organization and governance architecture described in the project plan will be put in place.* • *The project methodology [name it] will be used in the project.* • *Customer internal processes (such as purchasing) will be completed in a timely manner.* • *Systems components will be capable of being integrated with minimum rework.*
Budgetary Assumptions
• *The statistics used in preparing the estimates are accurate within a given percentage.* • *No travel and living expenses will be required.* • *No outside consulting will be required.*
Functionality Assumptions
• *The scope of the project is limited to that described in the project plan.* • *Formal scope change procedures will be in place.*

Project Scope

In Scope

Outside of the Boundary

People outside of IT
Processes outside of IT
Upstream and downstream systems outside of IT

Inside of the Boundary

People within IT
Processes within IT
Systems to be reengineered or architected

Life Cycle Coverage

Describe the coverage of the life cycle that the processes and systems will support.

Geographical

List the places where the processes and systems will be deployed and executed.

Out-of-Scope

Outside of the Boundary

People outside of IT
Processes outside of IT
Upstream and downstream systems outside of IT

Inside of the Boundary

People within IT
Processes within IT
Systems to be reengineered or architected

Life Cycle Coverage

Describe the coverage of life cycle that the processes and systems will support.

Geographical

List the places where the processes and systems will be deployed and executed.

Project Scope Statement

Deliverables

List the deliverables of the project here, for example:

Service oriented architecture-based product implementing identified use cases
User and support manuals
Source code
Help desk scripts
Trained support and operations staff or training

Project Objectives

Cost Objectives
Include cost objectives here.
Schedule Objectives
Include schedule objectives here.
Quality Objectives
To be established
Other Objectives

Project Scope Definition—Work Breakdown Structure

WBS Outline

The outline of the work breakdown structure (WBS) template is shown below.

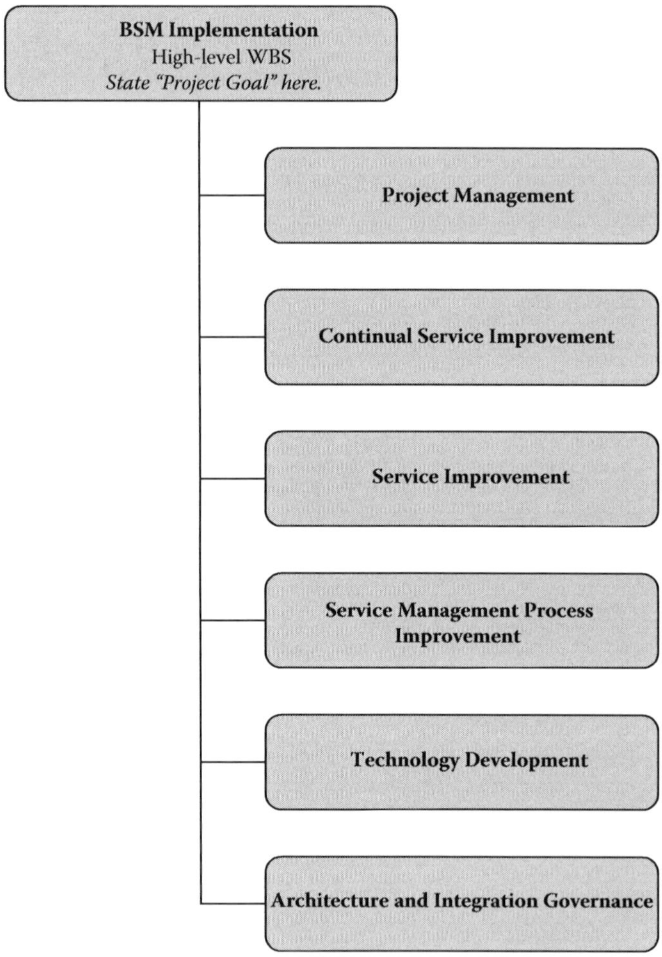

Detailed Work Breakdown Structure Template

Note that the following WBS is also available in an MS project template for each of the five phases of the IDLC. Also, since it is an iterative and incremental development, some activities from each of the following disciplines are repeated over the five phases (initiation, inception, elaboration, construction, and transition).

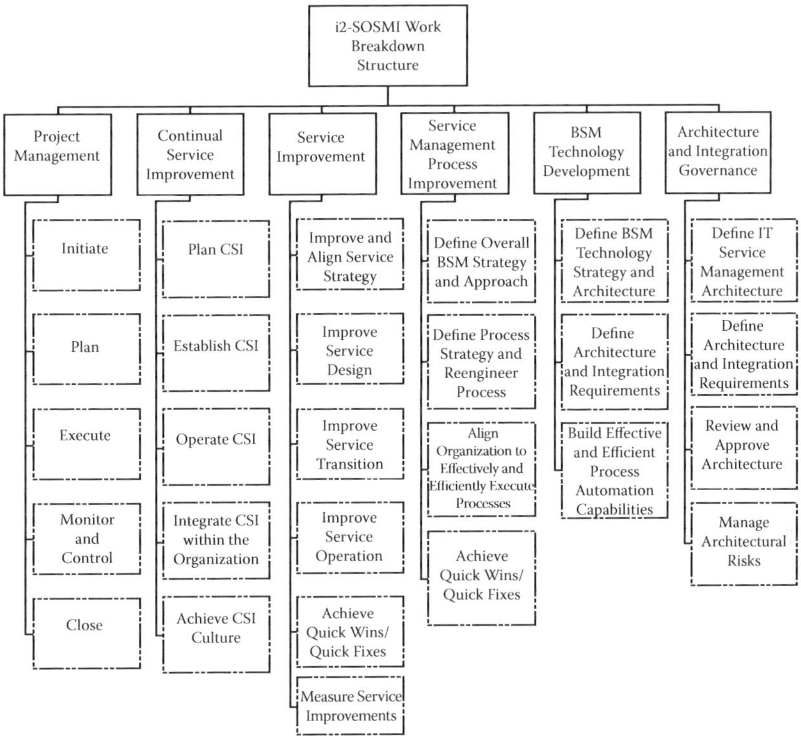

Phases and Iterations

Foundation Phase

Use the MS Project template, "Project Title—Initiation Phase," to plan for this phase.

Iteration Plan Reference	*Goals (Qualitative and Quantitative)*	*Deliverables*	*Evaluation Criteria*
Visualize Iteration Reference			
Architect Iteration Reference			
Realize Iteration Reference			

Design Phase

Use the MS Project file, *Project Title—Inception Iteration # N*, to plan for the iterations and assign resources to activities within the inception phase. Include the following details for each iteration. You may want to rename the template file to show unique iterations. For example, for WRS project's inception phase iteration # 1, template should be renamed to:

Iteration Plan Reference	*Goals*	*Artifact(s), Use Case(s), Feature(s), Process Definition(s)/ Refinement(s) etc.*	*Evaluation Criteria (to demonstrate that goals are met)*
Inception Iteration #1	*Ensure that all stakeholders have a common understanding of WRS requirements.*		

Please refer to the *Guide for Creating Phase and Iteration Plans* included in Appendix A for more information on defining goals.

Align Phase

Use the MS Project file, *Project Title—Elaboration Iteration # N*, to plan for the iterations and assign resources to activities within the elaboration phase. Include the following details for each iteration. You may want to rename the template file to show unique iterations. For example, for WRS project's Elaboration Phase Iteration # 1, the template should be renamed to:

Iteration Plan Reference	*Goals*	*Use Cases*	*Evaluation Criteria*
Elaboration Iteration #1			

Please refer to the *Guide for Creating Phase and Iteration Plans* included in Appendix A for more information on defining goals.

Integrate Phase

Use the MS Project file, *Project Title—Construction Iteration # N*, to plan for the iterations and assign resources to activities within the construction phase. Include the following details for each iteration. You may want to rename the template file to show unique iterations. For example, for WRS project's Construction Phase Iteration # 1, the template should be renamed to:

Iteration Plan Reference	*Goals*	*Use Cases*	*Evaluation Criteria*
Construction Iteration #1			

Please refer to the *Guide for Creating Phase and Iteration Plans* included in Appendix A for more information on defining goals.

Project Resources

Project Organization Chart

Include the project organization here. While you are organizing the team, keep in mind that you should identify resources that will work to accomplish the work identified in the "Work Breakdown Structure" section. For example, if we consider the WBS shown in the previous section, the resources will be allocated as follows:

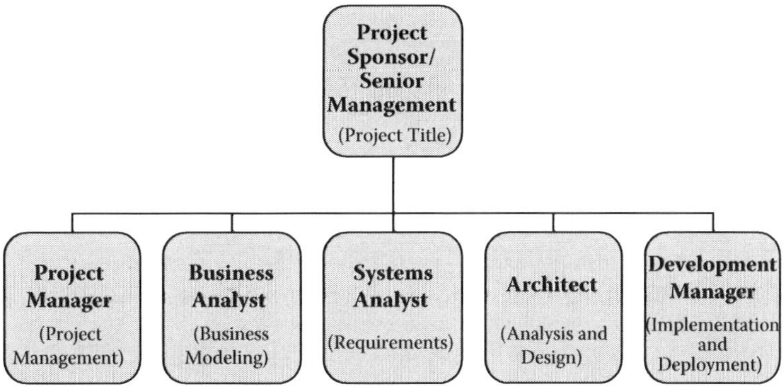

A detailed list of stakeholders should be included in the communications management plan.

Governance Architecture

Governance architecture illustrates how different internal and external bodies interact with the project. Such interactions are carried out through some form of interparty communications. There are two major parts involved in designing the governance architecture. These are:

Identifying the different bodies. A stakeholder list (created as a result of a stakeholder analysis) can be very helpful in identifying these bodies.
Identify what the project body (in the center) needs from them and what the external bodies need from the project body to ensure the success of this project.

Note that such architecture will also assist in planning and managing the communication (communication management plan).

Project organization (identified in the earlier section) forms the core of governance architecture, which represents the project team. Outside bodies are shown to illustrate the units that the project team will need to interact with over the life of the project to ensure success.

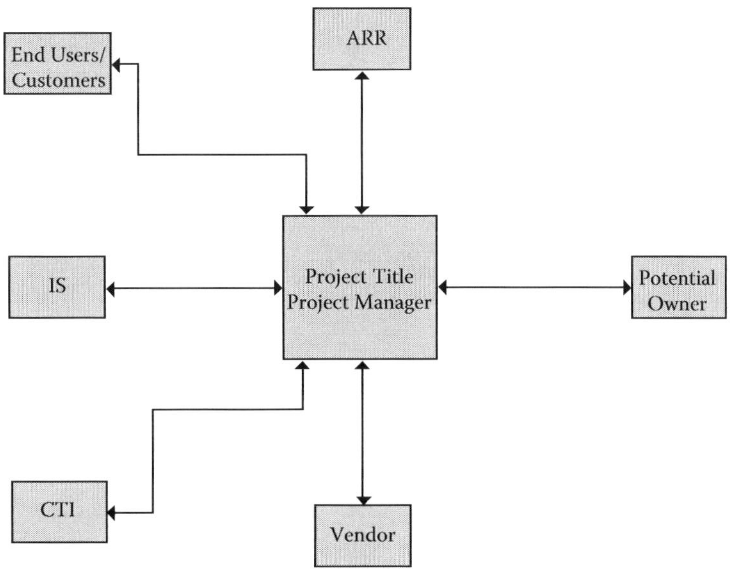

You need to list the responsibilities for each of the bodies identified above. Most of these bodies should have been identified during the stakeholder analysis. If there are new stakeholders identified during this session, you need to update the list of stakeholders and their goals.

Roles and Responsibilities

Since we have designed the project organization and the governance architecture, we are able to list in detail the roles and responsibilities of individual actors within these bodies.

Team/Individual	*Responsibility*

Project Resource and Effort Requirements

Human Resource Requirements

Assign tasks and activities at an appropriate level to resources. Note that these are the resources that will take ownership of these major project deliverables. These resources are mostly on the *manager* or *lead* level. They will be responsible for creating individual iteration plans within each of the major phases and for working as a team to ensure that the project successfully accomplishes the major milestones (LOM, LAM, IOCM, and PRM).

Activities/Tasks from WBS	*Specific Resources*
Project Management	
Business Modeling	
Requirements	
Analysis and Design	
Implementation	

Computing Requirements

Hardware Requirements
Software Requirements

Storage Requirements

Shelf and Space Requirements

Other Requirements

Major Milestones and Cost Estimates

L1 Estimates (–10% to +25%)

Major Milestones

Milestone	*Duration (in weeks)*
Life Cycle Objective Milestone (end of inception)	
Life Cycle Architecture Milestone (end of elaboration)	
Initial Operational Capability Milestone (end of construction)	
Product Release (end of transition)	

Cost Estimates

To produce L1 cost estimates, the following needs to be done:

Senior Management Review and Approval

____

Name
Formal Title appears here

____

Name
Formal Title appears here

L2 Estimates (–5% to +10%)

Major Milestones

Milestone	*Duration (in weeks)*
Life Cycle Architecture Milestone (end of elaboration)	
Initial Operational Capability Milestone (end of construction)	
Product Release (end of transition)	

Cost Estimates

Senior Management Review and Approval

Name
Formal Title appears here

Name
Formal Title appears here

APPENDIX

Project Monitoring and Control

Heavy Monitoring and Control activities are carried out after the project is baselined, which happens after the *elaboration phase* is concluded (i.e., during the construction and transition phases). Before the conclusion of the elaboration phase, you can make changes to the plan without needing to have the changes formally approved.

Project Communication Management and Reporting Plan

Taking project governance architecture as the base, it is recommended to carry out communications requirements (Communication Requirements Analysis Worksheet attached in Appendix A) and stakeholders analysis (Stakeholder Analysis Template attached in Appendix B) before creating the Communications Management Plan.

Key Stakeholders (Distribution Schedule)	*Stakeholder Issues*	*Key Messages to Communicate*	*Communication Methods to be Used (written, one-on-one, electronic, meetings, etc.)*	*Description of Specific Communications (content, format, level of detail, etc.)*	*Timing Issues (see also Bar Chart, Project Schedule)*	*Other*
Client						
Senior Management						
Sponsor						
Project team members						
Employees						
Subcontractors						
Suppliers						
Unions						
Government Agencies						
News Media						
Community						
Other						

Scope Management and Control Plan

This section describes how the project scope will be managed and an assessment of the expected stability of the project scope (i.e., how likely scope changes will be integrated into the project). It should also include whether it is to change, how frequently, and by how much. The scope management plan should also include a clear description of how scope changes will be identified and classified.

Project Scope Management

In this section, briefly describe how project scope will be managed.

Expected Stability of the Project Scope

In this section, assess the expected stability of the scope of this project (how likely is it to change, how frequently, and by how much).

Scope Change Identification

Briefly describe how project scope changes will be identified and classified.

Scope Change Integration

In this section, describe how scope changes will be integrated into the project.

Additional Remarks

Prepared by:

Preparation Date

Cost Management and Control Plan

Date:		
Person(s) authorized to request cost changes (see Cost Change Request):		
Name:	Title:	Location:
Name:	Title:	Location:
Name:	Title:	Location:

Person(s) to whom Cost Change Request forms must be submitted for approval:		
Name:	Title:	Location:
Name:	Title:	Location:
Name:	Title:	Location:
Acceptable reasons for changes in project cost *(e.g., approved scope changes, increased raw materials costs, etc.)*:		
Describe how you will calculate and report on the projected impact of any cost changes *(time, quality, etc.)*:		
Describe any other aspects of how changes to the project cost will be managed:		

Quality Management and Control Plan

Prepared by:
Date:
Description of project quality system:
Describe in as much detail as needed specifically what will be required in each of the following areas to manage quality on this project:
Organizational Structure
Roles and Responsibilities
Procedures
Processes
Resources
Describe how each of the following aspects of quality management will be addressed on this project:
Quality Control
Quality Assurance
Quality Improvement

Risk Response and Management Plan

Risk Management Plan

Prepared by:
Date:
Description of risk management methodology to be used:
Roles and Responsibilities:
Risk Management Action #1:
Team Leader
Team Members
Support
Risk Management Action #2:
Team Leader
Team Members
Support
[Add sections as needed]
Budget:
Timing: (Describe how risk management will relate to the project life cycle, and at what points it will be reviewed during the execution of the project)

Risk Response Plan

Risk response plan should provide the activities that should be performed in case the risk materializes, who the owner(s) of those activities should be and when those activities should be complemented.

Change Management

Changes can be made to a project in one of the following ways:

Scope changes
Schedule changes
Cost changes

Any one of these changes will affect one or both of the other two; if you change the scope of the system, it will certainly impact either the cost or schedule. Use the Change Request Form for submitting the change request and include the approved Change Request in this section.

Glossary

This Glossary should be revised to contain the key items the application deals with. For an insurance application, for example, define things such as claims, different types of policies, and so on. Also add common terminology that is used in the domain and that the team or stakeholders may not be familiar with. This glossary should help the participants agree on common terminology, as this is often a cause of miscommunication and misunderstanding.

Feature: A feature is a service provided by the system that can be observed by a user of the system and that directly fulfills a stakeholder need (Kroll and Kruchten, 2003).

Project Charter: A document issued by senior management that formally authorizes the existence of a project. And it provides the project manager with the authority to apply organizational resources to project activities (PMBOK, 2000).

Project Plan: A formal, approved document used to guide both project execution and project control. The primary uses of the project plan are to document planning assumptions and decisions, facilitate communication among stakeholders, and document approved scope, cost, and schedule baselines. A project plan may be a summary or detailed (PMBOK, 2000).

References

PMBOK. 2000. Project Management Body of Knowledge, Project Management Institute, www.pmi.org.

Kroll, P., and P. Kruchten. 2003. *The Rational Unified Process Made Easy: A Practitioner's Guide To The RUP*. Boston, MA: Addison-Wesley.

Kruchten, P. 2000. *The Rational Unified Process: An Introduction*. Boston, MA: Addison-Wesley.

Shuja, A. and K. Jochen. 2008. *Rational Unified Process Reference & Certification Guide*. Upper Saddle River, NJ: IBM Press.

Appendix C: <<Organization Name>> Business Service Management Implementation Project Communication Strategy and Plan Template

Please visit www.xceedure.com to download softcopies of templates, a full version of the service catalog, and further guidelines to support ITIL and business service management implementations.

Author: <<Name of author>>
Creation date: <<Date of creation>>

Table of Contents

Introduction

In this section, you should provide a brief background on the importance of communication for this project. A sample introduction is provided below.

Communication During Business Service Management Implementation

Business service management implementation is more about cultural change than any other single factor. Cultural change requires incremental changes in behaviors across the organization. Communication is the cornerstone of ensuring that the behavioral transition takes place in a smooth fashion with minimal organizational disruptions. Therefore, in the case of business service management implementation, communication is important not only to ensure that the project is successful but it is also critical to preventing it from failing.

Successful business service management implementation will require appropriate communications to:

- Keep employees informed about upcoming changes
- Create a sense of excitement about what benefits will be realized as a result of these changes
- Incrementally change attitudes and behaviors

Essential Components of Effective Communication

There are three key components that are essential to effective communication over the course of a project life cycle. These are:

Understanding communication needs and establishing business service management communication strategy
Developing a business service management communication plan
Assessing whether communication objectives have been achieved

This process of continually aligning communication to meet the business service management project needs, as well as stakeholder needs, is graphically represented in Figure I.

An overview of some of the key deliverables is provided in the next section. Each of these deliverables will be discussed in greater detail later in this template.

Business Service Management Communication Strategy

Before establishing a communication strategy, it is important to understand what the communication needs are. Key questions to be considered include:

What means and mode of communication is preferred by the stakeholders? Is this mode the right mode? Is there an element of educating the stakeholders on the means of communication that may be more effective?
*What do stakeholders already know about the project? Is this what we want them to know? Do we want to give a different message?
What would stakeholders like to know about the project?

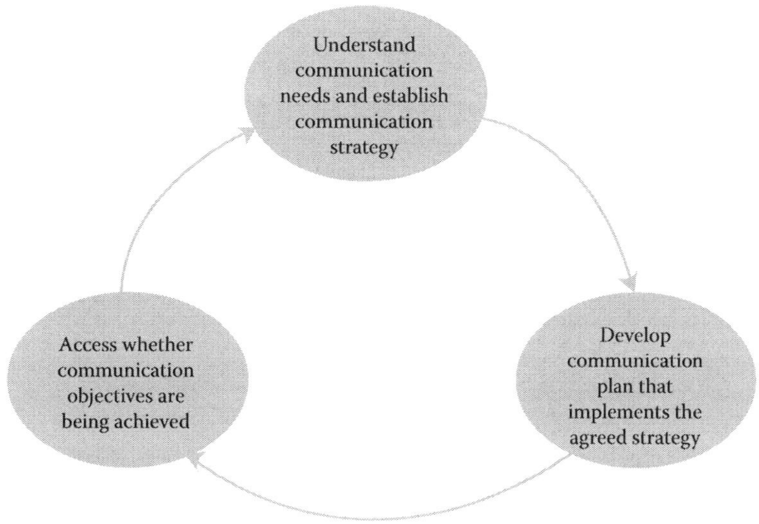

Figure I Continual business service management communication alignment.

Once communication needs are assessed, a communication strategy can be established on how those needs should be met.

A business service management communication strategy sets the long-term direction of how communication needs are to be managed to achieve the desired objectives. Key objectives of a business service management communication strategy are:

- Identify and assess stakeholders' communication needs.
- Identify key messages to be communicated.
- Provide relevant information in a timely manner to reduce any concerns related to cultural transformation and business service management implementation.
- Minimize room for damaging rumors.
- Achieve organizational readiness to embrace change.
- Instill trust in people during periods of disruption and uncertainty.

Business Service Management Communication Plan

A business service management communication plan lays out the communication-related activities that must be performed on an operational level. Key objectives are as follows:

- Implement the business service management communication strategy.
- Deliver specific, predetermined, targeted messages to respective stakeholders.
- Develop schedules and frequencies of messages to be delivered.
- Define a desired outcome as a result of executing the business service management communication plan.
- Identify and evaluate results of executing communications.

To have an actionable business service management communication plan, it is critical to analyze and document key messages that must be communicated and at what frequencies. Key questions to be considered include:

- Messages necessary to achieve the desired level of support and commitment from the stakeholders. These messages may include benefits to be realized as a result of implementing business service management.
- Once we have stakeholder commitment to implement the desired changes, what messages should be sent out to enable the respective stakeholders to migrate to new roles and to better enable them to understand and perform their activities in their new roles?

Communications Assessment

During this activity, a communications assessment is performed to determine whether communication objectives are being achieved or not.

Business Service Management Communication Strategy

The business service management communication strategy should be completed during the foundation (or initiation) phase of the project. Subsequently, depending on the size and complexity of the organization, this strategy may be revisited and refined at regular intervals (quarterly, annually, etc.). Refinement of this strategy should be based on the results of a *business service management communication effectiveness assessment*, discussed later in this document.

Introduction and Background

In this section, introduce the nature of changes that are expected as a result of implementing business service management. The following questions may be asked to complete this section of the strategy:

What is the name of the project or program?
What are the drivers for this change? Are there business changes that require IT to change how it operates or provides IT services?
How can this change be positioned in relation to other changes within IT or within the business?

Following this brief introduction to the change, comment on the importance of managing communications and relate it to the overall success of the project.

Purpose of Business Service Management Communication Strategy

Comment on the purpose of the business service management communication strategy. Some of the questions that should be asked may include the following:

What is the key reason for creating the business service management communication strategy?
Is there any existing strategy in place? If yes, then why is there a need to create this strategy?

Goals and Objectives

Document goals and supporting objectives here. This can be documented in a tree form or table format.

Objective	*Objective Description*	*Evaluation Criteria*

Benefits

List the benefits that are expected to be realized as a result of implementing the business service management communication strategy.

Communications Principles

Outline the core communication principles that must be followed during communications. Some of the common principles may include:

Accuracy: Accurate information must be communicated based on accurate data.
Confidentiality: Information must be accessible to relevant stakeholders only.
Availability: Information must be accessible to the relevant stakeholders when they need it.
Currency: Information provided must be up to date.
Consistency with objectives: Information provided must be consistent with the objective for delivering that information.

Overall Communication Approach

Describe the approach that will be taken to achieve communication objectives. This is the process that is followed to create key communication messages, get required approvals, and distribute these to the relevant stakeholders in a timely manner.

Key Messages

What are the key messages that must be delivered to the stakeholders?

Communication Channels

What are the communication channels that are available? Some of the common communication channels include the following:

Regular update presentations—Face-to-face meetings, team meetings, management meetings, Webcasts, and Webex
Project or program newsletters
E-mail
Voicemail
Notice boards
Video clips or Podcasts
Mass distribution letters
Team-building activities
Project workshops
Project posters or brochures

It is important to assess the most frequently used communication channels, whether they were effective, and if there is any need to make changes. The following table can be used to document the existing communication channels and their effectiveness:

Communication Channel *Name of communication channel should be documented here*	***Channel Effectiveness*** *Effectiveness of this channel is documented here. This may be categorized as high, medium, or low*	***Primary/Secondary*** *Document if this is going to be your primary communication channel*

Stakeholder Management

Describe how stakeholders will be managed in terms of satisfying their respective communication needs.

Project Stakeholders

List all stakeholders that have to contribute to the implementation of this strategy. Stakeholders should include all those individuals, groups, and departments that will either be impacted by the project or have the ability to impact the project. It is also important to document whether these stakeholders are internal or external. You may want to use the following table to capture this information:

Stakeholder/Stakeholder Group	*Internal/External*

After the project stakeholders are identified, the next step will be to establish what key messages will be sent through which channel.

Cultural and Organizational Issues

Before we discuss communication needs, it is important to clearly understand if there are any cultural or organizational issues involved here.

Stakeholder Communication Needs Analysis

Stakeholder/ Stakeholder Group *Name of the stakeholder/ stakeholder group*	***Group Size*** *If it is a stakeholder group, document the size of the group*	***Impact by the Change*** *Document the impact of this change on the stakeholder/ stakeholder group*	***Impact on the Change*** *Document the impact that the stakeholder/ stakeholder group can have on the change*	***Communication Objectives*** *Document the key objectives that will be satisfied as a result of this communication*	***Key Message*** *Document the key message that must be sent during this communication to achieve communication objectives*	***Proposed Channel*** *Document the channel(s) that will be used to communicate the key message*

Stakeholder Roles and Responsibilities

After completing the stakeholder communication analysis, stakeholder responsibilities should be documented. You may want to use the following table to document stakeholder responsibilities. Note that these responsibilities must enable the achievement of communication objectives.

Stakeholder/Stakeholder Group *What is the name of this stakeholder or stakeholder group?*	***Role*** *What is the role of this stakeholder in the project?*	***Responsibilities*** *What are the responsibilities of this stakeholder's role?*

Critical Success Factors

What key factors are critical to the overall success of the business service management communication strategy?

Business Service Management Communication Plan

Based on the business service management communication analysis and strategy, a business service management communication plan must be created. This plan should provide a list of actionable activities that must be executed to achieve the communication objectives. The communication plan must be continually assessed and improved to ensure that the intended communication objectives (approved and documented during the definition of communication strategy) are met. The following table may be used to develop a comprehensive communication plan.

Communication Effectiveness Assessment

It is critical to regularly and continually assess the effectiveness of your communication to ensure that the intended objectives are being achieved. The steps shown in Figure II may be performed to complete this assessment.

Communication assessments should be carried out at regular intervals during the project life cycle. It is important to ensure that your stakeholders clearly understand the purpose of this survey and the expected value. You may want to use introductions similar to the following:

> Success of the <<project name>> is critical to ensuring that our customers and business needs are met in the most effective and efficient manner. Timely and accurate information is critical to the overall success of <<project name>>. This assessment will enable us to assess the effectiveness of our communication channels, content, and messages. The information that will be gathered as a result of this survey will enable us to identify areas of improvement and to further enhance our communication approaches to ensure that your respective communication needs are addressed.

		RACI							
Communication Activity *Document the name of the communication activity*	**Key Message** *Document the key message that must be communicated to the stakeholders as a result of this communication*	**Responsible** *Who is responsible for ensuring that this activity is successful? Remember that there may be more than one person responsible.*	**Accountable** *Who is ultimately accountable for this activity? Remember that there must be only one person accountable.*	**Consulted** *Who must be consulted to perform this activity? Consulted also includes reviews and formal approvals.*	**Informed** *Who must be informed of this activity?*	**Channel** *What channel(s) will be used for this activity?*	**Audience** *Who is the audience for this communication?*	**Frequency** *How frequently is this communication going to be performed? It may be daily, weekly, monthly, quarterly, yearly, etc.*	**Timing** *When will this activity start and when will it end?*

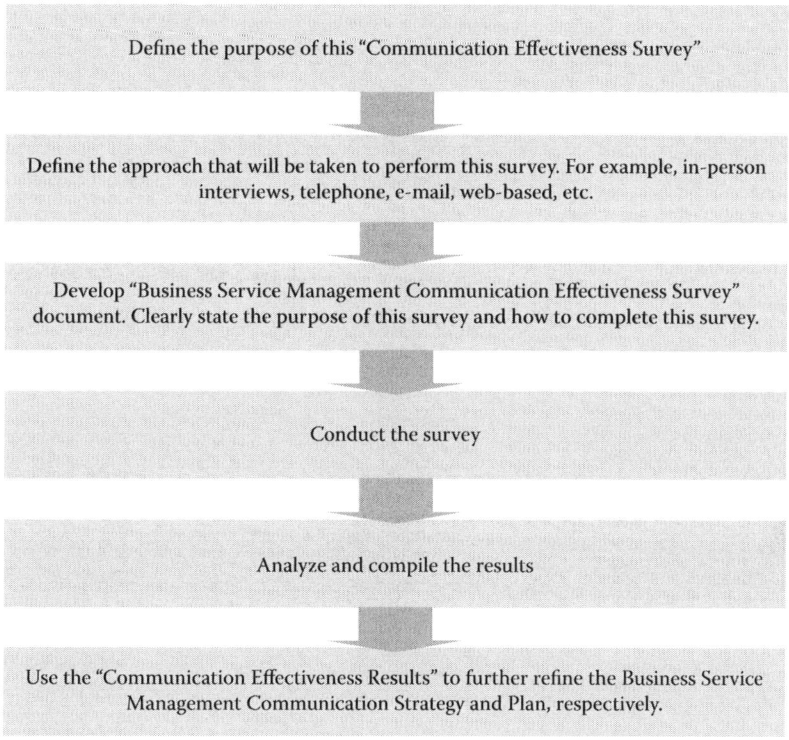

Figure II Business service management communication assessment steps.

Following the above introduction, you may want to provide the approximate time that it will take to complete this survey and provide any additional instructions required to complete it successfully.

You may want to consider questions across some of the following categories to complete this survey:

Stakeholder Information
- Ask for the stakeholder's or stakeholder group's name.
- Ask what department or team is involved.

Project Management
- Inquire whether the business case for this project was communication and whether this was clearly understood.
- Inquire if the decisions and issues have been clearly communicated.
- Gather comments on the overall effectiveness of the project team.

Communications
- Inquire about the types of communication channels used.
- Gather comments on the usefulness of these communication channels.
- Assess whether the information gained through these channels is useful. This is very important.
- Inquire whether there are any additional communication channels that may be beneficial to the overall project.

  - Ask stakeholders to rank the communication channels in the order of effectiveness (most effective to least effective).
- Stakeholder needs
  - Inquire whether the communications are meeting stakeholder objectives.
  - Inquire whether the information provided is sufficient to enable the stakeholder to effectively and efficiently perform their job responsibilities.
  - Inquire if there is a way in which stakeholders are able to provide their feedback and, if so, how effective that feedback process has been.
  - Inquire if the stakeholder's feedback is incorporated into the overall communication plan. In other words, ask if stakeholder feedback has concrete results.
- Open-ended questions for stakeholders to comment on items that may not have been covered in the survey.

Index

A

B

C

K

L

M

T